Business Objects:
The Complete Reference

Cindi Howson

McGraw-Hill/Osborne

New York Chicago San Francisco
Lisbon London Madrid Mexico City
Milan New Delhi San Juan
Seoul Singapore Sydney Toronto

The McGraw·Hill Companies

McGraw-Hill/Osborne
2100 Powell Street, Floor 10
Emeryville, California 94608
U.S.A.

To arrange bulk purchase discounts for sales promotions, premiums, or fund-raisers, please contact **McGraw-Hill**/Osborne at the above address. For information on translations or book distributors outside the U.S.A., please see the International Contact Information page immediately following the index of this book.

Business Objects: The Complete Reference

67890 CUS CUS 0198765

ISBN 0-07-222681-1

Publisher
  Brandon A. Nordin

Vice President & Associate Publisher
  Scott Rogers

Acquisitions Editor
  Lisa McClain

Project Editor
  Jennifer Malnick

Acquisitions Coordinator
  Athena Honore

Technical Editor
  Elizabeth Newbould

Copy Editor
  Robert Campbell

Proofreader
  Mike McGee

Indexer
  Jack Lewis

Computer Designers
  Apollo Publishing Services
  George Toma Charbak
  Lucie Ericksen

Illustrators
  Lyssa Wald
  Melinda Moore Lytle
  Michael Mueller

Series Design
  Peter F. Hancik

This book was composed with Corel VENTURA™ Publisher.

To Keith, Megan, and Samuel—
for teaching me everything about H.B., dragon flies,
front loaders, and unconditional love

About the Author

Cindi Howson is an independent consultant based in northern New Jersey, doing business as Analytic Solutions Know-How (ASK). She has worked with Fortune 500 companies, midsized, and small businesses to solve both technical and business application issues.

Cindi has 14 years' experience in information technology and has specialized in data warehousing and business intelligence tools for eight years. She has worked with BusinessObjects since 1994 and implemented it for thousands of users around the world. As an independent consultant, she writes for industry journals, speaks at user conferences, teaches for The Data Warehouse Institute, and consults with clients to select and optimize BI tools. Prior to working independently, she was a manager at Deloitte & Touche Management Solutions and Services, leading the Houston, TX, analytics practice.

With an MBA from Rice University in Houston, Texas, Cindi focuses on the business value of business intelligence. She was awarded Jones Scholar in 1999, an award to the top students in the school who have excelled in all aspects of business.

About the Technical Editor

Elizabeth Newbould is the director of Business Intelligence at Dataspace, Incorporated (www.dataspace.com), one of the U.S.'s foremost data warehousing consultancies. Elizabeth has more than 12 years' experience working with business intelligence and data warehousing solutions. Her e-mail address is enewbould@dataspace.com.

Contents

Part I

Getting Ready for BusinessObjects

Part II

A Better Universe

Part III

Reporting with BusinessObjects

Acknowledgments

So many people helped make this book what it is and I thank them for their help, commitment, and patience. The team at McGraw-Hill/Osborne took this book from concept to print, starting with Ann Sellers, who bought the idea and convinced me to publish under the Complete Reference line. It's never easy to inherit someone else's project, yet Lisa McClain followed through with enthusiasm and coached me to completion. Thank you to Athena Honore for keeping track of everything, and Jenny Malnick for her sense of humor and attention to detail. Elizabeth Newbould of Dataspace caught my technical inaccuracies and helped bring clarity to each chapter. She went beyond what was expected to answer all my "triple-check e-mails."

Without Business Objects—the company—there would be no book. I think back to the days when Business Objects was a small, privately held firm. At the time, selecting their tool was a risky decision. Now I can only cheer that they have turned into both a great company and best-selling product. Many of the original people have come and gone, but still, Mark Hayem, wherever he may be, taught me so much and provided a sturdy foundation. Thank you, Bernard Liautaud, for not laughing at my attempt at speaking French during our first introduction. I'm indebted to Sherry Lowe, who got the ball rolling, and Danielle Dawson, whose undying commitment to follow through with so many product managers and technical folks ensured this book is as accurate and complete as possible. I need to thank the people in tech support who made sure my cases were genuine problems and not just my bad habits, especially Marlene for her follow up and Dale Briggs, without whose support I would have cut coverage of Universal Drill Through Service. And thanks to John Care and Andre Lopez for making sure coverage of version 6 made it into this book.

A number of people helped shape this book and answered specific content questions. I thank Ed Heuser for providing inspiration and opinions; Joel Fedorko, DBA extraordinaire, who answered every question about every database; as well as Walter Müllner, Melanie Hoy, Mark McBride, Dave Rathbun, Steve Krandel, Greg Reitz, Tom Carson, Dan Vesset, Chuck Piercey, Bryan Motteram, Laura Vega, and Darren Cunningham. Keith Jaslow at Informatica was invaluable in making sure my ETL coverage was correct. Without the commitment from Dan Everett at Hyperion, I never would have been able to address incorporating Essbase into a BusinessObjects deployment. Mark Braunstein at eRobertParker and Julian Berkin at WineAlert.com provided the interesting data used for Part III of this book.

I never would have embarked on my career in business intelligence if it were not for the business people at Dow Chemical, including Fernand Kaufman, Dik Hoijer, Bob Lee, and Eddie Wilson, who kept me focused on the business goals in everything IT. They took me from the days of spreadsheet reports to landing on the moon at the push of a button! The original Access Tools Team, especially Armin Pressler, introduced me to the formal field of business intelligence. Of course, none of this technology makes a hoot of difference until people actually use it. I thank Kathy Krupp, Martin Cameron, and Gregg Reitz, for showing me just how worthwhile it can be.

Thank you to my professors at the Jones School at Rice University who rekindled my passion for business intelligence from a new perspective. In so many ways, this book is a product of what I learned while doing my MBA. Without all you taught me about entrepreneurship, marketing, power and politics, consulting, and the independent BI project, I never would have embarked on this project. Wayne Eckerson showed me the power of writing to help companies find the sweet spot of business intelligence. My friends and colleagues at Deloitte & Touche broadened my knowledge of consulting and business intelligence, especially Buck Ogilvie for his support and enthusiasm, Jeff Goodwin and the data team for putting up with my rantings, Harvey Michaels for allowing me so many opportunities, and Jennifer Vaughn and Jami Blake for being friends and mentors. So when are any of you going to relocate to NJ?

Last, but certainly not least, is my family. Writing a book is something that could not be accomplished during the course of a normal workday. They have all made so many sacrifices to allow me to write this book. I thank Megan for waiting patiently for a book of her own and who, at the age of seven, offered to proofread everything just so I would be done already! I thank Sam for cheering whenever I finished a chapter, and Keith for all those late-night cups of tea, neck rubs, and for still being my favorite user!

Introduction

The idea for this book started several years ago, when a client claimed he learned more about universe design and development from a single quality assurance review than all the classes he had taken and books he had read. For a consultant, there is no higher compliment. Let me set the record straight, though: I think the vendor training and documentation is excellent. What makes BusinessObjects uniquely challenging, however, is that for business intelligence, it is not enough to know the software; you have to know the business and the business users. In this respect, it's not enough to know how to create a universe object—for example, you have to know *why* users need objects defined a certain way, how certain SQL settings prevent or enable users to answer a business question. This book is my attempt at bridging what is often the great divide between IT and the business in their quest for better access to information. My hope is that it helps you take your implementation one step further.

Oddly enough, what pushed me to formalize a book proposal was seeing books on competitive BI tools. Despite Business Objects' market leadership, there was only one professionally published book, years out of date and addressing only document creation. The market needed a more up-to-date and comprehensive book. I confess this book had humble beginnings, with my primary goal to cover universe design, since universes are the heart of a BusinessObjects implementation. Do well in the universe, and reporting and analysis is easier. Build a cumbersome universe, and users will construct overly complex reports, or worse, find other ways to get to the data. In discussing the book concept with McGraw Hill/Osborne, I got a lesson in book brands. They suggested covering more functionality and publishing the book under the Complete Reference brand.

I take things quite literally. *Complete?* My definition of "complete" is the full set of vendor documentation that measures two feet on my bookshelf. So the work began to come up with an outline that would satisfy the majority of readers: business users, designers, supervisors, project managers, and sponsors. This book focuses on the business side of BusinessObjects and the core components that take you there: Designer, Supervisor, BusinessObjects, InfoView, WebIntelligence (referred to as WebI in the book), and Broadcast Agent. Therefore, it does not address installation, load balancing, and performance tuning techniques. Refer to the vendor documentation for these topics. Is the book, then, complete from the perspective of the full product offering from the company? No. But it is complete for a segment of readers? I hope so! If I've missed anything essential, please do let me know.

What's Inside

Part I, "Getting Ready for BusinessObjects," introduces Business Objects the company, the history of the product line, and the history of business intelligence. Project managers in particular will find Part I useful in understanding the people and communication issues that affect a BusinessObjects implementation. With the myriad of product choices and deployment approaches, Part I will help you stay focused on the users and the goals of your implementation.

Part II, "A Better Universe," covers universe design, maintenance, and integration with Supervisor. As you deploy BusinessObjects across the enterprise, there are choices about where to build the intelligence in relational tables, MOLAP cubes, the universe, and the reports. As well, the larger your company's deployment, the greater the need for test and production environments, a quality assurance process, and usage tracking. Part II gives you the tools to do this. Even if you are an end user, you will want to read sections of Part II to better drive the business requirements into the universe design.

Part III, "Reporting and Analysis with BusinessObjects," covers the end-user tools: BusinessObjects full client, InfoView portal, and WebIntelligence. Part III is when you finally get the return on your business intelligence investment as users explore and analyze data in ways never before possible. Part III covers the basics of accessing standard reports and exploring the data, as well as the advanced techniques of creating queries, defining complex conditions, and report formulas.

About halfway through the book, I learned that Business Objects would be releasing version 6.0 at about the same time this book would appear in print. Fortunately, much of the functionality in Designer and BusinessObjects is the same in version 6.0. The biggest changes are in WebIntelligence. After seeing the pre-beta, we decided these changes—and the breakthrough functionality—were significant enough to warrant inclusion. Chapter 24 introduces InfoView and WebIntelligence version 6.0. Even if you do not currently use WebIntelligence, you will want to read this chapter to see just how much Business Objects has closed the functionality gap between full-client and thin-client platforms. In the past, thin-client business intelligence often meant you had to sacrifice functionality for ubiquitous access. With WebIntelligence 6.0, the choice becomes largely an architectural one.

Conventions

This book uses the following conventions:

Convention	Used For
Bold	Information you enter in a dialog box
SMALL CAPS	Keys such as DELETE or BACKSPACE
Courier font	SQL syntax, BusinessObjects functions, or data source table and column names
Italics	Classes and object names as well as input variables
Business Objects	The company
BusinessObjects	The product

The Complete Reference

Part I

Getting Ready for BusinessObjects

The Complete Reference

Business Objects

Chapter 1

Introduction to Business Intelligence

"Study the past if you would divine the future."—Confucius

Business intelligence is a way of exploring data to improve business performance, whether to drive profitability or to manage costs. It is not a technology you implement and then put in maintenance mode; it is an approach that evolves, morphs, and starts over again as the business climate changes, the users discover new opportunities to leverage information, and technology changes. When you implement business intelligence tools, the focus of the project is not to finish, but rather, to deliver a certain amount of value and functionality within a predefined period.

The purpose of this chapter is to provide some insight as to how business intelligence evolved and is still evolving, so that you can assess where your company is in the implementation cycle, where your users are today, and where they are heading. You'll see how Business Objects, the company and the product, have evolved with their customers and the industry, bringing the dream of business intelligence to more users and beyond traditional corporate boundaries. In many cases, Business Object's innovations have shaped and re-defined the market.

The Background of Business Intelligence

The need to access information is not new. After all, people have always needed data to make informed decisions. As a type of technology, though, business intelligence is relatively young. Howard Dresner of the Gartner Group first coined the term "business intelligence" in 1989. Pre–business intelligence, it was expensive and time-consuming to get access to the right data. If you are just starting out on the journey of business intelligence, you may find it hard to believe there was a time when information access was yet more painful. But it was, and in some organizations, it still is.

In the 1980s, decision makers predominantly relied on the following sources of information:

- Printed reports, generated on a periodic basis by mainframe-based systems. If a critical measure were missing from the printed report, you had to wait months for IT to create a custom report.

- Spreadsheets, which provided a bit more flexibility than printed reports. Unlike today, when users may import data directly from a transaction system or data warehouse into a spreadsheet, in the late 1980s, field personnel would call in their sales figures to one accountant or analyst, who would manually enter the data into a spreadsheet. This allowed for some form of analysis on monthly data at best. With manual data entry, there was enormous room for human error.

- Gut feel still provided the best form of decision making, as managers were close to the markets and the customers, and markets did not change at the pace they do today. If a manager had access to quantitative numbers, there was a high degree of distrust of the numbers, and rightly so. After all, the data was stale and the manual collection processes fallible.

Caution   *As you deploy BusinessObjects, never underestimate the role and "hold" these legacy reporting systems continue to have over users. If you make BusinessObjects appear any more difficult than legacy reporting systems, your project risks failure. You are trying to change in a matter of months decision-making processes that have existed for decades. It's a little like crash dieting—everyone hates it and it's rarely successful over the long term.*

Custom-developed decision support systems (DSSs) and executive information systems (EISs) attempted to overcome some of the limitations of these original information sources. Decision support systems took the data from mainframe-based transaction systems and presented the results to users in a parameterized form. Users would enter a couple of parameters, such as time period, customer, country, and product. The DSS then displayed results in a tabular format. The beauty of this was that it was easy to use, significantly more so than wading through pages of paper-based reports. If you wanted to graph something, however, you had to re-key the data into a spreadsheet. If you wanted to view a different data subject, this was generally not possible. Decision support systems generally provided insight into only one subject of data at a time. Each function generally had its own custom transaction system (see Figure 1-1), making it almost impossible to share information across functions. When a customer placed an order, the order entry system maintained its own customer codes. To generate an invoice, the accounts receivable department would have to reenter the order into their own accounting system, which most likely used a different set of customer codes. If you wanted to combine actual sales data (accounts receivable) with shipment dates (orders), it was generally not possible.

Decision support systems with their proprietary nature gave way to executive information systems (EISs). Executive information systems were expensive to implement but provided graphical dashboards based on a broader set of information, sometimes with feeds from external data sources. At the time, products such as Pilot Software, Inc.'s, Lightship; Platinum Technology's Forest and Trees; and Comshare, Inc.'s, Commander Decision were breakthrough applications and in high demand.

The fundamental problem with EIS systems was that *E* stood for executive. Companies soon realized that not only executives needed access to information, but all decision makers. Some savvy marketing companies later would tout their products as *Everyone's* Information System. However, until organizations fixed the back-end data, the stale, silo-based information could not be actionable regardless of how pretty it looked in a dashboard or a briefing book. At the time, data warehousing was not a generally accepted technology, so moving beyond silo-based information systems was mission impossible.

Business Intelligence Is Born

In the early 1990s, a number of business and technological factors merged to drive and enable the creation of a new breed of tools, business intelligence, as shown in Figure 1-2.

Several factors drove the need for more information, faster. With increased free trade, the fall of the Berlin wall, the signing of NAFTA, the endless possibility of emerging markets, and economic prosperity, growth and globalization were the mantra for many organizations. However, to operate a global company, one needs access to global or

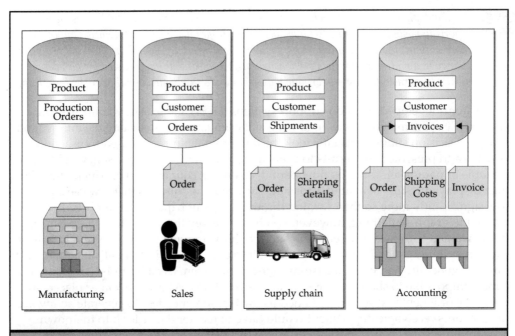

Figure 1-1.   *Each function had its own custom-built transaction system.*

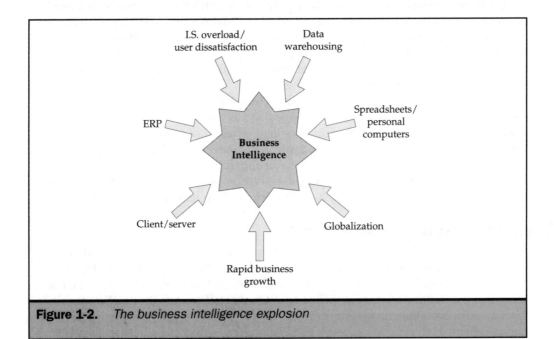

Figure 1-2.   *The business intelligence explosion*

multiregional data. The function- and region-based DSSs could no longer satisfy users' needs. Silo-based EISs broke. At the same time, PCs were becoming common office tools. Users were increasingly analyzing data via spreadsheets or PC-based graphic programs. With this limited data analysis, users put pressure on IT to deliver more robust reports. IT could not keep pace with the demand. Personal computing both drove business intelligence and enabled client/server computing.

A number of technological advances became enablers for business intelligence. First, large corporations began implementing enterprise resource planning (ERP) systems, such as SAP, PeopleSoft, Oracle Financials, and J.D. Edwards. With these implementations, companies hoped to: 1) reduce the number and complexity of custom transaction systems, 2) meet the business demands for growth and globalization, and 3) derive the productivity and cost benefits of business process reengineering. With ERP systems (Figure 1-3), companies implement modules that share common business data. Each module includes rules that ensure a company is following its intended business processes. For example, in generating a customer order, the shipment is not scheduled until a price has been agreed upon and inventory is available. Modules share information with one another. The same customer information used to process the order is used to invoice the customer. When a customer places the order and the product is shipped, this information is integrated with the accounts receivable module to generate an invoice. With the proprietary transaction systems shown in Figure 1-1, data was double-entered, and customer IDs were specific to each system. With an ERP system, an accountant no longer re-keys the information into a separate system; all reference data is shared across the multiple modules. If the productivity and business process reengineering savings were not enough to incite a company to replace their legacy systems with an ERP, then the threats of year 2000 issues were.

Initially, ERP vendors promised they would provide insight into a company's business. It was a false promise. ERP systems provide the infrastructure that makes the insight *possible*, but the insight comes only when business intelligence tools are implemented in *conjunction with* the ERP system. System integrators and consultants, eager to assist with ERP implementations, only fueled this misconception. Some companies recognized that the newly implemented ERP system would not be able to replace all the information requirements that custom reports and DSS systems provided. Although ERPs helped streamline operations and eliminate duplicate data entry, they did nothing to simplify data access.

Tip   *If you are deploying BusinessObjects directly against the ERP, you must reeducate users about new data nuances and new business terminology. Use the object descriptions in the universe or a help page in a standard report to ease this transition. You don't want BusinessObjects to take the blame for the confusion an ERP may introduce. Further, if you deploy BusinessObjects against a data warehouse, never underestimate the power of "promises" made during an ERP implementation. Users will want to know why they shouldn't get all their data from the ERP rather than BusinessObjects or the data warehouse. You may be perceived as the bearer of bad news, forcing them to learn yet another new tool when they were promised the ERP was the ultimate answer to all their information needs.*

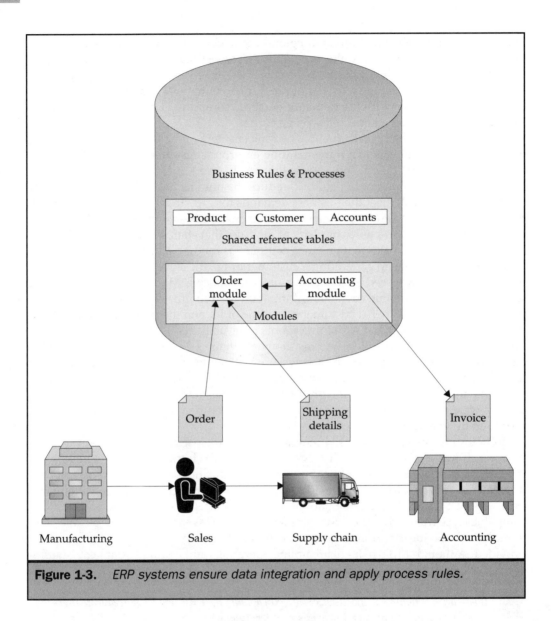

Figure 1-3. *ERP systems ensure data integration and apply process rules.*

The second key enabler to business intelligence was client/server computing. With PCs on many users' desktops, companies could shift much of the processing power from mainframes to PCs, at a significantly lower cost. All of the sexy charts that made EISs so appealing could easily be rendered on an MS Windows or Apple desktop. The user interface was much more intuitive than mainframe-based reports and programming languages. For the first time, companies could purchase best of breed products and the components worked together. Okay, so they needed some brute force and perhaps some aggressive vendor sessions, but they did work, a shock for many who previously had single-vendor solutions.

Data Warehouse Speeds BI Adoption

The data warehouse was the biggest enabler for powerful reporting and BI's rapid success. A data warehouse extracts information from the ERP and aggregates it to allow for fast analysis of vast amounts of data. Some initial data warehouse projects were deemed failures, costing millions of dollars and producing no measurable benefits after years of effort. Fortunately, industry consultants quickly remedied the data warehouse approach, proposing subject-oriented data marts that can be built in smaller time frames. Ideally, a central data warehouse still acts as the platform to populate the data marts. As a technology, data marts and data warehousing allow IT to safely isolate the transaction system from the reporting system. A slow query does not halt order processing. As a business application, data warehousing allows users to analyze broader sets of data with dimensional hierarchies. When analyzing data in either an ERP or a proprietary transaction system, the queries are still limited to a particular module or set of tables. With a data warehouse, the data is combined into one subject area or business view, allowing users to perform analyses that cut across multiple business processes. As the data is aggregated, data warehouses can contain years of history, allowing users to analyze trends and purchasing patterns; ERP and transaction systems often contain only current data at the most granular level of detail. Table 1-1 compares some of the different purposes and features of a transaction system with those of a data warehouse. Note that in the mid-1990s, you could easily replace the column heading "Data Warehouse" with "Business Intelligence." Now, business intelligence also applies to detailed, operational data, ideally in a data warehouse, but not necessarily.

ERP/Transaction System	Data Warehouse/Data Mart
Goal is to process orders, post journal entries	Goal is to provide access to information to improve revenues, manage costs, achieve strategic goals
Current information with very little history	Larger amounts of history allow five- to ten-year trend analysis, this year versus last year comparisons
Real-time information	Information extracted on a periodic basis (hourly, daily, weekly, and so on)

Table 1-1.   *Comparison of Transaction Systems with Data Warehouses*

ERP/Transaction System	Data Warehouse/Data Mart
Detailed data down to the line item or level of data entry	Aggregated data
Fast inputs, but slow queries	Read-only; tuned for fast queries
Rarely hierarchical groupings	Hierarchical groups of codes give level of time, chart of accounts, product groupings, customer groups, and so on
Fixed reports by one detailed dimension (cost center, plant, document)	Fixed or ad hoc reporting and analysis by multiple dimensions across all business functions
Historically awkward user interface, fixed reports only	Easy-to-use MS Windows or browser interface

Table 1-1. *Comparison of Transaction Systems with Data Warehouses* (continued)

With all the promises ERP-vendors and system integrators made about the ERP-providing business insight, Table 1-1 may become a necessary part of your training material, particularly for BusinessObjects users who also are ERP users (see Chapter 3 for more on user segments). Without this clear understanding, business users may rather have a custom, parameterized report against the ERP because they know the data is right (i.e., no transformations have messed it up) and it's real-time.

The Internet Influence

Business intelligence tools gradually grew from basic SQL generators to include advanced report formatting and scheduling, OLAP technology, and enterprise-wide deployment capabilities. However, some of the requirements that existed in the 1980s and early 1990s (refer to Table 1-2, "Then" column) still were not met. Executives are still looking for the dashboard-like interface, and former DSS users still want to be able to log onto any terminal and see their data at the push of a button (Table 1-2, "Now" column). I recall intense negotiations between Business Objects and the Fortune 500 company I worked for in 1995 in which we were ready to sign a global licensing agreement; if we could come up with a solution for executives who still wanted a push-button solution (à la the early EIS systems), our number of users would be tripled. Otherwise, we were solving only the problem of custom reports, previously developed by an overwhelmed IT department. At the time, few foresaw the profound impact the Internet would have on all BI tools and continues to have.

Then	Now
Information for executives only	Information for everyone, including external business partners
Dashboard-like interface	Dashboards and push-button access for key indicators, plus ad hoc access for deeper or different analyses
Fast access to strategic information with dimensions and history	Dimensions and history plus information from third-party data sources
Detailed operational reports via the transaction system / ERP interface	Via a Windows or browser interface, with more flexibility
Generic paper reports with too much information hand-delivered to the executive's desk	Personalized, electronic reports delivered via e-mail, intranet, or mobile device to everyone's desk, wherever their desk may be

Table 1-2.   *Today's Information Needs Are Extensions of the Same Needs in the Early 1990s*

With the Internet boom of the late 1990s, the industry has come full circle. In many respects, the latest BI innovations are trying to fulfill the needs of "Then" that were never met, in addition to fixing some of the problems that client/server computing introduced. With midtier application servers (such as WebIntelligence), companies are returning to a server-centric architecture and look to limit their product base. Initially, most BI vendors became Web-enabled by allowing users to save standard reports in HTML format. Finally, the executives once again had a kind of dashboard via corporate intranets! While client/ server architecture lowered computing costs and enabled a better user interface, it presented challenges for broad-scale deployments. Gluing together best of breed products from multiple vendors can get ugly. As BI vendors rearchitected their products to deliver interactive Web-based analysis via plug-ins, applets, or HTML scripts, the Internet promises to fulfill two very diverse needs: on a recurring basis, push-button access to key performance indicators, with the flexibility of interactive, ad hoc access when required. WebIntelligence's architecture enables business intelligence beyond the internal corporation to suppliers and external business partners. As a testimony to the company's profound impact on this type of BI innovation, CEO Bernard Liautaud published the business book *e-Business Intelligence: Turning Information into Knowledge into Profit* (McGraw-Hill, 2000), which highlights how companies are sharing information beyond traditional boundaries to drive profitability and generate new revenue opportunities.

Users may require much the same functionality they did in the 1990s but demand still more information, flexibility, personalization, and speed. The Internet again allows for ubiquitous deployments via an even easier-to-use interface: a web browser. Portals allow for mixed content and dashboard-like screens. Broadcast and push/pull technologies (such as Broadcast Agent Publisher) allow for highly personalized reports delivered to e-mail and mobile devices both within the corporation and beyond with suppliers and business partners.

Defining the Market

A successful BI implementation must be driven by business requirements and how well a tool can meet the architectural and functional needs of both IT and business users. However, it's helpful to understand the vendor's position in the marketplace as an indicator of financial stability, product innovation, and ability to drive and conform to industry standards. If you have implemented BusinessObjects at the departmental level and are now looking to deploy it across the enterprise, the company's position as an industry leader makes it easier to justify it as a corporate standard. Further, if your IT department is strapped for resources, Business Objects leadership position gives you greater flexibility in getting assistance from contractors, specialty consulting firms, and big-four management consultants. The sheer number of users means you have many third-party resources available to you, including regional user groups and a user-run discussion group, BOB (http://www.forumtopics.com/busobj/about.php).

As you evaluate market shares and leadership positions, it's important to understand in which context an analyst is speaking of BusinessObjects or its competitors. No two analysts define the market the same way. IDC defines the BI market as revenues from licenses and maintenance fees of query and reporting tools used in either a data warehouse environment or against a transaction system, OLAP, EIS, data mining, or packaged data marts such as SAP BW; it specifically excludes ETL tools and analytic applications. As shown in Figure 1-4, the BI market has grown from less than $1 billion in the early 1990s to close to $5 billion today, according to IDC. At its peak, the market grew at 38 percent per year from 1997 to 1998, but it has slowed significantly, to a meager 2 percent today. While Business Objects' growth has in part been due to general market growth, Figure 1-4 clearly shows that the company's growth has exceeded the market's. Business Objects' peak growth was also in 1997–1998, at 46 percent. However, even in 2002's economic downturn, Business Objects' revenue increased by 9 percent compared to the BI market's meager 2 percent growth and compared to other BI vendors who suffered declining revenues and losses.

Since its inception, the BI market has been highly fragmented. Companies that used to operate in only one segment now operate in several, making it harder to determine how much of a company's revenues account for a particular segment share. One thing that is clear is that business intelligence is Business Objects' sole focus. It is not in the

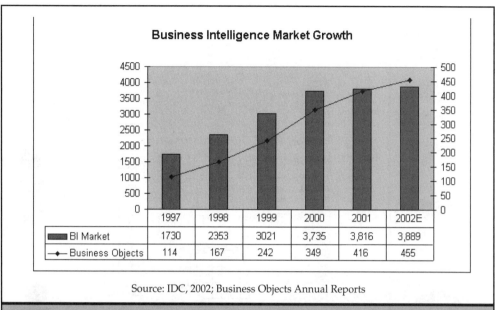

	1997	1998	1999	2000	2001	2002E
BI Market	1730	2353	3021	3,735	3,816	3,889
Business Objects	114	167	242	349	416	455

Source: IDC, 2002; Business Objects Annual Reports

Figure 1-4.   *Business Objects' growth has outpaced BI market growth.*

businesses of databases, ERPs, or operating systems, unlike other players in the BI space. While such a narrow focus could be a risk for small companies, Business Objects is financially solid. Its revenues for fiscal year 2002 were $454,800, comparable only to that of chief competitor Cognos and more than double the revenue of other BI-focused companies. While IDC does not publish exact market positions, it cites Business Objects as one of the top three, along with SAS and Cognos.

The sections that follow describe some of the main market segments. Figure 1-5 shows how some of the market segments relate to components of a BusinessObjects architecture.

Extract Transform Load (ETL)

Extract Transform Load (ETL) tools used to be a distinct tool set. Their job was to take the data from the source ERP or transaction system and then to cleanse and aggregate it to load in a data warehouse or data mart. Simply getting the data into a cube or RDBMS does not in itself provide business value. As business users attempt to answer questions with the data, often the ETL process changes, either to extract more data or to add robust business calculations. A tight integration between the ETL tool and end-user analysis has the potential to provide better business insight. Further, tired of gluing together products from multiple vendors, companies increasingly look to buy one product set from one vendor. Vendors from both sides of the divide, illustrated in Figure 1-5, have

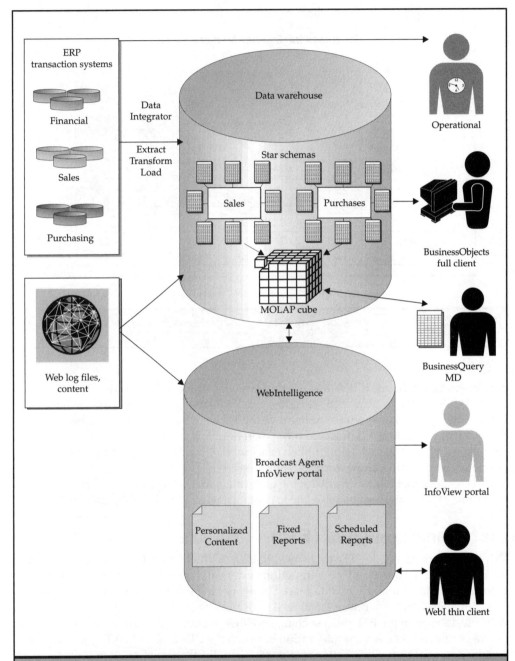

Figure 1-5.   *Business intelligence architecture*

expanded their tool sets. Oracle, traditionally an RDBMS and ERP vendor, offers Oracle Warehouse Builder as its ETL solution. In 1995, the company moved into the BI space with its acquisition of IRI's Express, a leading MOLAP tool and offers Oracle Discoverer, a query and reporting tool. In 1998, Cognos was one of the first major BI vendors to begin offering ETL functionality with DecisionStream. Informatica, long a leader in the ETL segment, began offering its own web-based BI tool, PowerAnalyzer, in 2002. In 2002, Business Objects acquired Acta Technology, another leading ETL vendor, and rebranded the product as BusinessObjects Data Integrator. While most ETL tools allow for scheduled extraction of data from the OLTP into a data warehouse, Data Integrator also facilitates real-time access. As of Q4 2002, sales from Data Integrator account for less than 5 percent of Business Objects' overall revenues but have been higher than expected. With Informatica and Business Objects both encroaching on one another's core market segments, there is bound to be some friction. However, Business Objects consistently claims it will continue to support integration with third-party ETL vendors such as Ascential and Informatica. Its goals for acquiring Acta were to offer a complete solution for companies that want to buy from one vendor and to provide turnkey analytic applications.

Query and Reporting

Query and reporting is the process of querying a database, then formatting it for readability and analysis. This is the segment in which Business Objects initially was launched and its origins help explain why its SQL generation is so robust. Within query and reporting, users may query a data mart or a data warehouse, or they may query a transaction system. Some industry analysts would say the latter is not really BI, it is simply operational reporting. Recall, though, that the purpose of BI is to explore and analyze data to improve profitability or manage costs. Companies can do this with summary data (data warehouse) or detail data (transaction system). Many mid-sized and small companies may not have the skills, budget, or time to implement a data warehouse. The robust functionality of BusinessObjects along with smaller data volumes allow these companies to accomplish BI directly against the transaction system. Further, ERP vendors are satisfying their users' demand for real-time, flexible reporting and analysis by embedding BI products into the ERP. For example, i2 and PeopleSoft embed BusinessObjects into their products.

Some define "reporting" as the process of formatting a report to enable analysis, while others define reporting as the delivery and distribution of standard reports throughout an organization. This latter definition would encompass Broadcast Agent and Broadcast Agent Publisher. In 1992, Business Objects was one of the first companies to have a repository that allowed users to store standard reports. Over time, this repository has grown to accommodate standard reports grouped by departments and navigatable by categories and subcategories.

On Line Analytical Processing (OLAP)

Many BI vendors provide both query and reporting solutions as well as an OLAP tool. Some BI vendors provide it via one integrated product; others offer separate products.

For example, Oracle Express is a MOLAP database; whereas Oracle Discoverer is a query and reporting tool; Cognos Powerplay is a MOLAP database, while Cognos Impromptu is a query and reporting tool. Business Objects provides query, reporting, and OLAP in one tool set, generating a dynamic microcube with each query that can reside on the desktop or the mid-tier server. BusinessObjects can also access server-based MOLAP and ROLAP cubes.

In its broadest sense, OLAP provides multidimensional analysis with different dimensions and different levels of detail. Functions such as drill-down, rotate, and swap are OLAP functions. OLAP, though, has some clear definitions set forth by E.F. Codd (the father of the RDBMS) in 1993. Arbor Software, the original makers of Essbase, later acquired by Hyperion, hired Codd to bring clarity to how Essbase was different from then-competing EISs. OLAP itself can be further divided into different approaches, either relational (ROLAP), multidimensional (MOLAP), or desktop (DOLAP). These approaches differ in where the aggregations, calculations, and processing are performed. The following table compares some of the vendors and their different approaches to OLAP:

Architecture	Primary Difference	Vendor
ROLAP	Calculations done in a relational database.	MicroStrategy, IBM DB2 OLAP. Microsoft Analysis Services can also act as ROLAP but most often uses MOLAP
MOLAP	Calculations performed in a server-based multidimensional database. Cubes provide write-access for inputting budget data or performing what-if analysis.	Hyperion Essbase, Cognos Powerplay, Oracle Express, MicroSoft Analysis Services
DOLAP	Calculations performed on the desktop or Web midtier to build a microcube. Cubes are read-only.	BusinessObjects/WebIntelligence (WebI)

Data Mining

Data mining is a particular kind of analysis that discovers patterns in data using specific algorithms. Whereas standard query and reporting tools require you to ask a specific question, data mining does not. A famous data mining discovery is that beer and diaper sales are closely correlated; a standard query tool would force a user to ask a more precise question such as, "what do beer consumers purchase in the same store visit?" Data mining is used in predictive analysis, fraud detection, customer scoring, and so on. Business Objects previously sold Business Miner, which used a decision tree algorithm to enable users to mine results from a standard query; this product was discontinued at the end of 2002. With Application Foundation 3.0, released in July 2002, the company embedding stronger mining capabilities from a third-party data mining company, KXEN. Results from other data mining packages, such as SAS and IBM, can also be passed to Application Foundation.

Analytic Applications

Henry Morris of International Data Corporation (IDC) coined the term *analytic application*. For software to be considered an analytic application, it must have the following characteristics:

- It must function independently of the transaction or source systems.

- It must extract, transform, and integrate data from multiple sources and allow for time-based analysis.

- It must automate a group of tasks related to optimizing particular business processes.

The hype around analytic applications has muddied the waters for BI vendors, and each has taken a slightly different approach.

With Application Foundation, Business Objects provides a development platform for companies to build their own analytic applications and management dashboards, specifying their own process rules and best practices. Although analysts like to refer to this as the "build versus buy" approach, I hesitate to use the term "build," as it is reminiscent of developing an application from scratch, coding in a programming language. The "build" approach with analytic applications is more like a "customize" approach in which developers choose objects and templates that generate underlying code. With Application Foundation, the "customized" applications still use the universe, BusinessObjects and WebI report engines to deliver the functionality. In addition, Application Foundation has five integrated analytic engines (Segmentation, Metrics, Rules and Alerts, Predictive, and Statistical Process Control) that allow for more sophisticated analysis.

IDC's Dan Vesset sees the "build" or "customize" strategy as a good one for BI vendors. He explains that analytic applications require a different selling process than straightforward BI tools, requiring much more process- and business-specific knowledge, and are sold directly to the business users. On the other hand, BI tools require less process-specific knowledge and are sold most often to IT. Frank Sparacino of First Analysis, a financial analyst who tracks the BI market for investors, believes "the pursuit of both strategies (buy and build) creates a number of inherent conflicts—for instance, in channel strategy and R&D focus that ultimately limit success.... Business Objects gives a greater focus—the right decision in our mind—on the build option." In 2002, Wayne Eckerson, Research Director for The Data Warehouse Institute, found that 62 percent of surveyed companies plan to build analytic applications, versus 34 percent who plan to buy. The biggest justification for building versus buying an analytic application is to obtain functionality (84 percent) that may not be available in a built application.

In addition to Application Foundation, Business Objects sells four analytic applications (the "buy" approach), all built with Application Foundation: Customer Intelligence, Product and Service Intelligence, Supply Chain Intelligence, and Operations Intelligence. A primary difference between these applications and applications from vendors that provide a buy-only approach is that Application Foundation allows customers to further customize the applications.

The History of Business Objects

Bernard Liautaud and Denis Payre cofounded Business Objects in France in 1990. Denis Payre left the company in 1996, and Bernard Liautaud has led the company since. Business Objects has dual headquarters in both Paris, France, and San Jose, California. While such a multicultural split in headquarters can create a "not invented here" attitude, Business Objects sees its transnational identity as a competitive advantage in a global marketplace.

In 1994, the company had an incredibly successful IPO at 17.5. With multiple stock splits, the stock today would be worth about five times the original IPO (trading at $16). Today, it is traded on both Nasdaq and Euronext Paris.

Customer focus is also one of the company's core values. Every employee's compensation is tied to a customer loyalty index that is measured on a quarterly basis. Since the index's inception in Q3 2001, customer loyalty has improved from 6.9 to 7.4 in Q3 2002. According to Bernard Liautaud, the company currently performs above average and is striving to be the best in the industry. To ensure a good customer relationship, customers with greater than $1 billion in revenue have a direct account manager. Smaller customers are handled through a newly formed General Business Group as well as by Business Objects' certified partners. Technical support is top-notch, with each problem assigned a case number and a priority, determined by the customer. Customers can log a case via a web site, search for similar resolutions, and track progress online. Engineers are quick to follow up even when customers themselves assign the case a low priority. A case can be closed only when the customer is satisfied with the resolution.

With the company focusing on enterprise-wide deployments and sales cycles that can take up to a year, customer loyalty is key. A number of the services that affect customer loyalty, such as maintenance and support, are superb. However, what once was a simple product line now is quite complex, making it difficult for customers to understand why and when they would benefit from new products. As in any company experiencing rapid growth, sales force turnover has been high and will prove a challenge in improving customer loyalty. If newly hired salespeople don't fully understand the Business Objects product line and are on a steep learning curve to build customer relationships, there is potential for missed opportunities on both sides. Business Objects is addressing these issues in a number of ways. First, there is a greater emphasis on hiring salespeople with more business knowledge, not just software experience. Second, new salespeople attend a Business Objects University program that provides training on the company, history, products, and partnerships. Finally, the company also has recently moved from a straight product selling orientation to Solution Selling methodology. This methodology requires the sales force first to focus on critical business issues faced by Business Objects' customers and then to match the products and solutions with the business issues.

Product Innovation

While early client/server computing allowed users to access data with SQL, in 1990, BusinessObjects provided a patented semantic layer that generated the SQL in friendly and familiar business terminology. Unlike in competing tools at the time, the SQL was completely open and could leverage each RDMS vendor's SQL extensions. Over the years, the company has actively sought to protect this patent, filing suits against competitors Brio, Cognos, and MicroStrategy for patent infringement. In 1999, Brio agreed to pay Business Objects a $10 million settlement; Cognos settled in 2002 for $24 million. As of this writing, no trial has been set for the MicroStrategy case.

In 1996, Business Objects completely rearchitected the product to:

- Move from a 16-bit application to 32-bit
- Provide OLAP functionality via a microcube architecture (previously, query results were stored as flat text files)
- Componentize the products to separate universe development, security, query, microcube, and analysis

By all accounts, BusinessObjects 4.0 was a major innovation. Whereas some companies were acquiring technologies to deliver integrated query, reporting, and OLAP, Business Objects was developing them. The company faced intense competition from Oracle, which had just acquired the MOLAP product Express, and Cognos, which had announced plans to integrate Impromptu (its query and reporting tool) with Powerplay (at the time, a desktop OLAP tool). The company rushed the release data and shipped an unstable product. Financial analysts issued stock warnings, and the Gartner Group, renowned for its conservatism and independence, warned customers not to implement 4.0. The product eventually stabilized, and the integration and seamlessness of the rearchitected product has been a key selling point ever since. However, 1996 and the struggles with 4.0 are something the company has not forgotten. Even as Hervé Couturier, Senior Group Vice President Products, demonstrated the prebeta of BusinessObjects 6.0 at the 2002 International User Conference, he firmly declared "the release date will be quality driven."

The dynamic microcube is just one of the Business Objects' breakthrough innovations. Figure 1-6 and the following bullets provide a timeline of some of the company's other major product innovations:

■ **1992**   The Slice and Dice Panel was introduced, allowing users to add multiple sorts, breaks, filters, and calculations through an easy interface as well as to pivot data into a crosstab report.

■ **1993**   Alerters were added to highlight exceptions and provide EIS-like functionality.

■ **1995**   BusinessQuery for Excel allowed users to launch a query directly from a spreadsheet and analyze the results in the spreadsheet.

■ **1996**   BusinessObjects was rearchitected as a 32-bit application and introduced the microcube technology.

■ **1996**   Support was added for Essbase, Metacube, and Oracle Express.

■ **1997**   BusinessMiner was first launched, a data mining product that allowed users to mine query results.

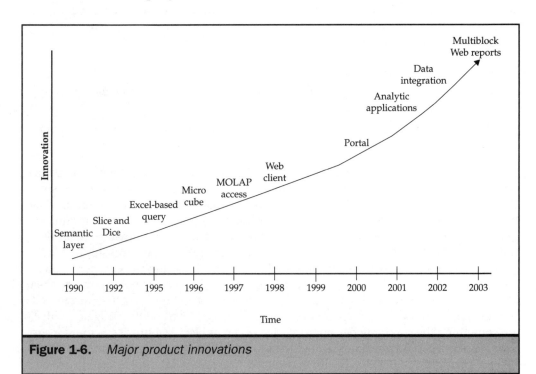

Figure 1-6.   *Major product innovations*

- **1997**   WebI thin client was released in December, enabling e-business intelligence in which customers shared information across an extranet with suppliers and external business partners.

- **2000**   InfoView Portal was released, along with BusinessObjects 5i, which offered full-client capabilities in three-tier mode.

- **2001**   Auditor was launched, allowing administrators to track use of documents, universes, and objects by users and groups.

- **2001**   Application Foundation and BusinessObjects Analytics were launched, providing companies with pre-built applications as well as a development environment for analytic applications that uses the BusinessObjects and WebI infrastructure.

- **2002**   WebI 2.7 was launched, providing thin-client drill-through from summary MOLAP cubes to details in relational databases.

- **2003**   BusinessObjects and WebI 6.0 were released, bringing more parity between the MS Windows and web platforms and offering a zero-footprint client via a D-HTML interface.

Because Business Objects has developed many of its leading technologies, the different products are highly integrated and use a consistent interface. To date, the company has acquired only four companies, all of whom were originally partners:

- **1999**   AnswerSets, later renamed Set Analyzer, was rolled into Application Foundation to enable time series– and set-based analysis, primarily in marketing applications.

- **2000**   OLAP@Work of Ottawa, Canada, offered powerful spreadsheet access and analysis to Microsoft Analysis Services cubes. The product has since been renamed BusinessQuery MD. The technology acquired has improved OLAP access via both BusinessObjects and WebI.

- **2002**   Blue Edge of Leeds, England, specialized in Web-based information delivery. The product, since rebranded and incorporated into BusinessObjects Broadcast Agent, allows personalized reports to be distributed via the Internet as PDF or HTML pages via report bursting. Broadcast Agent Publisher is one of Business Objects' top-selling products.

- **2002**   Acta, because of its ETL tools and packaged data marts, rebranded as Data Integrator and Rapid Marts. Within days of Business Objects' announcement of the acquisition, Informatica subsequently filed a lawsuit against Acta, claiming patent right infringement. The case is not yet settled. Despite the tensions between the two companies, Business Objects still views Informatica as an important partner and plans to continue interoperability (see Chapter 14).

The Future

Although the business intelligence boom of the 1990s has slowed, the business intelligence market continues to grow. Business Objects continues to innovate in several areas. When WebI was first introduced, there was an enormous difference in functionality between the thin client and the BusinessObjects full client. This is in part due to limitations of the Internet and the disparity between the platforms, something that has challenged many BI companies. BusinessObjects and WebI version 6, code-named Tosca, promises to close the functionality gap between the two platforms. The latest version of WebI provides new functionality that previously was available only in the full client:

- Wizards that guide you through report and query creation
- Ability to create formulas and variables
- Multiblock reports to mix tables and charts on one page
- Multiple report tabs in one document
- More powerful graphics and matrix reporting

In addition to bringing more parity between the platforms, WebI 6.0 provides a zero-footprint client via Dynamic HTML query panel, addressing security, and performance concerns, particularly in extranet deployments. Spreadsheet users will love the ability to save a report directly to Excel, with all the original formatting and ability to edit a chart.

Many analysts see collaboration as part of the future of BI. At the 2002 user conference, Business Objects announced and demonstrated a beta version of Sundance, the code name for collaborative business intelligence, expected to be released later in 2003. The goal with Sundance is to align the information practices with the underlying business processes and company initiatives. Upon reviewing a report, users can select from a number of predetermined actions. If monitoring a goal, users can annotate the report or initiate discussion threads for progress against the goal, establish a frequency for future alerts, and define thresholds for exceptions. Product release and launch has not been finalized at the time of this writing but is expected during the first half of 2003.

Besides the company's own innovations, you can expect the Internet and industry standards to continue to drive and enable further innovations. With WebI 6.0, Business Objects leverages third-party application servers. With BusinessObjects 6.0, users can select XML as another data provider. Just a few years ago, these standards did not even exist. In this respect, just as multiple forces led to the invention of business intelligence, so will multiple forces—the BI industry, emerging standards, technology, business events—cause it to continually evolve.

Summary

To borrow a phrase from a data warehouse vendor, business intelligence is not a destination but a journey. As the industry continues to introduce fiercer competition and invite ERP and RDBMS heavyweights, Business Objects will innovate to fortify its market leadership. While this book focuses on the company's core BI products, Business Objects now offers much more, extending its capabilities into ETL on the back end and analytic applications on the front end. Collaboration, which some industry analysts consider a key element to the future of BI, will be added to the product line in 2003. As customers look to buy a full BI solution from one vendor, Business Objects now encompasses the full breadth of a BI infrastructure, entering into what historically has been distinct market segments.

Emerging technologies and maturing Internet standards will also help drive innovation; so will demands from customers. What are the problems that have yet to be solved, and what are the pains not yet articulated? These are questions both you and the vendor must ask repeatedly. A BusinessObjects implementation is a project that you will never finish and is one in which the best you can do is to provide a *starting point* for users to make more informed decisions and discover opportunities. With so much product capability, you must stay focused on the business value of business intelligence. Your challenge will be to understand how the history of business intelligence in your company influences your users' attitudes, understanding, and receptiveness towards BusinessObjects. Perhaps you are still fighting some of the battles of just having implemented a new ERP. Perhaps your initial goal is a modest one of simply weaning users from printed reports to online reports. Perhaps your company will be one of the industry innovators to which many aspire, using BusinessObjects in ways never before anticipated and directly contributing to your firm's market position and profitability. Enjoy the journey!

The
Complete
Reference

Business
Objects

Chapter 2

Goals of Deploying BusinessObjects

Whether you are first implementing BusinessObjects or expanding an existing implementation, it's important to be clear about the goals of your deployment. BusinessObjects is often implemented as part of an IT effort or as part of a specific business initiative. The goals of these two different groups can be quite different. The goals may be driven by the following:

- IT to reduce infrastructure costs, limit custom report development, or replace a legacy reporting system
- A business unit to provide access to data to manage and measure the day-to-day business activities
- The corporation as part of a larger business performance management initiative, as a strategic tool that provides competitive advantage

The goals of different stakeholders may collide and impede progress or merge to make the implementation more successful. You may start out on the implementation with one set of goals only to discover a more important goal as you proceed. In some cases, good scope management will help the project stay on track. In other cases, recognize that business intelligence is not as exact as other technology projects and requires a degree of flexibility. Focusing on the goals of the project will help minimize the risk that the technology and latest product innovations become all-consuming.

IT Goals

Although BusinessObjects provides business insight, it is still a tool purchased primarily by the IT organization. IT controls the source systems and the data warehouse. The challenge here is in making sure the IT goals are a starting point and not an end point. For example, let's assume that your current approach to reports is for a custom programmer to develop them against the source system. The business users are reasonably happy because the report is customized with their view of the data; it's easy (no training required), and it's correct because the data came directly from the transaction system/ERP.

This approach to information access poses several problems:

- The report developer generally has to know the detailed ERP/OLTP schema and programming language.
- The cost to develop and maintain one report is high. Because the report developer is several steps removed from the business, it may take multiple iterations to get the report right. By the time it is right, however, the user requirements change.
- Reporting directly against the OLTP can affect response time both for inputting transactions and for executing a report.

Some users, though, are not satisfied because you can't develop more custom reports fast enough. Your company decides it needs an ad hoc query and reporting tool with the primary goal of reducing the time and cost to develop custom reports. You install BusinessObjects, build a few universes, and train the users on the tool. Users will now be able to create their own reports via BusinessObjects. Goal accomplished?

No. First, the skill set to build a BusinessObjects universe is often quite different than the programming skills to develop an ERP-based custom report. The roles of the existing report developers must be redefined, or they will impede implementation (see Chapter 3, "Influencers"). Is there still a need for custom reports against the ERP? Probably, yes, but ideally for a much smaller number. Second, you just went from a business user's having access to a fixed report (easy to use) to the user's starting at a blank Query Panel with no data. Part of the deployment effort must include replacing existing OLTP-based reports with standard BusinessObjects reports. IT may still develop these initial reports, since they know the data and current reporting requirements, or power users within the business may become the initial report authors. Don't let this step discourage you— providing standard reports with BusinessObjects is a starting point only. It ensures that users do not perceive that BusinessObjects is a step backward: theoretically empowered, but overwhelmed and with no data. At the same time, from the company perspective, it avoids a simple shift of report development costs from IT to the business.

Over time, as both power users and casual users work with the standard BusinessObjects reports, they can move on to modify, customize, and finally, create their own reports. It is this phase of the implementation in which IT realizes the cost benefit (and the business gains a lot of other benefits). Had you stayed in custom development mode, the programmers would still be hardcoding inflexible reports and users would only see a limited amount of data. While the goal to limiting custom report development may not sound as glorious and strategic as "business performance management," it is valid, with a measurable benefit of reduced costs. It also helps get BusinessObjects in the door and up and running. Use it, run with it, and soon it will hold strategic value.

Reporting Directly Against a Transaction System

When you replace custom report development with BusinessObjects, you may reduce report development costs, but you do nothing to improve query response time and transaction system performance. In fact, you run a high risk that you will make it significantly worse. The simple answer is to build a data warehouse or a data mart. After all, the fundamental difference between these two platforms is their sole purpose in life: automating a process versus providing business insight (see Table 1-1). Yet many companies still elect to implement BusinessObjects directly against the OLTP for several reasons:

- **Timing** A data warehouse may be a long-term goal, but in tough economic times, companies need to achieve immediate benefits. They don't have the time or resources to develop an enterprise information strategy. If you just implemented a new OLTP, then you need BusinessObjects reports right now, immediately, not six months from now.

- **Lack of sponsorship** A successful data warehouse project requires strong business sponsorship and agreement across departments and functions. In contrast, OLTP-based reporting is often deemed an IT responsibility, since IT programs the reports. IT can implement and control reporting in this environment, without having to gain the buy-in necessary for a data warehouse; the politics of a data warehouse project are deferred.

- **Cost and complexity** Data warehouse implementations range in price from $50,000 to millions of dollars. Poorly managed projects can take years to achieve measurable benefits, and even well-managed ones will take several months. In addition to selecting a BI tool, you will face a number of other choices in terms of architecture, servers, databases, ETL tools (if not Business Objects' Data Integrator), approach, and design. A data warehouse is a long-term investment, but be careful not to ignore the hidden costs associated with implementing BusinessObjects against the OLTP. Lack of dimensional or cross-functional data may limit the data's usability. The universes will be significantly more complex and take longer to develop, as transformations normally done in the ETL process must be performed to a degree in the universe.

- **Real-time access** In the last couple of years, there has been a lot of hype about real-time BI. Certain technologies allow a data warehouse to be updated in near real time as source data changes. Business Objects Data Integrator uniquely includes real-time BI. For some applications, users may indeed need access to real-time data with data feeds from multiple processes and functions. However, I think real-time BI also touches a nerve with OLTP users who need flexible access to transaction-level data. ERP vendors may excel in business process automation, but they have generally been weak at providing intuitive reporting tools. As long as the transaction processing time does not suffer, it makes perfect sense to integrate BusinessObjects with the OLTP. The vendor provides a number of Rapid Deployment Templates (RDTs) to facilitate this. An RDT is a set of prebuilt universes and reports that understand several leading ERP database schemas. Further, some of BusinessObjects features such as multipass SQL and multiple data providers per report make real-time BI against the OLTP achievable.

Whatever your reason for using BusinessObjects directly against the OLTP, you will need to take some precautions to ensure a successful deployment. Killer queries can cripple a system and prevent orders from being processed. It takes only a few times for this to happen before you will either a) fund a data warehouse or b) limit access to BusinessObjects.

If BusinessObjects is to become a strategic application, you do not want to limit access. However, you do want to deploy in a highly managed way, even more so when you are accessing an OLTP. Pay particular attention to the universe design, ensuring optimal joins and removing the ability to use nonindexed fields as condition objects (see Chapter 8, "Modify a Dimension"). Ensure the standard reports use prompts to limit the amount of data returned and to guarantee that the conditions are based on indexed fields. With custom OLTP reports, each user executes the query, placing an additional load on the OLTP. With BusinessObjects, use Corporate Documents for users to access one prerun report. Use Broadcast Agent to schedule more intensive reports during nonworking hours and Broadcast Agent Publisher to burst reports to individual users. Finally, ensure you use some tracking mechanism, whether the full-blown Auditor or the audit universe (see Chapter 15) to understand who is using certain reports, universes, or objects, and when.

Business Goals

Regardless whether you are starting out with a departmental implementation or with the simple goal of automating a legacy report process, the sweet spot of business intelligence is when it is aligned with the business goals. This is when BusinessObjects is not merely a productivity tool (for example, to get the same data faster) but a strategic tool that measurably affects company profitability, competitiveness, and market share. Even if you start out implementing BusinessObjects to fulfill IT goals, the road does not end there, as shown next. As long as users access BusinessObjects, its uses will evolve. It may take some heated discussions and a few reiterations of the universes, reports, and implementation approach for the goals to become realigned with the business, but eventually they must. That users will discover the value and all the opportunities to use BusinessObjects is not a sure thing. If its implementation is aligned with business goals, there is a higher chance users will be motivated to use it to its fullest potential.

If not, then IT or a business champion must continually promote and educate users on its effective uses (see Chapter 4).

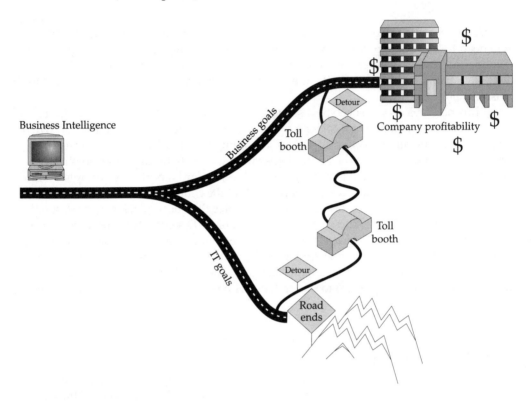

Okay, if you are a project manager or sponsor, then it's easier for you to keep the project aligned with the business goals. If you are a lone power user or universe developer, you may be thinking, "not me, that's for the higher-ups to do!" Perhaps. However, as the BusinessObjects expert, you are best suited to understand how the tool can be leveraged to fulfill the business goals. So often there is a disconnect between the opportunities and the technical capabilities. Keep your ear to the ground, and you will discover the opportunities. Read the company newsletters, and you will discern the company goals and come up with new ideas on how BusinessObjects can help achieve those goals. Most business units have individual business plans. Take a look at them. Which reports can you design to measure implementation of the business plan? Don't forget that some of the world's greatest innovations have come from the rank and file, not the executives!

Given the volume and breadth of data needed to fulfill broad company goals, BusinessObjects is often implemented in conjunction with a data warehouse or data mart. If the data warehouse is being implemented at the same time, many of the business goals in implementing and justifying the warehouse will be the same for implementing BusinessObjects.

The business goals may be fairly broad, such as:

- Stopping blind management without direct access to the data that shows the health of the day-to-day business

- Gaining insight into what was previously a black hole, caused by a closed transaction system that lacks robust reporting capabilities

- Providing data to support company-wide initiatives such as enterprise performance management, business process reengineering, and Six Sigma

Even when the goals are this broad, to achieve measurable benefits, you need to develop more precise goals and tie them in with the BusinessObjects development and implementation. Table 2-1 provides some typical goals by process. With each broad

Process	Goals	Measures
Sales and Marketing	Improve customer loyalty	• Customer sales over time • Customers who buy both products A and B • Customer purchases by channel
	Manage prices	• Price trend over time • Price versus manufacturing costs
	Increase market share	• Revenue versus competitors • Revenue trend versus industry trend
Supply Chain	On-time delivery	• Number/volume shipments shipped by requested data • Number of early, on-time, late orders over time • Inventory levels for top-selling products

Table 2-1.   *BusinessObjects Helps Measure Progress Toward Business Goals*

Process	Goals	Measures
Supply Chain	Low freight costs	• Orders fulfilled from most cost-effective shipping point • Freight costs • Volumes and discounts with freight suppliers
Finance	Reduce aging of accounts receivable Reduce budget variance	• Accounts receivable over time • Actual expense versus budget
Human Resources	Reduce employee turnover Competitive pay	• Employee turnover over time • Salary versus job level, job history, market salaries

Table 2-1.   *BusinessObjects Helps Measure Progress Toward Business Goals (continued)*

goal, as you implement BusinessObjects, identify what information elements help achieve or measure the goal. If the elements are in the data warehouse, then ensure these elements are exposed in the universe along with the necessary dimensions to provide context to the data.

While the goals in Table 1-1 are company-oriented, other business goals may be more narrowly defined yet still provide a measurable benefit. As you implement BusinessObjects in phases or by departments, look to align the implementation with achieving these specific business goals. For example, an oil and gas company wanted to reduce the number of days it took to invoice a customer. As invoicing is a transactional process, the manager never thought to use BusinessObjects to achieve this goal. The BusinessObjects development team modified the universe and created standard reports to provide the department a way of measuring the current number of days between product shipment and invoicing and monitoring that interval over time, by product and plant. In another case, a physical therapy office wanted to understand why it took longer to treat some patients than others. With flexible reports, they explored how multiple diagnosis or injuries affected the number of visits to recover and could better understand which treatments led to the fastest recovery.

In some cases, the elements may not be in the data warehouse, but you can still provide them with BusinessObjects. In this respect, implementing a data warehouse and BusinessObjects simultaneously poses a challenge for the data warehouse not to become a constraint that limits your ability to leverage BusinessObjects functionality.

Just because data isn't in the data warehouse doesn't mean you can't and shouldn't deliver data to users. If it helps achieve a business goal, do it. For example, many companies need access to external market data for benchmarking. Unless the data can be coded to conform to existing dimensions, third-party data often cannot be stored in the data warehouse. BusinessObjects, on the other hand, is much more flexible. It provides a number of ways to incorporate structured or unstructured external data:

- The document domain in the repository allows users to store non-BusinessObjects documents, so if the data comes in the form of an Excel spreadsheet, it can be stored in the repository.

- The microcube architecture allows users to merge corporate data with external data and display the results via one report or chart.

- Universe designers or report authors can embed HTML and web site addresses into standard reports, providing navigation through a thought or problem-resolution process.

- BusinessObjects version 6.0 allows XML as a new data provider.

Designing and building the dimensional models, ETL process, and warehouse infrastructure is resource intensive and complex. Short-staffed and nearing (or past) a project milestone, it's easy to devote 90 percent of the time to delivering the star schemas and only 10 percent of the time delivering BusinessObjects universes and reports. For the business, though, the universe and standard reports are the primary window to the data warehouse. Make it unwieldy and the business will not be able to focus on analyzing data for business benefit; they'll spend an inordinate amount of time figuring out how to use the tool. Fail to provide standard reports or dashboards, and the business may feel nothing was delivered. For each of the business goals, you must develop a corresponding standard report as part of the deployment effort. This standard report may act as a template that users then refresh with their own view of the data, or it may be automatically refreshed and sent to them. Even if you do not purchase BusinessObjects' Dashboard Manager, customizing the portal, My InfoView, can go a long way to providing users a pseudo-dashboard with their standard reports. If you are using the full client, you can leverage categories within Corporate Documents to help users track key indicators.

This all sounds pretty obvious, doesn't it? It should be! The issue is that while these business goals are often used to get project funding, with all the technological and organizational issues involved in delivering BusinessObjects, it's easy to forget why you started on this endeavor. The project team gets so focused on setting up the infrastructure, they leave it for the users to figure out what to do with these newfangled tools. In some rare organizations, where computer and data literacy is high, it may be a valid approach simply to deliver the tools. The business runs with it and exploits the value. Usually, though, users accustomed to no data or to inflexible, custom-developed reports do not immediately know how to approach a flexible BI tool. It's up to you as the BusinessObjects project manager, team leader, power user, or internal expert to show them the possibilities!

Measures of Success

How you measure success is determined, in part, by the goals you wish to achieve. On an intangible level, you know your implementation is successful when there are a number of ways to measure the success of a BusinessObjects implementation:

- People have heard of BusinessObjects (or the name of your BI project/ application).

- The business sees IT as a partner and not as a gatekeeper who holds the key to corporate data.

- Users feel empowered to get to the information they need to do their jobs.

- Analysts feel they spend less time collecting data and more time analyzing data, using it to make informed decisions.

It's a paradox that a tool that allows quantitative measurement of business goals is seldom measured itself. In some respects, this is true of many IT projects in which the measure of success is simply whether the application is delivered on time and on budget. In achieving IT goals, there are a number of ways to measure success:

- Several custom OLTP reports eliminated

- Reduction in IT overtime or contract programmers for developing custom reports

- Elimination of duplicate, competing report systems

- Number of users trained versus number of users who log into BusinessObjects

- Number of queries executed each month

- Number of standard reports accessed

Tip *Refer to Chapter 15, "Monitoring User Activity," for approaches to tracking BusinessObjects usage.*

In measuring achievement of business goals, the great debate is how much can be attributed to implementing BusinessObjects versus other variables that help achieve the goal. For example, in Table 2-1, one of the company's goals is to improve market share. This can be measured by changes in revenue over time or for particular market segments. BusinessObjects provides the *information* to measure progress and to do more targeted marketing. However, *achieving the goal* may require increased promotion, improved product support and innovation, better training of customer service personnel, reduced employee turnover, and so on. Exogenous change may remove a competitor from the market, allowing a company to improve market share without having taken any other action. When several variables contribute toward achieving that goal, then assign a reasonable percentage for how much BusinessObjects contributes toward achieving the goal. In the following table, BusinessObjects contributed 15 percent to increased market share. Is this an exact number? No. Can it ever be precisely measured? No.

Action to Improve Market Share	Percent Contribution
Increased promotion and modified ad campaign	30%
Improved product line	25%
Better employee training, customer service, reduced turnover	30%
BusinessObjects access to information to focus marketing efforts on most likely buyers, ensure order compliance, reduce product defect	15%

Table 2-2.   *BusinessObjects Contributes to the Cost Reduction or Revenue Improvement*

It is merely one measure of success. So if a five-billion-dollar company increases its revenues by 10 percent in an otherwise flat market, you can say BusinessObjects contributed $500,000 toward achieving this goal (10% × $5B × 15% = $500K).

With the more specific goals described earlier, the measure of success may be an improvement over the initial situation. For example, the oil and gas company wanted to ensure customers were invoiced within three days of shipment. If the current average was seven days, how much has the days-to-invoice improved since measuring progress with BusinessObjects? You can convert this goal to a financial impact, as the earlier the invoice is sent, the faster the money can be collected. What is the value of four days' worth of accounts receivable? For the physical therapy office, curing patients in fewer visits increases patient satisfaction and doctor referrals.

Some companies that have implemented BusinessObjects can cite individual cases where BusinessObjects directly affected the bottom line. A manufacturing company used BusinessObjects to do a gap analysis of production costs between two similar facilities; they identified $1 million in operating inefficiencies. Without BusinessObjects, they would not have had the data to identify this opportunity. So perhaps you would say BusinessObjects is 50 percent responsible for the cost savings; the remaining 50 percent can be attributed to eliminating the inefficiencies. The beauty of this example is that the company started implementing BusinessObjects as a follow-on to an ERP implementation. The goal was for IT to eliminate custom, disparate reporting systems, and now, BusinessObjects is a strategic asset that has helped the company achieve a number of business goals and measurable business benefit.

Owens and Minor was one of the early adopters of WebIntelligence (WebI) and is a frequent award winner in the business intelligence industry. As a medical supplies distributor, their data warehouse contains information on suppliers' delivery performance and hospitals' purchasing volumes. By providing both the hospitals and distributors access to this intermediary data, the company attributes $100 million in new business to their BusinessObjects extranet implementation. Their WebI implementation provides a competitive advantage and holds strategic value. Yet, it too had humble beginnings. According to Don Stoller, the director of information management, the original goal was to improve productivity of the field sellers who needed access to information while visiting clients. Four years after the initial WebI implementation, WebI not only offers a competitive advantage but is its own revenue stream, as external customers pay for access.

ROI as a Measure of Success

Return on investment (ROI) is another measure of success and one that is often used to fund the project. While it is fairly easy to measure the cost of the BusinessObjects implementation (the investment portion), it is not easy to measure the return. As you saw in the preceding section, it's debatable how much of a revenue increase you can attribute to BusinessObjects versus other factors. Even when ROI is used to fund a project, companies rarely go back and measure the actual ROI. It is a precise number derived from imprecise inputs. IDC first published a study on the ROI for data warehouses in 1996. IDC determined the average three-year ROI was 401 percent for the 62 projects measured. The Data Warehouse Institute published a study in 2000, showing an ROI of 300 percent. While 47 companies participated in the study, less than a quarter measured ROI. In December 2002, IDC released another ROI study focusing on the value of business analytics, the applications that reside on top of a data warehouse. The average ROI was 431 percent, and the median was 112 percent, with less than a year payback period. Some companies had returns of more than 2,000 percent, and IDC reported that the most successful projects were when the business analytics implementation corresponded with business process improvements.

The ROI being such an imprecise measure, it's not surprising many companies never go back and calculate it for a BusinessObjects implementation. You know your project is successful according to all the other measures of success described in the preceding sections. Nonetheless, it is a number that provides a basis for comparison to other BI implementations and IT initiatives. It also is a measure well understood by finance users, a significant group of BusinessObjects users. In this respect, knowing your approximate ROI is a useful tool in promoting BusinessObjects.

The basic formula for calculating ROI over a three-year period is

ROI = [(NPV Cost Reduction + Revenue Contribution)/Initial Investment] × 100

Net Present Value (NPV) considers the time value of money. In simplistic terms, if the company had one million dollars to deposit in a bank today, next year, assuming a meager five-percent interest, it would be worth $1,050,000. The formula to calculate NPV of a three-year cost or revenue is

$$NPV = F/(1 + r)+ F/(1 + r)^2 + F/(1 + r)^3$$

F is the future cash flow from the cost reductions and revenue contributions. R is the discount rate for your company. Five percent may be the interest a bank is willing to pay, but companies will have a different rate that takes into account the expected return for other investments and opportunity costs from investing in BusinessObjects versus other capital projects.

To take the earlier example of improved market share (Table 2-2), assuming

- $500,000 revenue contribution each year
- $400,000 annual savings by eliminating two custom report programmers @ $2 \times 2,000$ hours $\times$ $100 an hour
- 10 percent discount rate
- $1 million initial investment in hardware, software, training, and consulting to implement BusinessObjects

The projected ROI for a three-year period is

$$223\% = \left[\frac{\dfrac{400,000 + 500,000}{1.10} + \dfrac{400,000 + 500,000}{1.10^2} + \dfrac{400,000 + 500,000}{1.10^3}}{1,000,000} \right] \times 100$$

For additional information on evaluating the ROI for your implementation, William McKnight teaches an ROI course for The Data Warehouse Institute and provides a useful spreadsheet on his web site (www.mcknight-associates.com/downloads). Base Consulting provides a white paper and case study (www.baseconsulting.com) in the resources section of their web site.

The Complete Reference

Business Objects

Chapter 3

Segmenting Your Users

Different types of users will access BusinessObjects. One user may be logged into the system 90 percent of the workday and will actively ask for more data, more resources, faster query time, and more functionality. Another user may never directly log into BusinessObjects yet will make decisions from data delivered through BusinessObjects. Both users are your customers, yet they will have very different needs that affect how you develop, promote, and deploy the various products. Using the marketing concept of customer segmentation will help you determine who your user segments are and how they affect your deployment strategy. Chapter 3 defines possible segments, and Chapter 4 describes what you customize per segment.

What Is Segmentation?

Segmentation is a way of looking at one large user base—let's say, all employees in a company—and dividing it into smaller groups. Each segment, or smaller group, has similar characteristics, needs, or benefits. In different chapters in this book, I refer to two common segments, report authors and report readers. Your company may have more than these two segments. Segmentation provides you a way of better understanding your users and why their requirements are different. It will help you prioritize target user groups and provide the appropriate information and functionality to achieve the highest return on investment. As you define different segments, you will want to tailor your product offering, promotion, implementation schedule, and training for each segment. You also may use the segments to define groups and profiles in Supervisor. Following are some characteristics that will help you segment potential BusinessObjects users.

Computer Literacy Level   Potential users who have worked with personal computers since their inception will greet BusinessObjects differently than someone who only recently received a PC. Users who primarily surf the Web but do not use spreadsheets and other PC-based programs fall somewhere in the middle. With this characteristic, also evaluate a user's *attitude* toward computers. A user eager to learn but still a novice belongs in a different segment than an unwilling user who sees PCs as a waste of time and evil, and who would rather throw the ?@#!!*** thing out the window.

Primary vs. Secondary   Some users log into BusinessObjects to develop their own reports, refresh queries, and interactively analyze the data. These are *primary* users whom you will define in Supervisor and grant access to BusinessObjects resources and software modules. However, you will also have a *secondary* segment of users who consume the information provided by report authors and analysts. These secondary users may never log directly into BusinessObjects; in fact, they may not even know BusinessObjects exists (unless you do some positive promotion, covered in Chapter 4). They know only that they get a number or a report via e-mail or a corporate intranet. For all they know, the data came directly out of one ERP screen. It will be hard for you to estimate the size of this "secondary" user segment, but in many instances, some of your most important customers are in this secondary user segment. Let's say the VP of Marketing receives BusinessObjects-generated PDF files via e-mail on a regular basis. These standard reports are critical for the VP. The VP's administrative assistant is the one who developed the initial reports and scheduled them via Broadcast Agent. The assistant makes sure the reports are generated and delivered as needed. Meanwhile, as more users come onto the system, the Broadcast Agent server is getting overloaded. Some reports run much later than requested; some fail to execute. The primary user, the administrative assistant, may be the one to shout, but it is the secondary user, the VP of Marketing, that can most likely approve funding for an additional server. Also, it is this secondary customer—who has never logged directly into BusinessObjects—who will most likely see the business potential of products you have not yet implemented, such as one-to-one marketing with Broadcast Agent Publisher.

Job Level   A user's job level will affect the breadth of data the user wants to access (number of reports and universes) and the level of detail. Executive-level jobs may need a broad set of data but without a lot of detail. Analyzing the data is a minor part of these jobs, so these may be the people for whom you want to develop a dashboard with key performance indicators. Midlevel jobs may still need a broad set of data but with more detail. The combination of broad data requirements and more detailed data may make it hard to deliver one dashboard. They may need multiple documents and ad hoc access. Entry-level accounts payable clerks or customer service representatives may want to see only very detailed data. As their information requirements are narrow, these users may need one standard report with interactive prompts; they may access BusinessObjects often, constantly refreshing a document for a particular account, customer, date range, and so on.

Job Function   Supply chain users will all have similar information needs, which will be different from the information needs of users in the finance department. Administrative assistants may not be decision makers, but in many companies, their exceptional computer literacy and multitasking skills have led them to become pivotal users of BusinessObjects.

Degree of Analytic Job Content   Some jobs require a significant amount of data analysis. The analytic component also may relate to either the job level or the job function, or sometimes to both. For example, financial analysts may be fairly senior in a business; these jobs have a high analytic component. These are the number crunchers who will pound the system. They understand the different data nuances and even the potential data sources. It's easy to assume that these people are your only users, since they may have solutions implemented first, complain loudest when something is wrong, live and die by access to information, and control the information flow to secondary users. This may in fact be you! With all your demands for access to information, the company rewarded you with being the universe designer, report author, or BusinessObjects subject matter expert. Congratulations! Remember, though, that not everyone can spend all day collecting, manipulating, and exploring data. Some users need access to standard reports simply to know what is going on. They log into BusinessObjects for ten minutes a day (or week) just to make sure the business is running smoothly. If it's not, they call the business or financial analyst to figure out why not. Users whose job content requires a fair bit of data analysis may use more report variables, user-defined objects, drill by, and ad hoc queries; on the other hand, users with jobs with minimal analytic content may only refresh a standard query on a periodic basis.

ERP or Source System Use   Some of your BusinessObjects users may also enter data into the transaction or ERP system. Regardless whether you use BusinessObjects directly against the transaction system or an ERP-populated data warehouse, these users will be more familiar with the precise meanings of individual objects. At the same time, dimensional groupings and hierarchies that don't exist in the source system may be a completely new concept. These users may need additional explanation as to why there is a data warehouse and how the data has been transformed.

Level of Data Literacy   Source system users and users whose jobs have a high analytic content may understand the data well and have a high level of data literacy. However, you cannot assume that users with high levels of data literacy have equally high computer literacy. A transaction system user may know the data but be comfortably entering data only by following the exact same screens every time. Change the user interface and they are lost. Conversely, you cannot assume that users with high computer literacy understand the data well. Although these users may be comfortably learning a new software package, you will still need to devote an appropriate amount of time explaining the dimensions and measures.

Level of Spreadsheet Usage   Spreadsheet users deserve their own segment. They are loyal to the spreadsheet and think everything should be delivered in a spreadsheet. I used to underestimate the importance of this but was cured of my oversight in the early 1990s. After spending months developing a DSS system for a new transaction system, I waited with bated breath finally to train the users. The users balked at these inflexible, ugly mainframe-based reports and asked "Why do we need these reports? Just dump all the data into Excel." Indeed! Fortunately, BusinessObjects has a couple of solutions for these users. New in Version 6.0 is the ability to save a report directly to Excel; the save nicely preserves the charts, formatting, and breaks. BusinessQuery for Excel allows users to execute queries directly from a spreadsheet; it has some built-in features to handle formulas when the number of rows returned changes. If you use MS Analysis Services as an OLAP database, BusinessQuery MD provides the ability not only to retrieve data, but to create calculations and perform server-based rankings. However, running a query from BusinessQuery for Excel can be slower than running a query from BusinessObjects; the issue isn't the SQL, it's the overhead Excel introduces and the additional data/file format conversion. Further, what do users do when they have more than 64,000 rows of data? Is it better to teach these users how to export data or to get them to feel as passionate about BusinessObjects as they do about spreadsheets? Spreadsheet users can't take advantage of breaks; and while Excel may have some good pivot table capabilities, they bear no comparison to BusinessObjects functionality, which automatically adapts when the dimensions and rows change. Even though BusinessObjects offers a number of advantages over a spreadsheet, the issue is simply to recognize that regardless of those advantages, spreadsheet loyalists will want to do their analysis in a spreadsheet. The challenge for you is to recognize this user segment and figure out how best to meet their needs while simultaneously ensuring that the spreadsheets do not get out of hand and become alternative data sources.

Amount of Travel   Certain job types require more travel than others. Some BusinessObjects users may access the system only from their desktop; users who travel may want access via a palm pilot, a notebook computer, or if they travel to other offices, any web browser. They may want information broadcast to them or may want to work in offline mode, exploring previously refreshed queries and drilling in local microcubes.

Implementation Phase   As you ramp up your BusinessObjects implementation, you will offer different users access to the system at different points in time.

Internal vs. External Users   Consider the different needs of employees of the company and customers that you may provide information to via an extranet. Internal employees may be allowed to access whatever software module you have licensed, whereas external customers may not allow applets to cross the firewall, thus encouraging you to publish standard reports to InfoView and view them via HTML. Internal employees may have access to more data, whereas external users will only be allowed to see their data. For these users, you may use the row restrictions and object security levels in Supervisor.

Others Who Affect Implementation Efforts

In addition to your target BusinessObjects users (either primary or secondary), you need to be aware of gatekeepers, influencers, and deciders (Figure 3-1). These people may or may not be eventual BusinessObjects users, but they do affect project funding and your implementation efforts. For each type of stakeholder, I have provided an archetype. The individual job titles and dynamics will vary company to company. The important thing is to recognize that it is more than just the users that affect the success of your implementation and whose needs you must consider.

Gatekeepers

Gatekeepers control access to potential data sources, existing reports, or the users themselves. Gatekeepers can either help your implementation be a wild success or sabotage your efforts. Let's assume you want to use BusinessObjects to access a central data warehouse. IT had a vision of the central data warehouse being used to populate dependent data marts. Unfortunately, due to budget constraints, lack of understanding, and political issues, your individual business unit or function never built a dependent

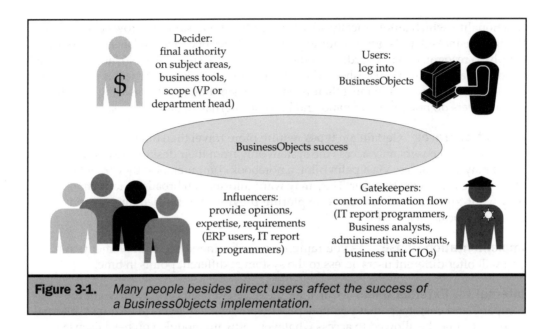

Figure 3-1.   *Many people besides direct users affect the success of a BusinessObjects implementation.*

data mart. The central data warehouse owner/project manager is a gatekeeper. The gatekeeper will either grant you ad hoc access, knowing you will only complain about the lousy response time (that's why they wanted you to sponsor a data mart!) or do everything to impede the BusinessObjects implementation. Thus, the infighting begins. Ideally, the two stakeholders work together to:

- Implement BusinessObjects in a controlled way.
- Understand usage to educate users/sponsors on the value of BI.
- Analyze access patterns and problems to fund and develop the dependent data mart.

The administrative assistant discussed in the preceding major section in connection with primary versus secondary status can also be a gatekeeper. As the BusinessObjects expert, you want to better understand the information flow and business value of the reports the assistant schedules on a regular basis. A conversation with the VP of Marketing would be invaluable. The assistant sees no need for such a meeting (nor does the VP of Marketing, since the VP has never even heard of BusinessObjects), as the assistant can tell you everything you want to know about how the department uses the tool anyway. At this point, you can rely exclusively on the feedback the assistant gives you, or you can ask the assistant for help by having a joint conversation with both the primary and secondary users. To make the BusinessObjects implementation more successful:

- Understand what the gatekeepers want.

- Recognize their efforts and role in the business intelligence process; look for ways to involve them or make them part of the implementation team.

- Identify the mutually exclusive goals.

- Identify the common goals.

- Build allegiances with the gatekeepers so that they work with you, not against you.

Influencers

Influencers are another set of people that affect how well your implementation proceeds. Influencers provide input to your users about how good the product is, whether it will really be useful, and how it is being deployed. The influencers often have some role in an existing reporting process and may have a vested interest in keeping the old reporting process running. They may be source system report programmers, source system experts (why do we need a data warehouse, anyway?), business analysts who have developed departmental databases, and power users. Positive influencers expedite your implementation and provide a lot of positive word-of-mouth promotion. ERP vendors that embed BusinessObjects are positive influencers, as are satisfied BusinessObjects users that were perhaps pilot users during development.

Unfortunately, you may encounter a degree of job protection or "not invented here" syndrome with negative influencers. These are the hurdles to overcome. If a business analyst has spent an inordinate amount of time creating queries to populate departmental databases and spreadsheets, then BusinessObjects will be perceived as a threat. It renders their data sources obsolete. Negative influencers may slow your implementation by seeding your new users with doubt, saying "Look how slow it is! The data is wrong!" For this reason, you need influencers on your side. If they know the data requirements, then get them to have a stake in BusinessObjects' success. While they may be proud of the departmental system they created, they will know too well the manual processes and reconciliation time they go through to keep the data current and accurate. If they cannot be directly part of the project team, ensure they are a focal point for implementation or a designated BusinessObjects expert.

Many companies have more than one BI tool; perhaps because individual departments proceeded with their own initiatives, business units were acquired, or ERP vendors offered an integrated BI tool. Of all the applications IT must deliver, BI standardization is the most contentious (next to spreadsheets, that is). If you are charged with reducing the number of different BI tools and converting users to the corporate standard of BusinessObjects, then the competing BI tool experts will be powerful influencers. They will be the first to spot how their tool is better and argue for standardizing on their BI tool. In some cases, competing BI tools may have better functionality in specific areas, so give them credit and save your breath. If you have followed an objective selection process, explain how the standard was selected, where BusinessObjects is stronger, and why it is a *better fit* for an enterprise-wide deployment (refer to Chapter 1 for some strategic reasons). You may have to do this multiple times before you gain acceptance.

If the decision to implement BusinessObjects as a corporate standard was autocratic, blame the decision maker and march onward. The bottom line is that the measure of success is not who agrees with the decision, but rather, that the standard is adopted and how well you use BusinessObjects to achieve a measurable benefit.

Deciders

Deciders are the final decision makers. A decider may be a project sponsor or an end user or both. Deciders are in a position of authority and can cast the final vote on funding the project, establishing an implementation strategy, or approving the initial set of BusinessObjects tools. In the preceding examples, the decider could be

■ The CIO who overrules the central data warehouse project manager and allows individual business units to proceed with a BusinessObjects implementation, regardless of the existence of a dependent data mart

■ The VP of Marketing who requires all marketing staff to at least be report readers who log into InfoView portal to retrieve their own reports, while the administrative assistant is empowered as a report author

■ The CFO who commits to phasing out the departmental spreadsheets/databases after an agreed-upon period of running BusinessObjects reports in parallel

Pre–business intelligence, I focused on work group computing tools. A new business unit VP was looking to improve productivity and computer literacy. In the late 1980s, this was the first time some people had ever seen a PC. Managers would scribble messages onto pieces of paper that secretaries typed and sent as e-mails. The secretaries printed incoming e-mails and manually distributed them. The new VP instructed managers to do their own e-mails and forbade the secretaries to type or print them any more. His mandate certainly expedited my implementation schedule! People were dismayed and aggravated. He was a decider. After everyone got over the shock of this radical change, productivity and computer literacy improved, and this same business unit eventually became an early adopter of business intelligence tools. I'd like to think that the Internet has drastically boosted everyone's enthusiasm for BI tools and direct access to information, but in those unusual cases where users, gatekeepers, and influencers are resistant to BusinessObjects, it helps to have a strong decider in your corner.

When to Analyze Segments

Ideally, the market segments should be identified early in the development process. As you will see in Chapter 4, market segments help you tailor deployment choices. Failure to agree on the target users or segment can quickly derail your project. As an example, a midsized maintenance supply company started out with a very clear scope: to enable senior marketing people to track monthly gross margin and sales by product, time, and region. They wanted a highly graphical tool with a dashboard. They selected a leading MOLAP and visualization tool, at the time a good decision for this user segment. At some point, field sellers voiced their information requirements. Field sellers needed a different level of detail than the senior marketing people, requiring daily sales figures down to the customer and order number. They didn't want graphics; they needed the detail numbers in a tabular report. Field sellers are a different user segment than senior marketing people, with different needs. Unfortunately, the scope of this project was not well managed. The project manager wanted to be responsive to *all users* and tried to cram a significant amount of detail into one big cube. Neither user segment was satisfied with the end product. Although the project had strong business sponsorship and was driven by business goals, it failed because the target user group was not well understood.

If the market segments had been clearly defined at the project scoping stage, the project manager would have recognized the diverse needs and could have either declared the requirements out of scope or more appropriately matched the solution with each user segment.

Project Roles

To deliver BusinessObjects functionality, the project team should include both IT and business personnel. As discussed in Chapter 1, business intelligence never ends. Therefore, many of these roles will continue beyond the project completion to provide ongoing support.

- **Sponsor**   When business goals drive the BusinessObjects implementation, the sponsor is usually from the business. It may be the CFO if you are trying to measure financial performance, or the VP of Marketing if you are trying to improve customer retention. If the goals of your implementation are IT-related (see Chapter 2), then the sponsor may be a senior person in the IT organization, such as the CIO, ERP manager, or data warehouse manager. The sponsor provides the funding for the project and resolves any scope issues the project team cannot resolve themselves.

- **Program manager**   The program manager ensures that BusinessObjects is deployed consistently across multiple projects and applications. The program manager sets the priorities for projects that vie for the same resources.

- **Project manager**   The project manager controls the budget, resources, and time to implement BusinessObjects. The project manager ensures that the deliverables are within the agreed-upon scope of the project and that the project stays focused on the intended goals.

- **Supervisor**   A supervisor defines users to BusinessObjects and grants access to the BusinessObjects universes, document domains, and software modules. It is primarily a security function that can be centralized or decentralized to allow one supervisor for each department or function. The supervisor must understand the data sources and software modules available, as well as staying informed about personnel changes to revoke or add access when employees change departments. The Supervisor module of BusinessObjects enables you to create profiles to add or remove functionality. These profiles should correspond to the different user segments you've identified.

- **Universe designer**   The universe designer provides the business view to the relational data in a transaction system or a data warehouse. The designer must understand SQL from a query and analysis viewpoint, database performance issues, and business requirements. It can be a challenge to find one person with these diverse skill sets. Some companies will train business analysts or power users in the more technical skills, finding this an easier approach than trying to teach an IT developer the business skills. The technical aspects required to build a universe sometimes lead a DBA to become the universe designer. The role of universe designer can also be split between two people, one who physically develops the universe and another who ensures the universe fulfills the business requirements. With larger deployments, there may be several designers across the organization, one for each business unit or function. In these circumstances, it's important to have an "ultimate" designer or quality assurance process to ensure the universes are deployed consistently (see Chapter 15, "Quality Assurance Check List").

- **Report author/pilot user**   A report author is typically a power user who both understands the data and is computer literate. Report authors may be business analysts who require ad hoc access to information or who previously created and maintained departmental data sources. Administrative assistants who are computer literate and who provide printed reports or compiled spreadsheets may also become report authors. When first deploying a new universe, pilot the universe with report authors. Not all users will be report authors.

- **Report readers**   Report readers access fixed reports that may include prompts to filter the data; report authors may prepare and distribute reports to readers via e-mail, the intranet, and so on. Report readers may not have a high degree of computer or data literacy, or the job type may have minimal information requirements.

- **BusinessObjects expert**   BusinessObjects experts know the end-user tool set and the different modules available, but they do not necessarily understand the data. They are good with software. Report authors may become BusinessObjects experts as they work more with the tool.

- **Data expert**   A data expert may be a business analyst, data modeler, or source system expert who knows where the data comes from, the quality of the data, and its different meanings. The data expert may not necessarily use BusinessObjects but can help resolve data discrepancies that are discovered when users start analyzing it with BusinessObjects. A data modeler designs the underlying star or snowflake schema in a data warehouse or data mart. That person can provide expertise on advanced business calculations and certain universe components such as aliases and shortcut joins. When you introduce aggregate awareness into the universe, the data modeler provides the dimensions by which to aggregate.

- **Database administrator (DBA)** A DBA may be the universe designer or may review the universe for optimal SQL. DBAs resolve query performance problems, build aggregate tables, or correct password synchronization problems between different data sources. The DBA will also help decide the technical deployment of the BusinessObjects repository.

- **Administrator** You may have a BusinessObjects administrator who installs and maintains the software applications (WebIntelligence, BusinessObjects, Broadcast Agent, Application Foundation, and so on). In small deployments, the BusinessObjects administrator and the designer are one and the same. In larger deployments, there may be multiple administrators. Whereas universe designers require a business background and SQL skills, administrators require more technical skills and may be systems engineers. In addition to software issues, the administrator deals with server performance and load balancing.

- **Trainer** The BusinessObjects trainer knows both the software and the data to a degree. Often, two people may provide the training to cover these two different aspects. Internal BusinessObjects experts may train end users, or they may use a Business Objects training partner.

- **Communication/marketing specialist** This person provides expertise on effective ways to communicate project plans, deliverables, and goals to the different user segments. He or she may write or review articles for company newsletters, coordinate internal user conferences, design logos used in project gifts or application screens, and help ensure that key messages are stated in terms of business benefits rather than technical features.

Summary

Segmentation is a way of grouping your users according to their needs and skill sets. These groupings will help you tailor deliverables and messages. Certain user groups will want only standard reports on an intermittent basis; others will need the flexibility of ad hoc access on a daily basis. Not all users will greet BusinessObjects with enthusiasm. Understanding these users' roles and objectives can help you minimize their disruption to your implementation efforts.

Chapter 4

Marketing BusinessObjects

In looking at the chapter title, you might respond, "Marketing BusinessObjects? That's something the vendor does! Nothing to do with my implementation." It's got everything to do with your implementation and is the one technique that will help you boost usage, user satisfaction, and ROI with little to no cash investment. It does, however, require an investment in attitude and in making sure a marketing approach gets incorporated into your project plan.

Many people assume they do not need to market BusinessObjects. It's easy to assume the tool should sell itself, especially if you are implementing it in response to users' requests. Keep in mind, though, that only a handful of users may have specifically requested BusinessObjects and been involved in the tool selection. For all the other users, you need a strategy of defining what you will deliver and how you will communicate those deliverables to your different user segments.

At the 2002 BusinessObjects user conference, participants said getting business users to use the data warehouse already built was their number one priority. Developing a marketing plan can help you achieve this goal. Still not convinced? In this chapter, I'll describe one case in which a marketing approach helped boost BusinessObjects usage five-fold within a three-month period. Marketing can be an uncomfortable concept for many IT people, so enlist help from your company's internal marketing or public relations department.

When to Develop a Marketing Plan

When I tell people I teach a course on marketing the data warehouse, they often laugh and say, "What's to teach? Marketing means just say yes." Ever the gullible consumer, I respond with, "That's selling!" Perhaps it's a minor distinction. The essence of marketing is understanding what users want and developing what they want. This sounds like the mantra of many IT organizations who want to be more aligned with the business. A marketing plan can give you the techniques to better accomplish this dialog and level of understanding. At a minimum, a marketing plan will help you develop a communication strategy and manage user expectations.

Therefore, you want to draft a market plan early in the project, often before project funding. A marketing plan will help you articulate what you intend to deliver and why. As discussed under "Product" in this chapter, a marketing approach ensures you get used to describing what you deliver in terms of the *benefits*, not the *features*. This difference in emphasis makes the funding and implementation process easier. What would your project sponsors rather invest in:

- **Feature** A three-tier BI tool
- **Benefit** A BI tool that will help improve profitability

As you develop the data sources and universes, and as you architect the BusinessObjects deployment, update the marketing plan to reflect changes in functionality. As you work with users to define requirements and preview the universe/reports/ training materials, gauge which elements of the plan are effective.

Elements of a Marketing Plan

A marketing plan consists of the following elements:

- **Situation analysis** Covers your current situation; offers competitive analysis; and includes a strengths, weaknesses, opportunities, and threats (SWOT) analysis.

- **Marketing mix** Involves the four Ps of marketing: product, price, promotion, and place.

- **Customer segments** Defines your user communities. Divide your users into different groups as described in Chapter 3. Once you have determined your user segments, tailor the marketing mix (product, promotion, price, and place) to each segment.

- **Objectives** Includes how you will measure your marketing and project effectiveness. Some of this may involve measurement of the goals described in Chapter 2, or it may include the marketing objectives: number of users trained, number of promotional efforts, and so on.

Situation Analysis

What is the current situation in your company? Have you just begun implementing BusinessObjects, or has it been available for a while but your implementation efforts have stalled? Are you trying to standardize on BusinessObjects, although you have multiple BI tools? If you have only just begun to implement BusinessObjects, then the current situation may describe the following:

- How users currently access information. Is information contained only in the transaction system, or have departments created their own spreadsheets and databases?

- How information is shared and distributed throughout the organization

- If you develop custom reports, the number of existing reports and the time backlog to fulfill new requests

- Attitudes toward the existing information flows. Are users frustrated, or do they think it's generally okay?

If BusinessObjects has been used in the company for a while, the current situation addresses

- What data sources are available and which universes are in use

- How much users create their own reports or the degree to which standard reports have been used

- Typical query response time

- System availability

■ Number of defined, trained, and active users

■ Product architecture and end-user tools to access the data (BusinessQuery for Excel, WebI, InfoView, BusinessObjects, PDF reports, corporate intranet, Application Foundation, and so on)

■ The degree to which the universe and standard reports can answer common business questions versus users having to create user-defined objects and report variables

■ User satisfaction with the current situation

Even if BusinessObjects is the only BI tool in your company, it faces competition. Your job is to identify and understand the competition to articulate why BusinessObjects is better. Recall from Chapter 1 the history of business intelligence. You are trying to change years of decision-making processes within a short time frame. Resistance to change is an automatic barrier. Users may be accustomed to accessing information via paper-based reports, hand-delivered to their desk. When information is difficult to get to, gut-feel decision-making is the competition. If you are deploying BusinessObjects against a data warehouse, then the ERP or transaction system may be the competition. If you are trying to get decision-makers to retrieve their own reports or to access key indicators via a dashboard, the competition is the phone call to a business analyst or to an assistant who can print the reports for them.

A SWOT analysis (strengths, weaknesses, opportunities, and threats) is an effective tool in evaluating the current situation in terms of BusinessObjects' internal competition. It is also a necessary first step in determining what product capabilities you can and should deliver and what benefits you will emphasize in promotions. Tables 4-1 and 4-2 give two sample SWOT analyses. The first one is a for a young data warehouse

SWOT	Analysis
Strengths	• Universes are small and focused, with access to global data.
	• Business definitions are consistent.
	• Self-serve access is available.
Weaknesses	• Queries are slow.
	• New terminology from a recent ERP implementation is confusing to users; universes contain no bridge to old transaction system terminology.
	• Standard reports are unavailable. The budget and IT mandate was to build the universe; users must develop their own reports.
	• The data warehouse is updated weekly; users want daily updates.

Table 4-1.   *SWOT Analysis for New Data Warehouse and BusinessObjects Implementation*

SWOT	Analysis
Opportunities	• Create summary table in data warehouse; include aggregate awareness in universe design to improve query performance. • Implement Broadcast Agent for scheduling slow queries. • Update objects' descriptions and modify training materials to bridge new and old terminology. • Ensure standard user reports are available via Corporate Documents; distribute some via intranet or e-mail. • Evaluate target user group, business goals for daily updates.
Threats	• To avoid slow response time, the department assistant prints reports and manually distributes them. • Another department is implementing a MOLAP server for faster queries, with a different BI tool.

Table 4-1. *SWOT Analysis for New Data Warehouse and BusinessObjects Implementation* (continued)

SWOT	Analysis
Strengths	• Complete data with three years of history is available. • A number of initial ETL problems have finally been resolved. • There are multiple subject areas.
Weaknesses	• Queries are slow. • The large universe is unwieldy for users to navigate. Users can create incorrect queries when they use the wrong object.
Opportunities	• Evaluate universe joins to improve query response time. • Evaluate the indexing strategy in data warehouse for most frequently used access paths. • Promote resolution of ETL problems and improved data quality. • Create smaller, more targeted universes.
Threats	• Since users perceive the data warehouse is always wrong, custom reports continue to be built against the ERP. • To avoid slow response time and the unwieldy universe, business units extract data into multiple MS Access databases and create custom Visual Basic front ends.

Table 4-2. *A Mature Data Warehouse and BusinessObjects Deployment that Has Stalled*

deployment in which BusinessObjects is not the only BI tool. The second one is for a mature BusinessObjects deployment that has stalled.

The goal with the situation analysis is to understand where you are today so that you can identify opportunities for improvement over the current situation and/or the competitive information sources. In both SWOT analyses, slow queries are a weakness that has caused a number of threats. Slow queries can be a major barrier for a successful implementation. In DataPro's 1999–2001 Business Intelligence and Data Warehousing User Survey, users rated performance as more important than ease of use when selecting a BI tool. I'm not surprised. Prior to BusinessObjects, users got their reports "instantaneously" via a DSS or a spreadsheet or a printout. Okay, so the data may have been stale or inaccurate, but users weren't twiddling their thumbs waiting for a query to execute. With the ever greater immediacy the Internet provides, users will want to wait even less time to refresh a query.

While it is true that the majority of response time issues can be blamed on the data warehouse and not specifically on BusinessObjects, failure to fix these problems directly affects the success of BusinessObjects. Users will blame the tool they see, not the technology behind the scenes. Further, while it is up to the DBA to ensure the database is well-tuned with efficient indexes and summary tables, it is up to the universe designer to leverage them. Ensure universe objects frequently used in conditions do not contain advanced SQL commands that cause the index to be bypassed. Report authors must ensure standard reports use condition objects from indexed fields. When you can't improve the data source performance, then use other deployment methods to bypass the problem. Use Broadcast Agent to schedule and distribute reports. Based on the SWOT analysis in Table 4-2, implementing a MOLAP source may be a good approach for response time issues as well as complex calculations. But is the additional BI tool also a right choice, or is it simply an oversight that BusinessObjects or WebIntelligence (WebI) is not being used as the front-end tool to the MOLAP database?

In Table 4-2, one of the identified weaknesses was a large, unwieldy universe. Even IT professionals struggled to know which object to use when. Once the deployment team developed a more targeted universe, offered some standard reports, and promoted the resolutions and enhancements, usage increased significantly within a short period.

Marketing Mix: The Four Ps

Marketing mix is a set of interdependent tools for increasing BusinessObjects usage and the impact it has within your company. If you speak to one of your internal marketing experts, he or she may give you a couple more Ps to add to the mix, but for business intelligence the most important Ps are product, price, promotion, and place.

Product

If you think the choice of product is predetermined (BusinessObjects or WebI), think again! In some circles and with some user segments, these product names may have meaning and recognition. Many business users, however, have never heard of them. In this respect, you will have to repeat, within your own organization, all the selling Business Objects the company had to go through to persuade you to buy their tool set.

As you do so, focus as much as possible on the *benefits* your implementation will deliver, not the technical *features* of the products. Consider some of the products you buy as a consumer. For example, Disney World emphasizes the magic and memories (the benefits), not the number of rides and attractions (the features). Particularly with business intelligence, a number of technical features will have little meaning to users, yet clearly, IT professionals are comfortable focusing on features. Restating the features in terms of the benefits is one of the hardest language barriers for the project team to overcome. Table 4-3 highlights some features that are better described to users in terms of the benefit they provide.

In a few instances, the feature and related benefit will be clear; but these instances are in the minority. For example, if you emphasize the ability to create graphs, spreadsheet users who have used graphs in their analysis will recognize that graphs provide the benefit of visual analysis and a faster ability to spot trends, problems, and opportunities. When you buy a car, you know that four-wheel or front-wheel drive (feature) will allow you to control your car better in snow (the benefit). When the benefit is not immediately clear, document it as part of your project plan. Then have the project team practice articulating the benefits so that they 1) stay focused on why you are implementing BusinessObjects and 2) can more effectively promote your efforts in both formal and casual conversations with users.

Feature	Benefit
Aggregate awareness	Fast queries
Corporate documents repository	Immediate access to key performance indicators; one version of the truth with no loss in time reconciling different reports
Offline access	Ability to work with reports while on the plane or at a customer site
Ad hoc queries	Explore the root cause of a problem, without waiting for an IT report developer
Exception-based reporting	Proactively manage the business when indicators fall below a certain threshold; fix a problem before it is out of control

Table 4-3.   *Emphasize Benefits, Not Features*

A second aspect to the product component of the market mix is, what will you call the product? Will you refer to it by the vendor-provided product names, or will you give it a different name that also reflects the business goals and data sources? The benefit of including the vendor-provided name is that you can leverage some of the vendor's marketing efforts. The downside is if the vendor changes product names, it can cause confusion. If you are suffering from a stalled implementation or if there were negative impressions early in the implementation, change the name! When you develop your own BI product name, be sure to consider the acronym created. If it is a global deployment, take into account the cultural impact of acronyms. Following are some clever product names:

- **WISDOM**   WebIntelligence Supporting Decisions, from Owens & Minor
- **OASIS**   Online Analysis Sales Information System
- **Risk Intelligence**   Used by Zurich North America for insurance claims and losses
- **Inventory Workbench**   Used by Lands' End for inventory information delivered via Application Foundation

Price

Internal pricing with business intelligence tools depends in large part on what you have done in the past with reporting systems and what you do with other information systems. Many companies do not charge end users for using BusinessObjects. It is reflected as an indirect cost, part of corporate overhead. Some companies will charge a flat fee when a user is first granted access to BusinessObjects or WebI. This approach may help you manage the implementation to ensure that the people who need access the most will also pay for it. However, let's assume your company has already bought 1,000 licenses. The company has already incurred the expense. Re-charging business units may help move the costs from the IT department to the business unit, but it has no material effect on company expenses. Your goal is to get the information closer to the decision-makers. You also need to recover your expenses, so you charge per trained user. This per-user fee may inadvertently cause the business unit manager to restrict the number of BusinessObjects users. Their budget is tight; they need to control expenses, no matter that it has no effect on company cash flow. The business stays stuck in the information flow of one central person running and distributing reports. The pricing strategy just caused you to fail to bring the information closer to the decision-maker.

Although BusinessObjects Auditor allows you to create reports for billing, the risk with direct charges that relate to usage is that you may also inadvertently discourage usage. The more expensive it is to analyze data, the less likely users will explore information. In determining a direct-billing approach, you need to evaluate how advanced your company is in terms of information literacy and where you want to get to. If the data warehouse or WebI servers are overloaded, then charging for usage may help you recover costs to pay for increasing capacity. If the servers are underutilized, don't charge by usage.

Companies are more likely to charge directly when the customers are external. Owens & Minor, for example, charges customers for access to WISDOM. Here, WebI is a source of revenue and the charges indicate WISDOM has exceptional value; if Owens & Minor offered it as a free service, customers might not have appreciated its value. An insurance company told me they began charging external customers only when they moved from mainframe reports to a data warehouse. Customers balked. They had never paid for reports in the past, why should they pay now? It didn't matter to them that they finally had more data and more flexibility than before. Nobody likes a price increase, especially if it has been forced upon them. If users had a free DSS or mainframe reports before, then don't charge for access to fixed reports. You can deploy the reports via InfoView, or you can create two different user profiles via Supervisor (see Chapter 12) for fixed reports versus ad hoc functionality. Charge only the ad hoc user group for the increased functionality.

Place

Place is where you deliver BusinessObjects or the reports. Somehow the place is a seldom-considered aspect of a business intelligence project, yet it is a component of the marketing mix that greatly affects which of the vendor's products you use. Table 4-4

Place	Product or Functionality
Palm pilot or other hand-held device	InfoView Mobile
E-mail with generic report	BusinessObjects, File | Save As | PDF
E-mail with personalized report	Broadcast Agent Publisher
Corporate intranet	BusinessObjects, File | Save As HTML; Broadcast Agent with reports distributed to a web server
Disconnected notebook	BusinessObjects offline mode
Web browser	InfoView, Application Foundation
Work group directory	BusinessObjects, File | Save As; Broadcast Agent with reports distributed to a network server
Remote dial-in	BusinessObjects with Citrix, or WebI
Corporate extranet	InfoView or WebI v6, HTML Report Panel

Table 4-4. *Place Affects Which Products You Deploy and How*

lists some of the places you may deliver standard reports or interactive analysis; each of these places affects the product functionality you will teach the users as well as the vendor products you choose to deploy.

Promotion

Many BI deployments focus on the product and capabilities they want to deliver and pay little attention to promotion. The project team, staffed primarily with IT people, focuses on development efforts and not on the promotion activities that should accompany an implementation plan. Changing from an old reporting environment or decision-making process to a new one requires promotion.

Users will go through an evolution as you promote BusinessObjects. During the funding and development stages of the project, you want to build *awareness* about what is coming. You want everyone—not just the power or primary users described in Chapter 3—to have heard of BusinessObjects or your BI product name. As you get closer to delivering capability, you want to increase *knowledge* as your target user segment learns when and how to use BusinessObjects. The third phase of promotion is to increase *usage,* in which people within all levels of the organization are *aware* of BusinessObjects, *know* when to use it, and *use* it as an invaluable tool to achieve business goals. You may use different media to achieve these different promotional stages. Different user segments will be at different stages simultaneously.

When to Promote

There is a comfort in waiting to promote BusinessObjects only when you are finished with the first phase of your BI development. If you wait until then, however, you are starting too late and it will take you longer to achieve any measurable benefits. Users must be aware of BusinessObjects long before they sign up for a training class. Clearly, you need to manage user expectations and not promise more functionality than what you can deliver. In early promotions, emphasize the high-level benefits, implementation waves, and broad time frames. Battered IT departments who have been criticized for being late in the past may truly cringe at this approach. I understand. I dreaded handing out promotional material on this book at the user conference, a full three months before I was due to finish writing it! Seeing the book already on Amazon.com while I am still writing the final chapters is enough to induce a panic attack. However, in order to build demand and excitement, you must promote early, well before you are ready for deployment. How far in advance did Business Objects begin promoting version 6? Months! Hervé Couturier, Business Objects VP of Products, demonstrated the pre-beta in front of thousands of users and appropriately likened the experience to bungee jumping. Yet these early promotions of a new product generated demand and excitement. He gave no exact release dates, so expectations were well managed. You don't have to *like* promoting early, but you do have to do it.

Key Messages

When you promote your BI solution, develop key messages that emphasize the benefits, not just the features. Look to emulate some of the most effective promotional campaigns, as shown in the following table. Business Objects recently trademarked their key message "Business Intelligence. If you have it, you know" and emphasizes "turning knowledge into information into profit" in many of their promotional media. The key messages you develop will depend a lot on the situation analysis. If users currently have to wait months to receive a custom report, a key message may be "information now." If one of the goals is to retain customers, a key message may be "helping you know our customers." If users access paper-based reports and there is a low level of computer literacy, then a key message like "good-bye paper-based reports" may cause a panic.

Product	Benefit	Key Message
Ford Trucks	Rugged enough to go anywhere	"Built tough"
Calgon Bath Crystals	Relaxation	"Calgon, take me away"
Bounty Paper Towels	Clean spills fast with fewer towels	"The quicker picker upper"
Miller Lite	Drink more beer	"Tastes great, less filling"
7-Up	Clear, refreshing, different from cola	"The un-cola"

Promotional Media

Choose the media according to the desired promotional frequency and target user segment. Promotion is not something you do once, but rather, it requires repetition. Do you ever see a commercial one time? No, you see and hear the same messages in magazines, on TV, and on radio. Remember, the goal with promotion is to move people from *awareness* of BusinessObjects to *usage*. It will take a number of repetitions, with different messages and media to get there.

Recall from Chapter 3 that only a portion of BusinessObjects users may actually log into the repository. Therefore, if you use the universe description or an InfoView sign-on page as your main communication medium, the message will not reach many user segments. You need an alternative medium such as staff meetings, newsletters, or e-mail campaigns to reach these secondary users.

Time your promotion efforts to certain project milestones. For example, if you give T-shirts away as project awards, have the team wear their T-shirts when you release a new universe or complete a software upgrade.

- **Road shows** When companies first start developing a business intelligence solution, many have corresponding information sessions about what is coming, when phase 1 will be available, and who will be trained first. The most successful "road shows" include business success stories and user testimonials on how BusinessObjects has had a measurable impact. For example, BlueCross BlueShield of North Carolina has an established data warehouse and BusinessObjects implementation. Even with a mature deployment, they still do two road shows a month for new groups of users. Their implementation is so successful that the project team is often now invited to speak at staff meetings to tell people about new functionality and how business units are benefiting from business intelligence.

- **Video** Some companies have created videos to use at road shows or staff meetings. The video may show the CEO, the project sponsor, or a business user giving a testimonial as to how BusinessObjects helps the business. While a video may be difficult to produce at first, it helps reduce travel costs and logistic issues in always getting the right people together.

- **Company newsletters** Existing corporate newsletters are excellent media for high-level messages to a broad audience. Given the readership of company newsletters, the primary purpose of these articles is to build awareness, not necessarily usage. These articles should include information about the business goals and project milestones. You do not need to get too detailed about functionality.

- **Industry journals** Companies often seem to have the attitude that user conferences and articles in industry journals help the careers of the project staff and not necessarily the company. Not true! Owens & Minor has received a number of industry awards, something that helped create enthusiasm internally and helped them win new contracts. As another example, my mother is the quintessential bargain-shopper, and I seem to have inherited her skill when it comes to rental cars. For me, the only way to find a rental car is to compare all the prices online, then dig through junk drawers to find stray coupons. After a few bad experiences in which I waited as long for a rental car as my flight time, I came across an article on how Avis is using business intelligence to improve customer service and loyalty. I do have an affinity to any company that uses business intelligence effectively, so I gave them a try and now I'm hooked. I went from standing in line, waiting up to an hour for a car, to being greeted with a smile, addressed by my name (instead of a gruff "NEXT!"), and driven directly to a warm, running car. This same level of service has been repeated at multiple airports. Avis didn't gain me as a customer by an advertisement, but rather, by an article about their business intelligence implementation in a business journal. Did this article help the careers of the development team? Perhaps, but it also directly added to the company's market share. There are a number of ways to get your project into an industry journal. You can author an article. You can volunteer to be interviewed by Business Objects for a press release. Your company's public relations department can issue a press release either to technical journals such as *Computer World, DM Review, Intelligent Enterprise*, or if it has more of a business slant, to industry journals.

- **Training classes** Training sessions should go beyond the straight how-tos and address the benefits and business application of the data and of sharing information. Some companies use a game-style approach to training to generate enthusiasm. For example, one company regularly holds group workshops in which they divide the group into two teams. There is a question and answer session in which the two teams compete to share tips and best practices.

- **Brown bag lunches**   A brown bag lunch is a casual information sharing session in which participants bring a bagged lunch and discuss BusinessObjects or the data warehouse. A facilitator may start the lunch with a success story, tip, or project update. These provide a useful follow-up to training and another opportunity to raise awareness about best practices, success stories, and benefits. In the earlier SWOT analysis, Table 4-2, one of the strengths was that the data warehouse was mature and a number of initial ETL problems had been resolved. In this same company, the data warehouse project team communicated each resolution via e-mail. Users became desensitized to repeated e-mails and no longer trusted the integrity of the data warehouse. They were convinced that if they used BusinessObjects again, they would find still more errors. It took several face-to-face discussions during brown bag lunches and a comparison of BusinessObjects reports with ERP-based reports to acknowledge the historical problems, explain how the problems had been resolved, and motivate the power users to trust the new reporting environment.

- **Internal user conferences**   Just as Business Objects and regional user groups host periodic user conferences, do the same in your organization. Kick off the meeting with a review of the benefits, project milestones, and a key success story. Then ask users to share tips and techniques on both the how-to of BusinessObjects and how it has helped them achieve business goals.

- **T-shirt days**   Many project teams give away T-shirts, sunglasses, and other promotional items to reward staff for their accomplishments. As both a motivational technique and a promotion opportunity, get the entire team to wear their giveaway on milestone dates. This works particularly well if the T-shirt is brightly colored. Seeing 50 yellow T-shirts in the company cafeteria will generate interest and curiosity about what's new.

- **Intranet**   The InfoView portal and universe description may be useful for promoting to existing users and keeping them informed; however, they are poor media for secondary and potential users. Secondary and potential users do not log into InfoView or BusinessObjects, so they will never see these messages. You can best reach these users through staff meetings and company newsletters. For primary users, the intranet and universe descriptions are ideal places to repeat key messages and project goals.

- **Staff meetings**   Most departments and business units have regularly scheduled staff meetings. Ask for five minutes on the agenda each quarter to give an update on new deliverables, problem resolution, and how other departments are benefiting from BusinessObjects. A real sign of success is when the department invites you and requests 30 minutes!

Approaches to Training

As you define your user segments, tailor the training accordingly. For report authors, you may have classroom or computer-based training; for report readers, training may consist only of a cheat-sheet with the quick steps to refresh a report. Following are some additional things to consider in developing a training approach:

- **Data vs. the tool**   A BI tool delivers no value without the underlying data users wish to analyze. If you train users only on BusinessObjects with the sample databases, users may not be able to translate the skills to their own data sets. Training users on their own universes and reports may be a logistical challenge if you don't have a sufficient number of users with common universe needs to fill a class. In these cases, you may want to offer tool training separately from data training. The bottom line is that you must do both, particularly for users who will create their own reports. Users who only refresh reports may not need data training, as in their view, there is only one meaning for an object.

- **Internal vs. third-party**   Business Objects and a number of certified training partners will train end users on the software. Some will customize the training material to include your universes, reports, and data in the screen shots. You also can buy the training material from Business Objects and incorporate your own screen shots.

- **Training method**   While classroom-style training is the most traditional, it can pose a logistical challenge when users are at different sites and have busy schedules. Some users may do quite well to read a book and then supplement that with computer-based training, on their own schedule and at their own pace. BusinessObjects Enterprise Desktop Education and Personal Trainer both offer computer-based training. Enterprise Desktop Education allows you to integrate your own data. Personal Trainer covers both WebI and BusinessObjects; however, it does not allow you to integrate your own data.

Regardless of the formal training method, for a successful implementation you must supplement scheduled training classes with other means to share tips, techniques, and uses.

Customizing per Segment

Chapter 3 defines different ways of segmenting potential users; this chapter covers developing a marketing strategy for BusinessObjects. Now you need to tie the two together and tailor the marketing strategy to each user segment. Table 4-5 shows three potential user segments. Table 4-6 shows how you would customize the marketing mix according to these segments.

Segment Characteristics	Accountant	VP Marketing	External Customer
Computer literacy level	High	Moderate	Unknown
Primary or secondary	Primary	Secondary	Primary
Job level	Mid	Upper	Unknown
Analytic job component	High	Low	Unknown
Spreadsheet user	Yes	No	Unknown
Amount of travel	Minimal	High	Minimal

Table 4-5. *Potential User Segments*

Marketing Mix	Accountant	VP Marketing	External Customer
Product(s)	BusinessObjects	InfoView, exception reports from Broadcast Agent	WebI
Product benefits to emphasize	Access to any information, ad hoc reporting	Monitor key indicators	Manage costs
Price	Overhead cost	Overhead cost	Per-report fee
Place	Desktop	PDA	Browser
Promotional media	E-mail, internal user conferences	Staff meetings, corporate newsletters	Fact sheet, site visit from salesperson
Training approach	Classroom, books	Reference card	Reference card

Table 4-6. *Customized Marketing Strategy per User Segment*

Summary

Applying a marketing strategy to your BusinessObjects implementation will help you speak the language of business users and speed your success. Marketing and promoting your efforts and accomplishments can be uncomfortable for many people, especially IT professionals. Enlist the help of your company's internal experts. Your best promoters will be the satisfied users themselves. Engage them to share their success stories in company newsletters, industry journals, and internal user conferences.

The
Complete
Reference

Business
Objects

Part II

A Better Universe

The
Complete
Reference

Business
Objects

Chapter 5

Universe Design
Principles

B usinessObjects is a powerful ad hoc reporting and analysis tool. The single greatest component of BusinessObjects that will make your implementation succeed or fail is the universe. A *universe* is a business representation of your data warehouse or transaction database. It shields users from the underlying complexities of the database schema. BusinessObjects often refers to this as the semantic or metadata layer. In all your development efforts, you must stay focused on that purpose: *business* representation. If your universe becomes a glorified entity relationship model, your project will fail. If your universe includes every data element any user may possibly want from now to eternity, your project will fail.

Universes can become unwieldy for end users. Poorly defined joins will result in unnecessarily slow queries. The universe is the most important component to get right.

Keep It Simple

I have worked with a universe that included thousands of objects and every table in the data warehouse. This universe was difficult for the administrator to maintain and was overwhelming even to expert BusinessObjects users. The result? End users often created invalid queries and blamed the data warehouse for bad data. Casual users would ask an IT expert to create MS Access data marts that were easier for them to use, thus defeating the flexibility and empowerment offered by an ad hoc query tool and causing unnecessary data reconciliation.

To build a successful universe, keep it simple. The universe should be useful for a clearly defined group of users and should not have much more than 200 objects in it. Bigger universes are technically feasible but not user friendly. Having more universes to build and maintain may result in slightly higher maintenance costs but will significantly increase end-user productivity and satisfaction. As your target user group expands, constantly ask yourself if the needs are distinct enough to justify a separate universe. If some users need only a handful of additional objects, keep it in the same universe. However, if they need many additional objects, create a separate universe.

Figure 5-1 illustrates how different user groups will need access to different information. Human resources is one group of users that needs access to salary details but does not need product sales and order information. Therefore, a Salary universe will only have information from this one fact table. Marketing people may need information on sales but will rarely need information on the individual order numbers that customer service representatives need; however, customer service representatives need both order detail and summary sales. This is an example in which it may make sense to have one universe that meets the needs of both user groups (marketing and customer service representatives). A director of the marketing group is most likely a people manager and may need salary and employee details; the director would use two universes, as including three subject areas in one big universe would potentially be overwhelming for the majority of users who don't need this information.

A BETTER UNIVERSE

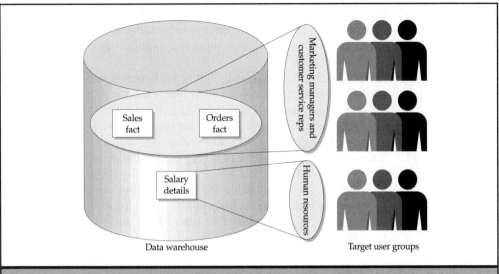

Sales fact

Orders fact

Marketing managers and customer service reps

Salary details

Human resources

Data warehouse

Target user groups

Figure 5-1. *A universe is a business representation of the database based on the needs of target user groups.*

Align with Business Goals

As discussed in Chapter 2, a data warehouse or business intelligence deployment should be carefully aligned with business goals. As you develop a universe, compare how this universe helps achieve the business goals. Sometimes, companies build new reporting solutions simply because the data is available or because a certain report always existed. However, old reports may no longer be meaningful in today's business climate.

The process of determining universe requirements will vary depending on whether your implementation is based on an existing data warehouse, a new data warehouse developed with BusinessObjects universes, or a transaction system.

Existing Data Warehouse

Just because information is in the data warehouse or data mart, that doesn't mean it needs to be in the universe. For example, data warehouses may contain dimension histories seldom used by end users. Likewise, data warehouses may contain only raw data elements that require a bit more intelligence in the universe. Likewise, just because users haven't specifically asked for something in a JAD session, that doesn't mean it shouldn't be in the universe. As an example, let's assume your company has a goal for on-time delivery performance. REQUESTED_DELIVERY_DATE and SHIP_DATE may be columns in an ORDER_FACT table. In evaluating how this universe is aligned with the company's business goals, a good universe designer will know to add an object called

Days Late that calculates the difference between the requested delivery date and actual ship date. Users may not know what SQL functionality can be added to database columns. A universe designer must be well versed in SQL reporting capabilities that can make the universe more robust.

I have worked with SQL-certified consultants who could create tables, optimize indexes, and input volumes of data quite efficiently. If I gave them a report request, it would take hours and days to get the desired results. The consultant may have been technically brilliant but was business-dumb. This mixed skill set can be a challenge in identifying the best universe designer in a company (refer to Chapter 3 for a discussion on project roles). It's often a DBA who has the SQL technical skills. A universe designed by a DBA with little knowledge of the business may be technically robust but lack the business functionality required. Universes designed by power users trained in SQL may have more robust business functionality, but with incorrect joins or objects that result in slow queries. Therefore, it's important that both a DBA and a power user review the initial universe.

New Data Warehouse

If you are building a new data warehouse or data mart in conjunction with your BusinessObjects implementation, ideally your development efforts are already driven by business goals. Requirements gathering in the development stage will drive the fact table design as well as the universe design. As discussed in Chapter 13, many of the issues at this stage will be where to put the intelligence—in the fact table or in the universe.

Transaction System

When your universe is based on a transaction system, some of your universe design choices will depend not only on the business goals and user requirements, but also on minimizing the impact on the source system. While users may want to search on customer name, a nonindexed field, such queries can cripple the source system (thus many organizations implement a data mart or data warehouse). If your company is not quite ready for a data warehouse, a quick alternative is to replicate the tables in the transaction system to a read-only instance of a database. This will better support detailed operational reporting requirements, without adversely affecting transaction processing. Even with this approach, a good designer needs to evaluate which business goals the universe is fulfilling. To follow on our supply chain example, customer phone numbers and contact details exist in the transaction system. This information is necessary for processing orders but useless for measuring on-time shipments. (If you are building a customer support system, then perhaps you need these details.) In building a user-friendly universe, the administrator must constantly evaluate objects that fall into the category of "I might need it one day." In an initial universe, defer adding the object to the universe.

Deployments against a transaction system generally fulfill the operational needs of a company but not the strategic goals of the business, as the data is not aggregated.

If the goal of the deployment is to provide a Windows- or Web-based, flexible, operational reporting environment, then your universe may indeed re-create fixed reports that exist in the source system. Another benefit of this approach is that the OLTP truly becomes the data entry/processing system, without detailed queries slowing down data inputs.

Lastly, if you are using WebIntelligence (WebI), administrators can now use Auditor to track how often universe objects are used. Prior to and without WebI, some companies use the SDK to create a small application that tracks universe, object, and report usage. You may still find scripts to do this in various discussion groups and system integrator web sites, although Business Objects has never officially provided a solution for tracking full client usage.

Universe Components

BusinessObjects administrators build universes using Designer. The key components of a universe are classes, objects, tables, joins, and contexts. As shown in Figure 5-2,

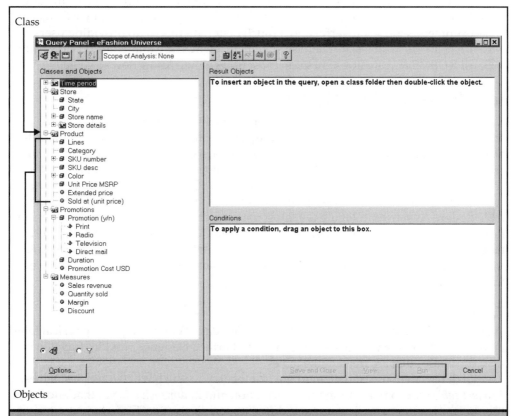

Figure 5-2. *Business users see classes and objects from the Query panel. The Price objects have been placed under the Product class but could also have been placed under Measures.*

classes and objects are the main items a business user sees when building a query. Objects become individual columns in a report; classes never appear in a report.

Classes

Classes are a way of grouping individual objects. In Figure 5-2, these appear with a folder icon. Sometimes these relate closely to the tables in a database but should be regrouped into business topics. In the sample EFASHION universe, the class *Product* is a more meaningful business term than *Article* and includes items from multiple tables ARTICLE_LOOKUP and ARTICLE_COLOR_LOOKUP.

Objects

Objects refer to columns of data. There are different types of objects (as explained further in Chapter 8) denoted with a square, sphere, or triangle icon in Figure 5-2. Objects can include a significant amount of intelligence and may not relate directly to one column in the database. For example, the object *Sold At (Unit Price)* includes a calculation of revenue/quantity. However, to avoid divide by 0 errors, it also includes an if-then-else statement to check for 0 quantities. This is one example of why Business Objects universes are so powerful and a much better alternative to providing users with direct access to tables; if-then-else statements in SQL are implemented differently for each RDBMS and are not something most users would know how to write.

Tables, Joins, and Contexts

Report authors never directly see several core elements of a universe: tables, joins, and contexts (see Figure 5-3). Universe designers use *tables* to map data from fields to objects in the universe. *Joins* allow the use of more than one table in a report, and *contexts* resolve which join path to take when more than one path is possible. All three of these components are then combined to dynamically build SQL statements in BusinessObjects.

Another strength of BusinessObjects is its ability to support almost any physical table design. As shown in Figure 5-4, most data warehouses use star schemas to ensure fast queries. However, some use snowflake schemas to make for smaller dimension tables. OLTPs use normalized schemas to eliminate data redundancy and speed data inputs (but which make for very slow queries). BusinessObjects supports all three of these designs, alone or in combination.

Tables

Tables are individual database tables that provide data. A table may be a physical table in the RDBMS, or it may be a view or synonym. Further, Designer provides functionality to create aliases that are treated like tables.

In a data warehouse or data mart environment, you will have two types of tables: 1) a *fact table* that contains numeric information and 2) *dimension tables* that allow a user to analyze the numeric data from different perspectives such as product, time, or geography. The fact table can have millions of detailed rows of data or can be smaller,

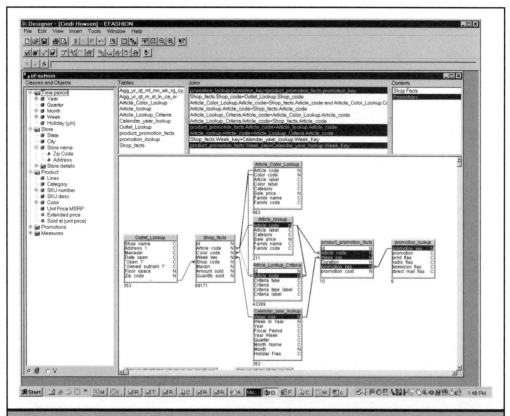

Figure 5-3.   *Tables, joins, and contexts are core elements of a universe that only the administrator sees in Designer.*

with summary numbers. One fact table together with its associated dimension tables is referred to as a *star schema*. There can be multiple fact tables and star schemas within a universe.

Dimension tables are also referred to as lookup tables or reference tables. The dimension tables can be broken into more than one table; for example, detailed material IDs may reside in a MATERIAL_ID table. The groupings and product hierarchy for the material IDs may reside in a separate table such as PRODUCT_GROUPING. This type of structure, referred to as a snowflake design, is used in some data warehouses that have extremely large dimensions as well as certain ROLAP tools.

In a normalized OLTP, both the fact tables and the dimension tables may be spread across many tables. For example, order information may exist in both an ORDER_HEADER table and an ORDER_LINES table. Dimensions and hierarchies often do not exist in the OLTP (note in Figure 5-4 that there is no Time or Plant table, just the individual facility that produced the product). Only the individual material IDs, customer IDs, and so on,

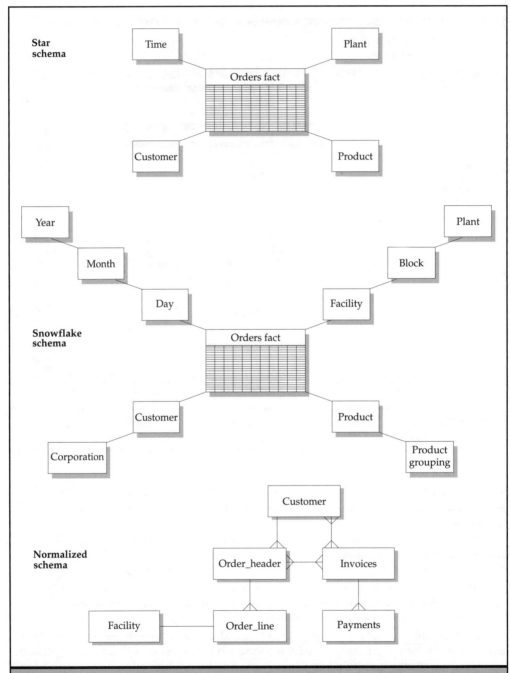

Figure 5-4. *Business Objects supports star schemas, snowflake schemas, and normalized table structures.*

are stored with detailed records. BusinessObjects does not allow a universe to point to two different databases, so having data that users want to analyze together generally calls for a data warehouse or data mart. However, if this is not immediately possible, BusinessObjects provides a workaround in the end-user tool. You, as the designer, can create two separate universes: one that points to the OLTP and one that points to the dimension database. Users then would have to build two queries; however, as long as the detailed key information is named consistently between the universes, the results will be nicely displayed in one table, without the user having to manually stitch the two result sets together. This technique is discussed further in Chapter 22.

When you build a universe, you are not replicating any data from these tables. Instead, you are basically creating pointers to tell BusinessObjects where to find the data; no data is stored in the universe itself. This is a drastically different approach than a full MOLAP tool such as Hyperion Essbase, Cognos Powerplay, or Microsoft Analysis Services. Data gets replicated only when a BusinessObjects user launches a report and the RDBMS sends results back to the report, populating a micro cube in a .rep file on either the WebI middle tier or the Windows client.

Joins

Joins specify how tables, views, synonyms, or aliases relate to one another. Joins allow a user to combine information from two or more tables. For example, in the following diagram, there are joins between ORDERS_FACT and the dimension table PLANT as well as between ORDERS_FACT and the dimension table PRODUCTS. There are no joins to the SUPPLIERS table. Without this join, a user is not able to determine which suppliers provide various products. There are many types of joins; they are discussed further in Chapter 7.

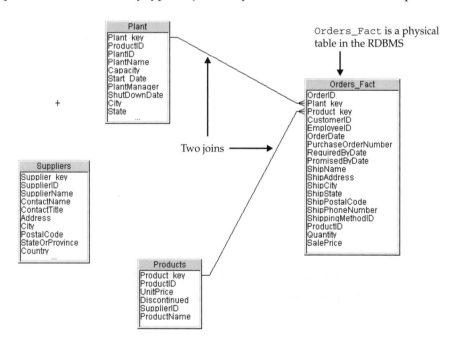

Contexts

Contexts group related joins. A context may group a set of joins together for each star schema. Without contexts, BusinessObjects would generate SQL that contained a loop. Loops generally result in incorrect queries with fewer rows returned than expected. Earlier versions of BusinessObjects supported queries that contained only one context. As contexts were generally confusing for end users, they were best avoided. BusinessObjects now allows one query to generate multiple SQL statements, one for each context. This allows users to query multiple star schemas to create powerful business reports. Two examples follow.

Days Sales Inventory (DSIs)   How many days worth of inventory do you have according to the daily sales volume? As shown in Figure 5-5, this query would

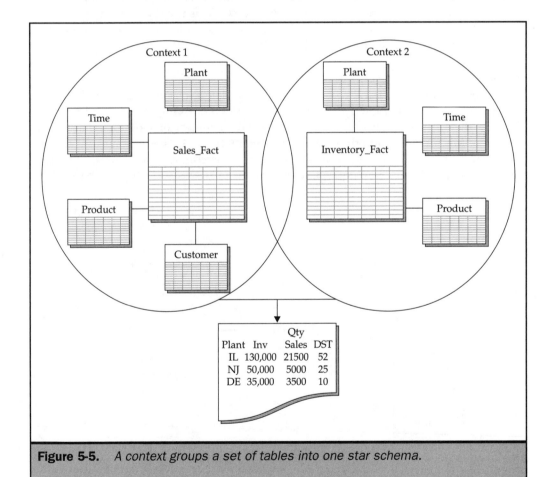

Figure 5-5.   *A context groups a set of tables into one star schema.*

involve two contexts, one with all the joins for the star schema with a SALES_FACT table and a second context with all the joins related to INVENTORY_FACT.

Account Balance/Debit/Credit   While MOLAP tools allow an administrator to specify measures that relate to one point in time versus a period in time, SQL-based tools cannot. Contexts provide a workaround, as a user can run a query, selecting individual month-end balances from an ACCOUNT_FACT table and then requesting summaries for all 30 days from a DAILY_DEBIT_CREDIT_FACT table. The results are again stitched together dynamically in the report. Contexts are discussed further in Chapter 7.

How Designer Works

Designer is a Windows client application that is installed on your PC, similar to Supervisor and BusinessObjects full client. Figure 5-6 illustrates how Designer interacts with the repository and the source data. When you modify universes, you are working offline on a copy of the universe. When you are finished with your changes, you export your copy of the universe to a repository that end users can access. Even if you are using BusinessObjects in Workgroup mode, without a repository, a designer still needs to put the modified universe (.unv file) in a shared folder that all users can access.

1. The universe designer logs on to the BusinessObjects repository. The repository checks if this person has the right to add a new universe or modify an existing one.

2. The designer either receives an error message or proceeds to the Designer Wizard screen. The designer can either create a new universe or modify an existing one.

3. The designer imports a copy of the existing universe as a .unv file into C:\ Program Files\Business Objects\BusinessObjects 5.0\Universe or whichever directory is specified under Tools | Options | Save.

4. The designer is logged onto the source system database specified as the connection for the universe. In modifying the universe or creating a new one, a SQL parameter file on the designer's hard disk reads the data dictionary for the RDBMS of the database specified in the connection (the data mart or OLTP).

5. The source database sends structure information (e.g., table names and column information) back to the designer's PC as part of the .unv file.

6. Once the designer is done modifying the universe, the designer must export the universe back to the repository for users to see the changes.

Designers (new, long-time, and rushed alike) sometimes forget this last step and inadvertently overwrite their changes the next day when they reimport a copy in step 3. The definitions for the universe are stored in relational tables in the repository, not as one .unv file. The relational tables in the repository are described further in Chapter 15.

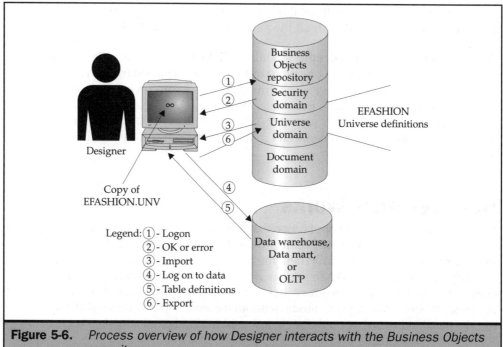

Figure 5-6. *Process overview of how Designer interacts with the Business Objects repository*

Universe Deployment Choices

Many companies have only one Business Objects repository and one universe domain. After all, the universe definitions are fairly small. Most universe interaction is not through the domain. It is either through a copy of the universe on the Windows full client PC or through the WebI midtier.

Having multiple universe domains may be helpful if you would like to have a test environment and a production environment or if you have geographically disbursed users that require different repository availability time. It is rarely useful to have multiple universe domains for network performance reasons. Geographic network bottlenecks will affect query execution more than universe uploads/downloads. In this case, both the data mart *and* the BusinessObjects repository will need to be located close to the user, as shown in Figure 5-7.

When a company has multiple universe domains, designers must pay particular attention to which domain they are exporting. This is not very obvious; it appears only on one drop-down box at the import/export stage (see Chapter 14).

A BETTER UNIVERSE

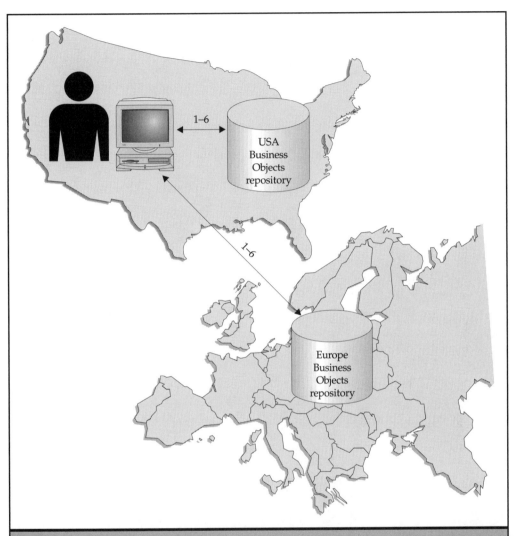

Figure 5-7.   *A company may have one person that modifies the universes globally but the BusinessObjects repositories are located in different regions.*

Note   *Companies may have multiple document domains, as documents can become quite large and resource intensive. Historically, companies may have had multiple security domains to decentralize security by region. However, with the introduction of Supervisor in version 4, this was no longer necessary, as security could be maintained by different security administrators in different regions or functional areas, yet still against one central domain.*

The
Complete
Reference

Business
Objects

Chapter 6

Using Designer to Build a Basic Universe

In Chapter 5, I discussed the importance of aligning the universe with business goals and reviewed the basic components of a universe. In this chapter, you will get much more technical and look at all the options and parameters that help you build the universe and manage the complexity of user queries.

Launching Designer

Administrators use Designer to build universes. If your BusinessObjects deployment includes a repository (which is not required), Designer presents you with a logon screen.

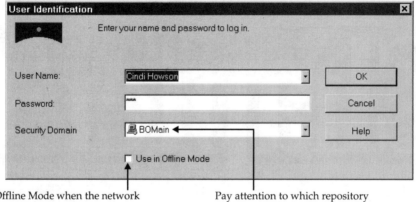

Select Offline Mode when the network or repository is unavailable

Pay attention to which repository you are working in

If your implementation has multiple repositories, then pay careful attention to which repository you log in to. Most large companies will have both a test and a production repository. Users may only ever see the production repository and may not necessarily have to select a repository; they access the production one automatically.

As a universe designer, though, it is easy to forget which repository you are working in, as the only time you see the repository name is when you first log in. Confusion between repositories may cause you to accidentally overwrite the wrong universe or to upload universes to a place that users cannot access.

Designer

As long as you have had one successful logon to Designer, Designer allows you to work in offline mode. This essentially means that you are not interacting with the repository. This may be useful if you wish to make changes to a universe while you are working on a notebook computer or if the repository database is otherwise unavailable for maintenance or due to a dreaded system failure. Personally, I have never used the offline option. Even if the repository is not available, it's unwise to make changes to a universe that is potentially out of date. Now, if you are the sole universe designer in your company and you know for an absolute fact that the universe on your hard disk is the latest version, then you may be thankful for the offline mode. If your company has multiple universe designers, working offline can be risky. Further, the offline mode applies only to the repository. Designer will still need to access the RDBMS to get current data dictionary information to create or modify classes and objects. If you are working on a notebook computer, offline, Designer will give you an error message when trying to refresh information about your data sources.

Designer maintains security in offline mode by the C:\Program Files\BusinessObjects\ BusinessObjects 5.0\LocData\sdac.lsi (secure data account, local security information). (Note: the .lsi file may actually be under ShData and may have an extension of .ssi for shared security information. These details are not important here; it matters only that one of the files exists, or offline access will not work.) Each time you log into one of the BusinessObjects modules, the .lsi file is updated with your user ID and password. When you log into Designer in offline mode, Designer checks that your user ID and password match what is in the .lsi file. If they do not match, you receive a message that your login is not valid.

Quick Design Wizard

Designer includes a wizard for basic universes. You probably will not be able to use a universe created with the wizard "as is," but it is a useful tool for creating a universe quickly and becoming more familiar with universe components. In the following example, you will create a new universe based on the MS Access database EFASHION.DB that BusinessObjects provides in the demo directory. For now, leave some options blank and at the default setting. The various options are explained further in this chapter.

1. To invoke the Quick Design Wizard, start Designer and choose File | New or click New Universe. Table 6-1 lists all buttons and shortcuts available in Designer.

Button/Key Combo	Name	Function
or CTRL-N	New Universe	Creates a new universe
or CTRL-O	Open Universe	Opens an existing universe
or CTRL-S	Save Universe	Saves the universe to disk in the .unv file. Does not export the universe to the repository

Table 6-1. *Designer Toolbar Buttons*

Button/Key Combo	Name	Function
or CTRL-P	Print	Prints the universe definitions and structure
	Print Preview	Previews what definitions will be printed
or CTRL-X	Cut	Cuts the selected item (table, join, object)
or CTRL-C	Copy	Puts the selected item into the MS Windows clipboard
or CTRL-V	Paste	Pastes the selected item
or CTRL-Z	Undo/Redo	Undoes or redoes the last action
	Quick Design Wizard	Launches the universe design wizard to build a new universe
	Parameters	Modifies the universe parameters such as connection information, SQL settings, strategies
	Hierarchies	Creates or modifies the universe hierarchies
	View List Mode	Views the join and context lists in statements as well as in the ERD
	Arrange Tables	Reorganizes the tables to make the structure pane easier to read
	Zoom Out	Makes tables in the structure window appear smaller
	Zoom In	Makes tables in the structure window appear larger
	Contextual Help	Launches the Designer Help

Table 6-1. *Designer Toolbar Buttons* (continued)

Button/Key Combo	Name	Function
	Insert Class	Inserts a new class
	Insert Object	Inserts a new object within a class
	Insert Condition	Inserts a condition object
	Show or Hide Item	Hides an object or class from users
	Table Browser	Shows a list of tables available to add to the universe
	Insert Join	Inserts a join between two tables
	Insert Alias	Creates an alias name for a table that already is used in the universe
	Insert Context	Creates a context to prevent loops in a universe
	Detect Joins	Checks the universe to determine if there are any tables not joined
	Detect Cardinalities	Detects cardinalities, or relationships between tables
	Detect Loops	Checks the universe to determine if there are any loops, and prompts for ways to resolve
	Detect Aliases	Checks the universe to determine if any tables create a loop that an alias could resolve
	Detect Contexts	Checks the universe for loops and determines if contexts would resolve the loops
	Check Integrity	Performs multiple universe integrity checks

Table 6-1.   *Designer Toolbar Buttons* (continued)

If the wizard does not appear, check that your default settings enable the wizard. From the Designer menu, select Tools | Options. On the General tab, click the check box File/ New Starts Quick Design Wizard.

2. The Wizard will present you with a welcome screen that gives you an overview of the steps to build a universe. Click Begin to proceed.

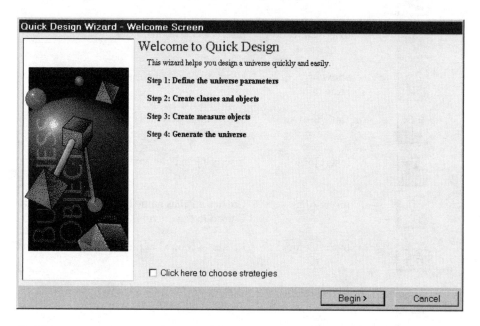

3. Give your universe a meaningful name such as **Test Fashion**. The universe name can be more than eight characters long and can contain spaces. The universe name is different from the PC filename that contains all the universe definitions. Test Fashion is what users will see when selecting a data source for a report.

4. Click New to create a connection to efashion.mdb.

5. Select ODBC Drivers from the list and click OK.

6. From the ODBC Drivers dialog box, give the connection a meaningful name such as **Fashion Database**.

Users will never see this connection name; only universe designers do.

This is the universe
name users see

BusinessObjects can pass through its username/
password to the OLTP or data mart

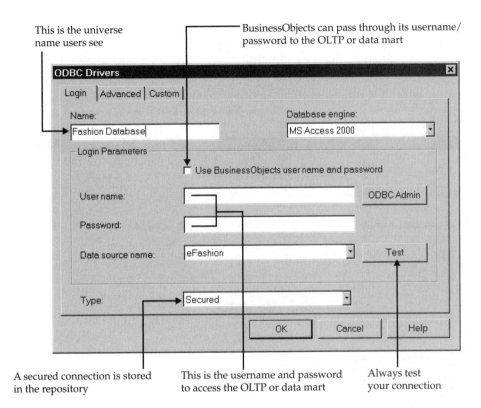

ODBC Drivers   ☒

Login | Advanced | Custom |

Name: Database engine:
Fashion Database| MS Access 2000   ▾

┌ Login Parameters ──
│
│   ☐ Use BusinessObjects user name and password
│
│   User name: [   ]   ODBC Admin
│
│   Password: [   ]
│
│   Data source name: eFashion   ▾   Test
│
│
│   Type: Secured   ▾
└──

                    OK   Cancel   Help

A secured connection is stored
in the repository

This is the username and password
to access the OLTP or data mart

Always test
your connection

7. Under Database Engine, select the version of MS Access used to create the database.

8. Under Data source name, select Efashion and then click OK. Test your connection. BusinessObjects should reply with "The Server Is Responding." If you do not receive this message, BusinessObjects cannot locate the MS Access database, because you selected either the wrong path or the wrong database driver. Click OK to return to the Quick Design Wizard.

9. Click Next to proceed to Step 2 of the wizard. In this step, you select either the full tables or individual data columns that will become universe classes and objects, respectively. By clicking the + sign next to the table name, you can choose individual columns from the table that will become objects. You may find it easier initially to add all the columns and delete the individual ones you don't want. Hold down the CTRL key while clicking the following three tables: ARTICLE_LOOKUP, CALENDAR_YEAR_LOOKUP, and SHOP_FACTS.

10. Click Add. If you click the + sign next to any of the individual classes, you will notice that Designer has added all the columns in each table with a blue box next to the item to denote a dimension. These symbols and object types are discussed further in Chapter 8.

A + indicates additional columns
to see in each table

The blue cube indicates
a dimension object

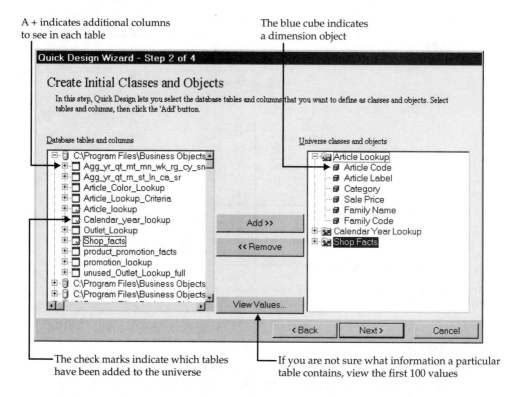

The check marks indicate which tables
have been added to the universe

If you are not sure what information a particular
table contains, view the first 100 values

11. Click Next to proceed to Step 3 of the wizard, in which you select objects that become measures. A measure is often referred to as a "fact" in a fact table in a data warehouse. It is numeric data that business users wish to analyze by different dimensions. In BusinessObjects, measures generally include a SQL aggregate function such as COUNT or SUM. These are also discussed further in Chapter 8. For now, click the + sign next to *Shop_Facts*, select *Article_Code*, then Count. Notice that the wizard will add a measure object called *Number Of Article Code* with a pink circle or sphere. Repeat the same steps for MARGIN, AMOUNT_SOLD, and QUANTITY_SOLD, using the Sum aggregate function for these objects.

A sphere or circle indicates a measure object

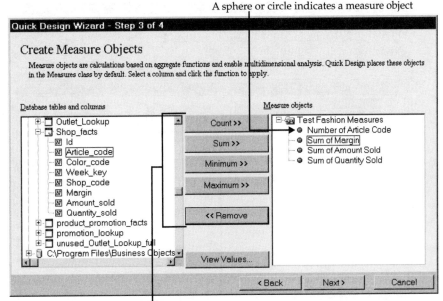

Designer provides several aggregate functions

Note

These measure objects are duplicates of objects created when you added the whole SHOP_FACTS table. The difference is that these objects contain a SQL SUM or COUNT command, whereas the ones in the Shop Facts class do not. You will eventually delete the duplicate objects from the Shop Facts class.

12. Click Next to proceed to Step 4 of the wizard. In this step, the wizard tells you how many classes, objects, and joins your initial universe contains. Click Finish to exit the wizard and view the universe in Designer.

13. Unfortunately, efashion.mdb has a small typo in the database that does not dynamically create one join you need. The default join strategy setting (discussed later in this chapter, in the section "The Strategies Tab") uses columns with the exact same names to create joins. The names are case sensitive. In the sample efashion.mdb database, "key" in the WEEK_KEY column is lowercase in the SHOP_FACTS table and initial caps in CALENDAR_YEAR_LOOKUP. You need to manually add this join. To create the join, click and drag CALENDAR_YEAR_ LOOKUP.WEEK_KEY to SHOP_FACTS.WEEK_KEY.

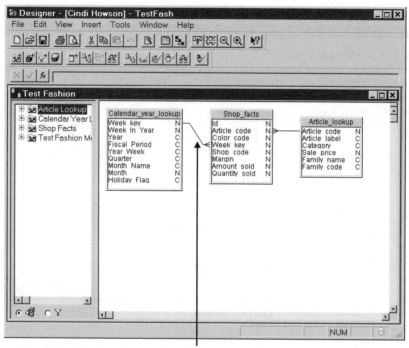

Insert a join by dragging and dropping between the two columns in each table

14. Click File | Save from the pull-down menu or click the Save button on the toolbar to save your universe. The first time you save a universe, BusinessObjects will propose an eight-character filename with .unv as the extension. This is different from the name of the universe you created in step 3. Universe files are saved to disk by default in BusinessObjects 5.0\Universe or in whatever folder is specified under Tools | Options | Save. Users working with the BusinessObjects full client may see the .unv file on their hard disks; otherwise, it is not something they need to be aware of.

15. If you are working with a Repository, you must click File | Export to export your universe to the repository and make it available to users. Users will not see the new universe until you complete this step.

Congratulations! You have just completed your initial universe. If only a real business universe could be this easy! In the following sections of this chapter, we will look at the settings and options that helped you build this universe.

Universe Parameters

The universe parameters provide information about your universe as well as allow you to change universe behavior such as how long a query can run and the type of SQL BusinessObjects generates. To modify the universe parameters, bring up the Universe Parameters dialog box by selecting File | Parameters.

Definition

From the Definition tab, you see the name of the universe as well as the connection you specified when building the universe through the wizard. The Description is an underutilized feature of BusinessObjects. Users see the description as a Help box whenever they create a new report and select a particular universe. Therefore, the Description box is an excellent place to provide users with information about the purpose of the universe and the target business user group, as well as timely information such as when data was last updated or if there are any data integrity issues.

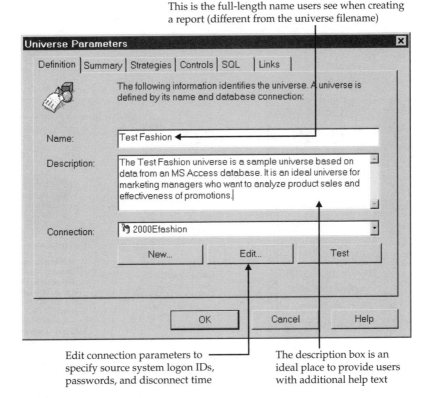

This is the full-length name users see when creating a report (different from the universe filename)

Edit connection parameters to specify source system logon IDs, passwords, and disconnect time

The description box is an ideal place to provide users with additional help text

Connections

Universe connections can be a great source of confusion for new universe administrators as well as DBAs. The connection in the universe parameters can be the same as or different from the connection used to validate your BusinessObjects logon (usually it is different). The parameters you specify will depend on how you decide to deploy BusinessObjects, where you store the repositories, and where your data sources are located. When you click the Edit button, BusinessObjects presents you with a dialog box that lets you customize the logon, advanced, and custom settings.

BusinessObjects Architecture

To understand how the universe connections work, you must first understand how BusinessObjects is deployed and how security in the various data sources, whether OLTPs or data marts, interact.

Scenario 1:   Let's assume that you are deploying BusinessObjects for a relatively small group of users who wish to access information in a source system—there is no data mart. As Figure 6-1 shows, the BusinessObjects repository resides in a PC database such as MS Access. The source system data resides in an enterprise-wide RDBMS such

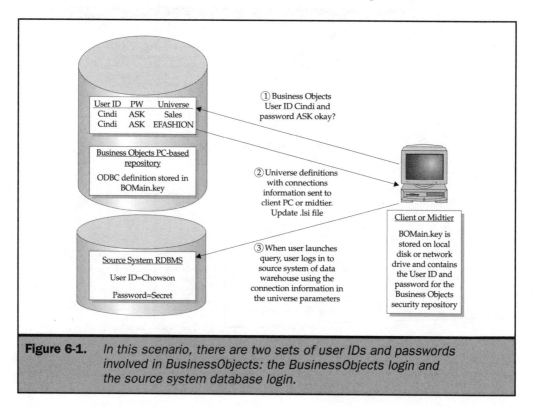

Figure 6-1.   *In this scenario, there are two sets of user IDs and passwords involved in BusinessObjects: the BusinessObjects login and the source system database login.*

as Oracle, DB2, or Teradata. When BusinessObjects was first installed, the supervisor created security and universe domains but did *not* specify a user ID and a password for the user. The only information stored in locdata\BOMain.key is the location of the PC database. The supervisor also granted each individual user a BusinessObjects user ID and password combination, Cindi/ASK, for example. The source system database has its own set of user IDs and passwords (Chowson/Secret). This leaves us with the potential of having three different sets of user IDs and passwords. Users need to know only two of them: the BusinessObjects user ID/password and the source system user ID/password.

Scenario 2:   As shown in Figure 6-2, many companies use a data warehouse environment rather than accessing data directly in an OLTP. The BusinessObjects repository tables may be physically installed on the same machine as the data

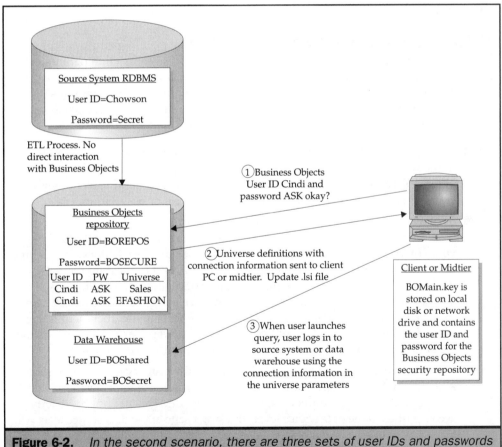

Figure 6-2.   *In the second scenario, there are three sets of user IDs and passwords involved: the repository connection, the BusinessObjects logon, and the data warehouse access.*

warehouse tables. Each set of tables may reside in its own database instance and may require a unique user ID and password combination. In Figure 6-2, the BOMain.key contains a generic logon user ID and password (BOREPOS/BOSECURE) as well as the name of the database instance.

Users never see the userid/password stored in BOMain.key; this user ID and password combination never appears to users (or universe designers) and is used only to log a user onto the BusinessObjects repository to determine which products, universe, and documents each user can access and modify. The BOMain.key file lets BusinessObjects connect to the physical repository.

In this respect, the BOMain.key file uses a shared logon to the repository. DBAs and enterprise security administrators get nervous about shared logons. However, if they understand the purpose of this particular user ID and password, they see that there is no reason ever to assign a unique logon to the repository. In fact, using anything other than a shared logon in BOMain.key is sure only to increase the number of error messages a user receives.

Which Connection to Use in a Universe

When you specify the user ID and password in the universe connection parameters, the administrator must understand how these IDs and passwords interact and carefully consider ease of use, security, usage tracking, and cost. Table 6-2 summarizes the alternatives and benefits/issues of each approach—the best alternative depends on ease of use, security, tracking requirements, and cost.

- **Ease of usage**   If users cannot remember any assigned password or if they put in the wrong password for either the BusinessObjects logon or the data access logon (OLTP or data warehouse) and their access becomes disabled, they will blame BusinessObjects for being too difficult to use or not working.

- **Security**   Much of what is in the BusinessObjects repository is not company confidential; it's not data. The exception to this is the document domain, which your company may or may not use. For many full client installations, the document domain essentially contains templates without data. Duplicating the data with the report templates can cause the document domain to become huge, so it is advisable only when you are trying to minimize access to the source system. In a WebIntelligence (WebI) implementation, reports in the document domain often do contain data and should be protected with a password. Clearly, data in the source system needs to be protected from unauthorized access.

- **Usage tracking**   Beyond these security aspects, the primary reason for requiring a BusinessObjects user ID and password is to track usage of BusinessObjects components: reports, universes, users, and so on. This cannot be strictly accomplished at the data source level. Tracking usage at the data source level will tell you how often a user accessed a particular table, but it will not tell you that the user had a report open for two hours and that the user actually combined data from two different source systems. Only BusinessObjects can do this. Conversely, if you decide to use a shared login from BusinessObjects to the source system database (alternative 3 in Table 6-2), it makes it harder to control runaway queries, particularly in a full client implementation. In a full client implementation, a source system DBA would have to kill the query and would not be able to identify the individual user who launched the query. In a WebI implementation, the WebI administrator would be able to see whose query has been running so long, as the rogue query would be consuming both WebI resources and source system database resources.

For this reason, many companies assign user IDs and passwords at both the BusinessObjects and data source levels. This also allows the source system RDBMS to handle row-level and column-level security.

Alternative	Business Objects ID	Source System Database	Issues
1	Cindi/ASK	Chowson/Secret	This approach appears secure but is not feasible. This situation may occur when the BusinessObjects administrator and source system DBAs do not cooperate. Passwords also can become out of synch when users change their BusinessObjects password and not the data warehouse or OLTP password.
2	Cindi/no password	Cindi/Secret	Easy to administer, and users do not need to remember different passwords. BusinessObjects usage tracking is accurate only if users do not share PCs or logon IDs. Security can be done only at the source system level, which is acceptable only if documents in the BusinessObjects repository do not contain confidential data.
3	Cindi/ASK	BOshared/ BOsecret	This is fairly easy to maintain and allows BusinessObjects administrators to track usage, but source system DBAs cannot track usage by individual user. Row- and column-level security must be done within BusinessObjects Supervisor.
4	Chowson/Secret	Chowson/Secret	This provides the most secure setup with the fullest usage tracking. However, it also increases maintenance, as user IDs and passwords must be manually maintained between the two systems. The BusinessObjects Supervisor should not allow users to change their passwords, or they may become out of synch with the source system. In defining the connection parameters, select the check box Use BusinessObjects User Name And Password.

Table 6-2.   *BusinessObjects Allows for Different User IDs and Passwords Between the Repository and the Data Source(s)*

■ **Cost**   Finally, another consideration in choosing between unique source system IDs or a shared one is your RDBMS licensing. If your license is by named user, then it is more cost effective to use a shared database logon for data access. You will still need to pay for the appropriate number of concurrent licenses, a price that, if your data warehouse is well tuned, can be relatively low with BusinessObjects. Many BI tools will keep the database connection active for longer period of times, thus increasing the number of RDBMS licenses required. Designer enables you to modify these settings to keep concurrency against the data source low.

In evaluating the ease of use, security, usage tracking issues, and cost issues, I prefer alternative 3 or 4 described in Table 6-2. Alternative 1 may happen inadvertently and will produce errors when users attempt to refresh a query. Alternative 2 is feasible when different source databases require different passwords. The BusinessObjects supervisor disables password checking; however, the password specified during BusinessObjects login still gets passed through to the RDBMS. Prior to refreshing a query for a second data source that requires a different password, the user must log out of BusinessObjects and login again to enter the password for the second data source.

Caution   *Always, always test your connection when changing the user ID, passwords, or database name. Just when you think you've typed it perfectly is when you make a mistake, rendering everyone's universe unusable!*

The Advanced tab of the Connection dialog box provides additional options that affect users during query execution. These options and their defaults will vary depending on which database you are using. Under Connection Properties, if you keep the connection active during the whole session, user queries are never slowed down for the source system/data warehouse logon and logoff process. This is great for users but can become expensive for RDBMS licensing and WebI overhead. Conversely, disconnecting after each transaction can make repeated querying for users appear unnecessarily slow as the logon process is added to each data refresh. A good balance is to allow the connection to be active for ten minutes.

In the vendor-provided database guides, Business Objects recommends avoiding the Use Asynchronous Mode option. Asynchronous mode allows a user to press ESC to cancel a query while the database is still analyzing the query (otherwise, users can cancel the query only during the fetch stage, when data is being sent across the network). Business Objects recommends disabling this, because while a user may cancel a query on his or her PC, the query will still be running on the database. However, if a user has been waiting an unexpectedly long time for the query to complete, the user may simply reboot his or her PC and start over; this essentially has the same effect on the source system database as if the user had simply pressed ESC to begin with. Therefore, I recommend using the asynchronous mode in conjunction with performing the cost estimate. In WebI, asynchronous mode is not supported. Connection Mode options are not available in ODBC.

The cost estimate feature is available in some databases and is database specific (at the time of this writing, Sybase and MS SQL do not have it). To enable cost estimates in Oracle, the DBA must first create a PLAN_TABLE using the Oracle-supplied utlxplan.sql file. Secondly, the DBA must analyze the database schema on a regular basis or whenever major changes are made to the database. Finally, the DBA must allow each individual user (or the shared BusinessObjects user ID as described in Table 6-2, Alternative 3) write access to the PLAN_TABLE. The BusinessObjects administrator also must enable two parameters:

- **Cost Estimate Feature**   Under Parameters | Connection | Advanced
- **Warn If Cost Estimate Exceeds**   Under Parameters | Controls

The last Advanced option you may want to change is the array fetch size. This setting determines how many rows of data can be shipped back to the client in one fetch. Increasing the fetch size may get the results to appear faster on the user's PC. However, higher settings consume more memory, and the actual response times also depend on network load and server load. If you are experiencing slow fetches, try increasing the number by increments of 10.

Synchronous mode allows users to cancel queries during the fetch stage

Higher minutes may increase data RDBMS license costs, but setting this number too low will slow user query time

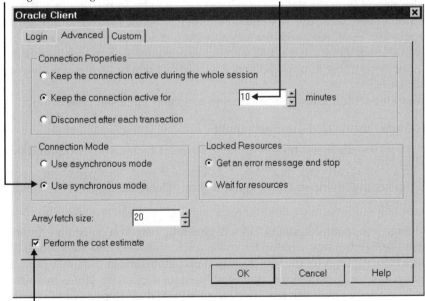

If the explain plan is set up by the DBA, the cost estimate gives users an idea of how long a query will take to run

The Custom tab enables you to make additional changes that are not available in the Advanced tab. They are database specific and rarely used. Your DBA may suggest changing certain custom parameters.

The Summary Tab

The Summary tab of the Universe Parameters dialog box provides information about the universe, such as the number of classes, objects, and joins. Additionally, it provides a last modification date, the name of the modifier, and a version number. Some companies will create one BusinessObjects administrator ID that people share (against the advice of security personnel). In order to take advantage of the revision information provided in the Universe parameters, it's important that administrators not share logon IDs.

 The Comments section in the Summary tab allows an administrator to include additional technical notes on the universe. BusinessObjects users do not see these notes. This makes the Comments section an excellent place to store detailed revision notes for change control purposes.

The Strategies Tab

The Strategies tab of the Universe Parameters dialog box defines how the universe uses information from the data dictionary to help you build the universe. Next to the Connection information, the Strategies can prove to be the greatest challenge in first developing universes. Although BusinessObjects provides some very powerful strategies to get you started, if you have a data warehouse or source system architecture that uses public synonyms (most do), you will need to modify them or Designer will never see those tables.

The strategy information is used during a number of Designer activities:

- During the wizard's universe build
- If you use the Insert button or menu to insert tables, joins, or candidate objects
- In automatically creating joins and objects, if your database options use this setting (discussed later in the section "Database Options that Relate to Strategies")

Although your source system DBA will generally help you customize these strategies, as a BusinessObjects administrator, the more you understand how they work, the better you can advise the DBA on the best approach to customization.

Strategies are SQL statements that read the data dictionary tables in your source system. The queries then use that dictionary information to present you with a list of initial classes, objects, joins, and tables. So if all your data warehouse tables start with DW, for example, then your initial proposed classes will also start with DW (such as

Dw Product). If you do not want the user to see this DW (not recommended), then you can modify your strategy file to drop the DW from the proposed classes.

The drop-down box lets you choose different strategies

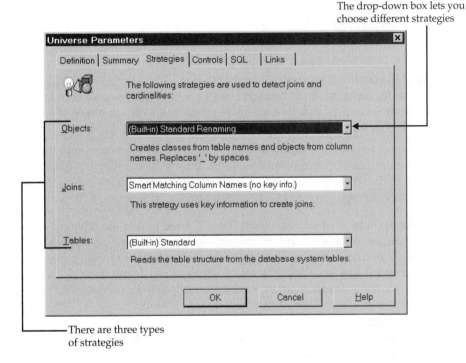

There are three types of strategies

There are three parts of a universe that strategies interact with: objects, joins, and tables.

- **Objects**   The object strategy determines how Designer reads the table and column information from the data dictionary to come up with some initial classes and objects (either when using the wizard or when inserting tables). By default, the table names become the proposed class names and the individual columns within each table become the objects in your universe. The default object strategy also converts all names to initial caps and removes the underscore (_) from any table and field names.

- **Joins**   Designer has three built-in approaches to automatically create joins, listed next.

- **Smart Matching Column Names (no key info)**   If the names of two columns match *exactly,* then Designer will propose a join between the two. Recall that the WEEK_KEY columns in our initial universe did not match exactly. Key was initial caps in one instance and lowercase in the second table. The columns must also be a primary key in each of their tables.

- **All Matching Column Names**   This strategy appears to work the same as the preceding one.

- **All Matching Numeric Column Names**   This strategy works well if your tables contain a lot of foreign keys. Designer will look for numeric columns that are named exactly the same and propose joins between the two.

- **Tables**   This part of the strategy is probably your most important part. If Designer cannot find your necessary tables, it can never move to the next step of creating objects and proposing joins. Information collected from the table part of the strategy is displayed in the structure window, such as the column name, data type (Numeric, Character, Date), and key.

In earlier versions of BusinessObjects, the SQL used to find the tables in the RDBMS was quite seamless. With version 4, BusinessObjects switched to this approach of built-in strategies and external strategies. Thus, the exact SQL of the built-in strategies is no longer viewable. However, Designer basically selects all physical tables owned by the individual user specified in the connection parameters. For example, if the owner of the tables in your Central Data Warehouse is CDW, then you must log on with the user ID CDW for Designer to find these tables.

You can change the OWNER=N parameter in your *database*.prm file. This will drop the owner name from your table prefix and will cause the built-in strategies to look for public synonyms and views (for example, the username specified in the connection parameters does not necessarily own the physical tables). However, setting OWNER=N without customizing an external strategy can also pick up a lot of clutter such as system tables. Therefore, you will still need to use or create an external strategy.

External Strategies

External strategies appear under each of the drop-down options for objects, joins, and tables. However, you create them outside of BusinessObjects with any text editor such as Notepad.

The parameter for your particular database contains a setting on the STG line that tells BusinessObjects where to find the SQL for these strategies. As an example, in an Oracle database, the file ora7EN.prm contains the line STG=STORA7EN. STORA7EN is the default strategy file. Parameter files are database specific and located in c:\Program Files\BusinessObjects\Data Access 5x*specific database*. The files use the following naming convention: St*nnnn*EN.txt where St means Strategy, *nnnn* is the database abbreviated name, and EN is the English language version.

The strategy file requires a particular format as shown in the example that follows. The TYPE must be OBJECT, JOIN, or STRUCT. STRUCT refers to strategy files that generate the table information. The NAME section is the name that will appear in your strategy drop-down menu—for example, "Smart Matching Columns." The SQL section is the core of the strategy. This is where, if you don't like DW appearing in each class name, you use LTRIM to cut it.

If your source system uses L33 for every column involving a customer, use REPLACE to replace L33 with CUSTOMER. The HELP section is optional and provides a more detailed explanation of how this strategy works. The Help information appears in the drop-down box of the strategy selection.

```
[STRATEGY]
TYPE=JOIN
NAME= External Strategy: Same Column Name
[SQL]
Enter your customized SQL statements here, ensuring the correct number
of columns are generated as shown in Figures 6-4 through 6-6.
[HELP]
HELP= This join strategy reads the database constraints and provides
a list of joins.
```

Figures 6-3 through 6-6 show how Designer reads information from the RDBMS' data dictionary tables to create objects and joins and to display information about tables in your universe. Figure 6-3 shows the raw data dictionary information. The example uses information about the demo SALES table in an Oracle database. The dictionary tables that provide the information are USER_TABLES, USER_TAB_COLUMNS, and USER_COL_COMMENTS. Figures 6-4 through 6-6 show the required output layouts for objects, joins, and tables. For your external strategies to work, you must use the exact output layout. If you forget a column or mix up the order, you will get unusual results or an error.

	A	B	C	D	E	F
	Owner	Table Name	Column Name	Null?	Type	Column Comments
1	DATA DICTIONARY INFORMATION					
3	SH	SALES	PROD_ID	NOT NULL	NUMBER(6)	FK to the products dimension table
4	SH	SALES	CUST_ID	NOT NULL	NUMBER	FK to the customers dimension table
5	SH	SALES	TIME_ID	NOT NULL	DATE	FK to the times dimension table
6	SH	SALES	CHANNEL_ID	NOT NULL	CHAR(1)	FK to the channels dimension table
7	SH	SALES	PROMO_ID	NOT NULL	NUMBER(6)	promotion identifier, without FK constraint (intentional
8	SH	SALES	QUANTITY_SOLD	NOT NULL	NUMBER(3)	product quantity sold with the transaction
9	SH	SALES	AMOUNT_SOLD	NOT NULL	NUMBER(10,2)	invoiced amount to the customer

sales_dictionary

Figure 6-3. *Strategies uses SQL to read the data dictionary tables.*

F06_3_6.xls

	H	I	J	K	L	M	N	O	P
1	OBJECT LAYOUT								
2	1.Table	2.Column	3.Class Name	4.Object Name	5.SQL Select (Table.Column)	6.SQL Where Clause	7.Object Type	8.Description	9.Object Type (D, M, I)
3	SALES	PROD_ID	Sales	Prod Id	SALES.PROD_ID		N	FK to the products dimension tal	D
4	SALES	CUST_ID	Sales	Cust Id	SALES.CUST_ID		N	FK to the customers dimension t	D
5	SALES	TIME_ID	Sales	Time Id	SALES.TIME_ID		D	FK to the times dimension table	D
6	SALES	CHANNEL_ID	Sales	Channel Id	SALES.CHANNEL_ID		C	FK to the channels dimension ta	D
7	SALES	PROMO_ID	Sales	Promo Id	SALES.PROMO_ID		N	promotion identifier, without FK c	D
8	SALES	QUANTITY_SOLD	Sales	Quanity Sold	SALES.QUANTITY_SOLD		N	product quantity sold with the tra	D
9	SALES	AMOUNT_SOLD	Sales	Amount Sold	SALES.AMOUNT_SOLD		N	invoiced amount to the customer	D
10									

sales_dictionary

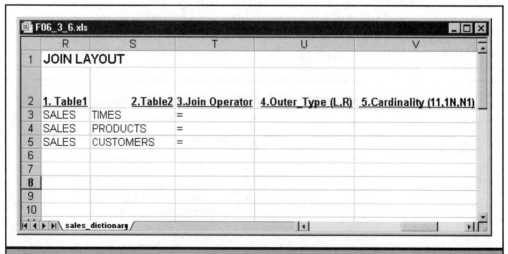

Figure 6-4. *Object strategies propose the initial classes and objects and require nine columns of information. Consider creating an object strategy using spreadsheet data from a JAD session.*

> **Note** *Accessing USER dictionary tables can be a problem in strategies if the username in the connection parameters is not the owner of the tables, views, or synonyms. Often synonyms are set up as PUBLIC. In such cases, use ALL_ dictionary tables to find synonyms and use WHERE clauses to find the appropriate database objects.*

Figure 6-4 shows the exact object layout that your SQL strategy must generate for Designer to propose initial classes and objects. As mentioned previously, it's rare to derive business-oriented classes and object names from data mart tables (and certainly not from OLTP tables). However, this section of an external strategy file is very helpful in ensuring your SQL statements are correct. Also, none of the built-in or sample strategies leverage

F06_3_6.xls

	R	S	T	U	V
1	JOIN LAYOUT				
2	1. Table1	2.Table2	3.Join Operator	4.Outer_Type (L,R)	5.Cardinality (11,1N,N1)
3	SALES	TIMES	=		
4	SALES	PRODUCTS	=		
5	SALES	CUSTOMERS	=		
6					
7					
8					
9					
10					

sales_dictionary

Figure 6-5. *Join strategies propose joins between tables and use five columns of information. Three are required, two are optional.*

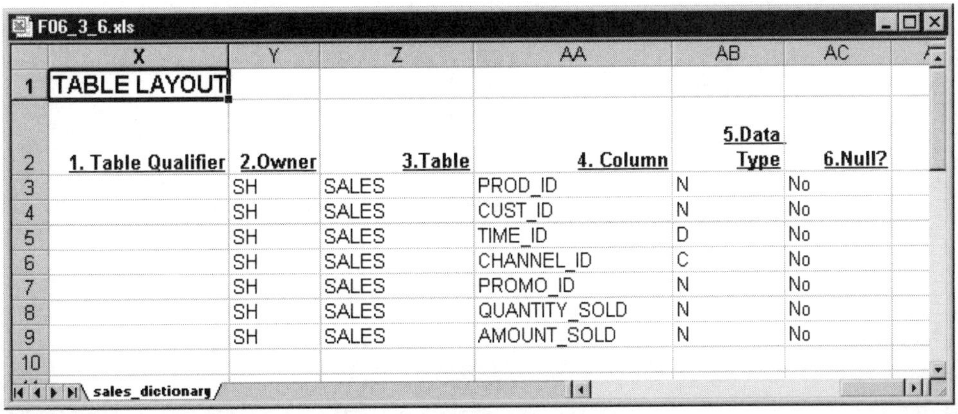

	X	Y	Z	AA	AB	AC	
1	TABLE LAYOUT						
2	1. Table Qualifier	2.Owner	3.Table	4. Column	5.Data Type	6.Null?	
3		SH	SALES	PROD_ID	N	No	
4		SH	SALES	CUST_ID	N	No	
5		SH	SALES	TIME_ID	D	No	
6		SH	SALES	CHANNEL_ID	C	No	
7		SH	SALES	PROMO_ID	N	No	
8		SH	SALES	QUANTITY_SOLD	N	No	
9		SH	SALES	AMOUNT_SOLD	N	No	
10							

sales_dictionary

Figure 6-6. *Table or structure strategies require six columns of information and are used to provide information in the structure window of the universe.*

the comments column in your RDBMS. If your DBA or ETL tool has used the comments column in your RDBMS, the comments column can be a good starting point to provide meaningful descriptions/help text for individual objects. Finally, the object strategy file is your best bet for recycling in a spreadsheet file that users can easily modify.

As an example, let's assume that following a JAD session, you have a documented list of initial universe requirements. Following the universe design guidelines discussed in Chapter 5, you carefully review this list to remove unwanted items and propose new ones. All these changes are documented in a spreadsheet. At this point, you, as the universe designer, can insert columns into the spreadsheet to get the physical table and column names and a formula (example: +A1&"."&B1) to generate the SQL SELECT statement. You can then create an external objects strategy that creates objects based on a text output of your JAD spreadsheet. This process can more quickly give you a working universe prototype than using the built-in strategy provided by BusinessObjects, simply because your new strategy uses business terms rather than generic OLTP or data warehouse terms.

The following table or STRUCT strategy was created by an oil and gas company that uses Public synonyms in its data warehouse. One of the risks of reading dictionary information from the ALL_TABLES, etc., dictionary tables is that the SQL will generate information about system tables, clearly information you do not need in a business universe. This strategy file does a good job of limiting the information generated, thus making structure refreshes faster.

```
[STRATEGY]
TYPE=STRUCT
NAME= DBLINK - To PRD5

[SQL]
```

```
SQL=SELECT
      'REPT', '|',
      S.TABLE_OWNER, '|',
      S.SYNONYM_NAME,'|',
      U1.column_name,'|',
      decode(SUBSTR(U1.DATA_TYPE,1,1),'N','N','F','N','D','D','C'),'|',
      '','|'
FROM ALL_TAB_COLUMNS U1, ALL_COL_COMMENTS U2, ALL_OBJECTS O, ALL_SYNONYMS S
WHERE
    S.table_owner=O.owner
AND  S.table_name=O.object_name
AND  (O.OBJECT_TYPE='TABLE' OR O.OBJECT_TYPE='VIEW')
AND  O.owner=U1.owner
AND  O.object_name=U1.table_name
AND  U1.owner=U2.owner
AND  U1.table_name=U2.table_name
AND  U1.column_name=U2.column_name
AND  S.table_owner NOT IN ('SYSTEM', 'MDSYS', 'ORDSYS', 'SYS')
AND  S.DB_LINK IS NULL
UNION
SELECT
      'PRD5','|',
      S.TABLE_OWNER, '|',
      S.SYNONYM_NAME,'|',
      U1.column_name,'|',
      decode(SUBSTR(U1.DATA_TYPE,1,1),'N','N','F','N','D','D','C'),'|',
      '','|'
FROM ALL_TAB_COLUMNS@PRD5.WORLD U1, ALL_COL_COMMENTS@PRD5.WORLD U2,
ALL_OBJECTS@PRD5.WORLD O, ALL_SYNONYMS S
WHERE
    S.table_owner=O.owner
AND  S.table_name=O.object_name
AND  (O.OBJECT_TYPE='TABLE' OR O.OBJECT_TYPE='VIEW')
AND  O.owner=U1.owner
AND  O.object_name=U1.table_name
AND  U1.owner=U2.owner
AND  U1.table_name=U2.table_name
AND  U1.column_name=U2.column_name
AND  S.table_owner NOT IN ('SYSTEM', 'MDSYS', 'ORDSYS', 'SYS')
AND  S.DB_LINK = 'PRD5.WORLD'
;
[HELP]
HELP= DBLINK - To PRD5
```

Database Options that Relate to Strategies

The settings on the Strategies tab also relate to the Designer's Database Options under Tools | Options | Database. In the Strategies tab, even if you tell BusinessObjects to use Smart Matching based on the column names, BusinessObjects will automatically create the joins in the universe only if you check the box Extract joins with tables in Options. (Yes, it would be more intuitive if this were in the same place as the Strategy settings!) The main difference between Parameters and Database Options is that Parameters are specific to the individual universe, whereas the Options apply to Designer, and, therefore, all universes created on the PC. But I confess that I still struggle to remember where each setting is because they are so interdependent!

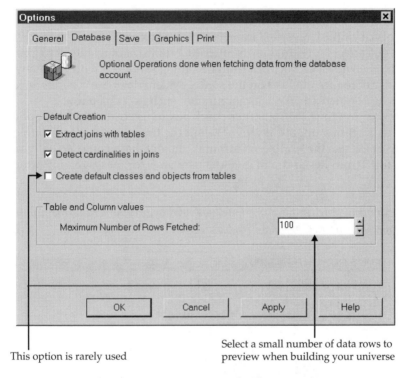

This option is rarely used

Select a small number of data rows to preview when building your universe

When Designer detects cardinalities, it analyzes the rows in each table to determine where the one-to-one, one-to-many, and many-to-many relationships are. Leaving the Detect Cardinalities In Joins box checked on large databases can cause a very slow structure creation. I'm fairly impatient, so I will leave the cardinalities unchecked during an initial build and will detect the cardinalities at a later point.

The last default creation option, Create default classes and objects from tables, should probably never be checked unless you have a very small star schema and you have modified your strategy to read only that schema. Additionally, your column names in your data mart must be based on business terminology, and even then, you will still need to delete a lot of extraneous objects and move them around to more meaningful classes. Otherwise, you will very quickly have a lot of garbage in your universe.

Table and column values is a useful feature to show you a sample of the data in your tables as you build objects in the universe. As a default, Designer will present you with the first 100 values in your database.

Controls

The Controls tab of the Universe Parameters dialog box enables you to specify additional limits that will affect individual users' queries. Limit size of result set to: prevents the user PC and the wide area network from becoming saturated with too many rows of data. It does not reduce the load on the source system database. Therefore, leave this box unchecked or increase it to a larger number such as 300,000 rows.

Limit execution time to: is another check box to use carefully. This option limits the time the PC is tied up, but it will not limit the time the database is affected. So if an administrator sets the limit to 60 minutes, the database could actually try to run the query for 70 minutes and will give the user an error message only after 70 minutes.

Note   *If your queries are running this long, you need to do some serious index optimization or encourage users to use the Broadcast Agent (refer to Chapter 20).*

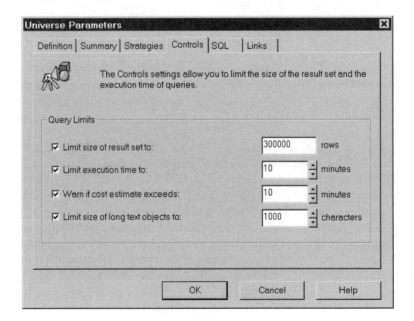

As described previously, Warn if cost estimate exceeds: is an excellent option for giving users a warning for long-running queries. As of this writing, BusinessObjects is the only BI tool that allows users to take advantage of this RDBMS capability. Users get to cancel the query before it hits the source system database and ties up resources unnecessarily. Set the time limit for this option high enough that users do not receive the following error message every time they refresh a query, yet low enough to allow them to receive a useful warning for particularly slow queries.

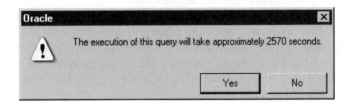

Limit size of long text objects to: is useful for blob fields or for very long variable-length fields. Users can adjust their column widths if they do not want to see the full text. However, if you as the administrator set this number too low, users cannot override it; they never can get to the data at the end of a long field.

SQL

When deploying BusinessObjects directly against an OLTP, you may want to limit complex SQL queries so that they do not affect response time for inputting data. Otherwise, I prefer to leave complex SQL enabled in pure reporting databases. Casual users will not know what to do with them and can ignore the options. However, if you disable advanced SQL, then power users may get frustrated. The following three options in the SQL tab of the Universe Parameters dialog box allow you to limit complex queries:

- **Allow Use Of Subqueries** Subqueries are a powerful type of query that allows users to nest one query within a main query (see Chapter 22). As these queries are complex and use additional RDBMS resources, administrators can remove this capability. By default, leave it enabled.

- **Allow Use Of Union, Intersect, And Minus Operators** These operators allow advanced users to combine multiple SQL statements into one report (see Chapter 22). By default, leave it enabled.

- **Allow Complex Operands In Query Panel** This option is similar to the preceding one but allows users to select the conditions from the query panel: Complex operands are Both and Except. Both generate an INTERSECT query, and Except generates a MINUS query.

The Multiple Paths options determine the kind of SQL generated behind the scenes. The users may not see the SQL, but they do affect the performance and accuracy of any given query.

Business Objects: The Complete Reference

■ **Multiple SQL Statements For Each Context**   Contexts were discussed briefly in Chapter 5 and are explained in detail in Chapter 7. This option should be checked so that a separate SQL statement is generated for each context or star schema. If your universe has multiple contexts and you do not enable this box, users will receive an error message when trying to create a query that contains measures from two different contexts. In the EFASHION universe, for example, one could not create a query that analyzes promotion costs and sales revenue for a given product.

■ **Multiple SQL Statements For Each Measure**   This box should always be enabled or queries from multiple fact tables may produce incorrect results. In the EFASHION universe, unit sales price and extended sales price are from two different tables. It's also useful to check this option even if you think you have one central fact table. For example, you may later create measures such as number of days or number of products that go against dimension tables. BusinessObjects will create a Cartesian product and give incorrect information if your measures come from more than one table (discussed further in Chapter 12).

■ **Allow Selection Of Multiple Contexts**   Enables users to create queries on objects from multiple contexts. This box should be enabled. In the EFASHION universe, it allows users to analyze sales and promotions in one report; sales and promotions are two different contexts.

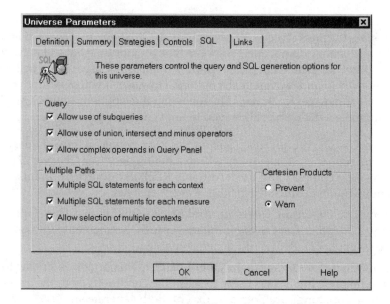

The Multiple SQL statements for each measure option has some nuances that are important to understand. First, even if this box is enabled, if the measures come from the same fact table, BusinessObjects will issue only one SQL statement. This is a good thing as it avoids tying up the database unnecessarily. Second, BusinessObjects will only issue two SQL statements if the object is a measure (discussed further in Chapter 8) and it contains an aggregate function (sum, count, and so on). The EFASHION universe is somewhat misleading, as a unit price should *never* contain a SUM. However, it still illustrates the risk of not splitting the measures when multiple fact tables are involved.

When SQL joins two tables together, it will repeat each row for each combination in the GROUP BY section. Figure 6-7 illustrates how this happens. The ARTICLE_LOOKUP table has only one row and shows a price of 114.55. The SHOP_FACTS table has six rows showing that this style blazer sold six times during week 8 of year 2000. When SQL joins ARTICLE_LOOKUP with SHOP_FACTS, the 114.55 unit price will get repeated six times and summed to 687.30; an incorrect result. This is not a problem of BusinessObjects; it is an issue of understanding how SQL works and ensuring that you have developed your underlying data mart and universe to give users correct results. The following

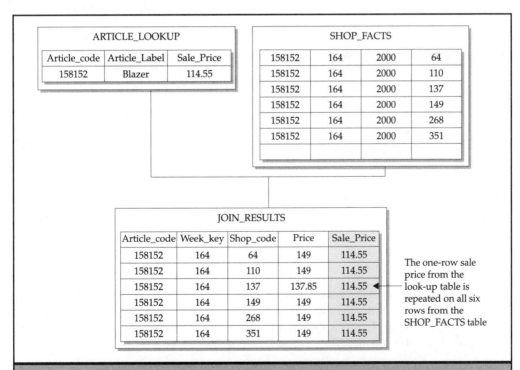

Figure 6-7.   *SQL may give incorrect results if you try to use a GROUP BY function such as SUM across two tables that have different numbers of rows. To prevent this inaccuracy, check the box Multiple Select Statements For Each Measure in the universe parameters.*

report shows the results depending on which option is set in the SQL universe parameters:

Splitting measures in the SQL
tab ensures correct results

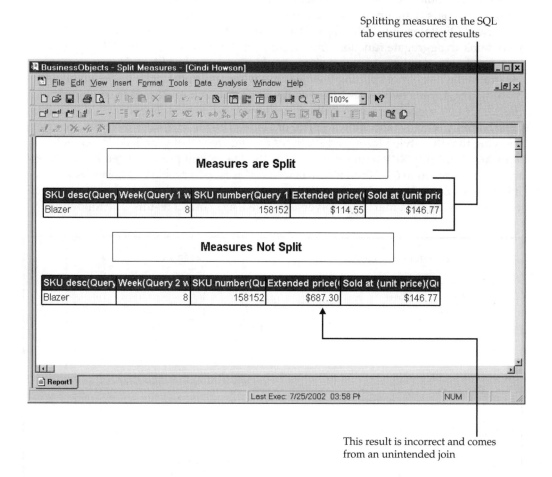

This result is incorrect and comes
from an unintended join

Links

The last tab of the Universe Parameters dialog box, Links, allows an administrator to create a master universe that is then linked to other universes. As this is an architecture and maintenance issue, links are described more fully in Chapter 14, "Linked Universes." By default, leave this tab blank.

The
Complete
Reference

Business
Objects

Chapter 7

Universe Joins

Joins define how two tables relate to one another. In Designer, your strategies (under File | Parameters) can automatically propose joins based on common names between two tables. Alternatively, you can manually define the joins. Most of the complexities around joins occur when your universe contains multiple star schemas or when you are using BusinessObjects against a normalized transaction system.

Join Graphics

In Designer, you can change the appearance of the join lines and the symbols used to display relationship cardinalities. You also can have Designer provide you with additional information that will help you create or modify the joins more accurately. These settings will apply to all universes (unlike parameter settings reviewed in Chapter 6 that are universe specific). Figure 7-1 shows the database structure for a sample Oracle Sales History (SH) database. A number of the graphic settings have been changed to make the structure easier to read.

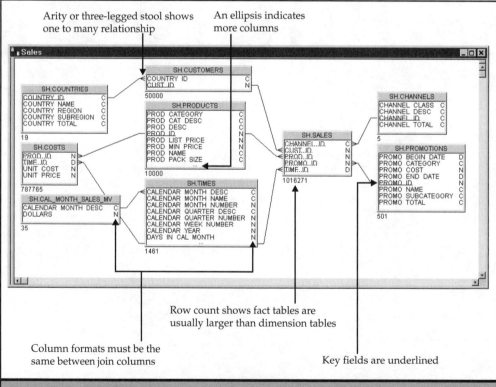

Figure 7-1. *This sample Oracle sales history universe shows table sizes, key names, and cardinalities. This information is useful in defining joins.*

To display this information in all universes, select Tools | Options | Graphics from the Designer menu.

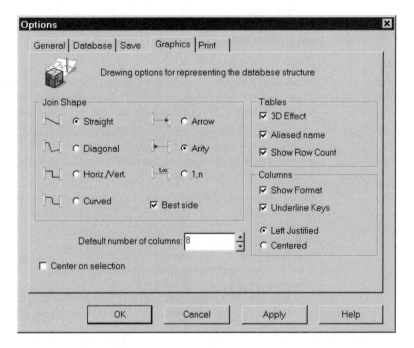

The Join Shape settings determine how you would like the join lines drawn. This is purely personal preference and does not affect your universe design. The Arrow join shape is the least helpful, as it does not provide any information about the cardinality of the join. Use either Arity or 1,n. Arity will give you a crow's foot for a many relationship, and 1,n will display numbers. The Best side check box merely has the line drawn from the side of the table that will make your entity relationship diagram appear less busy and easier to read. Table 7-1 summarizes other graphics options.

Show Row Count

Extracting row count information requires a full table scan against each table. It can be slow to generate this information for fact tables that contain millions of rows of data. Therefore, when you turn on the option to display the row counts, Designer does not automatically fetch these numbers. To fetch the numbers, ensure that your mouse is not on any one table, then select View | Number of Rows in Table. Designer will ask you if

Option	Purpose
Default number of columns	For tables with many columns, Designer will display the first n columns in the structure pane and use an ellipsis to indicate that more columns exist in the table.
3-D Effect	Displays a shadow box around the table name.
Aliased name	Aliases are described later in this chapter, in the section "Aliases." This checkbox will allow you to see both the alias name used in the universe as well as the physical table name in the underlying RDBMS.
Show Row Count	This option only works when you have separately extracted the row counts for each table. The row count will display the actual or expected number of rows in each table, useful for determining join order and outer join issues.
Show Format	Show Format will display the format of the column: C for character D for date N for number T for long text L for lob—all large binary objects (blob, clob, bfile, nblob in Oracle) Join fields are either character, date, or number. Most databases do not allow you to join between two columns that are a different format, even if the values are the same. For example, if the ARTICLE_CODE in SHOP_FACTS is character and ARTICLE_CODE in ARTICLE_LOOK_UP is numeric, the database will return an error during query execution and/or when you select Parse in editing the join statement. During the universe integrity check, quick parsing will not reveal this error, but thorough parsing will. Therefore, use thorough parsing.
Underline Keys	Joins between two tables are usually between key columns. For Designer to underline which columns are keys, check this box, and in addition, extract the key information via your strategies (see Chapter 6). Select File	Parameters	Strategies tab. In the Join box, select All Matching Column Names. Note that the first join strategy does not include key info. If Designer does not underline the key names in the structure pane, refresh your database structure by selecting View	Refresh Structure.
Left Justified or Centered	Left Justified and Centered affect the appearance of whether the column names are left aligned or centered beneath the table name in the structure pane.

Table 7-1.   *Designer Graphics Options Used in the Structure Pane*

you want to Set or detect row counts for all tables. Click OK. Select Refresh row count for all tables, as shown here:

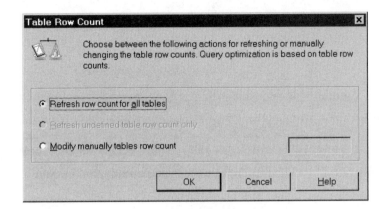

The Modify manually tables row count option allows you to enter manually the number of rows for an individual table. This can be useful if you are working with test data and you want to enter expected rows or if you know the approximate row counts for large fact tables and you do not want to wait for Designer to extract this information.

The row count information is used in two ways: First, it helps you as the designer understand when you are joining large tables together. Second, BusinessObjects lists the largest table first in the FROM section of a SQL statement to make queries run faster. Databases that do not have an optimizer will benefit from careful ordering of tables in the SQL statements. Databases such as Oracle and DB2 have an optimizer, so there is no need to spend time modifying row counts (unless you are using the Rule-based optimizer).

The row count information works in conjunction with the REVERSE_TABLE_WEIGHT parameter in the *database*.prm file. By default, this parameter is set to Y to list tables largest to smallest. Set this parameter to N for smallest to largest.

Basic Joins

Once you have set your graphics options, you can begin modifying or creating basic joins. Displaying the joins in list mode can be helpful in determining the order of the tables in the join statement as well as seeing long join statements. Click the View List Mode button on the toolbar or select View | List Mode from the pull-down menus.

Referring back to the Test Fashion universe we created in Chapter 6, the universe has two basic joins from SHOP_FACTS to CALENDAR_YEAR_LOOKUP and SHOP_FACTS to ARTICLE_LOOKUP. The arity or three-lined "crow's foot" indicates that the relationship between SHOP_FACTS and ARTICLE_LOOKUP is one to many. For every one article in ARTICLE_LOOKUP, there may be one or many sales transactions in SHOP_FACTS (for example, blazers can sell one or more times). View List Mode gives an overview of all join statements, as you can see here:

Modify the join statement in the formula bar

View List Mode button

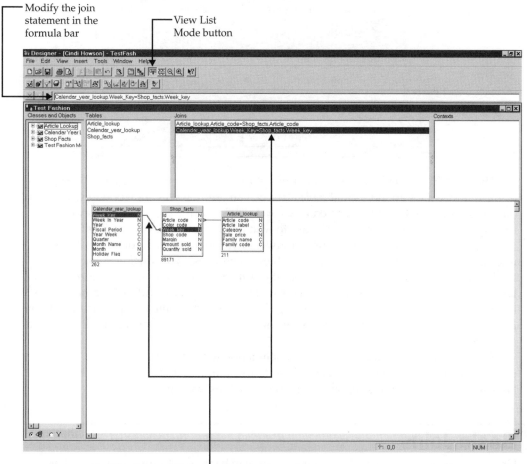

Double-click the join line or statement to modify it

There are several ways to modify the join statement:

■ Double-click the join line in the Structure pane.

■ Double-click the join line in the Join list.

■ Manually enter changes in the formula bar.

Modify the join between SHOP_FACTS and ARTICLE_LOOKUP. You are presented with the Edit Join dialog box. Keys are often used in joins. If your keys are not underlined in the structure pane, check File | Parameters | Strategies and refresh the structure.

Join type

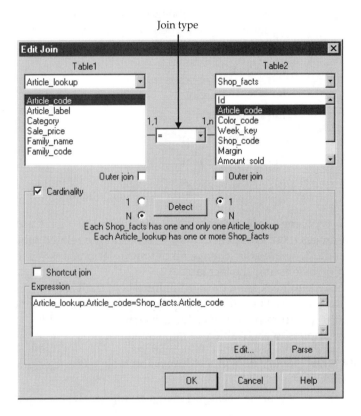

Table1, ARTICLE_LOOKUP, appears on the left-hand side and Table2, SHOP_FACTS, on the right. In some RDBMSs, which table is right or left does not matter, but in others, it can affect how quickly a query is processed. When Designer proposes joins via the Quick Design Wizard, it puts the smaller table on the left side of the join and the larger table on the right. This order may result in faster queries for certain databases, particularly for joins other than equi-joins (BETWEEN, >=, > !, =).

Note *When Oracle uses the cost-based optimizer, the order of the joins and the order of the tables in the FROM section of the SQL does not matter; however, if you are using the rule-based optimizer, it does.*

The first drop-down box lets you define the join operator:

Join Operator	Explanation
=	Equi-join. This is the most common and default join type. Two tables are related when every data value in the left table has an equivalent value in the right table
!=	Not equal
>	Greater than
<	Less than
>=	Greater than or equal
<=	Less than or equal

Cardinality

Above the join type, the cardinalities are indicated with 1,n = 1,1. Cardinality defines how many instances there are of each unique record in the related table: zero, one, or many. In a standard, single-star schema, all of your relationships will be one to many between the dimensions and the fact table.

If you remove the check from the cardinalities box, the 1,n and 1,1 are no longer displayed in the join panel beside the join operator. To change the appearance of the cardinality in the structure pane, select Tools I Database I Graphics.

Cardinality applies to each table in a join statement:

- **Table 1(1,n)**   Every item in the dimension table has one or more records in the fact table.

- **Table 2(1,1)**   For every record in the fact table, there is one and only one record in the lookup table.

Cardinality detection and display did not exist in earlier versions of BusinessObjects. According to the vendor-provided documentation, the sole purpose of cardinality detection is to warn you of possible loops. However, cardinality detection does not work reliably and has no effect on loop detection, though it does affect detection. As of this writing, Cardinality detection does not correctly detect many-to-many relationships, nor does it detect zero relationships (which would be quite useful in defining outer joins). According to BusinessObjects, the detection algorithm counts rows to determine the cardinality and does not catch anomalies that may affect cardinality. There are no plans to change this in version 6.

If you skip cardinality detection completely, Designer will still correctly detect loops but will not propose contexts. Therefore, you may want to skip this process entirely if

- Your universe will have only one star or snowflake schema.

- The cardinality between tables is not typical of star schemas. A star schema typically has one dimension to many facts. If your tables have many-to-many relationships and Designer correctly detects this (it normally doesn't), then Designer will falsely tell you "No New Contexts Needed." For more accurate context detection, manually set the cardinalities.

If your data is clean, however, and if your universe will have multiple schemas, cardinality detection can be helpful in later detecting contexts.

Outer Joins

Outer joins are a special join type and one that requires careful consideration before using. An outer join is a relationship between two tables in which records from one table do not have matching records in the other. BusinessObjects does not provide a sample universe that contains outer joins, but you can create one using ARTICLE_LOOKUP and SHOP_FACTS.

In the ARTICLE_LOOKUP table, you add a new record, ARTICLE_CODE 189480, a new sweatshirt for Leeds United Football Club. You know that there are no sales against this sweatshirt in the SHOP_FACTS table, because you just added it. If a user were to run a report for the sales category "Sweats," he/she would not see this sweatshirt listed if the universe contained a default equi-join. Therefore, you need an outer join on the ARTICLE_LOOKUP table.

This is a new record in the article lookup table for which there are no sales

Article_code	Article_label	Category	Sale_price	Family_name	Family_cc
185403	Starlet Jacket	Fancy fabric	$161.00	Jackets	F45
186108	Vivaldi Tunic	Long sleeve	$159.00	Shirt Waist	F20
186370	Flounced Collar Shirtdress	Long sleeve	$200.00	Shirt Waist	F20
187710	Africa Zipper Cardigan	Cardigan	$231.00	Sweaters	F25
187901	Fake Leopard Skin Gloves with Lurex Trim	Hats,gloves,scarves	$852.50	Accessories	F60
187904	Denim Front Button Dress	Casual dresses	$127.50	Dresses	F80
189479	Whisky Dancer T-Shirt	T-Shirts	$214.00	Sweat-T-Shirts	F36
189480	Leeds United Football Club	Sweats	$65.00	Sweat-T-Shirts	F36

A BETTER UNIVERSE

To change the existing equi-join to an outer join:

1. Double-click the join line between SHOP_FACTS and ARTICLE_LOOKUP or right-click and select Join Properties from the pop-up menu.

2. Under Table1, ARTICLE_LOOKUP, select the Outer join box.

3. Select Parse to ensure the join is valid.

4. Click OK to save the change to the join.

5. Click Save on the Designer toolbar to save the changes to the universe.

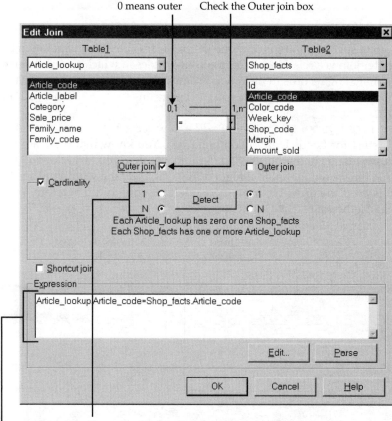

Note   *Designer version 5.1.3 has a bug that switches which table is Table1 in the Edit Join dialog box. Be sure that you are putting the outer join on the correct table.*

Now if you run a BusinessObjects report, you will see the Leeds United sweatshirt even though you have had no sales yet. The outer join allows this new ARTICLE_CODE to appear in the report, even though there are no corresponding rows in SHOP_FACTS.

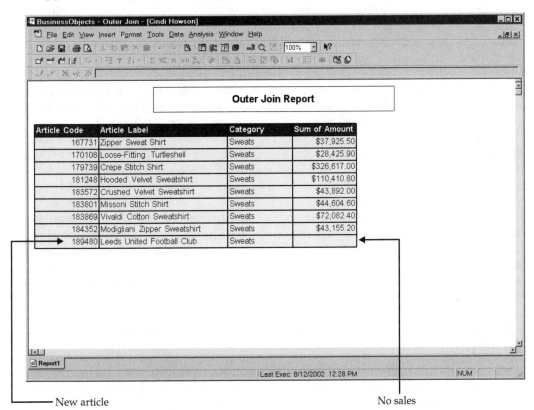

———— New article   No sales

The actual SQL syntax for outer joins will vary depending on which database and driver you are using. In the Edit Join dialog box, ODBC does not update the expression to show the outer join. Other RDBMs will adjust the join expression in the dialog box. The Microsoft Access SQL uses the following syntax:

```
oj Article_lookup LEFT OUTER JOIN Shop_facts ON
Article_lookup.Article_code=Shop_facts.Article_code
```

Oracle uses the + to indicate the outer join. The + always goes on the table that has fewer records (yes, it feels illogical to me, too!):

```
SHOP_FACTS.ARTICLE_CODE=ARTICLE_LOOKUP.ARTICLE_CODE(+)
```

You may now be thinking that it makes sense to put outer joins on all lookup tables, since you often have inventory before items have sold. However, it's also possible to have items in a fact table that do not have a corresponding record in the dimension table. As an example, imagine a frustrated sales clerk who keeps trying to scan a trendy new scarf for an impatient customer. The scanner does not ring up the product at the register, so the sales clerk manually enters the article code from the scarf's tag (let's avoid the worst scenario, when the clerk rings it up under a different article with the same unit price ... a common occurrence at my local department store). Why didn't the scarf scan? Who knows! Of course, the scarf should have been in inventory! And it should not have been on display without existing in the article master! But it happened, and unfortunately, it happens more than business people realize and more than data modelers wish.

In an ideal world, the sales transaction would automatically have added an entry in the article master. In an almost ideal world, the data warehouse will plug a number in the ARTICLE_KEY such as 999 or XXX to say the article description is not found.

In reality (such as a transaction system or poorly modeled data mart), you will need to use an outer join. Outer joins may not be a problem for small lookup tables, but they are best avoided for large lookup tables because the RDBMS cannot use the index to process the query because of lousy response times. Also, earlier versions of certain databases did not support outer joins.

Even when you use an outer join on a small lookup table, be sure to test the response time or analyze and explain the plan in your RDBMS. If the response time is slow, train the users to understand that if they want full product listings, full customer listings, or a list of customers who have not bought this year, analyze that data separately. Use of subqueries (discussed in Chapter 22) may help them answer the same questions more efficiently.

Loops

Loops occur when there are two different paths to accomplish one join. The following structure now includes PRODUCT_PROMOTION_FACTS in the Test Fashion universe. If users want to analyze articles versus time, there are now two join paths. BusinessObjects does not know which path to take, the one via SHOP_FACTS or the one via PRODUCT_ PROMOTION_FACTS.

The circular appearance of these four joins is a loop, which can give undesired SQL results.

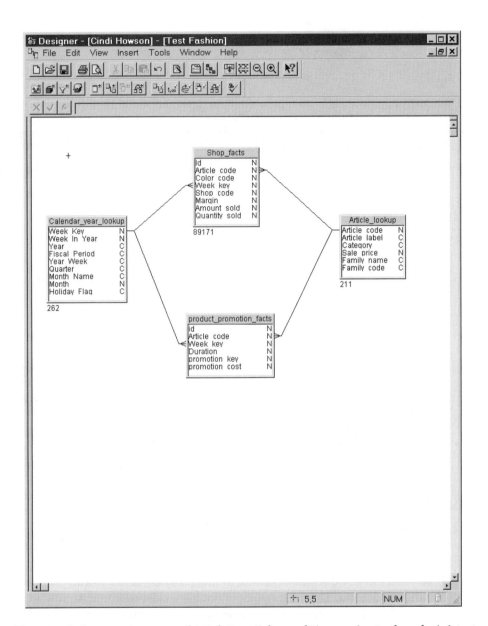

If users tried to create a query based on articles and time, prior to the administrator resolving this loop, they would receive the error message shown in Figure 7-2.

Contexts help break this loop into two sets of join statements, so the desired join path is always clear.

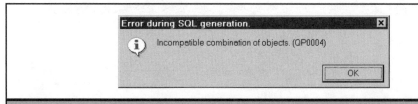

Figure 7-2. *Users receive this error message if you do not resolve loops or allow contexts in File I Parameters, SQL tab in Designer.*

Inserting a New Context

Designer can help you detect and resolve loops by using contexts. To enable this, we will first add a table to create a loop and then resolve the loop with a context.

1. Add the PRODUCT_PROMOTION_FACT table to your universe. From the pull-down menu, select Insert I Table or right-click in the Structure pane and select Insert Table from the pop-up menu.

2. From the table browser, select the PRODUCT_PROMOTION_FACT table and click Insert.

3. If your Database Options are set to extract joins with tables (the Options dialog box reached by choosing Tools I Options, Database tab) and if your universe parameters are set to propose joins based on matching column names (in File I Parameters, Strategies tab, see Chapter 6), Designer will automatically add the join between PRODUCT_PROMOTION_FACT and ARTICLE_LOOKUP. Recall also from Chapter 6 that the join names of the columns for WEEK_KEY do not have the same initial caps between the two tables. Therefore this join is not automatically detected and must be manually defined. Draw a join line between CALENDAR_YEAR_LOOKUP.WEEK_KEY and PRODUCT_PROMOTION_FACT.WEEK_KEY. This last join is what creates the loop and closes the circle just shown.

4. Click the Detect Loops button on the toolbar or select Tools I Detect Loops from the pull-down menus. Designer will highlight all the joins that create the loop or circle.

5. If you had already defined a context, at this point Designer would propose a Candidate Context. This universe does not have existing contexts, so you need to detect them. Designer will only detect contexts when the cardinalities have been set. Set them manually or click Detect Cardinalities. Designer will check the cardinality box in the join statement and show the relationships in the Structure pane.

If your data is not clean and the cardinalities do not follow the typical one-to-many for one-dimension-to-many facts, Detect Contexts will not work.

6. Select Detect Contexts from the toolbar or Candidate Context from the Loop Detection dialog. Designer will present you with a list of names as proposed contexts. These contexts include all the joins in each part of the loop or one set of joins. The proposed context name comes from whichever table name is at the center of the join path, in this case SHOP_FACTS and PRODUCTION_PROMOTION_FACTS.

7. Highlight each Candidate Context and select Add to include the two new contexts in the universe.

8. Click OK to close the Candidate Context box and Close to close the Loop Detection dialog. The universe Structure pane and List Mode should now appear as follows. Note that when a particular context is highlighted in the Contexts list, the join statements that belong to that context are also highlighted in the Joins list as well as the Structure pane.

Joins that comprise the context   New context

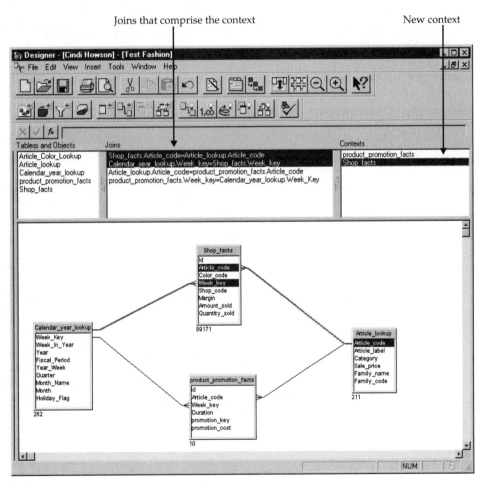

9. Click Save on the toolbar to save your universe changes.

Congratulations! You have resolved your first loop. Unfortunately, your real world universe may not be so easy. If your universe contains aggregates or is a snowflake design, Designer may propose more contexts than necessary. Likewise, as you add new tables to your universe, your contexts may become incomplete. If you leave the context name at its default and if your cardinalities are typical, Detect Contexts works very well and will help you identify isolated joins that do not yet belong to a context.

Modifying a Context

As a general rule, leave the context name as the default until you have added all tables, loops, and contexts. This makes the universe designer's life easier, as Designer will automatically add the table to an existing context, when you use Detect Contexts. With this semiautomatic insertion, you may never want to rename contexts. However, it is not the friendliest situation for users. When users launch a query involving a potential loop, users will have to select a context. If the context name uses the default table name, it may not be user friendly. It's always better to make life harder for one designer than for hundreds of users!

In the following example, I have renamed the context "Product Promotion Fact" to "Promotion." You can rename a context either while initially defining the context or after you have added the context to the universe. To rename the context after it has been defined:

1. Select the Context from the list.

2. Use the pull-down menu Edit | Context Properties or right-click the context name and select Context Properties.

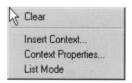

3. In the Context Name box, enter a business-oriented name; replace Product Promotion Facts with **Promotion**.

4. In the Description box, enter help text that will appear when users are prompted to select a context. For example, **BusinessObjects is not sure how to answer your question. If you want to know which articles were promoted in a certain time period, select the Promotion context. If you want to know which articles sold in a certain time period, select the Shop Facts context.**

Rename an existing context

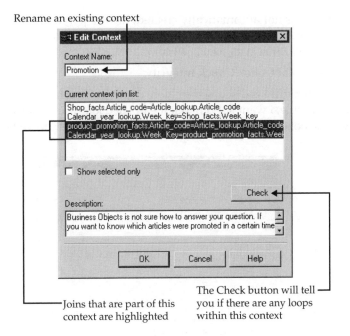

Joins that are part of this
context are highlighted

The Check button will tell
you if there are any loops
within this context

5. Click Check to verify that this particular context contains no loops; it does not
   check for other loops within the universe.

6. Click OK to close the Edit Context box.

Isolated Joins

Once you use contexts in a universe, you must keep using them and ensure they are
complete. As you add new tables to your universe, the joins between the tables must
be added to an existing context or included in a new context. In the following example,
you will add the PROMOTION_LOOKUP table to the universe and include it in an
existing context:

1. Add the table PROMOTION_LOOKUP to your universe. From the pull-down menu,
   select Insert | Table or right-click in the Structure pane and select Insert Table.

2. From the table browser, select the PROMOTION_LOOKUP table and click Insert.

3. If the join was not automatically created, draw a join line between PROMOTION_LOOKUP.PROMOTION_KEY and PRODUCT_PROMOTION_FACT.PROMOTION_KEY.

4. From the toolbar, click Check Integrity.

5. Universe integrity is discussed in more depth in Chapter 15. In this example, I want to point out the isolated join you just created. Check the boxes for cardinalities, loops, and contexts, as shown here:

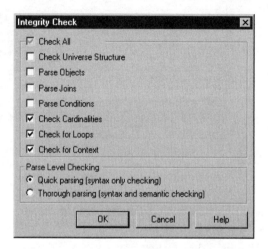

6. Click OK to run the Integrity Check. Designer will now go through and verify that all loops are resolved and any new joins belong to at least one context. The following screen shows that the newly added table PROMOTION_LOOKUP and its related join does not belong to a context:

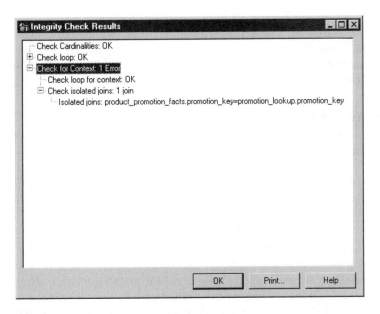

7. Click OK to close the Integrity Check Results box.

8. From the pull-down menu, select Tools | Detect Context or click
   Detect Context.

9. Designer will prompt you with the context product_promotion_facts, which
   includes the three joins to the fact table. If you did not rename this context
   Promotion in the last section, Designer will ask you if you want to overwrite
   your existing context.

10. Click OK and then Save to include this new context or additional join in the
    existing context.

Once you have created a context, it is also possible to add additional joins without
using the Detect Context command. You will need to do this if your cardinalities are
atypical (or if detection is slow and you know to which context new tables need to be
added). To modify a context, either double-click the context from the list pane or use
the pull-down menus to select Edit | Context Properties.

Once you start using Contexts, you must ensure all joins are included in at least one context. If you fail to do this, user queries are split into multiple SQL statements that may lead to inaccurate results or messages such as "Incompatible combination of objects." What happens depends on the universe Parameters | SQL | Multiple Paths settings.

How Contexts Are Used

Now that you have two contexts, all user queries will be affected in one of three ways, sometimes with user prompting and sometimes without prompting:

1. When a user selects objects from tables purely within one context (CALENDAR_ YEAR_LOOKUP, SHOP_FACTS, ARTICLE_LOOKUP), BusinessObjects is smart enough to know which context or join path to use to generate the SQL. The user is not prompted to choose a context.

2. When a user selects objects from both contexts, for example, sales and promotion costs by article and month, both contexts need to be used and BusinessObjects will intelligently generate two separate SQL statements and seamlessly stitch the results together in one report. Some vendors refer to this functionality as Multipass SQL. As the administrator, you must make sure you have the correct Parameters | SQL settings to allow this or users will see the error message shown earlier in Figure 7-2 (see Chapter 6 for correct settings).

Note   *The capability to generate multiple SQL statements and automatically stitch the results together is one of BusinessObjects most powerful features and one that sets it apart from other BI tools. Prior to this technology, users would have to follow such a process manually.*

The left side of Figure 7-3 shows the first SQL statement BusinessObjects generates to retrieve sales amounts. Select1 uses the Shop_Facts context. The right side shows the second SQL statement BusinessObjects generates to retrieve the promotion costs for the *same year and article IDs.* This is very important. The dimensions form the GROUP BY section of the SELECT statement. If these are not exactly the same, the query still executes but with additional rows of data, as BusinessObjects is not clear how to synchronize the results. For example, if I added a row Radio promotion to my query, it would only appear in Select2. The beauty of this synchronization feature is that users never see it; their business question is answered automatically and correctly.

3. When a user selects objects from the lookup tables without including objects from a fact table, BusinessObjects cannot determine automatically which context to use. Therefore, it prompts the user. In the next example, I created a query that includes Article Id and Year. BusinessObjects cannot determine if I want to know which articles sold (Shop_Facts context) within a certain year or which

articles had promotion costs (Product_Promotion_Fact context) within a certain year. Note in the following screen that users see the Description added in the earlier section "Modify a Context":

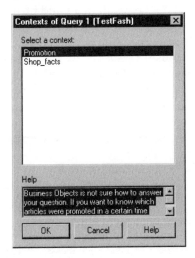

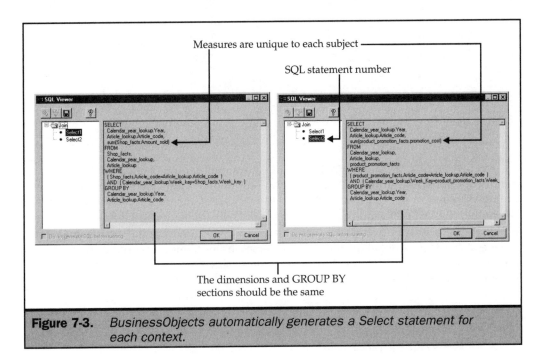

Figure 7-3. *BusinessObjects automatically generates a Select statement for each context.*

Are Loops a Bad Thing?

You have spent a lot of time identifying loops and getting rid of them with contexts. In many cases, a loop is unintended, caused by poorly written SQL against complex schemas. However, loops can be the result of a valid business question if users really want to know which articles and weeks are common between both the promotion fact table and the sales fact table.

Look at the following two BusinessObjects reports. The articles Polo Collared T-Shirt (166544), Whisky Dancer T-Shirt (166550), and Pomodore Lace T-Shirt (167695, week 33) had promotions but no shop sales, so they appear in the report labeled "Product Promotion Context" but not in the report labeled "Loop Report."

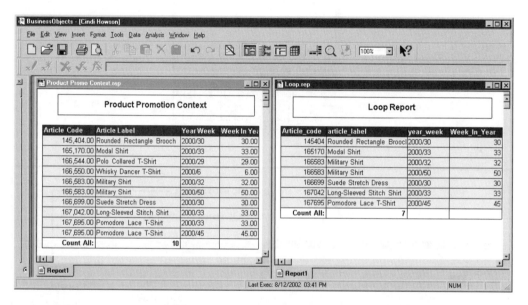

The first report, Product Promotion Context, contains ten rows of data for articles that had promotions during particular weeks. The second report, Loop Report, contains only seven rows of data and lists articles and weeks that are common between *both* the promotion fact table and the shop fact table. There are less rows in this second report because not all products had both promotions and sales in the exact same week. BusinessObjects does not allow loops in universes; users cannot run queries that contain an unresolved loop. The Loop Report was created using the following Free-hand SQL (discussed in Part III of this book):

```
SELECT
  Article_lookup.Article_code,
  Article_lookup.article_label,
  Calendar_year_lookup.Week_In_Year,
  Calendar_year_lookup.year_week
FROM
```

```
  Calendar_year_lookup,
  Article_lookup,
  product_promotion_facts,
shop_facts
WHERE
  ( Calendar_year_lookup.Week_Key=product_promotion_facts.Week_key  )
  AND  ( Article_lookup.Article_code=product_promotion_facts.Article_code  )
And
  ( Calendar_year_lookup.Week_Key=shop_facts.Week_key  )
  AND  ( Article_lookup.Article_code=shop_facts.Article_code  )
```

The bottom line? Designer does not allow loops and will force you to resolve them. One may consider this a limitation of BusinessObjects. However, most SQL that contains a loop is often unintentional; therefore, BusinessObjects forces designers to construct universes in a way that consistently provides correct answers. Similar business questions can be answered more efficiently in other ways, as described in Chapter 22.

Composite Keys and Complex Joins

Occasionally in resolving loops, Designer will suggest the loop can be resolved by an alias. This may happen when you are trying to join two tables together with two different fields, for example, SALES_FACT to CUSTOMER.SHIP_TO and SALES_FACT to CUSTOMER.SOLD_TO. Be careful not to confuse this with composite keys in which more than one column uniquely identifies a record.

Most fact tables have several columns that uniquely identify one row of data. In the BEACH or Island Resorts Marketing universe, the two columns CUST_ID and INV_ID uniquely identify the records in the SALES table. The two columns together are called a composite key. Lookup or dimension tables also may have a composite key. None of the BusinessObjects sample universes contain lookup tables with composite keys, and a recent, well-designed data warehouse also should not require them. However, first-generation data warehouses often used composite keys, and transaction systems still do.

For example, to track changes in customer reference data, the month and year often may be part of the composite key. Figure 7-4 shows multiple records for the customer IDs 106, 207, and 306.

■ Customer 106, Baker moved from Chicago, IL, to Sparta, NJ, in April 1997. The row from customer ID 106, MM_YY 04-1996 contains old data for the same customer.

■ Customer 207, Dupont divorced and reverted to her maiden name of Hayem in May 1997. The row from customer ID 207, MM_YY 05-1997 contains old data for the same customer.

■ Customer 306, Jones married and changed her name to Whitwell in January 2001. The row from customer ID 306, MM_YY 04-1996 contains old data for the same customer.

Composite key

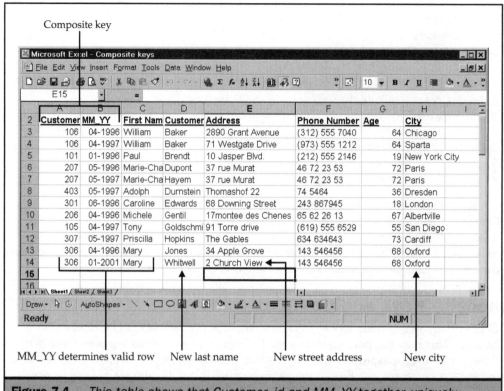

MM_YY determines valid row   New last name   New street address   New city

Figure 7-4. *This table shows that Customer_id and MM_YY together uniquely identify each record as customer names and addresses have changed over the years.*

When analyzing reservations by city or by last name, the join between CUSTOMER and RESERVATIONS must now include MM_YY to RES_DATE, *in addition to* the CUST_ID. In earlier versions of BusinessObjects, one could include these joins as separate line items (see Figure 7-5) since BusinessObjects automatically connects multiple join statements with an AND. In fact, when you use join detection or if your database options are set to extract joins with tables, Designer will incorrectly propose multiple join statements. However, with the addition of loop detection, these compound joins must be done in one join statement or Designer will falsely detect a loop.

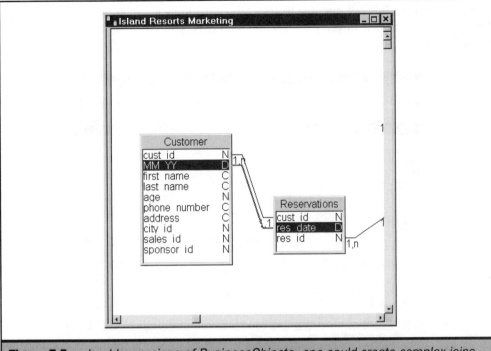

Figure 7-5.   *In older versions of BusinessObjects, one could create complex joins with multiple join statements. This kind of join will give a false loop detection in version 5.*

To correctly create a complex join, select the join on CUST_ID and double-click it to bring up the Edit Join box. In the Expression box, type **AND** at the end of the join statement. As soon as you enter AND, Designer changes the join type to Complex. You must continue to manually enter your join statement so that it reads

```
Customer.cust_id=Reservations.cust_id AND
Customer.MM_YY=Reservations.res_date
```

Unfortunately, it is not possible to select the additional join columns from the drop-down lists. As complex joins are manually entered, be sure to Parse these statements in particular.

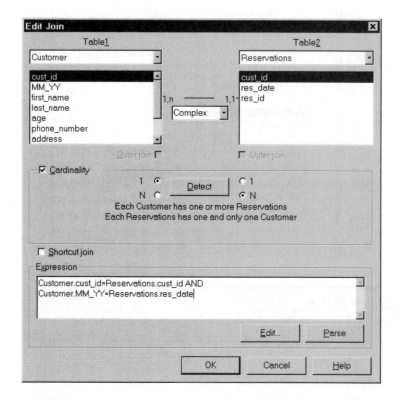

Aliases

When Designer sees two join statements between the same two tables, it often will propose an alias to resolve the loop. If your company has multiple SQL tools accessing a data warehouse, your DBA may have resolved many of these issues by creating synonyms or views in the RDBMS. For example, one physical CUSTOMER dimension table could be joined to a fact table two times as synonyms SHIP_TO_CUSTOMER or SOLD_TO_CUSTOMER. Synonyms in the source RDBMS appear to Designer as physical tables, even though they behave much like aliases. If such synonyms or views do not exist in your RDBMS, create an alias to use one physical table in different ways.

Laura Reeves, co-author of The Data Warehouse Lifecycle Toolkit *(John Wiley & Sons, 1998) and TDWI instructor, recommends using physical tables rather than views. Too many views can confuse database optimizers and result in slower query performance.*

When you insert a table that already exists in the universe, Designer will force you to create an alias and prompt you to give a new name to the table. Alternatively, you can ask Designer to detect potential aliases, or you can consciously choose tables that you know you want to use in multiple ways.

Detecting Aliases

The sample Island Resorts Marketing (BEACH.UNV) universe contains information about resorts and customers who visit those resorts. Resorts can be located in different countries, and customers can be located in different countries. If you were building this universe from scratch, Designer would have detected a join between the following tables:

```
COUNTRY.COUNTRY_ID=REGION.COUNTRY_ID (which eventually joins to CUSTOMER)
COUNTRY.COUNTRY_ID=RESORT.COUNTRY_ID.
RESORT.COUNTRY_ID=REGION.COUNTRY_ID
```

Note in the following screen that these joins cause a loop:

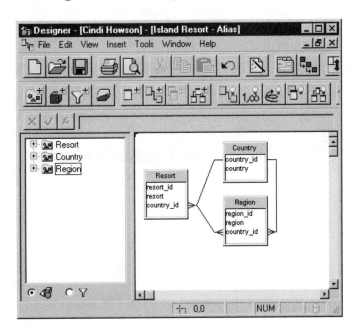

At this point, loop detection would suggest using aliases to resolve these loops. As you are a good data modeler who understands the business rules that "country" has multiple meanings, you agree and can move directly to alias detection.

1. Create a new universe that includes the three preceding tables.

2. From the pull-down menus, select Tools | Detect Aliases or click the Alias Detection button.

3. Designer suggests that an alias should be created for COUNTRY called COUNTRY_RESORT. Click Create.

4. Click OK to confirm the Alias creation. Note in the structure pane that Designer has inserted what appears to be a new table with the physical table name indicated below the alias (see Figure 7-6), if you have set your Join Graphics as described earlier in this chapter.

Inserting Aliases Manually

You may want to insert an alias manually if Designer does not propose an alias that makes business sense or if you know your business meanings in advance. For example, in the Evaluation Kit universe, the region alias is not correctly proposed. Designer proposes breaking the loop by creating an alias for SERVICE_LINE rather than COUNTRY.

1. Select the COUNTRY table from the structure pane.

2. Click the Insert Alias button or select Tools | Insert Alias.

3. When prompted, enter the name **Country_Resort** as the new alias name.

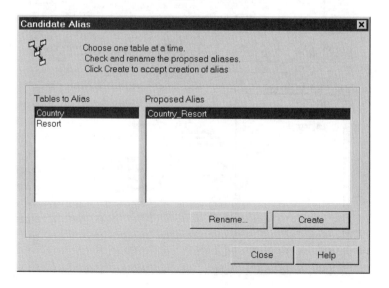

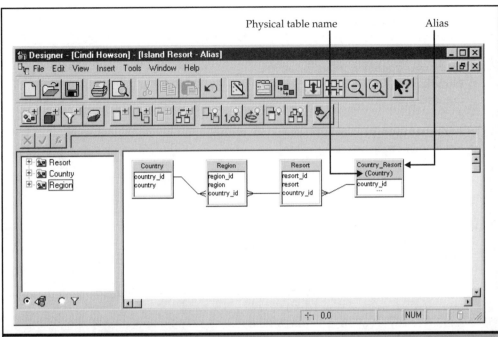

Figure 7-6.   *With aliases, the data model no longer contains a loop. The alias name replaces the physical table name in parentheses.*

4. Add a join between RESORT.COUNTRY_ID and the new alias, COUNTRY_RESORT.COUNTRY_ID.

Best practice is to name the alias using the first part of the underlying physical table to more easily keep track of related physical tables and aliases.

Although many DBAs and data modelers would prefer that the initial physical table also had an alias such as COUNTRY_CUSTOMER for consistency and clarity, Designer requires the physical table name in the universe. If you delete a physical table name that is used in aliases, all related aliases are also deleted.

Aliases in SQL

In generating the SQL, BusinessObjects will use the alias name in the column selection, join statements, and WHERE clause. In the FROM section, BusinessObjects rephrases the physical table name with the new alias name. This is standard SQL syntax and is not unique to BusinessObjects.

```
SELECT
   Country_Resort.country,
   Resort.resort,
```

```
     Customer.last_name,
     Country.country
  FROM
     Country  Country_Resort,
     Resort,
     Customer,
     Country,
     Reservations,
     Reservation_Line,
     Service,
     Service_Line,
     Region,
     City
  WHERE
     ( Service.sl_id=Service_Line.sl_id  )
     AND  ( Reservations.res_id=Reservation_Line.res_id  )
     AND  ( Reservations.cust_id=Customer.cust_id  )
     AND  ( Reservation_Line.service_id=Service.service_id  )
     AND  ( Customer.city_id=City.city_id  )
     AND  ( City.region_id=Region.region_id  )
     AND  ( Service_Line.resort_id=Resort.resort_id  )
     AND  ( Region.country_id=Country.country_id  )
     AND  ( Resort.country_id=Country_Resort.country_id  )
```

Self-Joins and Aliases

Self-joins are a way of joining a table to itself. You may need to use one as a way of restricting rows in a table or because the same values are used in two columns in the same table. A classic example is that of employees. Employees have managers. Thus, the employee ID in one column is also used in the manager ID in another column.

The following example uses data from Oracle's HR sample schema. In this schema, every employee has a supervisor, except for the main boss, Steven King (thus, you need an outer join for this one employee). Managers may supervise one or more employees.

As you see in Figure 7-7, the Employee Id is also used to indicate the Manager Id in the same table. So Employee ID 100, Steven King, manages Neena Kochhar (101) and Lex De Haan (102).

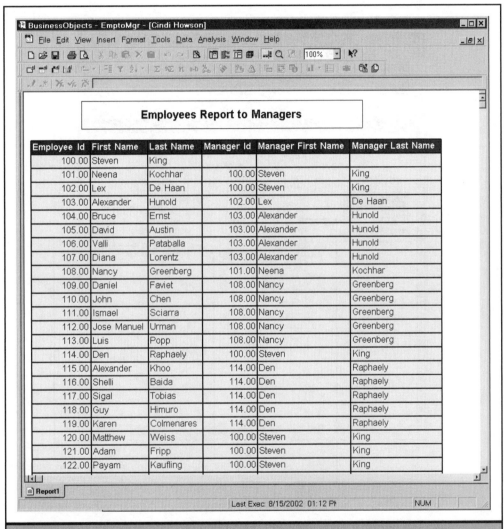

Employee Id	First Name	Last Name	Manager Id	Manager First Name	Manager Last Name
100.00	Steven	King			
101.00	Neena	Kochhar	100.00	Steven	King
102.00	Lex	De Haan	100.00	Steven	King
103.00	Alexander	Hunold	102.00	Lex	De Haan
104.00	Bruce	Ernst	103.00	Alexander	Hunold
105.00	David	Austin	103.00	Alexander	Hunold
106.00	Valli	Pataballa	103.00	Alexander	Hunold
107.00	Diana	Lorentz	103.00	Alexander	Hunold
108.00	Nancy	Greenberg	101.00	Neena	Kochhar
109.00	Daniel	Faviet	108.00	Nancy	Greenberg
110.00	John	Chen	108.00	Nancy	Greenberg
111.00	Ismael	Sciarra	108.00	Nancy	Greenberg
112.00	Jose Manuel	Urman	108.00	Nancy	Greenberg
113.00	Luis	Popp	108.00	Nancy	Greenberg
114.00	Den	Raphaely	100.00	Steven	King
115.00	Alexander	Khoo	114.00	Den	Raphaely
116.00	Shelli	Baida	114.00	Den	Raphaely
117.00	Sigal	Tobias	114.00	Den	Raphaely
118.00	Guy	Himuro	114.00	Den	Raphaely
119.00	Karen	Colmenares	114.00	Den	Raphaely
120.00	Matthew	Weiss	100.00	Steven	King
121.00	Adam	Fripp	100.00	Steven	King
122.00	Payam	Kaufling	100.00	Steven	King

Employees Report to Managers

Figure 7-7.   *Steven King does not report to a manager. Neena Kochhar, Lex De Haan, and others are managed by Steven King.*

To implement the self-join, first create an alias for the EMPLOYEE called EMP_MANAGER, as shown next. If you wanted to know the supervisor's job title and salary at the same time you wanted to know each reporting employee's job title and salary, you would also create an alias for JOB called JOB_MANAGER.

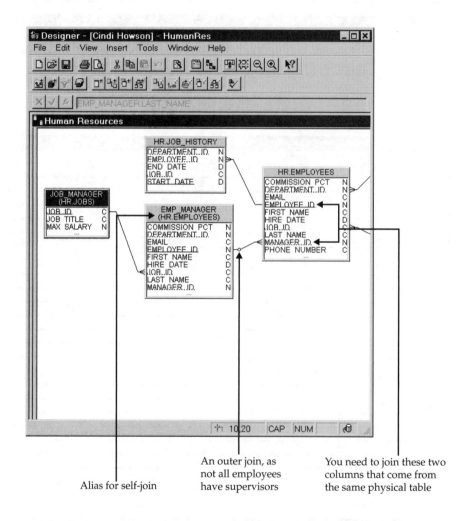

Alias for self-join

An outer join, as not all employees have supervisors

You need to join these two columns that come from the same physical table

Next, create the join that uses the alias. By using the alias, you are self-joining the EMPLOYEE_ID field in one table to the MANAGER_ID field in the same table; the alias makes it appear as if you are joining two different tables. To get a list of any employees that do not report to a manager, include an outer join on the EMP_MANAGER alias.

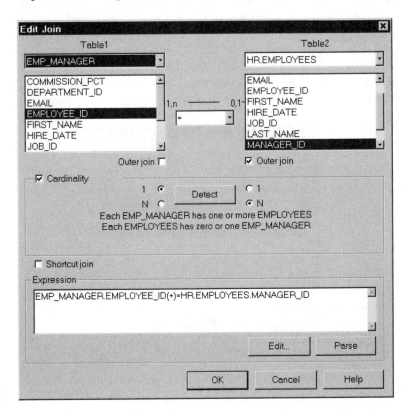

This last part is tricky. If you left the universe the way it is now, it would work fine as long as objects from EMP_MANAGER were never used in a report by itself. For example, if you tried to create a report that listed managers only, all employees would be listed on this report, as the self-join would not be activated: David Austin (105) would appear on the report, even though he is never listed in the EMLOYEE.MANAGER_ID column, as shown in Figure 7-6. To ensure that you get a list of managers only, you must force the self-join.

A BETTER UNIVERSE

Forcing a Join

There are two ways to ensure the self-join is activated any time you select objects from the EMP_MANAGER alias. The first, most obvious way is to include the join as a WHERE clause in each object definition. The second, less obvious way is to force the join by selecting EMPLOYEE as a Table in the object definition. This second way is preferable, as the join statement is added to the SQL statement once; with the WHERE clause in each object definition, the WHERE statement is added to the SQL statement multiple times according to how many objects contain the condition.

To force a join, modify the object definition. Click Tables and use CTRL-click to select the two tables EMP_MANAGER and EMPLOYEE.

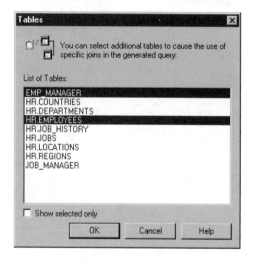

 Forcing a join to a table is also useful for security purposes, as discussed in Chapter 12.

Shortcut Joins

Shortcut joins are the best thing since chocolate chip cookies were invented (I know, the cliché is sliced bread, but I still buy whole loaves). Shortcut joins allow you to define an alternative, faster join path between two tables. Prior to shortcut joins, BusinessObjects would often have to go through a huge fact table to create simple reference lists. To the unsuspecting user, this query could take hours (and this was before time estimates existed, as well).

Figure 7-8 shows an example of a shortcut join between the PLANT table and the PRODUCTS table (line 1). If the shortcut join were a normal join, Designer would detect a loop. If you did not define a shortcut join and users wanted a list of which plants made which products, their query would be forced to join three tables together (join lines 2 and 3) and unnecessarily go through the large 30-million-row fact table. The shortcut join is a way of telling BusinessObjects that this is the fastest path to use for queries in which no objects come from the Orders_Fact table. Therefore, if users created a report to determine which suppliers ship to specific plants, the shortcut join is also used.

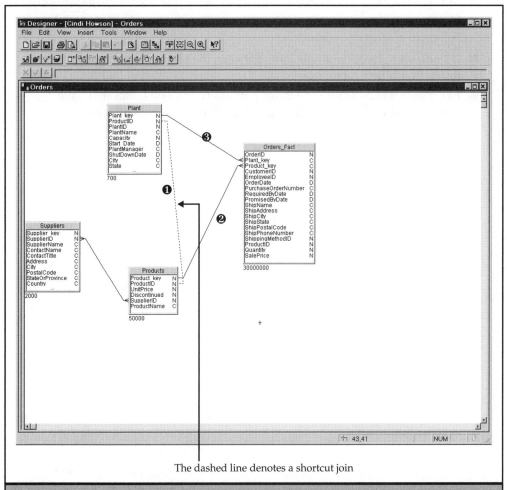

Figure 7-8. *Shortcut joins provide BusinessObjects with an alternate, faster join path without creating a loop.*

Summary

Joins can hardly be called an exciting, business-driven subject; however, if you correctly define the parameters covered in Chapter 6 and the joins covered in this chapter, you have built a sturdy foundation for a correct universe. The Classes and Objects covered in the next chapters become the familiar façade that users trust. If, on the other hand, you have made mistakes in the joins, then objects may not work with one another—or, worse, they give users incorrect results. To define joins correctly, keep in mind the following guidelines:

- Define joins based on the actual data and not just the logical business model.
- If you start using contexts, you must keep using them and ensure all tables belong to at least one context.
- Use aliases to create multiple joins between the same two tables that have different business meanings.
- Use shortcut joins to provide faster paths between two tables that have a direct relationship, rather than forcing a join through a fact table.

Chapter 8

Classes and Objects

C lasses and objects are the primary items a user sees when building a new query or working with an existing report. Classes allow you to organize objects into topics, similar to the way you organize documents into file folders. Objects correspond to columns of data in a database table. However, objects can be much more powerful than raw data lists, enabling you to add intelligence such as aggregations, transformations, variables, and formatting. Chapter 8 focuses on the basics of classes and objects, whereas Chapters 9 and 10 provide information to make your objects more robust.

The Universe Pane

The Universe pane provides information on the classes and objects. Unless an individual class or object is marked as hidden, Figure 8-1 is what users will see when they create a new query or insert a table or graph into an existing document.

Click the + sign to expand items in a class or the – sign to collapse the individual objects within a class.

You can have multiple levels of classes for classes that have a large number of objects such as *Store Details* within *Store*. These groupings are purely to ease navigation for the users. If you have a lot of detail information that is not used on a regular basis, placing these objects further within a subclass makes the universe appear less busy or difficult. However, if the information is used frequently, do not bury the objects.

In the EFASHION universe, the promotional media of *Print, Radio, Television*, or *Direct Mail* are details of the base object *Promotion (y/n)*. These details become organized in a separate folder within *Promotion (y/n)*, making the universe appear less cluttered. Specifying an object as a detail rather than a dimension also means it will not be available for multidimensional analyses. Some MOLAP tools differentiate between base dimensions and details (usually called attributes), which can greatly affect cube size and query performance. This is not true with BusinessObjects: denoting an object as a detail is more for organizational purposes and does not affect performance.

Note

In this example, a better business design would have been to have an object called Media in which the four different types are the data elements (print, radio, television, direct mail). This kind of design would reduce the number of objects as well as facilitate crosstab reporting and multidimensional analyses.

Within the Universe pane, you can specify if you want to display regular classes and objects or condition objects, a special object used to generate a SQL WHERE clause.

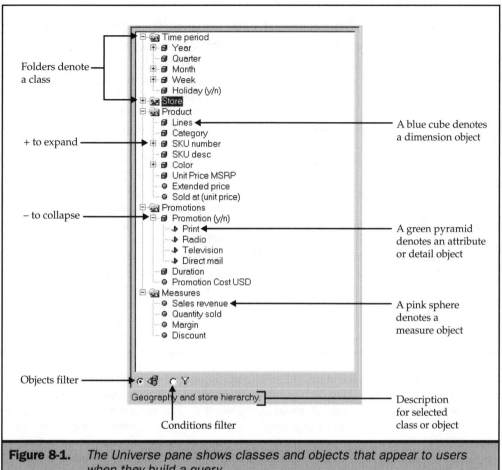

Figure 8-1.   *The Universe pane shows classes and objects that appear to users when they build a query.*

A BETTER UNIVERSE

Types of Objects

Objects can be one of three types: dimension, measure, or detail.

Dimension

A *dimension* object is denoted with a blue cube and is typically textual information by which users analyze numeric measures. A dimension object often comes from the lookup

Will queries run faster when, for example, a product ID points to the fact table rather than a dimension table?

In theory, if a user creates a query that contains a product ID and a sales amount, then this query could be answered via the one fact table. One would think that this would be a faster query than joining two tables together to fetch the product ID from a dimension table and the sales amount from a fact table. In practice, though, there is no impact on response time, assuming the product ID is an indexed field (if it's a joined field, it should be indexed!).

The other type of query that will run faster when the dimension object points to the dimension table is a list of values (discussed in Chapter 9). Lists of values are a particular kind of query that provides users with pick lists for their conditions. In providing the pick list, BusinessObjects runs a query against a dimension table to display a list of valid product IDs for which they can retrieve sales information. The list-of-values query should be fast (preferably instantaneous). However, if your product ID object points to a fact table, BusinessObjects must do a full table scan against the larger fact table to generate the pick list. This can be very, very slow, and I have seen users give up after an hour, thinking the system was unavailable.

If your particular database lacks an optimizer or has not been well indexed, then you may want to test the impact on your response time. In some rare cases, you may indeed find that it is faster to have a dimension object point to the fact table.

or reference tables within the universe. Dimensions are typically character or date information or numeric codes such as product numbers and customer numbers.

Some universe developers will mistakenly point their dimension object to the fact table.

If your data warehouse uses keys for reference information, then your dimension objects will point to a lookup table. However, if your universe accesses a transaction system or if meaningful codes and IDSs are stored in your fact table, you face a decision whether to point the dimension object to the dimension table or to the fact table. Some universe developers will mistakenly point the dimension object to the fact table, trying to reduce the number of joins. Others will duplicate the object for each occurrence in a different table. Don't do it. Create one dimension object that points to the lookup table.

 Have one object point to the dimension table.

Measure

A *measure* is a number that users wish to analyze; it is denoted by a pink sphere or circle. Measures often come from a fact table, but measures such as number of products or number of days could come from a dimension table. Measures are almost always aggregated in some form, such as sum, count, average, min, or max.

The only measure that is not aggregated is unit price. Price is a measure, but it applies to one particular product, and it is wrong from a business viewpoint to sum prices across

What if there were no sales for that particular product ID?

The other often-cited reason for pointing a dimension object to the fact table is a concern that it would be incorrect to show users a pick list of product IDs for which there may not have been sales in that period. However, there could have been sales; therefore, all potential product IDs should be displayed. If certain products have been discontinued, then the appropriate flags and time stamps should be built into your physical dimension table.

A large hospital system developed a novel approach to address these concerns: they created two objects for every dimension. For example, they had *Account number* pointing to the fact table and *ACCOUNT NUMBER* pointing to a dimension table. They trained users to use the uppercase object, *ACCOUNT NUMBER*, for conditions and the lowercase *Account number* object for result columns. This was unnecessarily confusing for the users and made the universe larger and more complex than necessary.

multiple product lines. *Average* price across multiple product lines would be a more appropriate aggregation; however, the universe should then contain two distinct price objects to ensure users can query both unit price and average price.

Universe designers may get confused about measures that apply to one point in time such as inventory quantity or account balances. Figure 8-2 gives an example from my consulting company bank account (purely fictitious). Inventory and account balances should *not* be aggregated across time. Unfortunately, BusinessObjects does not provide a solution to ensure that users do not aggregate inventory or balances across time; most server-based MOLAP tools do provide such functionality. In this case, many designers will think it is too risky to allow users to make the mistake of aggregating ending inventory/balances across time. How do users make this mistake? Using the data in Figure 8-2 as an example, let's assume that the universe references two fact tables: daily debits and credits and daily account balances. If a user builds one query that accesses both tables, the user will generally insert a condition where month equals September. BusinessObjects would tell the users that the ending account balance would be $129,955, rather than the correct number of $9,134. (If this were true, I would be vacationing in Hawaii rather than diligently writing this book!)

Hopefully, most users would recognize an inventory or account balance that is so blatantly wrong. However, good universe designers will take extra precautions in designing a universe to guarantee correct answers, no matter how users might construct a query. Some designers will remove the SUM aggregate from all inventory/account balance objects, ensuring users receive a correct value for every row for each day. However, this is not a good solution because now users cannot ask the question "What are my global inventories for a given product across all plants?" or "What is my total account balance across my various bank accounts?" Chapter 10 discusses other ways to prevent users from constructing an inaccurate query, but the best practice is to include the SUM.

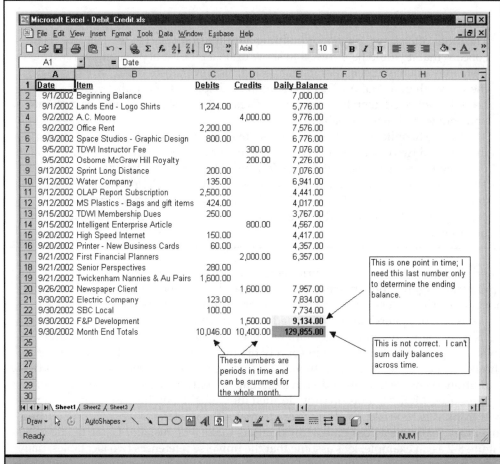

Figure 8-2.   *Inventory and account balances should be aggregated but not by time.*

    Always use an aggregate function on a measure object, unless that measure is a unit price or other similar number.

Detail

A *detail* object provides additional information about a particular dimension. Most BI and MOLAP vendors call these attributes, but BusinessObjects refers to them as Details. In Figure 8-1, *Print, Radio, Television,* and *Direct mail* are detail objects. Within a customer dimension, age, fax, phone number, street address, and notes are typical details. Details and attributes may supply users with additional ways to analyze the measures, or they may be purely informational. For example, users may want to analyze sales by customer age group, but they rarely want to analyze sales by the customers' individual street address. In this respect, the street address is purely informational.

Classifying an object as a dimension or as a detail has no impact on the query or micro cube size, unlike in some MOLAP tools. An object may be classed as a detail rather than a dimension for primarily visual reasons, to ease user querying. The main limitation with detail objects is that in BusinessObjects, they are not hierarchical (for example, if age is a detail, then ranges within age such as Youth, Adult, Senior cannot be grouped). Differentiating between dimensions and details or attributes allows BusinessObjects to work more consistently with MOLAP databases that do differentiate between these information types. For example, Hyperion Essbase distinguishes between a base dimension and an attribute. BusinessObjects understands this difference and correctly presents users with the two different types.

Object Ordering

If you use the Designer Wizard to build your universe, objects are added either in alphabetical order or in the order they are stored in the physical tables. In the *database*.sbo file, there is a parameter ColSort. The default for Oracle is ColSort=3, which means that columns in tables appear alphabetically in the table browser (shown in Figure 8-3 on the left) and therefore are alphabetical in the universe the wizard builds. If you change

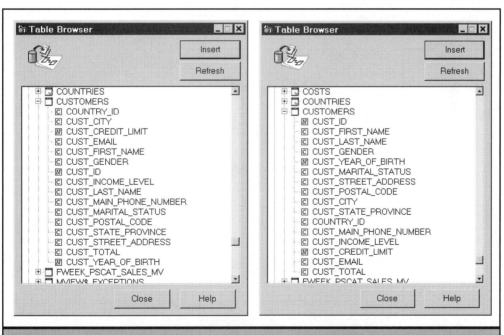

Figure 8-3.   *The parameter Colsort=3 sorts columns alphabetically (left), whereas the parameter Colsort=13 sorts columns by the order in which they exist in the physical table (right).*

the ColSort=13, then objects are sorted according to their physical order in the table (shown on the right). This is a much better sort order because join keys then appear at the top of the table browser, rather than being intermingled throughout the list.

In Informix, the default for ColSort is 2,3,7, causing the columns to be sorted by type. This may be okay as well, since most join keys will be numeric. In ODBC, the default and only possible value is ColSort=3 (physical).

The order of the columns in the table browser and the order of the objects that users see are only partially related; if your objects are automatically added to your universe when you insert a table (use the pull-down menus Tools | Options, select the Database tab and check Create default classes and objects from tables) or if you build your universe with the Quick Design Wizard, then the order of the tables and fields in the table browser will match the order of the classes and objects in the Universe pane. However, if you do not like this predetermined order, you can manually reorder the objects by dragging and dropping them. Notice in the following screen from the Test Fashion universe we created in Chapter 6 that objects in the *Calendar Year Lookup* class are in the same order as in the physical table CALENDAR_YEAR_LOOKUP:

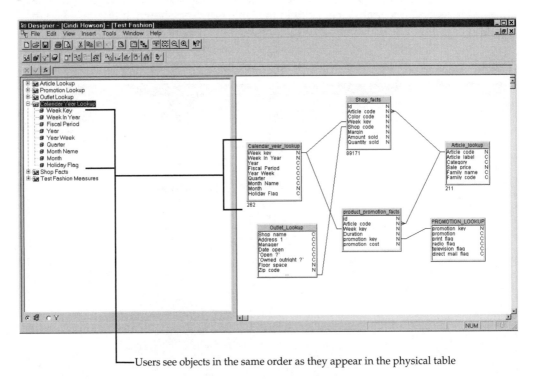

Users see objects in the same order as they appear in the physical table

This order is really not logical from a business viewpoint; *Week* is a smaller increment than *Year*, but then *Month* appears after *Quarter*. However, alphabetical is not logical either. Therefore, you must manually re-sort the objects into incremental order by dragging and dropping. The following screen shows how you want the sort order to follow time increments, running from *year* to *month* to *week*. As explained in Chapter 11, for multi-dimensional analysis, the larger increment or grouping should always appear at the top, the most detailed at the bottom. This sort order facilitates drill down.

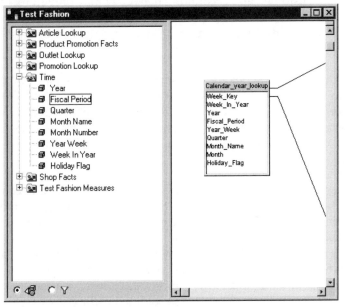

Sorted by business logic   Still sorted by
or time increment   physical storage

Naming Conventions

In creating your classes and objects, it's important to develop and follow a consistent naming convention, following a four Cs rule. They should be the following (listed in order of priority):

Customer Oriented   Your universe is for your internal and/or external customers, so you must use business terminology. Anything that reveals technical database-naming conventions does not belong in a universe.

Clear   The class and object names must be clear in their meaning. *Customer* is not clear if it could potentially mean *Ship To Customer* or *Sold To Customer*. Think back to the universe design principles discussed in Chapter 5. Who is the target user group for your universe? If these users know of only one type of customer, then *Customer* alone is acceptable as an object or class name. For example, supply chain personnel may only think of the ship to customer, and accounting personnel may only think of the invoiced or sold to customer. If these two groups of users will have separate universes, then *Customer* is acceptable; if they will share a universe, then the names must be clear and explicit.

Consistent   Object names should be consistent in two respects. First, use the same name when you mean the same thing. Always refer to the customer as the customer, and do not mix in other terminology such as client or business partner. Second, use the same clarifiers consistently. If your universe has columns that are IDs or codes and columns that are names or descriptions, then append these clarifiers consistently as Table 8-1 illustrates.

Concise   Object names should be concise, as they become the default column heading in a report. The bad thing about this is that *Article code* can be a long column heading if most of your article codes are only four characters long. In such a scenario, the abbreviated form *SKU* or *Gmid* may make for shorter and better column headings.

It would be a nice feature if Designer allowed you to centrally rename a column heading (just as SQL does), but unfortunately, it does not. Column headings can be renamed and wrapped within individual reports. Therefore, you can consider clear business terms a higher priority than concise column headings.

Warning: Object IDs

In early versions of BusinessObjects, object names within individual user queries and reports had to match object names within the universe. For example, in the Test Fashion universe, there is a *Month* object. Unless users look at the data, users are not sure whether this is the month name, a number, or a three-character abbreviation. As a universe designer, you can rename *Month* to *Month number* in the universe and all the user reports will automatically reflect this new object name. This is enabled through use of an object ID number that was introduced in BusinessObjects version 4. Prior to version 4, BusinessObjects would look for the *Month* object by name (which no longer existed) and give the users an error.

Table 8-2 shows how Designer stores object information in the UNI_OBJECT repository table. The BusinessObjects repository is discussed further in Chapter 15; here, however, it is important to note that the OBJECT_ID for Month is 14.

Often in renaming objects, a universe designer will make the mistake of cutting and pasting the original *Month* object to a new object titled *Month Number*, OBJECT_ID=59. The universe designer will then go back and delete the original *Month* object (after testing it or after a defined user acceptance period). Once the original *Month* object is deleted, all existing reports that previously used the *Month* object will generate an error that the

Initial Object Name	Potential Problem	Consistent Object Name
Article code	NA. This object name is consistent, assuming article is the generally used business term. The code name qualifer makes it clear.	Article code
Article name	NA. This object name is consistent, assuming article is the generally used business term. The code name qualifer makes it clear.	Article name
Article	It's not clear if this object refers to an article code or a description, unless all description fields have name or description appended at the end of the object name and, by default, everything else is a code or a number.	Article code
SKU	Duplicate of Article code and not the generally accepted business term. However, it is concise, which would make for a nice column heading in a report.	Article code
Product	Duplicate of Article code or SKU. Also, not clear if this is a code or a description object.	Article code
Gmid	Gmid is the abbreviation for global material identification used in the OLTP; data entry users know the term, but business users within the target universe group do not.	Article code

Table 8-1.   *Object Names Should Follow the Four Cs: Be Customer Oriented, Clear, Consistent, and Concise*

OBJECT_ID	UNIVERSE_ID	CLASS_ID	OBJ_NAME	OBJ_HIDDEN	OBJ_POSITION
14	11	2	Month	N	0
59	11	2	Month Number	N	1
13	11	2	Month Name	N	2
7	11	2	Week Key	N	3
8	11	2	Week In Year	N	4
11	11	2	Year Week	N	5
12	11	2	Quarter	N	6
10	11	2	Fiscal Period	N	7
9	11	2	Year	N	8
15	11	2	Holiday Flag	N	9

Table 8-2. *Object Names Are Assigned an OBJECT_ID Within the BusinessObjects Repository Tables*

Month object is missing. If the universe designer had modified the original *Month* object, OBJECT_ID=14, then the existing queries and reports would have automatically been updated with the new object information.

This use of OBJECT_IDS is also what allows BusinessObjects to handle changes to underlying SQL, help text, list of values, and so on, without the users knowing that the underlying metadata may have changed.

To minimize report errors, take these three precautions:

1. Maintain a printed copy of all object IDs.

2. Modify existing objects when you really wish to change the name or underlying SQL; avoid re-creating new objects to replace old ones.

3. Always make an offline, backup copy of a universe. One client I worked with deleted a number of objects accidentally. The designer thought he had fixed the problem by simply re-creating the objects with the exact same object names (which didn't work). A backup version of the universe allowed us to more quickly access and restore the original OBJECT_ID numbers.

Working with Classes and Objects

We have already seen how objects can be re-sorted within a class in the *Calendar Year Lookup* example. Classes and objects can also be renamed, deleted, hidden, and modified. In manipulating an object, you can access these actions in a number of ways:

- Use the Edit pull-down menu to clear, hide, or modify properties and formats.
- Select the item and then right-click to choose from various actions on the pop-up menu.

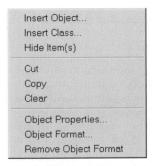

- Double-click the item to bring up the Edit Properties dialog box.

The modifications described in the remainder of this section will generally use the right-click approach.

Rename

Using the Test Fashion universe created in Chapter 6, you want to rename the class *Calendar Year Lookup* to *Time*.

1. Select the class *Calendar Year Lookup*.

2. Right-click and then choose Class Properties from the pop-up menu. The following
   screen shows the initial class definition:

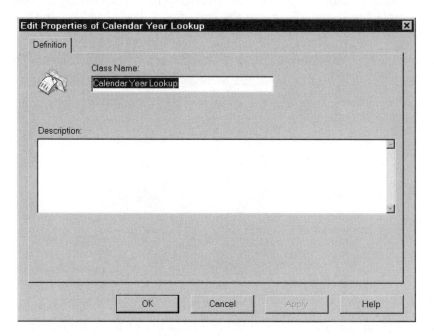

3. Once in the Edit Properties dialog box, replace the current name in the Name:
   box with **Time**.

4. Click OK.

   In the following screen, the *Calendar Year Lookup* class has been renamed *Time*,
and class description information has been added. Classes as well as objects can contain
meaningful help text in the Description box. Help text is an underutilized feature in most
universes, even though it is fairly easy to extract with an ETL tool. Power users or subject
matter experts can also provide description information via spreadsheet files and object
strategies (see Chapter 6) that can be easily imported into the universe.

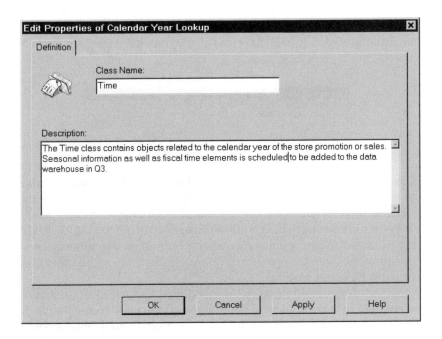

Delete

To delete a class or object, you can use the same three selection methods described earlier or two shortcut keys:

Key	Menu Equivalent	Explanation
DEL	Clear	This deletes the class or object. The only way to retrieve it again is to use the undo button.
CTRL-X	Cut	This cuts the class or object and puts it in the MS Windows clipboard. To retrieve the object again, use paste or CTRL-V.

Let's imagine the worst-case scenario: you accidentally deleted a class. When you delete a class, all the objects in that class will also be deleted. Designer warns you of this with the following error message:

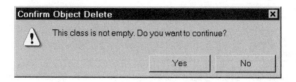

With Clear or DEL, the contents are not placed in the MS Windows clipboard. Undo allows you to undo only the last action. As the Clear was several steps ago, the undo button no longer can help you. All is not lost. Recall from Chapter 5 that you are working on only a copy of the universe. There is still a universe, with all the old object definitions, stored in the repository. When you make a catastrophic mistake like this, you can reimport a copy of the universe from the repository, although you will lose all other changes you made during this Designer session.

Given that DEL doesn't add items to the Windows clipboard, I suggest you use Cut as often as possible so that you have a better recovery process in case you accidentally delete something important. Keep in mind, though, that if you delete an object and recover it with the Paste command, the object will be assigned a new object ID and will generate errors in any existing user reports that reference the deleted object.

Hide

Hidden classes and objects are items that appear to you as the designer in italics but that users do not see when creating queries against this universe. Because the items still exist in the universe, they do take up space and will increase the size of the universe. Some designers will hide items so that all columns within the data mart appear to the designer but not to the user. I don't like this use of Hide because of the impact on universe size. However, Hide is useful when you want to hide "work in progress" or if you wish to remove an object but want a transition period to ensure that the removed object will not create problems for the users.

In the following example, I've added the table ARTICLE_COLOR_LOOKUP; Designer automatically added the corresponding class and objects. I don't want the users to see these items yet, as they are not in business terms, nor have I added my joins. To hide a class or object, select the item and then click the Hide/Show button. The Hide/Show button acts as a toggle. When I am ready for users to see this new class and its objects, I unhide or Show the items with the same button.

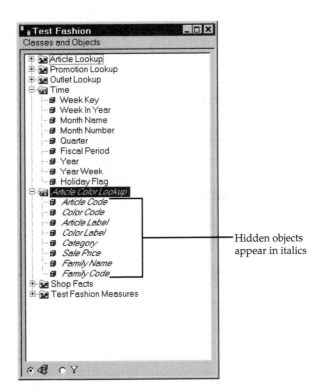

Hidden objects appear in italics

Modify a Dimension

If you have used the Quick Design Wizard to create your universe, or if you have made the setting to automatically create new classes and objects when you add a table to the universe (Tools | Options | Database), then much of your work now will be to modify those objects. In the next example, you will modify the dimension object Month, in the renamed *Time* class.

Definition

1. Select the object *Month* and double-click to bring up the Edit Properties dialog box. This dialog has three tabs: Definition, Properties, and Advanced. The Definition tab contains the object name, type, SQL, and description or help text.

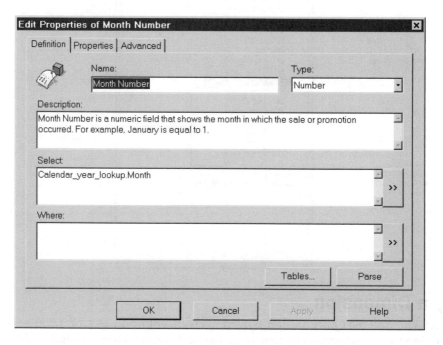

2. Change the object name from *Month* to **Month Number**.

3. The object type relates to the field format in the source database as well as to how users will choose to manipulate the object's data in a report. Leave the Type as Number.

4. In the Description box, enter help text that is meaningful for users. If users will use a field as part of a condition, I like to give them an indication of the format. Enter the following help text: **Month Number is a numeric field that shows the month in which the sale or promotion occurred. For example, January is equal to 1.**

5. The Select statement is the SQL used to dynamically build the user's query. If you are creating a new object, it is best to use the arrow button to launch the SQL Editor to select tables and columns to ensure the SQL is accurate.

6. The Where box is used to generate the WHERE clause within a SQL statement. It's important to remember, though, that BusinessObjects appends the WHERE clause to the entire query (assuming the particular object is used in the query). For example, if you have an object *Current Year Sales* with a WHERE clause of Year=2003 and a *Last Year Sales* where Year=2002 and a user selects both objects for one report, then no data will be returned; the two WHERE clauses are mutually exclusive. Therefore, this box is most often left blank or used for variable prompts discussed in Chapter 10.

Object Types vs. Database Field Format

As described in the preceding step 3, the object type and the data source field format do not necessarily have to be the same. In most cases, they are the same and should be. Table 8-3 summarizes the different types and their settings. There is only one instance in which I

Object Type	Explanation
Number	Any measure objects must have the object type of Number. Key fields and date fields may be numeric fields physically but should not be number objects in the universe. When they are number objects in the universe, BusinessObjects allows you to perform calculations such as sum, multiply, and divide that would not make sense from a business perspective.
Date	Fields that are in date format in the data source should be set to date type in the universe.
Character	Fields that are character in the data source should be set to character as the object type. Numeric fields that are not measures and that will not benefit from calculations may also be set to character.
Long Text	Long text fields are generally used for comments and note fields. The length of the long text object returned in a query can be controlled and is specific to each universe; it is set under File	Parameters	Controls.

Table 8-3. *Object Types Correspond to Physical Database Field Formats*

recommend changing the object type, and that is when your source system is a number field that you will never use as a measure. For example, product ID and customer number may be numeric fields in the source system, but you will rarely want to treat them as numbers (unless the coding has some meaningful sort or logic that you wish to manipulate). In this case, consider setting the object type to character.

When you specify an object as a number (whether or not you specify it as a measure), certain functionality within BusinessObjects is available to end users. Users will be able to do sums, divisions, averages, and so forth, on these numbers. From a business point of view, these calculations make no sense against most ID fields. The only calculation that makes sense is a count: How many new products sold this month? How many customers do I have? The count calculation is available to all objects, regardless of their types (number, date, character). Personally, I'd like to see BusinessObjects automatically disable nonsensical functionality for dimension objects, but they are more likely to consider an enhancement request from you than from me!

Except for changing from numeric to character types, be very careful about changing your field types. For example, in the Test Fashion universe, from a business point of view, I would much prefer that *Month Number* be a date type object. This would allow me to use all the wonderful date functions within BusinessObjects formulas. However, it is a numeric field in the database, and if I specify it as a date type in the universe, I will receive an #ERROR in my report if I try to use any of the date functions. So I need to use multiple functions to get my Month Number to generate a month name:

```
=Month(ToDate(FormatNumber(<Month Number> ,"00") ,"mm"))
```

If you change the object type to be different than the source data field type, formula functions within BusinessObjects will generate an error.

Clearly, having users do extra conversions for what should be a simple task is a poor universe design. To prevent users from having to do extra conversions, a business-oriented universe designer may try to help users by converting the number field to a date field (or number to character, and so on) in the objects' SQL select statement. This is a good practice in theory, but only if it does not affect the use of indexes. With most RDBMSs, if you change the appearance of a field, the index will not be used. Therefore, work closely with the DBA or analyze an explain plan anytime you use SQL functionality to convert field types. (See Chapter 10 for more on creating advanced objects.)

If you specify a character database field as a number and attempt to use it as a measure, BusinessObjects will drop any rows that contain characters from your report.

Properties

The Properties tab of the edit Properties dialog box sets the object qualification, the aggregates if it's a measure, and a list of values.

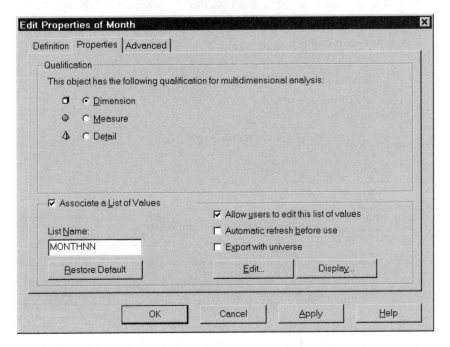

1. The Month Number is a dimension, so leave this box checked.

2. Change the list name of the associated list of values to **MonthNN**. List of values is explained in more detail in Chapter 9.

Advanced

The Advanced tab controls who can access the object, where the object can be used in a query, and date formats.

For the *Month Number*, leave all the settings at their defaults. Click OK to save the changes on the Definition and Properties tabs.

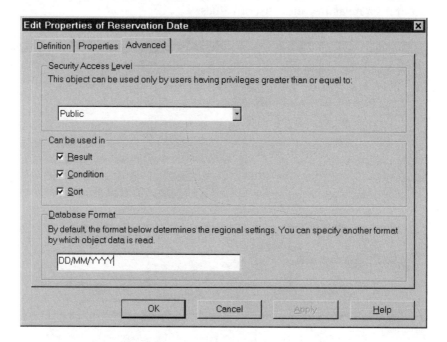

On the Advanced tab, security access level settings interact with Supervisor settings discussed in Chapter 12. The Public setting allows all users to access an object and is the default.

For each object, you can control whether the object can be used as a result, a condition, or a sort as described in Table 8-4.

Database Format applies only to date fields and will be dimmed for nondate fields. If you are an American, you may not realize that European countries write the date differently; if you are a European, I apologize that we are so ethnocentric! How do I know the different formats: I lived in Switzerland for eight years and am married to an English

Can Be Used As A	Explanation
Result	A result is a column in a query or a report. Most often, all objects are results.
Condition	Conditions relate to the WHERE clause of a SQL statement. If your universe accesses an OLTP, you may want to disallow nonindexed fields as conditions, as they may result in slow queries and bog down the source system. If you are in a data warehouse environment, I recommend allowing all objects as conditions. It's true that you may want users to search on the indexed CUSTOMER_CODE, for example, but what if there are several related customers that all start with the same first few letters, such as Deloitte & Touche? They could have the forms Deloitte Consulting, Deloitte & Touche Management Solutions, Deloitte Parsipanny office, and so on. By allowing *Customer Name* as a condition, a user could select everything starting with Deloitte.
Sort	Sort allows users to sort results on the server rather than on the client. As with conditions, I suggest allowing this on all objects. In most cases, users will sort their results within the report once they see the data. However, if users want to select Top 10 product sales, or Top 100 customers, the sort must be processed on the server.

Table 8-4.   *Objects Can Be Used in Three Different Ways in a Query*

A BETTER UNIVERSE

man. An American will refer to April 1 as 04/01. A European will write April 1 as 01/04. (You can imagine the confusion this causes when my husband and I attempt to share date-oriented passwords or book each other's dentist appointments!)

Note   *Concerned with response time issues, some DBAs may disagree with the recommendations in Table 8-4, but it provides the most user flexibility. You need to weigh the risk of users not being able to ask a valid business question with the impact on response time.*

By default, BusinessObjects uses the date format defined in the *database*.sbo file to generate the correct SQL syntax when a date is used in the WHERE clause. You can override this format in the Database Format box. For example, the ODBC.SBO file has the following parameter:

```
InputDateFormat={\d 'yyyy-mm-dd'}
```

In the Island Resorts Marketing universe, TIME.RESERVATION_DATE is stored in MS Access as YYYY-MM-DD HH:MM:SS. When a user places the *Reservation Date* object in the condition panel, BusinessObjects will automatically take the user's input and convert it to this format. Because this format is different from how the physical date values are stored (the ImputDateFormat is missing HH:MM:SS), the users will get no rows returned.

To ensure users get the correct results, specify a date format in the Object properties that corresponds with the date in the physical database. In this example, {\t\s 'yyyy-mm-dd HH:mm:ss'} is the correct Database Format. Note that ODBC requires the brackets and \t\s parameters; Oracle does not.

Now, if a user enters 1/12/96 as a condition value, BusinessObjects converts the SQL using the format specified in the Object Properties:

```
SELECT
  Reservations.res_date
FROM
  Reservations
WHERE
  (
  Reservations.res_date  =  {ts '1996-01-12 00:00:00'}
  )
```

Oracle uses the following default settings in the Oracle.sbo file. If any of your date fields in your database do not follow this format, you will need to modify the object properties to override the settings in the Oracle.sbo file.

```
InputDateFormat='DD-MM-YYYY HH:MM:SS'
InitDateFormat='DD-MM-YYYY HH24:MI:SS'
AuditTimeStampFormat='DD-MM-YYYY HH:MM:SS'
```

 Review the database.sbo *file to ensure it corresponds with the date values in your database.*

Modify a Detail or Attribute

Detail objects work much the same way that dimension objects work. The only difference is that you must associate a detail object with a dimension object. In the following example, the detail object *Street* is associated with the dimension object *Shop Name*. Once you have associated *Street* with *Shop Name*, *Street* and other details or attributes will now appear in a separate folder under *Shop Name*.

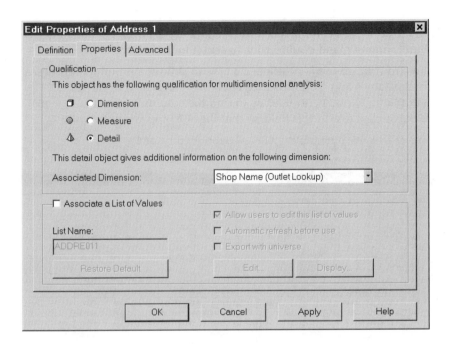

Insert a Measure

The previous section discussed modifying an existing object. You can also add new objects by clicking the Insert Object button or using the menu choice Insert | Object. In this section, you will add a measure object called *Promotion Cost*. This assumes that the table PRODUCT_PROMOTION_FACTS exists in your Universe pane.

1. Position your mouse in the *Test Fashion Measures* class. Click the Insert Object button.

2. Designer will present you with the same dialog boxes as when modifying objects. Enter the name **Promotion Cost** and set the object type to number.

3. Enter the object description as: **Promotion Cost is the dollar value spent on a given radio, newspaper or other media promotion. Promotion costs are unique for each individual product but are allocated across all stores**.

4. In the Select box, click the >> button to access the full select statement and SQL functions. The functions here relate to your specific database. Some popular functions are discussed further in Chapter 10.

5. In the Functions column, click the + sign next to Number functions. Scroll to the Sum() function and double-click to add it to the select statement.

6. Ensure your mouse is positioned in the middle of the Sum parentheses. In the Tables and Columns box, click the + sign next to the table PRODUCT_PROMOTION_FACTS to find the column PROMOTION_COST. Double-click to add this field so that the SQL appears as follows:

```
sum(product_promotion_facts.promotion_cost)
```

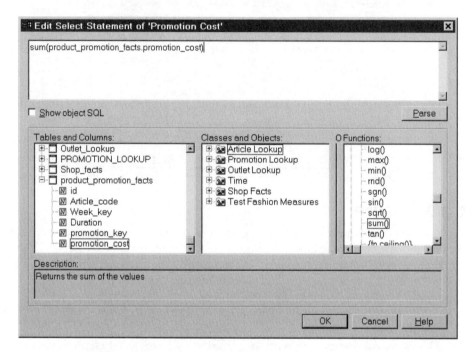

7. Click Parse to check that your SQL is correct.

You can wait to parse all objects when checking the universe integrity, but it is easier to diagnose problems if you parse objects as you build them.

8. Click OK to save your Select statement and return to the Definition tab.

9. Select the Properties tab and verify that the object qualification is a measure. The default qualification is Dimension, but this should have changed automatically when you selected the Sum function.

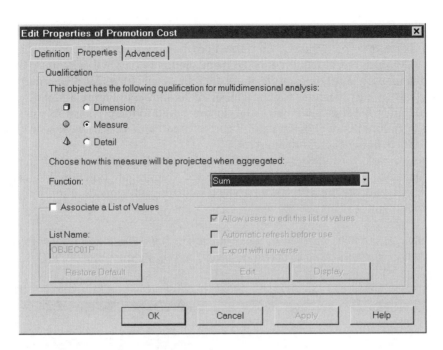

10. Select the Sum function as the projection aggregate.

11. There is no reason to have a list of values for measure objects, so leave the option Associate a List of Values unchecked.

12. Click OK to save your object changes.

13. Click Save to save the changes made to the universe.

14. Select File | Export. From the Export Universe dialog box, click OK to export the modified universe to the repository.

About Projection Aggregates

Two forms of aggregates are involved in a BusinessObjects universe: SQL functions and projection aggregates. Users can create a third aggregate called *calculations* within individual reports.

SQL Aggregates

SQL aggregates such as SUM, MIN, and MAX require a GROUP BY clause that BusinessObjects automatically includes in each SQL statement.

Refer back to Figure 8-2. There are 23 rows of data in the sample fact table. If I select debits and credits without the SQL sum function, then my report will display 23 rows. If I use the SUM function and request only debit and credits by day, SQL will group the debits and credits for each day. For example, there are four detail entries for September 12, 2002. SQL sums these into one entry for September 12, as shown in Figure 8-4. With the sum function, Figure 8-4 shows ten rows of data compared to the physical 23 rows from Figure 8-2. Failure to use SQL aggregates correctly can unnecessarily cause millions of rows of data to be sent across the network.

In this example, the number of rows returned to the client workstation or to the WebI midtier has gone from 21 to 10 through use of a SQL aggregate function. In a real-world example, this could be the difference between returning a few rows or millions of rows of data to a client.

Always use a SQL aggregate on a measure unless it involves a unit price or something similar; otherwise, you risk overloading your servers, network, and client PCs.

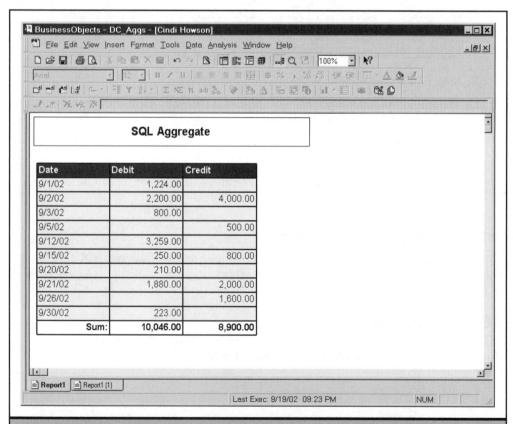

Figure 8-4.   *SQL groups individual rows into common columns, reducing the number of rows of data sent to the client.*

Projection Aggregate

The second form of aggregate is the *projection* aggregate, used in multidimensional analysis and when users remove dimension columns from a report or chart that still exist in the results set. In the following example, I only have a DATE column and not a MONTH column in the SQL statement; therefore, there are still ten rows in my result set. In Figure 8-5, I have created a month object in the report and removed the individual date. BusinessObjects now does the grouping in the report to yield one row of data for the entire month of September.

As a general rule, the SQL function you use will match your projection aggregate used on the individual object properties. As discussed earlier in connection with measures, price is one measure in which designers may not use a SQL aggregate; however, it would be useful to set the projection aggregate to Avg to allow further analysis. With inventory and ending balance, I recommend using the SQL SUM function but then setting the projection aggregate to None.

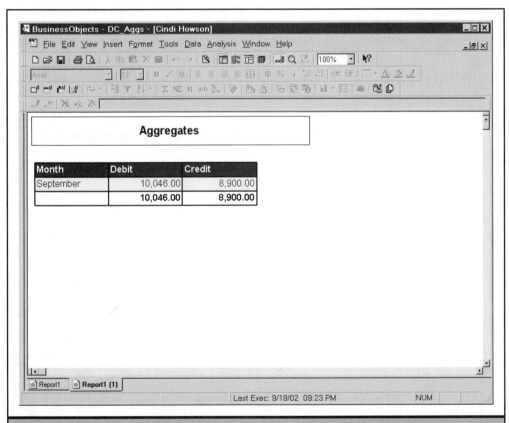

Figure 8-5. *A BusinessObjects projection aggregate groups records within the report.*

Object Formats

Object formats are a new feature in version 5. Previously, users had to modify the object formats in each individual report, which could be a very tedious process. Using object formats, the universe designer can centrally define a format that includes number, alignment, font, border, and shading. These formats are more frequently used in reports, discussed further in Part III of this book. In the following example, you will change the object format for *Promotion Cost*:

1. Select the object *Promotion Cost*.

2. Right-click to access the pop-up menu and select Object Format or choose Edit | Object Format.

3. Select the Number tab and specify the desired format. For many numeric fields and in particular, numeric fields that are not measures, set the number format to drop the decimal place. For example, with Month Number, by default, BusinessObjects will display a result for January as 1.00 unless you set 0 format.

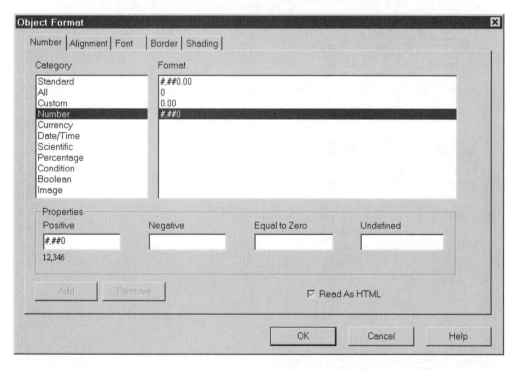

Other formatting options are described in Chapter 17, "Format a Cell."

Summary

Classes and objects act as the user interface to the physical columns in the data source. BusinessObjects provides three different types of objects (measures, dimensions, and details) to help users differentiate between types of information more easily. This chapter covered the basics of building different kinds of objects and highlighted some important design principles:

- Point dimension objects to look up tables.
- Always use SQL aggregates on measure objects.
- Sort dimension objects from biggest to smallest to facilitate drill down.
- Follow the four Cs in naming objects (customer-oriented, clear, consistent, concise).
- Ensure object types and data field types match the type in the physical database.

Following these principles will make your universe powerful yet ensure users consistently get correct results. In Chapters 9 and 10, you will add even more intelligence to the objects.

A BETTER UNIVERSE

Chapter 9

List of Values

T he *list of values* is a powerful feature that allows users to select from a pick list when setting conditions in a query. You as a designer determine which objects have lists of values via the object properties.

Because users can select conditions from a list of values, they do not need to enter conditions manually and therefore do not need to memorize lists of codes or guess how many leading zeros there may be in a particular field. Designer allows you to customize the default list of values even further to present meaningful names with the codes or to shorten particularly long lists into a more manageable size.

How List of Values Works

When a user adds a condition to a query, BusinessObjects essentially launches a second query and returns a list from the dimension or lookup table in the RDBMS, as shown in Figure 9-1.

The query file exists on either the full client's local disk or on the WebI midtier as \BusinessObjects\userdocs*universe**object*.lov, where *universe* is the name of the

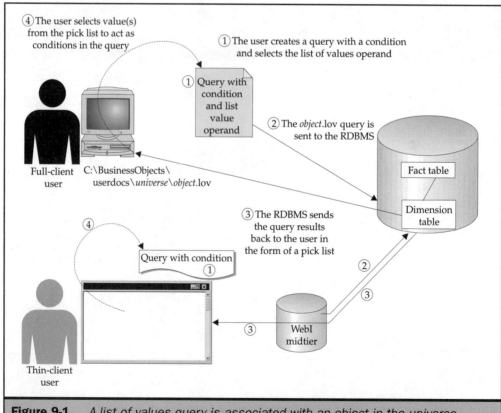

Figure 9-1. *A list of values query is associated with an object in the universe. It queries the dimension or lookup tables in the RDBMS to present users with a pick list for conditions in a user query.*

universe used in the query and *object* is the object used as a condition in a query. Designer automatically creates these query files whenever a universe designer enables a list of values on a universe object. Unless a designer customizes the list of values, the SQL generated is always:

```
SELECT DISTINCT
  Table.object
FROM
  Table
```

Notice that BusinessObjects adds a `DISTINCT` keyword to all list of values queries. This ensures that users receive only a single row for each distinct value. For example, a Customer dimension table may have multiple rows for each customer ID as changes to customer information are kept and time-stamped. In setting conditions in a query, users will need to see the unique customer ID only once.

The BusinessObjects repository, universe domain sends customized *object*.lov files to the client or midtier when the user accesses a new or modified universe (refer back to Figure 5-6, step 3). When users add a condition to a query, they must select an operand, as shown here:

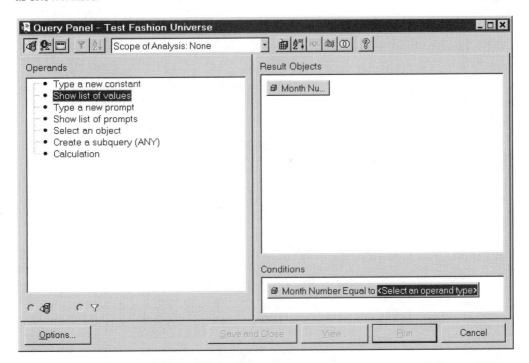

Users can either manually enter the value for the condition or select the operand Show list of values (Figure 9-1, step 1). This operand will send the *object*.lov query to the dimension table in the RDBMS (Figure 9-1, step 2). The RDBMS sends the query results back to the client (step 3). Users then select which condition value(s) they want in the original query condition (step 4). When the user launches the main query, the *object*.lov query is no longer involved.

Designers can customize the *object*.lov query to shorten long lists of values. For example, if you have millions of products, you may want to prompt users first to select a product category. If the users do not know the codes or spellings of the product categories, then BusinessObjects may first launch a prodcat.lov query. In this respect, steps 2 and 3 may be repeated multiple times until the user finally selects values to add to the query in step 4. The size of the *object*.lov files also may change over time as the number of products changes or as users select different product categories.

Once a user has accessed a particular *object*.lov file, the query results are permanently installed on the full-client PC or the thin-client midtier. The next time a user wants to use the same object as a query condition, the list of values or pick list is immediately available without having to query the RDBMS.

Basic List of Values

When you first create an object, Designer enables lists of values by default and assigns a name based on the object name. In the following example, you will modify the *Month Number* object that you used in Chapter 8:

1. Click the *Time* class.

2. Double-click the object *Month Number*.

3. Select the Properties tab. Notice that the check box Associate A List Of Values is enabled. By default, this check box is enabled on all objects, including details and measures. I will discuss why this makes no sense later in the chapter. The *Month Number* object is a dimension and should have a list of values.

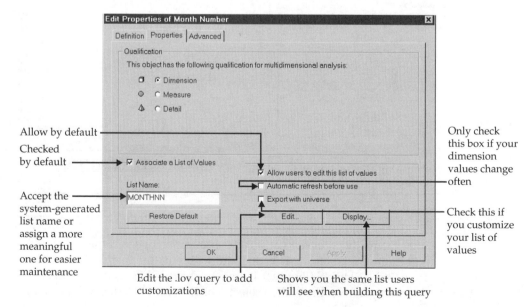

Allow by default

Checked by default

Accept the system-generated list name or assign a more meaningful one for easier maintenance

Edit the .lov query to add customizations

Shows you the same list users will see when building this query

Only check this box if your dimension values change often

Check this if you customize your list of values

4. You can accept Designer's default name, or you can modify the name to be more meaningful. If you did not change the system generated List Name (MONTHO5A), change it to a more meaningful name such as **MONTHNN**. I prefer to change the List Name, as it helps when using the same list of values for multiple objects and helps when you need to use Windows Explorer to clean up the files on your local disk.

5. The check box Allow users to edit this list of values is checked by default. Table 9-1 explains the purpose of each of these checkboxes.

6. Click Display to see the same list of values that users will see when using them in a query.

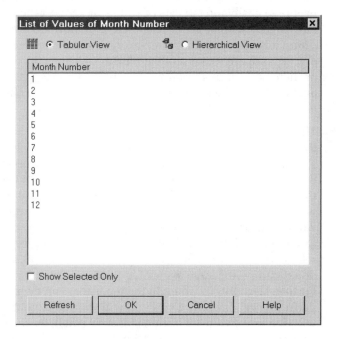

7. Click OK to return to the Object Properties panel.

8. Click OK to close the Object Properties panel.

When to Disable LOVS

By default, list of values is enabled on all objects, but there are instances in which it is better to disable it by removing the check from the checkbox Associate a List of Values.

Nonindexed Fields

One would think if you have disallowed an object to be used as a condition (Select Edit | Object Properties, then click the Advanced tab. [Refer to Table 8-6 for more information.]),

Option	Explanation
Allow users to edit list of values	This is allowed by default. This option lets users create their own custom lists, adding whatever filters, sorts, or personal data files they find most useful. I have rarely seen this used, even by power users, yet I find it an excellent feature. The main caveat here is that if the designer customizes and exports a .lov file, the universe .lov will overwrite the user's .lov, regardless of which is more recent.
Automatic refresh before use	This should rarely be checked and only for those objects in which the dimension information changes frequently. Otherwise, the users can easily refresh lists of values by request themselves. Particularly with large dimension lists or slow RDBMS response times, it is important not to force an automatic refresh. However, if your company has recently gone through a major reorganization, or there have been a number of RDBMS changes that would cause an old list of values to be massively out of date, you may want to enable the automatic refresh for a defined period.
Export with universe	This box should be checked only when the designer has customized the list of values with the universe. Leaving this checked for even simple lists that have not been customized will unnecessarily increase the size of the universe and slow user logon times. When you check this box, the query file *object*.lov gets exported to the repository with the universe. If you, as the designer, have refreshed the list of values, the data files get exported in addition to the query file. This can be a bad thing! It will almost always be faster for the users to refresh their list of values directly from the RDBMS, rather than downloading the large associated result set from the repository. Further, large lists of values in the repository can degrade repository performance. The only times you will want to export the result set with the list of values file are 1) for very small, frequently used lists, such as Time objects, and 2) when the results are coming from a personal data file or other source to which users may not have direct access.

Table 9-1.   *Options that Control List of Values Functionality*

it would automatically remove the list of values functionality from the object. It doesn't. So for many of the same reasons that you disallow an object to be used as a condition, you also may not want to associate a list of values. If the field is not indexed, you may not want to associate a list of values.

For example, let's assume that *Customer Name* is an object whose source system field is not indexed. It is still allowed as a condition because you want users to be able to search for all customers that start with the name Deloitte%. You want to discourage users from using *Customer Name* as a condition and encourage them to use *Customer Code* as a condition, since it's indexed. In this case, allow the list of values on *Customer Code* and disable it on *Customer Name*.

"Unfair! Unfriendly!" you say? Read the upcoming section "Simple Customization." You can still help users pick their customer codes according to customer name, but through a customized list of values.

Measure Objects

This is one of those times when I don't understand why the vendor doesn't make this functionality automatic: if an object is a measure, it should not have an associated list of values.

As discussed in Chapter 8, all measure objects (except things such as unit price) should have a SQL aggregate (SUM, COUNT, and so on). Therefore, if you have a list of values on a measure object, the list of values will always return only one row of data, since there is no GROUP BY clause in the SQL. For example, look at these two lists of values:

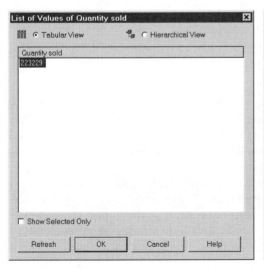 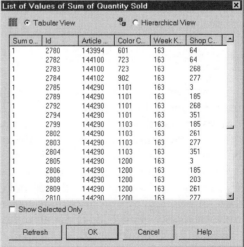

These are from the *Quantity Sold* object in the EFASHION universe. The left screen represents the default list of values. It is one row of data, 223229, because the SQL SUM aggregate will always return one grand total from the fact table unless there are dimensions in the GROUP BY section. The following SQL generated the single-row value:

```
SELECT DISTINCT
   sum(Shop_facts.Quantity_sold)
FROM
   Shop_facts
```

The screen on the right shows a list of values that I have customized to force a GROUP BY clause. As the query contains each key in the fact table, the list of values will display a row for every record in the fact table using the following SQL:

```
SELECT DISTINCT
   sum(Shop_facts.Quantity_sold),
   Shop_facts.Id,
   Shop_facts.Article_code,
   Shop_facts.Color_code,
   Shop_facts.Week_key,
   Shop_facts.Shop_code
FROM
   Shop_facts
GROUP BY
   Shop_facts.Id,
   Shop_facts.Article_code,
   Shop_facts.Color_code,
   Shop_facts.Week_key,
   Shop_facts.Shop_code
```

This is my long-winded way of showing you that lists of values against a measure make no sense. If users want to look for *Quantity Sold*, greater than a certain value, they can easily enter this manually and do not need to choose from a list that will never match the numbers in their particular query (because the GROUP BY in their query will generally be different than the GROUP BY in the list of values query).

The one exception to this rule continues to be unit price. Here, a list of values may make sense, and this measure should not contain a SQL aggregate. Users may want to look for products by unit price. In this case, my only concern is the impact on response time. Unit price is most likely not an indexed field, and some product dimension tables can be huge; therefore, test this list of values before enabling it for your users.

Details

Rarely will users want to use details as conditions in queries. For example, when users are looking for customer sales, do they use detail objects such as street address or phone number for the exact condition when it's unknown to them? No. If they knew the phone number, they may use it as a condition, but then they are usually entering the phone number manually and *not* choosing it from a pick list.

However, if you look at the EFASHION universe, it makes a lot of sense to allow a list of values for the object *ZIP code*. I would recommend customizing it to display the state; I would also have *ZIP code* as a dimension object, not a detail (refer to Chapter 8).

Simple Customization

A simple customization may involve adding a meaningful description next to the code or adding a prompt to shorten a long list. Each customization has three main steps:

1. Associate a list of values with an object.

2. Add additional information or conditions.

3. Export the customization with the universe.

Adding a Description Object to a Code Object

Some codes may have a logical meaning with which users are familiar. For example, many accountants know certain account ranges by sight. Power users also may know a number of account, product, and customer codes. However, in many cases, the codes are meaningless and users will only ever want to use names or descriptions as conditions.

 Keys are different from codes; they are generated during data warehouse or mart loads. They are often sequential by row and lack any business meaning. Unless there are response time problems, users should never see or use data warehouse–generated keys.

In large data warehouse environments or in OLTP systems, you want to encourage users to use indexed fields as condition objects whenever possible. This will speed their queries and improve overall response time. In many cases, the code or ID field is indexed but the description field may not be. Displaying a description next to the field in the list of values balances response time needs (searching on index field) while also making the universe more user friendly (letting users search on familiar names and descriptions). You also may want to add additional dimension objects in your list of values to facilitate sorting. Figure 9-2 shows that it may be meaningful to add *Country, Region,* and *City* to the *Customer Id* list of values.

In the following example, you will use the Island Resorts Marketing or BEACH universe. To ensure you do not affect the original universe, import the universe from the repository (choose File | Import and select Island Resorts Marketing). Then select File | Save As and enter the new name: **T_BEACH**, for Test Beach.

Users can select Customer Ids for France and Germany only | Displaying additional information such as country can be useful | The region refers to a region within a country

Customer Id	Customer	Country of origin	Region	City
201.00	Sartois	France	French Alps	Albertville
206.00	Gentil	France	French Alps	Albertville
204.00	Martin	France	French Alps	Grenoble
202.00	Michaud	France	French Alps	Lyon
207.00	Dupont	France	Paris	Paris
205.00	Piaget	France	Provence	Bordeaux
203.00	Robert	France	Provence	Marseilles
406.00	Titzman	Germany	Bavaria	Augsburg
402.00	Schiller	Germany	Bavaria	Munich
405.00	Schultz	Germany	East Germany	Berlin
407.00	Reinman	Germany	East Germany	Berlin
403.00	Durnstein	Germany	East Germany	Dresden
404.00	Weimar	Germany	East Germany	Magdeburg
401.00	Diemers	Germany	Ruhr	Cologne
501.00	Arai	Japan	East Japan	Tokyo
504.00	Makino	Japan	East Japan	Tokyo
506.00	Oneda	Japan	East Japan	Tokyo
502.00	Kamata	Japan	East Japan	Yokohama
507.00	Okumura	Japan	West Japan	Kobe
505.00	Mukumoto	Japan	West Japan	Kyoto
503.00	Kamimura	Japan	West Japan	Osaka
301.00	Edwards	UK	England	London
305.00	Keegan	UK	England	London
306.00	Jones	UK	England	Oxford

Sort order by country, not by Id or name

Figure 9-2. *Customers reside in cities that are part of countries. Marketing and sales personnel may manage more than one country.*

Associating a List of Values

1. Select the *Customer* class.
2. Select Insert | Object or click Insert Object.
3. Replace the default object name OBJECT1 with **Customer Id**. Complete the Description and SQL Select fields shown next:

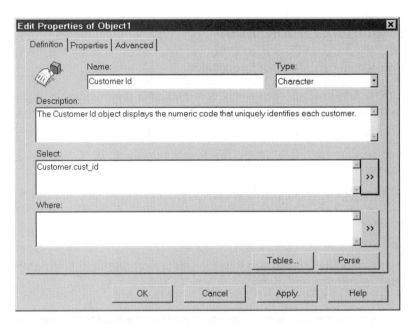

4. Select the Properties tab.

5. Change the list name to **CUSTID**.

6. Click Display. If the list is blank, click Refresh. Note that you are presented with a fairly meaningless list of codes to which you want to add the customer name.

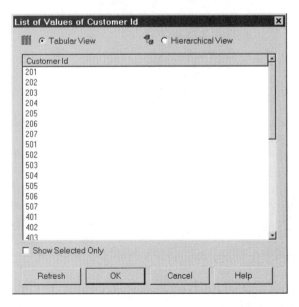

7. Click OK to return to the Object Properties tab.

Adding Additional Information

Now that the object has an associated list of values, you can modify the .lov query file to include an additional column of information.

1. From the Object Properties, select Edit. Designer presents you with a standard Query Panel. For more information on using the Query Panel, refer to Chapter 21.

2. Click the *Customer* class to expand the list of objects.

3. Drag the *Customer* (CUSTOMER.NAME) object to the right of the new *Customer Id* object.

4. The *Customer Id* has no sequence that is meaningful to users, so add a sort on *Customer* so that the names are sorted in alphabetical order. Click the Manage Sorts icon.

5. Expand the *Customer* class.

6. Double-click *Customer* to add it to the Query Sorts column. Leave the sort order at the default of Ascending.

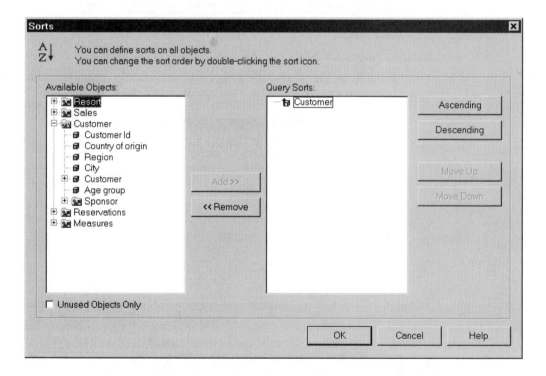

7. Click OK to return to the list of values Query Panel. The final query definitions should appear as follows:

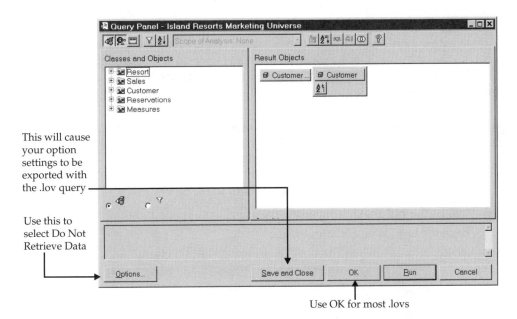

This will cause
your option
settings to be
exported with
the .lov query

Use this to
select Do Not
Retrieve Data

Use OK for most .lovs

8. Click OK to return to the Edit Properties of Customer Id panel.

9. Click Display and then Refresh to see the results of your customized list
   of values. Set the view to Tabular View (these views are explained later in
   "Tabular vs. Hierarchical Views"). This is what users will see when they
   access the list of values:

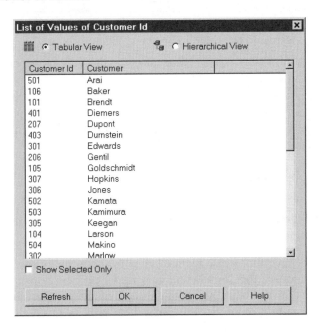

Exporting Customization with the Universe

Now that you are satisfied with the customization, you are ready to export the list of values with the universe. You do not want the data exported with the query definition (as explained in Table 9-1), so the following steps will purge the data and ensure only the query file gets exported:

 If you test your list of values (step 9 in the previous section), you must first purge the results or the data will be exported with the query customization. Exporting list of values data to the repository can slow universe imports unnecessarily.

1. From Object Properties, select Edit to return to the Query Panel.

2. From the Query Panel, select Options.

3. Check the box Do Not Retrieve Data.

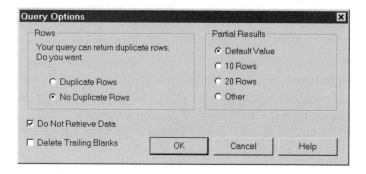

4. Click OK to return to the Query Panel.

5. From the Query Panel, select OK to return to the Edit Properties of Customer Id screen.

 If you select Save and Close rather than OK, the query option "Do Not Retrieve Data" is saved with the object.lov definition. You do not want this, as users also will not be able to retrieve data when using the list of values.

6. Check the box Export with universe.

7. Select OK to save the changes and exit the Edit Properties screen.

8. Select File | Save and then File | Export to save your universe changes and export them to the repository.

As an extra check, you may also want to view the size of the .lov file via Windows Explorer. The exact size of the .lov file will vary depending on how many columns of data, sorts, and conditions are in the list of values. The main point here is to make sure that no list of values files unintentionally have data with the query definitions.

Adding a Prompt to Filter a Long List of Values

The code table in the T_BEACH universe is quite small (35 rows); however, for many real-world data warehouses and OLTP systems, the customer tables and product tables are fairly large. For this reason, universe designers should customize the list of values to shorten the number of rows presented to the user. There is no fixed number as to how many rows are reasonable; it's more a question of reasonable response time. For lists of values, aim for seconds, not minutes, or users may incorrectly assume the system is down.

When adding prompts as part of your customized list of values, you must first be familiar with the dimension tables, how they relate, and which prompts will give a good response time without annoying the users. If a user is simply trying to find a customer code, the user does not want to be asked five questions in advance to arrive at the customer code; one or two levels of prompting should be the most you do. Whenever possible, strive to display more columns of information in the original list of values rather than adding a prompt as your first choice. The goal of the prompt is to shorten your list to guarantee a reasonable response time and navigatable size; the goal is not to generate the smallest list possible.

For customers, you may shorten the list by adding a prompt for customers beginning with a certain letter or a prompt for customers residing in a certain city or region. For products or SKUs, objects such as product category or line of business bring the list of values to a more manageable size.

In the following example, you will continue to work with the *Customer Id* object. First, study the dimension data. In looking at earlier Figure 9-2, notice which city and country each customer resides in. Additionally, each country is divided into multiple regions within the country; if your business users had not specifically told you this or if you had not studied the dimensional data, you may have incorrectly assumed that *Region* referred to *World Region* (such as North America, Europe, and so on). Ideally, users will tell you which customizations they want, but for them, the choices may not be clear, and the business definitions may not be obvious; it's up to you as the universe designer to give them your best guess for the friendliest, fastest customization.

Next, look at the tables involved, as shown in Figure 9-3. If you decide to prompt the users on *Country of Origin*, then four tables will be joined together to present the shortened list of *Customer Ids*. In this demo example, the tables are small, so the joins are not a problem. In a production implementation, carefully evaluate the impact on response time when your list of values customization involves more than one table. At this point, also see if a shortcut join is available, for example, to shorten the list of product IDs according to which plants make the products (see Chapter 7, "Shortcut Joins"). Prompting on *City* may result in a faster query, but it doesn't make sense from a business viewpoint; managers are organized by country.

1. Select the object *Customer Id* and double-click to bring up the Edit Properties box.

2. Select the Properties tab.

3. Select Edit to modify the CUSTID.LOV query and display the Query Panel.

4. Expand the *Customer* class and drag the object *Country of Origin* to the Conditions box.

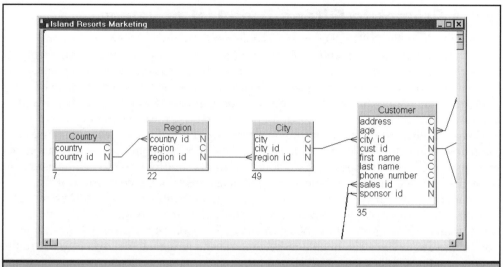

Figure 9-3. *Adding Country as a prompt in the Customer Id list of values involves four tables.*

5. When prompted, select the operator In List and the operand Type a New Prompt. In List allows users to select multiple countries. Operators and operands are explained more fully in Chapter 21. The customized list of values should appear as follows:

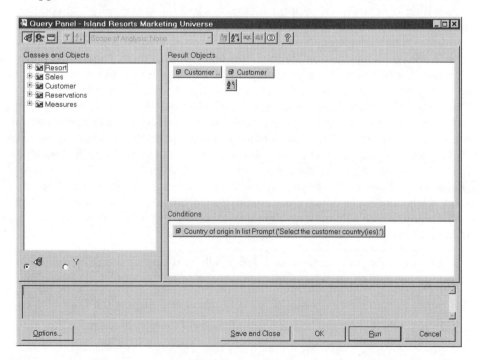

6. Follow the steps from the preceding section ("Export Customization with the Universe") to save the prompt into the list of values customization.

Tabular vs. Hierarchical Views

As you add more result columns in the customized list of values queries, users may wish to view customizations by hierarchy rather than in tabular form. As seen in most of the illustrations in this chapter, Tabular View presents the list of values information in a tabular or spreadsheet format. Hierarchical View provides drill-down functionality within the list of values.

In order for the hierarchical view to work correctly, BusinessObjects requires the columns be in a particular order. The list of values object must always be the first column. If the object is an ID or Code object, it would be intuitive if the description were the second column; but it's not! After the base object, the result objects run from left to right with the left-most object being the top of the hierarchy and the description or most detailed object being on the right side of the query. Each of the objects should have a corresponding sort order.

To continue with the customer example, *Customer Id* is the object whose list of values you are customizing. In the following screen, this is the left-most object. *Country of origin* is the top of the hierarchy and appears second. *Country of origin* is the primary sort order.

Base object whose values you want
in the condition is the first column   The top of the hierarchy   The lowest detail

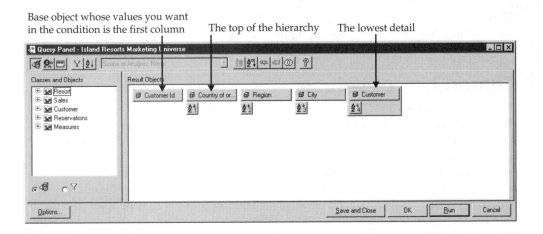

It is important to sort the objects according to the hierarchy levels, or the drill-down may appear nonsensical.

Now when users request to select a list of values, they can scroll through the possible values by drilling down through a hierarchy. My only complaint with the hierarchy view is that it does not work particularly well with code/description customizations. I would like it if the final drill-down displayed both the code and the description. Otherwise, this is a useful feature for helping users navigate long lists.

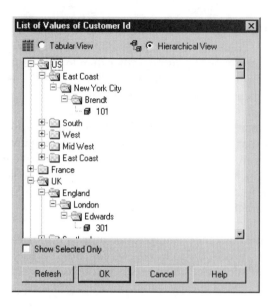

 As with prompts, be careful that the Hierarchical View does not require too many extra clicks. In the preceding example, the country hierarchy alone would have been sufficient, and I recommend leaving out the region and city columns.

Shared List of Values

As mentioned throughout this chapter, list of values are query files. As the files are stored separately from the object definition, it is easy to use one list of values query with multiple objects. Giving the lists meaningful names will make this process easier to maintain.

You may want to share the same list of values for objects used in multiple alias tables, regardless of whether they have been defined as aliases within the universe or synonyms within the RDBMS. For example, customer number may be used in both the *Ship To Customer* and the *Sold To Customer*. Both objects use the same customer numbers. In the next example, there is a *Sending Plant Id* and a *Receiving Plant Id* for a company that has plant-to-plant transfers. The list of plant IDs remains the same. Sharing the list of values query across the objects will mean less customization for you as the designer. For users, it results in faster universe updates and fewer list of values refreshes.

To share a list of values across multiple objects:

1. Select the object that contains the customization and double-click to edit the object properties.
2. Select the Properties tab.
3. Under List Name, assign a meaningful query name or note the system-generated name.
4. Customize the list of values query according to the instructions in the previous sections.
5. Ensure the box Export with universe is checked.
6. Select the second object that will share the query definition for the list of values.
7. Under List Name, fill in the same query name as in step 3. You do not need to check the box Export with universe on this secondary object. Figure 9-4 shows how two objects can share the same list of values customization.

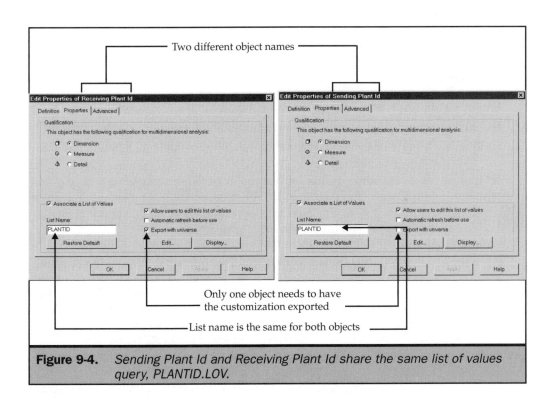

Figure 9-4. *Sending Plant Id and Receiving Plant Id share the same list of values query, PLANTID.LOV.*

Incorporating Personal Data Files

Throughout this chapter, I've warned against exporting data with the universe list of values, as it can unnecessarily slow universe updates. However, there are three instances in which you may want to break this rule:

1. The list is extremely small and it is faster for the repository to send the users a preexecuted query than it is for the users to execute the *object*.lov query themselves.

2. The dimensional data is not available in a central RDBMS to which all universe users have access.

3. The dimensional data in the data warehouse or OLTP is in transition, and new groupings and codes are not available in a central RDBMS.

For these last two reasons, a universe designer can incorporate personal data into the customized list of values and export it to the repository. Users may also do this on an individual basis. At this point, any data warehouse purist is cringing and rightly so. Of course, you want everyone viewing the same reference data! Of course, that reference data should be universally available! Sadly, this is not always the case. Remember, I am a business person at heart, so here is what you will need to do to keep business users happy (and to ensure you don't have dozens of them attempting this themselves!).

Personal data files can be text, spreadsheet, or database files. Each file must follow a specific layout:

- The condition column or pick list value must be in the first column.

- The remaining columns may contain additional information. Unlike standard customized list of values, these additional columns cannot be used for sorting once in BusinessObjects, so do the sorting first in the data file.

- It is okay to have column headings, but you must tell BusinessObjects they exist.

If your list of values is in a spreadsheet, create an Excel range name with just those columns and rows you want to appear as a list of values.

Using the EFASHION universe as an example, let's assume that you want to regroup certain SKU numbers into different product lines, as shown in Table 9-2, which contains a proposed product grouping that does not exist in the data warehouse or OLTP. The new groupings are available in a spreadsheet file that not all users can access. In the RDBMS, Lounge wear and Jewelry are grouped under the line Accessories. In the personal data file, they are regrouped into a newly created line, Jewelry. Other SKUs are moved into existing but different Proposed Lines such as 161363 Double-Breasted Silk Jacket from Accessories to Jackets.

Once you have ensured your data file is in the appropriate format, you can associate this data file with the object list of values:

1. From the pull-down menu, select Tools | List of Values.

SKU Number	SKU Description	Category	Proposed Lines	Current Lines
160812	Multicolored Pearl Necklace	Jewelry	Jewelry	Accessories
162520	Diamond Star Earrings	Jewelry	Jewelry	Accessories
168852	Silver Hoop Earrings	Jewelry	Jewelry	Accessories
185114	2 Row Pearl Necklace	Jewelry	Jewelry	Accessories
141406	Belted Tunic	Lounge wear	Sweat-T-Shirts	Accessories
150850	Zipper Vest	Lounge wear	Sweat-T-Shirts	Accessories
155576	Rudolph Shirt	Lounge wear	Sweat-T-Shirts	Accessories
159421	Striped Leggings	Lounge wear	Trousers	Accessories
160556	Spotty Leggings	Lounge wear	Trousers	Accessories
161363	Double-Breasted Silk Jacket	Lounge wear	Jackets	Accessories
167119	Jacquard T-Shirt	Lounge wear	Sweat-T-Shirts	Accessories
182379	Lurex Leotard	Lounge wear	Sweat-T-Shirts	Accessories
182488	Chenille Leotard T-Shirt	Lounge wear	Sweat-T-Shirts	Accessories
182880	Diamond Cigarette Holder	Lounge wear	Jewelry	Accessories
183861	Lycra Culotte Shorts	Lounge wear	Trousers	Accessories

Table 9-2. *List of Values Can Access Personal Data Files*

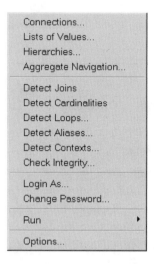

2. This will present you with a list of all objects in the universe that have an associated list of values. Expand the *Product* class, then select *SKU number*.

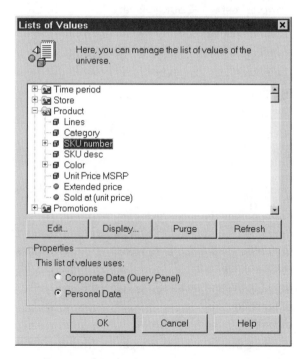

3. Change the radio button from Corporate Data to Personal Data. When you change this option, you will receive the following warning message:

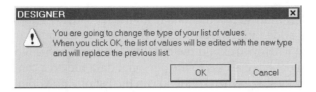

4. Click OK. Designer presents you with a Personal Data selection screen.

5. Specify the data file that contains your list of values and the format. If it is an Excel spreadsheet, you can specify a range name. An example using an MS Excel spreadsheet that uses a range name in which the first row contains column headings is shown here:

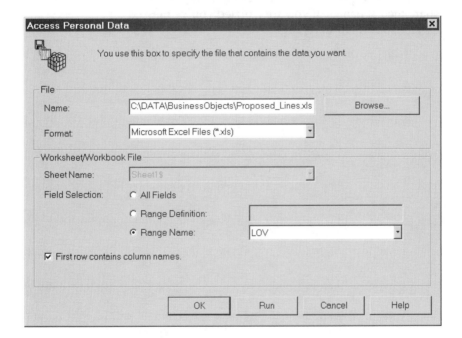

6. Click Run to have Business Objects access your personal data file and return to the List of Values dialog box.

7. Click Display to see this new list. Change your view from hierarchical to tabular. Designer displays the customized list of values in the format that will appear to users when they request a list of values for a condition object.

8. Click OK twice to close the display list and List of Values dialog box.

9. Modify the object properties for *SKU number* to mark the box Export with Universe.

When you click Run in step 6, the data from the spreadsheet (or other personal data file) is dynamically added into the custid.lov file. Designer exports this file with the universe definitions when you export the modified universe to the repository. If you skip step 6 and users do not have access to the personal data file on a central server, they will receive an error message when trying to run the list of values. Similarly, if users ever click Refresh, they will need access to the data file or will receive an error message.

Summary

It's true, list of values customizations can get out of hand. It can be difficult to manage which ones you are exporting, which ones have data in the *object*.lov file, and which objects share the list names. If you are worried you've messed up anywhere, check Chapter 15 for some helpful reports.

The Complete Reference

Chapter 10

Advanced Objects

In the previous chapters, you created some basic objects. In this chapter, you will add a significant amount of intelligence to columns of information. BusinessObjects provides two main categories of functionality to do this: internal BusinessObjects functions and SQL functions that are RDBMS specific. The first part of the chapter covers functionality that is specific to BusinessObjects but database independent. The second part of the chapter covers SQL commands that may be dependent on which RDBMS you use.

Reducing Maintenance with Base Objects and @Select

The @Select function is an internal BusinessObjects function that allows you, as the designer, to reuse universe objects without forcing you to repeat the entire SQL syntax. For example, take an initial object *Sales* that provides information on revenue in U.S. dollars. You can add a number of forms of intelligence to this object: *Sales in Local Currency, Sales in Euros, Sales Adjusted for Inflation, Sales with 10% Projected Increase,* and so on. These additional objects are not columns in the database; they are objects you create by using SQL commands described in the second part of this book. However, they all use the same initial column in the RDBMS. When building advanced objects with Designer, you can either select the RDBMS column or a universe object. Whenever possible, select an object. You will save time on maintenance. Imagine six months from now, the Sales column in the RDBMS is renamed. If all of the related Sales objects used the RDBMS column, that is how many objects you now must modify manually. However, if all the objects used @Select, you need to modify only the base object.

The syntax of @Select is @Select(*Class\Object*), where *Class* is the name of the class that contains the base object—for example, Measures, and *Object* is the name of the object that contains the base object—for example, Sales. When using @Select, you can still see the full SQL statement by clicking Show Object SQL in the SQL Editor. In all the examples in this chapter, I use @Select whenever possible but display the full SQL syntax.

Whenever possible, use objects rather than individual RDBMS columns. This will save you work if ever you rename an RDBMS column, as you will need to modify only the SQL of the base object; Designer will automatically update the SQL for all other objects that use the base column.

The @Where function is similar to @Select in that you can reuse a WHERE clause from an existing object.

The SQL Editor

When changing SQL statements, you can either enter the SELECT statements in the formula bar (to display, select View | Formula Bar), or you can use the SQL Editor to change either the SELECT statement or the WHERE clause. The SQL Editor also provides some help on BusinessObjects functions and SQL syntax (although I would like to see Business Objects provide more business-oriented examples in the online help).

Figure 10-1 shows the SQL Editor. You launch the SQL Editor by clicking the >> button from the Definition tab of the object properties. As you modify the SQL for an object, you can either point and click your way through it, or you can enter the functions, columns, and operators manually. Regardless of how you build the SQL Statement, be sure to Parse or Validate (formula editor) each object as you go. Parsing validates that your statement is correct and won't produce an error when a user launches a query. Parsing will not catch all SQL errors and may be slower for objects that use @Select (as multiple SQL statements must be checked), but it will catch the majority.

It would be nice if the vendor reordered the selection boxes as, in order to build a statement with point and click, you start with the Function box on the right. For example, to create the measure object from the Island Resorts Marketing universe, as shown in Figure 10-1:

1. Under Functions, expand the Number functions by clicking the + sign. Scroll to sum() and double-click. Notice that the mouse insertion point is correctly between the parentheses. If you had started with the Tables and Columns on the left, your mouse would be in the wrong place.

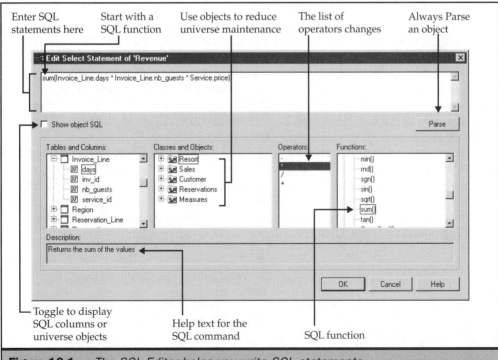

Figure 10-1. *The SQL Editor helps you write SQL statements.*

2. Under Tables and Columns, expand the INVOICE_LINE table by clicking the + sign. Double-click DAYS to insert INVOICE_LINE.DAYS into the statement.

3. Under Operators, double-click the multiplication sign (*). The list of available operators will change depending if you modify a SELECT statement or a WHERE clause.

4. Under Tables and Columns, double-click NB_GUESTS.

5. Under Operators, double-click * again.

6. Under Tables and Columns, scroll to the SERVICE table, click + to expand it, and double-click PRICE. The close parenthesis should still be in the correct place.

Proceed with Caution Using SQL

SQL contains a number of commands that are common to all databases. However, database vendors have added a number of extensions to make SQL more powerful. These extensions are not common for all databases. Some companies have a policy about ensuring that universes stay generic in case the underlying database changes; third-party vendors that use BusinessObjects as the reporting engine also may strive to keep their universes generic. However, when you avoid using database-specific SQL in the universe, you are generally forcing end users to do more work in the reports (see Chapter 13 for further discussion). My recommendation is to use your database SQL to its fullest. Your universe will be more powerful, and you will help save users time.

The big caveat is that you must understand how certain functions may affect query performance. As a general rule, if you change the appearance of a column, the database will not use that particular column's index to process the query. For example, if I convert a customer name field to uppercase, the name values in the index table are still stored in lowercase. If a user filters a query by UPPER(NAME), the lowercase name index cannot be used. Oracle 9i allows DBAs to create additional indexes that include the function, but there is no guarantee your DBA has done this.

The available SQL commands are stored in the *database*.prm file. Business Objects provides you with a default *database*.prm file that you may want to modify. These entries are for guidance only; if a command does not exist in the file, designers can manually enter it in the SQL statement. When you change the *database*.prm file, you must restart Designer for the change to take effect. Following is a section from the Ora7EN.prm file on the SQL UPPER function:

```
NAME= Uppercase
TRAD= String:
HELP= Returns a character string in upper case
```

```
TYPE=A
IN_MACRO=Y
GROUP=N
SQL=upper($A)
```

NAME corresponds to the name of the function that appears to you in the SQL Editor.

HELP is the help text that appears in the Description box in the SQL Editor.

TRAD acts like a prompt when users create their own objects. In the preceding example, users will be prompted to enter a String that then gets passed to $A as part of the SQL command. The prompt must end with a colon. If the SQL function requires more than one argument, a $ symbol must precede each subsequent prompt. For example, LTRIM trims characters from the left of a specified string. TRAD could be set to as follows:

```
TRAD=Enter the object to trim: $Enter the character at which to start trimming:
```

TYPE specifies if the output results are in an alphanumeric, date, or numeric column.

IN_MACRO indicates if users can access the SQL function to create their own objects. If you scroll through the file, note that by default, users cannot access the Oracle DECODE function. If you want them to be able to, set IN_MACRO=Y.

GROUP indicates if the use of the function should generate a GROUP BY clause in the SQL statement.

SQL shows the actual SQL syntax. If the SQL has any parameters, these are indicated with $A for character values, $N for numeric values, and $D for date values.

You may want to modify the *database*.prm file for the following reasons:

- To enable users to access SQL functions that have been disabled by default

- To improve the help text for frequently used functions, especially if your company has decentralized universe designers

- To add SQL functions that your RDBMS vendor has recently added but that Business Objects has not yet added in the *database*.prm file

Condition Objects

Condition objects are unique objects that allow users to access predefined conditions that the designer specifies in the WHERE clause. Condition objects are denoted with a filter symbol.

The Island Resorts Marketing universe, shown next, contains several predefined conditions. To access a condition object, click the Classes/Conditions filter in the lower-left corner. Click the + sign next to each class to see the Condition Objects.

Formula bar shows
the WHERE clause

Classes/conditions
filter

Classes/objects filter

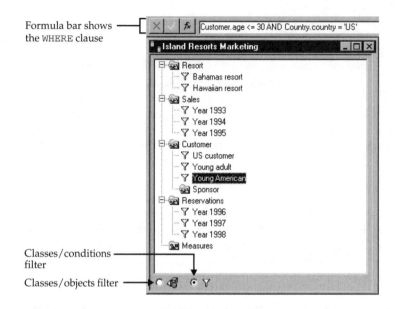

Most of these conditions are fairly simple. In building condition objects, you, as the designer, must evaluate if the objects add clutter or value. If it saves the users time, create the object. If it defines some unique groupings that do not otherwise exist in the dimension tables, create the object. Objects that contain one value such as *Year 1993* do not add much value; users probably could have added the condition themselves. *Young American,* on the other hand, contains two conditions (`Customer.age <= 30 AND Country.country = 'US'`). Nesting conditions can be confusing and cumbersome, so such an object would be very helpful to users.

In the following example, you will create a condition object, *Platinum Customers,* for customers who generate more than $100,000 in revenue in any given year. The next report shows seven customers who had revenues of $100,000 or more. You will add each customer code to the condition clause. Unfortunately, it is not possible to create condition objects based on measures (so you can't say `Where Revenue >= 100,000`) as doing so requires a different SQL clause. Conditions on measures use a HAVING clause (explained in Chapter 22) rather than a WHERE clause.

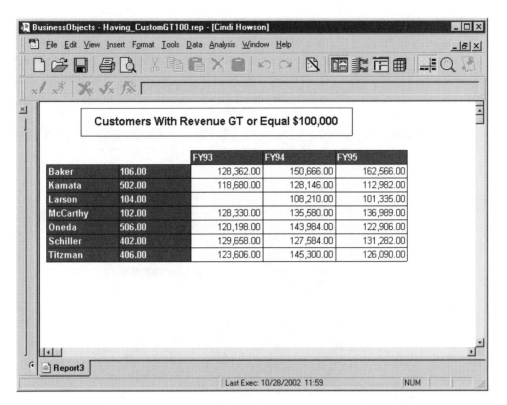

1. Using the Island Resorts Marketing universe, set the Classes and Objects pane to display the condition objects. Position your cursor in the class you want the new object to appear—in this example, *Customer*.

2. Click the Insert Condition button on the toolbar or select Insert | Condition from the pull-down menus.

3. In the Name box, enter **Platinum Customer**.

4. In the Description box, enter some meaningful help text such as: **A platinum customer is a predefined list of customer codes with revenues of $100,000 or more in any given year.**

5. In the Where box, click >> to call up SQL Editor.

6. At this point, you could manually enter the WHERE statement. Under Classes and Objects, scroll to the class that contains the object you want to use for the WHERE clause. In this example, click the + next to *Customer*.

7. For response time reasons, you want the WHERE clause on the indexed *Customer Id* object rather than the nonindexed *Customer Name*. Double-click *Customer Id* to have it added to the WHERE statement. Note that Designer uses the @Select function.

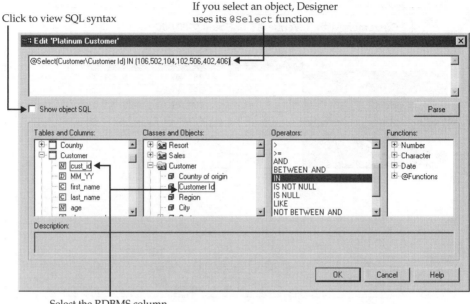

Click to view SQL syntax

If you select an object, Designer uses its @Select function

Select the RDBMS column or the universe object name

8. To view the SQL syntax, click the Show object SQL check-box, shown next. Notice that Designer grays the SQL statement box and does not allow you to edit the statement.

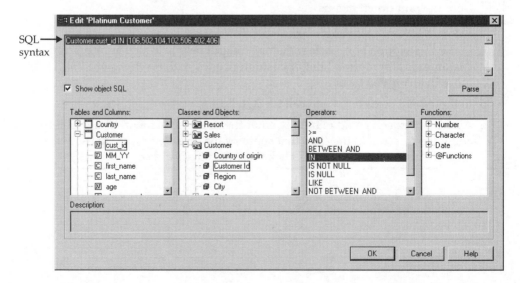

SQL syntax

9. In the Operators box, scroll to IN and double-click to add this to the SQL statement.

10. You do not need to transform your values, so you will not use any functions. Manually enter the list of customer IDs **(106,502,104,102,506,402,406)** generated by the preceding report. Because *Customer Id* is a numeric object, it does not require single quotes around each condition value.

11. *Always* click Parse to test the validity of the SQL statement.

12. Click OK to close the SQL Editor. The condition object properties should now look like this:

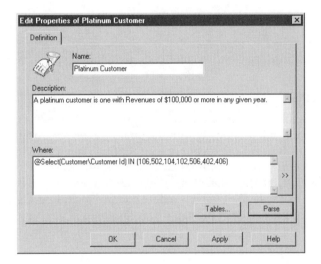

13. Click OK to close the object properties screen.

14. Click Save to save the universe changes. If necessary, export the changes to the repository with File | Export.

When users build a query, they can now add the condition object to the condition panel. To test this, select Tools | Run | BusinessObjects to launch the BusinessObjects user module. The next image shows how this new object appears to users in the Query Panel.

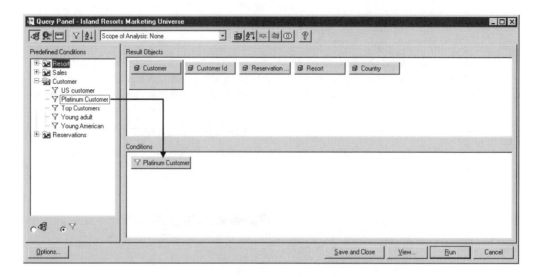

Time Conditions

Condition objects involving time functions are popular. Additionally, BusinessObjects does not allow users to add calculations within the query panel, so condition objects become the only way in which users can create rolling reports. The following objects use SYSDATE, which returns the current date according to the RDBMS.

The following SQL creates a *One Year Ago* condition object. The comparison column is in a date format. Because SYSDATE is a date column including the day of the year, you subtract 365 days to arrive at the same date last year.

```
TIMES.END_OF_CAL_YEAR=SYSDATE-365
```

If the comparison column is not in a date format but is numeric, then you must also convert the SYSDATE calculation to numeric with TO_NUMBER. The following SQL creates a *Last Year* object in which the year is four digits. To extract only the four digits, use the TO_CHAR function.

```
TIMES.CALENDAR_YEAR=TO_NUMBER(TO_CHAR(SYSDATE-365,'YYYY'))
```

You can further nest date functions to create a *Current 3 Months* condition object. In the following example, -3 shows that three months should be subtracted from the SYSDATE.

```
SH.TIMES.CALENDAR_MONTH_NUMBER  BETWEEN TO_NUMBER(TO_CHAR(ADD_MONTHS(SYSDATE,-
3),'MM') ) AND TO_NUMBER(TO_CHAR(SYSDATE,'MM') )
```

Caution   *The WHERE statements from each Condition Object and Row Restrictions set through Supervisor (Chapter 12) are appended to the entire SQL statement. If users combine incompatible condition objects, they may get no rows returned.*

Objects with Prompts: Interactive Objects

Business Objects refers to objects that contain prompts as *interactive objects*. Each time a user accesses an interactive object, BusinessObjects prompts the user for additional information that you, as the designer, build into the object. Prompts can be useful but also annoying if the user always wants the same values. For example, if a user always wants current year data, it can be aggravating if the object prompts the user for the year each time the user refreshes the query. In such a case, the user is better off placing a fixed condition in a report. Objects with prompts should be reserved for items in which some sort of condition is required either to limit the number of rows returned or to guarantee correct results.

In Chapter 8, Figure 8-2, you looked at the risk of constructing a query that involved a single point in time (account balance or ending inventory) and a period of time (debits and credits or movements in and out). One way to ensure users select one point in time for inventory or account balances is to prompt users to enter an individual date whenever they select month-end inventory, as shown in Figure 10-2. (It would be wrong to put

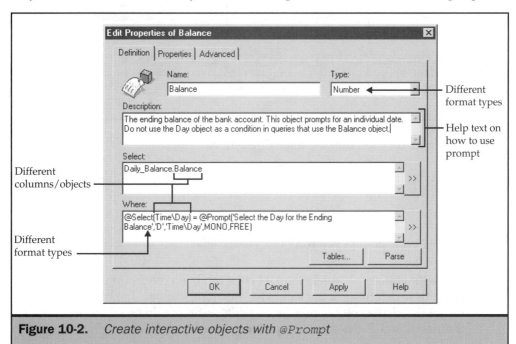

Figure 10-2.   *Create interactive objects with* `@Prompt`

the prompt on the *Day* object, because it would prevent users from analyzing debits and credits for more than one day.)

Notice in Figure 10-2 that the object or *TABLE.COLUMN* in the SELECT portion of the SQL can be different than the table.column in the WHERE clause. Because these two columns can be different, the format types also may be different. The *Balance* object uses the Type=Number, yet the @Prompt uses *D* to indicate the prompt answer will be in date format. Prompts are added in the WHERE clause of a new or existing object. Under Functions, double-click the @Prompt function to insert the syntax in the SQL statement, as shown here.

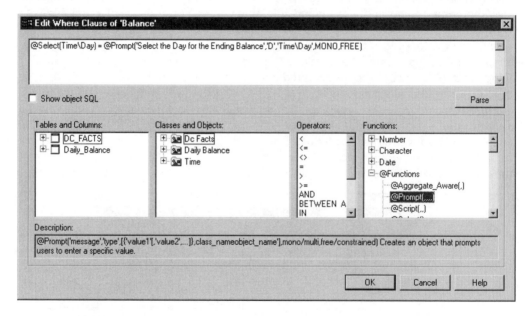

The @Prompt function uses the following syntax:

```
@Prompt('Message','type','object or list of values',MONO/MULTI,FREE/CONSTRAINED)
```

where

1. *Message* is the prompt you want users to see when they run a query that contains this object.

2. *Type* is the object type or field format for the condition column. BusinessObjects uses this to determine if the values require quotes or not. The base object and the WHERE clause column may be two different types. In this example, *Balance* is numeric and *Day* is date. Acceptable values are

   ■ *A* for alphanumeric

- *N* for number

- *D* for date

3. The `'object or list of values'` parameter can either be the individual objects whose list of values you want to use or a list of values you enter manually in the prompt. When entering a predetermined list of values, you must enclose the values in single quotes, separated by commas, and the complete list must be enclosed by brackets. For example, if I wanted to restrict users to the most recent two ending balances: `{'09/30/02','10/31/02'}`.

4. **MONO/MULTI**   If users can select only one value, use MONO. If users can enter more than one value, use MULTI. Note that the SQL operator must correspond to this setting. If users can enter more than one value, use the IN operator.

5. **FREE/CONSTRAINED**   If users must select a value from the list of values, use CONSTRAINED. If users can either select from a list of values or enter their own value, use FREE.

Caution   *The @Prompt function is very particular about commas, quotation marks, and matching object types. Be sure to Parse the object.*

When a user constructs a query that uses the *Balance* object, BusinessObjects will always prompt them to Select the Day for the Ending Balance. The following screen illustrates how prompts can become user *un*friendly. In the following query, the user wants to see daily balances and correctly includes the *Day* object as a result object:

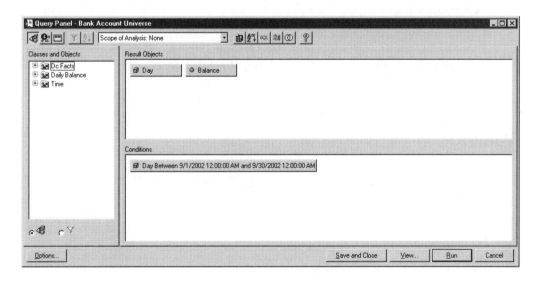

However, the *Balance* object also now includes the prompt. This generates the following SQL:

```
SELECT
  Daily_Balance.Date,
  Daily_Balance.Balance
FROM
  Daily_Balance
WHERE
( ( Daily_Balance.Date ) = @Prompt('Select the Day for the Ending
Balance','D','Time\Day',MONO,FREE)  )
  AND  (
  Daily_Balance.Date  BETWEEN  {d '2002-09-01'} AND {d
'2002-09-30'}
  )
```

First, from the user's viewpoint it seems nonsensical that BusinessObjects will prompt for information that the user has already included in the conditions. Second, users will only ever be able to retrieve balances for one day at a time when it is a valid business question for them to review daily balances over a period of time. In this respect, it is important in training and object descriptions to emphasize how these objects work and when to use them. As you build interactive objects, follow these guidelines:

- Use interactive objects only when the absence of a prompt could lead to inaccurate information.
- If the prompts are for user friendliness or automation, have two objects, one without a prompt for unrestricted information and one with the prompt. Differentiate between these two objects with clear names—for example, *Balance* and *Balance-Date Required.*
- Provide usage information in the object description or in training.

All Values

If you do not want the prompt to be mandatory to limit the number of rows, try the following technique, suggested by Walter Muellner of Mercury Business Solutions in Austria:

```
'ALL'  IN @Prompt('Enter City or ALL','A', 'Customer\City',multi,)
 OR
City.city IN @Prompt('Enter City or ALL','A', 'Customer\City',multi,)
```

This is a very creative approach to balancing user friendliness with prompting. When users enter ALL, the first part of the condition SQL gets used ('ALL' IN

'ALL'). Because the condition statement uses an OR clause, the second condition is not evaluated. Conversely, if users enter city names (or anything other than ALL), then the first part of the SQL is not true so it does not get used, while the second condition does. Of course, if ALL is a possible data value in the City column, this poses a problem. The alternative is to use a symbol such as * or %—however, the risk is that users mix up true uses of these symbols (wildcards in certain databases). Finally, in order for this to work, the prompt in both condition statements must be exactly the same or users will be prompted twice.

Reusing Interactive Objects with @Variable

BusinessObjects allows you to reuse the prompt as a variable that you can then use in other objects. The variable can be one that you create with @Prompt, or it can be a system variable. BusinessObjects provides the following system variables:

- **BOUSER**   The BusinessObjects user ID
- **BOPASS**   The BusinessObjects password

As an example, let's assume that a hierarchical PRODUCT table contains both products and employees responsible for those products. So that users automatically see information for their products, the *My Product* object could contain the following WHERE clause:

```
PRODUCT.PRODUCT_OWNER = @Variable('BOUSER')
```

Reusing Interactive Objects with @Where

As mentioned previously, @Where allows you to reuse a WHERE clause in multiple objects. There are two benefits to using @Where: the first is decreased maintenance. The second is decreased user prompting. If a query contains multiple occurrences of the exact same prompt, BusinessObjects will prompt the user only one time. For example, let's assume that users must filter Customer information by City to ensure only a limited amount of data is returned. The dimension object *City* contains a prompt. A designer could add @Where (Customer\City) to *Customer Name, Customer Id, Customer Age Group*. Even if a query contains all four of these objects in a query, the user is prompted only once to Select a City.

Prompts in Objects vs. Reports

Objects with prompts achieve a similar functionality as queries with prompts (Chapter 21, "Prompts"). In Chapter 13, you will look at the pros and cons of where to put this kind of intelligence. The main difference to consider with prompts is flexibility and maintenance. If you want to give the users flexibility, put the prompts in the reports. If you want to minimize your maintenance costs, keep the prompts centralized in the universe objects. The following table summarizes some of the key differences between prompts in objects versus prompts in a query.

Object with Prompt	Query with Prompt
Designer builds into universe	User builds in query
Centralized, so cost-effective to maintain because the designer creates the prompt once	Decentralized, so expensive to maintain because users must create the prompt in every document
Users cannot remove, so it can be inflexible, but error-proof, as it requires an answer	Users can remove, providing flexibility

Aggregate Awareness

An *aggregate table* is a summary table that DBAs build to execute queries faster. Aggregate tables are smaller than detail tables and can be aggregated in a number of ways. Most DBAs will strive for a certain compression ratio—for example, 10:1; the aggregate or summary table should be ten times smaller than the detail table or for every ten detail rows, there is one summary row.

Figure 10-3 shows two sample dimensions, Time and Product. In the Time dimension, there are five years of history, with four levels going from Year to Day. Within a given year, there are 365 days. If the Time dimension contains five years of history, this results in 1,825 rows of data. The Product dimension has four levels ranging from Total Product to SKU. There are 210 SKUs (this is a very small product dimension).

A DBA may create an aggregate table summarizing data to any of these levels, across any dimension, as shown in Figure 10-4. The SALES_FACT_DAY table contains daily sales figures for five years, at the SKU level for all customers. The SALES_FACT_ MONTH table aggregates sales by month and by product line. Customer is not aggregated in any way.

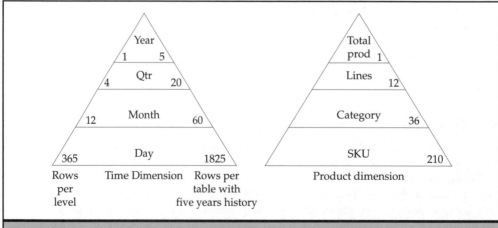

Figure 10-3.   *Two sample dimensions showing the number of potential rows at each level*

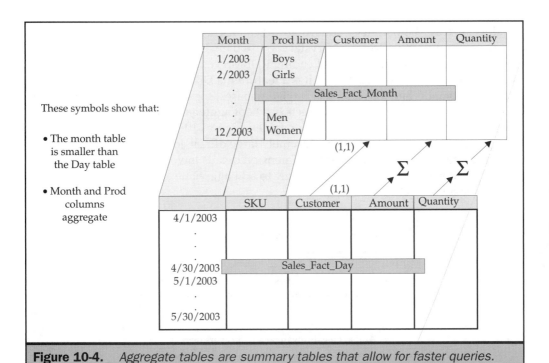

Figure 10-4.   *Aggregate tables are summary tables that allow for faster queries.*

The following table shows the potential number of rows in such a fact table, if you have 30,000 customers. Typically, not every product sells daily, nor does every customer buy every product on a daily basis, so the potential rows represent strictly a worse-case scenario. However, the table illustrates the purpose of using aggregate tables for faster queries. If a user wants to analyze customer or product line sales only on a monthly or quarterly basis, the queries will run much faster against a 21.6 million row table than an 11.497 billion row table.

	Time	Product	Customer	Potential Rows
Day, SKU	1825	210	30,000	11,497,500,000
Month, product line	60	12	30,000	21,600,000

The *existence* of aggregate tables does not help user queries. Users must *access* the summary tables, ideally automatically with awareness built into the BI tool or the RDBMS to force the query to be processed in the most efficient way. In recent years, BI vendors have debated if aggregate awareness belongs in the BI tool or in the RDBMS. BusinessObjects is the only BI tool that has built-in functionality to take advantage of RDBMS aggregate tables in a way that is seamless to users. Relational OLAP (ROLAP) vendors such as MicroStrategy and Microsoft can use aggregate tables, but tools such as Cognos Impromptu, Brio, and Crystal can use them only if a user specifically tells the tool to access a summary table. Leading RDBMS vendors now include an aggregate navigator in the database. However, it is a feature the DBA must tell the RDBMS to use; it is not automatic, and for extremely large databases, some customers have struggled to enable it. Fortunately, Business Objects has kept aggregate awareness in the tool and improved it to work also with dimension tables. Figures 10-1 and 10-2 focus on creating an aggregate for the fact tables. For extremely large dimensions, you also may have a smaller dimension table that removes dimension details lower than month and product line. The following example will show how to add aggregate awareness in both facts and dimension objects:

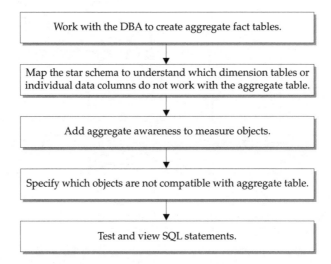

Creating Aggregate Fact Tables

Business Objects has provided two aggregate tables as part of the EFASHION.MDB. You will focus on the one table:

```
AGG_YR_QT_MT_MN_WK_RG_CY_SN_SR_QT_MA
```

The naming of the table is a bit cumbersome, so hereafter, I will refer to it as the aggregate fact table. The table name reveals some information on the contents of the table:

- **AGG**   Aggregate
- **YR**   Year
- **QT**   Quarter

- **MT** Month Text
- **MN** Month Number
- **WK** Week
- **RG** Maybe region was intended but not in the final table?
- **CY** City
- **SN** Store Name
- **SR** Sales Revenue
- **QT** Quantity
- **MA** Margin

I do have some concerns with the design of this table, but for demonstration purposes it will work fine. Notice that the number of rows for the aggregate table is 1,982 compared to 89,171 in the detailed SHOP_FACTS table. Whenever possible, you want queries to run against the smaller AGG_YR_QT_MT_MN_WK_RG_CY_SN_SR_QT_MA rather than the larger, detailed SHOP_FACTS.

Identifying Dimension Tables
Irrelevant to Aggregate Tables

In looking at Figure 10-5, you see that the aggregate table does not include any information on Articles. So these two dimension tables will become incompatible with the summary objects. The fact table includes a lot of dimensional information.

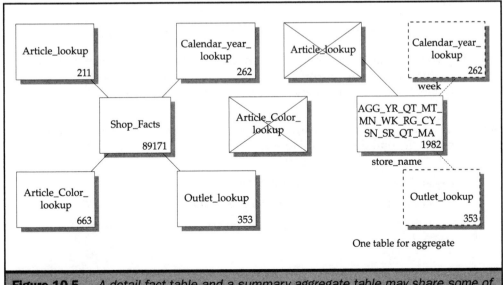

Figure 10-5. *A detail fact table and a summary aggregate table may share some of the same dimension tables.*

A BETTER UNIVERSE

Time information is aggregated to the week level. You can either retrieve dimensional information from CALENDAR_YEAR_LOOKUP or the aggregate fact table. Outlet information is not aggregated; the aggregate tables contain details on the STORE_NAME only.

Adding Aggregate Awareness to Measure Objects

You are now ready to define aggregate awareness to the individual measure objects *Sales Revenue, Quantity Sold,* and *Margin.* Aggregate awareness uses a BusinessObjects internal function:

```
@Aggregate_Aware(sum(smallest_table.column), sum(medium_table.column),
sum(biggest_table.column))
```

You can have multiple tables in the SELECT statement, with the smallest table first and the largest or most detailed table last. The @Aggregate_Aware function allows you to use any of the SQL Aggregate commands (SUM, COUNT, AVG, MIN, MAX); however, the aggregate command must be specified for each column as shown here.

Right:

```
@Aggregate_Aware(sum(Agg_yr_qt_mt_mn_wk_rg_cy_sn_sr_qt_ma.Sales_revenue),
sum(Shop_facts.Amount_sold))
```

Wrong:

```
@Aggregate_Aware(sum(Agg_yr_qt_mt_mn_wk_rg_cy_sn_sr_qt_ma.Sales_revenue,
Shop_facts.Amount_sold))
```

To follow the steps, use the Test Fashion universe created in earlier chapters.

1. If you normally have Designer automatically create objects when you add a table, turn this feature off for adding aggregate tables: Tools | Options | Database. Remove the check mark from Create Default Classes And Objects From Tables.

2. Insert the aggregate table into the universe structure. Click Table Browse or use the pull-down menu to select Insert | Table | AGG_YR_QT_MT_ MN_WK_RG_CY_SN_SR_QT_MA .

3. Expand the class *Test Fashion Measures.*

4. Select the object *Sum of Amount Sold* or *Revenue.*

5. Click the >> next to sum(Shop_facts.Amount_sold) to invoke the SQL Editor.

6. If you wish to save re-creating the SQL for the detail SHOP_FACTS table, ensure your mouse is positioned at the start of the SQL statement.

7. Under Functions, click the + sign next to @Functions to expand the group and display the BusinessObjects internal functions.

8. Double-click @Aggregate_Aware to insert the syntax in the SQL statement box.

9. Under Functions, click the + sign next to Number to display the SQL RDBMS functions. Scroll to sum() and click to insert the syntax into the SQL statement.

10. Under Tables, expand the aggregate table AGG_YR_QT_MT_MN_WK_RG_CY_ SN_SR_QT_MA and double-click SALES_REVENUE to insert the table .column between the sum().

11. Delete the right parenthesis and move it to the end to close the statement. Your SQL statement should appear as follows:

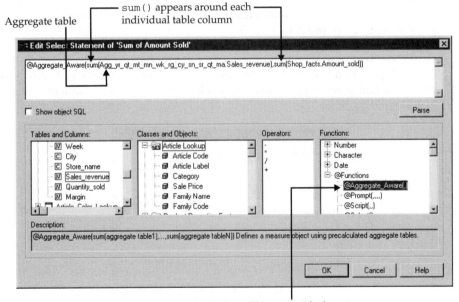

12. Click Parse to verify you have entered the correct syntax.

Note

According to Business Objects, Parse on aggregate aware objects only partially checks the SQL syntax. If you use @Select with @Aggregate_Aware, the parsing may be slower and less accurate. For complete universe integrity, be sure to test the objects by running queries and viewing the full SQL generated.

13. Click OK to close the SQL Editor then OK again to save the object definitions.

14. Repeat steps 4–13 for *Quantity Sold* and *Margin,* selecting the appropriate objects and columns.

15. At this point, there are no joins between the aggregate fact table and the dimension tables, nor is the aggregate part of a context. The aggregate table would normally have keys to join to the dimension tables that Designer may have detected; however, the design of this table is a bit unusual, so you must manually add the following two joins:

```
Agg_yr_qt_mt_mn_wk_rg_cy_sn_sr_qt_ma.Store_name=Outlet_Lookup.Shop_name

Calendar_year_lookup.Year=Agg_yr_qt_mt_mn_wk_rg_cy_sn_sr_qt_ma.Year And
Calendar_year_lookup.Week_in_Year=Agg_yr_qt_mt_mn_wk_rg_cy_sn_sr_qt_ma.Week
```

16. Either draw join lines between the respective tables and columns or use the pull-down menu Insert | Join. Note that the second join is a complex join that must be entered manually.

17. Add these two new joins to a new context. If you have correctly defined the complex join, you can use the Detect Context button or use the pull-down menu Insert | Context to include the two joins in a new context. Complete the entries as follows:

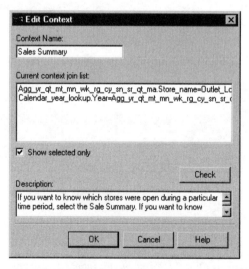

18. Click OK to accept the modified context.

19. From the pull-down menu, select File | Save or click Save to save the changes to the universe.

Specifying Which Objects Are Not Compatible with the Aggregate Table

The table now exists in the universe, and you have told BusinessObjects to use this table for certain measure objects. You now have to tell BusinessObjects that the aggregate table cannot be used when certain dimension objects exist in the query. This can be very confusing. Try to stay focused on two things:

1. You are essentially telling BusinessObjects when to use the detail table.

2. You need to worry about only one context or star schema.

Refer to Figure 10-4. Note that all article objects are incompatible with the aggregate table. If a user includes any article information in a query, it is not available in the aggregate table, and you must tell BusinessObjects to use the detail SHOP_FACTS table. You are only concerned with this one context and do not need to worry about the promotion objects. (Wouldn't it be a nice enhancement request if Designer only displayed those objects that were part of the relevant contexts!) This second point is especially confusing, because when Designer detects incompatibility, it unnecessarily and incorrectly marks objects from other contexts. If you mark promotion objects as incompatible here, you prevent users from constructing a query that compares sales by store (using the aggregate table) with promotions by store.

Remember *You only need to mark objects as incompatible that exist in the one context or star schema.*

1. To define incompatible objects, use the pull-down menu Tools | Aggregate Navigation.

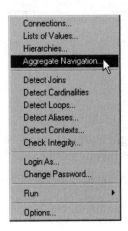

A BETTER UNIVERSE

2. Highlight the table for which you will define incompatible objects, AGG_YR_ QT_MT_MN_WK_RG_CY_SN_SR_QT_MA.

3. Under Associated Incompatible Objects, you can select entire classes or individual objects. Click the *Article Lookup* class.

4. If you created a measure *Number of Article Codes* in Chapter 6, set this object to incompatible as well.

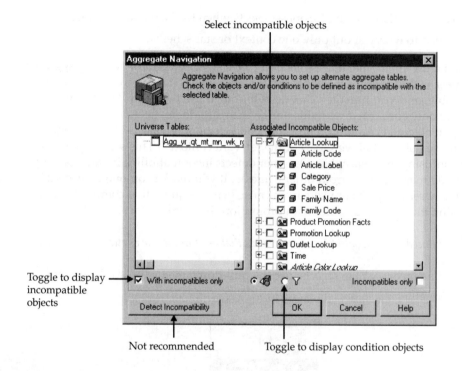

Select incompatible objects

Toggle to display incompatible objects

Not recommended   Toggle to display condition objects

If you toggle to display tables that contain incompatible objects, only aggregate tables should be displayed. If more than just the aggregates are displayed, you have a problem.

5. You can now use the toggle button Incompatibles Only to filter those objects that have been marked as incompatible against the aggregate table.

6. Click OK to close the Aggregate Navigation box.

7. From the pull-down menu, select File | Save or click Save to save the changes to the universe.

Testing and Viewing SQL Statements

Now that you have defined which objects are incompatible with the aggregate fact table, you need to make sure that BusinessObjects generates the correct SQL. To test this, use Figure 10-4 to develop a test plan as shown in Table 10-1. Take each measure that contains @Aggregate_Aware and add a dimension object from each of the dimension tables to the query. As you create a query for each scenario, verify that the SQL generated uses the appropriate table.

1. To view the BusinessObjects SQL statement, launch BusinessObjects from Designer by selecting Tools | Run | BusinessObjects.

2. When prompted, Select Generate A Standard Report and click Begin.

3. Select Universe as the way you want to access the data and click Next.

4. Choose the universe that contains the aggregate objects, Test Fashion, and click Finish.

Scenario	If Your Query Contains These Objects	BusinessObjects Should Use This Table
1	Sum of Amount Sold	AGG_YR_QT_MT_MN_WK_ RG_CY_SN_SR_QT_MA
2	Sum of Amount Sold, Month Name	AGG_YR_QT_MT_MN_WK_ RG_CY_SN_SR_QT_MA
3	Sum of Amount Sold, Month Name, Shop Name	AGG_YR_QT_MT_MN_WK_ RG_CY_SN_SR_QT_MA
4	Sum of Amount Sold, Promotion Cost, Month, Shop Name	2 SQL Select statements: AGG_YR_QT_MT_MN_WK_ RG_CY_SN_SR_QT_MA PRODUCT_PROMOTION_ FACTS
5	Sum of Amount Sold, Month Name, Store Name, Article	SHOP_FACTS
6	Sum of Amount Sold, Article Color	SHOP_FACTS
7	Sum of Amount Sold, Number of Article Code	SHOP_FACTS

Table 10-1.   *Test Plan for Aggregate Awareness*

5. Follow the test plan outlined in Table 10-1 to add the Result Objects to the query. The following screen shows a query based on Scenario 3 in Table 10-1:

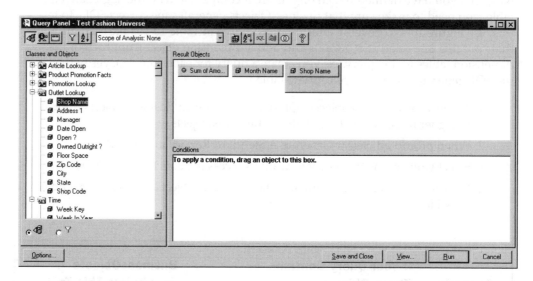

6. To verify the correct fact table is used in the SQL, click the SQL button on the Query Panel toolbar. Note that for Scenario 3, the aggregate fact table was correctly used.

```
SELECT
    sum(Agg_yr_qt_mt_mn_wk_rg_cy_sn_sr_qt_ma.Sales_revenue),
    Calendar_year_lookup.Month_Name,
    Outlet_Lookup.Shop_name
FROM
    Calendar_year_lookup,
    Agg_yr_qt_mt_mn_wk_rg_cy_sn_sr_qt_ma,
    Outlet_Lookup
WHERE
    ( Agg_yr_qt_mt_mn_wk_rg_cy_sn_sr_qt_ma.Store_name=Outlet_Lookup.Shop_name )
    AND ( Calendar_year_lookup.Year=Agg_yr_qt_mt_mn_wk_rg_cy_sn_sr_qt_ma.Year And
Calendar_year_lookup.Week_in_Year=Agg_yr_qt_mt_mn_wk_rg_cy_sn_sr_qt_ma.Week )

GROUP BY
    Calendar_year_lookup.Month_Name,
    Outlet_Lookup.Shop_name
```

7. When you add *Article Code* to the query as in Scenario 5, BusinessObjects automatically selects the SHOP_FACTS table without any user intervention. (Isn't it wonderful!)

```
SELECT
  sum(Shop_facts.Amount_sold),
  Calendar_year_lookup.Month_Name,
  Outlet_Lookup.Shop_name,
  Article_lookup.Article_code

FROM
  Shop_facts,
  Calendar_year_lookup,
  Article_lookup,
  Outlet_Lookup
WHERE
  ( Shop_facts.Article_code=Article_lookup.Article_code  )
  AND  ( Calendar_year_lookup.Week_key=Shop_facts.Week_key  )
  AND  ( Shop_facts.Shop_code=Outlet_Lookup.Shop_code  )
GROUP BY
  Calendar_year_lookup.Month_Name,
  Outlet_Lookup.Shop_name,
  Article_lookup.Article_code
```

For Scenario 4 in Table 10-1, BusinessObjects will generate two SQL statements and seamlessly stitch the results together in the report. This step can go wrong for two reasons: 1) if your File | Parameters, SQL tab, Multiple SQL statements for each context are not enabled, or 2) if you used Tools | Aggregate Navigation | Detect Incompatibility; in the latter case, Designer incorrectly marked objects from other contexts as being incompatible with an aggregate table.

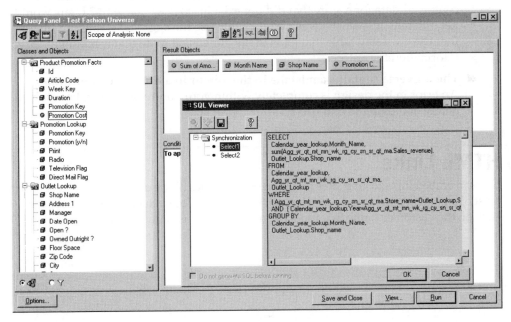

The most obvious error in this step of building aggregate awareness is if the wrong table is used in any instance. However, the ultimate goal is to get correct results. So as a final test, you should run a query to ensure that you get the same data when either the aggregate table or the detail table is used. In the preceding examples, Sales for September 2001 is $300,848, according to both the aggregate table and the SHOP_FACTS table.

There are a few reasons why you may not get the same result for an aggregate and a detail table:

- **One of the tables is incorrect**   If the DBA has not built the aggregate table correctly, you may not be able to fix it, but you must communicate this issue to both DBAs and end users. When something is wrong, BusinessObjects will always get the blame, because most end users don't know and don't care about which component in the information flow actually has the problem. If the summary table is incorrect in all circumstances, don't include it in the universe design. If it is correct in most circumstances and the DBA is working to resolve one minor inconsistency, use the table but clearly explain in the object description when the data may be incorrect.

- **The aggregate table contains dimensional information that is different from details in the lookup or dimension tables**   As a general rule, I don't like when dimensional information is stored in the fact table. It's even worse when there is a difference between dimensional information in a fact table and a dimension table. Yes, in a perfect world the data is clean and consistent. However, I've yet to see a company that had such clean data. In the example of AGG_YR_QT_ MT_MN_WK_RG_CY_SN_SR_QT_MA, the store name exists in both this aggregate fact table and the dimension table OUTLET_ LOOKUP. What if the fact table contained data for a store that did not exist in OUTLET_LOOKUP? Users would get different answers between queries that use the aggregate table and queries that use the detail table that joins to the dimension table that is missing information for a store.

- **The universe contains a mistake in the join or in a dimension definition** An error in the design is completely within your control and must be resolved before deploying to end users.

HTML Links

One can embed links to web sites based on object values. For example, if an object returns a list of customers and you know the web site address for each customer, a user can click on the customer name in a report to link to each customer's web site.

If SQL tests your patience, combing HTML into your SQL may cause you to lose your patience entirely! Pay careful attention to quotes and note that the syntax is different for each database.

About HTML

The basic syntax for a link to a web site is

- `<a>`   An HTML anchor element
- `Href`   The hot spot reference where you will provide the web site address or URL. You may display the URL to users or display different text
- `</a>`   Ends the HTML anchor element

BusinessObjects requires HTML elements to be enclosed in single quotes.

So, say you want to create a simple list of authors that may be visiting your book store:

```
<a href="www.website.com">Text to display to users </a>
<a href="www.jodipicoult.com">Jodi Picoult </a>
```

In the object, you need to add the single quotes around the HTML elements, the `<a>` and `</a>`.

```
'<a href="http://www.jodipicoult.com">'Jodi Picoult'</a>'
```

At this point, your object would not parse, because it lacks a `table.column`. To have BusinessObjects display the results of a column, the data must be concatenated with the HTML statement. Concatenation symbols vary from database to database; MS SQL Server and MS Access use a plus sign (+), whereas Oracle uses two vertical bars (||).

Therefore, your basic HTML syntax for MS Server or MS Access is

```
'<a href="http://www.website.com">'+TABLE.COLUMN+'</a>' for MS SQL Server
or MS Access
```

or for Oracle:

```
'<a href="http://www.website.com">'||TABLE.COLUMN||'</a>' for Oracle
```

If you want the website portion of the Select statement also to be dynamic, you can either access a column that provides a web site address or transform data from another column to form a web address. Concatenating HTML commands, with SQL data, with fixed text data can get messy pretty quickly. For all the concatenations to work correctly, you must use the RDMBS CONCAT function, rather than the + or || operators.

The following example is based on an MS Access database in which the web site address is a column in an Author lookup table:

```
{fn concat({fn concat('<A HREF='+ {fn char(34)}, '+Authors.Website+'+{fn
char(34)}+ '>')},{fn concat(
Authors.Author, '<A/>')})}
```

This second example is based on the sample Sales History database in which the web site address is derived from the city column. The web site address consists of three parts:

1. The prefix, www.

2. The city name, which comes from the SQL column SH.CUSTOMERS .CUST_CITY.

3. The end of the web address, .co.uk. Commercial web site addresses in the U.S. end in .com, while web site addresses in the U.K. end in .co.uk. For this object to work in a global deployment, one would need to add a DECODE or CASE function to test the Country as well.

```
Concat(concat('<A HREF=' || chr(34), 'www.'||SH.CUSTOMERS.CUST_CITY||'.co.uk' ||
 chr(34) || '>'),concat(
SH.CUSTOMERS.CUST_CITY , '<A/>'))
```

In order for BusinessObjects to generate the SQL statement correctly as an HTML link, you must set the Object Format to Read As HTML. Select the object and right-click to bring up the following pop-up menu:

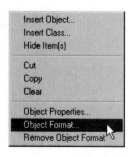

On the Object Format dialog, click the box Read As HTML.

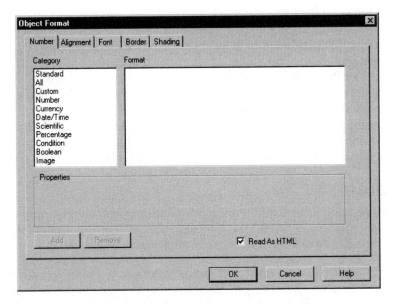

When users run a report, the object with the dynamic link to a web site address is displayed as a hyperlink. In the following screen, you also see the correctly formatted web site address that will take you to the web site for the city of Leeds (www.leeds.co.uk):

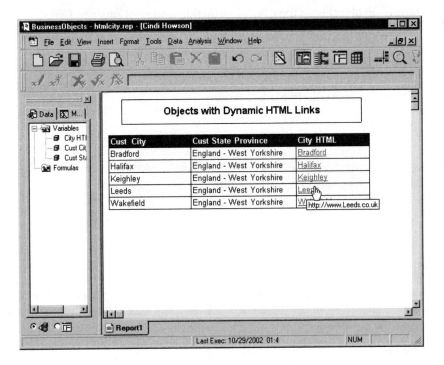

A BETTER UNIVERSE

Popular SQL Functions

Take a deep breath. If the BusinessObjects internal functions have overwhelmed you, get a latte, a glass of wine (at home, of course!) or do some yoga: SQL functions are ever more powerful and limited only by your creativity, but potentially, they are more overwhelming (especially if you have a nasty habit like me of putting commas and parentheses in all the wrong places). In the universe design process, this is when the power users, universe Designers, and DBAs must partner together to build a technically correct but business-robust universe.

There are entire books dedicated to SQL commands alone (refer to the Bibliography), so it is impossible to cover all of the functions here. What follows are just a few examples of some popular objects that use SQL functions to deliver business functionality.

Concatenated

Concatenated objects combine information from multiple fields. A common usage is to combine a customer or employee's *First Name* and *Last Name* into a new object, *Name*. Depending on your database, you have two ways to concatenate fields:

- The CONCAT function, which is database specific and allows you to combine two columns of data. One can nest CONCAT statements to combine multiple columns, but personally, I find the nested functions harder to read than an operator.

- An operator, which allows you to combine several columns into one. Microsoft databases use +, and Oracle uses | |.

The following object uses the CONCAT function and uses BusinessObjects @Select to reference existing objects in the universe:

```
CONCAT(@Select(Hr Employees\First Name),@Select(Hr Employees\Last Name))
```

The SQL statement will appear as follows:

```
CONCAT(HR.EMPLOYEES.FIRST_NAME,HR.EMPLOYEES.LAST_NAME)
```

Using an operator has the following syntax and allows you to combine more than two fields plus spaces between each column:

```
( HR.EMPLOYEES.EMPLOYEE_ID ) ||' '|| ( HR.EMPLOYEES.FIRST_NAME )||' ' || (
HR.EMPLOYEES.LAST_NAME )
```

Time Objects

If you look at any quarterly or annual report, it contains current period and Year-To-Date information as shown from the most current Business Objects 10Q filing, as in the following earnings statement:

	Three Months Ended December 31		YTD (Ended December 31)	
	2002	2001	2002	2001
License fees	66,129	72,688	243,955	249,594
Services	60,054	44,123	210,844	166,200
Total revenues	$126,183	$116,811	$454,799	$415,794

To create this functionality in BusinessObjects requires two steps. First, you must determine what is the definition of to-date: Is it whichever accounting month the books have closed? Is it the calendar day of today? The answer to this may depend on whether you are viewing accounting information or sales order information. Accountants may want *closed* accounting months, whereas salespeople will want the latest date possible. The second step involves grouping the information into columns of data as shown in the preceding table. Grouping information into columns of data is described in the section "If-Then-Else Logic with Decode and Case."

If users want to run rolling reports, you can provide them with condition objects that let them select current time periods or a rolling period. If you are looking for a closed accounting month, the best practice is to store the closed accounting month as a flag in the time dimension table. If this is not available, create an interactive object that prompts for the closed accounting month.

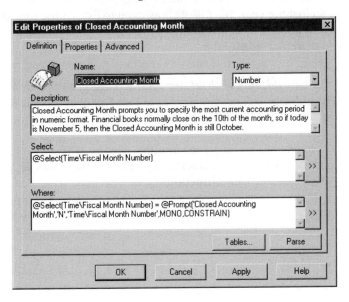

The prompt Closed Accounting Month can now be used as an @Variable in any Year- To-Date objects. For example, YTD Sales would include in the WHERE clause the following:

```
@Select(Time\Fiscal Month Number)<=@Variable('Closed Accounting Month')
```

If the interactive object *Closed Accounting Month* exists in the query or has been used during the report, then BusinessObjects will prompt the user and provide the list of values. If *Closed Accounting Month* is not in the current report, then when a user accesses *YTD Sales*, BusinessObjects will prompt the user for the *Closed Accounting Month* variable but does not know to link back to the interactive object to get the list of values. You can best resolve this quirk with user training and instructions in the Object Description.

So far, you have only asked the user to specify the month. You could include the accounting year in the prompt, or you could get the current year from the RDBMS's system date. Either users can include a *Current Year* condition in their query or you may have a compound WHERE clause in *Current YTD Sales*:

```
@Select(Time\Fiscal Month Number)<=@Variable('Closed Accounting Month')
AND
@Select(Time\Fiscal Year)=TO_NUMBER(TO_CHAR(SYSDATE,'YYYY') )
```

SYSDATE returns the system date on the RDBMS. It is a date field from which you want to extract just the year. TO_CHAR allows you to extract the four-digit year. However, your comparison object is numeric, so you must convert the character year to a numeric field using TO_NUMBER.

Be aware that with this type of object, the WHERE clause gets appended to the entire query and users will not be able to have Last Year objects in the same report. Refer to the next section for an alternative.

To allow users to create a rolling three months, use the ADD_MONTHS SQL command to subtract three months from the SYSDATE. Note that in this example, you only need the month or MM from the TO_CHAR function.

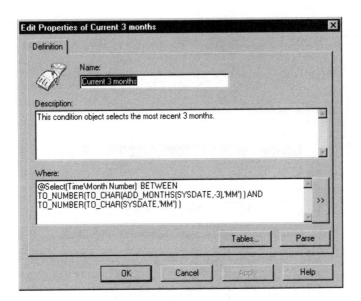

If-Then-Else Logic with Decode and Case

Oracle provides a SQL function DECODE that works like an If-Then-Else statement. The syntax is DECODE(@Select(Class\Object),'if_a','then_b'), where

- @Select(Class\Object) can either be the object whose value you want to change or the RDBMS *TABLE.COLUMN.*
- *if_a* is the value in the data column you wish to compare and replace.
- *then_b* is the replacement value.

In the sample Oracle SH.CUSTOMER table, the CUST_GENDER column contains only two values: F for Female and M for Male. The gender description is not stored in a column. DECODE can help you create a description:

```
decode(SH.CUSTOMERS.CUST_GENDER, 'F', 'Female', 'M', 'Male')
```

Current Period

DECODE is also quite powerful for creating *Current Period* and *Year-To-Date (YTD)* objects without the problem of WHERE clauses becoming appended to the entire query. To understand how to build this kind of object, look at the sample data in Figure 10-6.

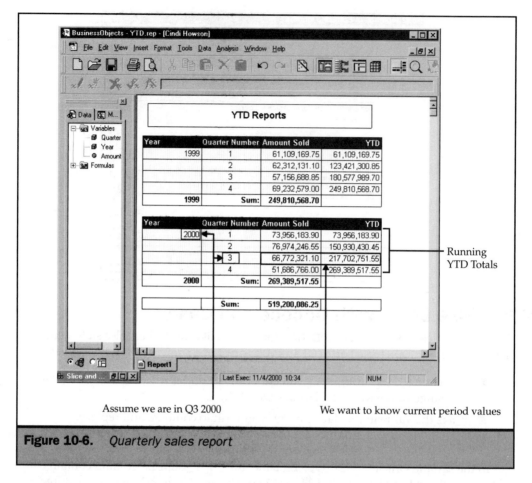

Figure 10-6.   *Quarterly sales report*

This is taken from the sample Oracle Sales History (SH) tables. Unfortunately, the data only goes through the year 2000, so for your purposes, you will have to imagine it is September 30, 2000 or Quarter 3 2000. You want to create two objects, one that retrieves the current period sales = 66,772,321 and one that retrieves the year-to-date sales = 217,702,751.

To determine which quarter you are in, you again use the SYSDATE and TO_CHAR commands. This time you want the date to be in YYYYQ format. The sample SH.TIMES table has the Year and Quarter in two separate columns, so you will concatenate the two together to get the same comparison from your SYSDATE. You want to create a *Current Quarter Sales* object that says: If the current calendar quarter matches the accounting quarter, then, for the same period in the database, show the sales; else, return null.

The corresponding SQL is

```
sum(decode(to_char(sysdate,'YYYYQ'),
'20003',DECODE(SH.TIMES.CALENDAR_YEAR||SH.TIMES.CALENDAR_QUARTER_NUMBER,'20003',SH
.SALES.AMOUNT_SOLD)))
```

When using DECODE in this way, it is important that the aggregate SUM function goes around the entire statement and is not nested between the DECODEs. The following table decomposes the DECODE portion of the SQL statement:

Part	Purpose	SQL Syntax
1	If the current calendar quarter	`decode(to_char(sysdate, 'YYYYQ')`
2	Matches the accounting quarter	`'20003'`
3	Then for the same period in the database	`DECODE(SH.TIMES.CALENDAR_YEAR||SH.TIMES.CALENDAR_QUARTER_NUMBER,'20003'`
4	Show the sales	`SH.SALES.AMOUNT_SOLD`
5	Else null	

Cumulative To-Date

There are a number of ways to create a *Current Year-To-Date Sales* object. While the comparison part of your SQL (parts 1–2) would remain the same, retrieving the values for a cumulative period in part 3 will be a bit more of a challenge. You can have three sums such as Q1+Q2+Q3, but if you ever try to create a *Current Week-To-Date* or *Current Month-To-Date* object, your SQL gets long and messy fast. What you really want is a way to retrieve a range of values or to test if the RDBMS accounting quarter is less than or equal to the SYSDATE quarter. With DECODE, one can do this in a complicated way using the SIGN function, or in Oracle 8i and 9i, the CASE command is an improved version of DECODE that allows comparisons.

The syntax for a simple CASE expression in Oracle 9i is **CASE** @Select(Class\ Object) when 'a' then 'b' else 'c' end. The else is optional but recommended. To take the gender example from earlier, the CASE equivalent is

```
CASE SH.CUSTOMERS.CUST_GENDER
      when 'F' then 'Female'
      when 'M' then 'Male'
      else 'Not Listed'
      End
```

The syntax for CASE in Oracle 8i is slightly different in that the comparison object or column must be repeated after each WHEN:

```
CASE
      When @Select(Class\Object)='A' then 'a'
      When @Select(Class\Object)='B' then 'b'
```

```
When @Select(Class\Object)='C' then 'c'
Else 'X'
END
```

The gender example would be as follows:

```
CASE
when SH.CUSTOMERS.CUST_GENDER= 'F' then 'Female'
when SH.CUSTOMERS.CUST_GENDER= 'M' then 'Male'
Else 'Not Listed'
END
```

Oracle 9i supports both syntaxes. The main difference is that the first simple CASE may be more efficient for simple translations (like DECODE), but the latter syntax provides more flexibility.

The *Current Quarter Sales* object using CASE instead of DECODE is as follows:

```
sum(
     CASE
     When SH.TIMES.CALENDAR_YEAR||SH.TIMES.CALENDAR_QUARTER_NUMBER
     =
     to_char(sysdate,'YYYYQ' )
     Then SH.SALES.AMOUNT_SOLD Else 0
     End
)
```

To create the *Year-To-Date* object, replace = with <= to get a cumulative total. The following SQL also contains a nested CASE statement to ensure that you add quarters from the same year:

```
sum(
     CASE
     When SH.TIMES.CALENDAR_YEAR=to_char(sysdate,'YYYY')
     Then (CASE When
SH.TIMES.CALENDAR_YEAR||SH.TIME.CALENDAR_QUARTER_NUMBER
          <=
          to_char(sysdate,'YYYYQ' )
          Then SH.SALES.AMOUNT_SOLD
          End)
     Else 0
     End
)
```

You can combine these automatic time period objects to create variances that compare sales trends between the two years or two quarters. The following report uses several time period objects to determine whether sales were 21 percent higher for the first three quarters of the year:

Automatic Dates				
Current Quarter Sales	Last Year Same Quarter	Current YTD Sales	Last Year YTD Sales	Variance
66,772,321.10	57,156,688.85	217,702,751.55	180,577,989.70	21%

One thing to be aware of with the *Current Year* and *YTD* objects is that users do not have to enter a *Year* as a condition. Everything is automatic. This can be great for users and for standard report maintenance, but it can be bad for the RDBMS if the queries result in a full table scan; the database will not use an index from any of the TIMES columns. If users will always select some other condition criteria such as Product or *Region*, then these indexes may be used to process the query. As a workaround, you may want to include a WHERE clause in the automatic objects that includes enough years for the results to be accurate, but also, for an index to be used. For example, if you have automatic objects for Current Year, Last Year, and 2 Years Ago, then include the following as a WHERE clause for each object:

```
@Select(Time\Year) IN ('2002','2001','2000')
```

To avoid having to update this each year, in theory one may be able to use <= SYSDATE-(365*3); however, this assumes that the base comparison year is also a date field. In the preceding example, it is not, in which case, one would need to convert the SYSDATE calculation using TO_CHAR. Once you add this kind of function to the SQL statement, the index is not used (unless the DBA creates a special function index).

As of this writing, CASE does not exist in the ora7EN.prm file. You can manually enter CASE statements in the SQL Editor, or to include some help, you may want to add the following entry:

```
NAME= If Then Else With Case
TRAD= String
HELP= Compares and replaces strings
TYPE=A
IN_MACRO=N
GROUP=N
SQL=CASE table.column when 'a' then 'b' else 'c' end
```

Count

In Chapter 8, you looked at using the SQL COUNT function in measure objects to count the number of products or the number of customers. COUNT can get a little more complex than this, as 1) what you want to count is not always obvious, and 2) COUNT may give unexpected results.

What to Count?

The business user says, "How many products do we have?" Easy, just count the unique product_ids in the dimension table! The following screen shows why this may not always be what the business user expects:

Prod Id	Prod Name	Supplier Id	Prod Min Price	Prod Pack Size	Prod Status
180.00	Potpourri Skirt	61.00	35.19	white paper bag	available, on stock
190.00	Potpourri Skirt	45.00	32.29	heavy duty box	available, on stock
195.00	Potpourri Skirt	77.00	32.29	brown envelope	available, on stock
200.00	Potpourri Skirt	77.00	32.29	heavy duty box	available, on stock
4,255.00	Potpourri Skirt	3.00	40.57	white paper bag	available, on stock
4,260.00	Potpourri Skirt	3.00	40.57	white paper bag	available, on stock
8,310.00	Potpourri Skirt	59.00	39.33	heavy duty box	available, on stock
8,315.00	Potpourri Skirt	105.00	39.33	heavy duty box	available, on stock
8,320.00	Potpourri Skirt	105.00	39.33	plastic bag	not available
8,325.00	Potpourri Skirt	105.00	39.33	heavy duty box	available, on stock
12,370.00	Potpourri Skirt	17.00	23.18	white paper bag	available, on stock
12,375.00	Potpourri Skirt	17.00	23.18	card box	ordered
12,390.00	Potpourri Skirt	17.00	33.53	white paper bag	available, on stock
12,395.00	Potpourri Skirt	47.00	33.53	water proof wrap	available, on stock
16,435.00	Potpourri Skirt	29.00	24.84	white paper bag	available, on stock
20,500.00	Potpourri Skirt	62.00	21.94	plastic bag	obsolete
20,515.00	Potpourri Skirt	62.00	40.99	heavy duty box	available, on stock
20,520.00	Potpourri Skirt	95.00	40.99	white paper bag	available, on stock
20,525.00	Potpourri Skirt	95.00	40.99	white paper bag	available, on stock
24,580.00	Potpourri Skirt	30.00	28.98	heavy duty box	available, on stock
24,590.00	Potpourri Skirt	83.00	26.43	plastic bag	ordered

A unique product_id is created for each combination of a product description, supplier, price, packaging, and availability. Note that the only difference between product_ids 195 and 200 is the packaging: brown envelope versus heavy-duty box. The business definition for number of products may in fact be according to the product ID, or it may be by product name. The SQL is different for each:

```
COUNT(PRODUCT_ID)
COUNT(DISTINCT PRODUCT_NAME)
```

Distinct Count

The COUNT function actually counts the number of rows returned; it does not count individual occurrences. In the preceding example, if you used COUNT(PRODUCT_ NAME), you would get the same result as with COUNT(PRODUCT_ID). If you want "Potpourri Skirt" to count as one product regardless of the number of times it occurs in the database, you must use COUNT(DISTINCT *TABLE.COLUMN*).

Recall from Chapter 8 that a dimension object should always come from the dimension or lookup table and not the fact table. With COUNT, this becomes even more important to guarantee correct results. There is a significant difference between counting the number of products versus the number of products sold in a particular period. The former must come from the dimension table; the later must come from the fact table. The following report shows how each count yields different results:

COUNT - NUMBER OF PRODUCTS					
Product Category	Number of Products	Number of Product Names		Number of Products Fact	Number of Products Fact Dist
Boys	2,428.00	85.00		227,102.00	1,091.00
Girls	1,926.00	73.00		177,538.00	901.00
Men	2,594.00	193.00		238,860.00	1,278.00
Women	3,052.00	411.00		372,771.00	1,752.00

Here is the SQL used to generate each column of data:

Object	SQL
Number of Products	COUNT(DISTINCT PRODUCTS.PROD_ID)
Number of Product Names	COUNT(DISTINCT PRODUCTS.PROD_NAME)
Number of Products Fact	COUNT(SH.SALES.PROD_ID)
Number of Products Fact Distinct	COUNT(DISTINCT SALES.PROD_ID)

For the Boys' product category, there are 2,428 unique product IDs or 85 different product names. These are both valid numbers. Users may want to see only one or both. If they want to see both, then the object name and the corresponding description must clearly convey what is being counted. Both columns come from the dimension table. The first object, *Number of Products*, includes the DISTINCT keyword, but only as a precaution; it is not strictly required. If the field you are counting is a unique ID or key field for the entire table, it is not required. Be careful about assuming that ID fields are always unique; some IDs may have an active/inactive flag or timestamp to indicate the latest record.

The next column in the report, Number of Products Fact, is misleading and meaningless. There are 227,102 occurrences of a `PRODUCT_ID` in the `SALES` fact table. When `DISTINCT` is used, there are 1,091 distinct occurrences of a `PRODUCT_ID` in the `SALES` fact table. This number has a business meaning in that 1,091 unique Boys' products were sold. Users may want to see one or all three types of counts.

Note	*Always use* `COUNT (DISTINCT TABLE.COLUMN)` *when counting items in a fact table. Otherwise, only use* `COUNT` *against columns with unique IDs or keys.*

Rank

The `RANK` function is one of the new analytic functions available in Oracle 8.1.6 or later and DB2 version 7.1 or later. At the time of this writing, a corresponding `RANK` function was not available in SQL Server. The `RANK` function allows you to rank a dimension (customer, product, salesperson) according to any metric (sales, profit, commission, and so on). The ranked dimension is determined by the user as result objects in the query. You, as the designer, specify the metric for the ranking. The basic syntax of `RANK` is

```
RANK() OVER(PARTITION BY DIMENSION_TABLE.COLUMN ORDER BY AGG(FACT_TABLE.COLUMN)
DESC
```

where `PARTITION BY DIMENSION_TABLE.COLUMN` is optional and is used to rank items within a subset of data.

`AGG(FACT_TABLE.COLUMN)` is the aggregated measure that forms the ranking. For example, products with the highest sales appear as `SUM(SALES.REVENUE)`. Customers with the highest average order price would use `AVG(SALES.ORDER_AMOUNT)`.

`DESC` is the sort order for the rank, either `DESC` for descending or `ASC` for ascending.

The next report shows how an object built with `RANK` appears to users. The Sales Amount column is not required in the report but is included to show how `RANK` works.

Prod Category	Prod Id	Prod Name	Amount Sold	Sales Rank
Women	1,805.00	Cole Huun Ashlyn	1,200,563.00	1.00
Women	1,065.00	Ukko X-Track High	1,001,952.00	2.00
Men	1,960.00	Ukko Track High	1,001,710.00	3.00
Women	1,250.00	Laundry Slim Skirt	1,000,196.40	4.00
Women	2,185.00	Laundry Ostrich-Texture Leath	913,702.60	5.00
Men	730.00	Fagonnable Windowpane Blaz	856,071.00	6.00
Women	585.00	T3 Faux Fur-Trimmed Sweatei	831,114.90	7.00
Men	415.00	Joseph Abboud Microfiber Tro	803,334.00	8.00
Men	930.00	Andrew D Yahoo Jacket	796,405.50	9.00
Women	735.00	Gurfield& Murks Slim Trousers	730,056.25	10.00
Women	830.00	Kenny Cool Leather Skirt	723,621.40	11.00
Women	1,085.00	Ukko X-Track High	692,532.00	12.00
Men	4,790.00	Fagonnable Windowpane Blaz	687,039.50	13.00
Women	1,070.00	Ukko X-Track High	668,898.00	14.00
Men	2,660.00	Yordsom Navy Blazer	659,743.50	15.00
Women	1,385.00	Yakster Monet	653,495.90	16.00
Women	330.00	Lamb Leather Jeans	650,863.20	17.00
Women	545.00	Embroidered Linen Trousers S	647,130.00	18.00
Women	4,885.00	Kenny Cool Leather Skirt	644,294.80	19.00
Women	620.00	Tiered-Hem Popover Dress	641,223.90	20.00
Men	1,560.00	Yordsom Cashmere Blazer	625,702.00	21.00
Men	4,800.00	Fagonnable Windowpane Blaz	622,690.00	22.00
Women	1,225.00	Kenny Cool Bye-Bye Birdy	620,450.00	23.00
Women	1,750.00	Stars-And-Stripes Cardigan	613,195.80	24.00

The SQL for the *Sales Rank* object is

```
RANK() OVER (ORDER BY sum(SH.SALES.AMOUNT_SOLD) DESC)
```

Note that this object did not use the PARTITION BY parameter. So in the preceding report, products are ranked regardless of the product category. If you want to see the rankings within a product category, the SQL would be as follows:

```
RANK() OVER (PARTITION BY SH.PRODUCTS.PROD_CATEGORY ORDER BY
sum(SH.SALES.AMOUNT_SOLD) DESC)
```

This generates the report shown next. Notice that the overall rank without the partition is different than the ranking within the product category. Within Men's products, Ukko Track High is the number one selling product but is the number-three selling product overall.

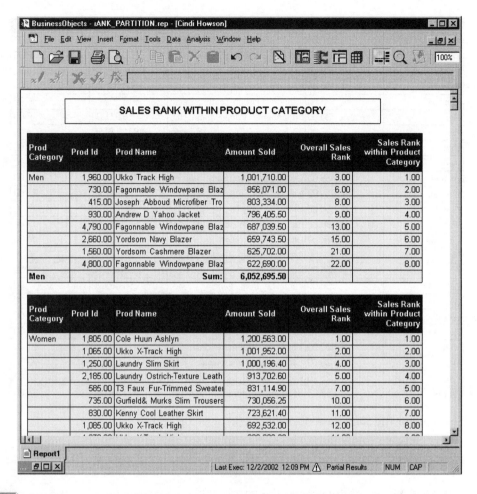

When you use the PARTITION BY *option, if your SQL settings are set to generate multiple SQL statements for each measure (File | Parameters | SQL), you will get two* SELECT *statements from the preceding report because both a dimension table and a fact table are involved in the SQL statement. Under normal circumstances, BusinessObjects generates multiple* SELECT *statements only when the measures come from two different fact tables.*

Summary

With BusinessObjects internal functions and SQL commands from your RDBMS, you can build powerful objects that make your universe more robust and business-oriented. In this part of the universe design and build process, it's important for SQL-savvy designers to have a close dialog with the business users. Just because a user did not specifically request an object, that doesn't mean users don't need the object; they simply may not realize it's possible and so easy to build.

While building advanced objects, you must constantly evaluate the impact on response time and user-friendliness. Certain objects may cause the RDBMS not to use a particular index to process a query. This is fine as long the RDBMS uses some other index. Objects with prompts and time-period intelligence may be incompatible with other objects and return unexpected query results. As the designer, be aware of these issues and ensure users understand when and how to use the objects to ensure accurate query results.

A BETTER UNIVERSE

Chapter 11

Multidimensional
Analysis

If you have designed a logical, business-oriented universe, designers need to do very little to provide users with multidimensional analysis capabilities. The power is mostly in the hands of the user at this stage. There is only minor tweaking for business users to do multidimensional analysis.

For WebIntelligence (WebI) users who access OLAP cubes, Business Objects recently released Universal Drill-Through Service (UDS). UDS allows you to drill from a summary MOLAP cube through to details in a relational database. It requires a bit more effort on the designer's part compared to standard multidimensional analysis within a BusinessObjects report; however, it is well-worth the effort given the seamless analysis UDS provides MOLAP users.

What Is Multidimensional Analysis?

As discussed in previous chapters, a dimension is often textual or time information by which users analyze numeric measures. Dimensional information may come from a lookup or reference table. Dimensions often have different levels or groupings associated with them called hierarchies. Figure 11-1 shows two sample dimensions.

The levels or hierarchies allow users to analyze data by different groups. Some hierarchies, such as Time, are very clear-cut. As reviewed in the section "Object Ordering" in Chapter 8, time objects typically go from Year to Quarter to Month to Week to Day. There is a natural order. Geography hierarchies may also be predetermined, starting with Continent, Country, State. However, when the geography applies to a marketing region, each company introduces its own variation. One company may group the Middle East and Africa together; another company may include Mexico as part of North America because it is part of NAFTA. Ideally, all these groupings should be agreed upon during your data warehouse design process and built into the dimension tables. However, as the universe designer, you may find that certain business units may want to view information according to different groupings. When the groupings change, do you provide users with the old grouping or new grouping or both?

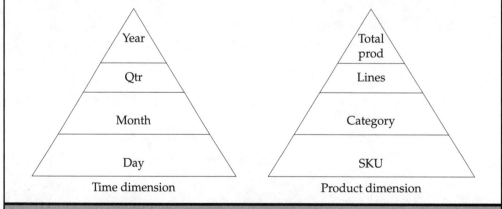

Figure 11-1. *The Time Dimension and the Product Dimension each have four levels that make up a hierarchy.*

For example, in Chapter 9, Table 9-2, you created a new product line, Jewelry. When you analyze historical sales at the product line level, do you analyze those products as if they were still part of Accessories, or part of the new line, Jewelry?

Time Hierarchy

BusinessObjects allows you to build one particular hierarchy, even if the upper-level groupings do not exist in the dimension tables: Time Periods. If you have a date column in the fact table and your database lacks a Time dimension table, Designer helps you build the hierarchy. If you have a Time dimension table, skip this section; you are better off using columns from the dimension table.

In order for the Time feature to be available, the database column and universe Object must be in date format. As an example, use the Island Resorts Marketing (BEACH.UNV) universe, *Reservation Date*. (Note: similar time objects already exist in this universe, so the following example is for instructional purposes only and not intended to replace the existing time objects.)

1. From Designer, open the universe Beach.unv. Expand the class *Reservations* by clicking + next to the class name.

2. Select the object *Reservation Date* and double-click to bring up the Edit Properties screen.

3. On the Definition tab, ensure that the Object Type is set to Date.

4. On the Properties tab, click Automatic Time Hierarchy.

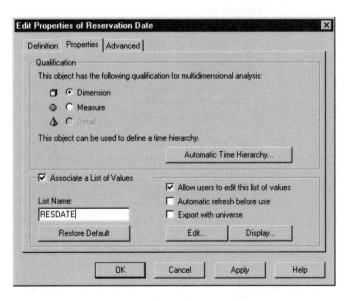

5. Designer presents you with an Automatic Time Hierarchy box, shown next. Click to choose which time levels you would like Designer to create. In the name box,

enter a name for each level. These become the names of the individual dimension objects.

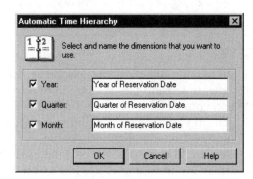

6. Click OK to close the Automatic Time Hierarchy box and OK again to save the Object changes.

Notice that Designer has created three dimension objects under *Reservation Date*, shown next. Once you Save and Export the universe, users can access the objects when building a query.

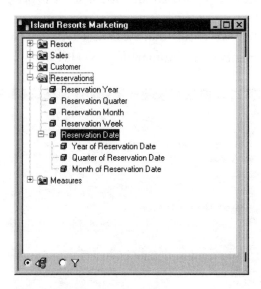

Limitations with Automatic Time Hierarchy

Chapter 19 discusses multidimensional analysis from the user's viewpoint in more depth; however, it is important for you, as the designer, to understand how these new time objects work. When a user constructs a query with these objects, BusinessObjects generates the following SQL:

```
SELECT
  DatePart('YYYY', Reservations.res_date),
  DatePart('Q', Reservations.res_date),
  DatePart('M', Reservations.res_date)
FROM
  Reservations
```

Using an Oracle data source, the SQL appears as follows:

```
SELECT
  TO_NUMBER(TO_CHAR(RESERVATIONS.RES_DATE,'YYYY')),
  TO_NUMBER(TO_CHAR(RESERVATIONS.RES_DATE,'Q')),
  TO_NUMBER(TO_CHAR(RESERVATIONS.RES_DATE,'MM'))
FROM
  RESERVATIONS
```

Notice that BusinessObjects is using the same advanced SQL that you learned about in Chapter 10. This poses two main problems: First, if a user tries to use one of the time objects as a condition, an index on RES_DATE will most likely not be used to process the query; Second, the SQL generated leaves the objects in numeric format. If a user tries to create a formula or variable using BusinessObjects' internal date functions, the user will first have to convert the object to date. Designers cannot modify the object properties for these objects.

Finally, when users build a query intended for multidimensional analysis, the users can specify a scope of analysis. For example, a user may want to start by analyzing reservations by Year and potentially drill down to the individual date. In the query panel, under Scope of Analysis, users tell BusinessObjects how much detail to retrieve and seamlessly store in the micro cube. Users can specify the Scope of Analysis by Class or by Hierarchy. The Automatic Time Hierarchy objects never appear under the Class selection (nor do other detail objects or subclasses), as shown in the next screen. This is counterintuitive for users; the objects are there and are ideal for multidimensional analysis, so why do the users suddenly not see them? If users toggle to display hierarchy objects, then you, as the designer, must have included these new time objects in your custom hierarchy. The following section on hierarchies explains how to do this.

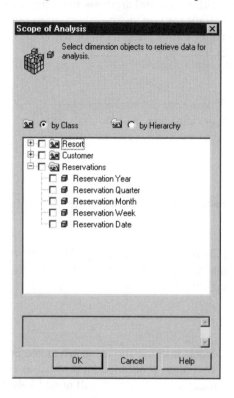

 My recommendation is to build the Year, Quarter, and Month objects yourself as regular dimension objects.

Hierarchies

BusinessObjects has two types of hierarchies: *default hierarchies* that are based on the order of the objects within a class, and *custom hierarchies* that you, as the designer, specify. If you have ordered your objects from largest to smallest increments, as discussed in Chapter 8, "Object Ordering," you may not need to define a custom hierarchy. The benefit of custom hierarchies is that you explicitly control the drill path. In the following example, you will use the Test Fashion universe (TESTFASH.UNV) created in earlier chapters:

1. From Designer, open the Test Fashion universe.

 2. From the pull-down menu, select Tools | Hierarchies or click the Hierarchies button on the toolbar.

3. Designer presents you with the list of classes and objects, as shown next. You will first build the drill path for Article. You can add either individual objects or entire classes. Select the *Article Lookup* class and click Add>>.

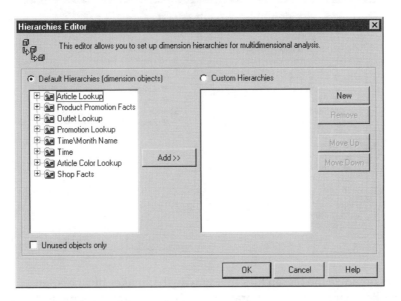

4. Under Custom Hierarchies, expand the *Article Lookup* class. Organize the objects so that they go from *Family Name* at the top to *Category* to *Article Name*. You can use drag and drop or select the objects and use the Move Up button.

5. In the drill path, it does not make sense to drill down from *Family Name* to *Family Code,* as they are at the same level. Therefore, remove *Family Code, Article Code,* and *Sales Price* by selecting each object and clicking Remove. The objects are only removed from the drill path. They still exist as dimension objects for query purposes.

6. Modify the hierarchy name *Article Lookup* to **Article Name** by clicking *Article Lookup* and typing over the name.

7. To create a separate hierarchy for the code objects, click New. Enter a hierarchy name **Article Code**.

So that users do not drill from a name object at one level to a code object at the same level, create two hierarchies, one for name objects and one for code objects.

8. Under Default Hierarchies, select the two objects *Article Code* and *Family Code* and click Add to add them under the new hierarchy *Article Code*. You may CTRL-click to select noncontiguous objects.

9. The custom hierarchies should appear as follows:

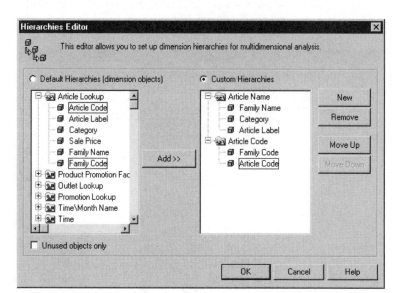

You can organize the hierarchies in any way that makes business sense. You may choose to follow agreed-upon corporate levels or incorporate groupings that are specific to various business units. For example, perhaps some business units want the drill path to be *Family* ⇒ *Category* ⇒ *Color* ⇒ *Article Name* ⇒ *Article Code*. It's perfectly reasonable for you, as the designer, to provide multiple drill paths. Users can also create the custom hierarchies per report. Therefore, you will want to reserve universe custom hierarchies for groupings that meet a broad set of users needs.

Once you begin using custom hierarchies, you must continue to use them for all dimension objects by which users will want to drill. In the preceding example, a Time Hierarchy has not yet been defined. When users begin drilling with BusinessObjects Explorer (see Chapter 19), no time objects would appear in either the Drill Through or the Scope of Analysis. Even if a user elects to view dimension objects by class versus by hierarchy, only those objects that exist in a custom hierarchy appear in the class view.

Drill Through from MOLAP to Relational

As part of WebI 2.7, released in the first half of 2002, Business Objects introduced a new component for multidimensional analysis: Universal Drill-Through Service (UDS). UDS allows WebI users to explore a MOLAP cube and drill through to details in relational tables. UDS is available for the following MOLAP servers: Essbase, DB2 OLAP, MS Analysis Services, and SAP/BW. This capability is available only for

WebI users and not for full-client users who access MOLAP cubes. According to Business Objects, they are considering functionality for which there is no formal time frame.

Figure 11-2 provides a conceptual overview of how drill-through works. A WebI user can drill down and rotate dimensions within an OLAP cube. The OLAP cube contains details down to the month and state. If the user would like details by week and by city, then the user can drill through to the underlying star schema that was used to populate the OLAP cube or to other detailed fact tables that share dimensions with the MOLAP cubes. This concept is quite different from the MOLAP vendor approaches. With Microsoft Analysis Services, users can only drill down to the star schema that built the initial cube and are presented with a "screen dump" of all the keys and columns for a particular cube intersection. Similarly, Hyperion's Integration Server also drills into a star schema used to populate the Essbase cube.

Once a WebI user clicks drill-through, the user then selects a predefined target document. This target document contains result columns that a user wants to see upon drill-through. UDS passes the intersection information to the WebI target report in the form of a WHERE clause.

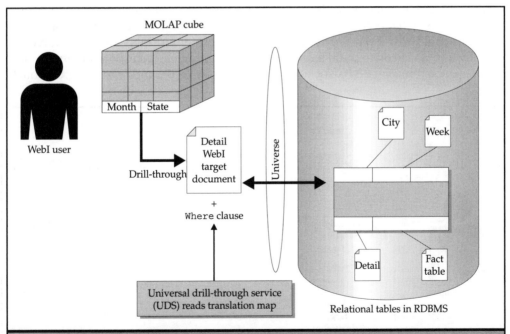

Figure 11-2. *When a WebI user drills through to the detail fact table, the user selects a document; the intersection in the MOLAP cube is passed into the WHERE clause of the query.*

Components of Drill-Through

The following components enable drill-through to function:

UDS Designer   In your Windows menu, this is called Map Developer, yet in the menu bar, it is called UDS Designer. This program allows you to define translations between a MOLAP cube and an existing universe, as shown in Figure 11-3. It is similar to Designer in that it is a full-client product.

UDS Maps   Translations between MOLAP cubes and BusinessObjects universes are called UDS Maps.

Originating Data Source   This is the MOLAP cube from which users will want to drill through to details. UDS Designer uses metadata information from the MOLAP cube to provide a link to a BusinessObjects universe. In Essbase, the metadata is the outline; in Analysis Services, it is the cube structure.

Target Universe   This is the BusinessObjects universe that contains the detailed fact tables to which users will drill through to get details from a summary cube. For MS Analysis Services, cubes must be populated from a star schema so that your Target universe is one that points to tables that were used to build the cube. For Essbase, the cube could have been populated from flat files and multiple relational sources. In this case, you need to build a relational data mart and a corresponding universe before proceeding. For SAP/BW, users may drill from Info Cubes into the operational

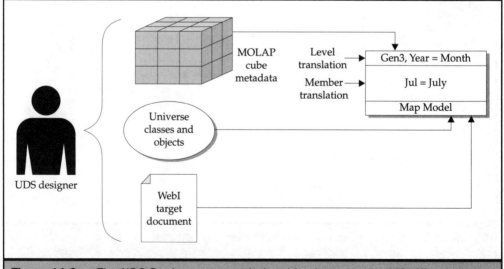

Figure 11-3.   *The UDS Designer maps relationships between the MOLAP cube metadata and the universe classes and objects.*

data store. Otherwise, the target universe can be an existing universe that contains dimensions similar to the ones in the MOLAP cube. The important thing is to ensure that the summary numbers in the cube will correspond (and ideally reconcile with) detail numbers when users run a relational report via a universe.

Target Database   The target database contains the relational tables that users will be drilling through to and is the same data source that is referenced by the target universe. The tables can contain more dimensions and details than the MOLAP cubes; however, the common dimensions must contain the same values (see Table 11-2 for more information). When the values are not exactly the same, they must be synchronized in the translation map. For example, if the cube refers to the month of July as Jul and the universe/target database refers to it as July, then you must create a member translation.

Target Document   These are prebuilt WebI reports that users can select from when drilling through to details. In one sense, these can contain all potential columns in the fact table, or you as a designer can provide users with multiple reports and varying result columns. UDS adds a WHERE clause to the SQL based on the point in the MOLAP cube from which users request drill-through. As shown in Figure 11-3, the UDS Designer links the target document with the translation maps.

 Target documents cannot be full-client documents, or the user will receive an I/O Exception error when attempting drill-through.

WebI Drill-Through Service (DTS) Manager   This is a new service that must be running in addition to WebI Manager. DTS handles the activity when a user drills from a MOLAP cube into a detail report. As you make changes to UDS maps, you must restart DTS for the changes to take effect. To enable drill-through, follow these steps:

1. Understand the data.
2. Build WebI documents.
3. Build UDS maps.
4. Add WebI documents to the map.
5. Restart DTS Manager.
6. Test the drill-through.

Understand the Data

In order to illustrate how UDS works, I will use the Hyperion Essbase Sample Basic application. This database contains revenue information for soft drink sales. A newly created MS Access database will be the Target database. As shown in Table 11-1, the two databases share four common dimensions: Year, Measures, Product, and Market.

Essbase Dimension	BusinessObjects Class
Year	*Time*
Measures	*Measures*
Product	*Product*
Market	*Geography Dimension*
Scenario	NA
... attribute dimensions	NA

Table 11-1.   *OLAP Dimensions Map to BusinessObjects Classes*

As shown in Figure 11-1, a dimension can have multiple levels. The terminologies of MOLAP products and of BusinessObjects universes do not correspond at this point. Normally in BusinessObjects, you think of levels as going from the top down. So *Year* would be level 1. This is the opposite in Hyperion Essbase. Hyperion refers to level 0 as the lowest level of detail; in Figure 11-1, this would be Day. Hyperion refers to top down as *generations*. So Generation 1 is Year. Next, in BusinessObjects, you see only the actual data values in the columns when you run a query; otherwise, all you need to know is that the object *Year* will give you a list of years (2000, 2001, 2002, 2003). MOLAP products refer to these individual data values as *members*. It is at these two levels of details that you start to see differences in how the MOLAP cube and BusinessObjects universe relate, as shown in Figure 11-4.

Notice in the Essbase outline at the Year dimension, Generation 3, you see the names of the individual months as Jul, Aug, Sep. In the BusinessObjects universe, you see only the object *Month*. You do not see the individual data values. As long as the member names and the data values are exactly the same between the MOLAP cube and the relational data source, you can map Essbase's Year,Gen3 directly to the BusinessObjects *Month* using a level translation. A *level translation,* which is the default translation, means that the individual member names within a particular generation match *exactly* the data values for a particular object. When they don't match, you use a *member translation.* In Table 11-2, the BusinessObjects *Month* object actually spells out the names of the month. Therefore, you will eventually create a member translation.

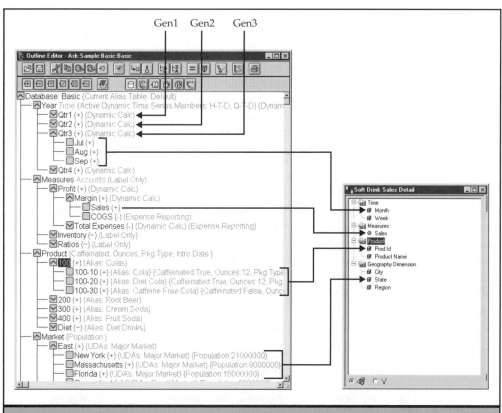

Figure 11-4.   *The Essbase Outline and the BusinessObjects Classes and Objects have common elements that become the Translation Map.*

Note

You could create a new object called Month MMM *using the SQL* LEFT *function to return the first three characters and ensure that your Essbase months match the months in the relational source. This is highly recommended, as maintaining UDS Maps is not automatic and can be cumbersome. The month member translation is purely for example purposes and is not a recommended approach.*

Recall from Table 11-1 that you do not have any universe classes that correspond to the Scenario dimension and the attribute dimensions. While you, as the UDS designer, may not need to define a specific translation, users must understand the data they are looking at. In this example, the fact table contains only actual sales figures. Other scenarios (budget) and measures (Cost of Goods Sold) are not available in the fact table. You do not define a translation, because there is no corresponding object to pass a WHERE clause to. Likewise, the objects *Week* and *City* are lower levels of detail that exist within the Target Universe and Target Data Source but do not require translations because they do not exist in the Original MOLAP source.

Building WebI Documents

In looking at Table 11-2, you can guess that users might have two drill-through reporting needs: 1) sales by product, region, and week or 2) sales by product, city, and month. Week and city are your lower levels of detail that are not available in the MOLAP cube and that must come from the detailed fact table. In order to make these reports available to the UDS Designer, you must first create them in WebI and publish them to Corporate Documents (refer to Chapter 23 for additional instructions). These documents should not contain any

Essbase Member	BusinessObjects Object (data value)	Translation Type
Gen3, Year: Jul, Aug, Sep	*Month* (July, August, September)	Member
	Week (27, 28, 29)	NA
Gen3, Measures: Sales	*Sales*	NA
Gen3, Product: (100-10, 100-20, 100-30)	*Prod Id* (100-10,100-20,100-30)	Level
Gen2, Market (East, West...)	*Region*	Level
Gen3, Market (New York, Florida...)	*State*	Level
	City (Orlando, Miami)	NA

Table 11-2.   *Translation Types Define How Essbase Members Map to Universe Object Values*

additional conditions or prompts, as WebI will replace them with the dimension member names from the MOLAP cube when a user drills through.

1. Log into InfoView.

2. Select Create Documents.

3. Select the target universe, or the universe that contains the star or snowflake schemas tables to which users will drill through.

4. Select the desired Sections, Result Objects.

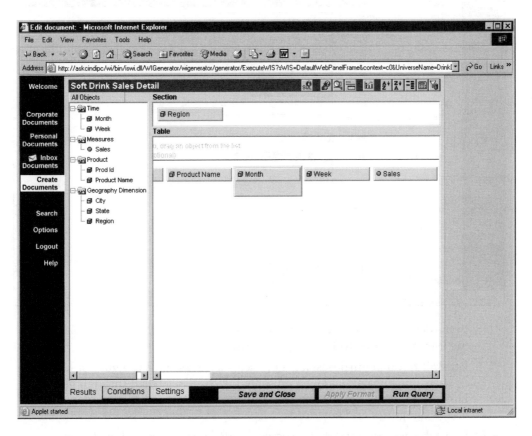

5. You do not need to run the query at this time, and you do not want to store the document in the repository with data. Click Save and Close.

6. From the top menu bar, click Publish.

A BETTER UNIVERSE

7. In the Publish As Corporate Document page, shown next, enter a document name: **Regional Sales by Week**.

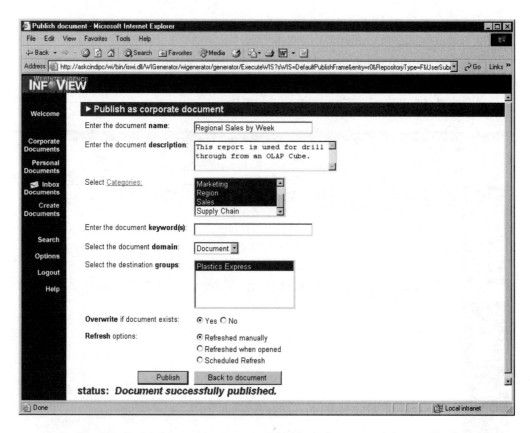

8. In the description box, you can enter help text; however, it is not displayed to the user during the drill-through process.

9. For drill-through purposes, it is not necessary to assign a category or keyword, as users will automatically be presented with a list of drill-through reports. However, if these reports are used outside of drill-through, you may wish to assign categories and keywords.

10. Select the user group(s) that accesses OLAP data sources and the target universe.

11. Set the Refresh option to Refreshed Manually.

12. Click Publish to store the new document as a Corporate Document in the Document domain of the repository.

Building the UDS Map

Building the UDS map has two main subprocesses: first, to define the MOLAP and Universe sources, and second, to create the translations.

Defining Source Information

1. From your desktop or the MS Windows Start menu, select Map Developer to start UDS Designer. If this option does not appear, you need to run the BusinessObjects Setup to install it as a separate component.

2. From the UDS Designer pull-down menu, select File | New. You will be prompted to provide OLAP Source Information.

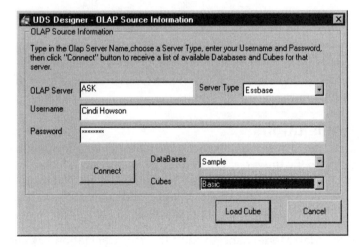

3. Enter the name of the OLAP Server and use the drop-down box to select the Server Type (Essbase, DB2OLAP, MSOLAP, or SAPBW).

4. In the Username box, enter a valid username for the MOLAP cube.

5. In the Password box, enter a valid password for the MOLAP cube.

A BETTER UNIVERSE

6. Click Connect so that the MOLAP server will generate a list of possible DataBases and Cubes. Use the drop-down box to select the desired sources—in this example, Sample Basic.

7. Click LoadCube for UDS Designer to read the MOLAP metadata and fill in the Originating Data Source Information.

8. You will immediately be prompted to log into the BusinessObjects repository so that UDS Designer can import the universe definitions. Enter your BusinessObjects username and password.

9. In the Universe Target Information dialog box, use the drop-down arrow to select the target universe. This is the universe that accesses the detailed data that will be used to generate drill-through reports.

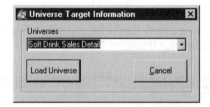

10. Click Load Universe. At this point, UDS Designer loads only the classes and objects; joins, contexts, and SQL statements are not needed for the translation and are not loaded.

Creating Translations

With translations, the primary goal is to tell WebI how cube information corresponds to object information in the universe. When there is no correspondence, the translation is disabled. UDS Designer initially displays the Map Model with all translations disabled, shown next. The red X indicates the translation is disabled for each hierarchy or dimension.

1. Under the Map Model pane, expand the Year translations by clicking the + sign. Select Gen3, Year. Recall from Table 11-2 that the month member names in Essbase are three characters, while in the BusinessObjects universe Month object, they are spelled out.

Document list   MOLAP structure or outline

Add to map

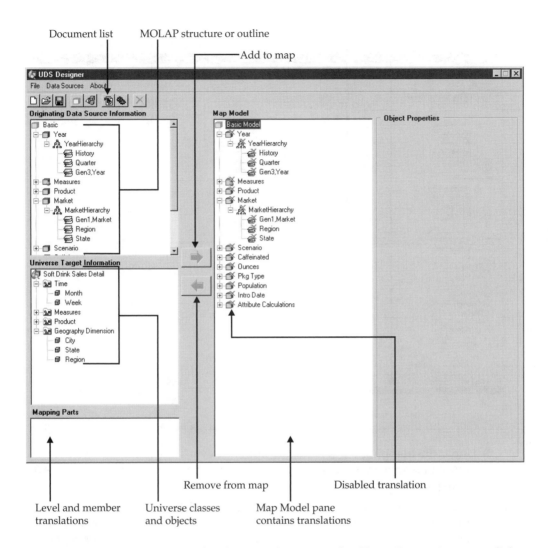

Remove from map   Disabled translation

Level and member   Universe classes   Map Model pane
translations   and objects   contains translations

2. To enable a translation for this Data Source, in the Object Properties pane, click Translation Enabled (step 1 in the next screen).

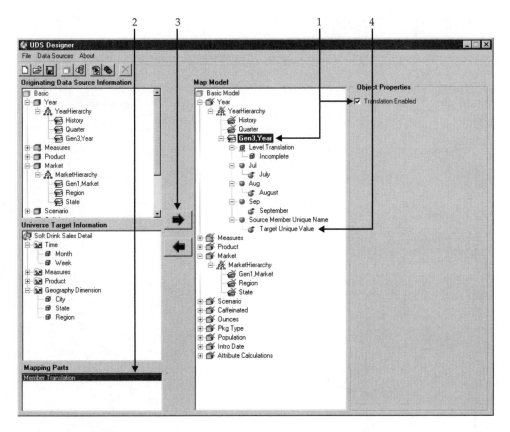

3. Under the Mapping Parts pane, the options Level Translation and Member Translation appear. Select the Member Translation (step 2), then click the Add To Map arrow (step 3).

4. UDS Designer automatically inserts both the Level Translation and the Member Translation. The Member Translation is set to a generic Source Member Unique Name and a Target Member Unique Name (step 4). In this example, replace the Source Member Unique Name by entering **Jul** (MOLAP member) in the Member Translation box, as shown in the following screen. Replace the generic Target Unique Value with **July** by typing this in the translation box.

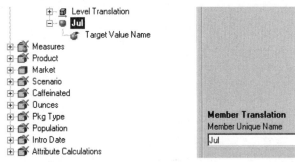

5. Repeat steps 1 through 4 for each member whose object value differs in the target relational database. Note that to add additional member translations, you must first select the translation point (step 1). At this point, it should be clear why you want to avoid member translations!

6. In the Map Model, under Gen3,Year, Level Translation, note that the translation is set to Incomplete. You need to tell the model that the Gen3,Year from the Essbase outline is the same as the *Month* object from the BusinessObjects universe.

7. Select Incomplete (step 1 in the following screen), then in the Universe Target Information, select the object Month (step 2).

8. Click the Add To Map arrow (step 3). Under Object Properties, UDS Designer fills in the Structure Translation for you. Gen3,Year in the Originating Data Source translates to the Universe Class *Time* and the Universe Object *Month* (step 4).

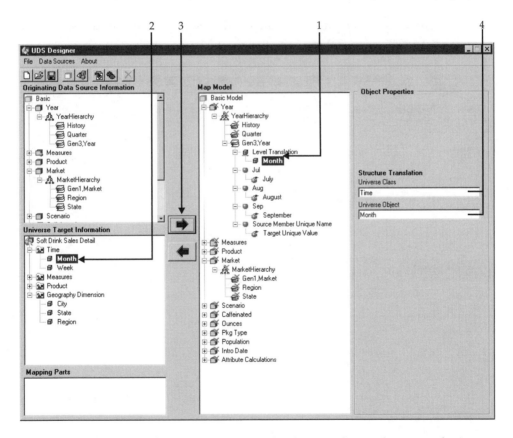

9. One final step in the translation to make the month translation work: Any upper-level translations must be enabled, even if the levels don't exist in the detail target database. In this example, set the Year and YearHierarchy Object Properties to Translation Enabled, as shown next.

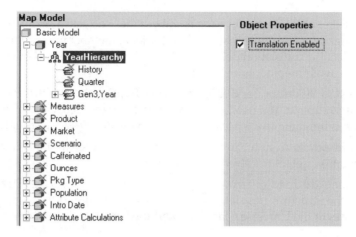

10. Click Save or use the pull-down menu File | Save to save your translation map.

11. Complete the map model for Market, Market Hierarchy as follows:

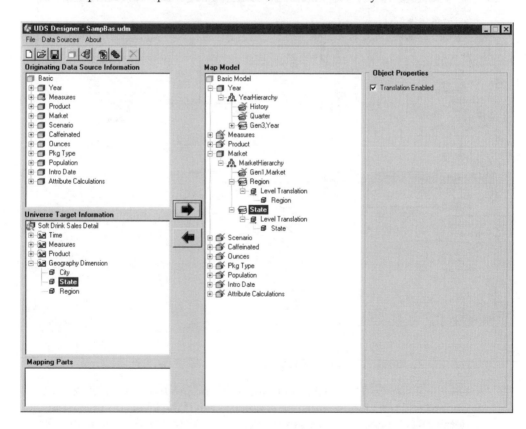

Adding Documents to the Map

These translation maps tell UDS when to pass a WHERE clause to a SQL statement
and what member/object data value to pass into the WHERE clause. You now need
to tell the UDS which documents users can access for the drill-through.

1. From within UDS Designer, select from the pull-down menu File | Add/Edit
   Target Docs or use the toolbar to select View/Modify List of Target documents.

2. UDS Designer presents you with a Document Information screen, shown next.
   Unfortunately, UDS Designer does not read the list of Corporate Documents
   from the Document domain. You have to remember the name *exactly*. This is the
   document you created in the earlier section "Building WebI Documents," step 7,
   Regional Sales by Week. Type in the Document Name: **Regional Sales by Week**.
   The Document Caption and Comments are optional and not displayed to the
   user. If you do enter a Document Caption, the caption, rather than the name,
   is displayed to the user when drilling through.

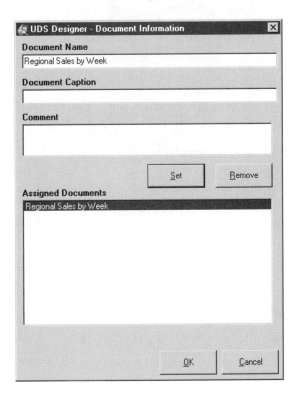

3. Click Add for the document to appear in the Assigned Documents box.

4. Click OK to close the Document Information screen.

5. Click Save or use File | Save from the pull-down menu.

Restarting DTS Manager

When you save a translation map, it is saved by default to C:\Program Files\
BusinessObjects\BusinessObjects 5.0\Data as a .udm file. Once the file is in the data
directory, the DTS Manager can read it. However, the changes take effect only when
DTS is first started. This is something your server administrator will most likely do
when you have completed the map.

1. From the Desktop, select My Computer.

2. Right-click to bring up the pop-up menu. Select Manage.

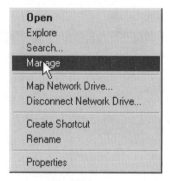

3. Under Services and Applications, double-click Services.

4. Scroll down to WebI DTS Manager, as shown next. Use the buttons on the
   toolbar to stop and restart the service.

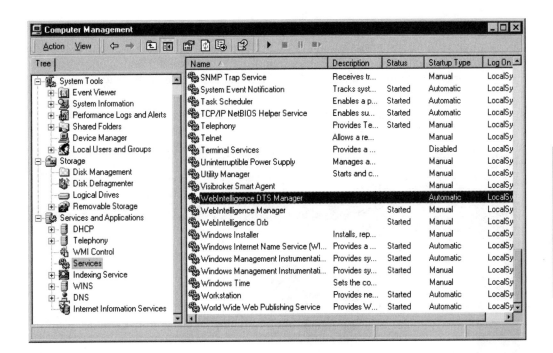

Testing the Drill-Through

The testing stage is the first place you find out if you have defined your translations correctly. If you have defined them incorrectly, users will receive either no data or too much data, as the drill context is not passed through to the WHERE clause. Chapter 23 provides additional information on creating documents in WebI.

1. Log into Infoview.

2. Select Create Documents.

3. Select OLAP Data Sources.

4. Select the data source for which you have enabled drill-through.

5. Within WebI, drill to the point in the cube for which you want to test the drill-through and for which you have defined translations. In this example, you want to test the drill-through from *State* to *City* detail. Note in the following screen that I have set my member selections to Scenario/Actual and Measures/Sales for members that do not have explicit translations to the BusinessObjects universe. If you want only the State name to get passed through to the WHERE clause, position

the cursor on a member value (such as Florida) and click the drill-through button. If you want all the possible intersections to be passed through to the WHERE clause, select the numeric cell (for example, 286.00) to tell DTS to use all available translations. In this example, both the Month and State translations will be used.

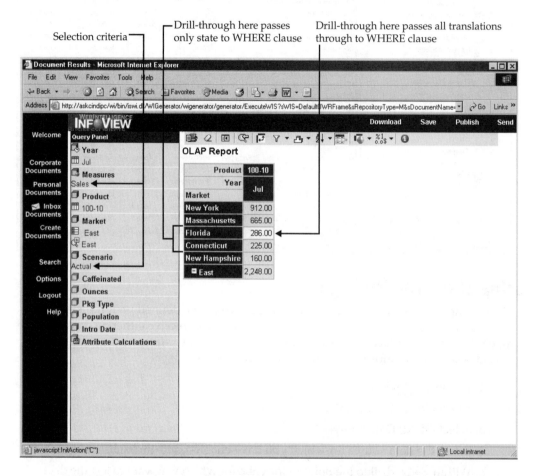

6. WebI displays a list of drill-through targets, as shown next. These are the WebI reports you added to the translation map. At the time of this writing, the list of available drill-through reports is not context-sensitive—for example, detail reports for Budget, Expense, and Product will also appear here. Select the name of the desired report and click OK.

7. WebI runs the query and displays the results. Select Edit, then SQL from the top menu bar to ensure DTS passed the drill context through to the WHERE clause. In this example, I drilled through while on a measure cell (286), so all valid translations were passed through. Notice that the Jul in the Essbase outline was converted to July:

```
WHERE
  ( Product.Prod_ID=Sales_Fact.Prod_ID  )
  AND  ( City.City=Sales_Fact.City  )
  AND  ( Time_Lookup.Week_Number=Sales_Fact.Week_Number  )
  AND  (
  City.State  =  'Florida'
  AND  Time_Lookup.Month_Name  =  'July'
  AND  Product.Prod_ID  =  '100-10'
  )
```

Summary

For standard multidimensional analysis within relational data sources, designers can create custom hierarchies that separate code drill paths from description drill paths. Otherwise, if you have sorted your objects within a class from largest to smallest increments, users are provided with a default drill path without any additional designer customization.

With the new UDS, designers build WebI reports and translation maps to enable users to drill seamlessly from a MOLAP cube to details in relational data sources. Any dimensions that are not similar between the MOLAP cube and the relational data source can easily be disabled in the translation map. To ensure your translations work correctly and the desired WebI reports appear when users select drill-through, follow these guidelines:

- When you modify a Target Universe, you must update the translation map.

- If the member names in the MOLAP cubes do not match the row values for objects in the universe, define member translations for each difference.

- Verify you have correctly entered WebI report names in UDS Designer, using the same uppercase letters, spaces, and so on.

- Restart the DTS Manager whenever you modify the translation map.

The
Complete
Reference

Business
Objects

Chapter 12

Incorporating Supervisor Settings into the Universe Design

Designer allows you to build and maintain a universe. Supervisor allows you to grant users access to the universe and other resources. This book assumes that most of your users have already been defined to Supervisor and focuses on the settings a universe designer, security administrator (Supervisor), or power user must understand that affect BusinessObjects functionality. It is not intended to cover the more technical start-up aspects of the Supervisor module.

While most of the work in Designer is done offline and then exported, Supervisor updates repository information in real time.

Security: A Philosophy

Security can be a touchy subject in many organizations. How much information should be public within a company? If information is overly restricted, how much will that impede decision-making? Bernard Liautaud, Business Objects CEO and author of *e-Business Intelligence: Turning Information into Knowledge into Profit* (McGraw-Hill, 2000), does an excellent job of describing the attitude toward information within organizations. Liautaud discusses four models:

1. Information dictatorship, in which few people have access to information

2. Information anarchy, in which data is duplicated in multiple forms, resulting in chaos

3. Information democracy, in which information flows in a free but managed way

4. Information embassies, in which information flows beyond the immediate organization to partners, suppliers, and customers

Unfortunately, many companies are stuck in an information dictatorship. They have not yet realized that to survive in today's competitive environment, decision makers need access to information now, not when the IT programmer can create the report or when the financial or business analyst can build a new query. Information dictatorships often result in data chaos; the financial controller will run a huge report and create an MS Access database so that decision makers within the business unit can access information. Bravo for the users (at least in the short term) and pity the poor IT person who has wasted so much time and effort building an overly secure reporting system.

Many business users would be happy if their company could at least reach the information democracy stage; information embassies are still a distant dream for most. As the BusinessObjects supervisor, it is probably beyond your control to change your company's security philosophy. However, you can make gaining access to information easier or harder. Supervisor allows you to restrict information down to the individual user, row, and column level. If you overly restrict access, the whole BusinessObjects implementation risks failure.

Ultimately, security philosophy should be driven by a cost-benefit analysis. It is costly and resource-intensive to secure data. The more granular the security, the more costly it is to implement and maintain. If the security impedes user productivity and decision making, you run a high risk of users' sharing passwords, ultimately rendering the security controls a failure. When restricting access to information, consider the following criteria:

- Are there legal reasons for securing the data (employee details, patient medical records, and so on)?
- What harm could be done if employees access the information? Is the cost to restrict access to a specific level higher than the potential harm an employee may cause?
- What opportunities may be missed if employees can't access the information?

Finally, if your data warehouse, data mart, or ERP system has its own restrictions, do not add any more in Supervisor; ensure you use individual data source login IDs (refer to Chapter 6, "Connections") to leverage that security. If you add a layer in BusinessObjects, you will be wasting your time and your company's money, as well as exhausting users' patience.

Understanding Your Company Organization

Before creating and modifying users and groups, you must understand your company's organization and how you want that to translate to your Supervisor definitions. What follows is an example of a matrix organization. Table 12-1 shows a partial list of employees for a company that has five functional departments. Figure 12-1 shows an organization chart for how this company may be represented in Supervisor.

Employee	Job Title	Finance	Human Resources	Manufacturing	Sales and Marketing	Supply Chain
Al Saraisky	CEO	√	√	√	√	√
Brendan McConnan	Supply Chain Manager					√
Jami Blake	Finance Director	√				
Lauren Saraisky	Legal Counsel	√	√		√	√
Mary Olen	HR Director		√			
Megan Michelle	VP Marketing				√	√
Peggy Eschbach	Medical Consultant		√			
Samuel Steven	Manufacturing Director			√		√

Table 12-1.   *Employees May Work Across Multiple Departments*

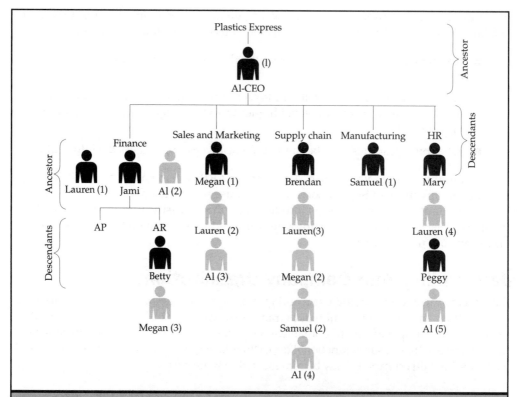

Figure 12-1. *A department at the upper level is called an ancestor, and its children are descendants. Each user can be defined to one or more groups; each copy of a user is called an instance.*

Each functional department translates to a separate group within Supervisor. The main group at the root level is the company, Plastics Express. This is referred to as an *ancestor* of all five departments, which are called *descendants*. In Figure 12-1, Finance has two additional subgroups, Accounts Payable (A/P) and Accounts Receivable (A/R). Both Plastics Express and Finance are ancestors to A/P and A/R. Understanding these relationships is critical for determining which rights get inherited.

As CEO of the company, Al Saraisky serves multiple roles within the organization and works across all departments. In Supervisor, each occurrence of Al within a group is called an *instance*. The first instance is denoted with a solid figure; each additional instance is gray. In Figure 12-1, there are five instances of Al. Lauren Saraisky is the chief legal counsel and so will need access to any information that may have legal implications. She needs access to employee contracts (Human Resources), customer credit records (Sales and Marketing), and material safety data sheets (Supply Chain), and so has three instances. Peggy Eschbach is the company's medical consultant and needs access only to employee records (Human Resources) and has one instance.

Resources

A universe is a resource that can be associated with the company, one or more groups, or the individual employee. Documents, stored procedures, configurations (software functionality), and domains are also resources that can be associated with each of these levels.

In Table 12-2, there are several universes. Some universes will be used by one and only one department. For example, Human Resources is the only group with access to the Human Resources universe. However, the Orders universe is associated with both the Manufacturing group and the Supply Chain group. Manufacturing personnel may want to know which orders are coming in for production planning, while Supply Chain personnel must keep track of on-time shipments. The test universes are used for training purposes and can be used by all employees in the company.

Figure 12-2 shows how these resources get linked to each individual group or to each individual user. The test universes TESTFASH and TBEACH are linked at the root, Plastics Express, level. All descendants will inherit access to these universes. The HUMANRES universe is linked to the Human Resources department only. Therefore, members of the other departments cannot use this universe unless it is specifically linked to the user. A document, Health Report, has been linked to the individual user Peggy. Only she can access this report; others within Human Resources cannot.

It is possible to *link* a universe at an ancestor level and then *disable* it at a descendant level. However, because of the way Supervisor stores these settings, your repository will be smaller if you use link rather than enable/disable.

Universe Name	Filename	Finance	Human Resources	Manufacturing	Sales and Marketing	Supply Chain
Orders	Orders.unv			√		√
Sales	Sales.unv				√	√
Bank Account	Debit_cre.unv	√				
Human Resources	Humanres.unv		√			
Test Fashion	Testfash.unv					
Island Resorts Marketing	Tbeach.unv					

Table 12-2. *Universes Can Be Associated with One or More Groups or Departments*

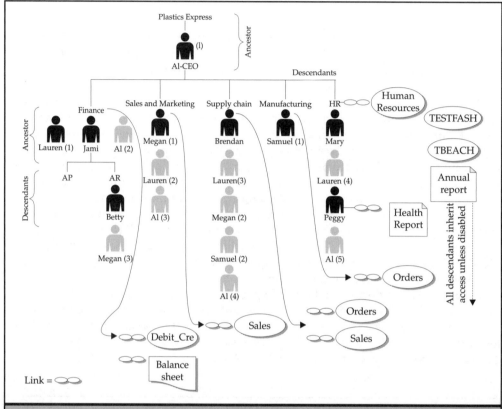

Figure 12-2.   *Resources such as universes, documents, stored procedures, and timestamp settings get linked at each group. The descendants inherit access to these resources.*

Caution   *When a designer exports a universe to the repository, if the designer is defined at the root level, the universe always gets exported to the root level. The general supervisor must always unlink the universe from the root group, or descendant groups may unintentionally gain access to data. Ideally, designers should also be defined within groups to ensure universes are correctly exported to the corresponding group.*

User Types and Profiles

The list of employees and available resources translates into the Supervisor settings shown in Figure 12-3. Notice also that each user has a different symbol or user type

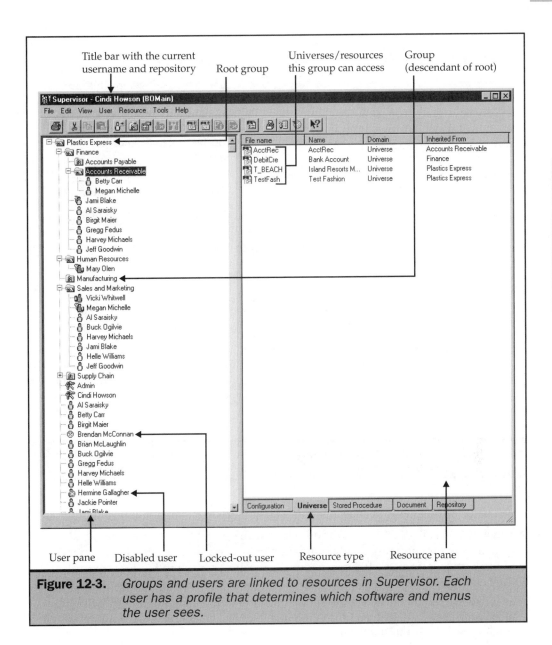

Figure 12-3.   *Groups and users are linked to resources in Supervisor. Each user has a profile that determines which software and menus the user sees.*

associated. The user type is determined by a profile assigned to each user. Table 12-3 explains each profile.

User Type	Products	Icon	Explanation
General Supervisor	All	Keys	Created during setup. This user cannot be disabled or deleted. The General Supervisor has access to everything and can control the BusinessObjects repository and its contents.
Supervisor	Supervisor, BusinessObjects	Green person	Creates and maintains individual users; grants access to resources.
Designer	Designer, BusinessObjects	Pink person	Creates and maintains universes.
Supervisor-Designer	Supervisor, Designer, BusinessObjects	Red person	Creates universes and users.
User	BusinessObjects	Blue person	Builds queries, reports and analyzes data using any of the end-user tools.
Versatile User	Initially a subset of BusinessObjects	White person	This profile can be customized by a supervisor to provide a subset of menus or end-user products to certain users. One can modify this user type to include access to other products.

Table 12-3. *Supervisor Allows You to Assign Profiles to Each User*

Supervisors may create additional profiles to restrict functionality. For example, Business Objects licenses its user modules in three parts: Reader, Reporter, and Explorer. The functionality is all in one executable, so if you license 100 Readers and ten Explorer licenses, 100 users could theoretically use the Explorer modules. Oddly enough, the company does not provide the corresponding profiles to restrict functionality to match product licensing; the supervisor has to create them. In this respect, command restrictions or menu items behave like resources that get assigned to each group or individual user.

Company vs. Department: Where to Create a User

Users can either be added at the root or company level or within a descendant group. For example, Plastics Express has a new customer service representative (CSR), Hermine Gallagher. As a CSR, Hermine will work within the Supply Chain organization. You can add Hermine directly to the Supply Chain group, or you can add her under Plastics Express and then specifically to Supply Chain. Where you initially define the user is a reflection of company organization, security policies, and how much power you want to give to BusinessObjects supervisors. It only minimally affects response time.

Centralized or Decentralized Security

Companies either centralize IT access or decentralize it by department, business unit, or function. Security definitions for all systems, not just BusinessObjects, are done centrally. In this case, the username most likely exists at the root; a BusinessObjects administrator may have done a mass import of all employees or potential BusinessObjects users from a company directory or ERP username table. In this situation, your role as supervisor is to ensure each existing user is correctly defined to each group or resource.

If security is decentralized by function or business unit, then a supervisor role should logically exist within each function or business unit. Decentralized supervisors may add users and may grant or deny privileges. However, it also means that one group's supervisor may unwittingly delete a user that also accesses another group. The general supervisor may have added the user to this secondary group. Deleting a user from the repository will also remove any historical usage information, generally going against most companies' retention policies.

 Add users centrally but decentralize control over resources.

Supervisor Control of Inherited Users: An Example

To better illustrate the practice just described, let's look at the fictitious Plastics Express. Jami Blake is the Finance Director. She has been designated a supervisor and designer for this group. Al Saraisky is the CEO but is a member of this group so that he can access Bank Account information. As the supervisor of the Finance group, Jami can change Al's profile to grant access to any Finance universes and can modify user definitions (disable login, reset password) that will affect Al's access, even to universes that do not belong to the Finance group. However, Jami cannot delete Al from the repository definitions because Al's ID was created at the root level. Only the BusinessObjects administrator or general supervisor can delete Al's ID, because he was defined at the corporate, or root, level.

If, however, a new employee joins the Finance department and Jami creates that user, then Jami can subsequently delete the user. Jami cannot add users to groups she does not control (such as Human Resources).

Should Supervisors Add Users?

Okay, now the smart, security-oriented BusinessObjects administrator will look for ways to make sure that decentralized supervisors cannot create users (perhaps under command set restrictions described later, in "Software Functionality: Command Restrictions"). Perhaps in some organizations, the individual functions or business units can patiently wait until the central group creates the user. However, in most cases, this is where the whole security model falls apart: If a new logon ID is not available immediately, business users will simply share their login IDs and passwords; they are under pressure to get the new employee productive as quickly as possible. Of course it's against policy! Of course they signed a form saying they would never give out their password! But it happens, and they do.

 A workaround is to allow group supervisors to add users, but ensure that the general supervisor or centralized security group periodically reviews which new users group departmental supervisors have created. The following screen shows that a new user, Hermine Gallagher, was created in a group and does not yet exist at the root, or company (Plastics Express), level. To access this screen, select the root group, then click User/Group Properties.

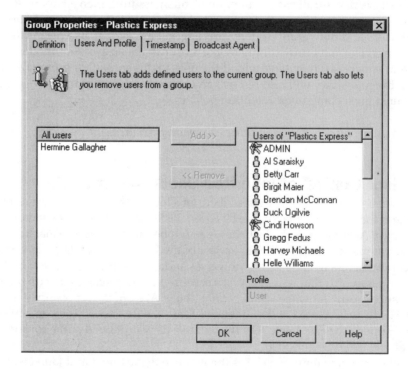

Adding a New User

During an initial installation, Supervisor allows you to import usernames from a text file or to create users individually. To create a new user individually:

1. Position your mouse on the root group or the member group where you want to add the user.

2. Click Create New User. Refer to Table 12-4 for a complete list of Supervisor button and shortcut keys.

3. Enter a name for the user.

4. Press F5 to refresh the list of groups and users or select View | Refresh.

Note *Version 5.1.5 of Supervisor has a bug such that the new username is not displayed until you close and restart Supervisor; it is, however, immediately defined in the repository tables. Supervisor 5.1.6 corrects this problem.*

Button/ Key Combo	Name	Function
or CTRL-P	Print	Print the user, group, resource definitions.
or CTRL-X	Cut	Cut the selected item (user, group, resource).
or CTRL-C	Copy	Put the selected item into the MS Windows clipboard.
or CTRL-V	Paste	Paste the selected item.
or CTRL-U	New User	Create a new user.
or CTRL-R	New Group	Create a new group.
	User/Group Properties	Modify the user or group properties, including passwords and login times.
	Disable/Enable User	Toggle to disable and enable user login. You may want to use this when employees may be absent for an extended period or if an employee leaves the company but you wish to keep that employee's usage history.
	Add to Group	Add the user to a group.
or CTRL-E	Link Universe	Grant a group or individual user access to a universe.
or CTRL-D	Link Document	Grant a group or individual user access to a document.

Table 12-4. *Supervisor Buttons and Shortcut Keys*

Button/ Key Combo	Name	Function
	Resource Properties	Modify the resource properties, similar to the universe parameters screen in Designer.
	Disable/Enable Resource	Toggle to disable a configuration, universe, stored procedure, document, or repository. Use this to make the resource temporarily unavailable to all users for system maintenance.
	Manage Categories	Create and modify categories to organize documents for searching.
	Repository	Manage the repository and available security, universe, and document domains.
	Connections	Add or maintain secure connections to data sources used in universes.
or F5	Refresh	Refresh the view. (Note: This doesn't work in 5.1.3.)
or SHIFT-F1	Contextual Help	Display contextual help.

Table 12-4.   *Supervisor Buttons and Shortcut Keys* (continued)

Modifying User Properties

User properties consists of three areas: user definitions that establish security levels and passwords, groups and profiles that control membership to groups and software, and timestamps that determine when a user can access the repository.

User Definition

To modify the user properties, select the user and click User/Group Properties.

The username is case-sensitive and can be modified here. It's important to understand that user properties are global and apply to all instances of a user. If a user belongs to more than one group and his property is set to Disable Login, then he will not be able to access any universe. Table 12-5 summarizes each of the properties that you can control.

Option	Description
Disable Login	Prevents the user from logging into the repository. Generally used when employees leave the company or if a user has been defined to the repository but not yet trained.
Enable Offline Login	Allows users to work offline in a full-client environment, either when the repository is unavailable or when disconnected from the network.
Enable Password Modification	Users can change their own passwords for their BusinessObjects login. Warning: If the universe passes the login ID to the data source (Table 6-2, alternative 4), then users should not modify their BusinessObjects password as it may become out of synch with the data source password.
Enable Real Time User Rights Update	This option significantly increases the load on the repository. Normally, the universe version and available documents is checked only upon the first access. With real-time updates, any changes to the universe/document list are sent to the client PC when the user edits the data provider/retrieves documents. Use this option with caution, as it will increase overhead and is necessary only if your universe changes frequently. Note: this option does not work for three-tier BusinessObjects/ZABO.
Enable Delete Document	This box should be checked, as it allows users to delete documents from their Personal Documents folder in InfoView or to remove Corporate Documents they have exported.

Table 12-5.   *User Properties Are Global and Apply to All Resources and Instances of the User*

A BETTER UNIVERSE

Object Level Security

In Chapter 8, you left all the object definitions as Public. BusinessObjects offers five levels of column security: Private, Controlled, Restricted, Confidential, and Public (numbered 1–5 in Table 12-6). Object-level security allows designers and supervisors to restrict access to

Object Name	Security Access Level	Priority	User
Social Security Number	Private	1	Mary Olen, Peggy Eschbach
Salary	Controlled	2	All VPs
Bank Balance	Restricted	3	Finance Users
Profit	Confidential	4	Users > Three months
Amount Sold	Public	5	All

Table 12-6.   *User Security Access Levels Interact with Universe Objects to Restrict Access to Columns of Information*

particular columns of data; it requires settings in both the universe's object properties and the user definitions. The user security settings are global and not universe-specific.

Private (priority 1) is considered the most restrictive; very few people would have access to such data, such as social security numbers or medical data. In Table 12-6, Mary Olen, the VP of Human Resources, and Peggy Eschbach, the Medical Director, are the only two users who have access to objects with a security access level equal to Private.

Salary objects have a security access level equal to Controlled. Users with an access level of Controlled or of a higher priority (Private) can access Salary objects. Profit-related objects are set to Confidential. Employees with their security access level set to Confidential (in this case, anyone who has been with the firm at least three months) can access the Profit objects, as can any users that have a higher-priority security level (Restricted, Controlled, Private).

These settings can be quite tedious to maintain. If you are not using them in your universe design or if you are restricted access at the database level, leave all settings in Supervisor Public.

To set the security access level on a universe object, use Designer, select Edit | Object Properties, and click the Advanced tab. Choose the desired restriction level from the drop-down box.

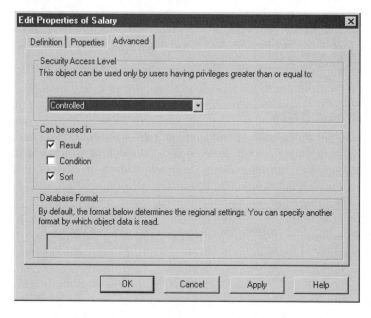

In Supervisor, set the security access level for each user that is allowed to access objects with security settings. In the following example, the VP of Sales and Marketing, Megan Michelle, has a security access level of Controlled. She will be able to see all objects except those with a setting equal to Private, as Private is a higher security level than Controlled. This applies only to universes to which she has access. For example, she still cannot see the Salary object, because it is part of a Human Resources universe that she cannot access.

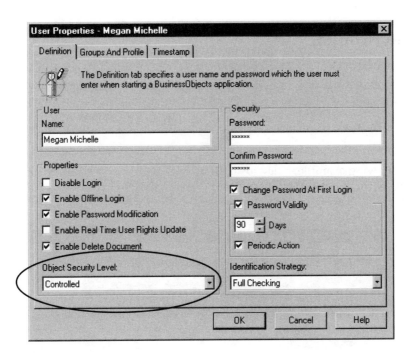

Password Settings

The degree to which you use password settings depends on whether or not you are using unique logon IDs at the data source level (see Chapter 6). Through the Supervisor Password settings, you can force users to log in with a unique BusinessObjects username and password. This may be in addition to a unique or shared user ID for the data source. If you have unique data source login IDs, then keep the BusinessObjects security and password settings to a minimum to avoid conflicts with synchronization of data source passwords. Set the box Identification Strategy to No Password Checking.

Alternatively, if you use a shared data source logon, then you will want to require passwords within BusinessObjects. Leave the Identification Strategy at its default of Full Checking and complete the password selections. The password is case-sensitive and will appear as *s as you enter an initial, default password. Supervisors should always provide a default password; otherwise, unauthorized users can start BusinessObjects without any password.

Change Password At First Logon will force users to change their password the first time they use BusinessObjects. This ensures the supervisor does not know a user's individual passwords. To force users to change their password periodically, click the box Password Validity and enter a frequency to force a password change—for example, 90 days. If a user enters an incorrect password three times, that user's login ID is disabled and a sad face appears next to his or her name. In Figure 12-3, Brendan McConnan's account has been disabled and he is locked out after he has entered his password incorrectly three times.

Groups and Profiles

Users can be associated with a group in one of two ways:

- Select the group, click User or Group Properties, and select the Users And Profile tab.

- Select the user, click User or Group Properties, and the Groups And Profile tab.

In the following example, a new user, Brian McLaughlin, was defined at the root or company level. He is a member of the group Plastics Express. To add Brian to another group, Sales and Marketing, select the name from Available Groups and click Add.

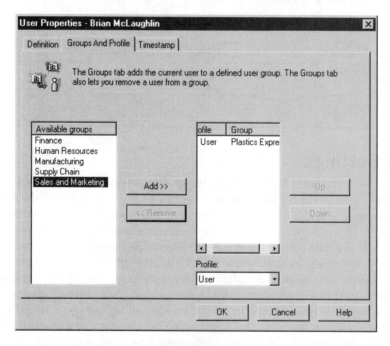

Users inherit a profile from the root level. Brian is automatically assigned a User profile within Sales and Marketing. To assign a different profile with access to the software modules listed in Table 12-3, use the Profile drop-down box to assign a different one.

Timestamp

Timestamps allow supervisors to control when users can access the BusinessObjects repository; users can continue to work offline with reports, but they are not able to create new queries or retrieve documents from the repository. Timestamps are best defined at the group level and not at the individual user level.

 Excessive use of timestamp control can slow repository performance in large deployments.

Disabling and Deleting a User

When you disable a user, the user cannot log into the repository. Many companies prefer to disable logins for new users until the user has attended training. Also, disabling a user retains all activity history even after a user leaves a company. Disabling is global and not group-specific.

To disable a user:

1. Select the username to be disabled.

2. Click Disable/Enable User.

3. Note the disabled symbol next to the user. In the Definition tab of the User Properties dialog box, the Disable Login check box is also now checked.

To reenable a user, follow the same steps.

I recommend only general supervisors delete users, as doing so removes all activity history and requires the supervisor to perform a repository scan and compact to physically remove the deleted user from the repository tables.

Tip *Refer to the section "Software Functionality: Command Restrictions" later in the chapter to learn how to prevent decentralized supervisors from deleting users.*

To delete a user:

1. Select the username to be deleted.

2. From the pull-down menu, select User | Delete User.

3. Supervisor will prompt you, "Do you really want to delete this user?" Click Yes.

4. The user will no longer appear in the Supervisor display; however, the user still exists in the Repository tables. To remove the user from the Repository tables, click the Repository button.

5. Select the Security domain and click Scan.

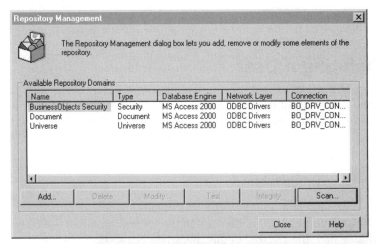

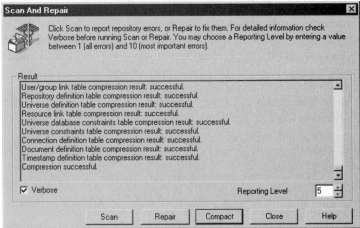

6. From the Scan and Repair dialog, click Compact to compress the repository tables and physically remove the deleted user from all tables.

7. Click Close to exit the Scan And Repair dialog.

8. Click Close to exit the Repository Management dialog.

Only delete users when you no longer need an activity history for that user. Only general supervisors should delete users, as it requires a repository scan.

Adding a Group

You may want to create a new group when a new department forms, an existing group becomes too large to manage, or access to resources could be better organized via a group. To create a new group:

1. Position your mouse on the root group or the member group where you want to add the group.

2. Click Create New Group.

3. Enter a name for the group.

4. Double-click or select User or Group Properties.

5. Select the Users And Profile tab.

6. The All Users column lists all users that do not directly belong to the newly created group. To add a new user to this group, select the username from the list. Note in the following screen that users do not automatically flow down to the subgroup. For example, Jami Blake is a user in Finance, but not in Accounts Payable. Betty Carr is in Accounts Payable and also in Finance. In this respect, Betty inherits access to universes and resources from Finance, but Finance does not inherit access from lower-level members.

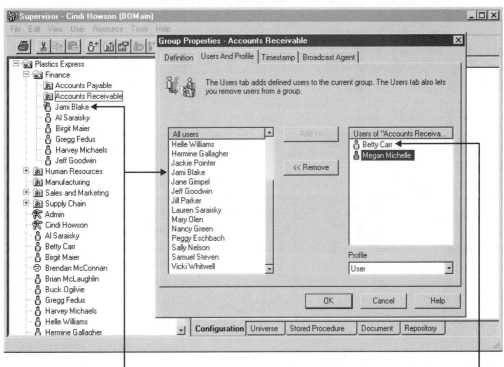

Jami Blake is in Finance, but not in Accounts Receivable

Betty Carr is in Accounts Receivable and inherits all resources and timestamps from Finance

7. Ensure the Profile is set to the desired setting.

8. Click Add>>.

9. Click OK to close the Properties dialog box.

To understand how the rights have flowed between the groups, look at Figures 12-4 and 12-5.

Group Timestamps

As mentioned previously, adding timestamps at the user level can significantly increase the size of the repository tables. It is best to use timestamps at the group level.

To modify a group's timestamps:

1. Select the group.

2. Click User or Group Properties.

3. Select the Timestamp tab.

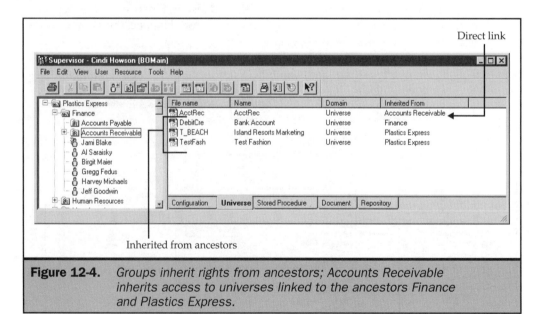

Figure 12-4.   *Groups inherit rights from ancestors; Accounts Receivable inherits access to universes linked to the ancestors Finance and Plastics Express.*

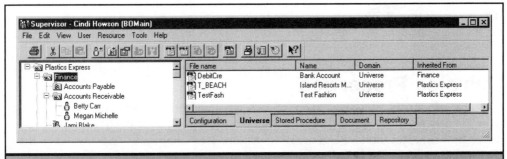

Figure 12-5.   *Ancestors do not inherit rights from descendants. The Finance group has not inherited a link to the universe ACCTREC.UNV.*

Note   *Timestamp restrictions do not affect the General Supervisor login times.*

Supervisor allows you to modify a timestamp in one of three ways:

Option	Description
Start/End Date	The calendar period the group is permitted to log into the repository or that the start/end times refer to.
Start/End Time	The start/end times a user can access the repository. This is according to the user's local time set, which is through MS Windows Control Panel. Therefore, this setting is not very secure.
How	The days of the week a user is permitted to log in.

These settings are global and apply to all resources. If more than one start/end date or start/end time is defined, the most permissive timestamp rules.

- **Scenario 1**   Plastics Express is at the root level. It has no timestamps. If I add a timestamp to allow login from 6 A.M. to 9 P.M. at any descendant level, it will be ignored; the timestamp at the root level is more permissive.

- **Scenario 2**   I add a timestamp at the root level that all users can log in from 6 A.M. to 7 P.M. I allow Finance users to log in from 6 A.M. to 9 P.M. Even though the timestamp is at a descendant level, it is more permissive.

A BETTER UNIVERSE

Timestamp restrictions are according to the user's local clock and date settings. Users can log in by changing their clock settings in the Control Panel.

Universe Properties

Universe properties allow you to override certain universe parameters that you may have already set in Designer (File | Parameters) such as the connection, controls for query time and size, and SQL generation options (see Chapter 6). In Supervisor, the Universe Properties also allow you to restrict data by column and row. Table Mappings allow you to replace table names in the default universe with group- or user-specific table names.

Universe Parameters: Definition, Controls, SQL

In Chapter 6, you set a number of parameters in the TESTFASH universe. In Supervisor, you can override certain parameters by group or by user. For example, the default result set for a universe may be 100,000 rows; in Supervisor, you could increase this to 300,000 rows for certain power users. Keep in mind that these controls are universe-specific.

For example, Al Saraisky is the CEO and has rights to all universes. Although he is a strong leader and CEO, he is new to computers. Al may unwittingly run resource-intensive queries. The Sales universe is widely used throughout the company and you need to make sure that inefficient queries do not affect response time. In the following example, the universe's default SQL Query settings allow complex SQL statements. You want to disable these settings for the casual users.

1. Scroll to the group that contains the instance of the user you wish to modify. In this example, Sales and Marketing, Al Saraisky.

2. Within the Resource pane, select the Universe tab at the bottom of the screen.

3. Select the Sales universe.

4. Click Resource Properties.

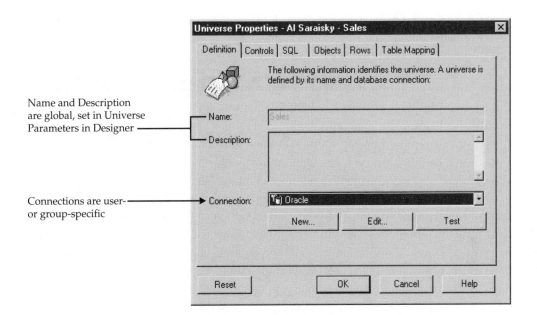

Name and Description are global, set in Universe Parameters in Designer

Connections are user- or group-specific

A BETTER UNIVERSE

5. If you wish, you can specify a unique connection for a user or group of users. This is useful if your database is replicated on two servers (for response time or security reasons). For example, a European group could have a connection to a database with just European Sales data that is physically located in Europe. A North American group could have a connection to a database with North American sales, physically located in North America.

6. Select the Controls tab, shown next. Supervisor displays the default settings from Universe Parameters set in Designer. Any changes you make for the specific user or group are highlighted in red. To restore the universe defaults, click Reset. As a general rule, you may want to increase the defaults for individual power users or information-intensive groups (financial analysts), but I do not

recommend decreasing the controls. These options are explained in more detail in Chapter 6.

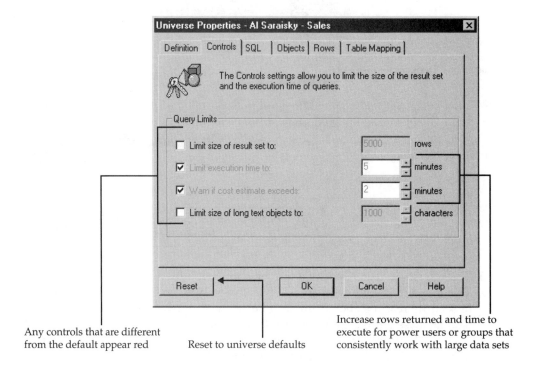

Any controls that are different from the default appear red

Reset to universe defaults

Increase rows returned and time to execute for power users or groups that consistently work with large data sets

7. Select the SQL tab to control how SQL is generated and which operators the individual user or group can control. In the next example, I have modified Al's rights to ensure he cannot generate complex SQL queries that may adversely affect response time.

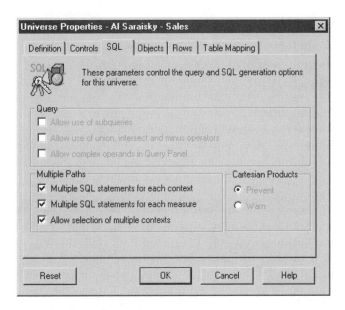

8. Click OK to save your changes and close the Universe Properties dialog box.

Data Restrictions

Earlier in this chapter, you saw how column-level security can be accomplished in User Definitions | Security Access Levels. Supervisor allows yet another way to control column-level access: through *object restrictions*. The following table summarizes the key differences between security access levels and object restrictions:

Security access level

- Global to all universes
- Requires corresponding settings in the universe
- Applies to an individual user (not a group)
- Varying security levels

Object restriction

- Universe-specific
- No universe modifications needed
- Applies to a group or all instances of a user
- Object is completely removed for the group or user— no priorities

1. To set object restrictions, scroll to the group or instance of the user you wish to modify—in this example, Sales and Marketing.

2. Within the Resource pane, select the Universe tab.

3. Select the Human Resources universe.

4. Click Resource Properties.

5. Select the Objects tab, shown here:

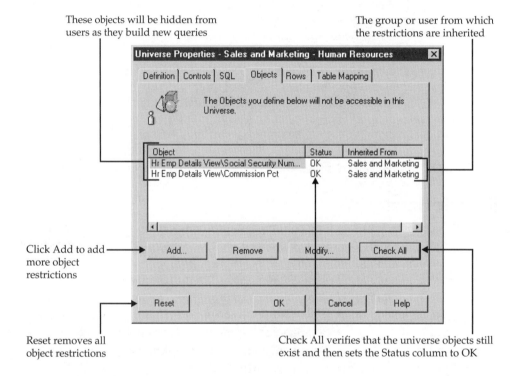

These objects will be hidden from users as they build new queries

The group or user from which the restrictions are inherited

Click Add to add more object restrictions

Reset removes all object restrictions

Check All verifies that the universe objects still exist and then sets the Status column to OK

6. Click Add.

7. Supervisor presents you with a New Restricted Object box. You can manually enter the *Class\Object* or click Select to use the Object Browser to expand any classes and select the individual object that you wish to restrict. In the next screen, I am adding a restriction on *Salary*.

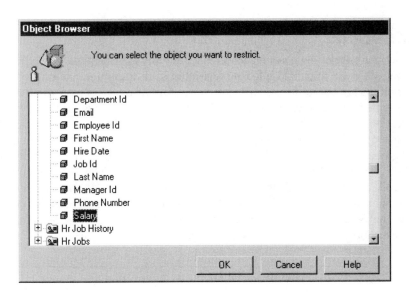

8. Click OK to return to the New Restricted Object dialog box.

9. Click OK to add the object to the list of restricted objects.

10. Click Check All to verify that the object still exists in the repository. This will set the Status to OK. If any objects have recently been deleted from the universe, the Status will show Invalid ID.

11. Click OK to save your changes and close the Universe Properties dialog box.

Note *Object restrictions apply to all instances of a user regardless of security access level and regardless of whether the restriction is inherited. If you have multiple instances of a user with different ways to inherit access to a universe, the objects will always be hidden, as the object restriction applies.*

When a user builds a query, the user will no longer see the restricted objects from the object list. If a user tries to refresh a query that contains a restricted object (or for which the user does not have sufficient security access), the user receives the following error message:

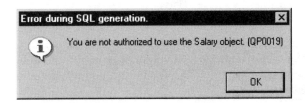

Row Restrictions

Row restrictions restrict the rows returned in a query by appending a SQL WHERE clause to every query a user runs. Multiple row restrictions are appended to the query with AND. Row restrictions are useful for security purposes, but also for user productivity. They save users time by automatically filtering the data according to what they need to see.

Figure 12-6 shows a more detailed organization for the Plastics Express, Sales and Marketing group. The group is organized by a combination of product managers who can view global information, and regional managers who can view sales information within their regions only. For example, Nancy is the Product Manager for children's clothes (product category = Girls, Boys). Nancy should be able to view all sales for these product categories, regardless of which country the customer resides in. Helle is the Regional Manager for Europe; she should be able to view sales for all product categories, but only where the region is Europe.

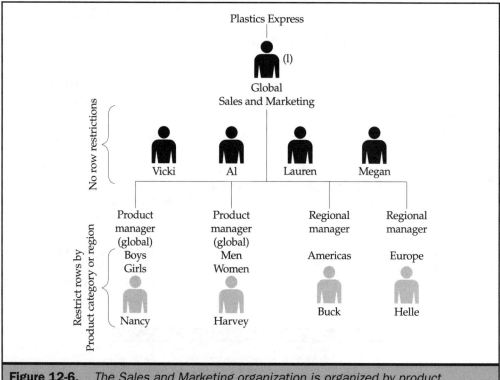

Figure 12-6. *The Sales and Marketing organization is organized by product categories and regions; row restrictions allow data to be automatically filtered according to this organization.*

Figure 12-7 shows all data rows available in the source system. In order to restrict which rows of data Nancy sees, you will add a restriction for SH.PRODUCTS.PROD_CATEGORY IN ('Girls','Boys'). Helle needs the restriction SH.COUNTRIES.COUNTRY_REGION = 'Europe'.

1. To add a row restriction, follow steps 1–4 from the preceding section to select the individual user and universe to which you want the restriction to apply.

2. Select the Rows tab.

3. Click Add.

4. Enter the WHERE clause to append to every query, or click >> in the Where box to call the Where Clause Definition box.

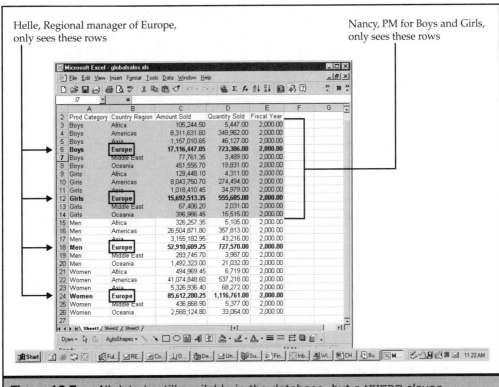

Figure 12-7. *All data is still available in the database, but a* WHERE *clause will filter the data so that each person sees only the rows he or she needs.*

A BETTER UNIVERSE

5. Under Tables and Columns, click + to expand the desired table name and double-click to select the individual column name you wish to restrict. In this example, SH.COUNTRIES.REGION_ID will be added to the first part of the WHERE clause.

The data value must be entered manually   Functions are optional

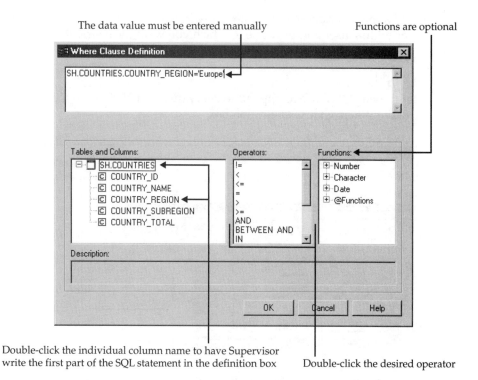

Double-click the individual column name to have Supervisor
write the first part of the SQL statement in the definition box   Double-click the desired operator

6. Select the operator and double-click to add it to the WHERE clause.

7. If necessary, select a function to convert the condition to a particular format. You must manually enter the restriction; there is no list of values available on this screen. If your restriction is on a character field, enclose the restriction in single quotes. If it is numeric, quotes are not required.

8. Click OK two times to return to the Universe Properties dialog box, shown in the next illustration.

9. Click Check All to verify that the object still exists in the universe.

User or group affected by the restrictions   Universe to which the row restrictions apply

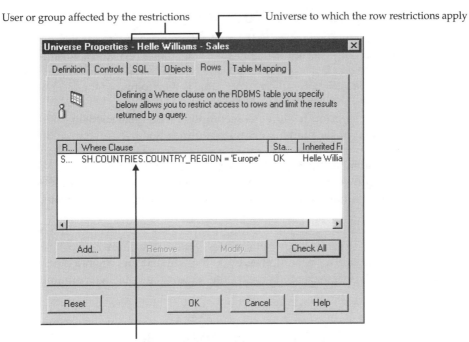

Universe Properties - Helle Williams - Sales

Definition | Controls | SQL | Objects | Rows | Table Mapping |

Defining a Where clause on the RDBMS table you specify below allows you to restrict access to rows and limit the results returned by a query.

R...	Where Clause	Sta...	Inherited Fr...
S...	SH.COUNTRIES.COUNTRY_REGION = 'Europe'	OK	Helle Willia

Add...   Remove   Modify...   Check All

Reset   OK   Cancel   Help

The WHERE clause will be appended to all queries that use the particular universe

Check All only verifies that the universe object exists in the repository; it does not verify SQL syntax or valid data values. If you enter either of these incorrectly, users will receive an error or no rows when a report or query is refreshed.

Row restrictions can be quite powerful but also problematic if restrictions are applied against multiple user instances and multiple groups. Row restrictions do not have priority levels; instead, all restrictions are used to generate the WHERE clause and are connected with AND. For example, if the Sales and Marketing group incorrectly contained a row restriction for REGION='Americas' and Helle's individual user restriction contained REGION='Europe', Helle would have no rows returned since the two conditions are appended to the query with an AND connector.

Database Views vs. Row Restrictions

Companies that have unique logins to the data source often create views for each user or group of users to accomplish the same thing as Supervisor's row restrictions. To implement this, the DBA would create a security table that contains each user and a column with the data values for each restriction. The security table is then joined to the fact or dimension tables to ensure users see only their own data.

There is no *best* solution for how to accomplish row-level security. Views may be easier to implement for many users with multiple security restrictions. Views are database-specific, so if your company uses more than one BI tool, the security model is open and independent of the tool. However, too many views may confuse a database optimizer, and queries may not be processed as efficiently. Unless the DBA creates an application to maintain the row restrictions, security becomes centralized with the DBA.

Simple WHERE clauses generated through Supervisor will leverage the optimizer. However, the security settings are not seamless and can be more difficult to maintain for larger user groups. The benefit, though, is that supervisors are often power users who know which data a user needs to see; the security may be better maintained.

Table Mappings

Table mappings provide another way to implement row-level security. Table mappings allow Supervisors to rename the base table in a universe with a different table name. In order for table mappings to work, the column names from the original table used in the universe must be exactly the same as the column names in the mapped table.

To follow on the preceding example, I could have multiple tables, either views or physical tables:

- SALES that contains all sales data
- CHILD_SALES that contains a subset of data for PRODUCT_CATEGORY IN ('Boys','Girls')
- EURO_SALES that contains sales for REGION='Europe'

1. To remap a table, select the individual user or group and the universe to which you want the restriction to apply and click Universe Properties.
2. Select the Table Mapping tab.
3. Click Add.
4. Use the Select button to launch the table browser or enter the original table name in the master universe. If you use the Table Browser, click OK to return to the New Table Mapping dialog box, shown next.
5. Position your mouse in the Replacement Table box. Use the Select button to select the new table or enter the new table name—in this example, SH.EURO_SALES.

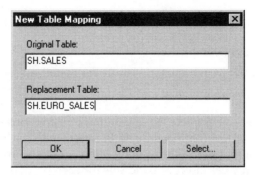

6. Click OK to return to the Universe Properties dialog box.

7. Click Check All to verify that the table names exist in the universe structure.

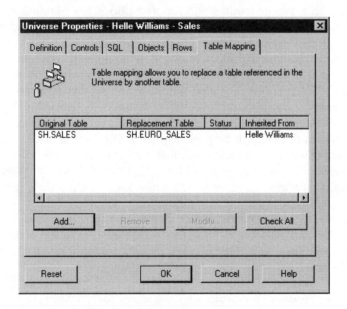

Software Functionality: Command Restrictions

As mentioned earlier in this chapter, Business Objects licenses product functionality by separate modules, even though the functionality is built into one set of software files. Table 12-3 showed how assigning different user profiles provides users with access to the main software products: Designer, Supervisor, BusinessObjects, and WebIntelligence. The Supervisor can further control what software functionality users have within the core products through *command restrictions*. In this respect, the software modules are treated as resources, similar to universes and documents.

There are a few main reasons you may want to modify command restrictions:

- To ensure licensing compliance
- To make the software more user-friendly for casual users
- To prevent users, Supervisors, and Designers from performing certain tasks

The vendor provides a complete list of command restrictions that correspond to each product module in the *Supervisor's Guide.* For users with the WebIntelligence profile, the vendor provides predefined settings that correspond to license options (Explorer, Reporter), including only certain command sets for each predefined setting. However, the same predefined settings are not provided for the BusinessObjects resource, or for the full client. The vendor recommends creating separate profiles based on each company's specific user segments. For example, many companies have at least two broad user segments: report readers and report authors. For maximum repository performance, the supervisor should create two new groups to correspond to these user segments. Second, they should create a new predefined setting for these user segments and apply the new setting to a group. Creating new predefined settings and applying them at the group level improves response time and reduces maintenance (versus modifying the default, vendor-provided settings on a user-by-user basis).

For casual users, fewer menu choices can go a long way toward making the product appear easier to use. In this respect, a Reader license allows users to read reports and refresh queries built by power users. Some companies allow all new users to be Readers without attending training; however, to be a full BusinessObjects user, companies may require full product training. In the following example, you will modify the BusinessObjects resource to add a new predefined setting called Reader.

Note *Supervisor allows you to restrict commands within existing predefined settings (Default, Novice, Standard). However, command restrictions apply to all user instances and are not universe- or group-specific. Therefore, I recommend creating a new profile when you wish to restrict commands.*

1. From the pull-down menu shown next, select Tools | Manage Predefined Settings. Under Select a resource, ensure that BusinessObjects is selected.

2. Click New.

3. Enter the name **Reader**.

4. Supervisor enables you to view command sets according to menu commands or families of functionality. Command set families are predefined by the vendor and based upon sets of functionality within the software. For example, Analysis includes Drill mode, Slice and Dice mode, and Business Miner. Command set families work for both BusinessObjects 4.*x* users and 5.*x* users. Menus do not. Menus also do not cancel functionality that can be activated by selecting a button on the toolbar. Therefore, you will use command sets to create the Reader profile. If command sets do not appear by default, click Options. Select Command Set and click OK to return to the Predefined Settings screen.

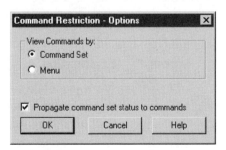

5. Within the Analysis command set family, select Work with BusinessMiner. In the Status drop-down box, select Hidden so that Reader users will never see this

menu option. A red traffic light will appear next to Work with BusinessMiner, as
shown next.

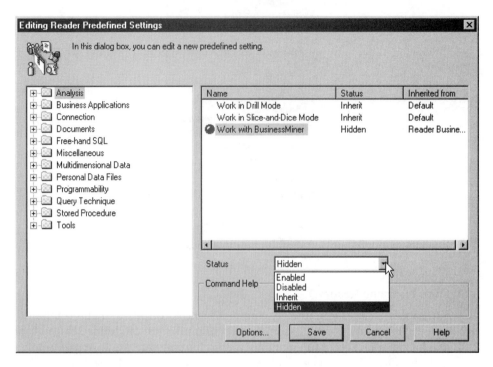

Supervisor enables you to set four different statuses. Similar to security access
levels, they have a range of priorities, with 1 or Hidden being the most restrictive.
When command sets are inherited through different groups and user permissions,
the most restrictive applies. For example, if the statuses for Analysis commands are
set to Enabled in one group and Hidden in another group and a user is a member
of both groups, the functionality for that user will be Hidden, as this Status has
a higher priority.

Priority	Traffic Light	Status	Explanation
1	Red	Hidden	The functionality is not available to the user and does not appear on either the toolbar or the pull-down menus.

Priority	Traffic Light	Status	Explanation
2	Yellow	Disabled	The functionality is not available to the user but *does* appear (but is grayed out) on the toolbar and menus.
3	Green	Enabled	The functionality is explicitly available.
4	None	Inherit	The functionality is available and inherited through a profile.

6. Follow the same process to set all the command sets in the following table to Hidden:

Command Set Family	Set the Following Functionality to Hidden
Analysis	Work With BusinessMiner
Documents	Change File Locations Conditional Formatting Copy To Clipboard Create Documents Create Templates Data Provider Manipulation Delete Corporate Documents Sent By Other Users Document Interactions Edit Euro Converter Rates Euro Converter Use Templates
Personal Data Files	Edit Personal Data Files Use Personal Data Files
Programmability	Set all functionality to hidden
Query Techniques	Edit Lists of Values Edit Query Edit Query SQL Use Queries Use User Objects View Query SQL

7. Click Save to save all the changes to the newly created profile.

8. The Reader profile can now be assigned to a particular user or group of users. Select the individual user or group. From the Managed Predefined Settings dialog box, click Apply to Users.

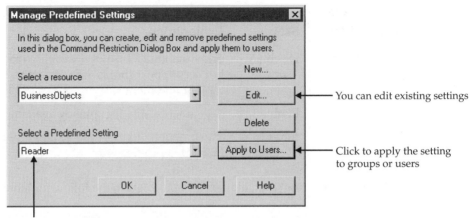

Verify the correct setting is selected before making changes or applying to user/groups

9. Select the desired user(s) from the list. Use CTRL-click to select more than one
user. Click OK two times to save your settings and close the dialog boxes.

Figure 12-8 compares two versions of the Data pull-down menus. In the menu
on the bottom, there are no command restrictions and all menu options appear. The
pull-down menu on the top is missing certain options.

*If you are using a BusinessObjects login name as well as a data source user ID
and password (Table 6-2, alternative 4), disable users' ability to change passwords in
BusinessObjects to prevent their login passwords from getting out of synch with their
data-source passwords. Edit the BusinessObjects and WebIntelligence Resources,
Default Predefined Settings and set Tools, Change Password to Hidden.*

Connections

In Chapter 6, you learned about how connections work within a universe and provide
access to either the source OLTP or a data warehouse. Secured connections are the only
ones that appear in Supervisor and are denoted with a yellow key. While Supervisor
allows many resources to be assigned to specific groups and users, connections are not
considered a resource and apply to all groups and users.

BusinessObjects supports three different types of connections, each denoted with
a unique symbol:

- *Personal* connections that users may create for free-hand SQL or that universe designers create when testing new data sources. The definitions reside in C:\Program Files\Business Objects\BusinessObjects 5.0\LocData\pdac.ssi (personal data account.shared security information).

- *Shared* connections that are shared via work group folders on a LAN server. The definitions reside in SDAC.SSI.

- *Secure* connections that reside in the BusinessObjects repository. Designers and supervisors create and modify secure connections, which are the most common in enterprise-wide deployments.

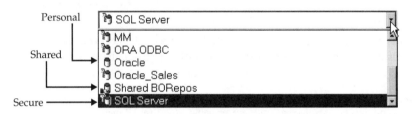

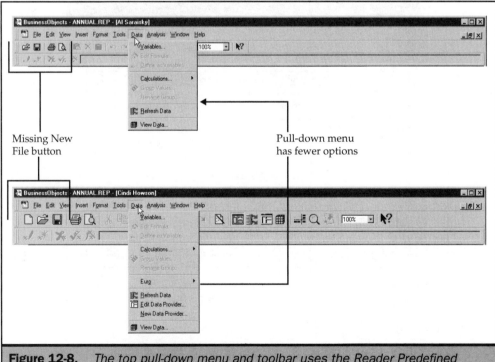

Figure 12-8.   *The top pull-down menu and toolbar uses the Reader Predefined setting and has fewer options than the bottom pull-down menu and toolbar, which uses the Default Predefined Setting.*

When you create a connection in Designer and set the connection type to secure, the definitions are immediately added to the repository security domain and appear in Supervisor. All the connection options and tabs (Login, Advanced, Custom) that exist in Designer appear in Supervisor. Because the connection information is global and affects all universes, I recommend you use Supervisor, not Designer, to review and maintain connections.

In the following example, you will create a secure connection for the BEACH.UNV or Island Resorts Marketing. Explanations for the various connection settings are in Chapter 6.

1. Log on to Supervisor. If you receive a message that you are not authorized to use Supervisor, contact your BusinessObjects administrator.

2. Select Tools | Connections or click the Connections button on the toolbar. See Table 12-1 for a complete list of buttons available in Supervisor.

The network layer controls which .prm and .sbo files BusinessObjects uses and thus what SQL commands are available

Database of the source data (OLTP, mart, or warehouse)

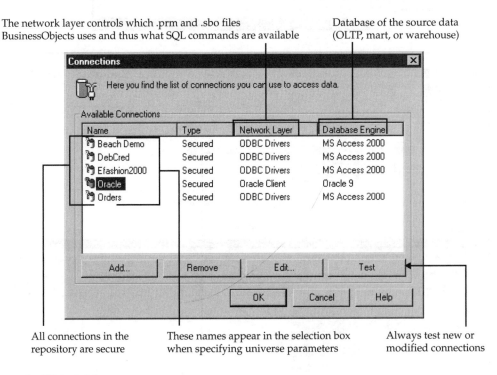

All connections in the repository are secure

These names appear in the selection box when specifying universe parameters

Always test new or modified connections

3. Click Add.

4. Select the network driver for this connection: ODBC Drivers. This becomes the Network Layer and determines which *database*.prm and *database*.sbo files BusinessObjects uses to build the universe and generate the SQL.

5. Enter the connection name **Beach DB**.

6. Select the database engine **MS Access 2000**.

7. I have selected alternative 3 (see Chapter 6, Table 6-2) for my security approach and so have entered a shared username and password.

8. For ODBC databases, the data source name comes from local ODBC definitions. For Oracle, the data source name may come from a TNSNAMES.ORA file. For other databases, the name may be manually entered.

9. *Always* test a new or modified database connection. If you have defined your login information correctly and the database is operational, Supervisor will confirm "The Server is Responding!"

10. If you click the Details button in the Test Connection dialog box, Supervisor will provide you with additional information on your connection settings. The following example shows information from testing an Oracle connection:

```
Database server version:
Oracle9i Release 9.0.1.1.1 - Production
PL/SQL Release 9.0.1.1.1 - Production
CORE    9.0.1.1.1      Production
TNS for 32-bit Windows: Version 9.0.1.1.0 - Production
NLSRTL Version 9.0.1.1.1 - Production
BusinessObjects configuration:
Network Layer: Oracle OCI
DBMS Engine: Oracle 8.1
DLL: C:\Program Files\Business Objects\Data Access 5.0\SQBOCI50.DLL
SBO: C:\Program Files\Business Objects\Data Access 5.0\Oracle\Oracle
PRM: C:\Program Files\Business Objects\Data Access 5.0\Oracle\ora7
RSS: C:\Program Files\Business Objects\Data Access 5.0\Oracle\oracle
```

11. Click OK twice to return and save your Connection.

Note

Changes to connection information are displayed instantaneously and are global. If one designer changes settings in the Advanced or Custom tab in one universe, these changes will immediately appear in Supervisor and affect all other universes that use the same Secure connection. They do not affect BusinessObjects users currently logged into the repository.

A BETTER UNIVERSE

Some Final Words: Response Time and Inheritance

This chapter presents a number of alternatives to control access by groups or individual users to different resources. While it is important to *understand* your organizational structure before defining users in Supervisor, trying to replicate a complex structure in Supervisor will negatively affect response time. As well, the more you use the Supervisor functionality, the more complex, and larger, your security repository tables, and the harder for you to determine what is actually happening. With all of these settings, you must consider the impact on response time as well as the net effect on user functionality and data access.

Response Time Effects

Each time you include a user in a group, Supervisor creates an additional row in the security tables. In looking back at Table 12-1, note that Plastics Express has five departments. Al Saraisky is defined at the main level and then added to each of the five departments. This creates six rows of data in the repository database. Supervisors of very large organizations with many groups need to be cognizant of this. However, even in very large organizations, membership to multiple groups does not have a strong impact on response time; long branches with sub groups and enabling/disabling does! For example, let's take a large global organization:

- **Number of users**   20,000
- **Number of business units**   15
- **Number of functional departments**   10

Of course, it makes no sense for every user to belong to every business unit or functional department, but if they do (perhaps due to constant reorganizations and never cleaning up security definitions) the largest our table would be is 20,000×15×10 + 20,000 (if users were initially created at the corporate level) = 3 million rows. This is not a relatively large table. However, by default, BusinessObjects includes only minimal indexes on the repository tables. Minimal indexes allow for faster updates and password changes but result in potentially slower login times with complex security rights. Integra Solutions, a consulting firm specializing in BusinessObjects, has some guidelines for indexes to improve login times (www.integrasolutions.net). These guidelines are not officially supported by the vendor, but Integra claims to have seen a 50–70 percent improvement in login time when these indexes are used.

Some Sweeping Generalizations

- Access to resources can be inherited from group settings.

- Access to resources can be explicitly assigned to a user and override inherited settings. Linking resources at lower levels for users within a subgroup means the users in the subgroup have more access than higher level users in a parent group; access does not flow up.

- If there is a conflict in inherited resources, the most permissive wins. For example, if the Human Resources universe is linked at the root or Plastics Express level and then disabled at the descendant, Sales and Marketing level, Sales and Marketing will still have access to Human Resources, as it is more permissive.

- Linking and unlinking resources is better than enabling and disabling resources. The inheritance is clearer and the repository tables will be smaller.

- For complex column and row-level restrictions, secure data at the database level.

- User definitions and command set restrictions are global. Timestamps and profiles are group-specific.

- Timestamps affect response time more than other restrictions and can easily be ignored by users changing their local clock settings.

- Row restrictions are per universe. Multiple restrictions from different groups that apply to the same universe will all be appended to each query.

- While universe, document, and stored procedure restrictions follow a "most permissive" flow, command restrictions do not. When determining command restrictions, the most restrictive are applied. For example, if a group or user has software functionality set to Hidden anywhere, the functionality will be hidden, as it is the most restrictive setting.

A BETTER UNIVERSE

Chapter 13

Design Principles: Where to Put the Intelligence

You have built your universe, made it more robust with advanced objects and hierarchies, and used Supervisor to grant users access to the universe. You are off to a good start. As your universe evolves, you will face a number of choices about where to put the intelligence, specifically the *business* intelligence. This chapter focuses on the alternatives and the pros and cons of each alternative. My goal is to help you understand the cost/benefit implications of the choices as you deploy BusinessObjects.

What Is Intelligence?

Intelligence is information with a *business* context. QUANTITY may be a physical column in a table. Add a time period such as month, then a context to the time period such as order month, and multiply the column by a price, and you arrive at *Sales Revenue*, something with meaning and value to business users.

Users will rarely want to analyze straight columns of data. If they did, the transaction or Enterprise Resource Planning (ERP) system would meet their needs just fine. To provide a business context, the raw data must be combined with other information, perhaps cleansed, transformed, and aggregated. Many transformations may be critical to the project's success and known to programmers and Extract Transform and Load (ETL) experts; however, they mean nothing to a business user. If a customer code is 306 in one system and 0306 in another system, the business person really doesn't care. The business person only cares and knows that this 306/0306 customer is Mrs. Whitwell. Transformations to make the data consistent are necessary to build the data warehouse or mart but are a given to the business user.

If the business user wants to do a promotion for newly married customers, then perhaps classifying this customer under a grouping such as Newlyweds would be a form of intelligence. At first glance, you may assume that this customer grouping should exist in a dimension table. A database is certainly one place to put the intelligence, but the customer grouping could also go in the universe or a user's report. Following are a few more examples of items that I would consider to be more than just straight calculations or transformations; they provide business intelligence:

- Measures that include time periods, such as *Sales Year To Date* or *Days Late*
- Variance analysis that compares the difference between two numbers, such as *Current Year Sales versus Last Year Sales, Percentage of On-time Shipments*
- Ratios, such as *Market Share, Patient Visits per Diagnosis, Gross Margin*
- Dimension groupings, such as customer age, income, product size, color

Places for Intelligence

A universe designer may naturally assume that the universe should contain all the intelligence. Power users may want user objects and report variables to contain all the intelligence. Depending on how much disk space and time a DBA has, the DBA may want the intelligence to be in the table design so that it is tool-independent. This is where a good Program Manager or Project Manager will work with the different stakeholders and determine the best place for intelligence considering a company's resources, time, and flexibility. Companies can build intelligence into MOLAP cubes, the data warehouse, the universe, or user objects and reports. If you are using BusinessObjects directly against a transaction system, your alternatives may be limited to the universe and reports.

Figure 13-1 shows these different places and where the intelligence gets processed. In Chapter 10, you built an object called *Current Year To Date Sales* as part of the universe. Stepping through Figure 13-1, you could have used a MOLAP cube to include the time period awareness in the sales column (place 1). The processing is done on the MOLAP server. The intelligence also could be a physical column in an aggregate fact table. The information is preprocessed by the RDBMS, so when a user runs a query, it is a simple fetch (place 2). If the object exists in either the universe or a user object, the RDBMS again does the work but does it upon query execution. The user may wait longer for the query to be processed, but the work is still done by the RDBMS.

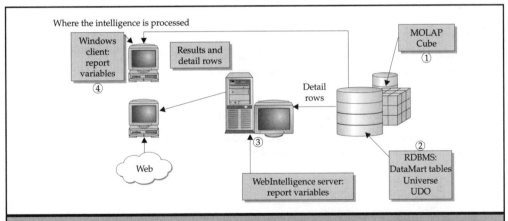

Figure 13-1.   *Intelligence can be built in a number of places in a BusinessObjects deployment.*

If a power user creates a report variable to calculate *Current Year To Date Sales,* then the RDBMS sends the detail rows to calculate that variable to either the WebI server in a thin-client environment or the user's desktop in a two- or three-tier environment (full client or ZABO, respectively). In a thin-client environment, the WebI midtier must calculate the variable and present the results to the user in HTML format (place 3). In two- or three-tier environment, all the detail rows travel the network to the desktop PC that then calculates the report variable (place 4).

Evaluating the Pros and Cons of Each Alternative

Occasionally, there is a single, clear-cut choice for where to put the intelligence. You are low on disk space, so you add it to the universe; the calculation is too complex for SQL, so you create a report variable. These are the easy answers. The not-so-easy answers are everything else in between. The best place for intelligence is the consultant's annoying but valid answer, "it depends." In the following sections, I give examples of business intelligence that are better suited to one place over another. Each alternative will have a cost associated. The question you must answer is whether the benefit outweighs the cost. Building intelligence into the fact table provides faster response time and consistent results; is this a strong enough benefit to justify the cost of redesigning the table, modifying the load routines, and buying more disk space? In some cases, absolutely. In other cases, no.

MOLAP Cubes

In presenting this topic at the BusinessObjects 2002 User Conference, I was disappointed (but not surprised) to see that only a small percentage of companies integrate MOLAP cubes with the BusinessObjects deployment.

MOLAP Cubes as Independent Applications

MOLAP cubes often are treated as separate applications for several reasons. First, each MOLAP vendor provides their own access tools:

- Hyperion and IBM provide Analyzer and a spreadsheet to access Essbase or DB2 OLAP cubes.
- Microsoft uses Excel to access MS Analysis Services cubes; Knosys' Proclarity is a third-party front end that is quite powerful.
- SAP/BW provides BW/Explorer as a front end to BW Info Cubes.

Just as data marts and BI implementations can be implemented departmentally, so can MOLAP databases. Unless a business sponsor and program management are in place to integrate the two, it seems rarely to happen. Vendors do little to help enterprises understand the integration possibilities. In a competitive sales situation, vendors will push customers to select one vendor and corresponding architecture. Faced with tight budgets and limited resources, customers too would also like to implement one BI tool. From a marketing perspective, Business Objects still lists Essbase as an *alternative* BI tool (that is, competitor), despite the company's efforts to improve the integration and treat it simply as another data source. Lastly, the MOLAP cubes may not be integrated with BusinessObjects, because until recently, the MOLAP vendors' access tools were generally better than BusinessObjects' OLAP access.

When Business Objects acquired OLAP@Work in 2000, it acquired a powerful spreadsheet add-in as well as technology that changed the way BusinessObjects OLAP access worked. The spreadsheet add-in, rebranded as Business Query for Excel MD, works only against MS Analysis Services cubes but is superior to what Microsoft itself offers. With OLAP access via BusinessObjects, users drill within a plain data access grid. This is not particularly appealing if users are accustomed to drilling within a chart or formatted report, as most MOLAP vendors' tools allow. Thus, users may have built large queries and analyzed, explored, and drilled within a standard BusinessObjects document (Figure 13-2). With the OLAP@Work acquisition, the work flow changed for MS Analysis and SAP/BW users; users no longer drill within a plain grid; they use the grid to build a query and then drill within the microcube. Essbase and DB2 users can still drill within the plain grid, but it's not for analysis purposes; it's mainly for filtering the data.

In Q1 2002, however, Business Objects released a new version of WebI that, for the first time, allowed formatted drilling, ranking, and sorting directly against a cube, similar to the way analysis tools from MOLAP vendors always worked (Figure 13-3). WebI now presents a formatted table or chart to a user. If the user double-clicks to drill down from Year to Quarter, this is done within the MOLAP cube, thus limiting network traffic and using the power of the MOLAP engine. The MOLAP server also performs sorts and nested rankings. At the same time, Business Objects also provided drill-through to details in WebI, by which users can be exploring a summary OLAP cube, then drill-through to details in a relational table (see Chapter 14, "Universal Drill-Through Service").

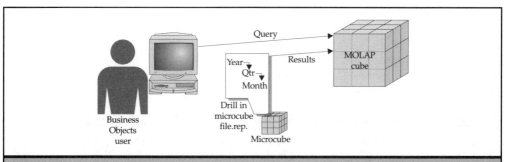

Figure 13-2.   *In a BusinessObjects full-client deployment, users drill within reports and not the MOLAP cube.*

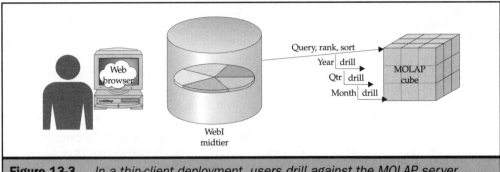

Figure 13-3.   *In a thin-client deployment, users drill against the MOLAP server via formatted reports and charts.*

Despite these improvements, BusinessObjects MOLAP access is still disjointed, with different functionality in the different user tools and MOLAP databases. First, WebI three-tier mode does not support access to MOLAP cubes at all. Second, compare how the functionality varies for each of the MOLAP capabilities listed here:

Functionality	Full Client	WebI Thin Client
Drill-in grid	Only for Essbase, DB2 OLAP, and Oracle Express; MS Analysis Services and SAP/BW use grid for query selection and not exploration	Yes
Drill-in formatted table or chart	Uses local report, not MOLAP server	Uses MOLAP server
Server-based sorts, rankings	Via Business Query MD only for MS Analysis Services	Yes
Write-access to cube for budgeting	Via Business Query MD only for MS Analysis Services	No

Business Objects has a number of improvements planned for OLAP access in the second half of 2003. Some of the enhancements will address the functionality differences between the thin, 3-tier, and full-client MOLAP access.

Advantages of Building Intelligence in MOLAP Cubes

Clearly, for this section to have any relevance, your goal is to integrate your MOLAP cube as another data source in your BusinessObjects deployment. The question becomes, then, when to build intelligence into the MOLAP cube. As shown in Figure 13-1, when the intelligence is put in a MOLAP cube, the server does the work (place 1), thus minimizing network traffic. In general, building intelligence into any server-based technology will also ensure consistent business definitions (compared to varying calculations in user reports and spreadsheets). Further, MOLAP tools have a better understanding of business analysis than most SQL-based reporting tools, so a number of functions are built into the OLAP engine. For time period calculations, Essbase includes dynamic period-to-date calculations with a toggle (Figure 13-4). Period-to-date calculations are not as straightforward in MS Analysis Services, but many developers find MDX coding easier than the SQL CASE and DECODE functions presented in Chapter 10. Recall from Figure 8-2 and Figure 10-2 the issue with comparing inventories and account balances (one point in time) with material movements and debit/credits (a period of time). BusinessObjects handles this through multiple SQL statements and user training; however, MOLAP tools again are aware of these issues and allow you to flag with a simple setting how the measure is used. In Figure 13-4, note how inventory is flagged with TB First, telling Essbase to choose the first occurrence of a value within a corresponding time period; the aggregation is never over time, but rather, just one value for one period.

MOLAP cubes also provide you with more control over the calculation order, something particularly important for ratios and percentages. As an example of calculation order, look at the calculations for profit as a percent of sales, as shown in Figure 13-5.

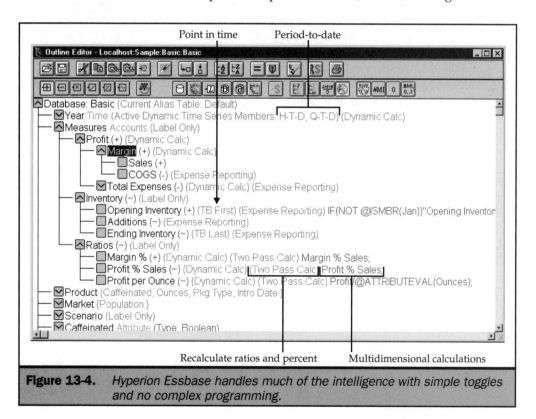

Figure 13-4.   *Hyperion Essbase handles much of the intelligence with simple toggles and no complex programming.*

	Product	Market	Actual			
	Oct	Nov	Dec	Q4		
Sales	48842	62758	73372	184972		
Profit	12686	17262.2	22316.8	52265		
Profit_% of Sales	**26**	**28**	**30**	**84**		

Sum across first

	Product	Market	Actual			
	Oct	Nov	Dec	Q4		
Sales	48842	62758	73372	184972		Calculate down
Profit	12686	17262.2	22316.8	52265		(profit/sales) to
Profit_% of Sales	**26**	**28**	**30**	**28**		correct ratios and %s

Figure 13-5.   *Percentages and ratios require a two-step calculation that MOLAP tools easily handle.*

To get sales and profit totals for quarter four, you correctly sum across the rows. However, for profit as a percent of sales, if you sum across, you get an incorrect percentage of 84. To calculate percentages and ratios, you need first to get the sums by quarter, and then calculate down to take profit / sales. This second calculation gives you the correct result of 28 percent.

Similar to this concept of a two-pass calculation are multidimensional and forward-looking calculations. In Figure 13-4, profit and sales are at two different levels within the accounts hierarchy. To calculate profit, one must first know the subtotals for Margin and Total Expenses, as shown in the next screen (first subtotal). Profit is not a simple sum, but rather, an aggregation of Subtotal Margin – Subtotal Expenses (second subtotal). To calculate profit as a percentage of sales, you must know both levels of subtotals as well as the detail Sales that is used to calculate the Margin Subtotal; the database must look "forward" to first calculate Profit before it can calculate Sales as a percentage of Profit.

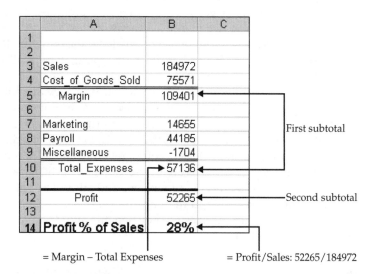

= Margin − Total Expenses   = Profit/Sales: 52265/184972

This is simple for MOLAP, which understands dimension members and levels (just say Profit % Sales!), but not so simple for SQL. Are there ways of doing this in the fact table, universe, or report? Of course! It's all a matter of the time and cost to implement and maintain the intelligence.

With the exception of MS Analysis Services, which does not directly support alternate rollups, MOLAP is also an ideal place to store dimensional information that needs to be aggregated in different ways. As discussed early in this chapter, a customer dimension could have groupings by physical region or by type of customer (newly married). Users are viewing the same measures but by different groupings. MOLAP tools allow dimensions to be aggregated in different ways, often without drastically increasing the size of the database.

Disadvantages of MOLAP

Before you rush out to buy the latest version of a MOLAP tool, note that they do have their disadvantages. First, they are another database and another data source. If your organization is strapped for IT resources, you may be forced to limit which technologies you can support. As a separate database, it is another copy of the data. However, if the MOLAP tool is integrated correctly with your data warehouse, I would argue that it is in fact another, smarter way to provide aggregate tables. MOLAP tools are famous for ensuring consistent response times on precalculated data; however, this requires smaller data sets than what an RDBMS can handle. Some MOLAP tools allow you to store data in relational tables (ROLAP) to increase capacity, yet this will have a performance impact. Although MOLAP tools are ideal for alternate roll-ups, they are not well suited for list analysis, and support for attribute analysis varies greatly. For example, if you want a list of customers above a certain age or a list of products packaged a particular way, MOLAP tools generally do not support this. The data would need to be stored in a relational table so that BusinessObjects could generate a tabular report; with MOLAP tools, all the information is stored as an intersection of a particular measure. In this way, it's possible to analyze measures by dimensions and attributes, but it may not be possible to generate lists of dimensions and their attributes.

The following table summarizes the key benefits and disadvantages to putting the intelligence in a MOLAP cube:

MOLAP Benefits	MOLAP Disadvantages
Built in period-to-date and point-in-time calculations	Additional cost and expertise
Control over calculation order for ratios and percentages	Risk of duplicate, inconsistent data if not integrated with data warehouse
Multidimensional and forward-looking calculations	Expertise generally comes from IT
Aggregated, so fast, consistent response times	
Server-based, so consistent business definitions and minimal network traffic	

Relational Tables

Building the intelligence into relational tables provides many of the same benefits as MOLAP cubes:

- Tables are preprocessed and so are generally faster than the dynamic SQL that a universe or user object would use.

- Tables involve server-based processing, so only limited data is sent across the network.

- Tables are server-based, so business definitions are consistent.

Again taking the example of *Current Year To Date Sales*, a DBA could build a fact table with the following structure:

product_key	customer_key	time_key	C_Month	LY_Month	C_YTD	L_YTD
123	111	102003	500	400	5000	3850
456	111	102003	200	180	2000	1800
123	333	102003	710	300	7100	3000
123	777	102003	900	1000	8000	10000

As the data is loaded into the fact table, each column represents a "bucket" of information with the time period intelligence built into each column. C_MONTH contains sales for just the current month; C_YTD contains sales for each month in the current year. If the month is October, it contains sales from January through October.

Many analytic applications that build data marts (including SAP BW's Info Cubes) use this kind of structure. However, if your company designs and builds your own fact tables, the DBA must program this kind of intelligence into the load routines; unlike in MOLAP cubes, there is no simple toggle to achieve time period intelligence. A robust ETL tool may help with the process. For example, Informatica's Warehouse includes a package on time dimensions that allows Power Center (their corresponding ETL tool) to build fact tables with these "buckets" of time period information. Power Center uses flags within the time dimension tables to do the year-to-date calculations. Even with an ETL tool, this kind of design requires more disk space and a stronger understanding of best practices in data warehouse designs. DBAs may not have the resources to implement this kind of design or the time (show me a DBA that is not overworked and overscheduled!).

Recall from the first section in this chapter that dimension groupings such as customer age, income, product size, and color are also forms of intelligence. Analyzing data by dimensions is the bread and butter of most businesses. Providing alternative groupings can help reveal previously hidden patterns. For example, let's take a wine merchant. Users can analyze sales by type of wine and rating. Users also can see which customers buy the most wine. Now break that customer list down by corporate customers versus individual consumers, and the analysis will reveal which group of customers generates the most business. If the dimension table contained income information for each corporate customer, the wine merchant can better understand if large corporate customers are more profitable than small business owners. The same logic applies to product information: what are sales for soft drinks in plastic bottles versus aluminum cans? Unfortunately, this kind of dimensional information is often not captured, or when it is captured, it is stored in departmental databases and spreadsheets. As discussed in Chapter 9, it is possible to incorporate personal lists of values into a universe; however, I would advocate that more dimensional information could be stored in the relational tables. If companies use a star or snowflake schema in data marts, then a data mart can contain both a standard customer dimension and a customer dimension with business-specific groupings and hierarchies. BusinessObjects can handle multiple dimensions with alternate hierarchies in each. Further, dimensional information in relational tables allows users to create lists and easily do attribute analysis with the information, something not all MOLAP tools support.

When Not to Store Intelligence in Relational Tables

Relational tables are not a good place to physically store ratios and variances, as the ratio always needs to be recalculated with an aggregated numerator and an aggregated denominator. To follow on the earlier example, let's say you want to calculate the percentage variance between the current year-to-date sales (C_YTD) and last year's year-to-date sales (LY_YTD). For each row in the database, you can correctly store the variance.

product_key	customer_key	time_key	C_YTD	L_YTD	% Variance
123	111	102003	5000	3850	29.87%
123	333	102003	7100	3000	136.67%
123	777	102003	8000	10000	–20.00%

However, recall that BusinessObjects users will create reports that dynamically group information by dimensions. Thus a business user may ask for a variance analysis by product. In order to allow this, the universe designer includes the SQL SUM aggregate in the object definition. This incorrectly sums the individual variance rows, suggesting that sales are 146.54 percent higher than last year sales. This is wrong!

product_key	customer_key	time_key	C_YTD	L_YTD	% Variance
123	111	102003	5000	3850	29.87%
123	333	102003	7100	3000	136.67%
123	777	102003	8000	10000	–20.00%
Subtotal for product 123:			20100	16850	146.54%

To arrive at a correct variance, you must get the subtotal for the C_YTD by product 123, and then the subtotal of L_YTD to arrive at a correct variance of sales being 19.29 percent higher than last year. MOLAP tools allow an administrator to control the calculation order; SQL tools do not. To guarantee correct results, the universe designer would ignore the variance column in the fact table and dynamically calculate the variance using a SQL statement in an object.

Summary

The following table summarizes when to store the intelligence in a fact table and when it poses disadvantages:

Relational Table Benefits	Relational Table Disadvantages
Precalculated in the table, so fast, consistent response times	Requires complex programming logic in the load routines
Server-based, so consistent business definitions and minimal network traffic	Fixed table design may limit flexibility
	IT/DBA must implement
	Requires additional disk space
	Not suitable for ratios and percentages

Universe

I confess I am biased: I prefer to put as much intelligence as possible in the universe. Of course there are exceptions, but let's start with the arguments for the universe. Intelligence in the universe offers much more flexibility than either a MOLAP cube or a relational table. When you add or modify an object, there is no need to restructure and recalculate a cube; there is no need to modify load routines and rebuild a table. The universe does not require the additional disk space that either MOLAP or RDBMS tables require. Because the universe is centralized, it enforces consistent business definitions. Further, as shown in Figure 13-1, the processing is done on the server, thus minimizing the impact on the network or WebI servers that user report formulas can overload. The universe allows partial control of the calculation order, necessary for ratios and variance analysis, something relational tables cannot offer in an ad hoc reporting environment. In the preceding example, you cannot aggregate the variance stored in a relational table or you get incorrect results. Within the universe, one uses the following syntax to control the calculation order:

```
(sum(C_YTD)-sum(L_YTD)) /sum(L_YTD)
```

A BETTER UNIVERSE

As users build queries that analyze the percent variance by different dimensions (product, time, geography), the variance for each row returned is always recalculated with the correct numerator and denominator. Problems may arise when users add breaks and subtotals within a report, but this can easily be corrected with report formulas.

Intelligence in the universe also does not necessarily require an overworked/ understaffed IT department to implement. New intelligence can be added quickly, as is critical in a changing business environment. Responsiveness and flexibility are the two main reasons I am biased toward building intelligence in the universe. If the BI deployment cannot respond as quickly as the business requirements change, it will be less successful. Requirements change not simply because users "overlooked" something, but more often, because they discovered a new or better way to explore information. Did anyone want to link click stream analysis with brick and mortar store sales before 1997?

The majority of companies put control of the universe in the hands of IT. This can be for the good, as IT staff have the skills to understand relationships between tables, joins, and index issues. They also can write complex SQL.

Note *Programmers and DBAs certified in SQL are not necessarily adept at SQL for business reporting; this is often a unique and hard-to-find skillset.*

However, unless the IT department has a close relationship with the business and an understanding of business reporting requirements, they may miss opportunities to add intelligence to the universe. Users do not know SQL and do not know what objects can be built with SQL; IT knows SQL but may not realize that the business would benefit from measures such as number of customers (COUNT function), number of late orders (COUNT and DAYS_BETWEEN functions), variance analysis ((SUM1-SUM2)/SUM2), and so on. Further, a recurring complaint about IT maintaining the universe is lack of flexibility. Users want something, and IT is either too busy to implement it or wants to keep the universe general.

This is when it makes sense to allow individual functions or business units to build and maintain their own universes. IT should still quality-assure these universes (see Chapter 15, "Quality Assurance Check List"), but it may be easier to teach a power user how to build a universe than to get IT resources to build the universe the way the business wants.

When a universe designer fails to build enough intelligence into the universe to satisfy the common business needs, end users are forced to create their own objects or to build the intelligence in the report. This approach may be fine for individual needs, but it can be a disaster for reports that are widely shared, as it can significantly increase maintenance costs and the risk of inconsistent business definitions.

Disadvantages of Intelligence in the Universe

Even though I prefer to build a robust universe, there are times when the universe is not the best place for the intelligence. Advanced objects will generally use complex SQL or BusinessObjects functions to create the objects. This can result in unpredictable query response times. Also, as the universe becomes more complex, there is a greater risk that certain objects do not work well together. For example, if a universe contains the two objects *Sales* and *Current YTD Sales*, will the user receive accurate information if the user places these objects in the same query? The first object, *Sales*, does not include any time-period constraints. The user therefore adds *Month*=10 and *Year*=2002 as conditions in the report. This makes the *Current YTD Sales* information wrong (it's now one month of data versus year-to-date) as BusinessObjects appends the WHERE clause to the entire query. Hopefully, users will recognize query results that are blatantly wrong; it's the not-so-obvious ones that pose a problem. In either case, a perfect universe would include only those objects that can be accurately combined together; a real-world universe accomplishes this most of the time and supplements it with good object descriptions and training!

Universe Benefits	Universe Disadvantages
Designers (IT or power users) can implement, so it is flexible	Use of complex business SQL is a unique skill
Server-based, so consistent business definitions and minimal network traffic	Unpredictable response times, as SQL is processed at query run time
Ratios and variances are correct	Individual objects may not be correct when combined with other objects with conflicting definitions

User Objects

Here is another bias: I prefer to avoid the use of user objects. User objects cannot be shared by other users. Rarely does only one person work with or view a report, so if the intelligence is lacking in the universe, either put it in the universe or put it in the report so that it can be shared.

The one problem that a user object solves and a report formula does not is that of too much data being sent across the network. If a user is using SQL for standard transformations (UPPER, TO_CHAR, and so on), then the same amount of traffic is sent across the network for a user-defined object versus a report formula. However, if a user builds an object to use CASE, DECODE, or RANK, then the database server processes the query, generating less network traffic than a report variable that gets processed locally on the client or WebI midtier. Similarly, if users want to limit the number of rows returned by a calculation, they can use only existing objects as a condition in a query. For example, if a user wants to run a report in which the order date is less than or equal to the order date minus 90 days, this can only be accomplished by a condition object the designer has built or a user object the user creates.

When users build objects with SQL functions, it may require a modification to the *database*.prm file (Chapter 10), increasing ownership costs. Another concern about both user objects and report formulas is that the business definition may no longer be consistent. One user's definition of *Current Month Sales* may be based on the accounting month the invoice was sent; another may define it with the calendar month, and yet another, the date the product was shipped.

The following table summarizes the pros and cons of user objects:

User Object Benefits	User Object Disadvantages
Users can implement, so flexible	Use of complex business SQL is a unique skill
Server-based processing minimizes network traffic	Unpredictable response times, as SQL is processed at query run time
	Objects cannot be shared with other users
	May require modification to the *database*.prm file to access certain SQL functions
	Not centrally maintained, so increases risk of inconsistent business definitions and higher costs

User Reports

With robust calculations and formulas, BusinessObjects offers users the ability to overcome many limitations in SQL. Users are familiar with formulas from spreadsheets and are comfortable building some quite powerful ones within the BusinessObjects documents. In some cases, users may have no choice but to create a formula in a report for the following reasons:

- It's an individual reporting need.
- The intelligence cannot be built with SQL.
- It's immediate and involves no politics.

If the report really is for individual use and the formula is not a common business one, then the intelligence does indeed belong in a report.

SQL Limitations

SQL does have limitations. MOLAP tool vendors often emphasize their solutions as a way to overcome a number of limitations of SQL (forward calculations, time period versus point in time, and so on). However, IBM and Oracle recently released a number of SQL extensions that make SQL more robust. Forward calculations such as rankings and percent market share are now possible with SQL.

But clearly, not everyone uses DB2 and Oracle, and not all intelligence can be solved with SQL; this is where many BI vendors have excelled. BusinessObjects in particular contains a number of formula functions that do not have a SQL equivalent. Variance Percentage, `Percentile`, and Euro conversions are just a few. Long before vendors added analytic functions to SQL, BusinessObjects offered a percent of sum calculation, as well as `Rank` and `RunningSum` functions. Recall the particular problems that variance and ratio calculations can cause; the calculation order is very important to get the correct answer. With report formulas, users control the calculation order either by specifically inserting a formula at each break level or with Calculation Context Operators (explained in detail in Chapter 18). To use the earlier example of the variance between `C_YTD` and `L_YTD`, look how the percent variance is correctly calculated, even for the break levels by product.

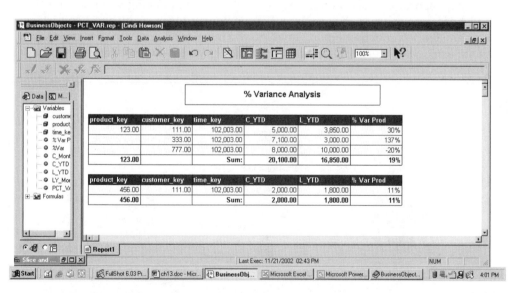

In some cases, it may be technically feasible to build the intelligence into an object, but the user needs it immediately. IT may maintain the universe and be unable to create a new object quickly enough; the user creates a report formula for time expediency. The user also may want to avoid the politics of having to get common buy-in for a universe modification.

Disadvantages of Intelligence in User Reports

Too many report formulas can be problematic over time. First, report variables are stored within a document and therefore are not centrally maintained. As formulas change, there is no way to track how many versions of the report have been shared and modified. Multiple versions of the formula will now exist. This problem becomes worse when the original formula creator changes jobs or leaves the company. There once was a statistic about 75 percent of spreadsheets containing errors. I wouldn't be surprised if report formulas have an equally high number of errors, or at the very least, cause a number of misunderstandings. One of my clients spent hours each month reconciling differences between two inventory reports: they both accessed the same universe in the data warehouse, but each contained different formulas. We eventually standardized on one report that became published and centrally maintained in the repository.

Second, report formulas contain a significant amount of intelligence that could, and should, be leveraged across the company. If a company is to ensure business consistency and capture the power of user report variables, you must develop a process to review and maintain formulas. Figure 13-6 shows one possible process. A user creates a standard

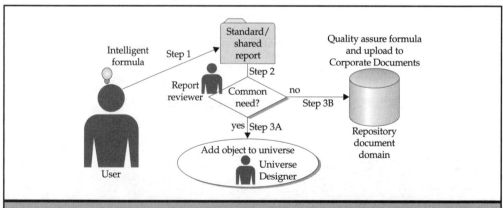

Figure 13-6.   *Creating a role of report reviewer can help companies minimize the risks of unnecessary and inconsistent report formulas.*

report that contains a number of formulas (step 1). A report reviewer, who may be a power user or a universe designer, reviews the report and looks for formulas that are common needs (step 2). When they fulfill common reporting requirements, the universe designer builds the intelligence into the universe (step 3A). If it is not a broad reporting requirement but only fulfills the needs of a few users, then the intelligence will remain as a report formula. The report reviewer quality-assures the formula and uploads the report to the repository (step 3B). Users may balk at this additional level of quality control, and the last thing a company wants to do is add barriers to sharing information. An alternative is to let users freely publish documents to the repository, but ensure a report reviewer and/or universe designer checks the reports periodically, after publishing.

Another major disadvantage of report variables is their effect on response time and system load. Overly complex reports can overload the WebI server. Formulas that require detail rows may cause too much data to be sent across the network. Let's look at the example of *Last Year YTD Sales*.

The following report formula looks at the computer's `CurrentDate` to determine which months are less than the current month. If it is less than the current month, then it displays the *Amount Sold*, else zero. The year must be one year ago.

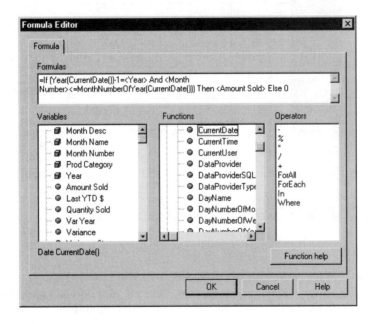

The report appears as follows (assuming the current date is October 31, 2000). Notice that while there were sales in November and December 1999, the rows for these months correctly display zeros.

Each year goes to a separate column

| Prod Ca Month Nu Year | | | Amount Sold | YTD $ | Last YTD $ |
Prod Ca Month Nu Year			Amount Sold	YTD $	Last YTD $
Boys	1.00	1,999.00	1,585,311.55	0.00	1,585,311.55
	1.00	2,000.00	1,976,772.00	1,976,772.00	0.00
	2.00	1,999.00	1,972,122.00	0.00	1,972,122.00
	2.00	2,000.00	2,680,488.60	2,680,488.60	0.00
	3.00	1,999.00	2,019,533.25	0.00	2,019,533.25
	3.00	2,000.00	2,558,275.15	2,558,275.15	0.00
	4.00	1,999.00	2,434,765.40	0.00	2,434,765.40
	4.00	2,000.00	2,862,946.00	2,862,946.00	0.00
	5.00	1,999.00	2,451,727.70	0.00	2,451,727.70
	5.00	2,000.00	3,207,527.00	3,207,527.00	0.00
	6.00	1,999.00	2,043,676.30	0.00	2,043,676.30
	6.00	2,000.00	2,443,540.10	2,443,540.10	0.00
	7.00	1,999.00	1,909,367.75	0.00	1,909,367.75
	7.00	2,000.00	2,344,933.00	2,344,933.00	0.00
	8.00	1,999.00	2,028,426.00	0.00	2,028,426.00
	8.00	2,000.00	2,368,214.45	2,368,214.45	0.00
	9.00	1,999.00	2,048,455.00	0.00	2,048,455.00
	9.00	2,000.00	2,535,076.55	2,535,076.55	0.00
	10.00	1,999.00	1,467,488.00	0.00	1,467,488.00
	10.00	2,000.00	1,777,547.00	1,777,547.00	0.00
	11.00	1,999.00	1,754,608.00	0.00	0.00
	11.00	2,000.00	2,184,936.00	0.00	0.00
	12.00	1,999.00	2,028,881.00	0.00	0.00

Only months < current month are used

Notice also that for every month, you need a row of data to be sent to the client. If you are analyzing sales for 20,000 products, then this kind of report requires 240,000 input rows (12 months times 20,000 product). You do not need the individual rows displayed in your final report, but as shown in the preceding report, BusinessObjects needs the detail month rows to process the formula.

The next table summarizes the advantages and disadvantages of putting the intelligence in a user report.

User Report Benefits	**User Report Disadvantages**
Users implement	Inconsistent business definitions
Flexible within an individual report	Increased maintenance costs, as reports and formulas are not centrally maintained
No politics to get defined centrally in the universe, RDBMS, or MOLAP cube	More rows than necessary shipped to client, slowing response time
Easy to build!	

I've presented different places in which to put the intelligence. As you can see, there is no clear-cut answer as to which place is best. I have said to end users, "What, are you crazy? That formula is much too complicated and important to be in a report!" I have also said to universe designers, "What, are you crazy? You can't build that object in the universe!" It all depends on the benefits you are hoping to achieve (robustness, flexibility, consistent business definitions), your constraints (cost, skills, technology), as well as the trade-offs (time to implement, politics, maintenance effort, costs). Figure 13-7 is a traffic light table that compares the different places with the trade-offs for each alternative.

Summary of alternatives and trade-offs

- Good
- Use with caution
- Not recommended

	MOLAP	RDBMS	Univ.	UDO	Report
Consistent business terms	Good	Good	Good	Not recommended	Use with caution
Fast queries	Good	Good	Use with caution	Use with caution	Use with caution
Flexibility vs. implementation time	Use with caution	Not recommended	Use with caution	Good	Good
User empowerment	Use with caution	Not recommended	Use with caution	Good	Good
Maintenance effort	Good	Use with caution	Good	Not recommended	Not recommended
Politics	Not recommended	Use with caution	Use with caution	Good	Good
Cost	Not recommended	Use with caution	Good	Good	Good
Skills	Use with caution	Not recommended	Use with caution	Use with caution	Good
Robustness	Good	Use with caution	Use with caution	Not recommended	Use with caution

Figure 13-7. *Deciding where to put the intelligence is a series of trade-offs.*

If a box shows a "good" circle, then the place is good for that criterion in deciding where to put the intelligence; if it shows a "use with caution" circle, then proceed with caution and be aware of the risks; and if it shows a "not recommended" circle, there may be significant risks. For example, putting the intelligence in the RDBMS is great for consistency of business definitions ("good") but is not very flexible ("not recommended"); however, when compared to a universe, the maintenance effort may be somewhat higher because of the effort to redo load programs and rebuild tables ("use with caution" versus "good").

While it is important to consider these design principles in deploying BusinessObjects, it's much more important that you add the intelligence *somewhere!*

The
Complete
Reference

Chapter 14

Minimizing Universe
Maintenance

As the number of universes in your deployment increases, there are a number of ways you can minimize universe maintenance. As users access multiple universes, built by different designers, you need to ensure that the interface is as consistent as possible. Linked universes may help with this. For large-scale deployments, you will want to establish a test environment, either through a test repository or a test universe domain. Finally, with so much meta data built in to the universe, extracting meta data from an ETL tool may minimize your maintenance efforts.

Linked Universes

Linked universes allow a designer to build one master universe called the *kernel* that then is used to build a subsequent universe called a *derived* universe. Companies generally use linked universes in one of several ways:

- A central universe designer builds a reference universe that contains common dimension classes that then get linked to other universes. In the derived universes, a second designer can add universe-specific tables. For example, in Figure 14-1, the tables and corresponding classes and objects for *Time, Products,* and *Customers* exist in the kernel universe. The designer for the Sales universe links to the Kernel

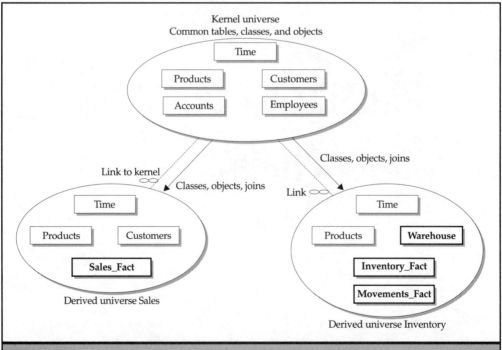

Figure 14-1.   *Linked universes help ensure consistent dimensions across universes.*

to use these common classes and objects. The Sales designer hides classes that sales users do not need (*Accounts, Employees*) and adds new tables to the derived universe (SALES_FACT). This approach can drastically reduce implementation and maintenance efforts, while ensuring a consistent universe interface across multiple universes.

■ A central universe designer maintains one kernel universe that contains all the star schemas in the data warehouse; business unit designers then create smaller *derived* universes that are focused on their individual user group (Figure 14-2). The business unit designer may hide many classes.

■ A derived universe can contain links to more than one kernel universe, so you may also have two small kernel universes that then link to larger derived universes. This approach is good for decentralized development, but unless your company follows some strict design principles, the derived universe may contain duplicates and/or you may find it hard to build a cohesive-looking derived universe. The problems faced with this kind of model are similar to the ones faced when trying to build a central data warehouse from independent data marts.

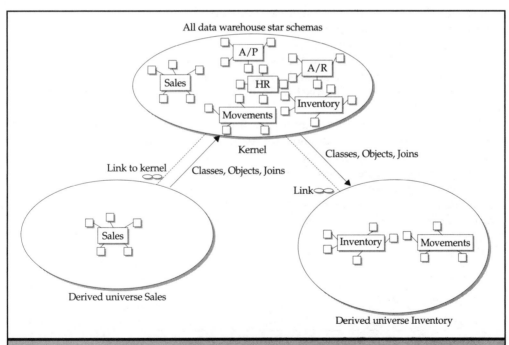

Figure 14-2. *Linked universes allow universe creation to be decentralized yet still consistent.*

What Gets Linked

There are a few gotchas with linked universe, and the first one is that not everything is linked. Not linking everything is both a help and a headache. Universe parameters are not linked. Therefore, within the derived universe, you still need to set Controls for query execution time and result-set size as well as SQL settings that determine if users can create complex queries or create queries that involve multiple fact tables.

Classes and objects generally get linked. However, within the object properties, list of values names, and therefore, customizations do not get linked. For example, if you rename the list of values on *Customer ID* to CUSTID, the derived universe shows a nonsensical name of ~00T0001. When a user tries to use a customized list of values that has been exported to the repository, the user gets an error "No data to fetch." For a list of values that has not been exported, the user can access the list of values. The physical query file (~00T0001.lov) is stored in UserDocs\Universe*DerivedUniverse*. As a workaround, create new objects that need customized lists of values within the derived universe (although even this approach is still somewhat buggy).

In a kernel universe, do not customize lists of values or use the Export with Universe setting.

Join definitions are linked to the derived universe, but not the contexts. The vendor argues that this is the correct procedure, as the derived universe may contain additional joins and contexts. This is true; however, the current approach builds an incorrect universe that contains loops. I would like to see the contexts brought into the derived universe. A universe designer could then add new joins to existing contexts or create new contexts altogether. With the current approach, all contexts must be re-created in the derived universe.

Aggregate navigation settings are linked. If you add a new aggregate table within the derived universe, you can define additional incompatibilities; all the original incompatibilities are still preserved.

Custom hierarchies are not linked. However, as you build new custom hierarchies in the derived universe, when an object name changes in the kernel universe, the new name is included in the derived universe's custom hierarchy. The following table summarizes which components get linked or not:

Universe Component	Linked	Not Linked
Universe parameters		√
Classes and objects	√	
List of values customizations		√
Joins	√	
Contexts		√
Aggregate navigation	√	
Custom hierarchies		√

How Linking Works

The linking works through the repository, so a key requirement for linked universes is that they use a *Secure* Connection. Recall from earlier chapters that there are three possible connection types:

1. *Personal* connections that individual users may create, whose definitions are stored in a local pdac.ssi file.

2. *Shared* connections that are shared via work group folders on a LAN server, whose definitions reside in sdac.ssi.

3. *Secure* connections that either supervisors or designers create and whose definitions reside in the BusinessObjects repository.

The kernel and derived universes must exist within the same universe domain. The kernel universe must have been exported to the repository at least once. This establishes a UNIVERSE_ID that then gets used in the link. You add the link within the derived universe. When you define a link, all the classes, objects, and joins get displayed within the derived universe; they appear gray to differentiate them from other items that you may add directly within the derived universe. The link is one-way and not bidirectional. When you export the derived universe to the repository, Designer updates the UNV_RELATIONS repository table to say the link exists. Table 14-1 shows that the Kernel universe with UNIVERSE_ID=19 is linked to a Derived universe with UNIVERSE_ID=20.

Be aware that linking does not save disk space in the repository. For each object, you will have two rows of data in the repository tables, each with a unique

UNIVERSE_ID	UNI_FILENAME	BASIC_UNV_ID	DERIV_UNV_ID
13	DebitCre		
15	Orders		
16	T_BEACH		
17	AcctRec		
12	Sales		
11	HumanRes		
14	TestFash		
18	DrinkDET		
19	Kernel	19	20
20	Derived		

Table 14-1. *Universe Links Are Defined in the Repository Tables*

UNIVERSE_ID. The *derived_universe*.unv will be somewhat smaller than if you did not link, but not by much. As an example, the size of my small kernel universe is 16K (46 objects, four tables) and the derived universe that contains only one additional table and two new objects is 11K. These sample files are exceedingly small. In a real-world implementation, *universe*.unv files get to be several megabytes. When a user accesses a derived universe, both the kernel universe and the derived universe get imported to the client PC, work group server, or WebIntelligence (WebI) midtier. (Refer to Figure 5-6 for an overview of how the universe gets imported.) If users have to wait patiently for two large *universe*.unv files to be imported (the kernel plus the derived universe), it is not user friendly. File size is more of a problem for companies trying to build a kernel universe with all the information in the data warehouse (Figure 14-2), as these *universe*.unv files are larger than files used in the other two approaches. To minimize this problem, universe designers can 1) move to scheduled modifications so that universe definitions change on a periodic (weekly or biweekly) basis or 2) push the *universe*.unv file to a work group directory for full-client installations or the WebI midtier; do not wait for the modified *derived_universe* .unv and *kernel_universe*.unv file to be downloaded during user login.

Note   *The size of the* universe.unv *file will be larger on a designer's PC than on a user's PC or WebI midtier, as it contains structure information from the data dictionary of the data source. To get the user size of the* universe.unv *file, export the universe to the repository, delete your local copy, and reimport the universe.*

If you are working with an existing universe or trying to combine two kernel universes into one bigger derived one, there are a few more caveats. First, class names must be unique. If the kernel universe contains a duplicate name as the derived universe, then Designer will rename this class upon linking. For example, if *Country* exists in both the derived universe and the kernel universe, it becomes renamed *Country2* in the derived universe. The object names within each class remain the same. The physical table, however, is another story. The table COUNTRY already existed within the derived universe structure. Upon linking, the table name remains the same, but unfortunately, the link table now takes priority and COUNTRY will appear dimmed. This will pose a problem only if you later decide you want to remove the link; you can't easily do this, as your existing *Country* class still needs the original COUNTRY table.

How to Add a Link

The following example uses Figure 14-1 as a model: the kernel universe contains common dimensions; the derived universe contains additional fact tables for a specific user group. For clarity, the kernel universe will be called Kernel and the derived universe will be called Derived. In an actual implementation, use the logical business names (for example, Dimensions and Sales).

As discussed earlier, the kernel universe must contain a secure connection and a designer must have exported the universe to the repository at least once.

1. Create a new universe by selecting File | New from the pull-down menu or clicking New Universe.

2. Designer displays the Universe Parameters. From the Definition tab, enter a universe Name and Description. In the Connection, select the same secure connection used in the kernel universe.

3. Select the Links tab from the Universe Parameters dialog box.

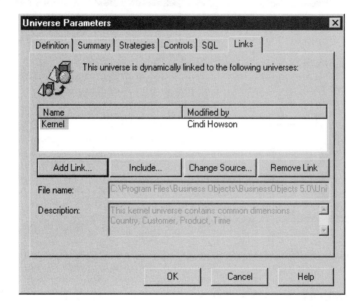

4. Click Add Link.

5. Select the *universe*.unv file to which you want to link. Click Open.

If you have not yet exported the kernel universe to the repository, you will receive an error message. The kernel universe must exist in the repository prior to linking to it.

6. Click OK to close the Universe Parameters dialog box. In the next screen, notice that any linked components are dimmed.

7. You can now re-create any necessary contexts and add new tables, joins, and objects. These items will not be dimmed but will appear as normal in the derived universe.

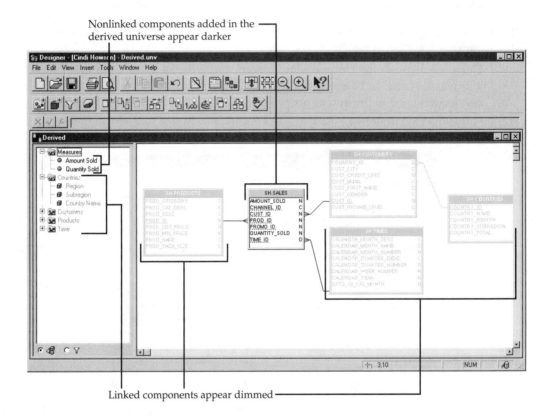

Nonlinked components added in the derived universe appear darker

Linked components appear dimmed

Even if strategies are set to create joins automatically between matching column names (set through File | Parameters, then selecting the Strategies tab), joins are not created automatically between tables in the derived universe and tables in the linked universe.

8. For the link to become active, you must save the universe and export it to the repository. From the pull-down menu, select File | Save, then File | Export, and click OK.

Permanently Importing Universe Components

With some of the pitfalls of linked universes, you may decide it is better to maintain two separate universes rather than linking. You may decide to do this in an initial build, in which case the link helps save time only in the build process and not in universe maintenance, or you may decide to do this after a period of time. Either way, you are essentially importing certain universe components (classes, objects, joins, aggregate navigation. . .not custom hierarchies, contexts) into a new universe. After the initial import, there is no relationship between the derived universe and the kernel universe. To import a kernel universe into a derived universe:

1. Select File | Parameters | Links.

2. If this is a previously linked universe, highlight the Name of the kernel universe you wish to import. If this is an initial build, click Add Link, then select the *universe*.unv file from which you wish to import components. Click Open.

3. Click Include.

All previously dimmed tables, classes, and objects now appear as regular components of the universe.

Once you break the link by clicking Include, you cannot switch back to a link. The Undo button is not available. If you need to recover the link, do not save the universe.

Removing a Link

Before removing a link, you must manually remove any newly created components from the derived universe that use a linked component. This may include

- Joins between linked tables and nonlinked tables
- Condition objects that use a linked object
- WHERE clauses in nonlinked objects that use a linked object
- Contexts that include joins from the kernel universe

To remove a link from a universe, use the pull-down menu to select File | Parameters, then select the Links tab. Highlight the link you wish to remove and click Remove Link. If you have not properly removed all the linked components that were integrated in the derived universe, Designer will give you the following error message:

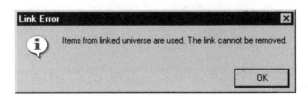

Object Sort Order

When two universes get linked, the initial sort order of the objects is the same in the derived universe and the kernel universe. If you reorder objects in the kernel universe, the sort order is not changed in the derived universe. If you add a class or an object in the derived universe, it stays in the order or position in which it was added.

If you want changes in the sort order in the kernel universe to be reflected in the derived universe, add the following to each *database*.prm file that uses linked universes:

```
[RDBMS]
(GENERAL)
CORE_ORDER_PRIORITY=Y
```

While this change helps synchronize sort orders, the downside is that it also adjusts the sort order for any new classes and objects added to the derived universe. New objects within a linked class get appended to the bottom of the class. New classes get appended to the bottom of any linked classes and cannot appear intermingled with the linked classes.

Approaches to Test and Production Universes

As business intelligence tools have matured, many companies are deploying them across the enterprise. However, all the version management that exists in a mainframe environment is still not quite as robust in the client/server environment. BusinessObjects offers two main approaches to separating development and production environments. The first is through the repository; the second is through domains.

Repository

The BusinessObjects General Supervisor has the capability to create two separate repositories, as shown in Figure 14-3. The benefit of this approach is that the environments are truly separate. Each repository can reside in a separate physical database. The connection string to each physical database is stored in a different key file, for example BOMain.key and Test.key. This can pose maintenance issues as users who need to access both repositories need to have both *repository*.key files installed locally or on a shared network drive. If you are using WebI, you are limited to one repository per cluster manager.

Designers and full-client test users select the appropriate repository/Security Domain during login:

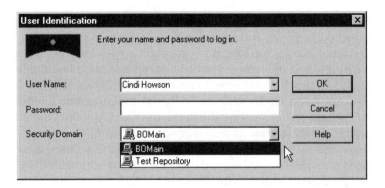

The main risk with the repository approach is that any work done on the PC is not clearly identified as test or production. Recall that all universe development is done via local files on the client PC (step 1, Build, in Figure 14-3). Let's assume you have a test version of the universe Sales.unv. This is stored in the default directory C:\ProgramFiles\ Business Objects\BusinessObjects 5.0\Universe*domain*, where *domain* is the name of the universe domain (the default is Universe). You export this to the test repository so that users can test the changes in the universe (step 2). When the universe is ready to go into production, you export the universe definition to the production repository (step 3). You may need to manually synchronize the connection definition in the new repository. As time goes on, you may make more changes to the

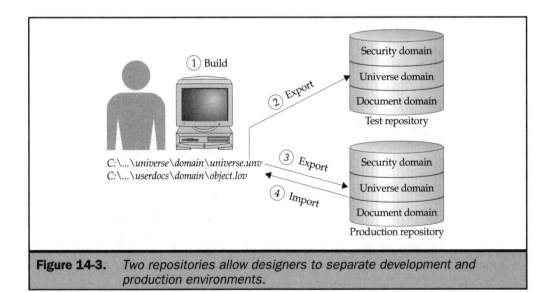

Figure 14-3.   *Two repositories allow designers to separate development and production environments.*

universe and export new versions to the test repository (step 2). However, while trying to solve a production problem, you stop working on the test universe and import the production universe (step 4). You forgot to export the revisions to the test universe to the test repository and just overwrote your test universe! The same thing happens with reports and lists of values. It's very easy to unintentionally overwrite the wrong files, especially as an import can happen automatically when logging into the BusinessObjects user modules. The universe names are the same; the file directory is the same; and the repository name is clearly displayed only during initial login.

Security personnel may like this approach because from the database viewpoint, the security domains must reside in different databases; the environments are truly separate. However, it is a potential nightmare for designers.

Domains

Years ago, the BusinessObjects repository contained everything from documents to user definitions to universe definitions. The concept of domains was introduced in version 4, allowing an administrator to divide more effectively the storage of various components. Large documents could be stored in a separate document domain, while smaller universe components could be stored in a universe domain. The existence of domains also allows an administrator to create separate domains for test and production (Figure 14-4). Each

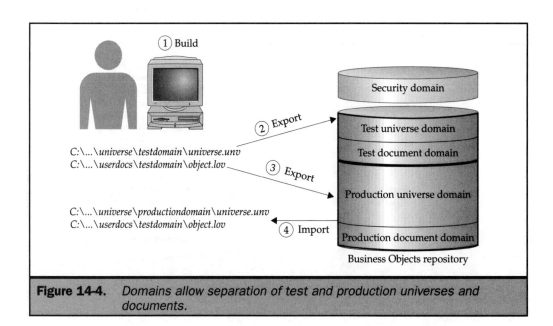

Figure 14-4.   *Domains allow separation of test and production universes and documents.*

domain has its own connection, thereby allowing test universe and document domains to be on one physical database while production universe and document domains can be on a separate database; however, the *security* domain is shared between the two, unlike in the repository approach. Alternatively, the test and production domains can also exist within the same database instance as long as the table owners are different.

The use of domains to separate test and production has some advantages over the use of repositories. First, domains do not require a separate .key file so this approach is also available for WebI users. Second, the domain name is appended to the default folders, minimizing the risk of unintentionally overwriting files. Each domain within a repository requires a unique name. Compare step 4 in Figures 14-3 and 14-4; the import from production goes to a separate folder with a unique domain name in the domain approach, whereas the same folder is used in the repository approach.

As an example, I have a test domain called the default, Universe, and a production domain called UniWeb. When I import the test Sales universe, the Sales.unv file gets stored in the following path:

```
C:\ProgramFiles\Business Objects\BusinessObjects5.0\Universe\Universe
```

The list of values files get stored in the following:

```
C:\Business Objects\BusinessObjects5.0\UserDocs\Universe\Sales
```

When I import the production Sales universe, the production domain name UniWeb gets included in the path:

```
C:\Business Objects\BusinessObjects5.0\Universe\UniWeb
C:\Business Objects\BusinessObjects5.0\UserDocs\UniWeb\Sales
```

Note   *You can modify the default path by selecting Tools | Options and the Save tab; however, the domain name will still get appended to the default path.*

When a designer is ready to export the test universe to production, you select the new domain name from the drop-down box while exporting (File | Export). It's important to pay careful attention to the domain name in the drop-down box as well as the path in the filename. In the next example, I am exporting a universe from the test domain (Universe) to the production domain (UniWeb). During development, or in cases in which you have not separated test and production, the domain name and file pathname

A BETTER UNIVERSE

will be the same; here you are moving from a test environment to production, so they are different.

Export to production domain ——————

Source is test domain ——————

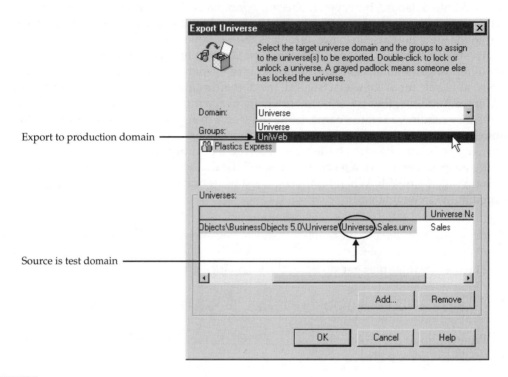

 Note   *If you are working with linked universes, you must manually update the link to reflect the new path of the production universe. Select File | Parameters | Links. Then click Change Source to specify the new production path.*

Documents in Test/Production Domains

When users create a report and there are two universes with the same name, the domain name gets reflected in [brackets]. In the next screen, there are test and production copies of the Kernel and Derived universes.

Domain names

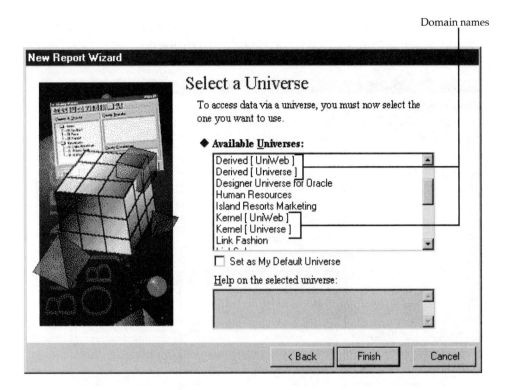

The actual document contains only the name of the universe and not the specific domain, making it easy to put reports into production. When a document finds only the production universe Sales.unv, it automatically uses this universe. There had been problems with earlier versions of WebI when the document still looked for the test universe file from the test domain. This problem existed only in derived universes and not in nonlinked universes; however, this bug was fixed in WebI version 2.6.

The slight exception is with a user or designer who continues to have access to both the test and production *universe*.unv files. These users must manually change the Universe Definition within the document Data Manager. From within the BusinessObjects user module, select Data | View Data and the Definition tab. Under the Definition setting, click the ellipsis button to modify which version of the universe the document should access:

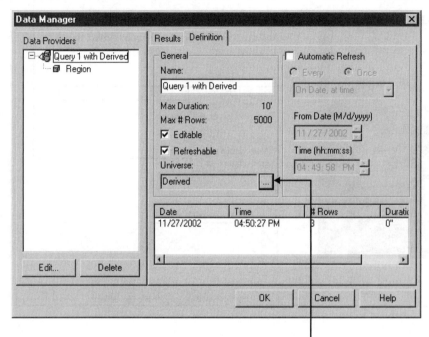

Click here to change the source universe

Multiple Designers

When working with a repository, Designer also allows universe development and maintenance to be distributed across several designers through a locking mechanism. As most development work is done locally on a client PC, it's possible for two designers to work on local copies of the same universe and overwrite each other's work when they export their changes. With the locking mechanism, each designer locks the universe for updates and unlocks it when he or she is finished making changes.

As an example, assume this is a global company with designers in Europe and the west coast of the U.S. There is a nine-hour time-zone difference between continental Europe and Pacific Standard Time. This essentially allows a company 16 hours of development time per day. The European designer imports the Human Resources universe (File | Import). To lock the universe for updates from other designers, the European designer *must* double-click the universe name. The padlock symbol appears next to the Human Resources universe to show it is locked, shown here:

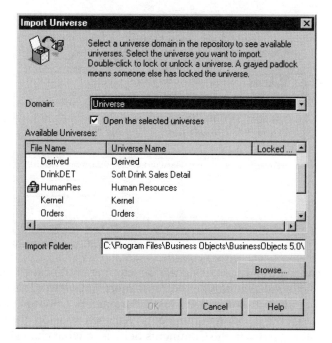

When any other designers log into Designer and try to import a universe, a dimmed padlock appears next to the locked universe. In the Locked column, the name of the designer who has locked the universe appears under the Locked by column. If you are the designer with the lock, your name is not displayed to you in the Locked by column. In the next screen, Cindi Howson has locked the Human Resources universe, and

Megan Michelle has locked the Sales universe. At this point, other designers may still import a copy of the universe, but they may not export changes to the universe.

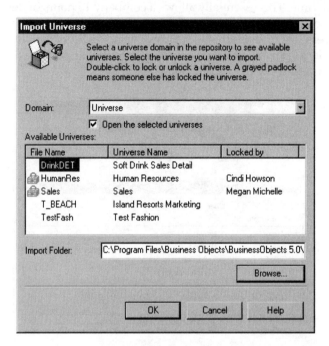

In environments with multiple designers developing and/or maintaining one universe, the universe revision number becomes more important. To see the revision number, select from the pull-down menu File | Parameters | Summary tab. Notice in the next screen that the revision number is 14. For each revision, the two universe designers have entered notes in the Comments field as to what changes were made in each revision. To enter a new line of text in the Comments field, use CTRL-ENTER. BusinessObjects assigns a new revision number each time the universe is exported to the repository, not necessarily each time the universe has been modified. Note in the following screen that revisions 4 and 6–8 contain no modification notes. It's possible that the universe was exported to the repository without either designer making changes to the universe.

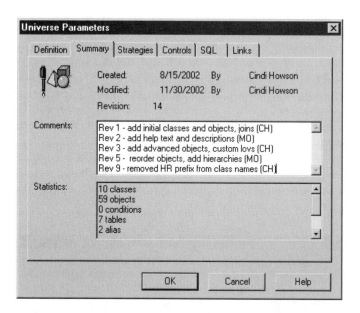

In the following example, when the designer in Europe finishes the workday and wants to allow the designer on the Pacific coast the ability to make additional changes, the initial designer must unlock the universe when exporting it to the repository. To unlock the universe, double-click the universe name; the padlock no longer appears next to the File Name.

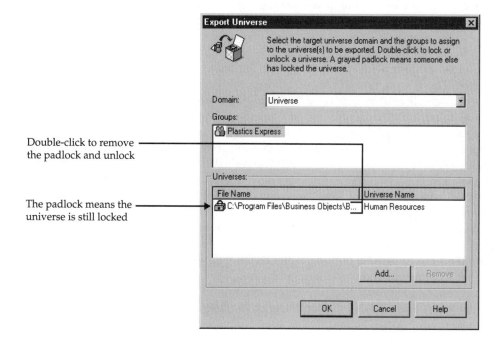

Double-click to remove the padlock and unlock

The padlock means the universe is still locked

A BETTER UNIVERSE

This last step can cause some frustration in distributed development environments. If the initial designer leaves for the day, without exporting changes to the universe, the second designer cannot make any changes. If the first designer exports the universe and forgets to unlock the universe, there is a workaround. The second designer can import the changes without a lock. Any changes the second designer makes must be e-mailed to the first designer, who has the lock. The first designer can then export the changes. Risky indeed! If you are fortunate enough to be in the same time zone, call the person to remove the lock.

BusinessObjects provides a safeguard in the event that the second designer tries to make changes on an older version of the universe. With each export to the repository, Designer will assign a new revision number. A universe with an older revision number cannot be exported to the repository. Designer generates the following error message:

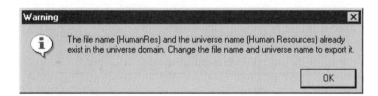

Incremental Export

Incremental export is one of those features that is great in theory but not-yet-great in practice. Proceed with caution if you decide to use this. As designers make changes to universes, the changes are tracked through the version number and through entries in a table in the repository UNV_AUDIT. With an extremely large universe, it's possible to export to the repository the most recent changes, rather than the entire universe. When either a user or designer imports a new version of the universe, only those changes get imported. This is wonderful if you are talking about a 5MB universe that only had a few minor changes. If you are generally dealing with small universes in which designer and user imports are fairly quick, then you can skip this discussion entirely.

Problems can arise when a user has a version of a universe that is two or more versions behind. For example, a user has version 10 of a universe, and the repository contains version 12. This may happen if the user did not log into BusinessObjects while version 11 was available. The user may receive an error "Could not import the universe," and other errors. In general, the user could delete the local *universe*.unv file to recover from the error.

However, a designer may also receive this error. For a designer to avoid this error, one must revert to a saved version of the *universe*.unv file and remove the incremental setting. This can cause a lot of rework. In this respect, with Designer 5.1.6, I recommend you limit incremental updates to large universes, while in development only. Once users begin accessing the production universe, force full updates. To enable incremental updates, select File | Tools | General. Check the Allow incremental export box, as shown next.

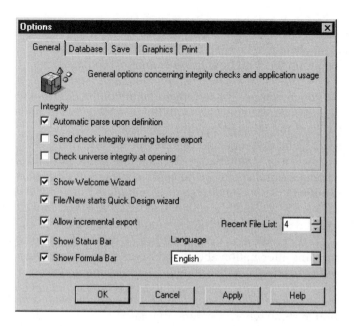

Integration with an ETL Tool

When your BusinessObjects implementation is part of an overall data warehouse initiative, you may be able to further minimize universe maintenance by integrating metadata from an ETL tool. An ETL tool has three primary goals:

- **Extract**   Get the information out of the source system.
- **Transform**   Cleanse the data and make it consistent regardless of where the information originated.
- **Load**   Load the data into data marts or data warehouses in a star or snowflake schema.

As ETL tools have matured, these three components have become easier, more graphical, and more robust. Many tools now include business and process intelligence to extract data from leading systems such as SAP, PeopleSoft, J.D. Edwards, or Lawson and to build corresponding data marts that focus on specific processes within an organization. What once was a nuts-and-bolts process of creating code to facilitate extracts, now is a complete set of tools to create interrelated procedures and to build business-oriented, dimensional views of the data. With this evolution, ETL tools contain more metadata: information about where the data originates, how it is transformed, business names, and uses. The BusinessObjects universe also contains metadata in the form of objects (meaningful business names), object descriptions (help text, calculations, and potentially, source system information), and joins (relationships between tables).

In an effort to ensure one consistent business definition, ETL and BI vendors have worked to enable metadata to be shared between the two platforms.

In order to better understand how this information is shared, refer to the definitions in Table 14-2.

The degree to which you use the full functionality of the ETL tool will affect how useful it is for you to integrate your tool with BusinessObjects. An initial build of the universe is fairly easy and straightforward. However, maintaining the universe as underlying physical tables change and understanding where the data originated can add a significant amount of maintenance. Recall in the discussion how linked universes help reduce maintenance and ensure consistent business definitions across universes that use the same objects. Theoretically, sharing metadata from an ETL tool brings this consistency and leverage to yet a higher level. In Chapter 6, you looked at how strategy files use SQL to read data dictionary information to build the initial classes and objects. With ETL tools, a BusinessObjects bridge reads ETL metadata to build the universe. ETL metadata contains information above and beyond what standard data dictionary tables contain and can be used in the following ways in the universe:

- The source system / ERP `TABLE.COLUMN` name is displayed in the object description to show where the data originated.

- Business names established in the ETL tools become the universe object names, thus ensuring consistent terminology across multiple BI tools and multiple universes.

Term	Explanation
CWM	The Common Warehouse Metamodel (CWM) is a specification that describes metadata interchange among data warehousing, business intelligence, knowledge management, and portal technologies.
XMI	XML Metadata Interchange. It allows tools to share metadata information through the XML file format. Also referred to as CWMI.
XML	The Extensible Markup Language is a file format for sharing data.
Metadata	Information about the data, including from which source system or ERP system it originates, how a number is calculated, transformation logic, and business terminology.
API	Application Programming Interface.
CWMI	XML-based file for exchanging metadata. Also referred to as XMI.

Table 14-2. *Glossary of Terms for Integrating Metadata Between ETL and BI Tools*

- As additional tables or columns become available in the data warehouse, their definitions can be imported into the BusinessObjects universes.
- Primary and foreign keys that form star and snowflake schemas build the joins.

With a bridge to the metadata, you can extract information from an ETL tool to build the universe. Business Objects offers two vendor-specific bridges and released a new Universal Metadata Bridge in Q1 2003.

Informatica and IBM Metadata Bridges

Business Objects offers vendor-specific bridges to Informatica's PowerMart and IBM's Data Warehouse Manager for DB2. Informatica's PowerMart and IBM's Data Warehouse Manager for DB2. The BusinessObjects Metadata Bridge accesses metadata within each ETL tool's repository. For Informatica, the Metadata Bridge communicates with the Informatica repository through an API, as shown in Figure 14-5. With DB2, IBM publishes its metadata in an Information Catalog that BI tools access through ODBC. The Metadata Bridge then allows a designer to use this information to build a new universe. In version 5.0 of the Informatica bridge, the universe object IDs (refer to Chapter 8, "Warning: Object IDs") were not preserved when the bridge was used to update a universe; this has been corrected in version 5.1. The IBM bridge does not allow universe updates and can only be used for the initial universe build.

Universal Metadata Bridge

While the preceding approach works, it puts the burden on Business Objects to develop and maintain a bridge for each ETL tool. Meanwhile, the Common Warehouse Metamodel (CWM) has been gaining industry acceptance. CWM uses a number of standards to determine how metadata can be exchanged between different tools. CWMI or XMI specifies how metadata can be exchanged via XML. In Q1 2003, BusinessObjects released Universal Metadata Bridge that will read XMI formats. As more ETL vendors support CWM and XMI, designers can use BusinessObjects' Universal Metadata Bridge to read metadata from ETL-generated XMI files and build universes. With Business Objects

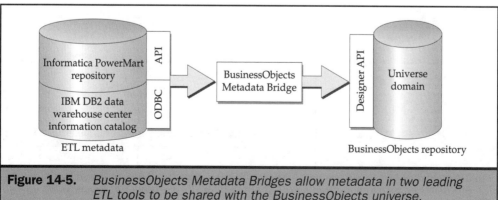

Figure 14-5.   *BusinessObjects Metadata Bridges allow metadata in two leading ETL tools to be shared with the BusinessObjects universe.*

acquisition of Acta, Data Integrator (the renamed and updated Acta ETL tool) will be the first ETL-tool to leverage the Universal Metadata Bridge. Figure 14-6 shows how the new bridge works.

The Universal Metadata Bridge has several new features lacking in the Informatica- and IBM-specific bridges, such as batch updates and improved update handling. Previously, a designer could only interactively update a universe. With the new bridge, universe updates can be run in batch mode on a scheduled basis. As well, designers could previously only specify whether or not to update object names and descriptions. With the Universal Metadata Bridge, a designer can specify *how* to update them, either to replace the descriptions or to combine existing object descriptions with new object descriptions from the ETL metadata. The bridge also allows you to compare the metadata from the ETL tool versus the universe before updating the universe.

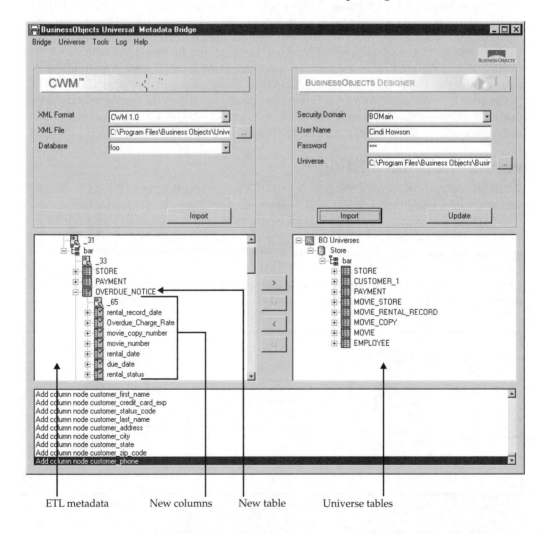

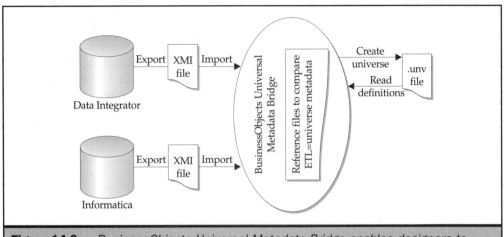

Figure 14-6.   *BusinessObjects Universal Metadata Bridge enables designers to build universes from any tool that supports XMI.*

With the Universal Metadata Bridge, BusinessObjects creates a reference file to specify how each TABLE.COLUMN in the ETL import file is associated with a universe class and object. As a designer updates the universe with a new XMI file, the Bridge compares information from the XMI file with information in the reference file to correctly update existing objects. This helps preserve the unique OBJECT_IDS and ensure that user reports continue to work correctly.

For companies that use Informatica as an ETL tool, designers can choose between either the Informatica Bridge that communicates with the Informatica repository via the API or the new Universal Metadata Bridge that works with an XMI file. With the former bridge, users can import the Business Name from the Informatica repository to be used as the object name in the universe. Unfortunately, the Business Name is not included in Informatica's XMI file as the Business Name is not part of the standard CWM specification. So while designers would benefit by using the Universal Bridge for batch scheduling and improved update handling, the lack of a Business Name will limit its usefulness.

Not surprisingly, the integration between Business Object's Data Integrator and the Universal Metadata Bridge is tighter and does include the Business Name. Here, Data Integrator has its own XML format, whereas Informatica uses the CWM format.

Summary

As the number of universes in your deployment increases, so does the cost and complexity to maintain the universes. Linking universes to reduce maintenance is great in theory, but problems around customized lists of values and confusion in remembering what is not linked makes it difficult in practice. As you modify the universe and want to test the changes with pilot users before making it widely available, you can create a test and production environment either through multiple repositories or multiple domains. Multiple domains are easier to handle. When you have multiple designers modifying the same universe, Designer offers a good check-in/check-out capability to tell you when a universe is being modified by another designer. If you use an ETL tool to build the data warehouse or marts, the Metadata Bridge products can help you reduce universe maintenance.

Chapter 15

Almost There

This is a bit of a loose-ends chapter in which you finalize and quality-assure the universe, prepare universe documentation, and monitor system usage. If you have had close conversations with the business users and parsed objects as you built them, you may find that some of these steps are perfunctory. If, on the other hand, you built the universe in isolation and didn't test along the way, you will find this is an intensive time to recycle the universe.

Universe Integrity

As you have built the universe, you have done a number of integrity checks. In modifying the SQL of individual objects, you should have Parsed each one. The Parse validates that you have entered the SQL correctly. In building joins, you have detected cardinalities and loops to create contexts and aliases.

The overall universe integrity check becomes a final chance to catch anything you may have missed in earlier stages. If you are using linked universes, it checks the integrity in both the kernel and derived universes. It also will determine if anything has changed in the data source structure that would make an existing object or join invalid.

To check the integrity of a universe, select the pull-down menu Tools | Check Integrity or select the Check Integrity button from the toolbar.

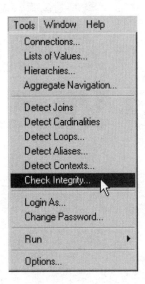

Designer presents you with the following dialog box:

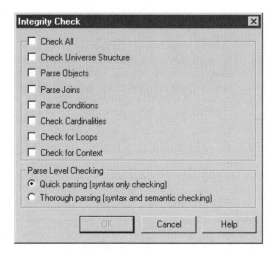

A BETTER UNIVERSE

At this point, you can choose Check All to have Designer perform all possible checks, or you can choose to check the integrity of individual components. Table 15-1 explains the purpose of each check.

Option	Purpose
Check All	Checks all components within the universe.
Check Universe Structure	Compares the structure information in the Structure pane with the tables and columns within the RDBMS. If there is a difference between the two, Designer will give a warning. Tables within the Table Browser that have been removed or renamed but that are not in the Structure pane will not cause an error. If you regularly refresh your structure with View | Refresh Structure, this check should return no errors.
Parse Objects	Similar to the Parse button within the Object definition, this verifies that the SQL SELECT and WHERE syntax is correct and that the *TABLE.COLUMN* for each object is valid.
Parse Conditions	Similar to Parse Objects but checks predefined conditions only. This does not check the WHERE clause of regular objects.
Check Cardinalities	This will check if the cardinality has been defined for each join. It will not detect the relationship between the tables.
Check For Loops	This will detect any loops and inform you if they were resolved with an alias or context. Designer will list any loops that have not been resolved.

Table 15-1.   *Settings to Check the Integrity of Universe Components*

Option	Purpose
Check For Context	When you start using contexts, you must ensure that all joins defined belong to a context. The one exception is a shortcut join. These do not need to belong to a context but will generate an integrity check error if they are not defined to one; you can ignore this error as it does not cause a problem during query execution.
Quick Parsing	Quick parsing checks the syntax only.
Thorough Parsing	This provides more extensive checking than quick parsing and can be slow to execute on very large universes. For example, it will check that the SQL statement format matches the object type. If the SQL statement includes a date field and the object type is set to character, the check will return an error.

Table 15-1.   *Settings to Check the Integrity of Universe Components* (continued)

To perform the check, select the desired components and click OK. The following screen shows the results from Check All with Quick Parsing. Designer groups each warning according to the component tested, as listed in Table 15-1. Next to each component, Designer will display an OK or an Error count. Initially, any warnings and errors are collapsed. To see the full error, click the + sign next to the component.

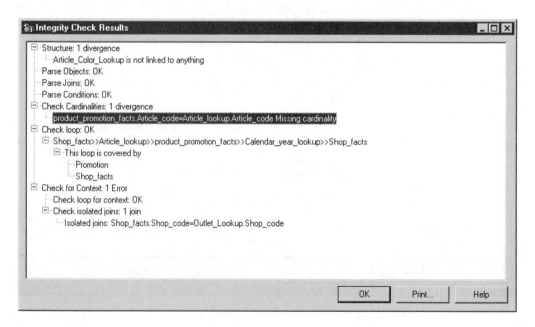

Under Structure, you have one divergence or potential problem. The table ARTICLE_COLOR_LOOKUP exists in the universe structure but is not joined to anything. Designer does not list this as an error, because it may be valid for one table to exist on its own. If there are no objects associated with this table, you can delete the table from the Structure pane. If there are objects that use this table, then you need to add a join from the ARTICLE_COLOR_LOOKUP to the fact table and then include it in the context.

Under Cardinalities, you have one divergence in that no cardinality was defined for the join from PRODUCT_PROMOTION_FACTS to ARTICLE_LOOKUP. Designer does not list this as an absolute error, because cardinality detection is used primarily to propose contexts. The absence of cardinality settings will not create an invalid universe or user error. To add the cardinality, you can double-click the join statement and Designer will present you with the Edit Join dialog box. Note that the cardinality has not been defined:

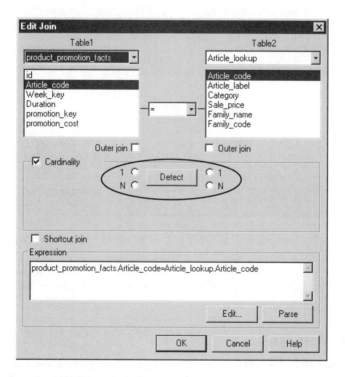

Under Check loop, Designer lists the status as OK. There are no errors within this component. You can expand this folder to display any loops and the contexts or aliases used to correct them.

Under the Context check, you have a genuine error that can cause errors when a user executes a query. There is a join between SHOP_FACTS and OUTLET_LOOKUP that does not belong to any context. Once you start using contexts, all joins must belong to at least one context. The exception is shortcut joins (see Chapter 7). By definition, these joins are most often used outside of fact tables and contexts. Therefore, even if they produce an error during the integrity check, they still work correctly, as the shortcut join is used only when a user builds a query that involves only the two tables.

In the following screen, Check All was selected with Thorough Parsing. Note that Designer reported four more errors over the preceding check. Thorough checking may take longer to run for large universes.

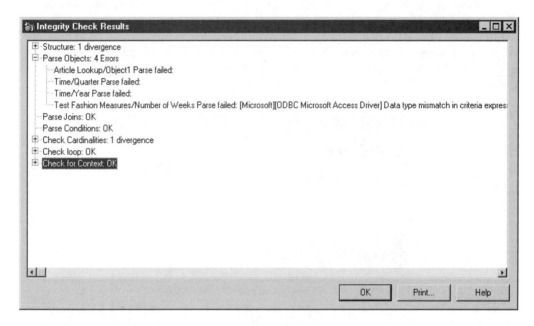

In some cases, the results will inform you of an error but not the cause. *Time/Year* Parse failed because the object type is set to Date although the physical database column is Character. The measure object *Number of Weeks* failed because it used a SUM on a character field. You must either use COUNT or convert the character field to a numeric field before using the SUM function.

Checking as You Go

With the preceding two object errors, had you clicked Parse during the object modification, you also would have received an error. Hence a very important lesson: unless you like solving many problems at once, check the universe integrity as you make modifications. Designer allows you to set options that will force you to adhere to this practice. These options are global for all universes you develop from this particular workstation. From the pull-down menu, select Tools | Options and the General tab.

In the Integrity box, set the option Automatic parse upon definition to have Designer check the SQL syntax whenever you add or modify an object or join. With this setting, you will not be able to add objects or joins that contain errors. Designer will not warn you about isolated joins when you create them, but it will prevent you from adding joins that contain an incorrect SQL statement (for example, if you define a complex join and skip a parenthesis or join operator).

The second setting, Send check integrity warning before export, will prompt you to do an integrity check prior to exporting the universe to the repository. The warning is not particularly intelligent; if you do an integrity check on all components but did not select the Check All option, Designer will still remind you to do an integrity check. With this setting, you cannot export a universe that has unrecoverable errors. For example, class and object names are limited to 35 characters. When you select File | Export, Designer automatically runs the integrity check and will not allow you to export the universe until this error is resolved. Other errors such as isolated joins or SQL errors can still be exported and corrected at a later time. Designer prompts you to check the universe integrity prior to export:

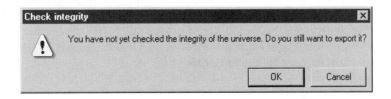

The last setting, Check universe integrity at opening, forces an integrity check
as soon as you open the universe. While this is a useful reminder to resolve errors,
I personally find it annoying when used in conjunction with the first two settings.

 *If you use either of these last two options, consider setting Quick Parse as the default.
Thorough Parsing can be slow on large universes and cannot be interrupted. You can
always set Thorough Parsing for checks as you specifically request them.*

Universe Documentation

Designer allows you to print a report to generate documentation on the universe. Years
ago, these printouts provided only limited information. Now they cover almost all
components of the universe. To select what information gets included in a particular
printout, use the pull-down menu to set Tools | Options | Print.

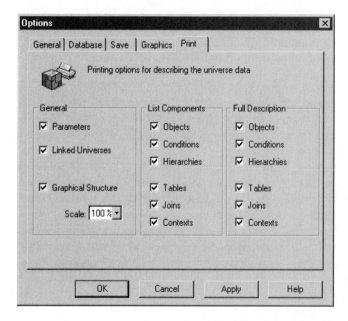

In general, options under List Component will generate a simple list (refer to Table 15-2).
Options under Full Description will give the complete SQL statements or Object Properties.
When you select items from the Full Description, it's advisable to set your print options
to landscape. Select File | Page Setup and then set the Orientation to Landscape. Sample
reports are shown in Figures 15-1 through 15-3.

A BETTER UNIVERSE

Print Option	Information Printed
Parameters	Universe-specific parameters set through File | Parameters such as the universe filename and description, revision number, total classes and objects, strategy settings, and SQL controls. Refer to Chapter 6 for more information on these settings.
Linked Universes	When set, the name of the kernel universe is displayed plus all relevant objects, joins, and tables. Each is marked with the name of the kernel universe.
Graphical Structure	Displays the tables and joins as they appear in the Structure pane.
List Components: Objects	Displays the class and each object name.
Full Description: Objects	Displays all the properties for each object including object type, SELECT statement, WHERE clause, list of values settings, and so on.
List Components: Conditions	Displays the class and object names for condition objects.
Full Description: Conditions	Gives the description defined for each condition object as well as the SQL statement.
List Components: Hierarchies	Displays the Class equivalent or dimension name of any custom hierarchies.
Full Description: Hierarchies	Displays the individual objects within the custom hierarchies.
List Component: Tables	Displays the physical table names that appear in the universe structure.
Full Description: Tables	Displays the columns and their field types for each physical table from the data source that appears in the universe structure.
List Components: Joins	Lists the simple join statements.
Full Description: Joins	Describes the cardinality between the tables and specifies whether or not the join is an outer join.
List Components: Contexts	Lists the names of the contexts, which are fairly meaningless without seeing which joins belong to which context (Full Description).
Full Description: Context	Displays the context name as well as each join that is included in the context.

Table 15-2. *Print Options to Document the Universe*

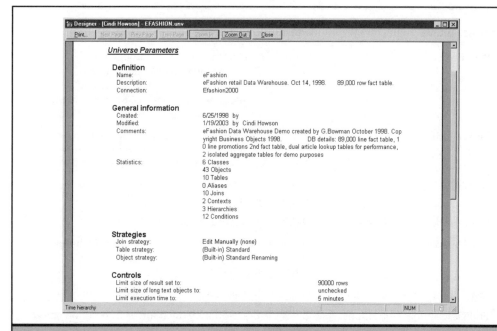

Figure 15-1. *Print parameters displays all the settings in File | Parameters.*

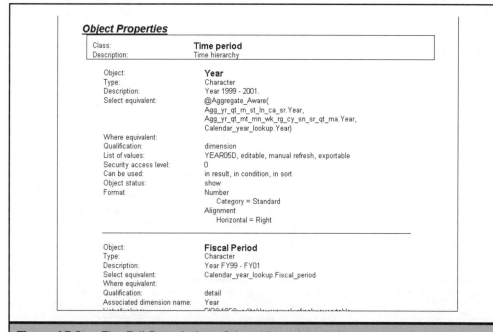

Figure 15-2. *The Full Description of the object shows object properties and object formats, whereas the list gives only the object name.*

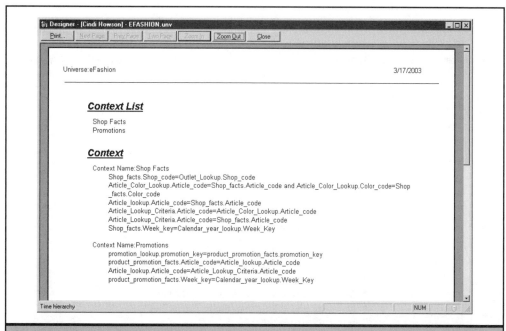

Figure 15-3.   *List Component Contexts gives a list of the context, whereas Full Description Context gives the joins that belong to the context.*

Quality Assurance Checklist

Before distributing the universe to the users, it is good to have a quality assurance session to review the universe. Table 15-3 provides a checklist that covers recommendations from the previous chapters. A review session is different from an integrity check; the integrity check ensures that the universe is technically correct but does nothing to ensure that the universe follows best practices or will be successful with the users.

Chapter	Category	Item	Date Reviewed	Comments and Exceptions
5	Overall Universe	• Subject area corresponds to business goal • Target user group identified • Number of objects appropriate for target user group		

Table 15-3.   *Quality Assurance Checklist*

Chapter	Category	Item	Date Reviewed	Comments and Exceptions
6	Universe Parameters	• Universe description clear and complete • Connection synchronized with database username and password • Controls adequate for query results • Incremental export disabled		
14		• Linked universe points to same domain • SQL settings generate correct results (recommend all enabled) • Query test for split SQL with multiple measures • Query test for split SQL with multiple contexts		
7	Joins	• Joined fields indexed • Join fields that contain nulls use an outer join • All loops are resolved with a context • Tables with multiple meanings have an alias • Joins belong to at least one context (excluding short-cut joins) • Joins with composite keys are entered as complex joins • Short-cut joins created for faster join paths not through fact table		
8	Objects	• Class names logical and meaningful • Classes sorted logically • Dimension objects point to lookup table • Objects not used for drill-down marked as Detail objects • Column format and object type match • Measure includes SQL aggregate function • Separate measure provided for *average* unit price, and so on • Objects include description • Objects sorted logically within class (top to bottom for drill-down) • Object names are customer-oriented, clear, consistent, and concise • Object format is set, particularly for numeric ID fields • Unnecessary hidden objects removed		
8 and 12		• Security access levels match Supervisor settings • Object uses are sensical (recommend all enabled)		

Table 15-3.   *Quality Assurance Checklist* (continued)

Chapter	Category	Item	Date Reviewed	Comments and Exceptions
9	List of Values	• List of values disabled for measure objects • List of values disabled for nonsensical detail objects • Long list of values are customized with prompt • Meaningless ID fields customized to include name or description • List of values access dimension table not fact table • Object.lov file does not unintentionally contain data • Export with universe set only for custom list of values • Shared list of values used for common dimension objects		
10	Advanced Objects	• Condition objects created for common conditions, particularly time • Condition objects use index or give satisfactory query performance • Objects with prompts are not overly restrictive • Prompted field is indexed or gives satisfactory query performance • Count objects point to key field or use Distinct • Ratios use SUM aggregate correctly SUM()/SUM()		
13		• Ratios in fact table recalculated in universe		
13		• Candidate objects for fact/dimension table insertion identified		
10	Aggregate Objects	• Aggregate table included in universe • Aggregate table has its own context • SUM function inserted correctly within Aggregate aware @ AGGREGATE_AWARE (SUM(AGG1)), SUM(AGG2), SUM(DETAIL)) • Incompatible objects set • Incompatible objects include only relevant context • Query test accesses aggregate table and detail table as intended • Query test verifies summary answers match answers from detail table		

Table 15-3. *Quality Assurance Checklist* (continued)

Chapter	Category	Item	Date Reviewed	Comments and Exceptions
11	Hierarchies	• Custom Hierarchies created • Hierarchies sorted from top to bottom • Separate hierarchies for ID and Description objects • UDS Maps enabled at correct levels • Standard reports created in WebI		
12	Supervisor	• Password synchronized with universe connection • Object level security matches universe object • Row restrictions do not cancel each other out • Resources linked at appropriate level so inheritance flows down • Linking resources is used more than disabling resources • Timestamps used on limited basis		
	Other	• Backup copy of universe available • Relevant documentation printed • Benchmark reports identified		

Table 15-3. *Quality Assurance Checklist* (continued)

The following people should ideally be involved in a quality assurance review:

■ **DBA**   The DBA will help verify the correctness of certain SQL statements, assess their impact on response time if there are advanced SQL functions, consider join strategies to generate the fastest queries possible, and identify opportunities to create aggregate tables and to tune indexes for popular condition objects.

■ **Data modeler/architect**   The data modeler or architect will help identify any possible problems with joins that arise from missing data—for example, if a particular field is not required. This person can also review business terminology, object descriptions, customized lists of values, and aliases (CUSTOMER versus CUSTOMER_SHIP_TO versus CUSTOMER_SOLD_TO). A source system expert may also be helpful in this role.

■ **Power user/report authors**   Power users and report authors will provide input on the overall appearance, organization, and functionality of the universe. Did you, as the designer, actually deliver what they hoped for? Will they be able to build the reports they need to build using the current design of the universe? Power users will also provide input on similar items to the data modeler.

■ **Other designers**   If your company has multiple universe designers, it's useful to get an objective opinion from another designer on the universe. This is an excellent way to share tips and techniques and to provide a consistent user interface across universes (as an alternative to linked universes).

A Universe about Universes: ManagerO

Prior to printed reports, one could get universe documentation only through another universe: managerO. With printed reports directly from Designer, Business Objects had intended to eliminate managerO. ManagerO is structured strictly for Oracle-based repositories, but you can modify it to work with other databases. While Oracle may be the predominant database in BusinessObjects deployments, the vendor would clearly have to update managerO for other databases if it were a more predominant offering. You'll notice that managerO is never discussed in any documentation. However, the vendor is kind enough to still supply it via the Freeware directory on the BusinessObjects installation CD. Despite greatly improved printed reports, I still find managerO a really useful tool. It contains information not available in the printed reports. Additionally, if you wish to print information about individual objects or classes, ad hoc reporting with this universe gives you more control over the output than do the standard Designer reports.

To install managerO, copy it from the Freeware directory to your Universe folder. Launch Designer and select File | Open | managerO. Select File | Parameters to modify the default connection to point to your particular Universe Domain.

ManagerO organizes information about the universe into the following classes:

■ *Universe Parameters*

■ *Class Details*

■ *Object Details*

■ *Condition Details*

■ *Universe Tables*

■ *Joins*

■ *Contexts*

■ *Hierarchies*

If your repository is not stored in an Oracle database, you will need to modify any objects that make use of nonstandard SQL functions. For example, *Object Security Access Level* uses DECODE to translate the numeric settings in the repository to match the meaningful descriptions you see in Designer. To identify these objects, print the Full Description for Objects and look for SQL your database does not support.

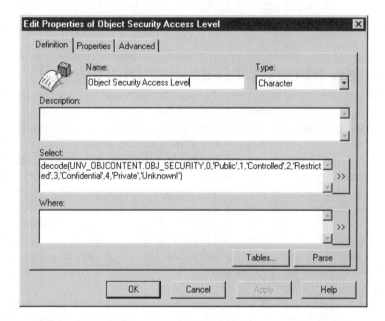

In Chapter 8 (Table 8-2), I warned that you must take care in renaming objects to ensure the OBJECT_ID is preserved. This is a great example of information that is accessible through managerO and not the standard Designer reports. Following are some additional objects that provide information not otherwise available through the printed reports:

- *Number of Universes*
- *Number of Linked Universes*
- *Universe ID*
- *Version* shows the revision number listed under File | Parameters | Summary
- *Linked Universe ID*
- *Incompatible Tables*, set through Tools | Aggregate Navigation (where there are incompatible objects)
- *Object Table Name*, set through Object Properties, Tables button. While the printed reports will show the table used in the SQL SELECT or WHERE statement, it will not show tables selected that may be used to force a join (see Chapter 7).

Evolving the Universe

For designers used to a waterfall development approach, welcome to the realities of business intelligence: it's all iterative. The universe is never finished. Your first universe is version 1, which will evolve as you elicit user input, the business environment changes, the applications evolve, the source systems/data marts change, and the technology changes. Figure 15-4 illustrates how a universe evolves over time.

You normally update the universe as the first users see it. Ideally, pilot users will *preview* the universe as you are developing it to ensure it will fulfill the intended business goals and requirements. This can be in a formal joint application development (JAD) session or with one user looking over the designer's shoulder. It is not a pilot! Until you have done a thorough quality assurance review, users do not access the universe. As a result of the quality assurance review, you may make more changes, perhaps to correct

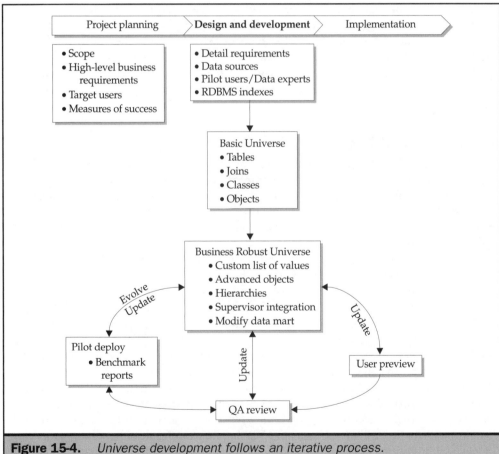

Figure 15-4.   *Universe development follows an iterative process.*

errors, tweak performance, or make classes and objects more meaningful. Following quality assurance, the universe goes to a pilot phase. The goal of the pilot is to identify errors or opportunities for improvement you could not uncover yourself; the goal of the preview is to tell you if the universe development looks as users expect.

Finally, users begin accessing the universe in a controlled way via a pilot. This is your first glimpse of payback for all your development efforts. If your company is new to ad hoc reporting, be sure to choose your pilot users wisely; casual users accustomed to fixed-screen DSS systems will be overwhelmed unless you provide them with parameterized reports. The pilot is typically a limited number of power users who understand the data and are fairly computer literate. For ad hoc access, they may be accountants or business analysts used to writing their own SQL or 4GL reports. The pilot uncovers more objects that you may need to build, modify, or remove hiccups in the supervisor/universe integration, and so on. Modify the universe following the pilot period and before you move to full-scale implementation.

As you make major changes to the universe, it's helpful to document these in the Comments (File | Parameters | Summary). Also, I recommend you keep a separate backup copy of the *universe*.unv file. In the event of a disk crash or other hardware failure, you will be able to restore the entire repository and the universes if you regularly back up the repository database. However, as you revise individual universes, there is no way to recover a particular version from the repository; keeping a copy of the *universe*.unv file allows you to do this.

Benchmark Reports

During the pilot, it is important that either the designer or the power users develop standard reports that can be used to benchmark universe performance. Clearly, the universe is only one component that affects performance. However, if BusinessObjects is the tool that accesses the data, it is all the users will see and, therefore, will get blamed entirely for performance issues. Users rarely say, "the data mart is slow," but frequently say "BusinessObjects is slow today."

Some companies do a formal stress test during the pilot phase. Although BusinessObjects does not provide integrated benchmarking tools, tools are available from third-party companies. For example, some companies use Compuware's *QA*Load to simulate user load on the system. One federal agency used it to simulate RDBMS and WebIntelligence (WebI) utilization for, initially, 25 concurrent users. As they neared 125 concurrent users, they experienced transaction failures; the RDBMS did not respond to WebI within specified time limits. Following the test, the agency went from one WebI server to a cluster manager with three nodes. This kind of controlled testing is much easier to manage than uncovering performance issues during actual implementation.

Figure 15-5 provides a conceptual overview of the phases of a user query, starting with the initial login and finishing with the presentation of a formatted report. In a full-client implementation, all the software and BOMain.key can reside either on the individual

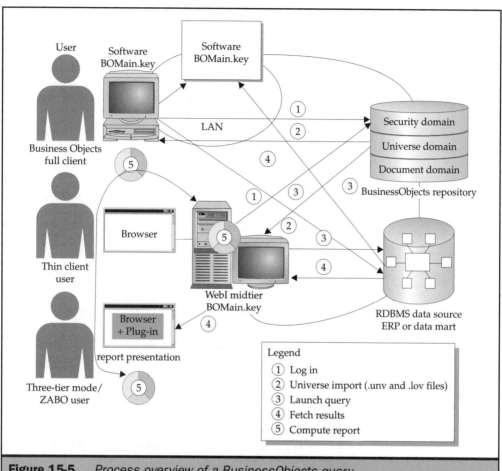

Figure 15-5.   *Process overview of a BusinessObjects query*

user PCs or on a workgroup application server. WebI can be deployed in either two-tier mode, in which all the software resides on the midtier and users access it via a browser, or in three-tier mode (ZABO), in which the software gets installed on the user PC via a plug-in. With three-tier mode, the WebI midtier still provides the connectivity to the source databases, whereas in full-client or two-tier mode, all the database drivers must also reside on the client PC. Figure 15-5 shows only one WebI server—although clearly, one could have a cluster manager and multiple nodes. With three-tier mode, the additional bottleneck becomes the initial software installation and subsequent software updates. Table 15-4 explains the potential bottlenecks during each of these phases in full-client and thin-client modes.

Phase	Description	Potential Bottlenecks
1	Repository Login	• For full client, LAN performance to access BOMain.key and software if not installed on local disk. • For full client, WAN performance for client PC to access Repository RDBMS; for thin client, WAN performance for WebI server to access repository RDBMS. • RDBMS load if a significant number of users simultaneously access repository, security domain. • Security domain if the security settings are complex and use timestamps, resources enabled and disabled • For WebI, load on WebI Cluster Manager.
2	Universe Import	• Size of universe and kernel universe if linked; the *universe*.unv files get imported to the client PC or WebI midtier. • Number of exported custom lists of values, as the *object*.lov files get imported for each user. • Size of exported custom lists of values that contain data, as this increases the size of each *object*.lov file. • Size of universe domain. • WAN performance to transport universe definitions. • For WebI and application servers: only the first user accessing the modified universe is affected.
3	Launch Query: Analyzing and Executing	• Number of users concurrently logging into RDBMS. • If using row-level security within data warehouse, complexity • of security model and number of views to implement. • If accessing source ERP, current load on system to update transactions. • Ability of RDBMS to execute SQL efficiently, using indexes whenever possible; subqueries can be slow. • For WebI: number of concurrent users, in particular those who open full-client documents.
4	Launch Query: Fetching	• WAN performance to deliver results from RDBMS back to user PC or WebI midtier, particularly for queries that contain a large number of rows (in other words, 100,000 or more).
5	Present Results: Computing	• Memory on user PC to convert text results to micro cube, display charts, formatted tables, link multiple SELECT statements. • For WebI: complexity of reports, conversion to HTML.

Table 15-4.   *Potential Bottlenecks that Affect BusinessObjects Response Time*

Debugging performance is a complex task. In a full-client environment, individual PCs and LAN performance are hard to control. In a WebI environment, utilization of different cluster nodes, a user mix of thin and full clients, and file conversions to different formats significantly add to the complexity. As the designer, the key thing within your control is the query execution time. While the RDBMS may largely affect this, the SQL generated is often the culprit of poor query performance.

Some BI tools do not allow users to see the exact SQL that gets submitted to the RDBMS; BusinessObjects does. There are a few exceptions, such as queries that contain prompts, but for the most part, you can copy the SQL from the BusinessObjects Query Panel and rerun it in another tool. The DBA can submit the same SQL directly to the RDBMS to isolate whether response time problems are RDBMS-related or not. This is reflected in step 3 in Figure 15-5 and Table 15-4. If the query executes within a similar time in the RDBMS as in the full client or WebI, then RDBMS load or query execution is most likely the source of the response time problem. DBAs or other support personnel can analyze the SQL against an explain plan to understand if the RDBMS executed the query efficiently with indexes or performed full-table scans.

To access the SQL from within the BusinessObjects full client, select Data | Edit Data Provider and click SQL to launch the SQL viewer.

From within the SQL viewer, click Save to save the SQL to a separate text file.

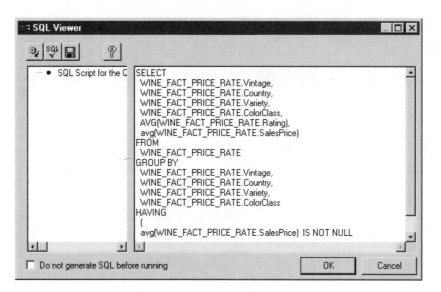

From within WebI, select Edit from the menu bar and then click SQL. The SQL viewer within WebI does not have a save to disk option. However, you can still highlight the SQL statement and use CTRL-C to copy and paste it to Notepad or another SQL or text editor.

BusinessObjects also tracks how long it takes to run the query and build the micro cube. In the full client, the elapsed time unfortunately does not distinguish between phases 3 (executing) and 4 (fetching), even though it does display this information on the status bar. To view the query execution time, open the Data Manager via the pull-down menus Data | View Data or select the Data Manager button from the toolbar. Select the Definition tab. The Duration column displays how long it took to execute the query, transport the raw data across the network, and build the reports. In the next example, the last query refresh finished in 16 seconds and contained 591 rows. The refresh at 4:20:58 P.M. finished in one second but contained 50,000 rows.

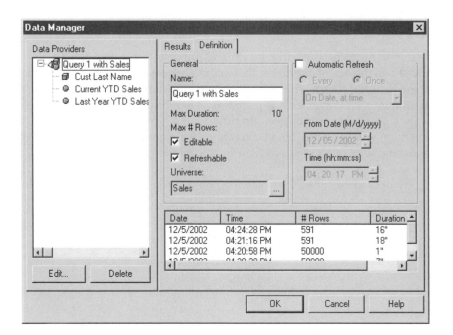

Monitoring User Activity

Unlike in the full client, WebI does not display the duration information to end users. However, WebI administrators can access this and more via the Audit Log. For WebI users and BusinessObjects three-tier mode (ZABO) users, you can monitor response time issues in three ways:

- Audit the log file.
- Audit a database that captures activity using the freeware Audit universe.
- Use the Auditor product.

All three are interrelated and must be explicitly enabled. All three approaches capture only activity that goes through the WebI midtier; therefore, no full-client activity is captured. Auditing is enabled via the BusinessObjects Services Administrator.

One can still capture full-client activity by creating a program with the BusinessObjects SDK and installing it on each full-client PC.

The Audit Log

The audit log captures activity in a text file using different event IDs to help you understand if it is the query execution that is a bottleneck or the report presentation. The audit log is useful for viewing recent, isolated incidents or interactively testing a benchmark query. However, as it is pure text, it is too cumbersome for debugging problems for a particular user or point in time.

As of version WebI version 2.6, you can launch Administrator as a desktop product. Alternatively and with older versions, you start it via the Notify icon from the Windows taskbar.

From the Notify icon, right-click to call the pop-up menu. Select Launch Administrator.

This starts a browser and a Java applet that lets you view and control the WebI server. From the menu bar, select View Log.

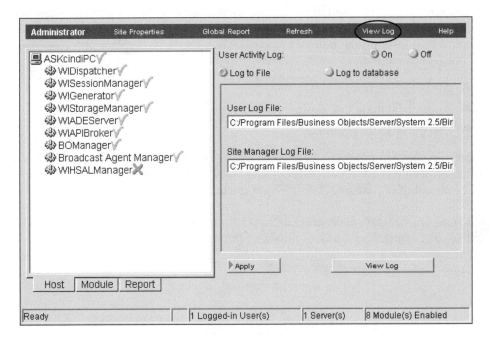

By default, user activity is not logged. To capture user activity, click the On button. The default is set to Log To File. Once enabled, user activity is captured in user.log and server activity is captured in sm.log. Unless you specify a different path, the default directory is C:\Program Files\Business Objects\Server\System 2.5\Bin\ on the WebI Cluster Manager, not on the individual nodes. Another log file, userdet.log, contains more detailed information such as the universes selected or the report refreshed. Information in this log file is not available through Administrator; however, you can view it with a text editor or the Audit universe.

To view user activity, click View Log. The initial log presented is System Activity. To switch to user activity, select the User Activity tab.

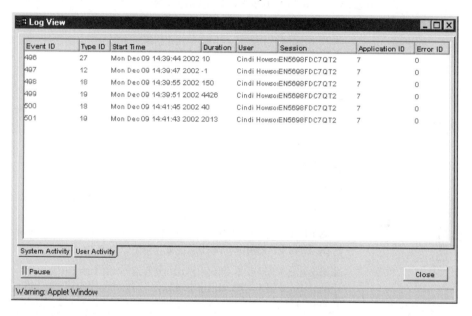

For each event, WebI records an ID, as described in Table 15-5. If you use the Audit universe, you do not need to be familiar with these IDs, as long names are stored in the database. WebI also records the Start Time, Duration in milliseconds, User, Session, Application ID, and an Error ID if applicable. Application IDs are listed in Table 15-6.

The activity log shows a partial activity log. In viewing a production activity log, you may see events scrolling by. Click Pause to analyze a particular set of events. In the preceding screen, compare events 499 and 501, both with the Event Type ID of 19 to refresh a document. The first query (event 499) took 4,426 milliseconds to execute. The second query (event 501) took 2,013 milliseconds to execute, roughly half the time. Well, this was a controlled event, so I know the cause of the difference in response time: in the first case, Oracle was running on the same machine as the WebI server, slowing the system down. With the second event, WebI was the only process running on the server. In a production environment, it is much harder to determine differences in response time. Here, the difference was in seconds; in the real world, it's the differences in minutes that can affect whether users are satisfied with the system or not.

Event Type	Event Description
1	Log into the repository
2	Failed logon
3	Log off from WebI. This event is not recorded when a user closes the browser without logging off
4	Get a list of inbox documents
5	Get a list of corporate documents
6	Get a list of universes to which the user has access
7	Send a document to users
8	Publish a document to a group
9	Save a document
10	Read inbox document
11	Read corporate document
12	Read personal document
13	Open the query panel
17	Login successful
18	Execute the query. The first time a user runs a query, event type 18 is generated without an event type 19
19	Refresh document. Once a query has been run once with Event Type ID = 18, there is always a corresponding Event Type ID = 19
20	Compute result after drill
21	List of values
22	Edit document
23	Get document generated by reporter
24	Get a Comma Separated Value (CSV) file, for downloading WebI documents into spreadsheets
25	Refresh document after a prompt
26	N/A

Table 15-5. *Events Are Captured in the WebI Activity Log*

Event Type	Event Description
27	Get list of personal documents
28	Apply format
29	N/A
30	Open report from cache
31	Execute macro (VB)
32	Execute script (4.1)
33	Download non-WebI and non-BusinessObject document
34	BusinessObjects three-tier mode started
35	Delete inbox documents
36	Delete corporate documents
37	Delete personal documents
38	Delete scheduled documents
39	Upload non-BusinessObjects documents

Table 15-5. *Events Are Captured in the WebI Activity Log* (continued)

Application ID	Description
1	Unknown application
2	WebI 2.5
3	BOManager invoked by WebI
4	BusinessObjects full client
5	BOManager invoked by Broadcast Agent
6	Three-tier BusinessObjects or ZABO
7	WebI 2.7

Table 15-6. *The Audit Log Captures Information According to these Applications*

The Audit Universe

With the audit universe, events are tracked in a relational database. There are several benefits to this approach. First, it is easier to analyze trends and sets of events, as you can create BusinessObjects or WebI reports. Second, a relational database can handle more transaction activity than a standard text file. Finally, the universe exposes meaningful event details. These details are captured in userdet.log but cannot be viewed via Administrator. Table 15-7 shows the classes and objects within the Audit universe.

In order to use the audit universe, you must do the following:

1. Create a connection to the audit database in Supervisor; you need to decide where you want to create the audit tables, either in the existing repository domain or a separate database instance.

2. Modify the activity log settings to capture to a relational database.

3. Copy and modify the Audit universe.

4. Create reports or modify default reports.

Modifying Activity Log Settings

A connection to an audit database must exist in the BusinessObjects repository for WebI to access it. Initially, the database will be empty. WebI creates the tables when you first

Class Name	Object Name	Object Description
Session details	*Event User*	This is the user who generated the event.
Session details	*Event Session*	This is the WebI session ID. It can be used to generate traces of the first and last event, and to break reports by the sessions a user generates.
Session details	*Session start time*	The time when the first action in the session took place.
Session details	*Session end time*	The time when the last action in the session took place.
Event Detail	*Event Object ID*	The is the ID value of the object used in the event. In the case of a universe, or object, this is the ID in the repository.

Table 15-7. *Classes and Objects in the Audit Universe*

Class Name	Object Name	Object Description
Event Detail	*Event Trace Name*	This is the text name that is used by the user—for example, a name of a universe, document, or object in a query.
Event Detail	*Event Trace Type Name*	This is the type of trace item that is being traced—for example, whether the value in the Event Trace Name/ID is a universe, or the name of a document, or the number of lines returned by a query.
Event Log	*Event ID*	This is the internal ID used to trace events.
Event Log	*Event Starttime*	This is a date/time field holding the start time of the event.
Event Log	*Event Type Name*	This is the type of the event—for example, to get the list of corporate docs, or to Edit a document.
Event Log	*Event Type ID*	This is the numeric type of the event that appears within the WebI log file.
Event Log	*Event Duration*	This is the duration of the event, in milliseconds.
Event Log	*Application Name*	This is the application inside of WebI that generated the event. This can be WebI 2.5, or if the document is a BusinessObjects 5.0 Document, the BOManager.
Event Log	*Event Error ID*	This will be used by Broadcast Agent to record the error codes.
Event Log	*Event Host*	This is the WebI server that generated the event.
Audit V2.5 Measures	*Number of lines*	
Audit V2.5 Measures	*Number of documents read*	The number of documents that have been read.
Audit V2.5 Measures	*Number of users*	The number of different user sessions that have been opened.
Audit V2.5 Measures	*Number of actions*	The number of actions recorded.

Table 15-7.   *Classes and Objects in the Audit Universe* (continued)

enable capturing to a database. (Refer to Chapter 12, "Connections," for more information on how to create a secure connection.) Once this is done, follow these steps:

1. From the WebI Administrator, select the View Log screen. Ensure that User Activity Log is set to On. Click Log To Database. Administrator will ask you to enter a General Supervisor user ID and password. Enter the Supervisor Login name and Password.

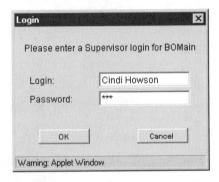

2. Click OK to close the Login window.

3. Use the Audit Database Connection drop-down box to select the newly created connection that will hold the audit tables.

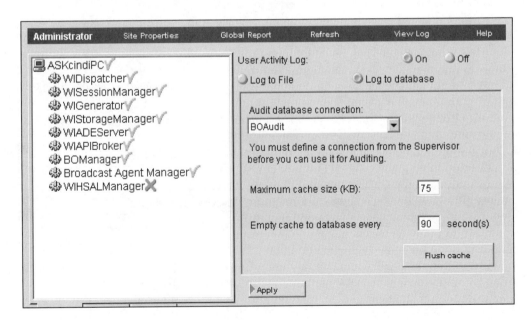

4. Click Apply to accept the changes.

Copying and Modifying Audit Universe

The Audit universe provides the semantic layer to access the information in the newly created audit database.

1. To install the Audit universe, copy it from the Freeware directory on the installation CDs to your Universe folder.

2. Launch Designer and select File | Open | Audit.unv.

3. In Designer, select File | Parameters to modify the default connection to point to the Audit connection.

4. I recommend making two changes to this universe. First, the universe contains a description of the Event Type but not the numeric Type_ID, useful for sorting and selection purposes. In the *Event Log* class, insert *Event Type ID* as follows:

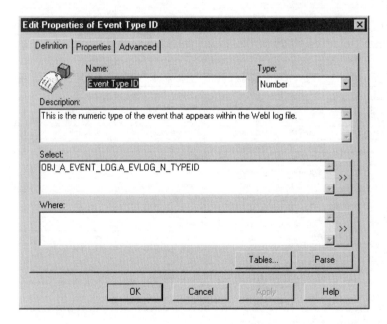

5. If you wish to aggregate duration times, modify the Event Duration object to include a SUM aggregate. Also, if you wish to see seconds rather than milliseconds, divide by 1,000:

```
SUM(OBJ_A_EVENT_LOG.A_EVLOG_N_DURATION) / 1000
```

Creating Reports

In the same Freeware directory on the installation CDs, Business Objects provides some sample WebI reports that use the Audit universe. You can also create your own reports, in either WebI or the BusinessObjects full client.

The following sample report shows how logging to a database provides more detailed information than the audit log. Under the columns *Event Trace Type Name* and *Event Trace Name,* you now can see the individual reports, universe, and objects associated with each event. With the audit log, this information is not easily available, as such details are stored in a separate detail log file. The audit universe is a valuable tool not only in monitoring response time issues, but also in identifying popular and/or seldom-used objects.

Event Id	Event Type ID	Event Type Name	Event Trace Type Name	Event Trace Name	Event Duration
498.00	18.00	Compute result	Document name	Highest Price Wine Austra	0.15
498.00	18.00	Compute result	Number of lines	7	0.15
498.00	18.00	Compute result	Object name	Country	0.15
498.00	18.00	Compute result	Object name	Highest Price	0.15
498.00	18.00	Compute result	Object name	Label Name	0.15
498.00	18.00	Compute result	Object name	Producer	0.15
498.00	18.00	Compute result	Object name	Varietal	0.15
498.00	18.00	Compute result	Object name	Vintage	0.15
498.00	18.00	Compute result	Repository name		0.15
498.00	18.00	Compute result	Universe name	Wine	0.15
499.00	19.00	Refresh document	Document name	Highest Price Wine Austra	4.43
499.00	19.00	Refresh document	Number of lines	7	4.43
499.00	19.00	Refresh document	Object name	Country	4.43
499.00	19.00	Refresh document	Object name	Highest Price	4.43
499.00	19.00	Refresh document	Object name	Label Name	4.43
499.00	19.00	Refresh document	Object name	Producer	4.43
499.00	19.00	Refresh document	Object name	Varietal	4.43
499.00	19.00	Refresh document	Object name	Vintage	4.43
499.00	19.00	Refresh document	Repository name		4.43
499.00	19.00	Refresh document	Universe name	Wine	4.43
500.00	18.00	Compute result	Document name	Highest Price Wine Austra	0.04
500.00	18.00	Compute result	Number of lines	7	0.04
500.00	18.00	Compute result	Object name	Country	0.04
500.00	18.00	Compute result	Object name	Highest Price	0.04
500.00	18.00	Compute result	Object name	Label Name	0.04
500.00	18.00	Compute result	Object name	Producer	0.04

The next graph shows how you can analyze query execution times for benchmark queries over different points in time.

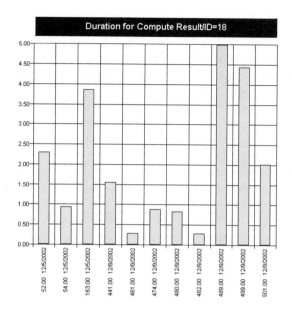

A BETTER UNIVERSE

Auditor

Auditor is a separate product but uses the same activity database to track user activity. In fact, the steps from the preceding two sections are preinstallation tasks for Auditor. However, Auditor is much more than a tracking database. Auditor contains four universes, about 50 reports with varying levels of detail, and key indicators organized into the following categories:

- User Information, such as number of users, most active users, users who never log out correctly, user profiles
- Document Management, 10 Least Downloaded documents, document size, average refresh time
- Universe Management, most popular universe, most popular objects, number of classes and objects in each
- Broadcast Agent
- System Information

While the freeware universes managero and Audit correspond loosely with the Auditor universe Universe Domain Analysis: Universe and System Information: Activity, Auditor provides two additional universes for which there are no alternatives: Broadcast Agent Analysis and Repository Analysis: Security. While you could build your own universe with security information from the repository in a similar fashion to managerO, this gets highly complex. Also, the Auditor universes will span multiple sources of information to deliver more meaningful reports. For example, the Repository Analysis: Security universe looks at both username information (stored in the security domain) and number of logins (stored in the activity/usage database).

For companies with enterprise-wide deployments, Auditor is ideal for optimizing and understanding the deployment. The two main limitations of Auditor are these:

- Auditor cannot incorporate full-client activity.
- For companies that have multiple WebI servers, Auditor can monitor only the one main server and nodes, as this generates the usage logs; merging multiple usage logs from multiple WebI cluster managers into one activity database is a manual task outside of Auditor. The vendor plans to improve this in a future version.

The
Complete
Reference

Business
Objects

Part III

Reporting with BusinessObjects

Chapter 16

Introduction
to Reporting

If you have read Parts I and II of this book, Part III is your reward; you finally get to report, explore, and analyze data in ways that improve your business. Although BusinessObjects has a powerful ad hoc query and reporting engine, most BusinessObjects deployments involve standard reports. These reports may be common information requirements with key business indicators that the majority of users refresh with their own view of the data. A typical deployment is geared to two types of users: report readers who access standard reports and report authors who build the standard reports. Report authors may also build ad hoc reports for individual and one-time analyses (refer to Chapter 3 for more information on different user segments). Starting with a blank screen and no data can be very discouraging. For this reason, Part III of this book is organized for users who start by viewing and analyzing a standard report and then evolve to modify the report and/or build new ones.

If you like to start off with your own data and dive right in, then skip ahead to Chapter 21 and flip back to Chapters 16–20 for formatting and analysis.

About the Sample Data

This section of the book uses a sample wine database for many of the reports and queries. As Business Objects is a French company, I thought it would be a way to pay homage to the company's origins by exploring one of France's premier exports (plus I am a true wine novice, and BusinessObjects provides an excellent way to uncover some good wine values!).

Rating and price data was provided compliments of eRobert Parker (www .erobertparker.com) and WineAlert (www.winealert.com), respectively. Robert Parker is the world's leading wine critic and founded the publication *The Wine Advocate*. He also is a contributing editor for *Food and Wine Magazine*. Wine Alert is an Internet company that surveys retailers, distributors, and wholesalers to help consumers find the best wine prices. The eRobert Parker site selected the wines at random, and I matched them with prices provided by Wine Alert. The wine database contains ratings for approximately 1,800 wines and prices for approximately 300 of the rated wines. Disclaimer: this database is provided purely for instructional purposes and should not be used to draw any conclusions about individual bottles of wine or wine markets. You can download a copy of the database and universe from www.osborne.com.

The vendor also provides a sample universe, EFASHION, and reports that are used in isolated instances for functionality not available in the wine database; contact your BusinessObjects administrator for access to this sample data set. The EFASHION universe is based on fictional data from a retail clothing store. It contains three years of sales and promotion costs for 211 clothing articles and 13 stores. Both the wine database and the EFASHION universe use MS Access as the database engine. In certain cases in which I want to demonstrate complex queries using Oracle, I use the sample Sales History tables provided by Oracle.

Starting BusinessObjects

Although it is possible to deploy BusinessObjects in work group mode, most companies deploy BusinessObjects with a repository and require you to log into the repository to verify:

- That you are authorized to use BusinessObjects
- Which universes and standard reports you are allowed to access
- Which program modules, such as Reporter, Explorer (Chapter 19), InfoView, or Business Query for Excel, you are authorized to access and what functionality within each program is enabled

The examples and login procedures in this chapter assume your deployment uses a repository.

Note *If you are using InfoView to start BusinessObjects in three-tier mode (ZABO), please refer to Chapter 23.*

Figure 16-1 gives an overview of what happens during this login process.

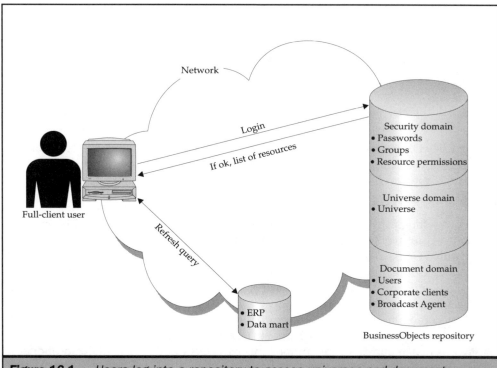

Figure 16-1. *Users log into a repository to access universes and documents.*

1. To start BusinessObjects, select the BusinessObjects icon from either your desktop or the MS Windows Start menu. Assuming a default menu structure, choose Start | Programs | BusinessObjects 5.1 | BusinessObjects.

2. BusinessObjects presents you with the User Identification dialog box. Enter your User Name. This is case sensitive and may be different from the login name you use to access other corporate resources such as the network and transaction systems. If you have logged into BusinessObjects at least once from this computer, then BusinessObjects will prompt you with the name of the user who last logged in. You can use the drop-down box to select the User Name.

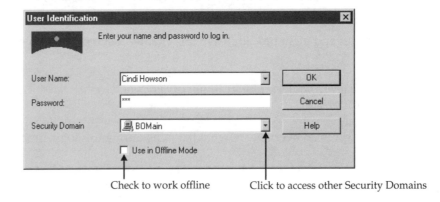

Check to work offline   Click to access other Security Domains

3. In the Password box, enter a password if required. BusinessObjects will display an asterisk for each letter you enter. Passwords are case sensitive and in some circumstances must match the password for the data source.

4. Select your default Security Domain. Leave the Offline Mode box unchecked. Security Domains and Offline Mode are explained further in this section.

5. Click OK to close the User Identification and enable BusinessObjects to validate your username and password against the repository.

About Passwords

Password settings are determined by the BusinessObjects supervisor (see Chapter 12). The supervisor may not require a unique BusinessObjects password but may use the password you enter at login for refreshing a query. This is called a data source password. If the supervisor requires both a BusinessObjects password and a data source password, these passwords must be one and the same. When they become out of synch, you will receive an error when refreshing a query.

Many corporate systems require your password to be a minimum length and do not allow passwords to match your first name or last name. At the current time, BusinessObjects passwords may require a certain number of characters but do not contain additional restrictions such as differing from your login ID. They are case sensitive, and there are certain symbols that you cannot use.

BusinessObjects allows you three attempts to enter the correct password. It warns you each time you enter an incorrect password with the following error message:

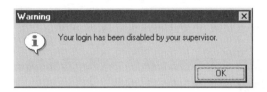

After the third incorrect attempt, your login account is disabled. You must contact your BusinessObjects supervisor to reenable it and to reset the password.

Changing the Password on First Login

The very first time you log into BusinessObjects, you may be prompted to change your password. You also may be prompted to change your password after so many days, for example, every 90 days. After you enter a valid username and password, BusinessObjects will tell you that your password has expired.

1. Click OK to acknowledge the message "Your password has expired."

2. BusinessObjects prompts you to change your password.

3. As passwords are case sensitive, verify that your CAPS LOCK is turned off if you want mixed or lowercase passwords or turn CAPS LOCK on for all-uppercase letters. In the box Enter Old Password, enter your existing BusinessObjects password.

4. Press TAB to move to the next box or use your mouse to click in Enter New Password.

5. In the Confirm New Password box, reenter your new password. BusinessObjects requires you to confirm the password change in case you mistyped anything the first time.

6. Click OK.

Security Domains

Your company may have one or more security domains. A security domain is a component of the BusinessObjects repository that contains BusinessObjects user IDs, passwords, and permissions. Some companies will have multiple security domains for:

- Different business units within a company
- Different regions within a worldwide deployment
- Test and production environments

In general, you will most often use the same security domain each time you log into BusinessObjects. In order to access each domain, you need to have access to the file *domain*.key under the folder \Business Objects 5.0\locdata. Even if your name is defined to more than one repository, you will not be able to access these repositories unless the *domain*.key file exists on your PC or network drive.

If you need to log into a different security domain, click the drop-down box from the User Identification screen and select the desired domain.

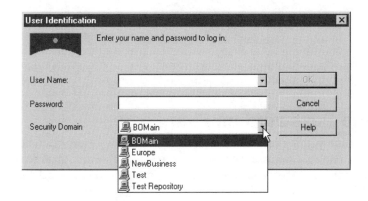

Online Mode vs. Offline Mode

There are two modes of working in BusinessObjects, online and offline. *Online mode* is the default mode and means you are connected to the BusinessObjects repository; *offline mode* means you are not connected to the repository.

With online mode, you can interact with the repository to retrieve new universe definitions and documents, as shown in Figure 16-1. As the designer changes the universe or creates new ones, you can access these changes via the repository in online mode. You can publish reports to Corporate Documents or use Broadcast Agent to schedule reports.

With offline mode, you do not interact with the repository, so you will not be able to do the following:

- Receive new or updated universe definitions
- Send documents to other users via the repository
- Schedule reports with Broadcast Agent
- Publish reports to Corporate Documents

In order to use offline mode, you must have successfully logged into BusinessObjects at least once, from the PC you currently are using. Each time you log in, BusinessObjects updates the following file with security information:

```
\BusinessObjects 5.0\LocData \sdac.lsi
```

This file allows you to log into BusinessObjects in offline mode. Notice in Figure 15-1 that the repository does not actually connect you to a data source. Therefore, you can in theory still refresh reports and build new queries while in offline mode. This may be useful if the BusinessObjects repository is unavailable due to maintenance or network problems. In order to work with universes and create new documents, however, the universe definitions must be stored on a local disk or accessible network drive, and you must still have connectivity to the data source.

In reality, you most often will use offline mode with notebook computers while you are traveling and not connected to the network. In this respect, you do not interact with either the BusinessObjects repository or the data sources.

Note   *The BusinessObjects supervisor must specifically grant you access to enable you to work in offline mode. Without this access, when you select offline mode, BusinessObjects will give you an error message that your login is not valid.*

Opening a Document

A *document* is a file that contains formatted reports, charts, query definitions, and a subset of data from one or more data sources. A document is your starting point for viewing and analyzing data or for modifying a standard report. BusinessObjects full-client documents use *document*.rep as the file naming convention, where *document* can be a long report name and .rep is always the extension. Other Business Objects products such as WebI documents and Business Query for Excel have different file extensions.

BusinessObjects documents can be stored in several places:

- A personal directory on your local computer's hard disk or a work group directory on a file server
- The document domain of the BusinessObjects repository
- E-mail

Where the document is stored affects how you open a document.

Specifying the Default Directory

When you open a document or retrieve a document from the repository, BusinessObjects looks first in a default directory. The default directory for BusinessObjects reports is

```
\Business Objects\BusinessObjects 5.0\UserDocs
```

You can change the default directory for storing and retrieving documents.

1. From the pull-down menu, select Tools | Options, then click the File Locations tab.

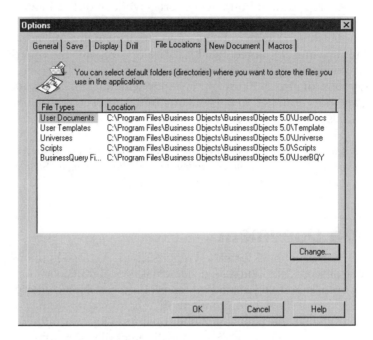

2. Under File Types, double-click User Documents or highlight User Documents and click Change. This launches a standard Browse For Folder dialog box. Click through the various directories and select the desired default folder.

3. Click OK to close the Browse For Folder dialog box, then OK again to close the Options.

Opening a Local Document

To open a document from the default directory:

1. Select File | Open from the pull-down menu.

2. When you use the pull-down menu, BusinessObjects will display the last five reports you accessed. Click the name of the report you want to open.

Alternatively, you can:

1. Click the Open button on the toolbar. BusinessObjects displays a standard Open dialog box.
2. Select the name of the file you wish to open. If you want to open more than one document at a time, CTRL-click to select multiple files.

Repository Documents

A report author may distribute documents via the repository, document domain in several ways. First, if there are only a few report readers for the document, the author may send the document to one or more users or groups of users. The report author may schedule the report to be refreshed and distributed on a periodic basis by Broadcast Agent (see Chapter 20). Once the query is refreshed, it gets stored in the document domain. Finally, the repository can contain a set of documents that an author has published for all users as Corporate Documents. In all cases, in order to access these documents, you must first retrieve them from the repository, then open your local copy, as shown in Figure 16-2.

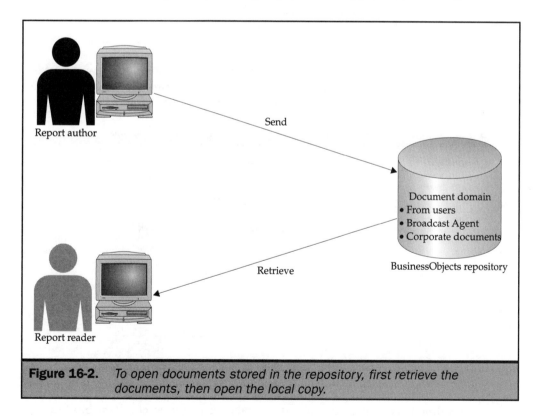

Figure 16-2. *To open documents stored in the repository, first retrieve the documents, then open the local copy.*

Documents from Users

1. To open a document a report author has sent you, select File | Retrieve From | Users.

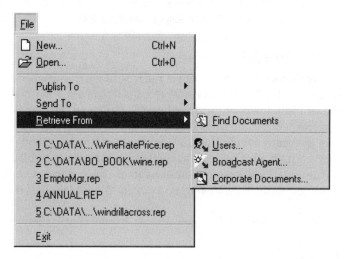

2. BusinessObjects displays a list of reports that users have sent you, who sent the report, the time exported to the repository, and the approximate file size. Note under the column Type that all Types are User documents.

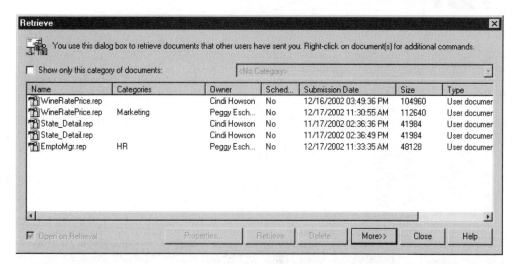

3. The list of available reports can become quite long. If you want to filter the list according to certain groups of reports, called Categories, check the box Show

Only This Category Of Documents. By default, BusinessObjects will initially display documents that have not been associated with a particular category, <No Category>. Use the drop-down box to select other categories.

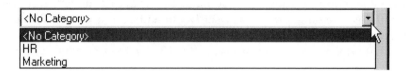

4. For additional search options, click More >>. BusinessObjects expands the Retrieve panel to include a Find Documents section. Within Find Documents, you can search for documents by the different ways it was exported to the repository, specific document domains, or particular document characteristics such as the size of the file or universe accessed.

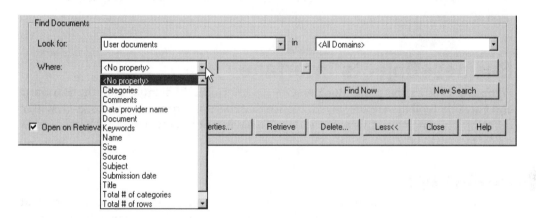

5. Highlight the name of the document you wish to retrieve and open. To retrieve and open multiple documents, CTRL-click.

At this point, you could also right-click the individual document to Retrieve Into a different default directory or to view additional properties about the document.

6. Check the box Open On Retrieval to have the document automatically opened once you have retrieved it from the repository.

7. Click Retrieve. BusinessObjects transfers the report from the repository to your local disk.

8. When the document has been transferred, BusinessObjects tells you the import was successful and opens the document. Click OK to acknowledge the message.

Scheduled Documents

Broadcast Agent (covered in Chapter 20) allows you or report authors to refresh documents on a periodic basis. Once the document has been refreshed, Broadcast Agent will store the results in the repository, document domain. To retrieve documents from Broadcast Agent, you follow the same process as User Documents, but use File | Retrieve From | Broadcast Agent as your first step. The document Type will display Processed documents, rather than User documents. Continue with steps 3–8 in the preceding section.

Corporate Documents

Corporate documents are documents that all users can access. Documents may be restricted to particular groups, but not to particular users. InfoView users also may access Corporate documents, so in this list, you may see different document types, including WebI documents. To retrieve a document from Corporate Documents, select File | Retrieve From | Corporate Documents, then follow steps 3–8 from the section "Documents from Users."

BusinessObjects Interface

Figure 16-3 shows the initial BusinessObjects interface. By default, only the Standard and Formula toolbars are displayed. Notice that there are three report tabs, each with a different report name and view to the data. To navigate to a new report, click the desired report tab.

The Status Bar

The status bar at the bottom of the BusinessObjects screen changes depending on what actions you perform on a document. If you refresh a query, it will display the progress of the query from analyzing to fetching. As you drag and drop cells or convert blocks to different formats, the lower-left corner of the status bar tells you what action will occur. The right side of the status bar tells you the last time the query executed and will warn you if the query did not run to completion.

View Options

You can modify view options to alter the way BusinessObjects displays documents. View | Page Layout will show the print header and footers. View | Structure will show the

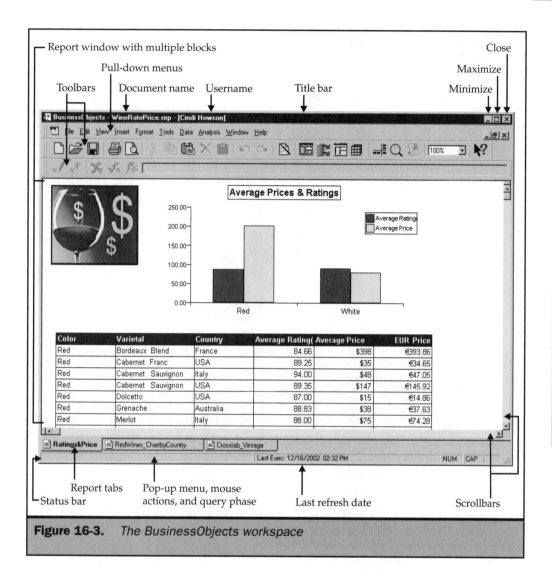

Figure 16-3. *The BusinessObjects workspace*

contents of a report with cells that contain formulas (see Figure 16-6 for an example). Structure mode is useful when you are trying to format large documents. View | Grid will display a grid behind the report components. This is useful for aligning different components. These different view options act as toggles to turn the modes on and off.

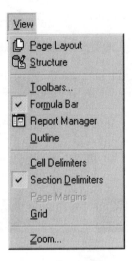

Toolbars

The toolbars enable you to access commonly used functions through buttons. By default, BusinessObjects displays the Standard and Formula toolbars. To have BusinessObjects display additional toolbars, select View | Toolbars and check the appropriate boxes.

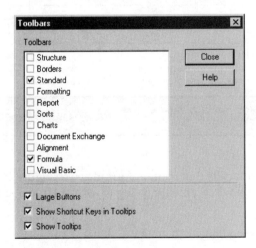

The option Large Buttons will increase the size of the icon on the toolbar. Show Shortcut Keys In Tooltips will display the keyboard shortcut when your mouse moves over a particular button. For example, in Table 16-1, CTRL-O is a shortcut to open a document. Tooltips display the purpose of a particular button. Notice in the next button that BusinessObjects shows the tooltip (Open) as well as the shortcut (CTRL-O).

Table 16-1 lists buttons on the Standard toolbar. Other toolbars are reviewed in different chapters as they are used.

Button/ Key Combo	Name	Function
or CTRL-N	New	Creates a new document.
or CTRL-O	Open	Opens an existing document already retrieved from the repository.
or CTRL-S	Save	Saves the current document to disk.
or CTRL-P	Print	Prints the current report within the document.
	Print Preview	Previews how the report will appear when printed.
or CTRL-X	Cut	Cuts the selected item. When you use Cut, you can undo the cut. Similar to delete.
or CTRL-C	Copy	Puts the selected item into the MS Windows clipboard.
or CTRL-V	Paste	Pastes the selected item.
	Delete	Deletes the selected item. You can undelete it with Undo.
or CTRL-SHIFT-V	Paste Format Only	Pastes the format selections, not the actual cell contents.
or CTRL-Z	Undo	Undoes the last action. You can undo up to ten actions.

Table 16-1.   *Buttons on the BusinessObjects Standard Toolbar*

Button/ Key Combo	Name	Function
or CTRL-Y	Redo	Redoes the last action. You can redo up to ten actions.
	New Report Wizard	Launches a wizard that helps you build a new document (not just a new report).
	Report Manager	Displays the Report Manager.
	Refresh Data	Executes the query.
	Edit Data Provider	Launches the Query Panel to modify a query.
	View Data	Shows the data columns in text format.
	Slice and Dice	Launches the Slice and Dice Panel for adding breaks, sorts, and filters.
	Drill	Launches Explorer for analyzing data from different dimensions and hierarchies.
100%	Zoom	Increases or decreases the display size. This does not affect the size of printed reports.
or SHIFT-F1	Contextual Help	Launches online help.

Table 16-1.   *Buttons on the BusinessObjects Standard Toolbar* (continued)

Components of a Document

One of the hardest concepts with BusinessObjects is the document itself. A document is not a simple report, but rather, a set of components that eventually present a report. A document contains the following components:

- One or more data providers that are typically SQL queries that extract information from source databases.

- A result set in which the results of the queries are stored as a microcube. You can view the results through Data Manager.

- One or more formatted reports. Each report may be a different type, such as a chart, table, or crosstab. One report may have multiple report types.

Figure 16-4 gives a conceptual overview of a document that is made up of two data sources: a SQL query and a spreadsheet. The document contains three reports, two that are tabular reports with a view to each result set and a third that displays a chart with data from both result sets. In many documents, you may have only one query, one result set, and one report. Alternatively, you may have one query, one result set, and multiple reports. Each report tab may contain a view with the full data set but in a different block type such as table, crosstab, or chart. Alternatively, each report may contain a limited number of columns or rows of data as you remove variables and apply filters. The structure of the BusinessObjects document allows you to explore information from multiple perspectives without ever having to requery the database. Similarly, the microcube technology allows

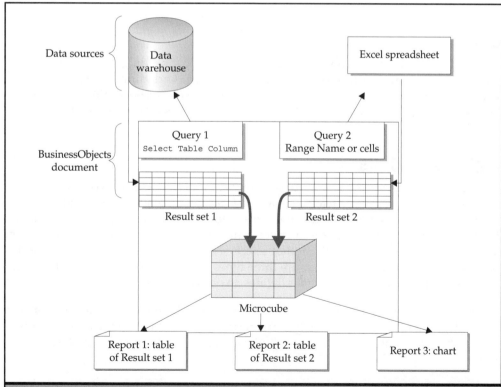

Figure 16-4.   *A BusinessObjects document is composed of several components.*

you to seamlessly combine information from multiple data sources into one report, even if you don't have a central data warehouse.

Components of a Report

Within a given report, you have several components: sections, blocks, and cells. As you explore information within a report, these components are not particularly important; as you try to format the report or add information to it, however, it's important to understand which component you are altering.

Sections

Every report has a main *section*. Within the main section, you can have a section header and a section footer; these are different from page headers and footers that appear in printed reports. Main section headers typically hold the title of the report but also may contain a picture or logo. Reports also may have subsections if you create a Master Detail report. Figure 16-5 shows a report with section headers for each different color of wine. The report title "Average Wine Ratings By Country and Decade" appears in the main section.

Blocks

A *block* is a set of data that contains column headings, row headings, and data values. A block also may contain titles for an individual table or chart, different from a title that applies to the entire report (main section). BusinessObjects supports different types of blocks such as a simple table, crosstab, or chart. A block is one component within a section.

Variables and Cells

A *cell* contains either fixed text, formulas, or report variables. Cells that contain fixed text such as a title or a picture are referred to as *constants*; the contents of the cell never change no matter which data you are viewing. Cells whose contents change may be either a formula or a report *variable*. Report variables are pointers to the columns of data. When a report author builds a query, the author selects *objects* from the universe. These objects become variables in a report. There are three types of report variables that correspond directly to how the universe designer defines an object:

■ A *dimension* object is denoted with a blue cube and is typically textual information by which you sort and analyze numeric measures. In the wine reports shown thus far, color, vintage, varietal, and country are all dimension variables.

- A *measure* is a number that you want to analyze; it is denoted by a pink sphere or circle. Average Rating and Average Price are measure variables.

- A *detail* provides additional information about a particular dimension. You may want to see the information in a list report but will not want to use it to analyze measures by. Phone number and street address are typical detail variables.

In a spreadsheet, each cell contains the actual value. In a BusinessObjects document, the cell contains either the constant value or a formula that tells BusinessObjects where to find the data value. By viewing the report structure, you can see the true contents of each cell, as shown in Figure 16-6. To view the report structure, use the pull-down menu to select View | Report Structure.

The first cell is a text cell whose contents do not change, referred to as a constant. All the other cells show formulas that are used to retrieve the data values for each report

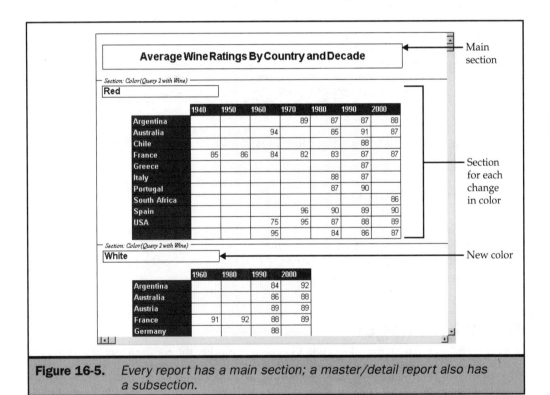

Figure 16-5.   *Every report has a main section; a master/detail report also has a subsection.*

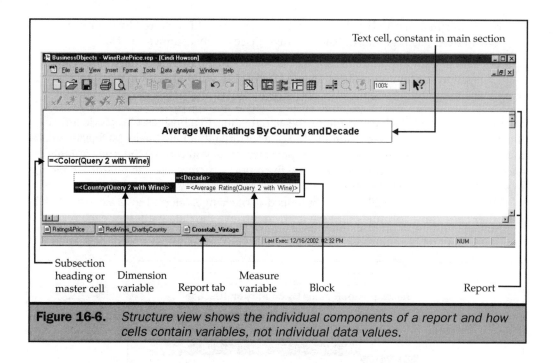

Figure 16-6. *Structure view shows the individual components of a report and how cells contain variables, not individual data values.*

variable. For example, the following formula will retrieve the individual colors of Red, White, and Rose:

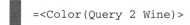

```
=<Color(Query 2 Wine)>
```

<Color> is the name of the report variable for this particular dimension object. The column and row headings (*<Decade>*, *<Country>*) as well as the measure variable that will display individual data values (*<Average Rating>*) make up the block. All these components together make up the report.

Report Manager

Report Manager is a tool that allows you to view and modify the components of each report. You can view the data variables, or you can view the structure of the report.

Data View

To display the Report Manager, click the Report Manager button from the toolbar or select View | Report Manager from the pull-down menu.

BusinessObjects displays the Report Manager in Data view. By default, Report Manager is anchored to the toolbar. You can drag and drop it to any place on the screen. Under Variables, all the variables in the microcube are listed alphabetically. Notice in the following screen that Vintage is a variable within the microcube, but Vintage is not displayed in the chart or table. You can add the variable to the block by dragging it from Report Manager to the block. Also, because this document contains two queries, there are two variables for Color, each from a different query. In this case, the contents for this variable are the same, but in other circumstances, they could be different. For example, Query 1 could contain a condition `Where Color=Red` and Query 2 could contain a condition `Where Color=White`.

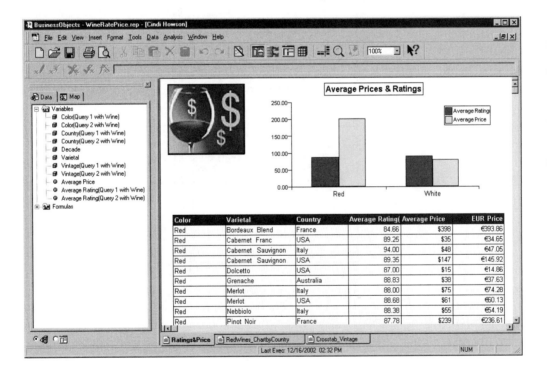

To sort the variables by data provider rather than alphabetically, click the Data Provider icon from within Report Manager.

Sort variables alphabetically   Sort by data provider

Map View

To switch to Map view, click the Map tab from within Report Manager. Initially, Report Manager shows a list that corresponds directly to the report tabs within the Report window. The Navigation icon in the bottom-left corner is selected. Navigation allows you to select individual reports within the document, or for master/detail reports, the individual sections.

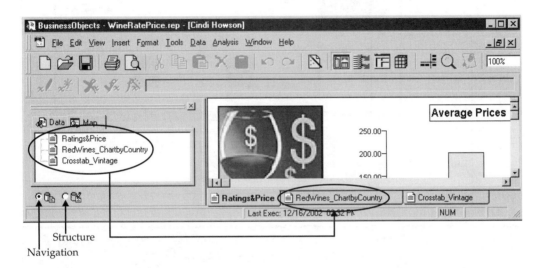

Navigation

Structure

To view the components of an individual report in Structure mode, click the Structure icon in the bottom-left corner. The Report Manager displays the structure of the first report tab, while keeping the WYSIWYG format in the Report window, as shown in Figure 16-7. Notice that this report has one main section. Within the main section, there are two blocks (a table and a chart) and one cell that contains the picture of the wine glass. The Map view shows the different block types of table, chart, and crosstab with unique icons and names. As you select each report component within Report Manager, BusinessObjects highlights the corresponding component within the Report window. This feature is excellent for formatting different report components. Within Report Manager, Map mode, you can right-click any component to call a pop-up menu with various formatting functions. Map mode also makes it clear which components belong to a block or to a section: note that within the chart block, there is a title, but it belongs to the individual chart and not the entire report; if you delete the chart, you delete the title as well.

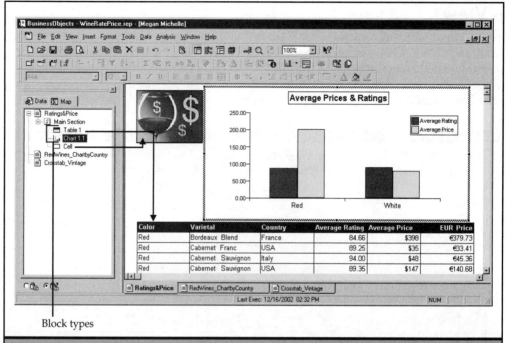

Block types

Figure 16-7. *In Map mode, Report Manager allows you to view the structure of a document while simultaneously viewing the WYSIWYG format in the Report window.*

Recall from the earlier discussion of sections that a master/detail report adds a subsection to the main section. This is more apparent when using Report Manager to view the structure, as shown in the following screen. The subsection name is based on a dimension variable for which you want a separate block (table, chart, crosstab); in this example, Color Section. Within the Color section there is a master cell that contains the contents for each new color; there is also a crosstab or details for each new color. In the Report window, you see two section cells and two crosstab reports, for Red and White; in the structure, there is only one "placeholder," regardless of how many different dimension values may exist for the master cell.

Used for report title or picture

Main section header

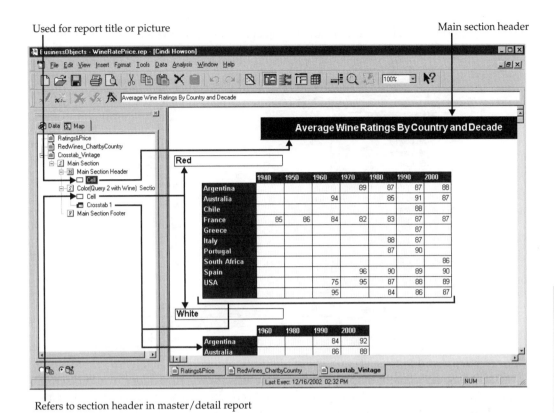

Refers to section header in master/detail report

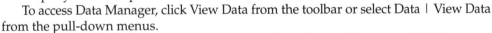

Data Manager

Data Manager allows you to view the components of a *query* in business terms as well as the query results in plain text.

To access Data Manager, click View Data from the toolbar or select Data | View Data from the pull-down menus.

In the next example, there are two queries within this one document. Click the + next to each data provider to see the columns included in the particular query. Notice that at this stage, you see only the result objects that make up the columns of data; you do not see the conditions that may be different for each query. Query 1 contains additional details by Varietal and Price that are not included in Query 2. Data providers are explained in more detail in Chapter 21.

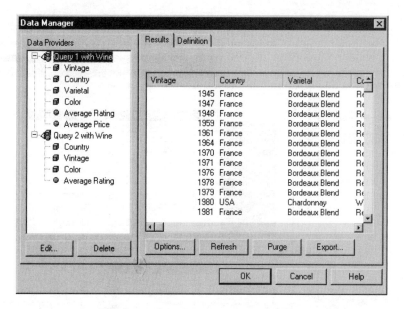

Data Manager initially displays the query results for the first query. You can scroll right and left to see more result columns. Alternatively, you can adjust the column widths. These column widths do not relate to column widths within a formatted report; they simply allow you to see more result columns within the Data Manager window. To adjust the column width, position your mouse on the crossbar between each column heading. The mouse turns to a column-sizing cursor.

Another point to notice in the Data Manager is that it contains detailed data. The reports, on the other hand, may contain summary information that uses Projection Aggregates set by the universe designer. For example, in Figure 16-3, the Average Rating for French Red wines is shown as 84.66. BusinessObjects calculates this average from all the individual rows for each Vintage, which exists in the result set but which is not displayed in Figure 16-3. When your summary reports appear incorrect, it's helpful to look at the raw details in the Data Manager to understand if there is an error in the source data, the query definition, or your report calculations. Data Manager allows you to export to Excel detail queries that may not otherwise be displayed in a formatted report.

The Definition tab of Data Manager displays additional information about each query, including the number of rows returned, time to refresh, and schedule information. When you select a variable rather than a query name, you see the variable type (dimension, measure, detail) and the values. You use Data Manager to link variables from multiple data providers, which is described in Chapter 22, "Link Dimensions."

Block Types

BusinessObjects allows three block types: table, crosstab, and chart. A master/detail is a type of report or section and not specifically a block style. Financial is a block type available in WebI; in BusinessObjects it is considered a way of formatting a table block. Frankly, this distinction is a little confusing, but it only matters when you are trying to format a block. A report can contain multiple block types. Figure 16-3, for example, has both a chart block and a table block within one report. The following table summarizes the different block types and when to use them:

Block Type	Use When. . .
Table	You want to detail information in a list or spreadsheet style. You may break the list into sections in a master/detail report or with breaks. Tables can contain additional columns for many dimensions, details, and measures.
Chart	You want to discover trends and patterns by exploring summary, not detail, numbers in a graphical format. Charts are ideal for analyzing a limited number of measures by a limited number of dimensions.
Crosstab	You want to compare measures by different points within a given dimension. A crosstab is a particular kind of table layout that lets you compare actual sales with budget sales, for example, or to compare data from one period to the next.

You can choose to add, modify, and delete blocks and reports either through the Report window or Report Manager. In the following examples, I will show how to use either approach.

Table

When you initially create a new document, BusinessObjects uses the default block type of table. A table is a spreadsheet-style block that lists data in rows and columns. When you are working with an existing document, you can choose to:

- Insert a table into a new report or report tab
- Convert a crosstab or chart block to a table
- Insert a table into an existing report

Inserting a Table into a New Report

In this example, you will create a new report and insert a table through the Report window.

1. Use the pull-down menu to select Insert | Report.

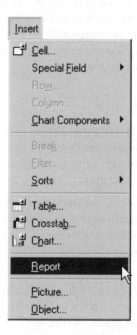

2. BusinessObjects inserts a new report tab, named ReportN, where N is a sequential number. If you have one report tab, BusinessObjects creates Report2. When your report tabs contain meaningful names, as in the following example, BusinessObjects restarts the numbering. To modify the name of the report tab, double-click the tab and enter a meaningful name.

3. The Report window is initially blank. From the pull-down menu, select Insert | Table. Or, if the report toolbar is displayed, click Insert Table.

4. BusinessObjects converts the mouse pointer to a table icon. Drag the mouse to indicate where you want to position the table.

5. BusinessObjects presents you with the New Table Wizard. From here, you can choose to insert a table with data from the existing document, a new query on the existing universe, or a new query with a new data source. Select Use Existing Data From The Document.

6. The New Table Wizard displays a list of variables from all data providers. When you have multiple data providers in a document, click By Data Provider to view the variables by query rather than alphabetically. Use CTRL-click to select which columns you want to appear in the report table. In the following example, I want a table listing the Country and Average Rating:

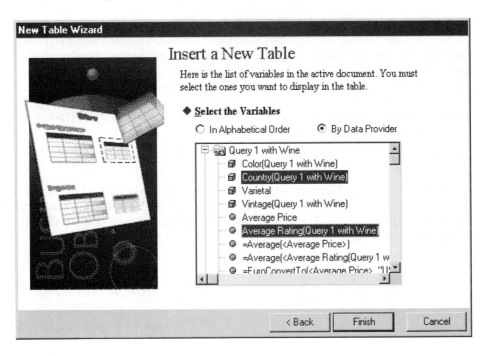

7. Click Finish to close the New Table Wizard and have BusinessObjects insert the new table. At this point, the table is fairly basic. Chapter 17 provides information on how to format the report.

Average Rating	Country
87.33	Argentina
88.95	Australia
89.02	Austria
87.75	Chile
87.72	France
88.45	Germany
87.00	Greece
87.32	Italy
86.67	New Zealand
88.00	Portugal
85.50	South Africa
89.45	Spain
87.77	USA

Converting an Existing Block to a Table

If you have a report that contains a block and you want to view the same data in a different format, you can convert the block to a different type. In the following example, you will convert a chart to a table. You can also convert a small table to a chart. Use the Report Manager to ensure you have selected the correct block.

1. From Report Manager, set the view to Structure by selecting the Map tab and clicking the Structure icon at the bottom.

2. Select the report tab that contains a chart—in this example, RedWinesChartByCountry.

3. Within the Report Manager Map, select Chart1. Note that the chart block is correspondingly selected in the Report window. Right-click to invoke the pop-up menu and select Turn To Table. Note that the status bar tells you it will turn the chart into a table.

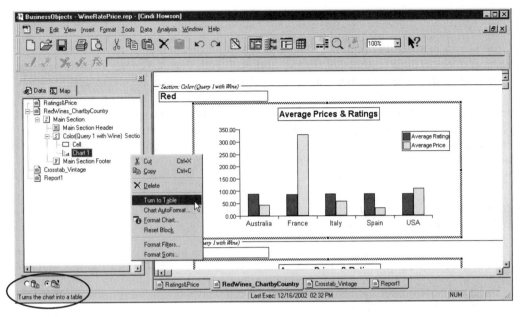

4. BusinessObjects replaces the chart block with a table block. The section headings by Color remain the same. Note that in the Report Manager window, the block type also now reflects Table 1.

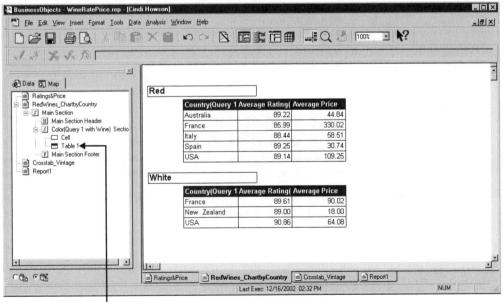

New block type

Chart

Charts are a powerful way to uncover trends and patterns in your data. In many BusinessObjects deployments, charts are underutilized. Perhaps this is in part because a number of deployments grew out of replacements of mainframe or transaction-based reporting systems that do not provide charts. Also, many times, report readers do need to see the individual numbers. However, I would argue that a corresponding chart can help you take your analysis one step further to uncover opportunities and potential improvements and, therefore, recommend that all standard reports contain at least one chart. Table 16-2 provides some sample business questions to show which block type best answers certain questions.

 As you build standard reports, make it a point to include at least one chart that shows an unusual pattern or trend.

Table	Chart
What is the average rating and price for wines by individual producer, varietal, and vintage?	How do ratings compare by different countries?
What are my inventory levels for individual products?	Are any of my inventory levels significantly different for certain products; have the levels increased or decreased over time?
What are the actual and budgeted expenses for each department and quarter?	How big is the variance between actual and budgeted expenses?
How much product did our top ten customers buy for the last three years?	Do any customers buy significantly more than others, and how have the buying patterns changed over time?

Table 16-2. *Sample Business Questions that Can Best Be Answered by a Particular Block Type*

Inserting a Chart

As with tables, you can convert an existing table or crosstab to a chart, or you can create a chart based on a new query. Because charts generally involve fewer variables than tables and crosstabs, I rarely use Convert and recommend using Insert | Chart.

In this example, you will create a new report and insert a chart through the Report window. You could also create a chart within an existing report to have multiple block types within the same report.

1. Use the pull-down menu to select Insert | Report. BusinessObjects inserts a new report tab. Or, if the Report toolbar is displayed, click Insert Chart.

2. Double-click the report tab to enter a meaningful name and press OK.

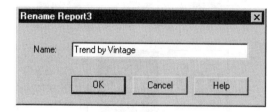

3. From the pull-down menu, select Insert | Chart.

4. BusinessObjects converts the mouse pointer to a chart icon. Drag the mouse to indicate where you want to position the chart.

Note   *With tables, BusinessObjects automatically resizes the box you initially draw to fit all the columns in the table. With charts, it does not resize the box, so ensure that the size of your box is adequate for the number of columns or data points.*

5. BusinessObjects presents you with the New Chart Wizard. Select the radio button Use existing data from the document.

6. The New Chart Wizard displays a list of variables from all data providers. When you have multiple data providers in a document, click By Data Provider to view the variables by query rather than alphabetically. Use CTRL-click to select which columns you want to appear in the chart. For most chart types, you want to limit the number of dimension objects but may have multiple measures.

REPORTING WITH
BUSINESSOBJECTS

7. The New Chart Wizard prompts you to select a chart type. For each chart type, there are different styles and settings, which are discussed further in Chapter 17. Select the desired type and style.

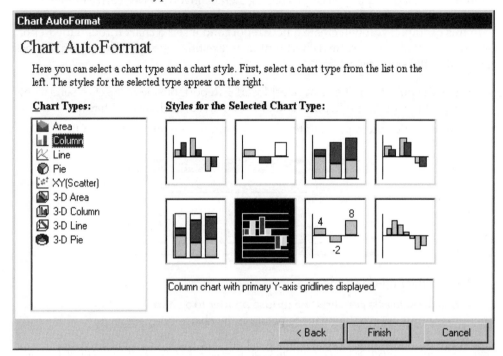

8. Click Finish to close the Wizard and see the newly inserted chart. The chart shown here is fairly basic. Chapter 17 describes how to add a title and legend, and format the X-axis descriptions.

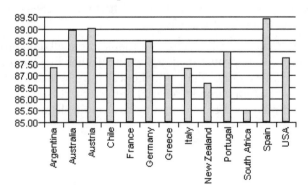

Crosstab

A crosstab block allows you to compare information by different groupings and transposes what may originally be rows in a tabular report to column headings. People frequently use crosstabs for the following types of analysis:

- Customers sales by year, quarter, or month
- Financial measures by actual and budget
- Product sales by region

Columns and Rows are mislabeled in the BusinessObjects Pivot tab. So if you really want Year to appear as column headings in your crosstab, then you place this variable under Rows. Because of this confusion, I recommend using the Slice and Dice Panel in which you drag and drop the variables to create a crosstab (Chapter 18).

The columns may have multiple levels. In Figure 16-8, both Year and Quarter are column headings.

You can either convert an existing table or chart to a crosstab or you can insert a new crosstab based on new data. In the next example, you will convert an existing table to a crosstab. The initial table contains the dimensions Color, Varietal, and Country and

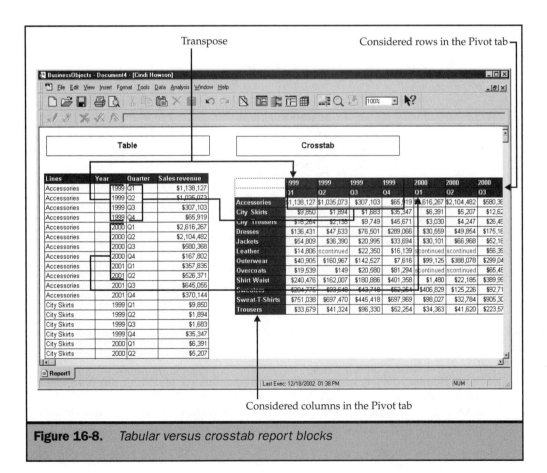

Figure 16-8. *Tabular versus crosstab report blocks*

the measure Average Price. You want to create a crosstab to compare how prices vary by country for each varietal.

1. From within the Report window or Report Manager, select the table block.

2. Right-click to call the pop-up menu and select Format Table. Alternatively, use the pull-down menu to select Format | Table.

3. Select the Pivot tab from the Table Format dialog box. Under Available Variables, BusinessObjects displays all the variables in the microcube. Under Used Variables, Body, BusinessObjects displays the columns from the existing table.

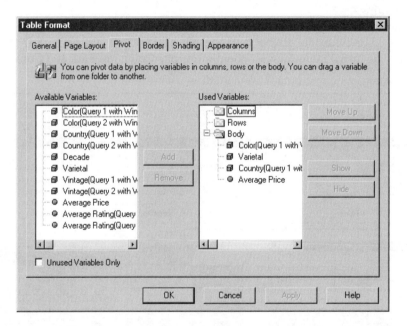

4. You want the Country as Columns in the crosstab. Under Body, select the Country variable and drag and drop it to the Rows folder (because you want it as a column heading!).

Move Up and Move Down work only within a specific part of the crosstab block, such as Columns. You cannot use Move Up and Move Down to move a variable from the Body of a crosstab to a Column heading.

5. Select Color and drag and drop it to the Columns folder (because you want it as a row!). Do the same for Varietal. Average Price and other measures remain in the Body folder. The Pivot definitions should be as follows:

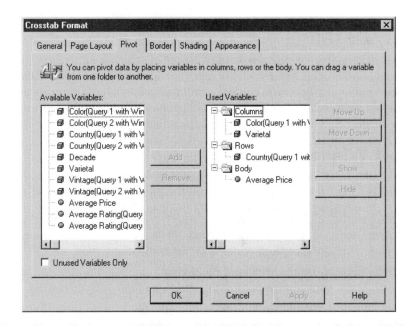

6. Click Apply. BusinessObjects converts the table to the following crosstab:

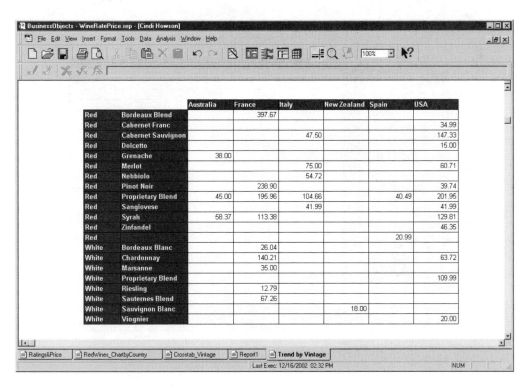

Master/Detail

A master/detail report is a particular kind of report in which a dimension value is used to separate different blocks. Master/detail reports allow you to analyze data within a particular subset. For example, you can have multiple tables, charts, or crosstabs for each color of wine. As discussed earlier in "Sections" and shown in Figure 16-5, BusinessObjects will insert a subsection when you create a master/detail report.

From Report Window

When your block already contains the data you want to use as a section heading, you can convert an existing column to a section heading called a *master cell*.

1. Right-click the cell that you want to convert to a section heading. In the following crosstab, you want color to become a section heading. There will be two sections, one for Red wines and one for White wines.

2. From the pop-up menu, select Set As Master.

New cell will appear as subsection

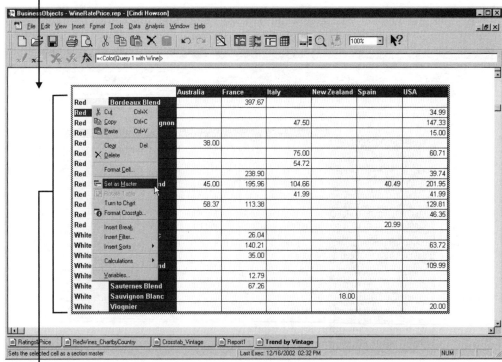

Color column will become master

3. BusinessObjects moves the cell from the block to a new cell that acts as a section heading.

From Report Manager

If you want the dimension column to remain in the block, but you want a section heading in addition, use the Report Manager to create the master/detail report.

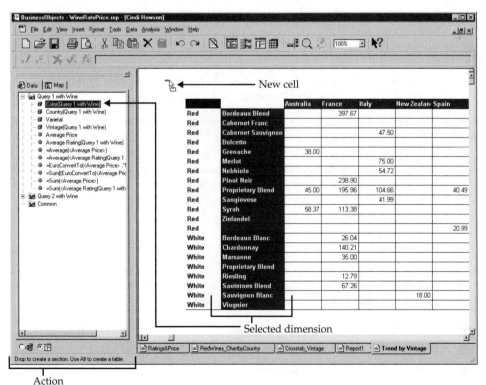

		Australia	France	Italy	Spain	USA
Red						
Bordeaux Blend			397.67			
Cabernet Franc						34.99
Cabernet Sauvignon				47.50		147.33
Dolcetto						15.00
Grenache		38.00				
Merlot				75.00		60.71
Nebbiolo				54.72		
Pinot Noir			238.90			39.74
Proprietary Blend		45.00	195.96	104.66	40.49	201.95
Sangiovese				41.99		41.99
Syrah		58.37	113.38			129.81
Zinfandel						46.35
					20.99	
White						

1. From the toolbar, click Report Manager or select View | Report Manager from the pull-down menu.

2. Ensure the Report Manager is set to Data view. If you have multiple data providers, click the Data Provider radio button at the bottom of Report Manager to sort the variables by query.

3. Under Variables, select the dimension object you want to become the section header and drag it to the Report window at the upper-left corner of the block. The mouse changes to an insert cell cursor, and the status bar indicates you are creating a new section.

Saving Documents

As you add and modify reports and their components, you should periodically save the document. To save a document, click the Save button on the toolbar or select File | Save from the pull-down menu. This saves the *document*.rep file to your local disk or work group directory. Any changes you make to a query, the results of the query, as well as the individual report tabs and blocks are saved in this one *document*.rep file. If you make a lot of changes to the document, you may want to use File | Save As to give the document an entirely new filename. This way, you can safely revert to a previous version of the document.

Save As

Using File | Save As also allows you to select a different file format for sharing data with other applications. In the Save As Type box, click the drop-down box to see the different file types. BusinessObjects will automatically replace the .rep extension with a new extension for the corresponding file type.

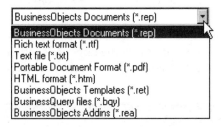

> **Note** *If you are looking for a Save As Excel format, you will not find it in version 5, but you will in version 6. To quickly export all information displayed in the current report including break values, use Edit | Copy All. To export the raw data values, use Data Manager (Data | View Data), then select the Export button.*

When you need to share documents with other users who may not have access to BusinessObjects, consider saving them as Portable Document Format or .pdf. This allows any users with Adobe Acrobat to read the report. Adobe Acrobat is a third-party software program that many people have installed and use for viewing and printing corporate and/or Internet documents. When you save a BusinessObjects document as a .pdf file, it converts the report tabs to Bookmarks in Adobe, allowing readers to easily navigate between the different reports.

Save As HTML

Save As HTML is useful for publishing corporate documents to an intranet, to InfoView, or to the Web. When you choose File | Save As HTML, BusinessObjects prompts you with additional options. These are the Save options:

- **Current Report**   Converts just the current report tab to an HTML page.
- **All Reports in Document**   Converts all report tabs to HTML.
- **Select Reports**   Interactively choose the report tabs to convert to HTML.

■ **BusinessObjects Document**   Allows BusinessObjects full client and three-tier mode (ZABO) users to download a copy of the *document*.rep file. Creates a Download hyperlink in the HTML page. Warning: it does not save the original document.

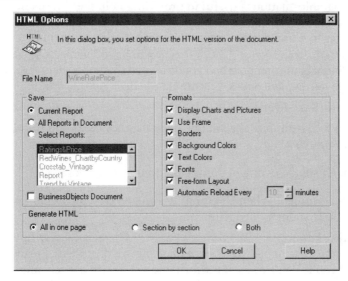

When you save a document as HTML format, BusinessObjects generates multiple folders and files. For each report you save as HTML, BusinessObjects adds a hyperlink within the HTML page.

Save Options

You can modify certain options for saving a document. Select Tools | Options, then the Save tab. Alternatively, select File | Save As and click Options.

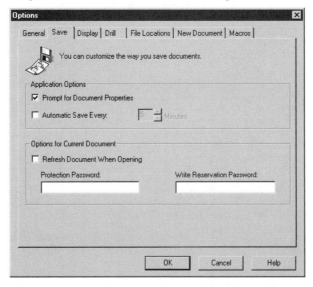

Application Options apply to all documents:

- **Prompt for Document Properties**   Document properties include a Title (which can be different from the filename), Subject, Keyword, and Comments. This additional information is useful in providing help and/or documentation about the reports that you can view through File | Properties. You also can use these properties to search for particular documents as described in the earlier section "Documents from Users." Check this box to have BusinessObjects prompt you for additional information when you first save a new document; it will not prompt you with subsequent saves. I recommend checking this option.

- **Automatic Save Every**

- **Minutes**   Use this if you want BusinessObjects to save your work automatically, after *N* minutes.

Options for Current Document apply only to the active document:

- **Refresh Document When Opening**   Causes all data providers/queries to refresh when you first open the document.

- **Protection Password**   If you enter a password here in the save options, you will be prompted to enter a password prior to opening a document. BusinessObjects will prompt you to confirm the password you enter. I do not recommend file-level password protection, as you will have no way to recover the document if you forget the password.

- **Write Reservation Password**   Report readers can open password-protected documents as read-only. If you want them to be able to save formatting changes or refreshed result sets, then you must also assign a write reservation password.

The Complete Reference

Business Objects

Chapter 17

Report and Chart Formatting

A s you work with standard reports, you can format different report components to make your report easier to read and to better enable you to identify patterns and exceptions. Many of the formatting options in BusinessObjects are standard for MS Windows–compliant products.

The Formatting Toolbar

While formatting reports, you may want to display the formatting toolbar. From the pull-down menu, select View | Toolbars | Formatting. BusinessObjects automatically anchors the formatting toolbar to the Standard toolbar or other toolbars already displayed. If you wish, you can drag the formatting toolbar to other parts of the screen. Table 17-1 shows the formatting buttons. These commands are also available via the pull-down menus Format | Cell and various tabs.

Button	Name	Function	Cell Format Tab
B	Bold	Formats the selected cell as bold.	Font
I	Italics	Formats the selected cell as italics.	Font
U	Underline	Underlines the text or numbers in the selected cell.	Font
≣	Align Left	Aligns text and numbers to the left within a particular cell.	Alignment
≣	Center	Centers the text and numbers.	Alignment
≣	Align Right	Aligns text and numbers to the right. It is often easier to view numbers right-aligned. When you do this, be sure to align the corresponding column headings to the right as well.	Alignment

Table 17-1.   *Buttons on the BusinessObjects Formatting Toolbar*

Button	Name	Function	Cell Format Tab
	Justify	Spreads the cell contents across the width of the column. This may be useful for cells with a lot of text and/or comments.	Alignment
	Center Across Break	When a dimension is used as a break header, you can format the cell to display one break value, centered across the rows in a table. See Chapter 18, "Breaks."	NA
	Currency Style	Formats a numeric cell to display the $ symbol.	Number
	Percentage Style	Formats a numeric cell to display a % symbol.	Number
	Million Style	Formats a numeric cell to include a comma as a thousands separator.	Number
	Add a Decimal Place	For each time you click this button, adds one decimal place to the existing cell. If your current cell has two decimal places, it adds on to set the cell format to display three decimal places.	Number
	Remove a Decimal Place	Removes one decimal place from the cell format.	Number
	Decrease Indent	Decreases the left alignment of a text cell by one character position.	Alignment
	Increase Indent	Indents the left alignment of a text cell by one character position. Indents are useful for showing subitems within a dimension.	Alignment

Table 17-1. *Buttons on the BusinessObjects Formatting Toolbar* (continued)

Button	Name	Function	Cell Format Tab
	Border Toolbar	You can customize the border button to display a border format you most frequently use. Alternatively, click the DOWN ARROW to launch a smaller toolbar to format the cell border.	Border
A	Font Color	Launches a color dialog box to allow you to change the font color for the current cell.	Font
	Background Color	Launches a color dialog box to allow you to change the background color of the current cell.	Shading
	Border Color	Launches a color dialog box to change the border color. The default border color is black.	Shading

Table 17-1.   *Buttons on the BusinessObjects Formatting Toolbar* (continued)

You can customize the border button to display a frequently used border format. For example, the following toolbar shows a button that adds an outside border. To display a button that removes all borders from a cell, click the drop-down box next to the border button and select the last cell that displays the tooltip No Border. The No Border button now appears on the formatting toolbar.

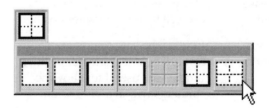

What and How to Format

Within a BusinessObjects document, you can format individual report components ranging from a single cell to an entire block or a section. You can format the different report areas using the formatting toolbar for common format changes. If you want to modify multiple formats at once, you may choose to use the formatting pull-down menus that display the full range of possible formats. When you develop a particular format or style that most effectively presents a report, you can save these styles as a standard report style or as a template to reuse in other documents.

Formatting a Cell

An individual cell is the lowest level of detail in a BusinessObjects report. It may contain a variable that displays information from a data source, a formula that calculates additional information, or a constant that shows a report title. Most often, you will want to format a cell when it contains a constant. Otherwise, it is more efficient to format a block or a section.

Via the Toolbar

To select an individual cell, you can click the cell in the report window or select the cell within the Report Manager, Map, Structure view. In the following example, a cell in the Main Section Header is selected. This cell acts as the report title for all tables, crosstabs, and charts within the current report tab.

The toolbar buttons will change to reflect the cell's current format. If the font is bolded, then the bold button on the toolbar is highlighted. In the following example, the current font is Arial, Regular, 12 point. The text is centered. The cell has a border. You will change it to Times New Roman, bold, italic, 18 point, left aligned, with no cell border.

1. Select the cell either in the Report Manager or the Report window.

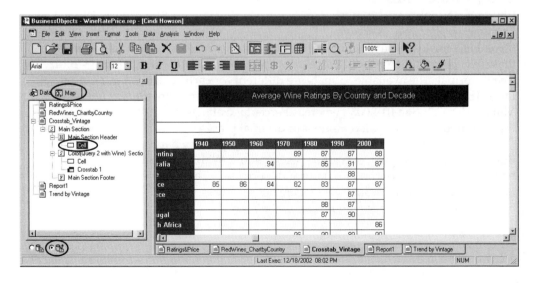

2. From the Formatting toolbar, use the Font drop-down box to change the font from Arial to Times New Roman.

3. Use the Font Size drop-down box to change the font from 12 point to 18 point.

4. Click the desired formats, shown at left, on the toolbar. In this example, Bold, Italic, Left Aligned, No Border. The final cell format should appear as shown next. Notice that the left alignment applies only to the particular cell's contents and not to the cell's position in the report. To position a cell within a report, use Format | Cell, then select the Appearance tab.

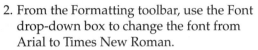
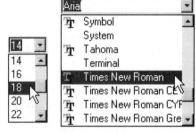

__Average Wine Ratings By Country and Decade__

The Cell Format Pull-Down Menu

The pull-down menu Format | Cell allows you to change formats similar to those in the toolbar but provides more options. Ideally, the BusinessObjects universe designer will have specified default object formats in the universe that make sense for most of the data values. If you find yourself often reformatting certain columns of data, ask the designer to apply a format to the object definition in the universe. Several of the tabs that allow you to format an individual cell serve the same purpose when formatting a table or a chart; common tabs are described only under the present section, "Formatting a Cell"; they are not repeated under "Formatting a Table" and "Formatting a Chart."

The Number Tab

Within the Number tab, there are multiple categories such as Standard, Custom, Date, Number, and Boolean, as shown in Figure 17-1. Don't let the name of the dialog box tab, "Number," mislead you; the different categories allow you to format individual cells that are character, number, or date. Under each category, you can further customize a cell's format. The available formats are different for each category. For example, Date/Time allows you to display a date object as dd/Mmm/yy (01/Jan/03) or as Mmm-dd-YYYY (Jan-01-2003), whereas Percentage allows you to choose to include the % symbol and a specified number of decimal places.

Unless the universe designer or report author applies a particular number format, BusinessObjects interprets everything as Standard. With Standard, numeric values will have two decimal places and no thousands separator. This can look messy for numeric fields such as Years or Product IDs that are not measures, in which case the object should be formatted as a Number with no decimal places.

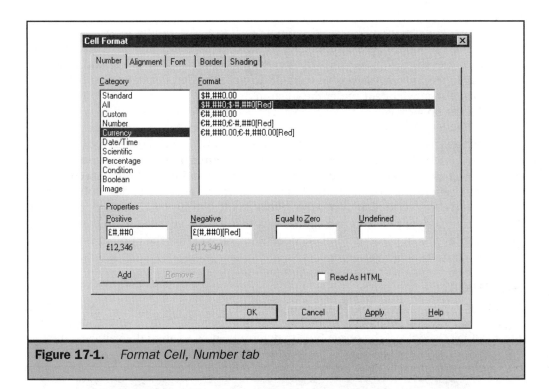

Figure 17-1.   *Format Cell, Number tab*

> **Tip**   *Format numeric fields that are not measures as Number, 0 format. Request the universe designer to do this at the object level. For example, a Year object may indeed be a number, but 2003.00 is not a correct representation of the year, whereas 2003 is. However, the cell format must match the object type. If you format a numeric column as Date with YYYY as the format, BusinessObjects displays all 0's. To correctly format numeric columns without the decimal places, use the Category Number, with the Format 0 (no decimal places, no thousands separator). You can also create a new Number format to precede the year display with FY to indicate Fiscal Year.*

The Custom category contains formats that you have added. The Number category contains settings for numeric fields that specify the number of decimal places, thousands separators, zero treatment, and negative values. For example, you can have positive numbers formatted in black with negative numbers formatted in red. To specify a color format, insert the color in brackets—for example, [Red] to display a negative number in red. In the Currency category, BusinessObjects provides U.S. dollars ($) and Euros as standard symbols. To create a format for British Pounds, as shown in Figure 17-1, enter the following in each box:

Positive	£#,##0
Negative	£(#,##0)[Red]

Note that you can use either the # symbol or a 0 as a placeholder for each digit. In the preceding example, there is a comma for a thousands separator and no decimal places. Negative values display in red and with parenthesis around them. Click Add to add the format to the Currency category, then OK to close the Cell Format dialog box. This format will also now appear under the Custom category.

Under the Boolean category, you can alter the format for cells that display 0's and 1's; unfortunately, the Boolean format does not work for cells that contain other Boolean types such as yes/no, true/false. The format provided will convert a cell containing 1 to True and 0 to False. The information in the data source may use a Boolean field to flag products as stock items or order items; valid or discontinued. While you could use an if-then-else formula to convert the 0's and 1's to more meaningful descriptions, it is easier to add a format to display Yes/No, Stock/Order, Valid/Discontinued, and so on. The Condition category works in a similar way to the Boolean category in that it allows you to display text in place of numbers depending on whether the number is positive, negative, zero, or undefined.

Alignment

Within the Alignment tab, you have additional options over the toolbar, as shown in Figure 17-2. Here you see that the default alignment is General. With a General alignment, BusinessObjects looks at the object type to determine how to align the values. If they

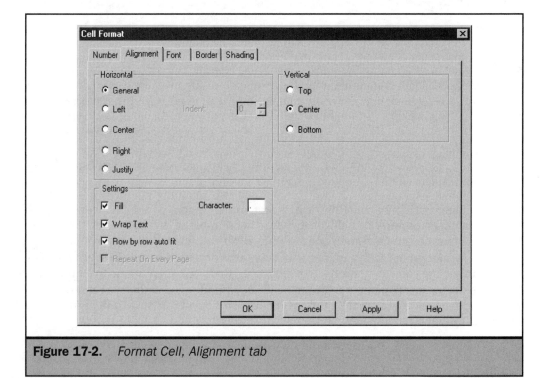

Figure 17-2.   *Format Cell, Alignment tab*

are text values such as dimensions and details, they are aligned left; numeric values align right unless you specify a different alignment.

Under the Settings section of the Alignment tab, you can specify how to treat text:

- **Fill**   When you select Fill, the Character box becomes enabled. You can append a column with a character such as a period or dashes to fill the cell as in the following example:

Label Name	Unit Price
Barbaresco Bric Balin................................	56.24

- **Wrap Text**   For columns with long text names, you can choose to wrap the text rather than truncate the display. When you choose Wrap text, the row height does *not* automatically adjust to accommodate the number of rows. In order to adjust the row height, also select the option Row by row auto fit.

- **Row by row auto fit**   Check this when you use Wrap Text so that the row height automatically adjusts to display all available text, as shown next. The cells in the table on the left are truncated and do not have the format Wrap Text. The cells on the right used the settings Wrap Text and Row by row auto fit.

Label Name	Unit Price
Beaune les Greves Vignes	52.09
Chateauneuf du Pape Hom	646.90
Coteaux D'Aix Domaine de	94.99

Label Name	Unit Price
Beaune les Greves Vignes de L'Enfant Jesus	52.09
Chateauneuf du Pape Hommage A Jacques Perrin	646.90
Coteaux D'Aix Domaine des Beates Terra D'Or	94.99

- **Repeat On Every Page**   This option is enabled for individual cells only and not cells within a table block. Use this to have a cell within the main section, such as a title or picture, appear on every page.

Font

When you want to change the font and font size for certain cells, you can use the formatting toolbar as described earlier. Within the Font tab, you can make similar changes, but in addition, there are options to select a strikethrough format to put hatch marks over a particular cell.

Border

The border buttons on the border toolbar allow you to select where to place a border within a given cell. By default, BusinessObjects uses a single-line box border around free-standing cells that you use as either titles or master cells in a master/detail report. The Border tab allows you also to specify a line format and a border color within a range of cells as shown in Figure 17-3. The Border box shows the borders for the current cell range.

1. To use a particular line format, select the line format under Style. In Figure 17-3, the double line is selected.

2. Within the Border box, click the cell position within the grid. This is the bottom line in Figure 17-3, as indicated by the two triangles.

3. Click Apply.

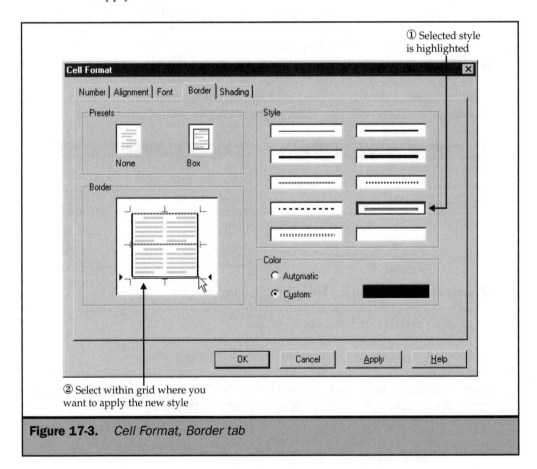

Figure 17-3. *Cell Format, Border tab*

Shading

The Shading tab allows you to specify if the background of a cell contains any shading. By default, BusinessObjects uses the following shading for the different types of cells:

- **Free-standing**   None
- **Block Header**   Solid dark blue
- **Block Body**   25 percent yellow

If you want to permanently modify the default shading for these cells, refer to the section "Standard Report Styles" at the end of this chapter.

Appearance

The Appearance tab appears only for free-standing cells, sections, or entire blocks; it will not appear if you have selected a range of cells within a table. Name allows you to specify a name for an individual cell that will then appear in the Report Manager, Map, Structure view. In Figure 17-4, the cell is renamed Title Cell.

When you insert an initial cell, BusinessObjects inserts the cell relative to the section delimiters. To have the position relative to another component, click the drop-down

REPORTING WITH BUSINESSOBJECTS

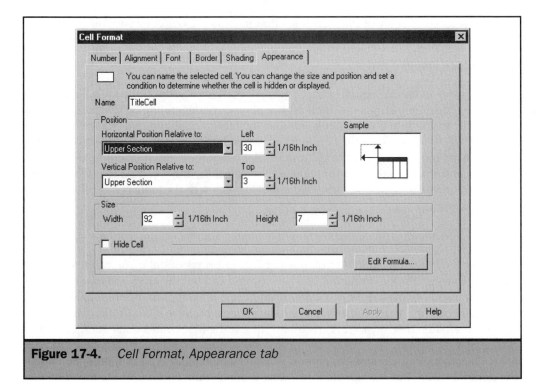

Figure 17-4.   *Cell Format, Appearance tab*

box next to Horizontal Position Relative to: From here, you can have the title cell placed next to the left margin or centered across the page. As your margins change, the cell position will automatically move with the margin. You can also vertically position cells, tables, and charts. This is particularly important when you have multiple blocks within a document. If the size of your table increases as new rows appear in a table, you must position objects beneath the table relative to one another; otherwise, the block on top will overwrite the block beneath.

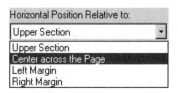

Formatting a Table

Many of the formats you applied to individual cells can also be applied to a set of cells that make up the table block. Within a table block, there are three types of cells:

- **Block Header**   Column headings that usually are object or variable names
- **Block Body**   Values from the variables
- **Block Footer**   Any subtotals

You can select the individual header, footer, or body, or else the entire table. Figure 17-5 shows how the mouse cursor and table highlights change depending on which component you select. As you move your mouse around the table, the shape will change to a right-pointing arrow when you select either the header, body, or footer. To select only one column, hold the mouse over the column until it becomes a down-pointing arrow. To select the entire table, you may find it easiest to select the table component with Report Manager, Structure view. When the entire table is selected, the table border shows black square markers.

Alerters

An *alerter* is a type of formatting you use to highlight rows of data. You can use different fonts and colors to highlight a row, or you can tell the alerter to display certain text. In Figure 17-6, the alerter displays different text messages in different colors based on the wine rating. Alerters are evaluated from top to bottom: if the first condition of >= 95 is met, then this formatting/result applies; if the first condition is not met, then BusinessObjects proceeds to evaluate the second condition. If none of the conditions are met, then the cell content and format remain unaffected. An alerter also can display the original values but change the formatting when certain conditions are met. For example, an alerter may highlight expenses that are 10 percent over budget in red and when they are on or under budget, display them in green. Working with alerters

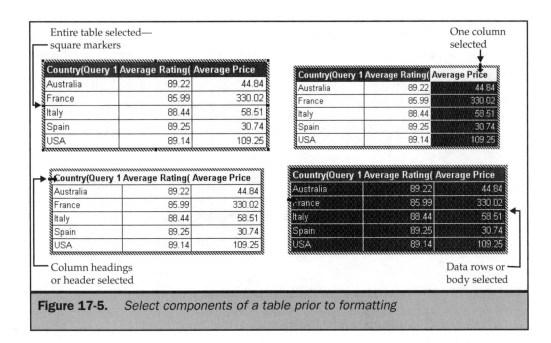

Entire table selected—
square markers

One column
selected

Column headings
or header selected

Data rows or
body selected

Figure 17-5. *Select components of a table prior to formatting*

requires two steps: first, select the column(s) to which you will apply the alerter; then create the alerter.

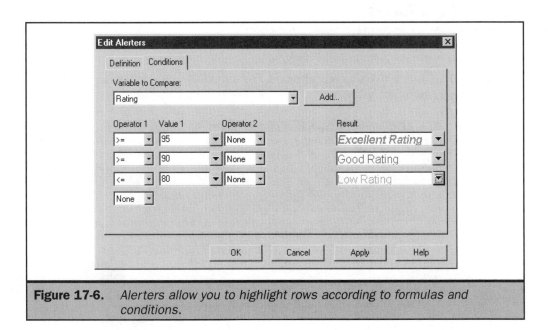

Figure 17-6. *Alerters allow you to highlight rows according to formulas and conditions.*

Inserting a Column for Text Alerters

If you want to highlight certain values in a different color or format, select the column within the table and then create the alerter. However, if you want the alerter to display a particular text or a different variable as shown in the preceding figure, you must first insert a new, blank column.

1. Position the cursor in the column next to where you want to insert a new column.

2. From the pull-down menu, select Insert | Column. BusinessObjects asks you if you want to insert the column to the right or left of the current column.

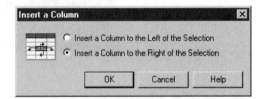

3. Choose an option and click OK.

4. Click on the new column where you will apply an alerter.

BusinessObjects uses a contextual formatting technique so that the new column uses the same formatting as the surrounding columns.

Creating the Alerter

To create the alerter as displayed in Figure 17-6:

1. Select Format | Alerters and click Add.

2. The Edit Alerters dialog box appears. From the Definition tab, enter a name and a description for the alerter.

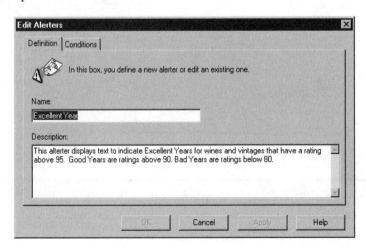

3. Select the Conditions tab shown in Figure 17-6.

4. Under Variable To Compare, select the variable that will determine if the row should be highlighted or not. This is most often a measure variable—for example, Expense Variance, or in this example, Rating. You also can click Add to create a new variable for comparison.

5. Under Operator 1, click the DOWN ARROW to specify equal to, greater than, and so on. In this example, select >=.

6. Once you specify an Operator, a Value box appears. Enter a value or click the drop-down box to select from a List Of Values. In this example, enter **95** to alter the format for wines greater than or equal to 95.

7. In the Result Column, the default display is Cell Content formatted with red text. With Cell Content, the formatted table displays the values of the cell but allows you to change the color, font, border, and shading. For example, it will continue to display the wine rating (or an expense variance) but will highlight it in red. To specify a format for this condition, click the drop-down arrow and select Format.

8. To have it display text such as Over Budget or Excellent Rating, use the same drop-down arrow and select Text. When you select Text, you will be prompted to Enter Your Text. In this example, enter **Excellent Rating**.

9. Continue entering additional conditions and results. Click OK to close the Edit Alerters dialog box.

10. From the Alerters dialog box, click Apply to apply the alerter to the currently selected column.

11. Click OK to close the dialog box and see the effects of the alerter, shown here:

Country	Producer	Varietal	Vintage	Rating	
France	Angelus	Bordeaux Blend	1990	Excellent Rating	96.00
France	Angelus	Bordeaux Blend	1990	Excellent Rating	96.00
France	Angelus	Bordeaux Blend	1993	Good Rating	92.00
France	Ausone	Bordeaux Blend	1926	Low Rating	65.00
France	Ausone	Bordeaux Blend	1978		88.00
France	Ausone	Bordeaux Blend	1982	Excellent Rating	95.00
France	Ausone	Bordeaux Blend	1988	Good Rating	90.00
France	Ausone	Bordeaux Blend	1993		87.00
France	Ausone	Bordeaux Blend	2000	Excellent Rating	96.00
France	Balestard-la-Tonn	Bordeaux Blend	1995		86.00
France	Baret	Bordeaux Blend	1996	Low Rating	80.00
France	Batailley	Bordeaux Blend	1998		82.00
France	Beaulieu Comtes	Bordeaux Blend	2000		88.00
France	Beaumont	Bordeaux Blend	1989		85.00
France	Beaumont	Bordeaux Blend	1997		84.00
France	Beauregard	Bordeaux Blend	1999		88.00
France	Beauregard	Bordeaux Blend	2001		85.00
France	Beauregard	Bordeaux Blend	2001		85.00
France	Beau-Sejour-Becc	Bordeaux Blend	1995		89.00
France	Beau-Sejour-Becc	Bordeaux Blend	1998	Good Rating	92.00

Column Headings

In formatting cells that are column headings, you can change the contents of the cell to shorten the column heading as well as format the headings. In a standard tabular report, the column headings are in the first row of the table. If you create a financial table with Format | Rotate Table or if you create a crosstab report, the column names may also be in the first column.

Long Column Names

Sometimes the name of the variable is much longer than the values the column will contain. For example, if your product codes are only six digits and the object name is *Global Material Identification*, the column heading and width is unusually long for what would otherwise be a small column. By default, BusinessObjects will use the following formula for a column heading:

```
=NameOf(<Variable(Query N with Universe)>)
```

Where
> *Variable* is the name of the object.
> *N* is the query number within the document.
> *Universe* is the name of the data source.

The *N* and *Universe* options appear only when there is more than one variable with the same name in a document.

You can modify the name of the column heading to show a smaller name.

1. Select the cell that contains the long column heading.

2. Type the shorter name directly over the formula. You can do this in the cell within the Report window or within the formula bar if the formula toolbar is displayed.

Formatting Header or Column Headings

In the following example, you will change the header part of the table so that the font is automatic (black), the border shows a darker line, and the cells contain no shading. Recall that by default, BusinessObjects aligns text cells left. This is fine for columns that contain text values, but for column headers that display measures, you want them to be right-aligned along with the numeric values that appear below them.

1. Move your cursor to the left of the table until it becomes a right-pointing arrow.

2. Click next to the row that contains the column headings. The row of header values changes color to show you selected the entire row.

3. Use the pull-down menu Format | Cell, then select the Font tab.

4. The default font is Custom (white). This is legible with a dark blue background but not with no background. Set the Color to automatic and then click Apply.

5. Still within the Cell Format dialog, select the Border tab.

6. Under Style, select a thick line style.

7. Under Presets, select Box. Then select a thin or dashed-line style and click the middle cell border to have a dashed line separate each column heading.

8. Click Apply to reflect the Border formatting.

9. Select the Shading tab.

10. Set Fill to None and Background and Foreground Colors to Automatic. Click OK to accept the Shading changes and close the Table Format dialog box.

11. To align the column headings for the measure columns, select the two measure columns. From the toolbar, click Align Right.

If you have properly selected the full row for steps 1–10 and just the measure column for step 11, your column headings should appear as follows:

Country	Avg Rating	Avg Price
Australia	89.22	44.84
France	85.99	330.02
Italy	88.44	58.51
Spain	89.25	30.74
USA	89.14	109.25

Additional Table Format Options

In the preceding examples, you selected individual cells and components of a table to display the different tabs from the Format dialog box shown in Figures 17-1 through 17-4. When you select the entire table, you have two additional tabs in the Table Format dialog box: General and Page Layout. If you are working with a crosstab report, you also have a Pivot tab.

The General Tab

The General tab contains the following options, as shown in Figure 17-7.

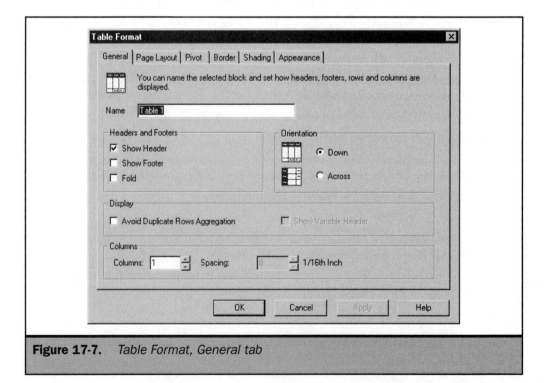

Figure 17-7.   *Table Format, General tab*

- **Show Header** This box is enabled by default to display column headings.

- **Show Footer** When you add a calculation on a column (discussed in Chapter 18), this box is automatically checked and the table shows an additional row with the subtotals.

- **Fold** This hides the body of the table, similar to working in Outline view (discussed in Chapter 18).

- **Avoid Duplicate Rows Aggregation** When the universe designer sets an object to use a projection aggregate, BusinessObjects automatically shows the aggregate for the dimension and level of detail displayed in the table. You generally want to check this box only if you are trying to see the individual rows of a result set to identify calculation issues.

- **Columns** When you want to print one long table on a page, you can specify a number of column sets or groups; this is useful only for narrow columns. In the following example, Label Name and Unit Price fill up only half the page:

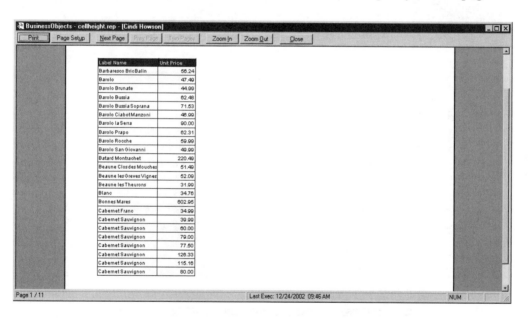

You can specify three column sets to have BusinessObjects repeat the number of columns three times across the page. When you modify the number in Column, you must also specify the Spacing between the column sets. The next example uses 4/16ths of an inch between columns. To have the column headings repeated on each column, select the Page Layout tab, then click Repeat header on every page. Use Print Preview to see the effect of this setting.

Note *If you select more columns than actually fit on the page, BusinessObjects will display only what fits and will continue the next column set on another page.*

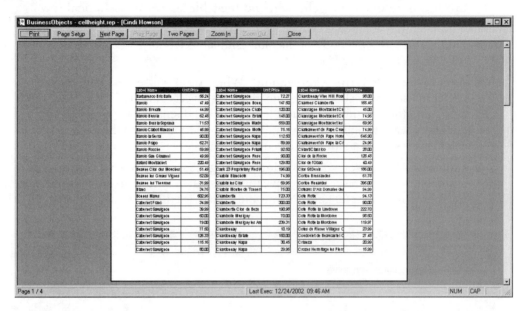

- **Orientation/Across** By default, the column headings run across the page. If you want to rotate them down, select Down. This option may be useful for reports that contain only a few rows of data but many dimensions and measures. Changing this setting to Down has the same effect as selecting Format | Rotate Table. In WebI, this block style is referred to as a Financial block.

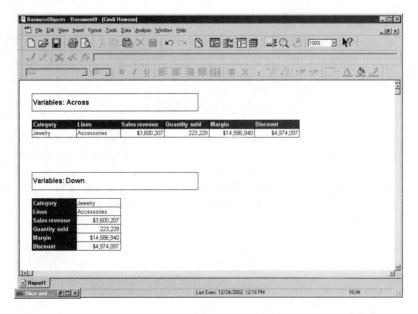

Page Layout

Most of the options in the Page Layout tab (Figure 17-8) affect what happens when you print a report. To see the effect of these settings, select View | Page Layout.

The New Page options are useful only for very small tables. Start On A New Page will insert a page break between each table. Repeat Block On Every Page repeats a small table on top of every new page. For example, if you have a small summary table at the top of a report and a long detail table beneath, select Repeat Block On Every Page to have the summary table repeated at the top of each page as the details change beneath.

Under Page Break, Avoid Page Break In Block is useful when you have multiple tables in a report. This option will force BusinessObjects to print the block on a new page so that the second table starts on a new page, or if possible, prints on one page. This option is superfluous for reports that contain only one long table that spans more than one page and will cause a blank page to print before the block.

Remember that a master/detail report may appear to have multiple tables, but in reality, they are one table with multiple sections. If you want each new section in a master/detail report to start on a new page, then select Format | Section, then Page Layout.

The Repeat Header and Repeat Footer options are very useful for long tables that span multiple pages. The header or footer must already exist in the table for these options to have an effect. By default, all tables display headers. For a table to display

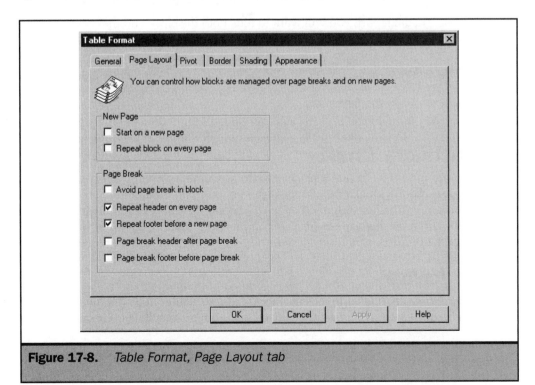

Figure 17-8.   *Table Format, Page Layout tab*

REPORTING WITH
BUSINESSOBJECTS

a footer, you must insert calculations (see Chapter 18) or select Table Format, then the General tab, and check the Show Footer box. Headers refer to the column headings or variable names; the footer refers to the additional row used for subtotal calculations.

Hiding a Table

The Appearance tab, shown in Figure 17-4, is similar to the Appearance tab for formatting a table or section. However, the Hide Cell option will change to a Hide Block or Hide Section Header depending upon which component you selected. This option is quite powerful for multiblock reports and master/detail reports. For example, if you have a report that contains a chart for trend analysis and a detail table beneath to show budget variance, you may only want to show the detail table when the total variance exceeds a certain value. To conditionally hide the block:

1. From the Table Format dialog box, select the Appearance tab.

2. Check the box Hide Block.

3. Enter a formula or click Edit Formula to launch the Formula Editor. You do not need to specify an If statement. For example, to hide a block when the total variance for the block is less than $1,000, enter:

   = <Variance> < 1000

4. Click Apply to see the effect of this setting, then OK to close the dialog box.

In a master/detail report, you will want to hide both the block and the corresponding section header so be sure to use the same options and formula for both report components.

 The Hide Block setting evaluates the entire table or mini table in a master/detail report. It will not hide individual break levels or rows. To hide these, you need to use Filters, which are covered in Chapter 18.

Formatting a Chart

Just as you can format particular parts of a table, so can you format particular parts of a chart. As you click individual components, BusinessObjects adds black markers to indicate what component you have selected. When you double-click a component, BusinessObjects launches the correct menu and tab for that component. Figure 17-9 shows the various chart components. The Y axis is selected as indicated with the black markers.

The Chart Toolbar

When formatting a chart, enable the chart toolbar by selecting View | Toolbars, then checking the Charts box. BusinessObjects adds the next toolbar to the menu.

The chart toolbar allows you to change the entire chart type. For example, you can change a bar chart to a pie chart. To change the entire chart type, be sure you have selected the entire chart block. To change only one of the series to a line chart (as shown later in Figure 17-12), select the individual data series.

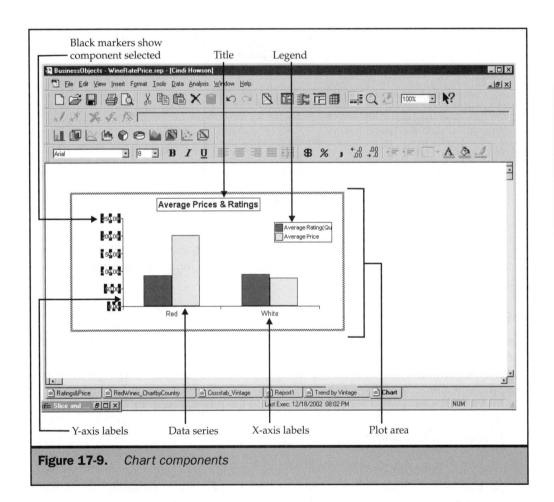

Figure 17-9.   *Chart components*

The Chart Pop-Up Menu

The chart pop-up menu allows you to format and insert individual chart components. To invoke the pop-up menu, click anywhere within a chart block and right-click to invoke the pop-up menu. The middle menu option changes depending on which individual component you have selected; for example, if you have selected a title, the middle menu option changes to show Format Chart Title. If you have selected a data series, the middle menu option displays Format Data Series. In previous Figure 17-9, the Y-axis label is selected, and the following pop-up menu shows Format Axis Label:

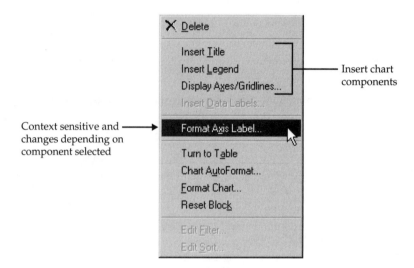

From the pop-up menu, you can insert a title, a legend, axes, or data labels. You can also insert these via the pull-down menu Insert | Chart Components or via various tabs within the Chart Format dialog box.

Chart AutoFormat

For each chart type displayed in the toolbar, BusinessObjects provides several default formats. For example, within the Line chart type, you can choose if you want each data point to be marked with a square, a diamond, or nothing; you can specify gridlines or not. You can manually set these options via the Chart Format dialog box shown in Figure 17-10; however, the Chart AutoFormat dialog box automates the most useful options.

To apply a default format:

1. Within your report, select the chart block.

2. Use the pull-down menu Format | Chart AutoFormat or right-click to invoke the pop-up menu and select Chart AutoFormat.

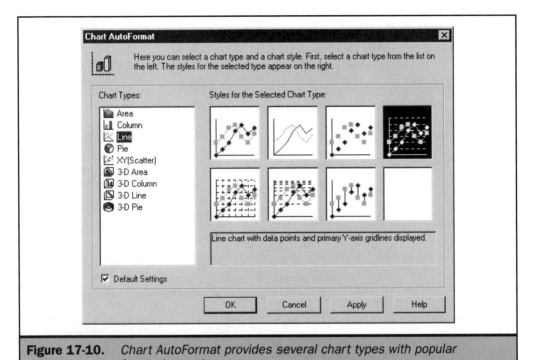

Figure 17-10.   *Chart AutoFormat provides several chart types with popular
formatting options.*

3. Select a Chart Type.

4. Select a particular style for the chart type. BusinessObjects displays a detailed
   description for each chart type.

5. Click Apply to apply the autoformat to the chart. You will be able to see the
   effect of your selections in the background.

6. Click OK to close the Chart AutoFormat dialog box.

*When you use Chart AutoFormat, it resets any other formats you have applied to
titles and legends. Be sure to use AutoFormat first to avoid having to reformat other
chart components. If you change the chart type via the toolbar, formatting for other chart
components is preserved.*

Chart Format

Some of the options in the Chart Format dialog box are similar to the Cell Format and
Table Format dialog box. The General, Series, and Pivot tabs contain the most differences.

The General Tab

Table 17-2 explains each of the options on the General tab.

Titles	Needed
Name	Enter a name for the chart. This will be displayed in Report Manager and will become the title if you click the Title box. If you rename a chart after clicking the Title box, you may need to remove the check mark next to the Title box and then reenable it to get BusinessObjects to reflect the new name.
X-Axis	Displays values on the X axis.
Z-Axis	If you select a 3-D Chart Type, then this box is automatically enabled. What you otherwise may have displayed as legends become the Z-axis labels.
Primary Y-Axis	Displays labels on the Y axis. BusinessObjects sets default increments that you can override through Format	Axis Label, then the Scale tab.
Secondary Y-Axis	When you chart two measures that have different numeric ranges, it may be more meaningful to display two Y axes.
Back Wall, Left Wall, Floor	These options apply to 3-D charts and determine if you want walls displayed along each of the axes of the chart.
Legend	Displays the variable names for the measures as a legend. You format the legend via Format	Legend Text.
Title	Creates a cell within the Chart to display a chart title. By default, it uses the text from the Name field.
Start on a new page	If your report contains only one chart, do not select this option. If you have multiple charts and block types, check this to have the chart printed on a new page.
Repeat on a new page	If you have a summary chart within a report and a long, detailed table beneath the chart, use this option to print the chart on each page.

Table 17-2. *Chart Format Options in the General Tab*

Titles	Needed
Avoid page break in block	When you have multiple blocks in a report, check this to ensure the chart is printed on one page and that the chart does not get fragmented across multiple pages.
Adjust plot area to chart size	The plot area is one component within a chart, as shown earlier in Figure 17-9. By checking this box, you tell BusinessObjects to resize the bars, lines, or pie shape within the chart. This box does not remain checked.
Adjust scale to value range	Check this box for master/detail charts so that the Y-axis labels are rescaled according to the values. For example, French wines have a wider price range than American wines. By default, the Y-axis label shows 0 to 250. When this option is checked, the scale for French wines shows 0 to $400, and American wines shows 0 to $200.

Table 17-2.   *Chart Format Options in the General Tab* (continued)

The Series Tab

The Chart Format, Series tab defines how you want to display the numeric values in the chart. A *group* refers to one measure or a set of measures that are graphed using the same Chart Type. By default, a chart contains one group and one chart type. However, you can create multiple groups to select a different chart type for each group. The new group can either use the same Y axis or a secondary Y axis. In Figure 17-11, Group 1 is a line chart that displays the Average Rating in a line. Group 2 is a bar chart that displays the Average Price in a bar, along a secondary Y axis. Note that the chart type icon is different next to each Group number.

The check boxes and buttons in the Group Type section will change depending on the type of chart you choose for a particular group. For example, with the line chart shown in Figure 17-11, you can choose if you want to display drop lines, high-low lines, or up-down bars. With the Chart type set to Column, you can choose how much of a gap you want between the different bars.

Labels

Data Labels correspond to each data series and may be a numeric value for a particular data point, a percentage, or a description of the measure. From the Series tab, click Labels to launch the Data Labels dialog box. You also can access Data Labels by selecting a series within the plot area of the chart, then right-clicking to call the pop-up menu and

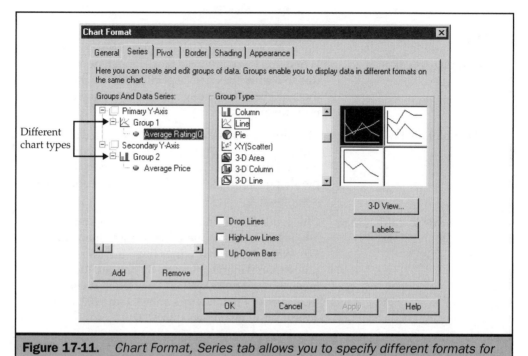

Figure 17-11. *Chart Format, Series tab allows you to specify different formats for each measure.*

selecting Insert Data Labels. This dialog allows you to choose the following options to add to the plot area of the chart:

- **None**   By default, no label is added to the series.
- **Show Value**   Display the numeric value above the data point, bar, or pie wedge.
- **Show Percent**   For pie charts, display the percentage.
- **Show Label**   When there are multiple measures, display the name of the variable. This acts like a legend.
- **Show Label And Percent**   For pie charts, display the name of the measure as well as the percentage value.

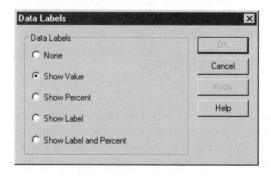

To modify the labels number format (for example, no decimal places, red if negative), alignment, or font, select the labels within the plot area and then right-click to call the pop-up menu or use Format | Data Labels. For charts, the Alignment tab has an additional option for Orientation. This affects how you want the labels rotated above each data point. Otherwise, BusinessObjects does not allow you to modify where the data label appears and all other Alignment options are grayed out.

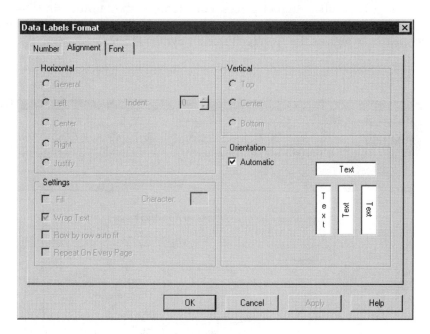

Adding a Group to a Secondary Y Axis

Within the Series tab, you can specify a secondary Y axis when you are charting two measures that will have different numeric ranges. For example, wine ratings will only go to 100, whereas wine prices can go into the thousands. By displaying two different Y axes, the chart displays the different measures more effectively. In the following example, you will add a group to a secondary Y axis, as shown in Figure 17-12:

1. From within the Chart Format, Series tab, select Secondary Y Axis (Figure 17-11).

2. Right-click to call the pop-up menu shown here.

3. Select Add. BusinessObjects inserts a new group number.

4. With your mouse still positioned on the group number, choose the desired chart type for this group.

5. Right-click to call the pop-up menu and select Variables.

6. From the Variables dialog box, choose the measure that you want to associate with this group and click Insert.

7. With the secondary variable highlighted, click Labels and select Show Value.

Figure 17-12 shows a sample chart with two Y axes. Note that each axis has its own scale. By splitting the measures into two Y axes, you more clearly see when higher ratings do not necessarily result in higher prices. For example, the Merlot wines have high average ratings, as do the Syrahs. However, the Average Price for American Merlots at $61 is not nearly as high as the Average Price for Syrahs at $97.

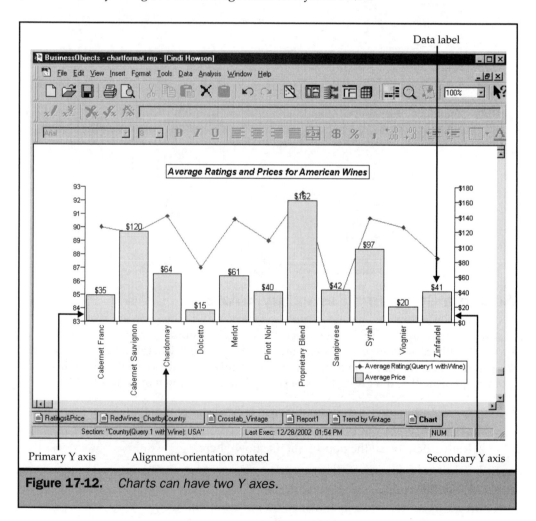

Figure 17-12. *Charts can have two Y axes.*

The Pivot Tab

Within the Chart Format dialog box, the Pivot tab allows you to select which variables you want to display along the X axis, Z axis (for 3-D charts), and Y axis.

The Appearance Tab

The Appearance tab is similar to the one shown in Figure 17-4 that also applies to free-standing cells and tables. When you have a report with multiple blocks such as charts and tables, it is important to set the position of the blocks relative to one another. If you leave the blocks relative to a section or margin and the size of the block changes (for example, when the number of rows in a table expands), the two blocks may run into and overwrite one another.

When you position a chart to the right of a table block:

1. Select Format | Chart from the pull-down menu, then click the Appearance tab.

2. Click the drop-down box for Horizontal Position Relative To and select Table 1.

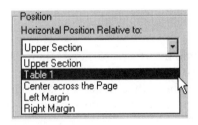

3. Enter a number for how many 1/16ths of an inch you want between the table and the chart.

4. Click OK.

Templates and Standard Report Styles

Templates and standard report styles allow you to format documents with pre-defined settings. A *template* is a particular kind of file within BusinessObjects that allows you to include a company logo and a document classification (confidential, public information, and so on) in headers and footers. Templates have a .ret extension and are stored in \Business Objects\BusinessObjects 5.0\Template. Templates also allow you to specify an initial block type and formatting options when creating a new document.

Standard report styles exist within a global template file, default.ret. They control the formatting of the different report components (section headers, table block, crosstab block) described in Chapter 16. Unless your administrator has provided you with a modified default.ret file, the settings in this file create the standard yellow table with blue column headings. Once you are comfortable formatting the various components of a report, modifying the standard report styles is the best way to apply a consistent format to all reports you create. When you modify standard report styles, BusinessObjects automatically saves the changes to default.ret.

If you are the BusinessObjects administrator and want the standard report styles applied to all users' reports, you must modify your default.ret file and ensure the modified version is installed for all full-client users.

In order to ensure a consistent appearance to all documents, you need to create at least two files, a template that contains the desired header and footer and a modified default.ret that contains report components with the desired color and font settings.

Templates

In the following example, you want to modify the default header and footer to include a company logo, a document refresh date, and page numbers. The default initial block type is a crosstab and a master/detail report. In developing a template, you work with an existing document.

Company Logos

To insert a company logo, you insert a picture cell. Therefore, you must first have access to your company logo as a bitmap or tagged image format file. When you insert a picture into a report, the path to the report is also inserted; BusinessObjects then looks for a separate picture file in the specific path. This can pose problems when sharing documents with other users. To force BusinessObjects to look for the picture file in the same directory as the document, remove the path from the cell. As an alternative, if the size of the logo in the .bmp or .tif file corresponds to the actual logo size, use Insert | Object, Create From File. This directly imports the picture into the report. The downside is the report file becomes larger, but the benefit is that the report no longer looks for a separate image file.

1. Open an existing document by selecting File | Open or clicking the Open button from the toolbar.

2. Be sure Report Manager is open and in Map/Structure mode. Select Report Manager from the standard toolbar, then click the Map tab. From within the Map tab, select the Structure icon.

3. Select the report tab that contains the desired block layout—in this example, Crosstab_Vintage.

4. Select View | Page Layout so that you see the Page Header and Page Footer.

5. Select Insert | Picture.

6. The mouse cursor becomes an insert picture cell icon (looks a bit like a mountain). Position it in the Header section and drag it to create a cell the approximate size of your company logo.

Note *The size of the cell is important in preserving the shape of the logo. BusinessObjects provides no way to preserve aspect ratios as other graphics programs do.*

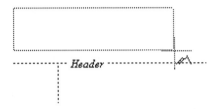

7. BusinessObjects will prompt you to select a bitmap or tagged image file. Select the desired file and click Open. In the Report window, BusinessObjects displays the logo. Report Manager shows a new cell under Page Header.

New cell for picture

Logo appears

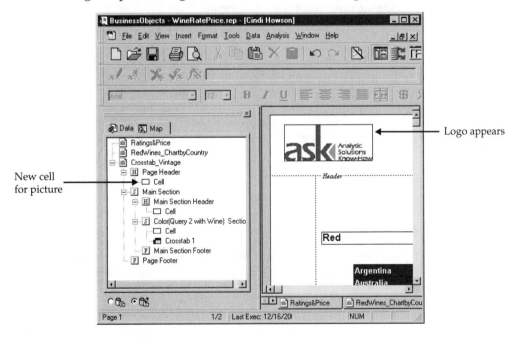

8. The default cell format for a Page Header includes a border. Click the No Border button from the formatting toolbar.

Special Fields

BusinessObjects allows you to insert *special fields* for commonly used document information such as current date, last refresh date, and page numbers. You can access additional information through report formulas. With report formulas, for example, you can create a formula to display either the original document author (DocumentAuthor) or the user logged into the repository (CurrentUser). Refer to Chapter 18 for additional instructions on report formulas. In the following example, you will add two cells to display a last refresh date and a page number.

1. Within the Report window, scroll to the Page Footer. Alternatively, from within Report Manager, in Map/Structure view, select Page Footer.

2. From the pull-down menu, select Insert | Special Field | Date and Time | Last Refresh. If you have more than one data source, BusinessObjects prompts you to select a query for the refresh date.

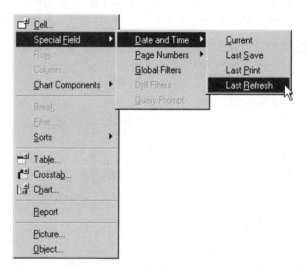

3. The mouse pointer becomes an insert cell cursor. Position your cursor to the left-hand side of the footer and drag the mouse to the desired cell size.

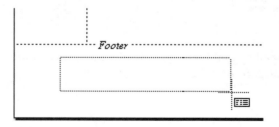

4. Select Insert | Special Field | Page Numbers | Page # of #. The mouse pointer again becomes an insert cell cursor. Position the cursor to the right-hand side of the footer. Your footer should now appear as follows:

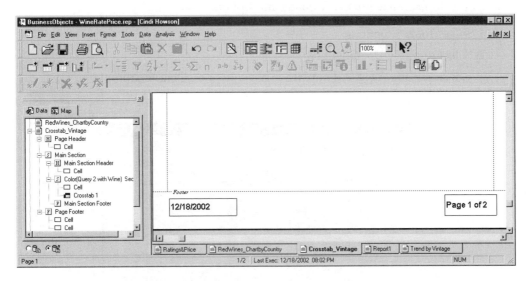

5. You can remove the cell borders by selecting both cells in the Report window (use CTRL-click to select both footer cells); from within Report Manager, you can select and format only one cell at a time.

6. From the toolbar, click the No Border button.

Save As Template

Once you have included the desired headers and footers, save the document as a template to be applied to other reports.

1. From the pull-down menu, select File | Save As.

2. Give the template a meaningful name: **Table with Logo**.

3. Click the drop-down menu Save As Type and select BusinessObjects Templates.

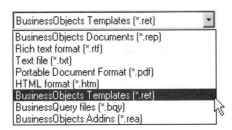

4. Click OK.

Apply Template

You can apply the template to existing reports by selecting Format | Report | Apply Template. Additionally, when you create a new document, you can have BusinessObjects prompt you to select a template. To enable this option:

1. Select Tools | Options.

2. Select the New Document tab.

3. Check the box Select A Template to have BusinessObjects prompt you for a template name.

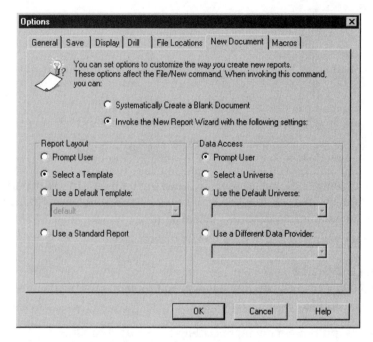

4. Click OK to close the Options dialog box.

Standard Report Styles

To modify the standard report styles, select Format | Standard Report Styles (see Figure 17-13). Under Report Components, BusinessObjects displays the different block types and sections of a report. The tabs General, Page Layout, Border, and Shading are similar to those for individual cells and tables.

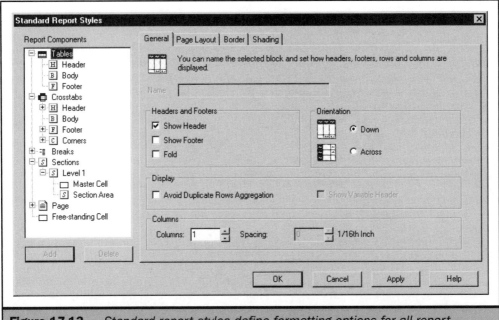

Figure 17-13.   *Standard report styles define formatting options for all report components.*

Summary

BusinessObjects provides formatting options above and beyond what appears in a standard MS Windows product. You can spend a lot of time formatting reports rather than analyzing data. The key is to fiddle with the formatting options just enough to ensure the formatting aids your analysis and provides the kind of print layouts you want. As you become more comfortable with the different formatting options, try to avoid repetitive formatting tasks and standardize on a consistent format via templates and/or standard report styles.

Summary

Chapter 18

Analyzing the Data:
the Slice and Dice Panel

The Slice and Dice Panel is your key to analyzing data. It allows you to sort information, group it, create calculations on groups, and filter the data to further analyze a subset of information. While many options in the Slice and Dice Panel are also available via separate pull-down menus and toolbars, the Slice and Dice Panel is more intuitive and allows you to apply multiple options simultaneously. Once you have added different sorts, breaks, and filters, you may find that you want to take your analysis further by creating custom variables and formulas. The formula syntax BusinessObjects provides is quite powerful and overcomes many of the limitations in SQL; it thus provides you with functionality that the universe and query may not otherwise provide.

The Slice and Dice Panel

To launch the Slice and Dice Panel, click the Slice and Dice button from the Standard toolbar or use the pull-down menu Analysis | Slice and Dice.

Figure 18-1 shows the Slice and Dice Panel. Unlike when using other panels within BusinessObjects, you can leave the Slice and Dice Panel active while you view the effects of your analysis. You can minimize, maximize, and resize the panel.

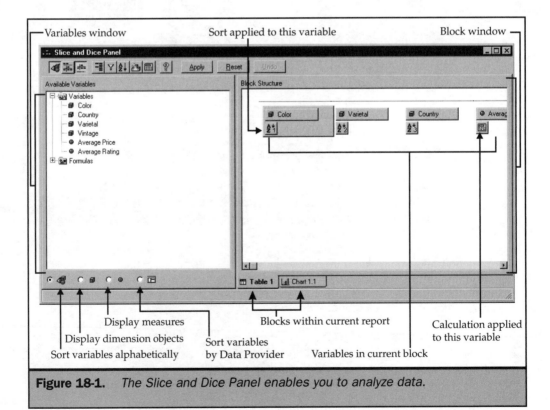

Figure 18-1. *The Slice and Dice Panel enables you to analyze data.*

The Slice and Dice Panel also contains its own toolbar. The buttons it contains are described in Table 18-1. You can also access some of these options within the main Report window via the Report toolbar (View | Toolbars, then select Report). The Slice and Dice Panel allows you to apply multiple functions to multiple columns at the same time. When you are working with large data sets, this approach is faster than applying functions one column at a time via the Report toolbar.

Button	Name	Function
	Show/Hide Available Variables	Within the Slice and Dice Panel, all available variables from all data sources are displayed in the Variable window, whether or not they exist in the current block. If you do not want to see all the variables, click this button to hide the Variables window.
	Show/Hide Section	In a master/detail report, this displays the Master Cell(s).
	Show/Hide Status Bar	Hides the status bar.
	Apply Break	Apply a break to a dimension within the existing block.
	Apply Filter	Apply a filter to a dimension within the existing block.
	Apply Sort	Sort the data values. Once you add a sort to a column, double-click to set the sort to descending.
	Apply Ranking	Rank the data to display only the top or bottom values for a particular measure—for example, top-selling products or worst-selling products.
	Insert Calculation	Insert a sum, average, count, and so on, for a column of data. Note: variance calculations are not available via the Slice and Dice Panel; use the pull-down menus or Report toolbar.

Table 18-1.   *Buttons Within the Slice and Dice Panel*

Button	Name	Function
<img Help icon>	Help	Display contextual help.
Apply	Apply	Apply the changes added in the Slice and Dice Panel to the block within the Report window.
Reset	Reset	Remove all formatting and reset to the default style.
Undo	Undo	Undo the last change set through the Slice and Dice Panel.

Table 18-1.   *Buttons Within the Slice and Dice Panel* (continued)

Available Variables displays all the dimensions, measures, details, and formulas in the current document. When you first create a report, the Available Variables and the variables in the right in the Block Structure are one and the same. By default, these are sorted alphabetically. If you want to sort them by Data Provider, click the radio button in the bottom-left corner.

The Block window displays the variable names within the current block. If you have more than one block, such as a table and a chart as shown in Figure 18-1, the block types and names are displayed across the bottom. Click a block tab to switch the display to another block within the same report.

Sort

Sorting data within a report allows you to rearrange the rows alphabetically, or if your sort is on a measure column, numerically. For example, you can use Sort to find wines with the highest rating. When you want to analyze data within a subset by using Breaks, the breaks take priority over the sorts. In the following example, you will sort the data by Country and then by Rating to further analyze ratings within each country:

1. Select the column within the Block Structure. BusinessObjects adds a gray box to the column selected. Here Country is selected; Varietal is not.

2. Click Apply Sort from the Slice and Dice Panel toolbar.

3. The first sort you add applies to all the rows within the existing block. The sort icon shows a number 1 to indicate that Country is the primary sort order.

4. Select the column Average Rating.

5. Click Apply Sort. The sort icon shows a number 2. When you apply a Sort to a column, the default sort order is ascending and the button shows AZ. In this case, you want to see the highest wine ratings within a particular country, so the sort order should be from highest to lowest. To change the sort order to descending, double-click the sort icon beneath the variable name; it turns to ZA. If you have the status bar displayed, it informs you the action will invert the sort order.

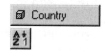 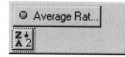

Note

You can see above that the sort icon is highlighted with a dotted line. This means the icon or function is selected, not the entire column. When you have just the function selected, you can use DEL to remove the function from that column.

6. Click Apply to have the data in the block sorted. Until you click Apply, the data in the Report window does not change.

7. Minimize the Slice and Dice Panel to view the results of the new sort order.

The following table shows the results of these two sorts. Without the breaks, the sorts may not be particularly clear. Sorts and breaks together more clearly divide the report in a way that facilitates analysis by different groups of data.

First sort ↓   Second sort ↓   Sorted descending within Country

Country	Color	Varietal	Average Rating
Australia	Red	Syrah	90.71
Australia	Red	Proprietary Blend	88.50
Australia	Red	Grenache	88.83
France	White	Sauternes Blend	91.13
France	Red	Syrah	90.26
France	Red	Proprietary Blend	88.60
France	White	Chardonnay	89.03
France	White	Riesling	89.33
France	White	Marsanne	89.17
France	White	Bordeaux Blanc	89.00
France	Red	Pinot Noir	87.78
France	Red	Bordeaux Blend	84.66
Italy	Red	Cabernet Sauvignon	94.00
Italy	Red	Proprietary Blend	88.00
Italy	Red	Merlot	88.00
Italy	Red	Nebbiolo	88.38
Italy	Red	Sangiovese	87.65

REPORTING WITH BUSINESSOBJECTS

Breaks

A break will break the table into multiple pieces so that you can better analyze the data within a group. A master/detail report is somewhat similar, except that a break does not create a separate master cell. Once you create a break, you then use Calculations to generate subtotals. The first break column becomes the primary sort order. Often, this is the first column in the table, but it does not have to be.

Using the same sample table from the preceding section, add a break to the Country column:

1. From the Slice and Dice Panel, select the Country column.

2. Click Apply Break. Just as with sorts, you can have multiple breaks. When you apply a break, the break icon indicates that this is the primary break column by preceding the break icon with a number 1. The Country column should now contain both a sort and a break, like this:

3. Click Apply to have the break applied to the data in the block.

4. Minimize the Slice and Dice Panel to see the effect of the break.

In the table in Figure 18-2, it is much easier to see that the data is sorted by country. For each country, there is now a separate mini-table. Visually, you can now more clearly see a set of wines for each country and can tell that the highest-rated wines (the second sort variable) are not necessarily the highest-priced wines.

 Although breaks make the data appear *as if they are in separate mini-tables, in the strict sense, BusinessObjects still treats the table as one block, an important nuance when formatting the table. In Figure 18-2, the Table Format options will be the same for both the France and Italy mini-tables.*

Break Options

Figure 18-2 shows the break options, break header, break footer, and remove duplicates. To modify these options, return to the Slice and Dice Panel, and double-click the break icon beneath the Country variable. Alternatively, you can use the pull-down menu Format | Breaks.

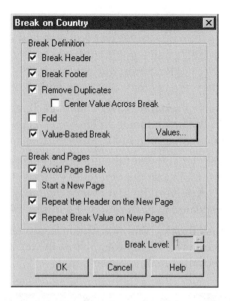

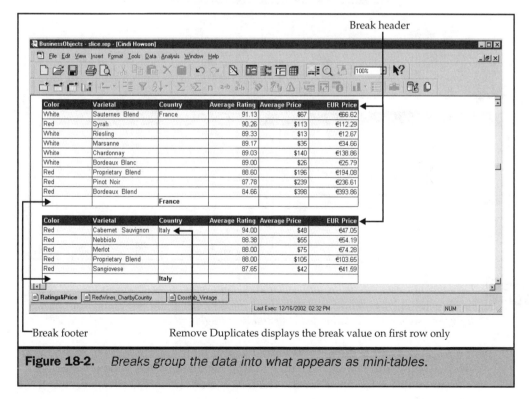

Figure 18-2.   *Breaks group the data into what appears as mini-tables.*

■ **Break Header** Repeats the column headings within each mini-table. If your table contains more than one break and you enable the Break Header for each break, certain mini-tables will contain multiple rows of column headings. To avoid this, set the Break Header on the last break only (or on the lowest level detail for which you want to create a separate mini-table).

■ **Break Footer** Inserts a separate row beneath each mini-table. The calculation subtotals appear in the break footer. In Figure 18-2, the break values (France, Italy) appear in the break footer, but the report does not yet contain subtotals.

■ **Remove Duplicates** If you want the break value repeated only once in the first row of the mini-table, use this option. As shown in Figure 18-2, the country name France appears only in the first row of the table. Without this option set, France would be repeated in each row of the mini-table.

■ **Center Value Across Break** Works with the Remove Duplicates option so that the break value is centered within the rows of the table. The following screen shows an example of the break value centered:

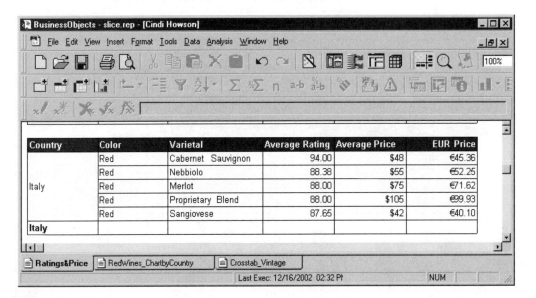

 Do not confuse a break value with calculation values that may appear in the row of a break footer. A break value is the value from the dimension—in this example, France, Italy, and so on. A calculation value would be the subtotals.

■ **Fold** Hides all the detail rows within a mini-table and displays only the footer. This is a powerful feature that, after adding calculations, lets you better analyze the subtotals for the break levels. The next screen shows the effect of folding the break on Country.

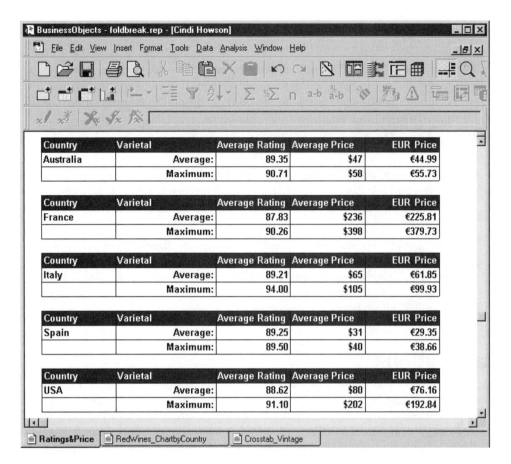

- **Value-Based Break** By default, BusinessObjects creates a mini-table for each value within a dimension. By selecting a value-based break, you create a mini-table only for the individual dimension values you select. For example, if you want Italian wines in one mini-table and all other countries in a separate table, select the Value-Based Break option. The Values button then becomes enabled, through which you select the break values for which you want to create a mini-table.

Chapter 17, "Page Layout," discusses formatting a table to improve the layout when you print a report. Breaks have similar options that affect the mini-tables when you print a report:

- **Avoid Page Break** Use this option to force BusinessObjects to start the break or mini-table on a new page. For breaks that contain many rows of data, particularly long tables, it may not be possible to avoid a break in the middle of the mini-table. If the grouping of data is longer than a page and not the first grouping of data in the block, a page break will occur before the break and the mini-table will span multiple pages.

- **Start a New Page**   For each break level, print the mini-table on a new page. This print setting is useful when you intend to distribute each break level to a different person—for example, if you have different product managers and have a break on product.

- **Repeat the Header on the New Page**   For each page break, repeat the column headings.

- **Repeat Break Value on New Page**   For mini-tables that span multiple pages, repeat the break value in the first row of each page. If you choose to repeat the header as well, then the row with the break value is repeated beneath the column headings.

- **Break Level**   Within the Slice and Dice Panel, the Break Level displays a grayed-out number to indicate which break number this dimension is. You cannot modify the Break Level from this screen. To change the Break Level, you would re-sort the break icons within the Slice and Dice Panel, or use the pull-down menu Format | Breaks.

Calculations

Calculations allow you to add subtotals to a table that contains breaks. If the table does not contain any breaks, then the calculations are grand totals for the entire block. In most instances, if you add a calculation to one measure, you will want them on all measures in a report. The subtotals are inserted as formulas in the break footer. Table 18-2 lists the calculations available in the Slice and Dice Panel as well as the formula syntax inserted in the break footer.

The Calculation dialog box is somewhat context-sensitive, depending on the object type (character, date, number); however, it does not consider the object qualification (dimension, measure, detail). For example, SUM appears for numeric dimension objects. This does not make sense from a business perspective; you may want to COUNT the number of products or number of wines, but it is not something you will want to SUM. Therefore, pay attention to which column you have selected before inserting the calculation function.

Using the same sample table from the preceding section, add AVERAGES and MAXIMUMS to the three measure columns:

1. From the Slice and Dice Panel, select the Average Rating column.

2. Click Insert Calculation.

3. To select the type of calculation, double-click the Calculation icon beneath the Average Rating column. This opens the Calculations dialog box.

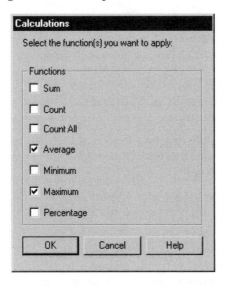

4. Remove the check from Sum and select Average and Maximum. Click OK to close the dialog box.

5. Repeat steps 1–4 for the remaining measure columns.

6. Click Apply to insert the calculations into the table.

7. Minimize the Slice and Dice Panel to see the effect of the break.

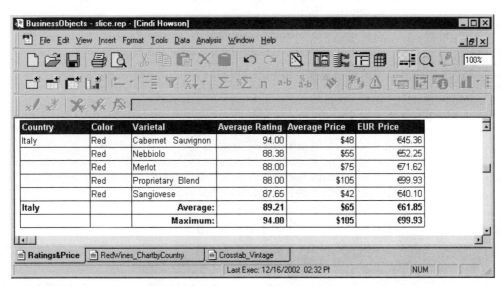

Calculation	Explanation	Formula
Sum	Adds the values for a particular measure. SUM is the default calculation when you first apply a calculation to a variable. However, SUM may not make sense for certain measures such as ratios and percentages.	=SUM(<*Measure Variable*>)
Count	Counts the unique values within a break. Use this with dimension or detail objects.	=COUNT(<*Dimension Variable*>)
Count All	If you want a row count, rather than just the unique values, use Count All.	=COUNTALL(<*Dimension Variable*>)
Average	Calculates the average based on the individual measures displayed in the table. If you hide certain rows of data through a filter, the values from the hidden rows do not, by default, affect the subtotal. Average is not a weighted average, so for things like average price, you may want to create a formula to get a weighted average or use extended syntax, discussed later in this chapter.	=AVERAGE(<*Measure Variable*>)
Minimum	Displays the minimum value for a particular measure within the break.	=MIN(<*Measure Variable*>)
Maximum	Displays the maximum value for a particular measure within the break.	=MAX(<*Measure Variable*>)
Percentage	Calculates the percentage contribution a particular break level makes to the grand total. In addition, it inserts a new column in the table that shows the percentage each row contributes to the individual break level. This calculation uses the Context Operator ForAll described later in this chapter.	=<*Measure Variable*>/SUM(<*Measure Variable*>) ForAll (<*Dimension Variable*>)

Table 18-2.   *Calculations Available from the Slice and Dice Panel*

> **Note**
> *If you do not have your break options set to include a break footer, the calculations are inserted only as grand totals at the end of the report. Also, if you apply a break after you have inserted calculations, the calculations are not repeated in the break footer and remain as grand totals. To have them appear as subtotals in the break footer, first set the break, then insert the calculations.*

BusinessObjects inserts row descriptions for each different calculation you insert. This can sometimes be quirky—for example, averages may appear on multiple rows; the break value may be overwritten; the calculation description may be missing. The calculation description gets inserted in the column immediately preceding the first calculation, so you are less likely to encounter problems when this column is not the break column. To fix these problems, you can click Reset within the Slice and Dice Panel, but then you lose other formatting changes.

An alternative is to drag and drop the different break values and/or calculation descriptions to make the break footers more visually appealing. If you are uncertain about which calculation appears in the various columns and rows, use View | Structure to see all the formulas. In the following example, the Average calculation description has been modified to concatenate the country name; concatenation is described later in this chapter, in "Concatanation." The calculation descriptions for the grand totals have been moved to the first column; the generic Average cell text has been replaced with Average for ALL Countries to more clearly identify it as a grand total.

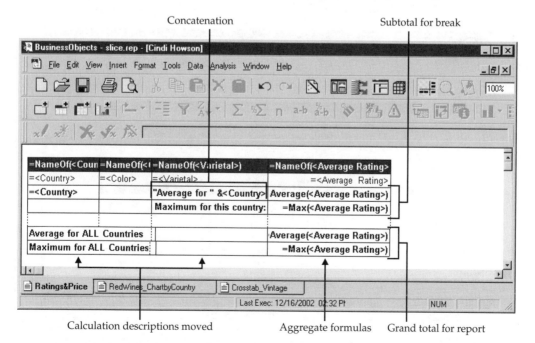

Multiple Sorts, Breaks, and Calculations

As you insert sorts and breaks, you may find the tables are easier to read if the order of the columns reflects the sort and break order. You can easily reorder columns within the Slice and Dice Panel by selecting a column and dragging it to a new position within the Block Structure. Figure 18-3 shows a sample structure using data from the

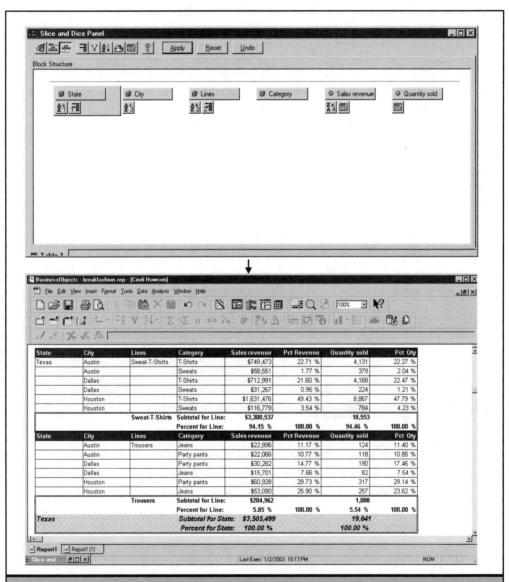

Figure 18-3.   *The Slice and Dice Panel and a formatted report with multiple sorts, breaks, and calculations*

EFASHION universe. The leftmost column, State, is the primary sort order and primary break. Cities is the second sort column but does not contain a break. Clothing Line is the third sort column and contains a break. In actuality, the Sorts on State and Clothing Line are redundant as the breaks force a sort; however, they more clearly and accurately reflect that City is the third sort priority. Clothing Line, the third column, contains the break header so that the column headings are repeated for each change in clothing line. The State break does not contain a break header; otherwise, an additional row of column heading would appear for each change in State. Sales Revenue and Quantity Sold have two calculations, Sum and Percent. The bottom of Figure 18-3 shows a corresponding sample report in which the break footer rows have been formatted to make the subtotals more apparent. Refer to Chapter 17 for instructions on formatting a section of the table.

Filter

As you apply breaks, sorts, and calculations, you may find that you want to focus on one or more subsets within the report. Filters allow you to restrict the number of rows displayed in the report. They do not affect the query results; they affect only the data currently displayed in the block. It's important to understand that the calculations will also change to reflect only what is displayed. In Figure 18-2, the table displayed both Red and White French wines. To focus only on White wines, insert a filter on Color.

1. From the Slice and Dice Panel, select the Color variable in the Block Structure.

2. Click Apply Filter.

3. BusinessObjects displays a list of values from data in the microcube. Select the desired values. Use CTRL-click to select multiple values. Click OK to close the Apply A Filter dialog box and return to the Slice and Dice Panel.

4. Click Apply to see the effect of the filter.

Complex Filters

In the preceding example, BusinessObjects displayed a simple list of values upon which you based the filter. This filter applied to the current block. In reports that contain multiple blocks, you can apply a global filter that filters data from both the chart and the table, for example. Complex filters also allow you to filter values based on a formula rather than a list of values. For example, you can select all products that start with a particular ID sequence, character string, or the like. If it's likely that the filter values change as the query is updated, you also want the filter to be based on a formula, rather than fixed values. This is particularly true when you filter by measures. For example, if you want to identify customers that have bought more than $1,000 worth of products, the precise values and corresponding customer list will change each quarter as customers buy more products; Customer A may buy $1,010 by Q2 and then $1,200 by Q3. For these instances, you want to create a filter based on a formula rather than a fixed list of values. You do this within the Report window and pull-down menu, not in the Slice and Dice Panel. In the following example, add a filter to identify wines with an average rating of 90 or higher:

1. From the Report window, position your cursor within the desired block.

2. Select Format | Filters. (Note that Insert | Filter and the Filter button from the Report toolbar only allows you to apply simple filters).

3. BusinessObjects displays a Filter dialog box (see Figure 18-4) that shows you any existing filters added via the Slice and Dice Panel. Filters under Global apply to all blocks in the existing report. Filters under Table 1 apply just to the particular table. Select Table 1.

4. To define a new filter, click Add.

5. You will be prompted to choose a variable upon which to filter. In this case, select the measure Average Rating and click OK.

6. You are returned to the Filters dialog box shown in Figure 18-4. Click Define to create a filter formula. BusinessObjects displays the following Filter Editor. This editor is similar to the Formula Editor discussed later in this chapter, in "Formulas."

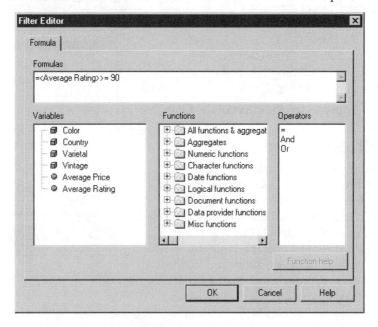

7. Under Variables, select the comparison variable, Average Rating, and double-click to have it inserted in the Formula box.

8. Under Operators, select a comparison operator, >=, and double-click to have it inserted in the Formula box.

9. In the Formula box, enter a comparison value, **90**.

10. Click OK to close the Filter Editor.

11. In the Filters dialog box, the asterisk next to the Filter Variable indicates it is based upon a formula. If you click Apply, the dialog box displays which values are selected by the filter. Because it is a formula, this selection list is not fixed; if a value of 90.1 appears in the next query refresh, this new value also will be selected because it is >= 90.

12. Click OK to close the Filters dialog box and see the table with the new filter.

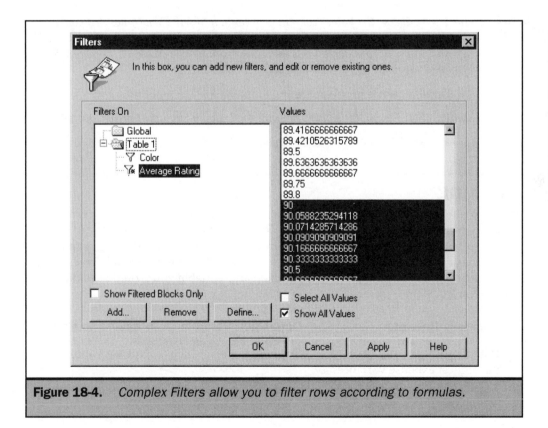

Figure 18-4.   *Complex Filters allow you to filter rows according to formulas.*

Caution   *From within the Filter Editor, you can in theory select a different variable for comparison than the one selected in step 7; however, BusinessObjects ignores any part of the formula that deals with a different variable, which is rather misleading. For example, suppose you wanted to create a filter:*

`=<Country>="France" And <Average Rating> >= 90`

If the variable selected in step 7 is Average Rating, then the `<Country>="France"` part of the formula is ignored; if the variable selected in step 7 is Country, then `<Average Rating> >= 90` is ignored. In order to accomplish the preceding selection criteria, you must create multiple filters for each variable. In certain circumstances, you may want to nest the filters—for example, wines with a Rating >=90 And with an Average Price <=100. In order to do this, you would first create a formula to identify these rows, and then filter on the formula result. Refer to the section "Formulas," later in the chapter. Version 6 allows you to add multiple variables in one complex filter.

Tip   *In the Filters dialog, the Values column may contain #EMPTY for rows that contain null values. You also can click Define and use the Filter Editor to create a formula to select null values or to suppress null values. For example, to create a list of wines for which there are no prices, use the logical function `IsNull`:*

`= IsNull(<Average Price>)`

To create a list of wines for which prices are available, incorporate the `Not` operator:

`= Not IsNull(<Average Price>)`

Ranking

Whereas filters limit the rows returned in accordance with specific selection criteria, normally from dimension variables, Apply Ranking enables you to limit the rows according to top or bottom values of measures. When you apply a ranking, you apply it in terms of the dimension you are trying to analyze. The following table gives some business questions that show which dimension and variable you would base the ranking on:

Business Question	Dimension Variable	Measure to Rank
Which business units have the highest expense variance?	Business Unit	Expense Variance
What are the top-selling products?	Product	Sales Quantity

Business Question	Dimension Variable	Measure to Rank
Which customers generate the most revenues?	Customer	Sales Revenue
Which warehouses have the most product on hand?	Warehouse	Inventory
Which wine producers produce the highest-rated wines?	Producer	Rating
Which years have yielded the highest-rated wines?	Vintage	Rating

In the following steps, you learn which producers make the highest-rated wines:

1. From the Slice and Dice Panel, select the Producer variable within the Block Structure.

2. Click Apply Ranking.

3. BusinessObjects displays a Select Top/Bottom for Producer dialog box. Select Top and enter a number. For example, to see the Top 10 Producers, enter **10**. If you wanted to select the lowest-rated wines, or the lowest-priced wines, you would choose Bottom and change the Based On value.

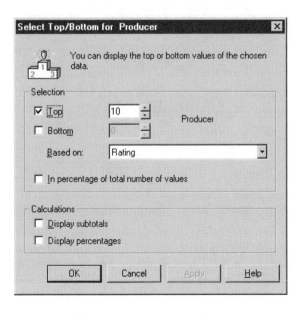

4. In the drop-down box Based On, BusinessObjects displays only measure variables. Select which measure variable you want the ranking to be based on—in this example, Rating.

5. If you have already added calculations in the report, such as Average and Maximum, BusinessObjects will continue to display these. If you want sums and percentages added to the report, select these two options. With Ratings, sums have no meaning, so leave these options blank.

6. Click OK to close the Select Top/Bottom dialog box.

7. From within the Slice and Dice Panel, click Apply to filter the number of rows according to the ranking.

As shown in the following report, if there is a tie for the 10th ranking (or whichever value you specified), then BusinessObjects displays more than ten rows—in this example, 12 Producers:

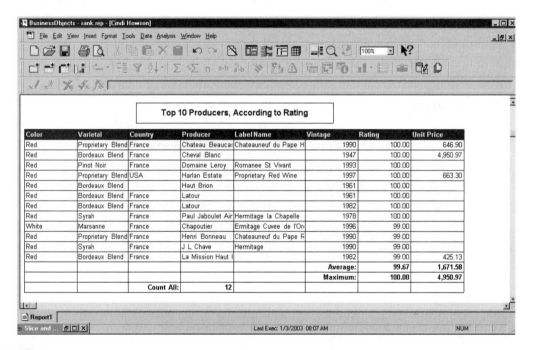

Top 10 Producers, According to Rating

Color	Varietal	Country	Producer	Label Name	Vintage	Rating	Unit Price
Red	Proprietary Blend	France	Chateau Beaucas	Chateauneuf du Pape H	1990	100.00	646.90
Red	Bordeaux Blend	France	Cheval Blanc		1947	100.00	4,950.97
Red	Pinot Noir	France	Domaine Leroy	Romanee St Vivant	1993	100.00	
Red	Proprietary Blend	USA	Harlan Estate	Proprietary Red Wine	1997	100.00	663.30
Red	Bordeaux Blend		Haut Brion		1961	100.00	
Red	Bordeaux Blend	France	Latour		1961	100.00	
Red	Bordeaux Blend	France	Latour		1982	100.00	
Red	Syrah	France	Paul Jaboulet Air	Hermitage la Chapelle	1978	100.00	
White	Marsanne	France	Chapoutier	Ermitage Cuvee de l'Or	1996	99.00	
Red	Proprietary Blend	France	Henri Bonneau	Chateauneuf du Pape F	1990	99.00	
Red	Syrah	France	J L Chave	Hermitage	1990	99.00	
Red	Bordeaux Blend	France	La Mission Haut I		1982	99.00	425.13
					Average:	99.67	1,671.58
					Maximum:	100.00	4,950.97
		Count All:	12				

The Apply Ranking function works only on the rows within the local document, so it is a ranking within a subset of data. If you want a genuine ranking based on all the data in the source data, this must be set up at query time either via an advanced object that includes the Rank function, or as a workaround, by limiting the number of rows returned in the query. Refer to Chapter 10 or Chapter 22 for more information.

About Ranking Calculations

In applying rankings, you can elect to display the ranking according to a percentage. This percentage relates to the number of values in the dimension you are applying the ranking. It does not relate the percentage contribution from a particular measure column (for example, which products generate 10 percent of the revenues). This is quite different to the way a measure object that uses the RANK function works. For example, if you have a list of 100 wine producers, ten percent of this is 10 producers. If your document contains 200,000 product IDs, one percent of this is 2000 product IDs. To apply ranking by a percentage of the dimensional values, select the option In percentage total number of values in the Select Top/Bottom dialog box.

As an example, refer to the first few rows in the following table. The table on the left contains 20 Category items. Ten percent of this is two, so only two category items will be selected when a ranking is added according to the percentage total number of values. The top two categories according to sales revenue are shown in the top right report. Jewelry accounts for 76 percent of the top-ranked sales or 36 percent of all sales in the report. Belts, bags, wallets is the second highest-ranked category. In the bottom-right table, the ranking is by quantity sold. Jewelry is still the top ranked, but the percentage from quantity sold is now 35 percent. Evening wear replaces Belts, bags, wallets as the number-two-ranked category according to the quantity sold.

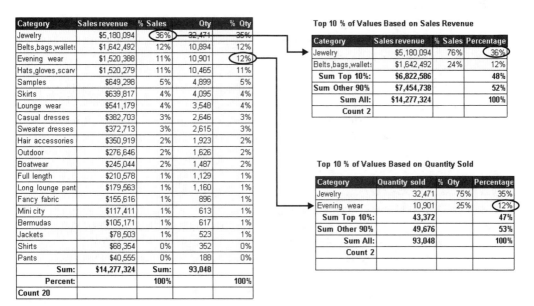

REPORTING WITH BUSINESSOBJECTS

 In certain circumstances in BusinessObjects versions 5.1.4–5.1.6, Ranking may return incorrect results. This has been identified as a bug, with a fix scheduled for patch 5.1.7.

The preceding table makes it fairly easy to understand how ranking works. However, the ranking feature becomes even more powerful when it is incorporated into a table that contains multiple break levels in which it is not so easy to immediately identify the top performers. For example, refer back to Figure 18-3. If the same Ranking is applied to this report, then only the rows containing T-Shirts and Jewelry for all the break levels would be displayed.

In the Select Top/Bottom dialog box, you can choose to display subtotals and display percentages. When you display percentages, BusinessObjects inserts a new column in the block report to calculate the percentages for each row of data. In the preceding ranking reports, the % Sales and % Qty columns were created by applying a Calculation to the columns. The last Percentage column in each ranked-block was inserted by selecting the Display percentages option from the Select Top/Bottom dialog box. Notice that it corresponds to the percent values from the full data set on the left. In this way, you can say that the top two products account for 48 percent of Sales Revenue while the rest account for 52 percent of the Sales Revenue. The following calculations get inserted into the column or break footer:

- Column:

  ```
  =Sum(<Sales revenue>)/NoFilter(Sum(<Sales revenue>) ForAll <Category>)
  ```

- Break Footer:

  ```
  =Sum(<Sales revenue>)
  =(NoFilter(Sum(<Sales revenue>)))-Sum(<Sales revenue>))
  =NoFilter(Sum(<Sales revenue>))
  ```

The first subtotal in the break footer reflects the sum of the values for only the rows of data displayed. The second subtotal calculates the subtotal for the values not displayed—that is, the clothing categories that do not account for ten percent of the number of categories. The third subtotal gives the grand total of $14,277,324, as shown earlier.

Master/Detail

Chapter 16 showed how you can select an existing column in a block to become a master cell. You also can create master/detail reports via the Slice and Dice Panel by dragging variables into the Section window. I find this approach more intuitive, as it shows you the report layout before you apply the change. It also gives you more control in creating reports with multiple sections. In the following example, you will create a master/detail report using Country as a section heading:

1. From the Slice and Dice Panel, select Show/Hide Section to display the Section window in the top-right portion of the screen.

2. If you want the variable to remain as a column within the table block, select the variable from the Available Variables window and drag it to the Section

window. If you want to remove the variable from the block so that it
appears only as a master cell, drag it from the block to the Section window.
BusinessObjects automatically adds a Sort to the Section header.

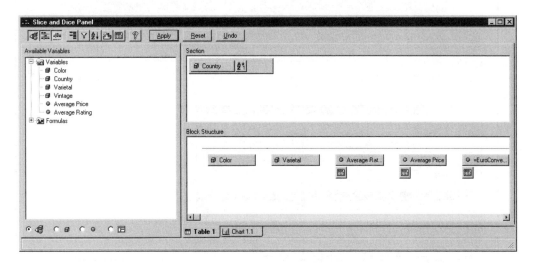

3. To have multiple sections, drag the second variable to the Section window. For
   example, to create a section on Color within each Country, BusinessObjects will
   automatically readjust the sort priority so that the top section is always the first
   sort order.

4. Click Apply to see the new report layout.

Outline View

Once you have defined the breaks, calculations, and sections, use Outline view to
interactively explore the different mini-tables within your report; this feature is
particularly useful for long reports that contain several sections. While Outline view
may not be as robust as the BusinessObjects Explorer module with its drill-down
capabilities (see Chapter 19), it is an overlooked functionality that can facilitate
analysis. Earlier versions of BusinessObjects allowed you to use Outline view with
break levels; the latest version works only with section headings, which I find a bit
of a drawback.

To enable Outline view, select View | Outline from the pull-down menus.
BusinessObjects adds buttons to the bottom of the report that correspond to the number
of sections. In Figure 18-5, there is a main section, indicated with the S button, a first
section for Color, and a second section for Country. The downward triangles on the left
of the Report window allow you to collapse one particular section. For example, to
hide the details just for Australian wines, click the triangle next to Australia to fold this
section. To hide all the level 2 section details, click the 2 button in the bottom-left corner.

Click to collapse this color

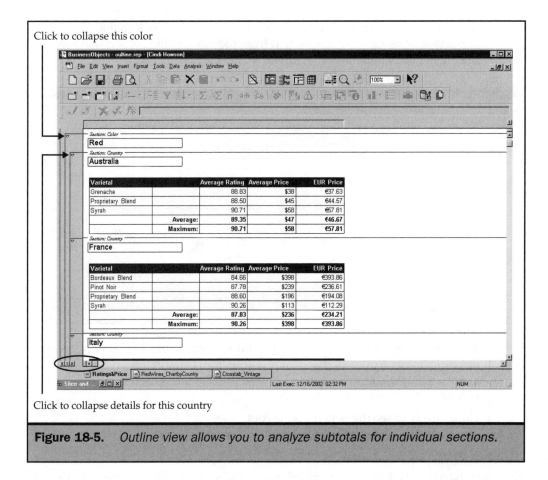

Click to collapse details for this country

Figure 18-5.   *Outline view allows you to analyze subtotals for individual sections.*

To make this feature more useful, insert subtotals next to the master cells. For example, insert subtotals next to each Country and Color. Then, when you fold/hide each section, you still see the subtotals and can get a quick overview of the business.

Crosstab

Recall from Chapter 16, "Crosstab" (Format | Table, Pivot tab), the confusion with what is considered a column and what is considered a row. Building a crosstab report in the Slice and Dice Panel is also much more intuitive.

To create a crosstab, drag the variable that you want to display as column headings so that it is above the first measure. If you position it above a second or third measure, the crosstab will not be built properly. The cursor changes to a crosstab insertion. The status bar informs you of the action "Moves *Variable* and builds Crosstab." You also can stack the column headings, as shown in Figure 18-6.

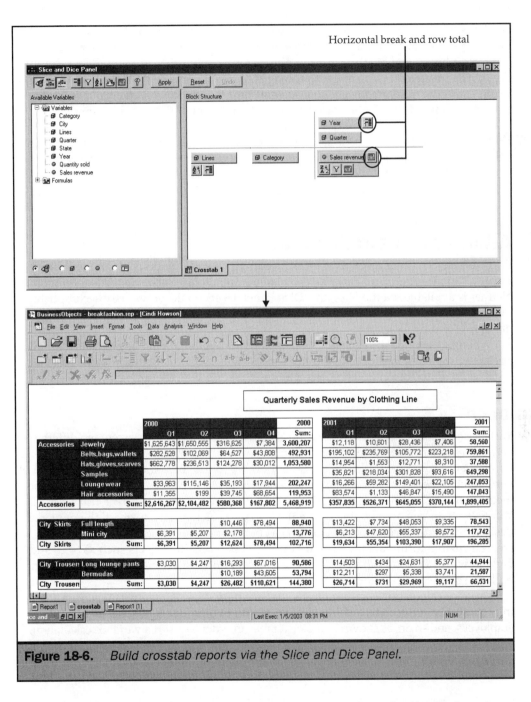

Figure 18-6.   *Build crosstab reports via the Slice and Dice Panel.*

With crosstab reports, you also can have horizontal breaks and subtotals. In order to ensure the subtotals appear correctly, it's important to apply the break first and the calculation second. For example, if your report has Quarter and Year as column headings, you can sum the quarters across to show a yearly subtotal, as shown in Figure 18-6. The last column of the table would show the grand total for both years. To create a horizontal break, select the dimension or column heading and click Apply Break. The break icon will appear to the right of the variable name. To calculate row totals, select the measure for which you want the row total and click Apply Calculation from the toolbar. The calculator icon appears to the right of the variable name.

 When a crosstab table contains multiple measures, by default, the column headings do not display the measure names in the column headings. To display the measure names as column headings, select Format | Crosstab, then select the General tab. Under the Display section, select the option Show Variable Header.

Additional Calculations

With version 5.1, BusinessObjects introduced two new calculations via the pull-down menus, Variance and Euro. Variance calculations are also available via the Report toolbar. Neither is available via the Slice and Dice Panel. Users could previously accomplish these calculations only via custom formulas that you would need to create for each detail row and break level.

Whereas the calculations in the Slice and Dice Panel deal with aggregates that appear as subtotals in a footer, variances are additional rows or columns in a table or crosstab. Euro conversions replace values in an existing column.

Variance

Variance calculations calculate either the absolute difference or the percentage difference between two dimension values; they will not allow you to calculate the difference between two measure columns. In this respect, your ability to use these built-in calculations will very much depend on how the universe and/or data mart tables are structured. If the measure objects contain built-in time period intelligence such as *Current Year Sales, Last Year Sales*, then you are not able to use the Variance calculations. Instead, the universe designer should provide variance objects as part of the universe or you will need to create a custom formula. However, if your universe contains objects such as *Sales* and *Time*, in which *Time* contains rows for current year and last year, then you may use the built-in Variance calculations.

Variance calculations are not limited to time periods; you can create the variance in profitability between two stores, sales between two products, salaries between two employees, and so on, as shown in the next table. In order to insert a variance calculation, you select the dimension values you wish to compare. The variance is inserted for all measures within a report. You can insert a variance calculation into a table block, in which case BusinessObjects will insert a new row in the table; however, you may find the variance analysis easier to read in a crosstab report.

If you want to know the variance for a measure such as:	Then select these dimension values:
Sales between two quarters	Q1, Q2
Salary between genders	Male, Female
Profitability between stores	Store1, Store2
Sales between products	Product1, Product2
Expenses between scenarios	Actual, Budget

The next example uses the same crosstab report shown in Figure 18-7. You can access the Variance calculations via the pull-down menu or the Report toolbar. To enable the Report toolbar, select View | Toolbars, then choose Report.

Variance Difference

In the following example, you will calculate the difference in sales between two quarters:

1. Within the table, select the dimension values you wish to compare. In this example, Q1, Q2. Use CTRL-click to select multiple cells. If you are working with a crosstab report, these may be the column headings, as shown on the left or the individual rows, as shown on the right.

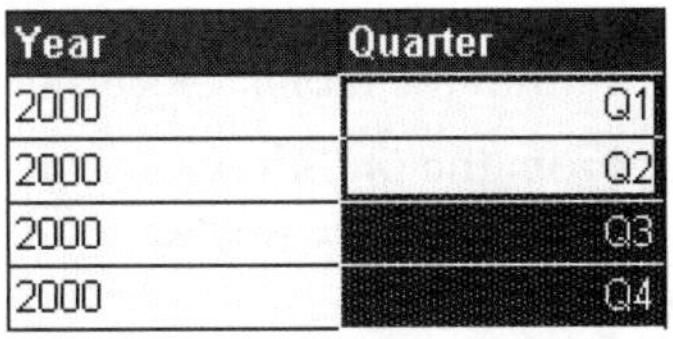

2. From the pull-down menu, select Data | Calculations | a-b Variance or click a-b from the Report toolbar. If you have not properly selected two and only two dimension values, these menu options and buttons will remain grayed out.

3. BusinessObjects inserts a new column labeled Q1-Q2. If you inserted the variance into a table block, then a new row labeled Q1-Q2 is inserted in the Quarter column.

New variance column

		2000					2000
		Q1	Q2	Q1-Q2	Q3	Q4	Sum:
Accessories	Jewelry	$1,625,643	$1,650,555	$-24,912	$316,625	$7,384	3,600,207
	Belts,bags,wallets	$282,528	$102,069	$180,459	$64,527	$43,808	492,931
	Hats,gloves,scarves	$662,778	$236,513	$426,266	$124,278	$30,012	1,053,580
	Samples						
	Lounge wear	$33,963	$115,146	$-81,184	$35,193	$17,945	202,247
	Hair accessories	$11,355	$199	$11,156	$39,745	$68,654	119,953
Accessories	Sum:	$2,616,267	$2,104,482	$511,785	$580,368	$167,802	5,468,919

Within the body of the block, Variance inserts the following formula:

```
=<Sales revenue> Where (<Quarter>="Q1")
- <Sales revenue> Where (<Quarter>="Q2")
```

Within the footer of the block, variance creates the following formula. Note that this calculation contains the aggregate SUM function:

```
=(Sum(<Sales revenue>)) Where (<Quarter>="Q1")
- (Sum(<Sales revenue>)) Where (<Quarter>="Q2")
```

Percentage Variance

To insert a percentage variance:

1. Within the table, select the dimension values you wish to compare.

2. From the pull-down menu, select Data | Calculations | %a-b Variance or click %a-b from the Report toolbar. If you have not properly selected two and only two dimension values, these menu options and buttons will remain grayed out.

3. In a crosstab report, BusinessObjects inserts a new column labeled Q1-Q2. If the table contains both variance differences and percentage variances, relabel this column **%Q1-Q2**. You can either double-click the column heading and insert a % symbol or, if the Formula toolbar is displayed, select the column heading and insert a % in the formula toolbar.

The % Variance calculation inserts the following formulas in the body and footer of the block, respectively:

```
=(<Sales revenue> Where (<Quarter>="Q1")
<Sales revenue> Where (<Quarter>="Q2"))
/ (<Sales revenue> Where (<Quarter>="Q2"))

=((Sum(<Sales revenue>)) Where (<Quarter>="Q1")
 - (Sum(<Sales revenue>)) Where (<Quarter>="Q2"))
 / ((Sum(<Sales revenue>)) Where (<Quarter>="Q2"))
```

Euro

Although the Euro has been an active trading currency for many years, the European Union fixed the exchange rates for all participating countries January 1, 1999. The Euro coin and notes went into circulation later, on January 1, 2002. Not all members of the European Union agreed to participate in the Euro currency; for example, Greece only began participating in mid-2001, and Great Britain still uses pounds as the official currency. If you are accustomed to seeing measures stated in a local currency, it may not be easy to identify trends or fluctuations when viewing data in the relatively new Euro. Because the exchange rates for Euros are fixed, BusinessObjects provides you with an exchange rate table. You can use this table to add new currencies. You also can use it to convert from other foreign currencies to the Euro; however, this exchange rate will be valid only for a particular time period.

Exchange Rate Table

The internal exchange rate table (Figure 18-7) is always stated in terms of 1 Euro to a foreign currency. To display the exchange rate table, select Data | Euro | Display Conversion Rates. These rates are fixed for countries that participate in the Euro currency. You also can add other exchange rates, such as U.S. Dollars, but they refer to a rate for a particular time period. BusinessObjects does not provide a way of storing rates for various periods, although you could create a formula to do so. The rate for 1 Euro to U.S. Dollars is 1.04724 as of January 6, 2003.

In Figure 18-7, the Euro to Greek Drachma conversion is missing, as Greece joined the currency participation at a later date. To add Greek Drachmas to the conversion table, select Add from the Conversion Rate table. Enter the following information:

- **Currency**   The three-digit trading symbol, GRD.
- **Rate**   Either the rate at which the Euro is fixed for participating countries or the exchange rate for 1 Euro that applies to a particular time period for nonparticipating countries. The rate for Drachmas is fixed at 340.75.

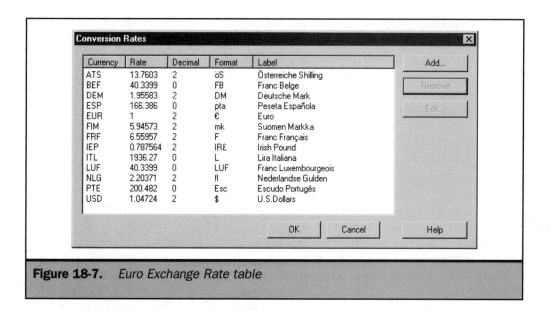

Figure 18-7. *Euro Exchange Rate table*

- **Decimals** The number of decimal places that you want to display when you convert a column in a report to Euros.
- **Format** The currency symbol to display for the values or an abbreviation.
- **Label** A long description for the currency.

Click OK to close the Add Conversion Rate dialog box. The new rate is displayed in the Conversion Rate table. Click OK to accept the new rate. This rate is now available in all reports and documents.

Converting to/from Euros

You can convert an existing measure column to Euros, or if the measure column is stated in Euros, you can convert the values to a local currency. When you convert a column to or from Euros, the values in the column are replaced. Therefore, if you want to display both the Euro value and the local currency value, first insert a new column and then convert. In the following table, you will convert Wine prices that are stated in U.S. Dollars to Euros and then to French Francs:

1. From within the Report window, select the measure column you wish to convert. In this example, Unit Price.

2. From the pull-down menu, select Insert | Column. When prompted, select Insert Column to the Right of the Selection and click OK. Alternatively, you can display the Structure toolbar (View | Toolbars, then select Structure) and select the Insert Column After button.

3. Copy the Unit Price column to the newly created blank column by selecting Copy and Paste from the Standard toolbar.

4. You should now have two columns that display the same values. Ensure that the second column is still selected. Select Data | Euro | Convert to Euros.

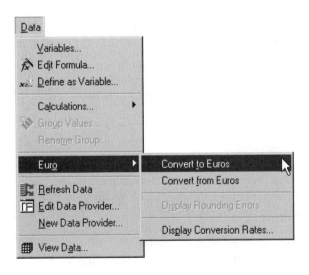

5. BusinessObjects prompts you to Select A Currency. Click the drop-down arrow to select a currency and click OK.

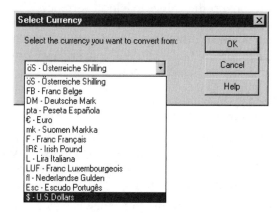

6. Enter a column heading to reflect the correct currency name: **Euro Unit Price**.

Converting from Euros

If your original measure is displayed in Euros, then you can use Data I Euro I Convert From Euros to another currency in the exchange rate table. In some cases, however, BusinessObjects may not prompt you to select a target currency. In this case, you need to create a formula to finish the conversion. The following formula first converts a Unit Price in dollars to Euros, then to French Francs:

```
=(EuroConvertFrom(EuroConvertTo(<Unit Price> ,"USD" ,2) ,"FRF" ,2))
```

Formulas

Most of the data you have manipulated in this chapter comes from results that a data provider returns to the microcube, which is then called a *variable*. As you added Calculations to the report, BusinessObjects automatically inserted formulas. Formulas allow you to manipulate the raw variable data in a number of ways. Because the manipulation is against the local report variables, they can use a proprietary BusinessObjects syntax that overcomes many limitations of SQL. You can use formulas to create new variables. The disadvantage to formulas and created variables, though, is that they are document-specific. In this respect, you must re-create formulas for each new document, a process that can be maintenance-intensive. While I like the power and flexibility formulas provide, I caution you to evaluate whether you really should create an individual report formula or work with the universe designer to create more powerful objects. See Chapter 13, "User Reports," for a more thorough discussion of this issue.

When you create or modify a formula, the formula is available to all reports within a document. BusinessObjects provides several sets of formula functions that allow you to manipulate different types of data. For example, the calculations via the Slice and Dice Panel are referred to as *aggregate functions*; they allow you to create different types of subtotals (SUM, AVERAGE, MIN, MAX, and so on). Aggregate functions also allow you to create running totals, averages, and others. The conversions to Euro were accomplished through a *numeric function* (EuroConvertTo); numeric functions allow you to manipulate columns of numbers. In addition, there are character, date, logical, document, and data provider functions. The Formula Editor, shown in Figure 18-8, also provides operators for straightforward calculations such as subtraction and division as well as more complex manipulations with If-Then-Else and Where.

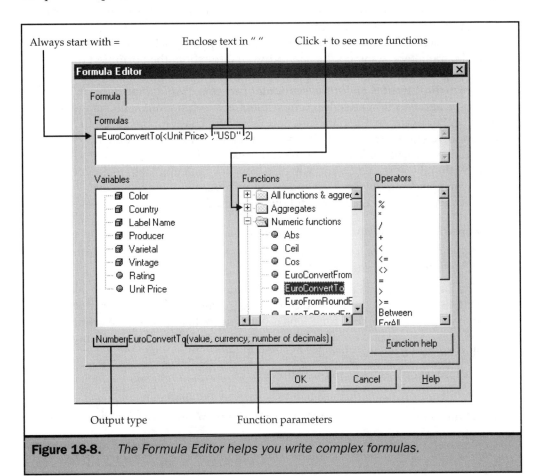

Figure 18-8.   *The Formula Editor helps you write complex formulas.*

There are multiple ways to launch the Formula Editor and to insert a formula into a block:

- Insert a blank column in a report and then select Data | Edit Formula.

- Display the Formula bar with View | Formula Bar, then click the Formula Editor button from the bar.

- Select the pull-down menus Data | Variables, then select Add to launch the Variable Editor and Formula Editor. If you do not give the variable a name, it is treated as a formula and not a variable.

Once you have created a formula or variable, you can select it either from the Report Manager or the Slice and Dice Panel to insert it into an existing block. With this approach, BusinessObjects will automatically insert a new column for the new formula.

As you work with the Formula Editor, you can perform simple calculations such as = <Unit Price>*1.06 or you can work with functions. When you work with functions, you insert the function first, then the variable to which it applies and any additional parameters. As you select an individual function, the Formula Editor displays the syntax at the bottom of the dialog box. Notice in Figure 18-8 that it also displays the output type for the particular function; this is important, as the variable type and function must be compatible. Certain functions will change the output type. For example, the date function Year will change a date type field to number; once it is converted to number, you can no longer use other date functions against the new variable unless you convert it back again.

From within the Formula Editor, you also can click Function Help to access more information about the function and see examples.

As you create your own formulas, follow these guidelines:

- Always start the formula with an = sign.

- When you reference a variable name, enclose it in brackets <>. In Figure 18-8, <Unit Price> is the variable.

- The formula function must correspond to the variable type. For example, Unit Price is numeric; therefore, you can use aggregate and numeric functions with this variable. Often, date functions can pose a challenge when the original column is stored as a number—for example, year. In this case, first convert the year to a date, then use the date functions.

- Enclose text parameters in quotation marks.

- Do not enclose numeric parameters in quotation marks.

- If you want to use an alerter on a formula column, you must first convert the formula to a variable.

Using Formulas as Variables

When you want to reuse a formula in different reports or perhaps in another formula, you can either explicitly create the formula as a variable or convert an existing formula to a variable. By identifying a formula as a variable, you also can apply alerters to the new variable or store the formula as a dimension to use for drill-down analysis.

Creating a New Variable

To create a variable from a new formula:

1. Select Data | Variables.

2. The Variables dialog box lists the current variables, formulas, and constants. From the Variables dialog box, click Add.

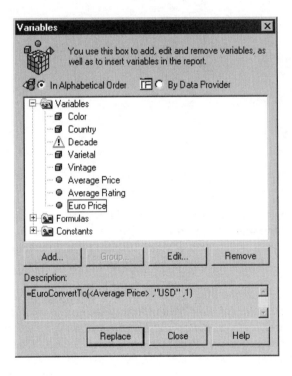

REPORTING WITH
BUSINESSOBJECTS

3. BusinessObjects displays the Variable Editor. On the Definition tab, you specify a name and a qualification. The variable name becomes the column headings in reports and is displayed in the Slice and Dice Panel and the Report Manager.

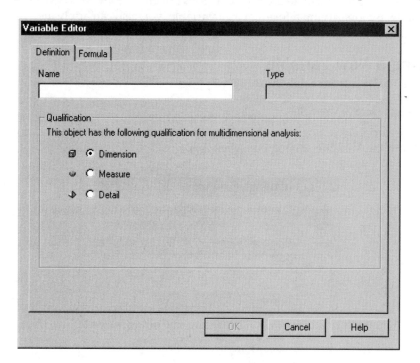

4. Select Dimension for Character, Date, and Numeric fields that you may want to sort and drill by; select Detail for detailed information such as phone numbers and street addresses that you will not use in drill down; select Measure for numeric values that you want to analyze and aggregate.

Tip   *As you define the formula, BusinessObjects will propose a qualification based on the variables you use in the formula. If your formula contains a measure variable, it proposes that the new variable also be a measure. The proposed qualification may not always be correct. For example, if you want to flag highly rated wines (If <Average Rating> > 90 Then "High" Else "Normal"), then BusinessObjects will interpret it as a measure, when it should be a dimension given the result of the formula. Also, after you select a variable to use in the formula, the Type box in the preceding screen is also filled in according to the type of variable used in the formula (Character, Date, Numeric). While you cannot change the type, it is useful to know the variable type to ensure the function you use is compatible, or you will receive an error.*

5. The formula tab displays the formula editor shown earlier in Figure 18-8.

6. Once you have defined the variable and the formula, click OK. The new variable now exists in the document or microcube. To display it in the report, use the Slice and Dice Panel to drag it to a new column.

Converting an Existing Formula to a Variable

If your report already contains a formula, you can convert the formula to a variable.

1. Select the column that contains the formula.

2. From the pull-down menu, select Data | Define As Variable or click the Define As Variable button from the Formula bar.

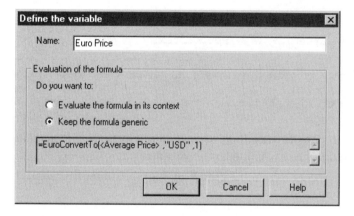

3. Enter a Name. This name becomes the variable name displayed in the Slice and Dice Panel and Report Manager.

4. You can choose to keep the formula generic or to fix the context in which the formula is evaluated. Contexts are explained in the next section.

5. Click OK to close the Define The Variable dialog box and return to the report. While the results of the calculation in the report may not have changed, the cell formula has changed to =<*Variable*> or, in this example, =<Euro Price>.

6. BusinessObjects will have automatically assigned a qualification (dimension, detail, or measure). If you want to change the qualification, choose Data | Variables, then Edit.

Calculation Contexts and Extended Syntax

With calculations and formulas you build yourself, BusinessObjects reevaluates the formula to give results based on the data displayed in the current block. This reevaluation happens automatically and is referred to as a *context*. In a typical formula, you never see the context. In certain circumstances, however, you may want to control the calculation context by using extended formula syntax.

As an example, refer to the rows in the report in Figure 18-9. The second mini-table in the report contains seven rows of data with individual unit prices for French wines produced by Chapoutier. Even though there are multiple wines for a particular vintage, the automatic aggregation has been temporarily disabled to further illustrate the dynamic nature of calculations (Format | Table, select the General tab and the option Avoid Duplicate Rows Aggregation). The Average Price for these wines is $112.34.

An *input context* defines which variables or subtotals within a report go into the calculation; the input context controls the level of detail in the calculation; therefore, these contexts are critical in calculating correct averages and counts. The *output context* determines at which point a subtotal should be calculated. A formula with extended syntax is written as follows:

```
=Function(<Variable> In  InputContext) In OutputContext
```

BusinessObjects provides three operators that allow you to control the contexts:

- **In** Works with context keywords such as `Body`, `Block`, `Report`, and `CurrentPage`
- **ForEach** Works with dimension names to indicate the calculation should happen for each new value within a dimension
- **ForAll** Indicates that the grand total for the dimension should be used in the calculation

Average Price for All French Wines: $163

Country	Varietal	Producer	Vintage	Average Price
France	Bordeaux Blend	Carbonnieux	1998	23.93
		Carbonnieux	**Average:**	**23.93**

Country	Varietal	Producer	Vintage	Average Price
France	Marsanne	Chapoutier	1999	35.00
France	Proprietary Blend		1998	94.99
France	Syrah		1992	98.50
France	Syrah		1996	94.13
France	Syrah		1996	119.97
France	Syrah		1996	171.19
France	Syrah		1999	172.60
		Chapoutier	**Average:**	**112.34**

Average=128.43

			Average:	**101.29**

Figure 18-9. *Calculations in columns and footers are reevaluated according to their context.*

The following table summarizes the different components of an input context that affect your calculations:

Context Keyword	Area of Report
Body	The data displayed in the body of the table. By default, BusinessObjects reevaluates calculations according to what is displayed in the body.
Block	The individual row values; these may not be displayed in the body of the report, but they exist in the document. In order to get "weighted" averages, replace the Body input context with Block.
Report	The entire report. This component is relevant only for reports that contain multiple blocks.
CurrentPage	The current page within a report. Use this when you want to get a subtotal for one page in a multipage report.
<Variable>	*<Variable>* contexts specify at which point a new subtotal should be calculated. If you are using a cumulative aggregate function such as RunningSum, you can specify the context to be reset at a particular break level by inserting a semicolon before the break variable: *CumulativeAggregate(<measure>; <dimension variable>).*

Displaying Extended Syntax

To see the extended syntax of a formula with the explicit contexts:

1. Display the Formula bar (View | Formula Bar).

2. Select the measure column or the break footer that contains the subtotal calculation. In the Formula's text box, the simple formula is displayed as:

```
=<Average Price>
```

3. Position the mouse over the Formula bar in the text box (but do not click in the text box). The full formula with the context is displayed as a tool tip.

The full formula with contexts for the Average Price column is

```
=<Average Price> In (<Producer>, = RowIndex(), <Country>,
<Varietal>, <Vintage>)
```

In the Producer break footer, the full context for Average Price in Figure 18-9 is

```
=Average(<Average Price> In  Body) In <Producer>
```

The extended syntax for Average Price for the entire report replaces the
`In <Producer>` output context with `In Report`:

```
=Average(<Average Price> In  Body) In Report
```

Dynamic Contexts in Action

When automatic aggregation is re-enabled, the Average Price in Figure 18-9 is
automatically calculated from the four dimensions displayed in the current table.
The three rows for the vintage 1996 are collapsed, and the average of $128.43 is
calculated; the individual rows still exist in the *block* but not in the *body* of the report;
by default, BusinessObjects recalculates the averages from the numbers displayed or
what appears in the body of the report.

This now poses a problem with the footer averages. Is the average price for Chapoutier
wines $112.34, as shown in Figure 18-9, or is it a new result of $105.90 because one row
at $128.43 replaced three rows for the Vintage 1996? Also note the new total average
of $92.24 for the report ((23.93+105.90)/2) versus the former $101.29; the new average
reflects a new input row of $128.43 rather than the three detail rows for 1996.

Country	Varietal	Producer	Vintage	Average Price
France	Bordeaux Blend	Carbonnieux	1998	23.93
		Carbonnieux	**Average:**	**23.93**

Country	Varietal	Producer	Vintage	Average Price
France	Marsanne	Chapoutier	1999	35.00
France	Proprietary Blend		1998	94.99
France	Syrah		1992	98.50
France	Syrah		1996	128.43
France	Syrah		1999	172.60
		Chapoutier	**Average:**	**105.90**

One row for three variables

			Average:	92.24

If you want to use the eight individual rows from Figure 18-9, rather than the six
rows displayed in the body in the preceding table, to calculate the average, then change
the input context from `In Body` to `In Block` .

To reflect an average price of $112.34 for Chapoutier wines, the formula at the break
footer should be

```
=Average(<Average Price> In  Block) In <Producer>
```

To reflect a total average price for both producers, the formula in the global footer should be

> `=Average(<Average Price> In  Block) In Report`

So far, these calculations have been affected by the columns that appear in the report. Another feature that affects the calculations are filters. So if you were to filter the report in Figure 18-9 by Varietal or by Vintage, all the footer averages would be recalculated. If you do not want them to be recalculated, then insert a `NoFilter` function into the formula:

> `=NoFilter(Average(<Average Price> In  Block) In Report)`

Tip   *You can copy a cell with a subtotal calculation to the main section of a report. This cell will reflect the grand total or overall averages for the entire report, regardless of the columns displayed and the rows filtered. The Average Price of $163 in Figure 18-9 is for all French wines, not just the two producers displayed in the table. Inserting NoFilter into the footer calculation has the same effect.*

Final Advice about Contexts

Extended syntax and contexts can be a painful concept to understand. So I want to make some sweeping generalizations to ease the process:

- Do not worry about contexts for rows within a table that deal with straightforward sums.
- Understand input contexts for averages, min, max, and count for break footers.
- For rows within a table that use averages, min, max, or running aggregates, understand variable contexts and resets.
- Leave output contexts at their default.

Some Popular Formulas

BusinessObjects provides dozens of functions that allow you to manipulate and better analyze the data. Some of the more frequently used functions are covered in the next sections.

If Then Else

`If Then Else` syntax appears in the Operator box of the Formula Editor. Use If Then Else logic to create complex formulas and powerful alerters.

The following formula describes a wine as Highly Rated if the Average Rating is > 90:

```
=If <Average Rating> > 90 Then "Highly Rated" Else "Normal"
```

To combine multiple comparisons in the `If` statement, enclose the comparison in parentheses. The following formula describes a wine as a Good Value if both the rating is above 90 and the Average Price is less than $100:

```
=If (<Average Rating> > 90 And <Average Price> < 100) Then "Good
Value" Else "Normal"
```

Ratios

In calculating ratios, pay attention to the calculation order to get a correct subtotal. If your universe contains objects that are ratios, you must ensure that you create a calculation to recalculate the ratios at each subtotal or break level:

```
=Sum(<Sales revenue>)/Sum(<Quantity sold>)
```

If the universe does not already contain a ratio or price object, you may want to create a formula that calculates the price row by row:

```
=<Sales revenue>)/<Quantity sold>
```

As long as you do not convert this formula to a variable, you can reuse this same formula in the break footer. This is where dynamic contexts are truly wonderful, as BusinessObjects does not require you to create a new calculation for each subtotal; it does it automatically for you. There was a time in early versions in BusinessObjects in which you had to explicitly define which subtotal and break level to use; some other BI tools still require you to do this. As you added and removed breaks, you would have to manually redo the ratio/price formulas at each break level. For example, if you have a table that contains breaks at clothing line and year, you can insert the same formula `=<Sales revenue>)/<Quantity sold>` in the two break footers; the extended syntax is different for each footer, as shown in the following table. If you remove or add breaks, the new context is automatically specified. Awesome, isn't it?

Break Level	Formula with Extended Syntax
Second, Year	`=(<Sales revenue> / <Quantity sold>) In (<Lines>, <Year>)`
First, Clothing Line	`=(<Sales revenue> / <Quantity sold>) In <Lines>`
Grand Total	`=(<Sales revenue> / <Quantity sold>) In Report`

To ensure that you do not receive a divide by 0 error, include an `If` statement to test the denominator for zero values.

```
=If Sum(<Quantity sold>)>0 Then Sum(<Sales revenue>)/Sum(<Quantity sold>)
```

As part of the formula, you cannot specify a text value such as "NA" to display for those rows in which the Quantity Sold was 0, as "NA" is a text value and all other values are numeric. However, you can format the cells to display NA for Undefined values. Select Format | Cell, then choose Number. Select a desired format and in the Undefined box, enter NA.

Year-to-Date Measures

Within the Date functions, BusinessObjects provides several functions that allow you to interpret date columns. In certain circumstances, the function converts a date variable to a numeric type variable. It's important to pay attention to this nuance to avoid calculation errors.

- `CurrentDate` reads the current date according to your computer and returns a date type.
- `Year` formats a date variable to a four-digit year and returns a numeric value.
- `MonthNumberOfYear` assigns a numeric value of 1–12 for a date field.

The following formula creates a Last Year Sales variable. If the year of the date on the computer minus 1 (last year) is equal to the year in the report, then display the amount sold; else, return 0.

```
=If (Year(CurrentDate())-1=<Year>) Then <Amount Sold> Else 0
```

To incorporate data up to and including the current month, include the month comparisons as well.

```
=If (Year(CurrentDate())-1=<Year> And <Month
Number><=MonthNumberOfYear(CurrentDate())) Then <Amount Sold> Else 0
```

Concatenation

In certain circumstances, you may want to combine the values of two variables into one via the Character function `Concatenation`. This is useful for creating one formatted field that has both a first name and a last name in a form letter. Alternatively, you may have a column that contains an order number and an order line number. The order line number in itself is not a unique identifier unless it is combined with the order number.

`Concatenation` does not automatically trim blank spaces in fields, nor does it add spaces to make the newly combined cell legible—for example, to leave a space between a first name and a last name. To accomplish this, you can use `RightTrim` to trim blank spaces from a variable, and you can nest `Concatenations` to insert spaces between variables.

The following example creates a newly combined column that has both first name and last name. The " " in the formula inserts a space between the two variables:

```
=Concatenation(Concatenation(<Cust First Name> ," ") ,<Cust Last Name>)
```

A similar structure for order number and order line would be

```
=Concatenation(<Order Number> ,<Order Line>)
```

You do not want too many spaces between the first name and the last name. If the first name variable has extraneous blank spaces at the end of the field, then incorporate `RightTrim` to remove the blanks as follows:

```
=Concatenation(Concatenation(RightTrim(<Cust First Name>) ," ")
 ,<Cust Last Name>)
```

An alternative to the `Concatenation` function is the ampersand (`&`) operator. The ampersand allows you to combine several fields at once and so may be easier to read than nesting multiple `Concatenation` functions. The preceding formula would be restated:

```
=<Cust First Name>&" "&<Cust Last Name>
```

The following formula shows how you can incorporate multiple ampersands with other functions. The `Substr` function allows you to display part of a field starting in a particular position. To display the first initial of someone's name, start in the first position and display one character:

```
=<Salutation>&". "&Substr(<Cust First Name>,1,1)&". "&<Cust Last Name>
```

Cumulative Aggregates

Cumulative aggregates incrementally aggregate each row of data within a report. By default, BusinessObjects will keep adding data through each break level in a report. If you want to create a running subtotal for a particular break level or mini-table, then insert a semicolon and a dimension variable to reset the calculation context:

```
CumulativeAggregate(<measure>; <dimension variable>)
```

`RunningAverage` calculates a running average for each row of data in the report. Compare the differences in `RunningAverages` in the following report. The first measure column uses the standard syntax. The last column in the report resets the average for each break in Producer. Business Objects refers to this variable as a *reset context*:

```
=RunningAverage(<Average Price>;<Producer>)
```

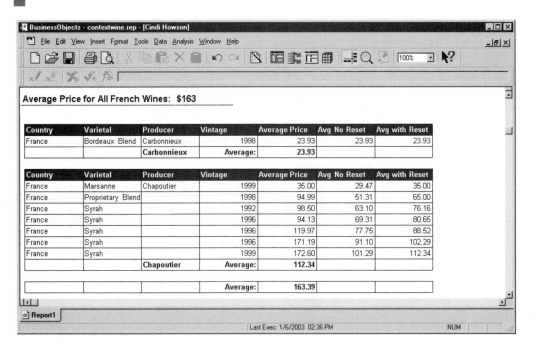

Summary

The Slice and Dice Panel is the heart of many of the analysis functions within BusinessObjects, allowing you to add multiple sorts, breaks, filters, and calculations simultaneously. You can take your analysis further by using internal BusinessObjects functions to create powerful formulas and variables. The formula's extended syntax ensures that the break formulas are dynamically adjusted whenever you redo the breaks and filters. The main caveat with report formulas and variables is to understand that they are report-specific, potentially posing a maintenance issue. For formulas that many users require, work with the universe designer to incorporate some of the intelligence in the universe objects.

REPORTING WITH
BUSINESSOBJECTS

The Complete Reference

Business Objects

Chapter 19

Exploring the Data: Multidimensional Analysis

In Chapter 18, you added many meaningful breaks, sorts, and calculations. With multidimensional analysis, you look at the same data but from different viewpoints. The viewpoints may be from different dimensions or different levels of detail, often called granularity. Multidimensional analysis requires the BusinessObjects Explorer module, licensed as a separate product.

BusinessObjects Explorer first became available with version 4 of the product and, at the time, was a breakthrough in the market place. Prior to Explorer, companies could accomplish multidimensional analysis only through dedicated MOLAP or ROLAP servers. As these servers require a DBA or Administrator to build the cube in advance of the analysis, one had to predict the user requirements in advance. With version 4, Business Objects overhauled the product and changed the file formats from multiple files with results stored in a plain text file to a microcube. BusinessObjects builds this microcube as a file format, seamlessly and regardless of whether you plan to drill in the cube. With this breakthrough approach, users no longer had to define their requirements in advance; multiple users can create multiple personalized queries and drill within their own microcubes.

What Is Multidimensional Analysis?

As discussed in previous chapters, a *dimension* is a kind of object by which you analyze numeric measures. Dimensions often have different levels or groupings associated with them called *hierarchies*. Multidimensional analysis is the process of analyzing data by different dimensions and levels within the dimensions. Within BusinessObjects, one can perform multidimensional analysis only with Dimension objects, not with objects the designer has created as Detail objects (see Chapter 8).

Hierarchies allow you to analyze data by different levels of detail. Some hierarchies are very clear-cut, such as Time, going from Year to Quarter to Month to Week to Day. There is a natural order. Geography hierarchies may also be predetermined, running from Continent to Country to State. When the geography applies to a marketing region, however, each company introduces its own variation. One company may group the Middle East and Africa together; another company may include Mexico as part of North America because it is part of NAFTA or will group it under a different management region such as Latin America. Many of these groupings are fixed as part of your company's reference data and built into the ERP or data warehouse. The universe designer uses the hierarchies to build the default drill paths you use for multidimensional analysis. You can also override the standard drill paths and create your own (see the later section "Hierarchy Editor").

With BusinessObjects Explorer, you can drill *down* within a hierarchy, for example from year to quarter to month. You also can drill *across* by analyzing the current year or the past year; you are at the same level of detail, year, but you are changing the selection value that you are analyzing. You can analyze data by one dimension at a time (Time) or by several at once (Time, Geography, Product). You can also drill against multiple report formats including tables, crosstabs, and charts.

Fixed reports often deal with standard, recurring information needs and give you an overview of *what* is going on in your business. Multidimensional analysis is more exploratory and answers *why*, *where*, and *when*. For example, you may start with a standard management report that shows product sales for this year and last year. Sales for one product is lower this year than last year. You need to know *why*. So you begin to explore: were the sales bad for a particular region, salesperson, or quarter?

Understanding the Data

You can easily get lost when drilling within a report. Therefore, it's helpful to first understand how the different universe objects relate to one another and where you are drilling from and to. Figure 19-1 shows two sample hierarchies for the Wine universe. Compare that with earlier Figure 11-1, which shows two hierarchies for a product dimension and time dimension used in the EFASHION universe.

It's also important to understand that most drilling occurs within a local microcube. You are not requerying the database. Figure 19-2 shows how this works. For simplicity, I will use an example of a Time dimension that contains Year, Quarter, Month. When you construct a query, you first specify which columns of data you want to retrieve from the database. Initially, the default report displays all columns of data. However, as you format the report and/or slice and dice the data, you may hide certain columns. These columns still exist in the query and therefore in the microcube, but they are not displayed in the initial report. In Figure 19-2, Quarter and Month exist in the microcube but are not displayed in the report. This allows you to drill from Year to Quarter to Month without having to execute a new query.

REPORTING WITH BUSINESSOBJECTS

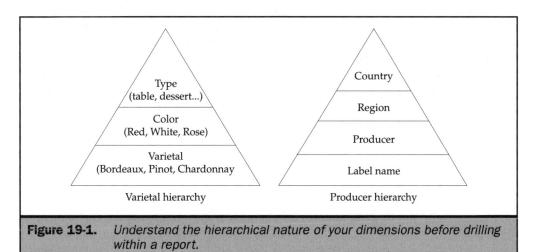

Figure 19-1.   *Understand the hierarchical nature of your dimensions before drilling within a report.*

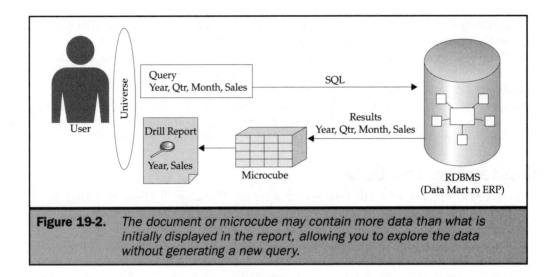

Figure 19-2. *The document or microcube may contain more data than what is initially displayed in the report, allowing you to explore the data without generating a new query.*

How Is the Data Aggregated?

BusinessObjects aggregates measures in two ways: SQL functions and projection aggregates. SQL functions affect the number of rows returned in the initial query. When you drill within a document, BusinessObjects uses projection aggregates. Projection aggregates are set by the universe designer (see Chapter 8, "About Projection Aggregates," for more information). Figure 19-3 shows a summary table of wine ratings and prices by Color and Country. The averages for Australian Red wines are 91.86 and $51, respectively. When drilling, BusinessObjects calculates these two numbers from all the details in the document. The document or microcube contains additional details by Dryness, Type, Vintage, Varietal, Producer, Label Name. The bottom table in Figure 19-3 displays seven rows of detail numbers for Australian wines that were used to calculate the one row in the summary table. For these particular objects, the universe designer specified a projection aggregate of Average, as it would be incorrect from a business viewpoint to sum prices and ratings. Often, projection aggregates use the SUM function—for example, sales, expenses, and available inventory are summed across various dimensions.

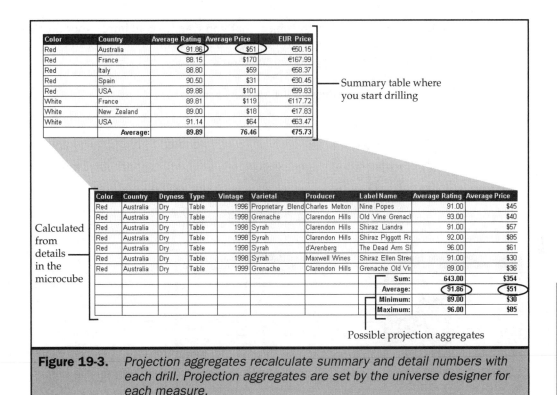

Figure 19-3. *Projection aggregates recalculate summary and detail numbers with each drill. Projection aggregates are set by the universe designer for each measure.*

Drill Down

With *drill down,* you are looking for lower levels of detail within an existing hierarchy. In the following example, you will use Explorer to understand which specific wines have higher prices and ratings. In looking at Figure 19-1, start at the second level, Color, from the Varietal hierarchy and the top level, Country, in the Producer hierarchy. Additional columns of data such as Dryness, Type, Vintage, Varietal, Producer, Label Name exist in the microcube but are not displayed in the initial report. The business question is: Wine ratings and prices vary by color and country; do they vary as much or more for particular varietals?

1. To begin drill down, first select the object that you want to drill into, either the table, crosstab, or chart. This first step simply enables drill mode. It doesn't matter where in the table you position the mouse.

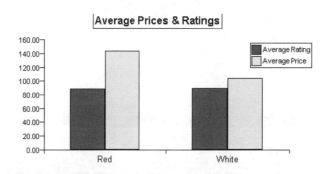

Average Prices & Ratings

Color	Country	Average Rating	Average Price	EUR Price
Red	Australia	91.86	$51	€50.15
Red	France	88.15	$170	€167.99
Red	Italy	88.80	$59	€58.37
Red	Spain	90.50	$31	€30.45
Red	USA	89.88	$101	€99.83
White	France	89.81	$119	€117.72
White	New Zealand	89.00	$18	€17.83
White	USA	91.14	$64	€63.47
	Average:	89.89	76.46	€75.73

The hatched box indicates the table, not the chart, is selected for drilling

2. Click the Drill button from the toolbar, or select Analysis I Drill from the pull-down menu. If you have not first selected the object you want to drill into, the cursor becomes a drill icon or magnifying glass with a question mark. Click on the table.

 If the Drill button does not appear on your toolbar, you may need to ask the BusinessObjects Supervisor to include it in your profile, or your company may not have purchased this software module.

3. BusinessObjects inserts another report tab, naming it *Report (1)*, where *Report* is the name of the first report tab (assuming this Drill option is enabled via Tools I Options). In the next screen, I have not changed the default report name, so Report (1) appears with a drill icon to indicate Report (1) is in Drill mode. If your Drill options are set to Add A Sum On Measures, BusinessObjects adds a sum row to the end of the table. For ratings and prices, a sum is nonsensical

and should be removed. If the initial report includes other Calculations, such as Average, then these are also added to the report.

Caution   *The report totals are based on data displayed, not on contents in the cube. For this reason, report averages in particular may appear misleading, as they are not genuine averages for the entire data set. If you are not satisfied with the totals as they appear, refer to Chapter 18, "Calculation Contexts and Extended Syntax," for ways to correct them.*

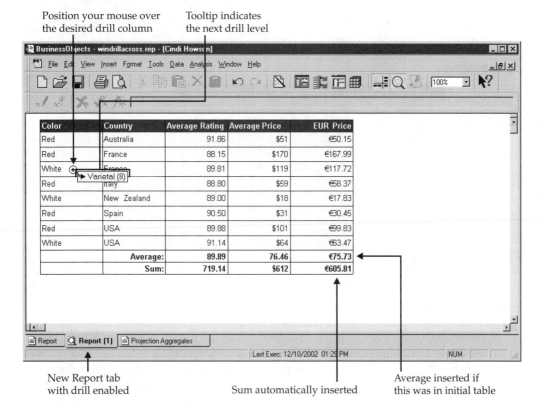

Position your mouse over the desired drill column

Tooltip indicates the next drill level

New Report tab with drill enabled

Sum automatically inserted

Average inserted if this was in initial table

4. Once in Drill mode, position your mouse in the column and cell value that you wish to move to the next level of detail. As shown in Figure 19-1, to move from the *Color* to *Varietal*, position the mouse over any cell that contains a Color value. If you want to see only Red varietals, position the mouse over Red; if you want to see only White varietals, position the mouse over White.

The tooltip tells us that the next drill level is Varietal. Double-click to drill down to the next level of detail.

Selection added to Drill toolbar
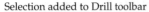

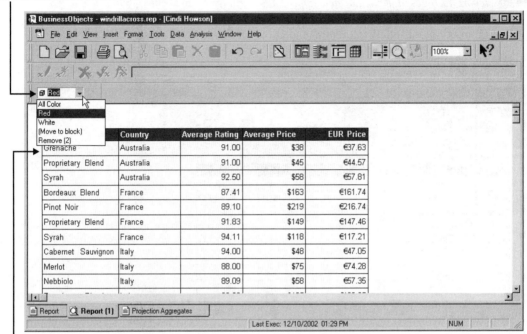

Next level in hierarchy inserted as new column

5. BusinessObjects inserts the detail column into the report table and moves the drill selection to the toolbar. You can drag and drop the Drill toolbar to any place on the screen. By default, it appears with the other toolbars. From the Drill toolbar, you can use the drop-down box to filter the selection to All Colors, Red, or White only. Move to block will insert the color indicator into the table. Remove will remove the filter and close the drill toolbar.

In step 1, you selected the table for drill down. Drilling within a chart works in a similar fashion, except that the next level of detail appears on the X axis. The next screen shows the results of drilling from Color to Varietal. Details by country do not appear in the chart, as they were not in the initial bar chart.

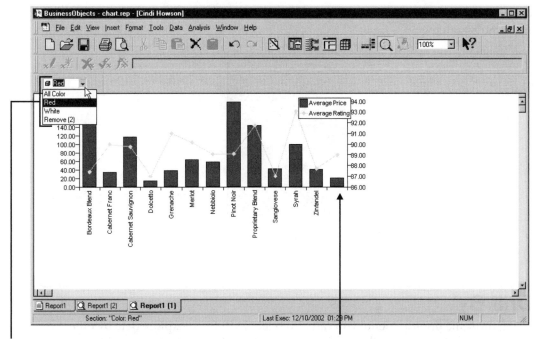

Selection added to Drill toolbar   Next level in hierarchy inserted into X axis

Drill down has helped uncover some interesting patterns. The initial summary report displayed some differences in average wine ratings by country but greater differences in prices. French Red wines are the most expensive. When you drill down, you see that it is the varietals Bordeaux Blend and Pinot Noir that are the most expensive, yet with lower average ratings than other varietals.

Drill Up

As you drill down, you may decide that the particular level of detail did not provide meaningful insight into the business trends or that you want to explore details by other dimensions. You can *drill up* to the preceding summary level.

To move back up the hierarchy by one level, right-click the desired dimension to invoke the pop-up menu, and select Drill Up, as shown next. This will remove the detail column from the report and replace it with a column of data from one level up in the hierarchy.

Drill By

Using the same pop-up menu, you can also select Drill By to explore data by other dimensions that exist in the document or microcube but that are not currently displayed in the report. In the following pop-up menu, Varietal and Vintage are additional columns of information that one can Drill By without generating a new query. Selecting Drill By to Varietal produces the same results as drilling down from Color to Varietal. However, setting Drill By to Vintage creates an entirely new perspective on the data. BusinessObjects will automatically move the current column to the Drill toolbar and replace it with the Drill By column.

With the Drill By Vintage, you can see that there are a few fairly old, very high-priced, French, Bordeaux Blend, Red wines that will affect the average price.

France - Bordeaux Blend

Color	Vintage	Average Rating	Average Price	EUR Price
Red	1945	93.00	$1,750	€1,733.24
Red	1947	89.75	$4,951	€4,903.55
Red	1948	84.50	$772	€764.25
Red	1959	86.00	$577	€570.98
Red	1961	85.00	$1,000	€990.42
Red	1964	83.40	$254	€251.20
Red	1970	82.50	$62	€61.48
Red	1971	84.00	$410	€406.07
Red	1976	78.00	$60	€59.43
Red	1978	80.40	$110	€108.51
Red	1979	89.40	$323	€320.31
Red	1981	65.00	$62	€61.42
Red	1982	88.63	$249	€246.59

The Drill By is contextual and becomes more powerful when more details and columns of data are available in the microcube but not displayed in the report. For example, the EFASHION universe contains three classes: *Store, Product, Time Period*. A user can start by analyzing Sales revenue at the top level for each of these dimensions. If all the details for each dimension are included in the query, then the Drill By displays these additional levels, as shown in the following screen. When a user Drills By State from the *Store* class, you can drill to the next level of City or to the lowest level of detail, Store name.

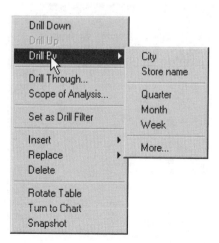

When you select Drill By from the Product dimension or Lines column, then the pop-up menu changes to reflect additional columns of data and levels of detail.

BusinessObjects groups the variables by class or hierarchy and sorts the variables from biggest to smallest within the hierarchy. The "Hierarchy Editor" section later in this chapter describes how you can customize this.

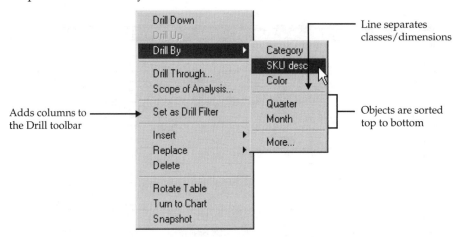

Adds columns to the Drill toolbar

Line separates classes/dimensions

Objects are sorted top to bottom

The Drill By pop-up menu will display only a few lines of available dimensions. You can elect to display more dimensions by changing your Drill options (Tools | Options, Drill tab). When more dimensions or levels of detail are available, select More to display the Drill By – All Available Dimensions dialog box. Within the dialog box, dimensions currently displayed in the report appear dimmed. All other variables that exist in the document appear in the Drill By list and appear in a regular font. The universe may contain still more columns by which to explore the data; however, if they do not exist in the local document, Drill By does not display them. Scope of Analysis and Drill Through do.

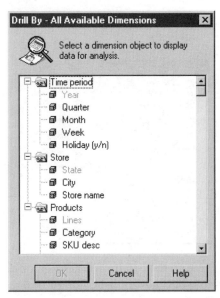

Drill Across

Drill *across* is the process of moving within the same dimension level but changing your selection criteria. You saw by drilling down that French Red Wines, Bordeaux Blend are higher priced, but not necessarily higher rated. Is the same true for Australian Red wines?

You use the Drill toolbar to select different values to drill across. Dimensions get added to the Drill toolbar in two ways:

■ As you drill down or choose to drill by different levels within the same hierarchy, the higher-level selection gets added to the Drill toolbar.

■ You can also specifically select a column, right-click, and choose Set as Drill Filter.

In the following example, you can drill across on wine Color, Country, and Dryness by using the drop-down menus for each. Using drill across, you see that the Average Rating and Price for Australian dry, red wines are 90.87 and $45.23, respectively. The lowest-priced year is 1999.

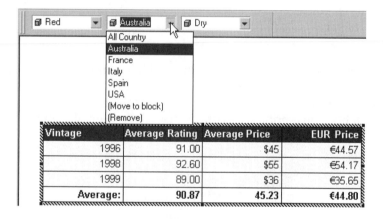

Note   *This report illustrates how report averages can be misleading unless you modify the calculation input context. You have seen in other reports that the average rating for the entire cube for Australian Red wines is actually 91.86. In this report, BusinessObjects determines the report average by averaging the three rows (91,92.60,89), not by averaging the entire cube contents. The default formula for the footer is =Average(<Average Rating> In Body) In Report when a more accurate formula would be =Average(<Average Rating> In Block) In Report. Refer to Chapter 18 for further explanation.*

You drill across to the Country USA, keeping the color and dryness selections the same. You can see next that while the ratings are only slightly lower, the average prices are significantly higher.

| | Red ▼ | USA ▼ | Dry ▼ | |

All Country
Australia
France
Italy
Spain
USA
(Move to block)
(Remove)

Vintage	Average Rating	Average Price	EUR Price
1984	90.00	$148	€146.09
1985	81.00	$130	€128.56
1986	90.00	$120	€118.85
1989	90.00	$101	€100.28
1991	90.80	$82	€81.46
1993	91.33	$141	€139.65
1994	89.57	$94	€92.77
1995	91.00	$76	€75.11
1996	88.80	$87	€86.40
1997	92.20	$265	€262.74
1998	90.50	$113	€111.53
1999	89.00	$49	€48.45
2000	90.00	$41	€40.93
	89.55	111.28	€110.22

In previous releases of BusinessObjects, the drill filters did not exist as part of the toolbar and acted as a section header. The toolbar is a nice improvement for intuitive, multidimensional drilling; however, it requires an extra step for printed reports. To include the drill filters in a printed report, insert a cell by using the pull-down menus Insert | Special Field | Drill Filters.

This will insert a cell that displays all the drill filter selections, shown next. As the data in the drill selections change, so do the contents of this cell.

Snapshot

Snapshots allow you to save a picture of your drill at a particular level of detail or point within your exploration. BusinessObjects inserts a new report tab with the drill selections as section headers. To create a snapshot, use the pull-down menu to select Analysis | Snapshot. Figure 19-4 shows an example of a snapshot. Note in the Slice and Dice Panel that the drill selections are converted to section headings with the same filters.

REPORTING WITH
BUSINESSOBJECTS

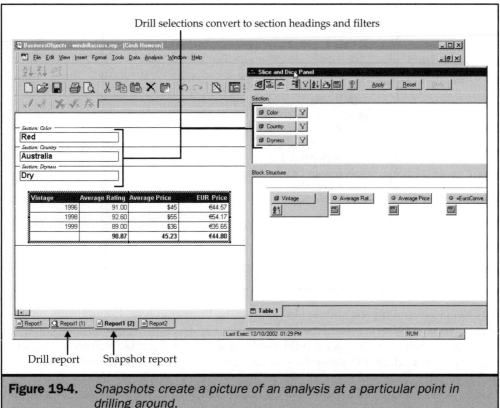

Figure 19-4. *Snapshots create a picture of an analysis at a particular point in drilling around.*

Note   *If you insert a special field with your drill selections prior to creating a snapshot, the snapshot will contain an extraneous empty cell.*

The Hierarchy Editor

The default drill path is determined by either the order of the objects as they appear in each class or the existence of a hierarchy. The universe designer must explicitly build a custom hierarchy. If no hierarchy exists in the universe, then BusinessObjects will use the order of the objects as they appear in each class as the drill path. Once the universe designer builds a custom hierarchy, then only the custom hierarchies are enabled for drilling.

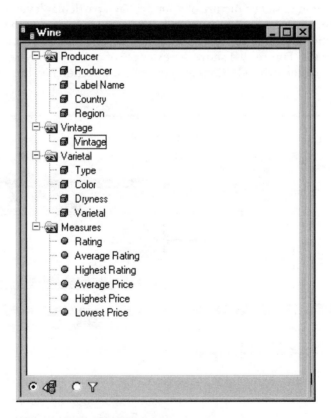

The classes and objects shown next exist in the Wine universe. Compare the order of the objects in each class with the hierarchies in Figure 19-1. For multidimensional analysis, the universe designer should ideally reorder the objects within each class to go from top to bottom. However, for standard ad hoc reporting, the designer may decide to sort objects alphabetically, or according to most frequently used, and would create custom hierarchies to provide a meaningful drill path. If you are not satisfied with the way the designer has defined the hierarchies, you, as the user, can modify them for each individual report via the Hierarchy Editor.

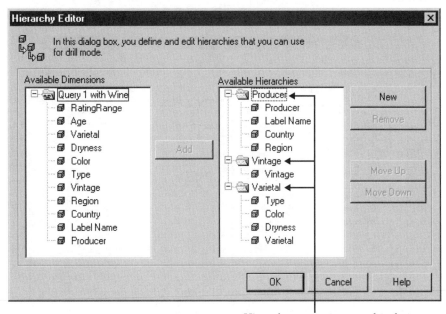

Hierarchy names correspond to class names

1. To invoke the Hierarchy Editor, select from the pull-down menu Analysis | Hierarchies.

2. Under Available Dimensions, click the + sign to expand the folder and see all dimension objects within the specified query. Under Available Hierarchies, BusinessObjects displays either the default classes and dimension objects within the current query or the custom hierarchies the designer created. In the preceding example, the class names and hierarchy names are the same; the universe contains no custom hierarchies.

3. To remove a hierarchy or individual dimension object from the drill path, select the object and click Remove.

4. To add objects that appear in the query but not in a hierarchy, select the object under Available Dimensions, then select the Hierarchy name to which you want to add the object and click Add. RatingRange and Age are two dimension objects created within the report using formulas. They exist within the document but do not belong to any hierarchy. To add Age to the Vintage dimension, under Available Dimensions highlight Age. Under Available Hierarchies, highlight Vintage and click Add.

5. To create a New hierarchy, click New. BusinessObjects will insert a generic *Hierarchy #*, where # is the number of the hierarchy. Type over the *Hierarchy #* with the dimension name and press ENTER. In the following, I have added Rating as a new hierarchy and added Rating Range as a member of the hierarchy:

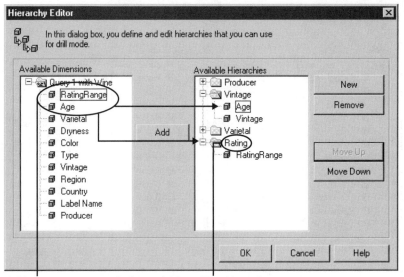

Add objects in query to the hierarchies   New hierarchy

6. To reorder the objects from top to bottom or biggest to smallest, select the object, then select Move Up or Move Down. Reorder the objects within the Producer hierarchy to go from Country ⇒ Region ⇒ Producer ⇒ Label Name to match the drill path specified in Figure 19-1.

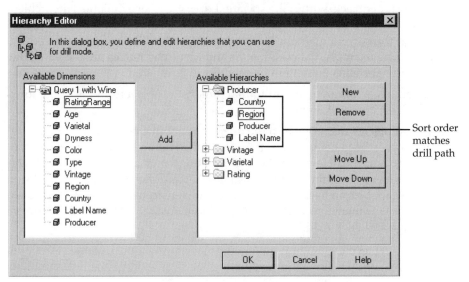

7. Click OK to close the Hierarchy Editor and save all changes to the Hierarchies.

Scope of Analysis

As shown in Figures 19-2 and 19-3, the initial drill screen does not necessarily contain all the dimensions or levels by which you can drill; more data may exist within the microcube. Ideally, these additional drill-by details are still at a reasonably aggregated level for the most frequently performed analysis. With Scope of Analysis, you can further expand the data in the microcube while drilling. In this respect, Scope of Analysis lets you expand the cube with still more detail rows or less frequently used drill-by dimensions than what was stored in the original cube. Scope of Analysis modifies the query and retrieves a new full set of data; the microcube is rebuilt. Therefore, you want to reserve Scope of Analysis for retrieving less frequently used details and dimensions.

To invoke the Scope of Analysis, right-click within the drill table and select Scope of Analysis from the pop-up menu.

Figure 19-5 shows the Scope of Analysis dialog box and how it relates to the data in the drill table as well as the microcube. Note that only dimension objects appear under Scope of Analysis; detail and measure objects do not appear. Any objects in the existing query definition and microcube have a check mark next to them. Objects that are currently displayed in the table are dimmed; Country and Color are in the drill table and so are dimmed under Scope of Analysis. Region is included in the query and the microcube but not in the current table; this appears in black.

When you modify the Scope of Analysis, you can choose whether or not the query should return all rows for all selections within the dimension or if the selection should get translated as a condition in the query. The current drill selections are marked with filter icons, similar to condition objects. The filter values come from either the Drill toolbar or the position of your mouse within the drill table. This is a wonderful new feature that is not available from the BusinessObjects Query Panel. For example, in

Currently displayed columns are dimmed   Select additional objects to include in query

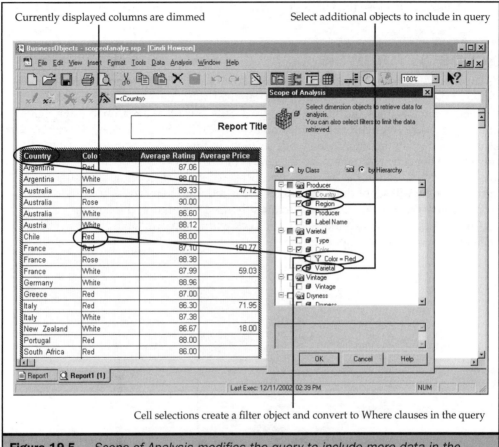

Cell selections create a filter object and convert to Where clauses in the query

Figure 19-5.   *Scope of Analysis modifies the query to include more data in the microcube for drilling.*

Figure 19-5, the mouse selection is on Red wines. Color=Red appears as a filter in the Scope of Analysis. If additional selections existed on the Drill toolbar, these also would appear as filters in the Scope of Analysis. Varietal is the next level of detail within the dimension and has been added to the Scope of Analysis. If you want to limit the rows returned, and thus the size of the microcube, click the filter object to retrieve Varietals for Red wines only. Compare the difference in the SQL generated. The first SQL statement has no WHERE clause and with large databases can return a large number of rows.

Be careful about including too much data in your Scope of Analysis; use filters for large dimensions. Drilling times within a cube will vary depending on your computer's resources but will become slower with larger result sets. Selecting the lowest level within a product or customer dimension without additional conditions may return millions of rows of data.

```
SELECT
  WINE_FACT_PRICE_RATE.Country,
  WINE_FACT_PRICE_RATE.ColorClass,
  AVG(WINE_FACT_PRICE_RATE.Rating),
  avg(WINE_FACT_PRICE_RATE.SalesPrice),
  WINE_FACT_PRICE_RATE.Region,
  WINE_FACT_PRICE_RATE.Variety
FROM
  WINE_FACT_PRICE_RATE
GROUP BY
  WINE_FACT_PRICE_RATE.Country,
  WINE_FACT_PRICE_RATE.ColorClass,
  WINE_FACT_PRICE_RATE.Region,
  WINE_FACT_PRICE_RATE.Variety
```

This second SQL statement includes the Filter Color=Red in the Scope of Analysis. For extremely large databases, and in particular, product and customer dimensions that may contain thousands and millions of rows of data, select the Filter objects.

```
SELECT
  WINE_FACT_PRICE_RATE.Country,
  WINE_FACT_PRICE_RATE.ColorClass,
  AVG(WINE_FACT_PRICE_RATE.Rating),
  avg(WINE_FACT_PRICE_RATE.SalesPrice),
  WINE_FACT_PRICE_RATE.Region,
  WINE_FACT_PRICE_RATE.Variety
FROM
  WINE_FACT_PRICE_RATE
WHERE
  WINE_FACT_PRICE_RATE.ColorClass  =  'Red'
GROUP BY
  WINE_FACT_PRICE_RATE.Country,
  WINE_FACT_PRICE_RATE.ColorClass,
  WINE_FACT_PRICE_RATE.Region,
  WINE_FACT_PRICE_RATE.Variety
```

Note   *Changing the Scope of Analysis does not affect the columns displayed in the table. You must use Drill By to insert a new column in the table.*

Drill Through

Drill *Through* is quite similar to Scope of Analysis in that it modifies the query and expands the content of the microcube. It is different from Scope of Analysis in the following ways:

- Drill Through automatically inserts the drill-through object into the drill table; Scope of Analysis retrieves the data but the additional data is displayed only when you select Drill By.

- Drill Through moves all other dimension objects to the Drill toolbar and sets the drill selections.

- You can select only one dimension object for the drill through; Scope of Analysis allows you to select multiple dimension objects and levels of detail.

- The Drill options (Tools | Options, the Drill tab) determine whether or not the drill filter is used as a condition in the query. Either all filters are appended or no filters are appended to the query conditions; with Scope of Analysis, you can pick and choose which filters you want to append to the query.

Use Drill Through when you want additional details for a particular set of data. Use Scope of Analysis when you want to explore data in a broader way.

1. To launch Drill Through, position your mouse in the table at a point for which you want additional details. If you position your mouse in a measure cell, all corresponding dimension objects will appear as selections in the Drill toolbar; this is referred to as the intersection of all dimensions. For example, in the next image, the mouse is at the Average Rating for Australian Red wines. If you want the Country=Australian *and* the Color=Red to be used as drill filters, then position the mouse on one of the measure objects. If you *only* want Country=Australian to be used as a drill filter, then position and select the cell that contains Australia.

2. Right-click to call the pop-up menu. Select Drill Through. Compare the Drill Through screen to the Scope of Analysis dialog box in Figure 19-5. The dimensions currently in the microcube appear dimmed, as in Scope of Analysis. However, there are no filter icons next to any objects. Also, there are no check boxes next to individual objects; you can drill through to only one dimension object.

These will become drill
selections in the Drill toolbar   Drill-through point   Drill-through column

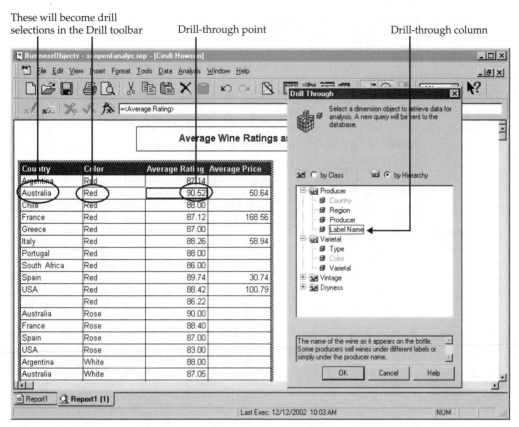

3. If you choose to Drill Through to Label Name, the lowest level of detail in the
   Producer dimension, Label Name gets inserted into the drill table. Select the
   dimension object for which you want to see the details and click OK.

4. Notice in the next screen that BusinessObjects added to both Australia and
   Red as selections in the Drill toolbar. Because the drill options were not set to

Apply Drill Filters, data for all countries and all wine colors still exist in the microcube.

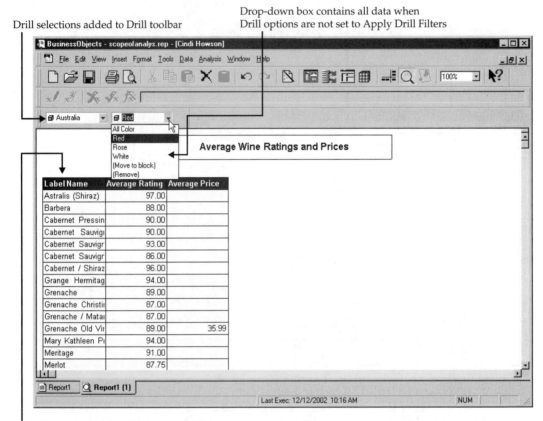

Drill selections added to Drill toolbar

Drop-down box contains all data when Drill options are not set to Apply Drill Filters

Drill-through column inserted in drill table

Drill Through with Drill Filters Applied

With Drill Through, you can elect to have the drill filters appended to the query as a condition or WHERE clause. This is an ideal way to limit the amount of data in the microcube and keep the queries small and fast. However, it also means that with each Drill Through in which you change the drill filters, BusinessObjects executes another query. The best approach will vary greatly depending on several factors, such as the speed and available memory on your computer, initial size of the document, response time of the source RDBMS, and number of rows returned for each selection.

In the following example, Tool | Options | Drill are set to Apply Drill Filters. I have included the dimension object Dryness as additional information in the drill table. Color and Country appear as drill filters on the Drill toolbar.

Note

In order to pass the drill filters as conditions, they must appear as drill filters in the Drill toolbar or your mouse must be on the individual cell that contains the desired dimension value. This is somewhat inconsistent from when you first set the Drill filters because, when you select a measure object, BusinessObjects will not use the intersection of all dimensions as conditions.

Use the following report to select different drill-through points. Notice that the Drill selections (and therefore the microcube) currently contain data for all Countries.

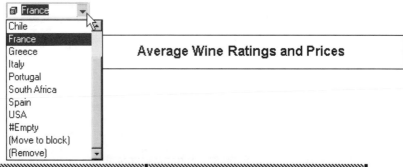

You want to know who produces French Sweet Red wines. Position your mouse on the cell that contains Sweet so that this will be used in the query conditions as well as the drill filters on the Drill toolbar. Right-click to invoke the pop-up menu and select Drill Through To Producer, shown next. The Drill Through dialog box shows us that Color=Red, Country=France, and Dryness=Sweet will get used as conditions in the query. The filter objects appear dimmed and cannot be modified from this screen. They can be modified only via Scope of Analysis.

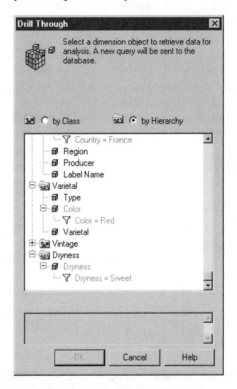

BusinessObjects displays a list of Producers of French, Sweet, Red wines. Notice that the list for the Country filter now displays France only, since BusinessObjects used Country=France as a query condition; it modified the contents of the microcube. To return to a full list of Countries, use Scope of Analysis to remove the filter from Country=France.

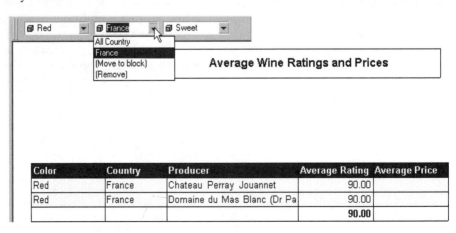

Color	Country	Producer	Average Rating	Average Price
Red	France	Chateau Perray Jouannet	90.00	
Red	France	Domaine du Mas Blanc (Dr Pa	90.00	
			90.00	

Drill Options

BusinessObjects allows you to specify several drill options. Use the pull-down menu Tools | Options and then select the Drill tab.

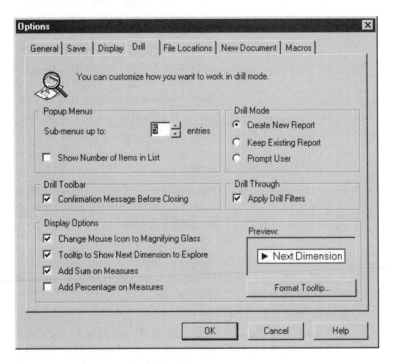

Table 19-1 summarizes each option.

Option Type	Option	Explanation
Pop-up Menus	Submenus Up To *N* Entries	By default, BusinessObjects displays up to five dimension objects to drill by. If ten dimensions are available in the microcube, the pop-up menu displays the first five only and adds a More option to the menu. Increase this number to show more drill-by dimensions.

Table 19-1.   *Drill Options*

Option Type	Option	Explanation
Pop-up Menus	Show Number Of Items In List	Check this box if you want BusinessObjects to display a count of the number of rows for a particular dimension within the microcube. The number of rows appears next to the dimension object in both the tooltips and the pop-up menus. This option is useful for identifying a drill procedure that will display a large number of rows.
Drill Toolbar	Confirmation Message Before Closing	When the Drill toolbar is undocked, BusinessObjects warns you that you are ending a drill session if you close the toolbar.
Display Options	Change Mouse Icon To Magnifying Glass	When in Drill mode, BusinessObjects will change the mouse pointer to a magnifying glass.
	Tooltip To Show Next Dimensions To Explore	Tooltips help you understand where you are drilling to when you double-click to drill down.
	Add Sum On Measures	This Sum is different from a projection aggregate used when drilling around a report. Check this box if you want to add a Sum to each of the measures in a table. Note: Sums may not make sense on certain measures such as unit prices and ratings. If you do not check this box, you can manually add Sums to each measure through the Slice and Dice panel.
	Add Percentages On Measures	This Percentage is different from a projection aggregate used when drilling around a report. Check this box if you want to add a Percentage to each of the measures in a table.
Drill Mode	Create New Report	When first enabling Drill mode, BusinessObjects will insert a new report.

Table 19-1.   *Drill Options* (continued)

Option Type	Option	Explanation
Drill Mode	Keep Existing Report	If you do not want a separate Drill mode report inserted, check this option. Warning: When you enable Drill mode with this setting, BusinessObjects will remove all but the current block from the report. If your initial report has multiple blocks, do not use this option.
	Prompt User	By default, BusinessObjects inserts a new report tab with the current report tab name and a sequential number. Check this box if you want to be prompted to create a new report when first enabling Drill mode.
Drill Through	Apply Drill Filters	As you drill through to details, check this box if you want the drill selections in the Drill toolbar and the current cell selection to be passed as a condition in the query. This limits the size of the microcube but may cause you to run multiple queries for each drill operation.

Table 19-1.   *Drill Options* (continued)

REPORTING WITH BUSINESSOBJECTS

Summary

Drilling within a report requires the software module Explorer. Use the drill functionality to explore data by additional levels of detail and different dimensions. Whereas a standard report may give you an overview of *what* is going on, multidimensional analysis helps you uncover why, when, and where. Use the Drill bar to navigate different dimensions and select different members within a hierarchy. Drill Up is only available in the pop-up menu. In drilling around a report, it's important to understand how data is aggregated. As you explore the data, you may find that you need additional details not within the microcube. Use Scope of Analysis or Drill Through to retrieve additional information from the data source and re-execute the entire query. Scope of Analysis allows you to add new hierarchies to the query, whereas Drill Through allows you to add additional levels of detail within existing hierarchies. The universe designer sets the default drill path through the organization of objects within a class or through custom hierarchies. You can modify the drill path with the Hierarchy Editor.

The Complete Reference

Chapter 20

Accessing New Data

The previous chapters have shown that you can do quite a lot with a report without ever having to requery the data source. If you want to work with more current data, however, you need to refresh a query in which you retrieve a new result set from the data source. Because the size of documents in the BusinessObjects repository can become quite large, some companies use Corporate Documents to store empty standard reports that you must immediately refresh. This chapter reviews different ways to refresh a document and how to handle prompts that may appear when you execute a query.

Refreshing a Document

As discussed in Chapter 16, a document contains multiple components that deliver the formatted reports and analysis. When you want to retrieve new data from a data source, you are sending a query to a database, as shown in Figure 20-1. The data source may be a relational database such as the transaction system, an enterprise resource planning (ERP) system, or a data mart or data warehouse. When it is a relational data source, a SQL statement from your PC gets submitted to the source database. Therefore, you must have all database connectivity files installed on your PC. At this point, you do not go through the repository at all (unless you are using BusinessObjects in three-tier/ ZABO mode). The data source could also be a MOLAP cube such as Essbase or Microsoft Analysis Services. Local spreadsheets and departmental databases also are valid data sources.

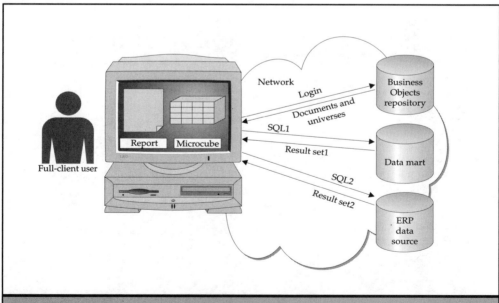

Figure 20-1.   *Refreshing a query sends SQL to the data source.*

To refresh a query, select the Refresh button from the standard toolbar or select Data | Refresh Data.

One document may have one or more data sources. Depending on how the universe designer established the connection settings for each data source, your BusinessObjects login ID may automatically be used to log you into each data source. Therefore, if you change your password for one system, you may inadvertently cause them to get out of synch.

In Figure 20-1, you may have one password for the data mart and a different ID/password for the ERP data source. This is clearly not ideal and is very user unfriendly. Preferably, the universe and BusinessObjects login parameters should be designed in such a way that the different systems work seamlessly together. Unfortunately, that isn't always possible, and when the two become out of synch, you will receive an error message similar to the following:

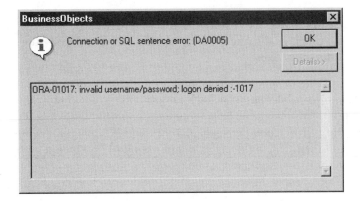

If your company requires a different username for each data source, you also may have multiple BusinessObjects logins. If you have different passwords, you should try to synchronize the passwords. To change your BusinessObjects password to match the data source password, select Tools | Change Password.

Query Phases

When BusinessObjects refreshes a query, it refreshes the entire result set. For example, let's assume you have a document that shows year-to-date sales. The data source is from a data warehouse updated on a daily basis. A report author originally ran the query last week and sent you the results. Your version of the report is therefore out of date by a week. You refresh the query. This rebuilds the entire microcube (refer back to Figure 16-4); the microcube does not incrementally add one week of data. For smaller queries, this is not important, as the results may be returned in a few seconds. Other queries, however, may take quite a long time to run. Ideally, the report author warns you of this in the File | Properties, Comments box. For exceedingly long queries, the universe designer may also elect to have the database warn you of long-running queries based on estimates from previously run queries. These estimates can be wildly inaccurate and depend on a number of factors; they are useful, though, to tell you whether a query will be instantaneous or long. If the estimated time is acceptable to you, click Yes; if it is too long and you want to submit it to Broadcast Agent to run later, click No. The time estimate will remain displayed during the query refresh.

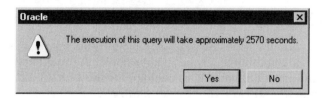

   Although you are able to work with other MS Windows products while a slow query is executing, you cannot continue to work with BusinessObjects.

The status bar in the Report Window displays when a data provider was last refreshed and also displays the query's progress. For slow-running queries, it's useful to monitor the different phases.

Connecting, Analyzing, Fetching phases displayed here

During query refresh, displays rows and time counters

- **Connecting** Logs you into the data sources. The universe designer determines if you log in for only the first query refresh and log out when the query is finished, or if you stay logged into the data source for the entire BusinessObjects session. For extremely busy databases, repeatedly connecting and disconnecting for each query can slow down query refreshes and add unnecessary delays.

- **Analyzing** When the database reads the SQL statement and performs the sorts and aggregations. If the query is poorly designed or the database is not well-tuned, the Analyze phase can take hours. During the Analyze phase, you generally cannot cancel the query (although the status bar displays a message "Press Esc to cancel"). The only way to interrupt the query at this stage is to contact the DBA. You also can terminate the BusinessObjects session, by starting the MS Windows Task Manager with CTRL-ALT-DELETE, selecting the BusinessObjects process, and choosing End Task. You will lose any unsaved work and the query will still be executing on the data source database, so this is not something you want to do casually.

■ **Fetching**   When the database is finished processing the query and begins sending the rows of data from the database across the network, as shown in Figure 20-1. The status bar displays the rows and time counters once the Fetch phase begins. At this point, you can press ESC to cancel the query (if the designer has enabled this parameter for this data source connection).

When you choose to cancel a query, you have several choices of what to do with the results sent thus far:

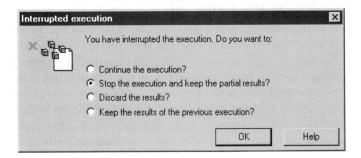

■ **Continue the execution**   Continues the Fetch phase of the query. Remember that pressing ESC during the Analyze phase does not interrupt the query. So if you have a slow-running query and you have gotten this far, I recommend continuing the execution. If, however, you suspect you have constructed an incorrect query with the wrong condition statement and the query is returning too many rows of data, stop the execution.

■ **Stop the execution and keep the partial results**   As shown in the earlier status bar, if you interrupt a query and keep the partial results, the status bar warns you the result set is incomplete. If this is the first time you are running the query, seeing the partial results may be useful in diagnosing query problems.

■ **Discard the results**   With this option, you stop the Fetch phase, the microcube is purged, and the report displays only the column headings.

■ **Keep the results of the previous execution**   If you opened a document that was previously refreshed successfully, this option stops the Fetch phase and reverts to the previous result set. Even though you are keeping an old result set, the status bar shows a new Last Execution time.

Time Limit Interruptions

If the universe designer has set time limits for query execution time, you also may receive only partial results of the query. There are two issues to understand with time limits. First, the time limit takes over only during the Fetch phase. So if the universe contains a query execution time limit of 60 minutes, and the Analyze phase takes 90 minutes, the time limit in the universe controls will interrupt only after 90 minutes, after the Analyze phase has completed. If the Analyze phase takes 55 minutes and the Fetch phase takes ten minutes, you will receive approximately half the result set (or five minutes worth of Fetch). Second, when a time limit interrupts a query before any rows have been returned, you may receive an erroneous error message, "No Data To Fetch." This is somewhat misleading, as you receive the same error message when you construct an incorrect query, with mutually exclusive conditions.

Refreshing and Regenerating SQL

When you refresh a query from the Report window, BusinessObjects uses the last version of the SQL statement. If the universe has been modified since you last refreshed the query, you may need to regenerate the SQL. This particular nuance is important only on rare occasions, such as when an object is incorrectly defined in the universe or the designer has modified objects to point to new table names. For example, let's assume that the universe contained an incorrect calculation for the selling price. The SQL for this should be SUM(revenue) / SUM(quantity), but the object was initially defined as SUM(revenue/quantity). The universe designer corrects the object definition.

Even though you have the latest version of the universe via your local disk or work group directory, the SQL file on your PC still reads SUM(revenue/quantity). Only when you build a new query or run a query from the Query Panel does BusinessObjects read the new object definition and regenerate the SQL with SUM(revenue) / SUM(quantity).

To regenerate the SQL and run a query from the Query Panel:

1. Select Data | Edit Data Provider or click the Edit Data Provider button on the standard toolbar to launch the Query Panel.

2. Click Run.

BusinessObjects generates a new SELECT statement and refreshes the results.

Handling Prompts and Lists of Values

When you refresh a query, you may be asked to select additional information to ensure the correct data is returned to you. You can enter the values yourself, or in many cases, you can choose from a list of values. Choosing from a list of values ensures you have entered the possible values correctly (either uppercase or lowercase, with leading zeros or not) and therefore ensures you retrieve the desired results. Often, if you receive an error message "No data to fetch," it is because you have entered invalid values in a query condition.

A list of values is a pick-list generated from a query your PC sends to the data source (for more information on how these are built into the universe, refer to Chapter 9). The query file is stored as *object*.lov in \Business Objects 5.0\UserDocs*domain**universe*, where *object* is the name of the query file related to the object, *domain* is the name of the universe domain, and *universe* is the universe to which the object belongs. Because the list of values is specific to each universe, even if you have similar objects such as *Product* or *Customer* in multiple universes, you will have multiple list of values query files. Most often, these query files are initially empty and contain no values. Therefore, the first time you access a particular list of values, you need to refresh the query. Once you have accessed a list of values the first time, the results are permanently stored on your PC. You should periodically refresh the list of values, as values in a dimension may change—for example, as new products or customers are added.

1. In the following example, the query refresh prompts you to enter a Closed Accounting Month. The dialog box displays Enter or Select Values, and the Values button is available. Click Values to display the list of Closed Accounting Months.

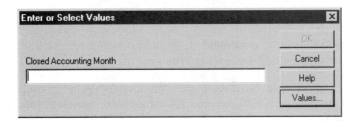

2. The first time you access a particular list of values, the List of Values screen will be empty. Click Refresh to launch the list of values query and then select the desired month. Click OK to close the List of Values dialog box, shown here:

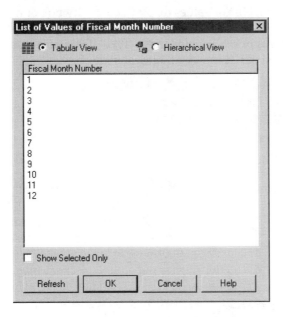

3. BusinessObjects returns you to the prompt and fills in the selected value.

4. From the prompt, click OK to execute the query and refresh the data.

Customized List of Values

For particularly long dimension lists such as customers or products, you may be prompted to further narrow the desired list of values. In this respect, the universe designer has customized the list of values query to include a prompt. If the dimension object displays an ID or code, the designer may customize the list of values to display the name or description in the list of values (refer to Chapter 9). For long lists of values, you can enter a letter or number to scroll to the corresponding section of the list, assuming the first column is the sort column. For example, to scroll to Customer Names beginning with *H*, press H while viewing the long list of values. The universe designer also may allow you to modify your own list of values. Refer to Chapters 9 and 21 for further instructions on how to do this.

If you modify your list of values and the universe designer makes another modification, the designer's change will always overwrite your changes.

In the following example, the data source contains a long list of customers. In order to work with a manageable list of customer IDs, you must first select a country in which the customer resides.

1. When you click Refresh, you are prompted to enter a Customer ID. If you knew the ID, you could enter it in the box provided. You don't, so click Values to choose from a list.

2. The Customer ID list of values displays an empty box or a previously refreshed list of values. Click Refresh. The list of values query prompts you to select a Country. At this point, you now have three dialog boxes open. Click Values to display a list of Customer Countries.

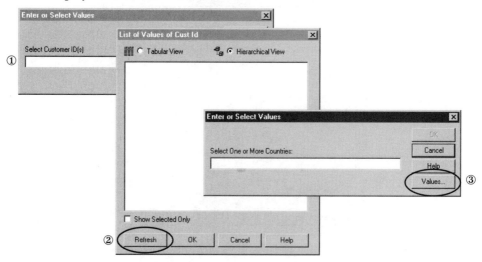

3. To select multiple values, use CTRL-click. In some cases, the report author may have built the prompt so that you can select only one value. Click OK.

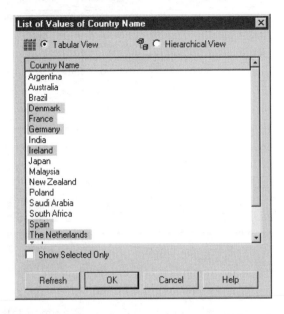

4. When you select multiple values, BusinessObjects fills in the values in the prompt box, separated by semicolons. Click OK to launch the query that will finally retrieve the Customer ID list of values (box 2 in step 2).

5. When a list of values has additional columns of information, you can navigate the list in Tabular View or Hierarchical View, as shown in Figure 20-2. In Tabular View, the first column contains the detail values that you want to use in the conditions or prompt. Tabular View displays the column headings and allows you to adjust the width for each. In Hierarchical View, each column is displayed as a folder. Click the + next to a value to expand the group and display the next level. The lowest level that you want to enter in the prompt box will be marked with a dimension (blue cube) or a detail qualification (green triangle). Select the values and click OK to close the List Of Values dialog box.

6. From the Prompt dialog box, click OK to execute the query.

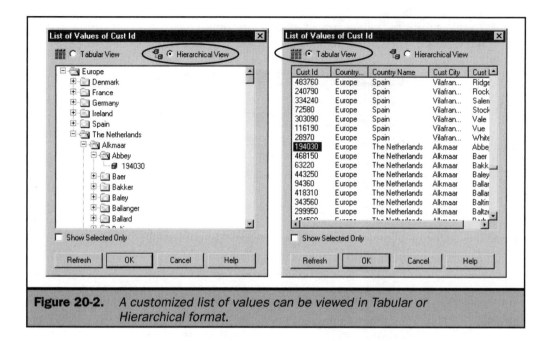

Figure 20-2. *A customized list of values can be viewed in Tabular or Hierarchical format.*

Notice in Figure 20-2 that the list of values displays customer IDs only for countries that you selected in step 3.

Multiple Prompts

Sometimes when you refresh a query, you may need to answer multiple prompts. The report author should ideally sort them in a logical order; for example, the earliest vintage prompt precedes the latest vintage prompt. By default, BusinessObjects displays them in alphabetical order. When this sort order is not intuitive, the report author may number the prompts as shown in the following screen. Once you have refreshed a query at least once from this computer, BusinessObjects displays the last values selected each time you refresh the query.

Refreshing Queries with Broadcast Agent

For slow-running queries and queries that you wish to refresh on a regular basis, you can refresh or schedule them through Broadcast Agent (BCA). BCA is a document scheduler that allows you to publish the finished results in a number of ways. When you schedule a document via BCA, there are a number of scheduling, output, and distribution choices. In working with BCA, you may want to display the Document Exchange toolbar. Select View | Toolbars, then choose Document Exchange to display the following toolbar:

Quick Steps to Using BCA

If you want to submit a slow-running query to BCA for immediate processing, follow these quick steps:

1. Select File | Send To | Broadcast Agent or click the Send To Broadcast Agent botton on the toolbar.

2. From the dialog box, select the Actions tab. Under Available Actions, select Refresh, and Click Add>>.

3. Select the Distribution tab and click Add My Name To The List.

4. Click OK to submit the document for scheduling and close the BCA dialog box. If your document contains any prompts, you will be prompted to fill in the conditions once you have specified the BCA options.

Whenever you first log into BusinessObjects, you will receive a message if you have received any new documents from BCA. You then select File | Retrieve From or click the Retrieve From Broadcast Agent button via the toolbar. Alternatively, you can monitor the progress of your report through the BCA Console. The next sections explain the different tabs from the Send Document To Broadcast Agent dialog box.

The BCA General Tab

A company may have multiple Broadcast Agent servers. From the General tab of the Send Document To Broadcast Agent dialog box, you specify the Server. The Priority allows you to select a Priority of Normal, High, or Low. The default is Normal. When the server is trying to process two queries at the same instant, one with a High Priority setting will be processed first. In the Description box, you can enter information about how often the query is scheduled and to whom it is distributed.

REPORTING WITH BUSINESSOBJECTS

The BCA Actions Tab

The Actions tab shown in Figure 20-3 enables you to choose how the query is refreshed and if it should be saved in additional formats. You may schedule a query for yourself or to be distributed to other users. When you schedule a query for other users, you can elect to have the query executed with each user's profile. If the BusinessObjects supervisor has restricted the objects and rows of data different users can access (refer to Chapter 12, "Data Restrictions"), then Broadcast Agent executes multiple queries for each different user profile. Use this option with caution. If you are scheduling a report for 100 users, the query will be executed 100 times, even if the users all have the same profile. This can put an unnecessary load on the source RDBMS. The benefit of this, though, is that, when you use Supervisor's row restrictions, each user will see only the data that is relevant to that user. The downside is when the supervisor is not using data restrictions through BusinessObjects and 100 queries are executed unnecessarily.

Note	*The vendor refers to this functionality as report bursting, although other BI vendors refer to bursting as one query execution that is then parsed into 100 smaller documents. Business Objects provides another product that works with BCA to provide true bursting, Broadcast Agent Publisher. Broadcast Agent Publisher refreshes the query once, then filters the data according to separate profiles and distributes the filtered reports via HTML pages in InfoView or e-mail.*

When you choose Refresh with the profile of each recipient, Standard Actions is grayed out. If you are not using report bursting, then under Standard Actions, choose Refresh and click Add>>. The Refresh action appears under Selected actions, as shown in Figure 20-3. Otherwise, you can also choose to execute custom macros or VBA scripts; publish to a channel; or save the document as RTF, text, or PDF.

The Condition box allows you to refresh the query only when certain conditions are met. For example, you may set a condition to refresh a Late Orders document when Orders are more than five days late. You may have a Budget Alert report when expenses exceed more than 10 percent of actual versus budget variance. After setting the condition, you still must schedule the report to tell Broadcast Agent how often to evaluate whether the condition is met. You can manually enter a condition, or you can select Editor to launch the Formula Editor.

The BCA Categories Tab

When you schedule a document, you can automatically assign it to categories. As described in Chapter 16, categories provide meaningful groupings to documents and enable you to view standard reports by category.

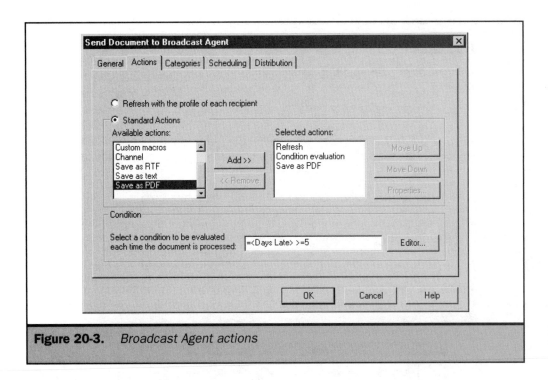

Figure 20-3.   *Broadcast Agent actions*

The BCA Scheduling Tab

From the Scheduling tab, you determine if the document will be refreshed one time or on a periodic basis, as shown in Figure 20-4. In this figure, the document is scheduled to refresh on a weekly basis, each Monday morning at 4:00 A.M. Scheduling the document to run early in the morning means that the document is refreshed after weekly data warehouse updates and at a time of day when the server is not so busy. The Start date on the Scheduling tab refers to when the Broadcast Agent will start monitoring this refresh. By default, this date is the date you first scheduled a document. You only need to ensure that the Start date is earlier than the scheduled date and time. The expiration date, by default, is one year from the date you submitted the request to BCA. So in this example, the document will be refreshed every week at 4:00 A.M. up until January 10, 2004. After that, the document will no longer automatically refresh.

When you first send a document to BCA, it schedules the document to refresh only once as soon as possible. To change the frequency and time to refresh the query, click Change. This launches the Change Schedule dialog box, as shown at the bottom of Figure 20-4. If you are running the query only once, use the up and down buttons to set the start date and hour, or enter the date and hour in the corresponding box. When you select a different run option, the options in the Start At section change appropriately. When you choose to refresh a document hourly, you then specify how many minutes after each hour. When you refresh a document on a daily basis, you can then choose which days of the week and what time of day.

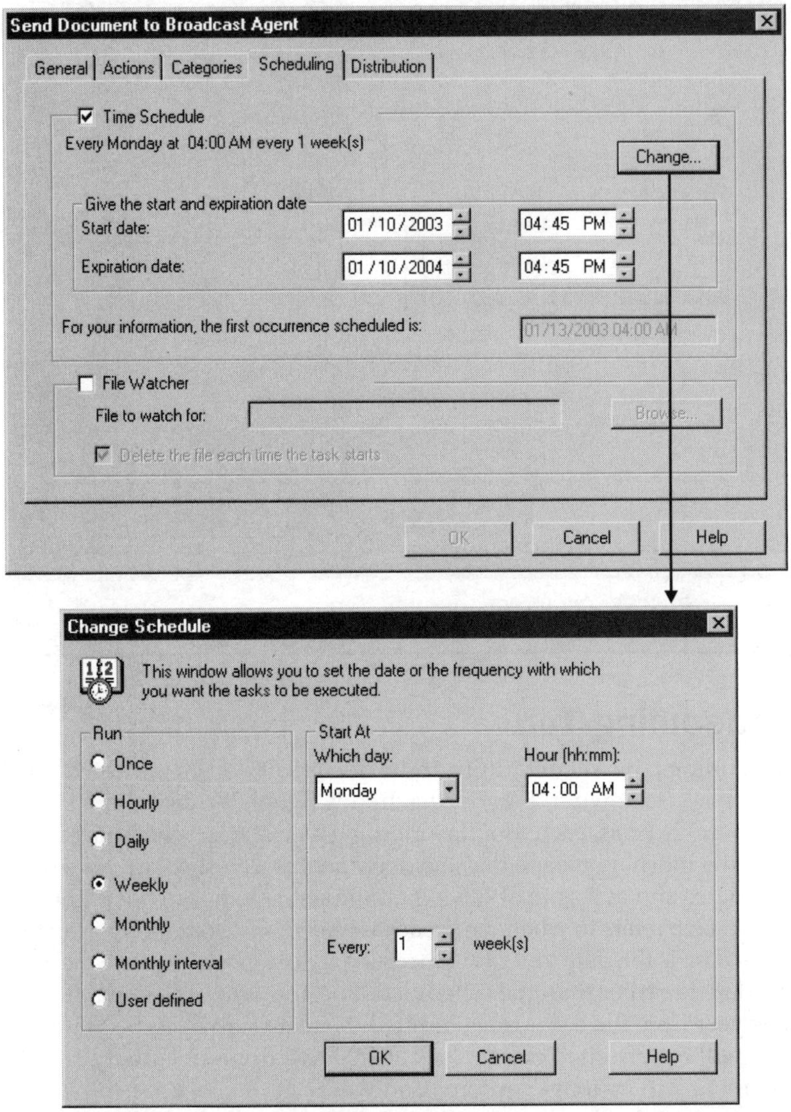

Figure 20-4. BCA scheduling options

File Watcher allows you to tell the query to refresh only when a particular file appears. This is ideal for documents that are dependent upon other updates. In a data warehouse environment, this may be a file to indicate that the data warehouse update routines are complete. If you schedule the document to refresh on Monday at 4:00 A.M., for example, but the file appears only at 6:00 A.M., BCA will continue checking for the presence of the file and will refresh the document at 6:00 A.M. The process that launches the query refresh (BOManager) must have read access to the specified server and directory. If you also want BCA to delete the file once the document refresh starts, then BCA must also have write access to the file. Once you check the File Watcher option, specify a file to watch for in the text box:

```
\\report_server\updates\weeklyload.txt
```

The BCA Distribution Tab

From the Distribution tab shown in Figure 20-5, you can specify how you should receive the report and if you want to distribute it to other groups and users. If you are scheduling the report just for yourself, click Add My Name To The List. Your name will appear in the To: column, and you can later retrieve the report from the repository (refer to Chapter 16, "Scheduled Documents"). If you wish to send the refreshed document to other users, click To and select the desired groups or individuals.

Sending the document to multiple users and groups does not cause the query to execute multiple times. Only one copy of the document is stored in the BusinessObjects repository, document domain. However, if you also select the option Refresh with the profile of each recipient from the Actions tab, the query will be executed for as many users as are listed in the To box.

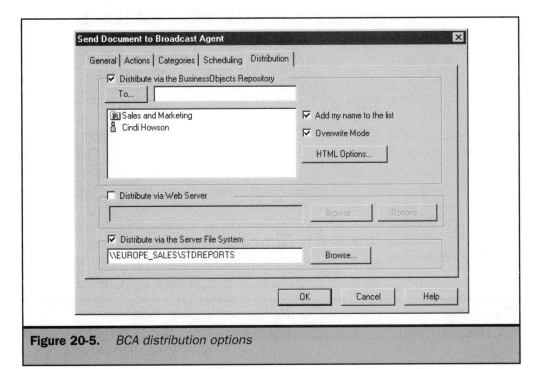

Figure 20-5.   *BCA distribution options*

By default, Overwrite Mode is enabled. When you refresh a document on a periodic basis, the latest version of the document overwrites older versions in the repository. You can disable Overwrite Mode to have a new document created for each refresh. I recommend against this, as you will unnecessarily, and very quickly, increase the size of the document domain.

You can also choose to have the refreshed document sent to a web server or a work group file server. Click Browse to select the server name and path. For the web server, select Options to choose different HTML output options described in Chapter 16, "Save As HTML." In Figure 20-5, the document will be distributed both to users via the repository and to a work group directory for users that do not have fast access to the repository.

Monitoring Status Through the Console

The Console allows you to view both scheduled documents and refreshed documents (see Figure 20-6). To access the console, select Tools | Console. Under Document Name, you can select an individual document and click Properties to see the selected Actions, Categories, and Distribution. From here, you also can delete a scheduled document. To view completed documents, click the View Processed Tasks radio button. If a document did not complete because it exceeded its time limit or there was some other error, the status column will display "Failed."

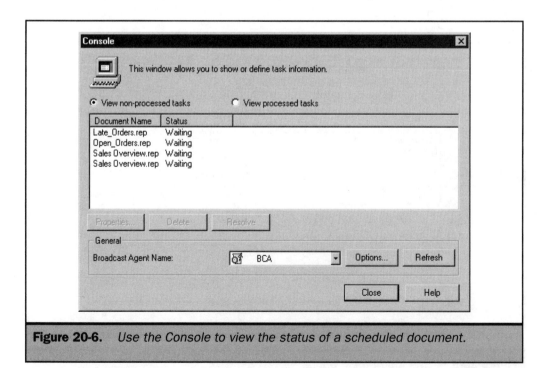

Figure 20-6.   *Use the Console to view the status of a scheduled document.*

The Complete Reference

Business Objects

Chapter 21

Creating a New Query

W hether you are creating a new query or modifying an existing query to add a new result column or change a condition, you use the Query Panel. The Query Panel lets you select columns to display in a report and specify conditions to limit the rows returned to the microcube, all without your knowing SQL. The universe's semantic layer displays business names and dynamically generates complex SQL behind the scenes. Chapter 5 gives a more thorough discussion of how the universe accomplishes this. This chapter provides a strategy for turning a business question into a query, how to use the BusinessObjects Query Panel, and analyzing data in OLAP databases.

Formulating a Business Question

Before you begin to create a new document through BusinessObjects, it's important to formulate the business question to help you construct a query that returns your desired information. If you do not do this, you may retrieve more data than necessary, making it difficult to uncover patterns and opportunities. You also may have to execute a query multiple times before you achieve the desired report. With large databases, this can be inefficient and frustrating. To formulate a business question in query terms, answer the following questions:

1. Where is the data?
2. What measures do I want to analyze?
3. By which dimensions do I want to analyze the measures? After viewing a high-level report, do I want to drill down or explore by other dimensions?
4. Do I want to see additional details for taking action on the information?
5. If the data source contains more data than I am interested in, how can I narrow my results to pertain to my area of interest or responsibility?

As an example, assume you are a product manager. You want to analyze sales. That's a pretty broad business question. Table 21-1 maps how you use these questions to refine a broad question into more specific details that help you formulate a query.

Broad Question	Refined Answers	Query Component
1. Where is the data?	If you want to analyze sales for just your products, the data may be in a departmental data mart. If you want to compare your sales with other products, it may be in the central data warehouse. Actual sales may be in the central data warehouse; forecast sales may only be in a personal database.	Data source or universe

Table 21-1. *Refine a Business Question to Construct a Query*

Broad Question	Refined Answers	Query Component
2. What measures?	Sales could be stated in terms of revenues, quantity sold, and selling price.	Measure result objects
3. Which dimensions?	Do you want to analyze sales by product only or also by salesperson, region, customer, scenario (actual vs. budget), and time period?	Dimension result objects
4. Additional details?	If sales are falling from one quarter to the next, do you want the salesperson's phone number or e-mail address to follow up? Perhaps you want the customer web site address to view more information about new customers.	Detail result objects
5. Your area of interest?	A departmental data mart may already provide a number of conditions to limit the information returned to you. You may want to limit the data by time to the current three months, current year, and last year. If you are accessing a data warehouse, you may have to select your products only. You may choose to limit results according to new salespeople or to sales that are more than 10 percent lower than forecast.	Conditions

Table 21-1.   *Refine a Business Question to Construct a Query* (continued)

Types of Data Providers

BusinessObjects enables you to create documents based on one or more data providers. When the document contains multiple data providers, BusinessObjects automatically links the multiple result sets by dimensions that share the same values. In addition to universes, a data provider can access data from the following sources:

- **Free-hand SQL**   Enables you to create your own SQL statements against data sources for which no universe has been built. The SQL Editor from this panel is quite basic and requires in-depth knowledge of SQL syntax. Therefore, the BusinessObjects supervisor may not enable this type of data provider for all users.

- **Personal data files**   Enable you to access Excel spreadsheet, text, and dBase files and then analyze the results using the full set of BusinessObjects Reporter (the Slice and Dice Panel) and Explorer (drill-down) functionality. This is a powerful feature that enables you to access departmental data in a spreadsheet, for example, and combine it with corporate data from a universe. The settings for accessing personal data files as a data provider are similar to those for using them for a list of values, described in Chapter 9, "Incorporating Personal Data Files."

- **Stored procedures**   Sets of SQL statements defined by the DBA. The BusinessObjects supervisor must grant you access to the stored procedures.

- **Visual Basic procedures**   Programs that a BusinessObjects developer builds with the Software Development Kit (SDK). A Visual Basic procedure can perform many functions—for example, refresh data, build reports, and then e-mail the results to multiple users. When using Visual Basic procedures as a data provider, you can either create a new procedure or select an existing one.

- **OLAP**   Enables you to access data in a multidimensional database. To access OLAP data sources, your company must have purchased an OLAP Access Pack for the specific MOLAP cubes. BusinessObjects can access MS Analysis Services, Hyperion Essbase, IBM's DB2 OLAP, SAP BW, and Oracle Express. Each OLAP Access Pack must be installed on your local disk for full-client use or on the WebI midtier for thin-client use.

New Document Options

New Document Options determine what happens when you first create a new document. To specify these options, select Tools | Options, then select the New Document tab, as shown in Figure 21-1. When you select File | New to create a new document, you can elect to invoke the New Report Wizard to guide you through the process of creating a document, or you can have a blank screen displayed in which you would then insert a block and create a data provider. Under Report Layout, you can choose the following:

- **Prompt User**   Prompts you with two options, to choose a standard report table block or to select a template that then presents more options to create a number of other report styles such as master/detail, cross/tab, or chart. If you most often use a tabular report style but occasionally use other styles, then select this option.

- **Select a Template**   Automatically prompts you to select a template. For beginning users, it may be overwhelming to set this option as the default as you are presented with multiple template styles.

- **Use a Default Template**   Allows you to set a corporate template as the default report style or to select a default other than the standard table style. To choose a template other than the default, click the drop-down box to see a list of available templates.

- **Use a Standard Report**   If tabular is your most frequently used report style, then select this option. You can easily change the report style after the results are retrieved, as described in Chapter 16.

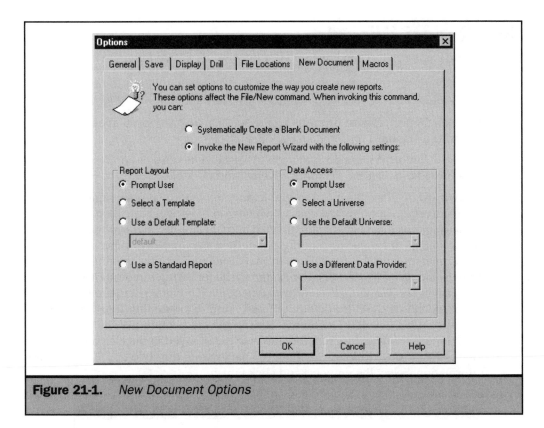

Figure 21-1. *New Document Options*

The Data Access options allow you to choose different types of data providers as a default.

- **Prompt User** Enables you either to choose a universe or to choose another data provider such as MOLAP, Stored Procedure, or Free-hand SQL.

- **Select a Universe** Will automatically prompt you to select a universe. The option to choose other data sources is not displayed.

- **Use the Default Universe** If you most often will work with one universe, then set this option and use the drop-down box to specify the default universe.

- **Use a Different Data Provider** If you most often do not access data through the universe, set this option and click the drop-down box to specify a different data source. For example, if you most often work with Stored Procedures or Personal Data Files, check this option and then click the drop-down box to specify the default type of data provider.

New Report Wizard

The following steps assume you have set your options, as shown in Figure 21-1.
To create a new document:

1. Select File | New or click New from the standard toolbar.

2. The New Report Wizard prompts you to select an initial report layout. Select Generate a standard report, then click Begin >.

3. The New Report Wizard prompts you to select a Universe or another type of data provider. Select the default, Universe, and click Next >.

4. The wizard displays the list of available universes. Your company may have more universes, but only the ones to which you have access are displayed. Some companies have multiple universe domains for test and production environments or for geographically distributed deployments. When there are two universes with the same name in two different domains, the repository name is indicated in brackets. For example, the following screen shows a Sales universe in the [UniWeb] domain and one in the [Universe] domain. From this screen, you also can set the default universe, similar to selecting Tools | Options, then specifying the New Document default universe setting. As you select each universe, a description of the universe is displayed in the Help box. For long universe descriptions, use the scroll bars within the Help box to view more information. Select the universe and click Finish.

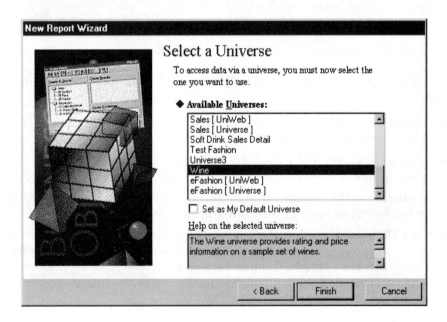

5. The New Report Wizard launches the Query Panel.

The Query Panel

The Query Panel (Figure 21-2) works similar to the Slice and Dice Panel. Classes and Objects are displayed along the left side of the screen. These are the objects that are available to use to display columns of information called *Result Objects* or to filter rows of data called *Conditions*. The objects in the Result window and those in the Condition window can be different. For example, you can create a query to display a list of customers in NJ. *Customer* would be a result object and *State* would be a condition object. In Figure 21-2, *Color*, *Country*, *Varietal*, and *Average Price* are the result objects. *Color* is a condition object.

The Query Panel has its own buttons that allow you to modify the way the SQL is generated. Table 21-2 provides an overview of each of these buttons.

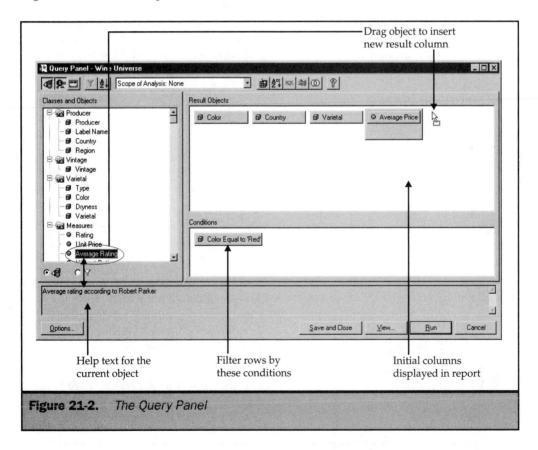

Figure 21-2.   *The Query Panel*

Button	Description	Purpose
	Show/Hide All Classes	By default, the classes and objects are displayed. If you have a large query with many result columns, you may want to momentarily hide the classes and objects to see more result objects.
	Show/Hide Help on Selected Item	The universe designer adds help text or a description to each universe object. The help text is displayed in the bottom window, as shown in Figure 20-2.
	Wrap Result Objects	For queries that have many result columns, you may want to wrap the result objects so that they all appear on one screen in the Query Panel; you do not need to scroll right to see the additional columns. This does not affect how the SQL or default report is generated.
	Simple Condition	A simple condition allows you to add a filter on the currently selected result object and presents you with a list of values. The object is then added in the Condition window.
	Sort	Apply a sort to the current result object. This sort is done on the server, not in the local report, as described in Chapter 18.
	Scope of Analysis	Modify the query to retrieve more levels of details in the microcube, but display only summary levels in the initial report. Scope of Analysis is discussed in Chapter 19.
	Manage Sorts	When you want to have multiple sort levels performed on the server, Manage Sorts allows you to specify a sort order across multiple objects.

Table 21-2.   *Buttons in the Query Panel*

Button	Description	Purpose
SQL	View SQL	View the SQL syntax.
	User Objects	Create a user object or formula that is processed by the server rather than the local report.
	Combine Queries	Create queries that are combined with the SQL operators UNION, INTERSECT, and MINUS. These are discussed in Chapter 22.
	Help	Display contextual help.

Table 21-2.   *Buttons in the Query Panel* (continued)

From the Query Panel, you can

■ **Run**   Execute the query and present the results in the previously selected template or report style.

■ **View**   Execute the query and display the raw results via the Data Manager.

■ **Save and Close**   Save the query definition and SQL statement but do not execute the query. Use this option when you are building standard reports that you will publish to Corporate Documents or send to other users and you do not want the initial report to contain data.

■ **Cancel**   Cancel changes made in the Query Panel. Depending on how you launched the Query Panel, you will be returned to either the New Report Wizard or the Report Window.

Result Objects

To see individual objects within each class, click the + next to the class. To add columns of data to the report, drag the individual object from the Classes and Objects window to the Results Objects window or double-click the object name. When you drag an object, the cursor changes, as shown in Figure 21-2. You also can drag an entire class of objects to the results pane. Ideally, you should sort the order of the result objects from left to right by how you want them to appear in the initial report. This is typically from largest dimension to smallest dimension, with the measures rightmost. Once you execute a query, the order of the result objects and that of the variable columns in a report do not necessarily match. As you add additional dimension or detail result objects to the query, the variable columns are inserted preceding the measure columns in a report. Reordering the columns via the Slice and Dice Panel does not affect the order of the columns in the query.

To remove a result object, select the object and press DELETE. Alternatively, you can drag an object from the Result Objects window back to the Classes and Objects listing.

Scope of Analysis

As discussed in Chapter 19, "Scope of Analysis," the Scope of Analysis button enables you to retrieve additional columns of data for multidimensional analysis without immediately displaying the results in the report. The details exist in the microcube and become available when you select Drill By or Drill Down. The Scope of Analysis dialog box called from the Query Panel is the same as the Scope of Analysis box called from the Explorer pop-up menu. However, the Query Panel also allows you to specify a scope of analysis by levels.

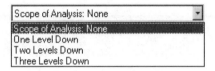

The data retrieved by the microcube directly corresponds to the result objects in your query. In this respect, the levels are relative and not fixed. For example, look at the sample hierarchies in Figure 21-3 and the currently displayed result objects in Figure 21-2. From the Producer hierarchy, *Country* is a result object in the query. If you change the Scope of Analysis to Two Levels Down, then the query will also retrieve results for *Region* and *Producer. Color* and *Varietal* are also result objects in Figure 21-2. Varietal is the lowest level of detail within the Varietal hierarchy, so the Two Levels Down specification has no effect on additional query columns. The levels selection applies only to dimensions currently used as result objects; therefore, changing the Scope of Analysis to Two Levels Down does not retrieve additional columns from the Vintage hierarchy, as the query contains no objects from the hierarchy.

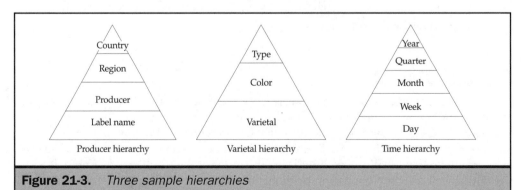

Figure 21-3. *Three sample hierarchies*

The following table shows another example of how the levels are relative using the time hierarchy from Figure 21-3. For each example, assume that the Scope of Analysis is changed to Two Levels Down.

If the current result object is	Then the query also retrieves
Year	Quarter, Month
Quarter	Month, Week
Month	Week, Day
Week	Day
Day	No additional columns, as it is the lowest level of detail in the hierarchy

Conditions

You use conditions to narrow your analysis to show information only for your particular subset of data. If you are a product manager, you may limit your analysis to certain products. If you are a regional manager, you may limit your analysis to certain countries. If you are a supervisor, you may limit your analysis to the employees you manage. You limit your analysis by adding *conditions* to a query. Conditions generate a WHERE clause in the SQL SELECT statement. In some cases, these conditions may be applied automatically through security settings in your database or in the BusinessObjects Supervisor settings. Usually, it is a combination of both. For example, if the transaction system or data warehouse contains information for multiple legal entities, the DBA may restrict your access to show you data only for the legal entity by which you are employed; you do not need to add an extra condition in your query. However, you will still need to add conditions in the query to restrict your analysis to particular products, regions, employees, and so on, within your legal entity.

When you add a condition to the query, you need to consider the impact on response time, particularly if you are accessing a transaction system or a very large data warehouse. Ideally, it is better to apply conditions to objects that have shorter values such as *Product ID* or *Product Code*, as these columns are more often indexed in the source database, rather than longer values such as *Product Name* or *Product Description*, which may not be indexed.

The Query Panel provides you with three ways to add a condition to your query:

- You can apply a simple condition by selecting a result object, then clicking the Simple Condition button. You are prompted to select from a list of values. Simple conditions use only EQUAL TO or IN LIST operators. You apply simple conditions only to dimension or detail objects that have an associated list of values.

- You can drag an object from the list of Classes and Objects to the Condition window of the Query Panel to create what Business Objects refers to as a *complex condition.* This object does not need to be a result object and can also be a measure object. The object does not have to have an associated list of values. In reality, the conditions you create this way can be fairly simple, so don't let the terminology of *complex condition* mislead you.

■ You can apply a predefined condition that is created by the universe designer and includes the operators and possible values.

Adding a Complex Condition

There are four steps needed to add a complex condition to a query. In the following example, you will add a complex condition on *Country,* using the initial query displayed in Figure 21-2 as a starting point:

1. Select the *Country* object and drag it to the Condition window.

2. Specify an operator to evaluate the condition. In the Condition window, BusinessObjects prompts you to <Select an operator>. You must move your cursor to the left screen that displays the list of operators. Select In List by double-clicking.

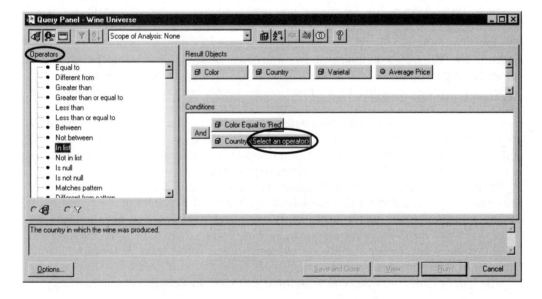

3. <Select an operator> is replaced by the In List operator, and you are prompted to <Specify an operand> for entering, selecting, or generating a potential list of values. Select Show List Of Values and double-click to launch the list of values.

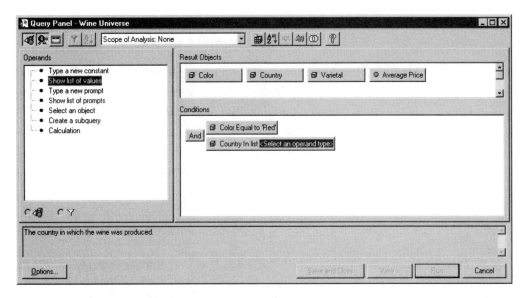

4. Choose Australia, New Zealand, South Africa. Use CTRL-click to select multiple values. Click OK to close the list of values dialog box and see the complex condition statement, as shown next. Notice that in this dialog box, commas separate multiple values, whereas in prompts discussed in Chapter 20, you used semicolons. Both conditions are connected with an AND.

To view the SQL generated, click the SQL button from the Query Panel. The conditions on color and country are connected with an AND. Because the object types are characters, the values are enclosed in single quotes automatically. If they were numeric values, they would not use quotes.

```
WHERE
  (
  WINE_FACT_PRICE_RATE.ColorClass  =  'Red'
  AND  WINE_FACT_PRICE_RATE.Country  IN  ('Australia', 'New Zealand', 'South
Africa')
  )
```

Operators

Operators form the basis of comparison for the object and the values you specify. Table 21-3 lists the possible operators. Some SQL equivalents are different for specific RDBMSs. The SQL equivalents listed in Table 21-3 are Oracle-based.

Operator	SQL Equivalent	Explanation
Equal to	=	Exactly equal to one value
Different from	<> or !=	Not equal to or different from one value
Greater than	>	Greater than a particular number, date, or character
Greater than or equal to	>=	Greater than or equal to a particular number, date, or character
Less than	<	Less than a particular number, date, or character
Less than or equal to	<=	Less than or equal to a particular number, date, or character
Between	BETWEEN	Records between and including the two values— for example, *Age* Between 20 And 30; *Price* Between 100 and 150; *Date* Between January 1 And January 23
Not Between	NOT BETWEEN	All values outside a particular range
In List	IN	Equal to multiple values, generally to select multiple character values in a noncontiguous list
Not In List	NOT IN	Different from multiple values
Is Null	IS NULL	Rows in which no value has been entered. Null is different from zero or blank spaces
Is Not Null	IS NOT NULL	Records that do not contain a null

Table 21-3. *Operators Available in the Query Panel Conditions*

Operator	SQL Equivalent	Explanation
Matches Pattern	Like	This allows you to use a wildcard character such as % in Oracle or * in SQL Server to find all records that contain or begin with a particular string. Use underscore (_) to match one particular space. For example, B% is everything that starts with B, %B% contains a B somewhere in the string, and _B% has B as the second position. Warning: this type of condition means an index for the particular column will not be used
Different from Pattern	Not Like	Does not match the pattern specified. Warning: this type of condition means an index will not be used
Both	INTERSECT	Retrieves records in which the two values overlap. Discussed in Chapter 22
Except	MINUS	Removes records from a main query. Discussed in Chapter 22

Table 21-3.   *Operators Available in the Query Panel Conditions* (continued)

Operands

Operands allow you to specify the values to which you want to compare the object. The list of available operands may change depending on the operator you specify in step 2. Table 21-4 describes the standard operands.

This Operand	Enables You To ...
Type a new constant	Manually enter one or more values. If you enter multiple values, connect them with a comma. Note that in answering a prompt, you connect them with a semicolon. For character values, you do not need to enclose the values in single quotes. BusinessObjects adds the quotes directly to the SQL.
Show list of values	Pick from a list of possible values that will remain fixed for each query refresh.
Type a new prompt	Execute the query and be prompted to enter or select values at refresh time. Create a prompt for standard reports that will be used by users with varying information requirements.
Show list of prompts	Select from a list of available prompts. Use this when you have already defined a prompt and want to reuse the same prompt for another data provider.
Select an object	Specify another object as the operand—for example, to select a list of customers that are both the sold to and ship to customers. This operation generates another join statement.
Create a subquery (ANY)	Specify another query to dynamically determine the comparison values. Discussed in Chapter 22.
Calculation	Launches a calculation wizard to create a particular kind of subquery. Discussed in Chapter 22.

Table 21-4.   *Operands for Specifying Comparison Values in a Complex Condition*

Predefined Conditions

In the Classes and Objects window, there are also two radio buttons that allow you to filter which objects appear in the window. By default, standard classes and objects appear. Click the Predefined Conditions radio button to display *predefined conditions*, as shown in Figure 21-4. *Predefined conditions* are a particular kind of object that have built-in operators and values to restrict the number of rows returned to the microcube and to display only the data you are interested in analyzing. For example, your universe may contain a predefined condition called *Current 3 Months* that automatically filters your data to retrieve the latest three months worth of information. The conditions and SQL in a predefined condition can be quite complex, performing multiple SQL translations and comparisons. See Chapter 10, "Condition Objects," for a more thorough discussion.

As shown in Figure 21-4, predefined conditions are denoted with a filter icon. To add a predefined condition to the query:

1. Click the Predefined Conditions radio button to display the condition objects. Note that any classes that do not have predefined conditions are not displayed.

2. Double-click the predefined condition to add it to the condition pane or drag the object to the condition pane.

In Figure 21-4, the predefined condition *New World Wines* has the same filtering effect as selecting the three countries, as shown in the earlier complex condition.

Prompts

As seen in Chapter 20, "Handling Prompts and List of Values," prompts allow you to refresh a query interactively. Prompts are useful when the conditions of your query change periodically or if you are a report author creating a document for other users. In developing prompts, follow these guidelines:

- If a list of values is available, start the prompt question with **Select**.
- If a list of values is not available, start the prompt question with **Enter**.

REPORTING WITH BUSINESSOBJECTS

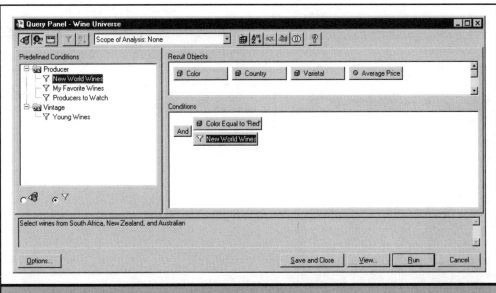

Figure 21-4.   *Predefined conditions are special universe objects that apply complex conditions with one mouse click.*

- Prompts are sorted alphabetically. If the conditions require a logical sort order, precede the question with a numeric value to force a logical sort order.

- If a document will contain multiple data providers, use the operand Show List of Prompts to select an existing prompt. For example, in Figure 21-5, you have two data providers that each contain a condition on *Year*; if you use the same *exact* prompt for each condition, when you refresh a document, you will be prompted to select a year only one time. The prompt is case sensitive, so use Show List of Prompts to select the prompt from a list of ones you have already created. The same condition value is then filled in for each of the conditions / data providers.

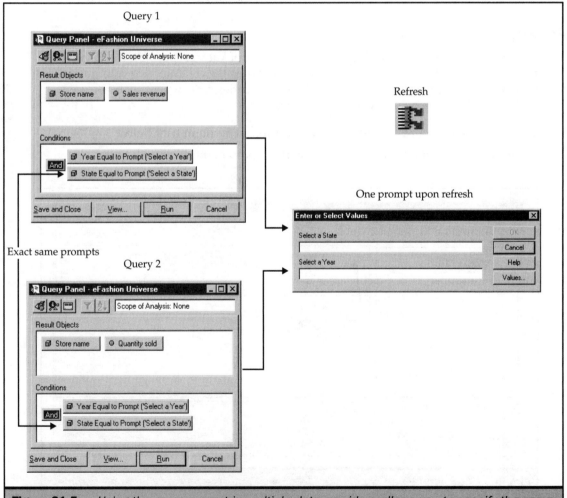

Figure 21-5. *Using the same prompt in multiple data providers allows you to specify the same condition for each query.*

To create a prompt on the wine's country:

1. Select the *Country* object and drag it to the Condition window.

2. In the Condition window, BusinessObjects prompts you to <Select an operator>. Move the cursor to the Operator list and select In List by double-clicking.

3. <Specify an operand> by moving your cursor to the Operand list and double-clicking Type a New Prompt. The value box changes to an insertion cursor. Create the prompt as **Select wine country(s)**. Press ENTER. This prompt will now be available for other queries in this document.

> 🗐 Country In list Prompt ('Select wine country (s)')

A prompt generates the following SQL, which gets evaluated when you execute the query or schedule it via BCA:

```
WINE_FACT_PRICE_RATE.Country   IN   @variable('Select wine country (s)')
```

Sorts on the Server vs. in the Report

You can either sort the results on the RDBMS server or in the document via the Slice and Dice Panel. As a general rule, I recommend sorting in the local report. Sorting on the server may take additional time to execute a query on what is already a potentially highly utilized database. The desktop, on the other hand, is typically underutilized with spare processing power.

The exception to this is if you also use the Query Options to limit the result set, and the sort order is important. For example, let's say you want to retrieve a list of newest 100 customers. You can do this via a subquery, or you can do this by including a descending sort on *Customer Creation Date* and limiting the result set to 100 customers. Likewise, ranking is a SQL analytic functional available in only some databases. If you want to get a list of the top ten selling products or top ten customers with the highest revenues, insert a descending sort on *Revenue,* and set the Query Options, Partial Results to 10.

Query Options

To access Query Options (shown in Figure 21-6), select Options from the Query Panel. These options relate to the individual query, and unlike New Document Options, they are not global for all subsequent documents.

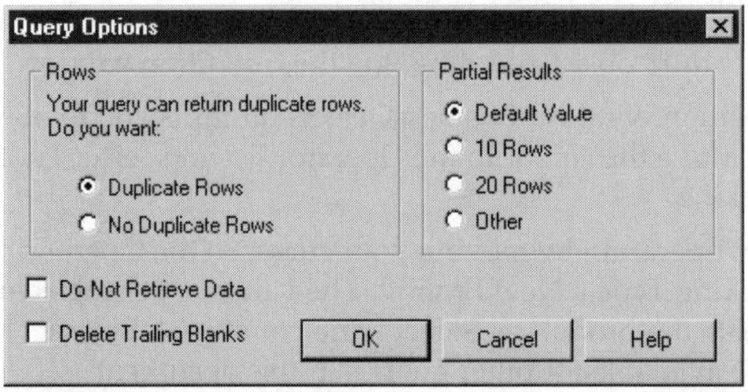

Figure 21-6. *Query Options*

If you are accessing dimensional data in which there are multiple rows for the exact same value, select No Duplicate Rows to add a DISTINCT to the SQL Select statement. For example, if you have a CUSTOMER or PRODUCT table in which there are multiple records with different valid to/from dates for the same customers or products, by default, you will receive multiple rows of information in a list report. BusinessObjects generates the following SQL:

```
SELECT CUSTOMER.CUSTOMER_ID, CUSTOMER.CUSTOMER_NAME FROM CUSTOMER
```

When you select the option No Duplicate Rows, BusinessObjects modifies the SQL statement:

```
SELECT DISTINCT CUSTOMER.CUSTOMER_ID, CUSTOMER.CUSTOMER_NAME FROM CUSTOMER
```

By default, all list of values queries contain the DISTINCT qualifier. This option is not important for queries that contain a measure that uses a GROUP BY function, as all rows are aggregated and grouped by each unique row identifier.

In earlier versions of BusinessObjects, when you modified a query, you could only Cancel or Run it. If you had a particularly complex query with nested conditions that you either wanted to schedule via BCA or to continue modifying at a later point in time, you could select the option Do Not Retrieve Data, click OK, then Run, and save a blank document. With the addition of the Query Panel's Save and Close button, the Do Not Retrieve Data option is no longer necessary.

Delete Trailing Blanks trims blank values from individual rows of data. The values are not trimmed for each column, but just for an individual row.

Partial Results allows you to retrieve a limited number of rows from the data source, ideally for testing complex queries or selecting top ten values, as described earlier. The Default Value is the maximum number of rows you can retrieve as specified by the universe designer. To enter a different value, select Other.

OLAP Access

In order to access MOLAP cubes such as Hyperion Essbase or Microsoft Analysis Services, you must have the corresponding OLAP Access Pack installed on your hard disk. You must also have access to the cube itself. Your BusinessObjects access rights do not flow through to MOLAP cubes, as they have their own security settings.

The query process is slightly different depending on which MOLAP server you are accessing. BusinessObjects acquired some of the OLAP access technology with its acquisition of OLAP@Work in 2000. With this acquisition, the OLAP Panel for MS Analysis Services and SAP/BW moved to acting solely as a selection screen, similar to the universe Query Panel; the OLAP Panel does not display any data values. However, with Hyperion Essbase and DB2 OLAP, the OLAP Panel still displays a grid of values. This grid makes it helpful to preview and drill around the data before running the query that returns the results to a BusinessObjects formatted report. Once you return the OLAP data to the BusinessObjects microcube, all the standard reporting and analysis features reviewed in earlier chapters are available to you. To better understand this workflow, refer to Figure 13-2.

Microsoft Analysis Services

The following example uses Microsoft Analysis Services as the OLAP data source. To access an MS Analysis Services data source:

1. Select File | New or click New to launch the New Report Wizard.
2. At the first Wizard screen, select Begin >. When the wizard prompts you to specify data access, select Others, then click the drop-down box to select an OLAP data source. For MS Analysis Services, select OLAP Connect.

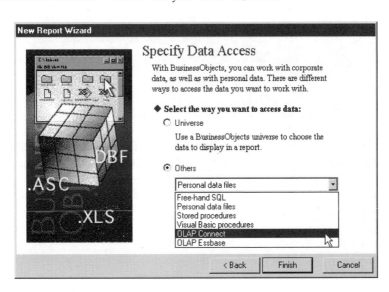

3. If this is the first time you are accessing an MS Analysis Services cube from this computer, you must define an OLAP connection. If you are not prompted to define a connection, skip to step 5. You can connect to either a server-based cube or a local cube file that you exported from MS Analysis Services. To access the server-based cube, select the desired server name under Computer. Click Next >.

4. BusinessObjects displays the Customize Connection Information dialog box. Here you specify a connection name and an optional description. Enter a name and description, then click Finish.

5. BusinessObjects displays the Select Connection dialog box. Once you have defined at least one connection to an MS Analysis Services cube from this PC, you will immediately be presented with this dialog box when you create a new document. From the Select Connection dialog, you can click New to define connections to other servers or local cubes. Select Next > to proceed with building a query.

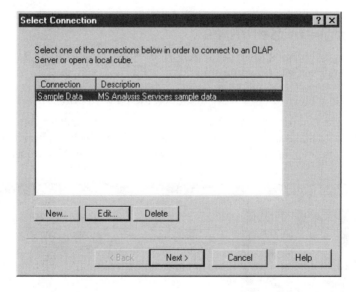

6. With MS Analysis Services, each server may have multiple databases. Each database may have multiple cubes. In the Select Cube to Open dialog box, click the + sign next to the database that contains the cube you wish to access. In the next example, Foodmart 2000 is a sample database that contains six cubes. Select the Sales cube and click Finish.

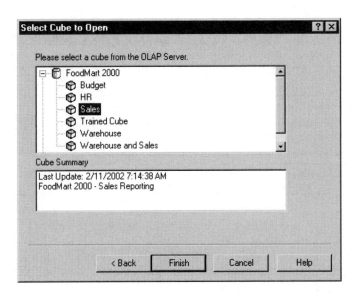

7. BusinessObjects displays the OLAP Panel shown in Figure 21-7. Specify your selection criteria and select OK to execute the query and display the results in a BusinessObjects report.

The MS Analysis Services OLAP Panel

Within the OLAP Panel, the available cube dimensions are displayed in the top window. The bottom window is where you specify which dimensions and members you want to display in the report. To add a dimension to the report, drag it from the top window and place it in the grid. As you move across the dimensions in the grid, a tool tip appears to show which relationships or individual member values you have specified. For example, in Figure 21-7, the tool tip shows that the individual measure values Unit Sales, Profit, and Sales Average have been selected.

Dimension Properties

When you first drag a dimension to the grid, BusinessObjects automatically launches a Properties dialog box for the particular dimension. Figure 21-8 shows the Properties of Customers Dimension dialog box. By default, the actual member or data value information is displayed. Select the Levels tab to view the values by levels—for example, Country, State, City, and Individual Customer Name.

From the Properties Dimension dialog box, you can select the Filters tab to perform server-based ranking such as Top 10 Customers according to Sales Average or to select dimension values (Country, State, or Individual Customer) with a Sales Average above a certain value. You also can apply a filter according to a particular attribute of the

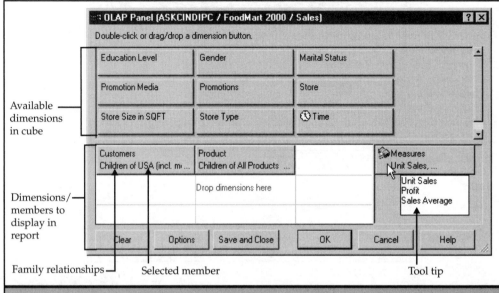

Figure 21-7. OLAP Panel for MS Analysis Services, Sales cube

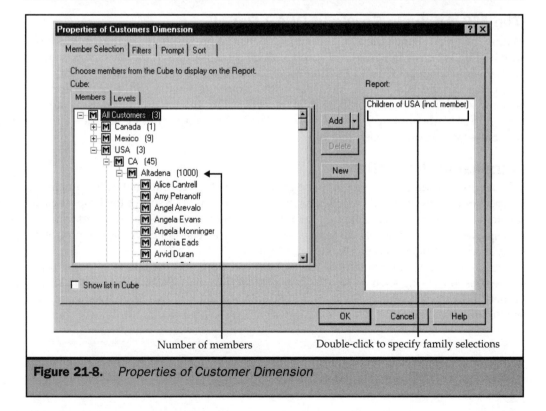

Figure 21-8. Properties of Customer Dimension

Customer dimension. For example, to display sales for only male or female customers, add a Filter on the Gender attribute. Similar to the prompt operand for queries against BusinessObjects universes, the Prompt tab allows you to prompt users at run time to select a value from the customer dimension. The Sort tab allows you to sort dimension values alphabetically, hierarchically, or by a measure value. This sort option has the server perform the sort, but you can override the sort order in the local report via the Slice and Dice Panel.

If you want to see a particular dimension value or level in your report, select the value—for example, USA, and click Add. This adds the member name to the Report column, as shown in Figure 21-8.

Family Relationships

In MOLAP cubes, all the dimensional information is hierarchical. Within BusinessObjects classes, the hierarchies are optional. As the information is hierarchical, you can select specific member values such as USA, or you can select values in terms of a relationship. To specify additional selection options relative to USA, double-click USA to invoke the Family dialog box shown in Figure 21-9. Alternatively, you can right-click USA, then select Family.

Figure 21-9 shows the Family selections for USA. Refer to the member values listed in Figure 21-8 to understand the relationships. By default, the family selection is the

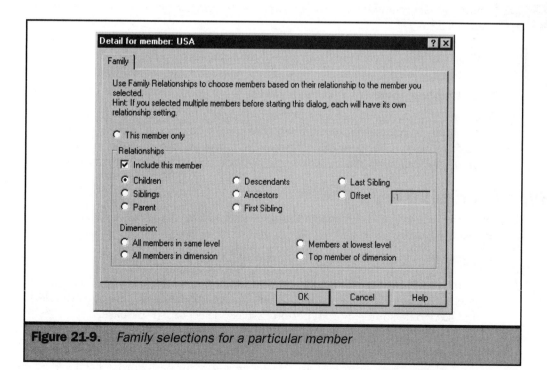

Figure 21-9.   *Family selections for a particular member*

current value and the box This member only is checked. From the Family tab, you can select these additional relationships:

■ **Include this member** Becomes available when you select any other relationships. Once you select additional relationships, click this box to display USA *in addition to* the other relationships.

■ **Children** Displays the immediate children or next level in the dimension. The children of USA are the states.

■ **Siblings** Displays other countries on the same level as USA.

■ **Parent** Displays the grand total for All Customers.

■ **Descendants** Displays all the children, grandchildren, and so forth, for USA. In this example, all states, cities, and individual customers within USA would be displayed. Use caution when you select descendants, as some dimensions can contain thousands of members, making for a slow query and potentially returning too much data. For each dimension level, the Properties Dimension screen shows the number of members within each level.

■ **Ancestors** Selects all the grandparents and upper-level selections. If Alice Cantrell (the first customer in Figure 12-8) were selected, then the Ancestors are Altadena, CA, USA, and All Customers.

Caution *Although there are additional sibling selections, the following do not work correctly in version 5.1.6.*

■ **First Sibling** Selects the first value at the same level in the list—in this example, Canada.

■ **Last Sibling** Selects the last value at the same level.

■ **Offset** Allows you to enter a number to specify the position of the sibling. Negative numbers refer to members that appear before the selected value. Positive numbers appear after the selected value. In this example, an Offset of –1 would select Mexico, as it is one position before USA in the member list.

Hyperion Essbase

The following example uses Hyperion Essbase as the OLAP data source. To access an Essbase MOLAP cube:

1. Select File | New or click New to launch the New Report Wizard.

2. At the first New Report Wizard screen, select Begin >. When the wizard prompts you to specify data access, select Others, then click the drop-down box to select an OLAP data source. For Hyperion Essbase, select OLAP Essbase.

3. If this is the first time you are accessing Essbase from BusinessObjects from this computer, you are prompted to define an OLAP connection. Enter the name of the Essbase server, your Essbase username, and your password. Click Next >.

4. An Essbase server can have multiple applications and within an application, multiple databases. Use the drop-down menus to select the application and database. From this screen, you also have the option to load the outline members only when needed. Members in an Essbase outline correspond to the data values within a dimension column—for example, Customer Names or Product IDs. Therefore, the number of members within a dimension can be quite long. Leave this option set to expedite navigation within the OLAP Panel.

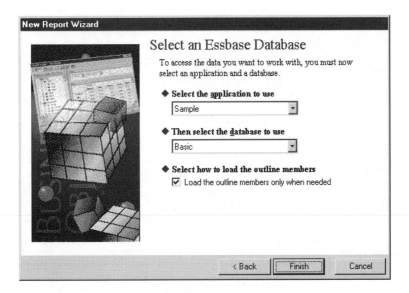

5. From within the New Report Wizard, click Finish. BusinessObjects displays the OLAP Panel shown in Figure 21-10.

The Essbase OLAP Panel

The OLAP Panel for Essbase is quite different than the OLAP Panel for MS Analysis Services shown in Figure 21-7. With the Essbase OLAP Panel, the dimensions and measures are displayed along the left side, similar to universe classes and objects. To expand a dimension, click the + next to the dimension folder. Some of the buttons within the OLAP Panel are similar to those in the standard Query Panel. The other big difference between the Microsoft OLAP Panel and the Essbase OLAP Panel is that the Essbase OLAP Panel displays the values whereas the Microsoft OLAP Panel displays the structure only. This allows you to do a limited amount of server-based analysis and drilling within the OLAP Panel before executing the query to generate a formatted report.

Note *The object qualifications as dimension, measure, and detail are not correctly displayed in the OLAP Panel; everything is denoted as a dimension object. Once you select Continue and generate a BusinessObjects report, measures are accurately denoted with a sphere. For example, Profit is denoted with a blue dimension cube in the OLAP Panel, but with a pink measure sphere within a report.*

REPORTING WITH BUSINESSOBJECTS

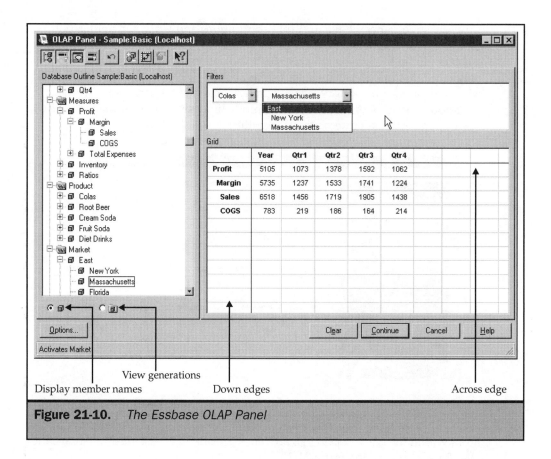

Figure 21-10.   *The Essbase OLAP Panel*

You build your initial query by dragging and dropping members from the outline to the grid. You can select an entire hierarchy or individual members. If you want to select an entire generation, view the hierarchies by generations by selecting the generations radio button in the bottom left of the OLAP Panel. To view the aliases (for example, that Product 100 is Colas) for the dimensions, select Options from the OLAP Panel. From the OLAP Panel Options dialog, select the General tab and under Aliases, check the box Use Table.

The Filters window of the panel enables you to define query conditions. Anything you add to the Filters window will later become section headers in a master/detail report. You can have multiple levels within the filters. For example, in Figure 21-10, the filter East will retrieve the totals for the Eastern region; the filters New York and Florida, which are children within East, will retrieve the data for these individual states. Once you begin analyzing the data offline in a report (rather than the server-based grid), you will still have the subtotal for East even though in the query you did not select all the states within East.

Items that you add to the Grid window become the column headings and rows of data. You can drill up and down within the grid. For example, the dimension member

Margin has two children, Sales and COGS, displayed in the grid. To remove Sales and COGS from the grid:

1. Select Margin from within the grid, then right-click to invoke the following pop-up menu:

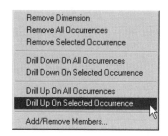

2. Select Drill Up on Selected Occurrence.

3. To drill down, double-click Margin.

Within the Grid, you can insert multiple column levels, similar to stacking column headings within a crosstab report. For example, to analyze Actual versus Budget within a particular Year or Quarter, drag the member Actual to appear below Year. The status bar informs you that the action adds Actual to the edge. If your status bar is not displayed, click the Show/Hide Status Bar button. Ensure that you position your mouse below the Year column so that the drag-and-drop insertion shape corresponds to that in the following screen. If a full gray box appears, then you may be replacing a member rather than inserting an additional member to the grid.

REPORTING WITH
BUSINESSOBJECTS

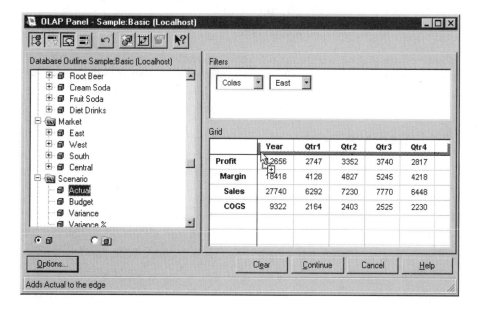

Drag and drop the Budget to appear next to the Actual column. The final grid appears as follows:

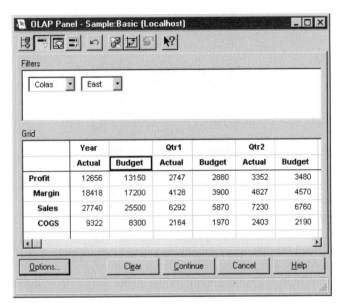

To delete an object from the grid, you can either drag it away from the grid to the outline view or

1. Select the member in the grid.
2. Right-click to invoke the pop-up menu.
3. Select Remove Selected Occurrence.

Once you are satisfied with your filter and grid selections, click Continue from within the OLAP Panel to execute the query and return the results to the BusinessObjects document. You can then begin using the standard BusinessObjects reporting and analysis features.

The Add/Remove Panel

You can further refine the filter and grid selections through the Add/Remove Panel shown in Figure 21-11. You do not use this panel to select initial dimensions. It has three tabs:

- **Filters**   Allow you to specify the filters for existing dimensions in the filter window.
- **Down Edge**   Allows you to select individual members in the down edge of the grid.
- **Across Edge**   Allows you to select members in the across edge of the grid.

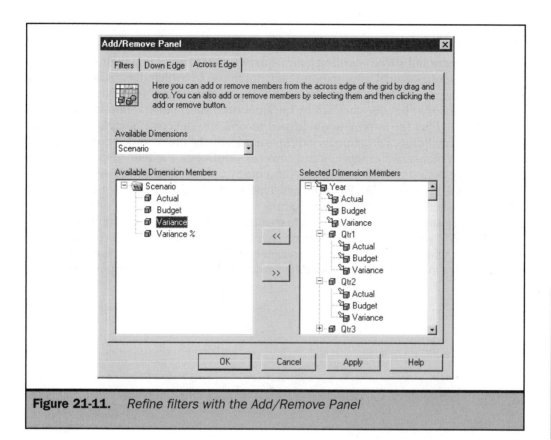

Figure 21-11. *Refine filters with the Add/Remove Panel*

Under Available Dimensions in Figure 21-11, Year and Scenario appear. These are currently the only dimensions displayed in the columns in the grid. In the earlier screen, you added the scenarios Actual and Budget to the grid through drag-and-drop. Now that Scenario exists in the grid, you can use the Add/Remove Panel to add the Variance member.

1. Launch the Add/Remove Panel by selecting the button from the toolbar. You also can right-click a dimension member within the grid and select Add/Remove Members from the pop-up menu.

2. Select the Across Edge tab.

3. From Available Dimensions, select the drop-down box, then Scenario.

4. From Available Dimension Members, expand the Scenario folder and select Variance. Click >> to add Variance to Selected Dimension Members.

5. Click Apply to close the dialog box and see the new member in the grid.

Summary

The most important step in creating a new query is first formulating your business question in terms of what information you want to see, by which dimensions you want to explore the results, and which subsets of data you want to analyze. If the question is too broad, you may be overwhelmed by the amount of information returned. Conditions enable you to filter the information returned to you. You can create simple conditions or complex conditions. Predefined conditions are set by the universe designer and enable you to select predefined groupings and complex conditions. Predefined conditions that involve time periods enable you to execute a query that automatically selects the most recent period, such as the last 90 days or current month. If you are building a report that will be refreshed by other users, use prompts to allow report readers to select their own conditions. BusinessObjects enables you to create documents that contain multiple queries and multiple data providers. This feature enables you to create one report to analyze information that comes from a data warehouse and an OLAP database, for example. Construct the individual queries per data provider, then create the formatted report.

Chapter 22

Complex Queries

Ohne of BusinessObjects' greatest strengths is its query engine. Its powerful semantic layer lets you create complex SQL statements, without your ever having to know or write SQL. I refer to complex queries as any query that contains SQL that

- Not all BI tools can handle
- Potentially have an adverse effect on response time
- May lead you to incorrect results the first time if you lack a clear understanding of the functionality or logic

You may not always realize when you generate a complex query; it's quite simple to add result objects to the Query Panel that, unbeknownst to you, come from two different star schemas. In other cases, you may struggle to define conditions in a way that gives you the desired results—for example, you may be forced to use nested conditions or subqueries in which building the query with the attendant thought process and tasks *feels* complex.

Multipass Queries

As I help clients select BI tools, some BI vendors claim they can do multipass SQL because they built reports in multiple stages. This is misleading, as it is not the generally accepted definition of multipass SQL. Multipass SQL means the BI tool can generate multiple SQL statements and thus perform multiple passes against the database to generate correct query results. From the user perspective, there is only one data provider; it appears you are building one query. The BI tool generates multiple SQL statements and dynamically stitches the results together, often unbeknownst to the user. Standard SQL cannot do this. BusinessObjects has been able to perform multipass SQL since version 4. It is one of the features that allow you to use BusinessObjects against complex data models such as those in a transaction system or against data warehouses that contain multiple start schemas. BusinessObjects will generate multiple SQL statements whenever there are measures in a query that come from more than one fact table. If the dimensions or GROUP BY clause for the two queries are exactly the same, BusinessObjects will automatically display the result set in one table and you will never know that multiple SQL statements were generated to create the report.

Following are some sample business questions for which BusinessObjects may generate multiple SQL statements to answer:

Information Requirement	Explanation
Debits, Credits, Month End Balance	Debits and credits are aggregated over a period of time, while balances are one point in time.
Movements In/Out, Inventory	Material movements are aggregated over a period of time, while inventory is one point in time.

Information Requirement	Explanation
Days Sales Inventory (DSI)	Sales are aggregated over a period of time, while inventory is one point in time.
Product Sales, Promotion	Sales come from one fact table, while promotion costs come from another fact table.

In order for multipass SQL to work correctly, the universe designer must set specific SQL parameters and define contexts for each set of joins that make up a star schema. These options are discussed in Chapters 6 and 7, respectively. Refer to Figure 6-7 and Figure 7-3 for examples of multipass SQL in action. From a user viewpoint, you only need to worry about multipass SQL if you think you are getting incorrect results or if BusinessObjects splits the results into two tables. For example, in Figure 22-1, the table on the left shows the desired results; the report on the right shows two tables, undesired results. BusinessObjects creates two tables, one for each SQL statement, when there is an additional dimension object that does not apply to both measures. The left-hand table displays the Sales Revenue and Promotion Cost by Year, SKU Description, and SKU number. These three dimensions are common to both Sales Revenue and Promotion Cost. The report on the right includes another dimension, State, that relates only to Sales Revenue. Promotion Costs are not tracked by State, so BusinessObjects creates two separate tables.

Figure 22-2 shows the two SQL statements used to generate the undesired report on the right in Figure 22-1. The problem appears in Select1. The dimension object *State* (OUTLET_LOOKUP.STATE) applies only to sales; it does not apply to promotions and is not defined as part of the promotion star schema or context. Therefore, OUTLET_LOOKUP.STATE does not appear in either the SELECT or GROUP BY sections of Select2 in Figure 22-2. When a dimension does not apply to both measures, BusinessObjects

Correct table

Year	SKU desc	SKU number	Sales revenue	Promotion Cost
2000	Belted Pocket Shirt	164962	$42,313	
2000	Chenille Leotard T-Shirt	166136	$20,252	
2000	Cotton Leotard T-Shirt	165197	$17,143	
2000	Diamond Patterned Vest	173117	$8,665	
2000	Long-Sleeved Stitch Shirt	167042	$265,788	$8,050
2000	Long-Sleeved Torn Stitch T-Sh	166553	$252,853	
2000	Military Shirt	166583	$125,554	$12,650
2000	Milkyway Pocket Shirt	146379	$1,480	
2000	Modal Shirt	165170	$286,935	$1,200
2000	Orange Short-sleeved Shirt	170875	$7,698	
2000	Tailored Short-sleeved Shirt	173608	$1,614	
2000	Whisky Dancer T-Shirt	166550	$348,839	$9,500

Undesired results

Section: Year
2000

Section: SKU desc
Long-Sleeved Stitch Shirt

SKU number	State	Sales revenue		SKU number	Promotion Cost
167042	California	$51,813		167042	$8,050
167042	Colorado	$17,464			
167042	DC	$23,172			
167042	Florida	$10,742			
167042	Illinois	$16,885			
167042	Massachusetts	$13,587			
167042	New York	$46,447			
167042	Texas	$85,678			

Figure 22-1. *Sample reports built by multipass SQL*

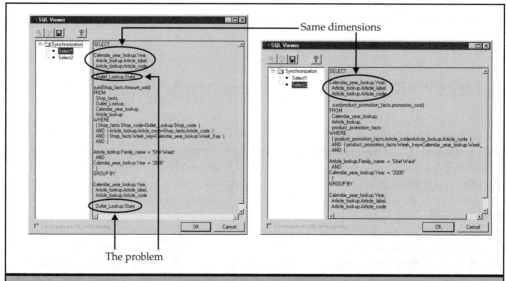

Figure 22-2. *One query generates two SQL statements. Select1 has an extra GROUP BY dimension.*

automatically creates a master detail report with two tables. The section header contains the Year and SKU Description dimensions that are common to both measures.

Multiple Data Providers

Multipass SQL automatically synchronizes result sets by common dimensions within the same universe. The synchronization happens even when you have multiple data providers from different star schemas, as shown in the previous section. For example, in the EFASHION universe, Sales is one star schema and Promotions is in a second star schema. They both share common dimensions such as Time and Articles. However, let's assume they are in two separate universes; you can no longer build one query or one data provider to create the report shown in Figure 22-1. You need to create a data provider for each universe. If the data providers and/or dimension names are different between the two result sets, you must manually synchronize the common dimensions by linking them.

BusinessObjects will allow you to build one table with variables from both data providers; however, until you link the common dimensions, the results will be incorrect. Also, this procedure works only with the reports that contain measure objects with an aggregate function; when the measures do not contain aggregate functions, BusinessObjects displays null values.

In Chapter 18, you saw a ranking of the top ten wine producers according to Robert Parker's rating. In the following example, you will insert a report from a second data provider and link the common dimensions. The second data provider is a spreadsheet that contains ratings and prices for the top ten wines, according to Wine Spectator. In this example, you want to use the second data provider to see if the ratings are different between the two sources. The original wine database has prices for only a small number of total wines rated, so the personal data source provides price information not otherwise available.

1. To insert a second data provider, you can either create a new report and insert another table or insert a second data provider into the main report by selecting Data | New Data Provider.

2. When prompted by the New Table Wizard, select Access new data in a different way and click Begin >.

3. Under Specify Data Access, select Others, select Personal data files and click Finish. BusinessObjects displays the Access Personal Data dialog box. (This dialog is explained in Chapter 9, "Incorporating Personal Data Files.") Complete the selections and click Run.

Synchronizing Data Providers

When you insert a new data provider, BusinessObjects does not automatically affect the data displayed in the report or current table block; the data has only been retrieved into the local microcube. In order to display the results in the table, you insert the new variables via the Report Manager or the Slice and Dice Panel. In order to ensure the data is correctly displayed, you must first synchronize the common dimensions via the Data Manager shown in Figure 22-3.

 To access the Data Manager, select Data | View Data or select View Data from the standard toolbar, then select the Definition tab. Under Data Providers, the name of each data provider is assigned according to the type of data provider (Query from a universe, PD from a personal data file, and so on) and a sequential number. In Figure 22-3, note the link symbol next to Producer and WS_Producer. This indicates that the two variables represent the same dimensions and content, even though the variable names are different. When you select a variable that is not linked, the Unlink button becomes a Link button.

Even if you display only one dimension in your report, you must link all dimensions to ensure you continue to get correct results. If you fail to do this correctly, you will get incorrect results in any block that accesses both data providers. If you are working with a personal data file, freehand SQL, or another data provider that does not accurately qualify dimension objects, you also must first modify the qualification for the object. In this example, Vintage in the spreadsheet contains numeric values. BusinessObjects incorrectly classifies this as measure. Also, BusinessObjects automatically aggregates measures by applying a SUM projection aggregate. For ratings and price, these should be converted to AVERAGE.

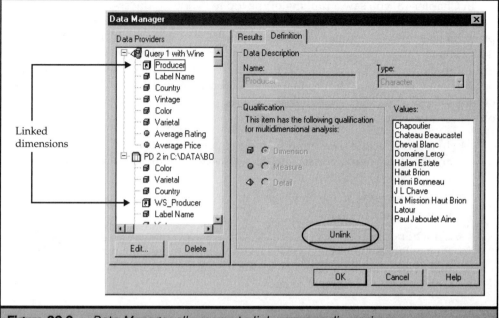

Figure 22-3. *Data Manager allows you to link common dimensions.*

Modifying Object Qualifications

To modify the object qualifications:

1. Launch Data Manager by selecting Data | View Data or click View Data, then select the Definition tab.

2. Select the variable from the non-universe data provider. In this example, Vintage.

3. When you select an object from a non-universe data provider, the Name, Type, and Qualification settings that are grayed out in Figure 22-3 become available. Change the qualification from measure to dimension by clicking dimension radio.

4. Now correct the projection aggregate for any measures. Select the measure variable whose projection aggregate you wish to change. In this example, select WS_Rate from the Data Provider pane.

5. In the drop-down box Select the function to aggregate this measure, change the setting from Sum to Average.

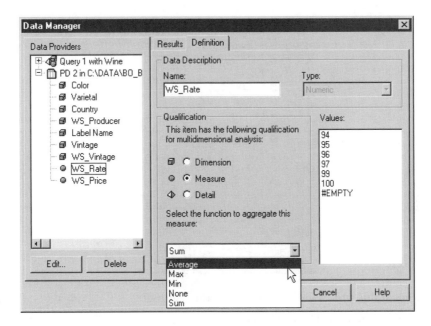

Leave the Data Manager open so you can continue linking the dimensions in the next section.

Linking Dimensions

Once you have corrected the object qualifications and aggregates, you continue to use the Data Manager to link the dimensions:

1. Select the variable in the first data provider. In this example, Query 1 with Wine, Label Name.

2. Click Link to.

3. The Define link Between dimensions dialog box displays a list of dimension objects from the second data provider (in this case, from a Personal Data File). Note that only the dimensions that do not have an existing link appear

(WS_Producer does not appear, as the link was previously defined). Select the common dimension, Label Name, and click OK.

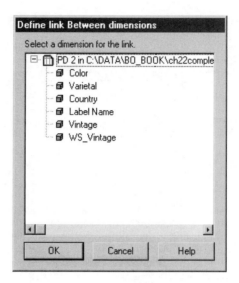

4. Repeat this process for all common dimensions.

5. Click OK to close Data Manager.

6. Use Report Manager to drag the new measure from the second data provider to the report table.

Figure 22-4 shows the combined results. Notice that data from the two sources has nicely been merged into one table; it is not split into two tables as in the report on the right in Figure 22-1.

Data Mismatches

When you synchronize data between two different data sources, there is a strong likelihood that the dimensional values will not match exactly. BusinessObjects will nicely merge whatever data does match and display null values in the measure column for which there is no data. As shown in Figure 22-4, there are data rows in both data providers that do not share the same dimensional values. For example, the Producer Chateau Beaucastel has three different vintages in data provider two (the personal data file) that do not exist in data provider one (the query), displayed in rows 9–11; Producer Caymus does not exist at all in the query results, row 17. For these rows, BusinessObjects displays null values in the measure column that comes from data

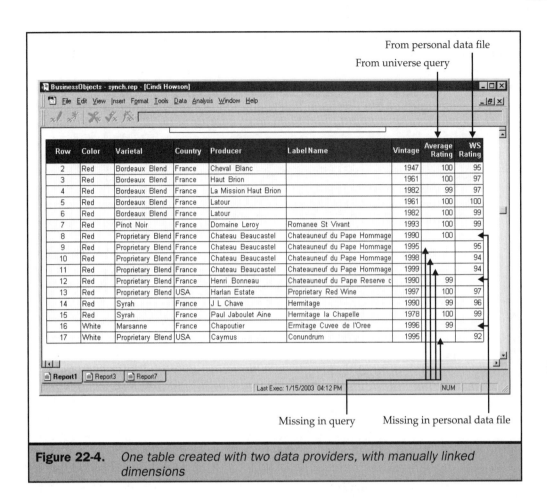

From personal data file

From universe query

Row	Color	Varietal	Country	Producer	Label Name	Vintage	Average Rating	WS Rating
2	Red	Bordeaux Blend	France	Cheval Blanc		1947	100	95
3	Red	Bordeaux Blend	France	Haut Brion		1961	100	97
4	Red	Bordeaux Blend	France	La Mission Haut Brion		1982	99	97
5	Red	Bordeaux Blend	France	Latour		1961	100	100
6	Red	Bordeaux Blend	France	Latour		1982	100	99
7	Red	Pinot Noir	France	Domaine Leroy	Romanee St Vivant	1993	100	99
8	Red	Proprietary Blend	France	Chateau Beaucastel	Chateauneuf du Pape Hommage	1990	100	
9	Red	Proprietary Blend	France	Chateau Beaucastel	Chateauneuf du Pape Hommage	1995		95
10	Red	Proprietary Blend	France	Chateau Beaucastel	Chateauneuf du Pape Hommage	1998		94
11	Red	Proprietary Blend	France	Chateau Beaucastel	Chateauneuf du Pape Hommage	1999		94
12	Red	Proprietary Blend	France	Henri Bonneau	Chateauneuf du Pape Reserve c	1990	99	
13	Red	Proprietary Blend	USA	Harlan Estate	Proprietary Red Wine	1997	100	97
14	Red	Syrah	France	J L Chave	Hermitage	1990	99	96
15	Red	Syrah	France	Paul Jaboulet Aine	Hermitage la Chapelle	1978	100	99
16	White	Marsanne	France	Chapoutier	Ermitage Cuvee de l'Oree	1996	99	
17	White	Proprietary Blend	USA	Caymus	Conundrum	1995		92

Missing in query   Missing in personal data file

Figure 22-4. *One table created with two data providers, with manually linked dimensions*

provider one (Average Price). Conversely, Producer Chapoutier and Chateau Beaucastel, Vintage 1990 exists in data provider 1 but not in the second data provider data file, displayed in rows 8, 12, and 16; for these rows null values appear in the measure column from the second data provider (WS Rating).

Measure Conditions/Having Clause

When you place a condition on a measure object that uses an aggregate function, BusinessObjects does not generate a straightforward WHERE clause, but rather, it generates a HAVING clause. The RDBMS performs the aggregations and GROUP BY first, then returns only those results that satisfy the HAVING condition. In the following example, the query returns rows for which the SUM of SHOP_FACTS.MARGIN is less than or equal to 0:

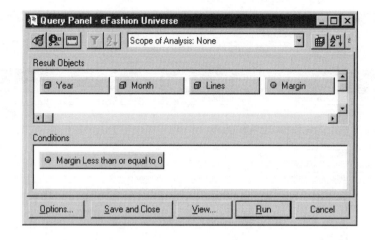

```
SELECT
  Calendar_year_lookup.Year,
  Calendar_year_lookup.Month,
  Article_lookup.Family_name,
  sum(Shop_facts.Margin)
FROM
  Shop_facts,
  Calendar_year_lookup,
  Article_lookup
WHERE
  ( Article_lookup.Article_code=Shop_facts.Article_code  )
  AND  ( Shop_facts.Week_key=Calendar_year_lookup.Week_Key  )
GROUP BY
  Calendar_year_lookup.Year,
  Calendar_year_lookup.Month,
  Article_lookup.Family_name
HAVING
  ( sum(Shop_facts.Margin)  <=  0  )
```

The problem here is that many users are deceived into thinking this is a simple query, as it returns few results. It is true that there may not be many article families/ lines that have a negative margin for a particular month. However, to answer the query, the database must do a full table scan on the fact table. In the sample database, the fact table is quite small; however, in real-world databases, the fact table can be millions of rows of data. To minimize the risk of this, consider adding conditions on any other dimension objects that will generate a WHERE clause. For example, a condition on *Year* in addition to *Margin* will allow the database first to select only those rows for a particular year. The database then performs the GROUP BY and HAVING on a smaller set of data (possibly retrieved via an index).

 If you use measures as conditions, ensure you include other conditions on dimension objects to improve the query processing time.

Specifying Sets of Data

To understand how the AND, OR, UNION, INTERSECT, and MINUS operators work, it's useful to review a bit of set theory. Figure 22-5 shows a Venn diagram with three sets of criteria: Country, Color, and Vintage. When you enter conditions in the Query Panel, the conditions are joined by a default operator, AND. All conditions must be met for the query to return results. You can say this is the intersection, or solid triangle, in Figure 22-5 where all three sets of criteria are met. For example, if you set the conditions as shown in the following screen, the query will return only American Red wines produced before 1980. Given the sample data in Table 22-1, only record 8 is selected.

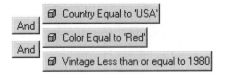

OR Operand and Nested Conditions

The complexity arises when you want to join one set of conditions with an OR and the other with an AND. For example, you may want to select only Red wines produced

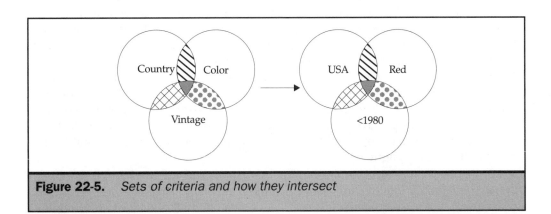

Figure 22-5. *Sets of criteria and how they intersect*

Record	Producer	Country	Vintage	Color	Varietal
1	Haut Brion	France	1961	Red	Bordeaux Blend
2	Chateau Ste Michelle	USA	1995	White	Chardonnay
3	De Fieuzal	France	1978	Red	Bordeaux Blend
4	Vega Sicilia	Spain	1970	Red	Proprietary Blend
5	Storybook Mountain	USA	1995	Red	Zinfandel
6	Oxford Landing	Australia	1997	White	Sauvignon Blanc
7	Ramonet	France	1978	White	Proprietary Blend
8	Robert Mondavi	USA	1966	Red	Cabernet Sauvignon

Table 22-1.   *Sample Wine Data for Complex Conditions*

before the year 1980 but want all wines for USA regardless of the color and regardless of the Vintage. Based on the sample data shown in Table 22-1, you want records 2, 5, 8, where the Country = USA, and only 1, 3, and 4, where the Color = Red and the Vintage <= 1980. Record 6 is not selected, because it satisfies none of the conditions; record 7 is not selected, because while the vintage is < 1980, the color is White, not Red. As shown in Figure 22-5, you want the intersection between color and vintage, shown with the dot-filled intersection; for the country criterion, you want the full circle with no intersection.

To change a condition connector from an AND to an OR, select the AND and double-click to change it to an OR. BusinessObjects will automatically indent two of the conditions. The indent has the same effect as putting a parenthesis around your condition statements. Unfortunately, it usually does not nest the conditions the way you want it to, and getting them exactly right can be a lesson in patience. I find it helpful to periodically look at the SQL (by clicking the SQL button from the Query Panel) to ensure the parentheses are in the right place. To change the indent in the Query Panel and thereby adjust the parenthesis in the SQL, right-click the operand to invoke the pop-up menu shown next and select Indent Left or Indent Right as needed.

Tip *To nest two conditions with an AND and one condition with an OR, as shown in the following screen, first set all operators to OR, then correct the indents:*

```
WHERE
  ( WINE_FACT_PRICE_RATE.Country  =  'USA'
  OR  ( WINE_FACT_PRICE_RATE.ColorClass  =  'Red'
     AND WINE_FACT_PRICE_RATE.Vintage  <=  1980 )
  )
```

In the preceding example, the OR operator allowed you to change one particular criterion. You also can use OR to search for the same value across multiple fields. For example, in SAP, the bill of lading may appear in several fields. With the following conditions, the OR operator allows you to search in multiple fields. By using the exact same prompt for each of the conditions, you only need to enter one bill of lading number and it is filled in each of the conditions.

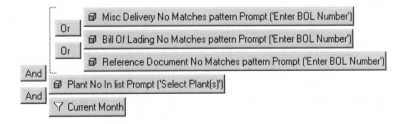

UNION/INTERSECT/MINUS

In some cases, nesting the conditions will still not give you the desired results. This often happens when you want to test for multiple values against the same dimension object. For example, let's say you are looking for wine producers who make both red wines and white wines. If you use the In List operator, you will get a list of producers that make *either* red *or* white wines. If you create two conditions and join them with

AND, you will get no rows returned, as the conditions in the WHERE clause are mutually exclusive.

```
WHERE
  (  WINE_FACT_PRICE_RATE.ColorClass  =  'Red'
  AND  WINE_FACT_PRICE_RATE.ColorClass  =  'White' )
```

To retrieve the desired results, you need to create two queries within one data provider. BusinessObjects is one of the few BI tools that allows you to create multiple queries using the RDBMS's set operators: UNION, INTERSECT, and MINUS. Table 22-2 shows the different operator icons and their purposes. In order to use these operators, the number of result columns and the data type for each of the columns must be the same. Often when using INTERSECT, the result objects are exactly the same and only the conditions change between the two queries. Chapter 7 discussed some of the problems with queries that contain loops, a join path that BusinessObjects does not allow; INTERSECT is a better alternative to answer a query that otherwise would contain a loop. For UNION and MINUS, you may want to change the measure column. It's possible to do this, but in the report, BusinessObjects will use the variable name from the first query. MINUS is also useful for determining if there are data quality issues between a fact table and dimension table, rather than using an outer join (see Chapter 7). For example, if you want a list of products for which there are no corresponding sales transactions, the main query would contain products from the dimension table and the minus query would contain products from the fact table. The result set is a list of products for which there are no records in the fact table. Table 22-2 describes the available operators and combined query icons within the Query Panel. You can use these operators to combine two or more queries.

To create a combined query, first evaluate the result objects in your main query. If you are using INTERSECT, ensure that it does not contain any result objects for dimensions that you will use as a condition. Select the Combine Queries button from the Query Panel. BusinessObjects inserts a new query with the same results objects as those in Query 1. The icon on the Query 2 tab indicates the type of operator. In Figure 22-6, Query 2 is combined with an INTERSECT operator as indicated with the U symbol. To change the type of operator, double-click the operator icon on the query tab or right-click the tab to invoke a pop-up menu.

Note that the dimension for which you want to retrieve multiple values, *Color,* appears only in the conditions. If it appeared in the result objects, no rows would return, as these values are mutually exclusive. Table 22-3 gives sample records to show how the different set operators work. The intersection between the two queries, as

Query Tab	Operator	Explanation
U Query 2	UNION	Combines the results of multiple queries. When the query contains a measure, the common rows are aggregated.
∩ Query 2	INTERSECT	Selects the rows that intersect or overlap between the two queries. This is not recommended for use with measures as a result object. When the query contains a measure object, unless the measure values are exactly the same, there is no intersection.
— Query 2	MINUS	Subtracts the rows in the second query from the main query. When a measure is included and the measure objects are the same, the aggregate from the subquery is subtracted from the main query measure.

Table 22-2.   *Set Operators to Combine Queries*

shown in Figure 22-6, consists of records 1, 2, 3, 4, 6, and 7. Record 5, Harlan Estates, is not selected, because they do not make both red and white wines. If Vintage were added to the result column, then only records 6 and 7 would be selected, as these are

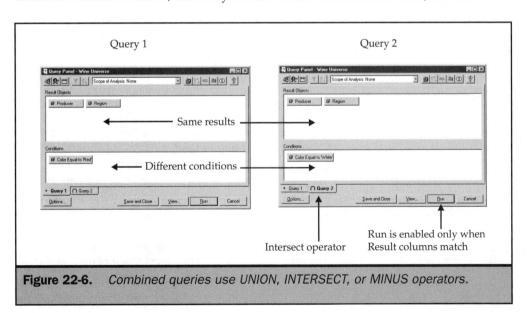

Figure 22-6.   *Combined queries use UNION, INTERSECT, or MINUS operators.*

Record No.	Producer	Color	Varietal	Region	Vintage
1	Beringer	Red	Cabernet Sauvignon	California	1987
2	Beringer	Red	Merlot	California	1998
3	Beringer	White	Chardonnay	California	1996
4	Beringer	White	Sauvignon Blanc	California	2000
5	Harlan Estate	Red	Proprietary Blend	California	1997
6	Arrowood	Red	Malbec	California	1993
7	Arrowood	White	Chardonnay	California	1993

Table 22-3.   *Sample Wine Data for Combined Queries*

the only two records in which there is an intersection for all three results columns. If Varietal were added as a result object, no rows would be returned, as there is no Red and White Varietal that is the same (if available, it may return producers who make Red and White Zinfandel, as the varietal name Zinfandel would be the same on multiple rows).

In the preceding example, if you change the operator to MINUS, the main query returns a list of producers of red wine and then removes the rows for those who also produce white wine. Therefore, only record 5 from Table 22-3 will be selected. Using the UNION operator in this example has the same effect as using IN List as the condition. With queries that contain multiple OR statements that are nested, you may find the query runs faster with UNION.

Caution   *You can change the result objects to aggregate two different measures using UNION. For example, you could use a UNION query to aggregate fixed cost + variable cost or if you have sales figures for two different companies that come from two different fact tables. However, when you use a MINUS operator and the measure objects are different, the rows from the second query are simply removed; the values are not subtracted unless the field names in the second query are the same.*

Tip   *You also can use the condition operators BOTH or EXCEPT to generate the INTERSECT and MINUS queries. Remember when using BOTH / INTERSECT not to include the same condition objects as result objects or you will get no rows returned.*

Subqueries

A subquery is a query that the main SELECT statement calls to determine the condition values. For example, in the EFASHION universe, certain clothing articles (SKU number) were promoted during various months in the year 2000. You would like to know sales for these articles by store in 2001. Did the promotions increase sales in the following year? Store does not directly apply to product promotions, so if you tried to retrieve all this information in one query, the results would be split into separate tables, as shown on the right in Figure 22-1. The solution is to use a subquery to retrieve a list of articles that were promoted in 2000 and see the effect on sales in 2001.

Creating a Subquery

When you specify a condition operand Create A Subquery ANY, BusinessObjects automatically inserts a new query tab named Subquery 1.1, as shown in Figure 22-7. When you create a subquery, there should be one, and only one, result object. The result object in the subquery must be the same object as the condition object in the main query. In Figure 22-7, this is *SKU number.* The conditions are what will vary between the main query and subquery. Notice in Figure 22-7 that the year conditions are different. The subquery looks for products that were promoted in 2000, but the main query displays sales for the products for a particular state in the subsequent year. Notice in the following SQL that there is another SELECT statement nested within the main query:

```
SELECT
Calendar_year_lookup.Year,
{fn concat('Q',Calendar_year_lookup.Quarter)},
Outlet_Lookup.Shop_name,
Article_lookup.Article_code,
Article_lookup.Article_label,
sum(Shop_facts.Amount_sold)
FROM Shop_facts,  Outlet_Lookup,  Calendar_year_lookup,  Article_lookup
WHERE
  ( Shop_facts.Shop_code=Outlet_Lookup.Shop_code  )
  AND  ( Article_lookup.Article_code=Shop_facts.Article_code  )
  AND  ( Shop_facts.Week_key=Calendar_year_lookup.Week_Key  )
  AND  (  Outlet_Lookup.State  =  'New York'
  AND  Calendar_year_lookup.Year  =  '2001'
  AND  Article_lookup.Article_code
  =  ANY
    (SELECT
    Article_lookup.Article_code
    FROM  Calendar_year_lookup,  Article_lookup,  product_promotion_facts,
          promotion_lookup
    WHERE
```

```
        (
promotion_lookup.promotion_key=product_promotion_facts.promotion_key  )
      AND  (
product_promotion_facts.Article_code=Article_lookup.Article_code  )
      AND  (
product_promotion_facts.Week_key=Calendar_year_lookup.Week_Key  )
      AND  (Calendar_year_lookup.Year  =  '2000'
      AND  promotion_lookup.promotion  =  'y'  ))
 )
GROUP BY
    Calendar_year_lookup.Year,
    {fn concat('Q',Calendar_year_lookup.Quarter)},
    Outlet_Lookup.Shop_name,
    Article_lookup.Article_code,
    Article_lookup.Article_label
```

Calculation Subquery

The Calculation operand launches a Complex Condition Wizard that creates a particular kind of subquery using aggregate functions. For example, you want to know which particular wines are lower than the average wine price for each country. Recall that a standard subquery can contain only one result object. To generate a GROUP BY clause for country, you need two result objects, *Average Price* and *Country*. Therefore, you cannot answer this question with a standard subquery; the Calculation operand allows you to generate a GROUP BY clause while still comparing only one result

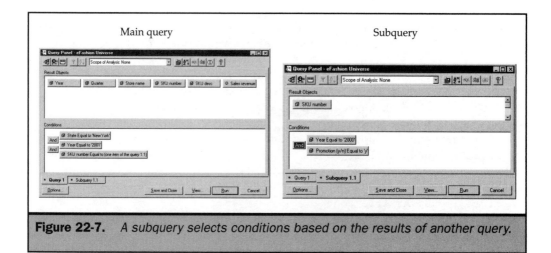

Figure 22-7. *A subquery selects conditions based on the results of another query.*

column. By combining an aggregate function with a dimension, you can answer a number of complex business questions such as:

- Which products had lower sales this year versus last year (assuming year is a dimension and there are no time period objects)?
- When was the last order date for a particular customer?
- Which employees have higher than average travel expenses?
- Which customers take longer than the average number of days to pay?

For some of these questions, there may be better, more efficient ways to answer the question. If your universe contains time period objects such as *This Year Sales* and *Last Year Sales*, you can more easily calculate the variance between these two objects to determine which products had lower sales this year. If the universe designer includes an object *Last Order Date,* then you do not need a calculation subquery to retrieve this information. In fact, the calculation query is much less efficient than the universe designer creating a simple object MAX(ORDER_DATE). The example in this section focuses on finding wines priced lower than the average, a question not easily answered by other means.

Before launching the Complex Condition Wizard, it's helpful to understand how some of the options work. Refer to Figure 22-8 for sample data retrieved from a main query on the left based on the possible values in the subquery on the right.

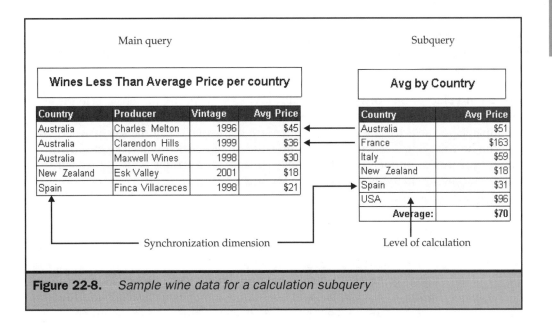

Figure 22-8. *Sample wine data for a calculation subquery*

Level of Calculation

For the level of calculation, you have two choices:

Global   Retrieves one grand total and does not generate a GROUP BY clause. The query reads the entire database and presents one average price, regardless of country or any other dimensions. In Figure 22-8, a single value of $70, the average price for all wines, would form the condition.

By one or more objects   When you select this option, you then specify the dimension objects for which you want to generate the GROUP BY. In this example, Country is the object for which you want to set the calculation level. In Figure 22-8, the subquery generates a list of average prices by country. These then will become the comparison values for the main query. If you wanted the query to be more precise—for example, to determine which wines are lower than the average price by Country as well as Varietal—you would specify these two dimension objects for the level of calculation.

Synchronizing the Calculation

If you choose a global level of calculation, the settings on this screen have no effect on the query, as you are always comparing only one value. I wish BusinessObjects would skip this screen when you select Global in the preceding step, as it only makes it more confusing! If you select a level of calculation by certain dimensions, however, then you must synchronize the calculation by the same dimension you specified for the level of calculation.

Independently of your objects   When you choose this option, you are selecting *any* wines from the main query that have an average price less than or equal to *any* country average. The values are compared regardless of, or independent of, any dimension values.

For each value of one or more objects   When you specify dimensions in the level of calculation, you should synchronize the calculation with the same dimension. For example, if you selected the Country dimension in the preceding section, you should select it here as well. Normally, the synchronization dimension would be exactly the same, because this option generates a join statement between the table in the main query and the subquery, as shown in the following SQL:

```
HAVING (
     avg(WINE_FACT_PRICE_RATE.SalesPrice)  <=  ANY
        ( SELECT
          avg(SubAlias__2.SalesPrice)
        FROM  WINE_FACT_PRICE_RATE  SubAlias__2
        WHERE
          SubAlias__2.Country = WINE_FACT_PRICE_RATE.Country
```

```
GROUP BY
   SubAlias__2.Country )
)
```

In this respect, the subquery is executed for each Country in the main query until the subquery has retrieved a comparison value for each Country. When you specify "Independently," the subquery is executed once. If you have two dimensions that are similar, such as *Ship To Customer / Sold To Customer* or *Sending Plant / Receiving Plant*, then it may be valid to specify one as the level of calculation and a different (but similar) object as the dimension upon which to synchronize.

Values to Compare

Finally, you select whether you want to compare one value (ALL) or any value (ANY). In this specific example, in which the comparison values are synchronized, using ALL or ANY has the same effect on the query results, as there is only one value to compare per country. In other examples, however, you may have multiple values from the subquery. For example, if the synchronization level is independently, then in Figure 22-8, there would be six average prices, one for each country. Selecting the option At Least One Value means that any prices that are less than ANY of the country averages will be retrieved. This is not too difficult, given the highest average price in the right-hand table is $163 for French wines. Selecting the option All Values means that only wines with a price less than the lowest one in the subquery, $18 in this case, would be retrieved.

Complex Condition Wizard

Having reviewed the different options in creating a calculation subquery, you are ready to use it in a condition. The purpose is to find wines with prices lower than the average for each country.

1. First create a query that contains the result objects, as shown in the left-hand table in Figure 22-8. Add the *Average Price* as a condition. Set the Operator to Less than or equal to.

2. From the list of Operands, double-click the Calculation operand. This launches the Complex Condition Wizard. You also may want to launch the wizard to later modify the condition selections.

3. When prompted, select an Object to use for comparison. In this example, *Average Price*, Click Begin >.

4. Define the level of calculation by one or more objects. Specify *Country* as the dimension object. Click Next >.

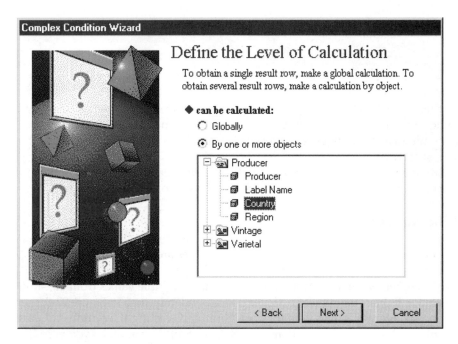

5. Synchronize the calculation by selecting For each value of one or more objects. Then select the same dimension specified in step 4. In this example, select the *Country* object. Click Next >.

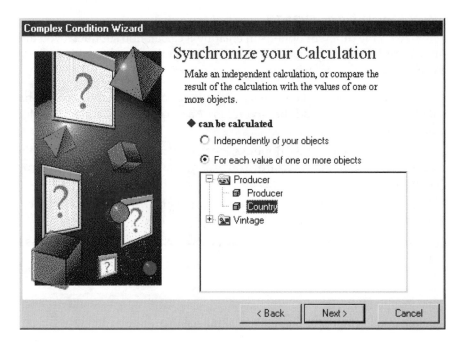

6. At the next wizard prompt, select the number of values to compare to at least one value.

7. Click Finish and then Run to execute the query.

Note *In the preceding example, Average Price was an existing object and allowed you to easily identify wines below the average. In many universes, the measure objects use the aggregate SUM, such as Store Sales, Margin, and Quantity Sold. If you wish to use a subquery to build queries based on the average, maximum, minimum, and so on, of particular measure objects, you must first ask the universe designer to create these objects either with the desired aggregate or as simple columns with no aggregate function. If the object exists in the universe without an aggregate function, the Complex Condition Wizard will prompt you to select an aggregate, thus giving you the most flexibility.*

User-Defined Objects

User-defined objects (UDOs) are objects that a user creates. They are available only for the particular user and from the PC in which the objects were defined. The definitions for user-defined objects are stored in a local file in the universe folder as *universe*.udo, where universe is the name of the universe to which the objects belong. Because the objects are stored in a local file, they cannot be shared with other users and you cannot schedule documents that contain UDOs via the BCA. For this reason, I recommend keeping user-defined objects to a minimum and prefer that the universe designer create a common object or that you use a report formula or variable (see Chapter 13 for a discussion of where to build the intelligence).

A user-defined object gets converted to SQL, so any transformations or calculations are performed on the server. With report formulas and variables, the transformations and calculations occur on the local PC. For this reason, if the universe designer has not included certain objects in the universe, you may need to create a user-defined object to minimize the number of rows of data sent across the network. For example, let's assume you want to get a count of the number of orders for each month. To use the BusinessObjects COUNTALL function in a report, you would need to retrieve all the individual orders. For companies with high order volumes, this may be millions of rows of data, and therefore, not possible. If you use the SQL COUNT function, then the server counts the number of orders and returns only one row per month.

 You create a UDO by either selecting User Objects from within the Query Panel or selecting Tools | Universes, then selecting User Objects. Once you create a UDO, the objects are stored in a separate class, *User objects*. As the objects are universe-specific, you can reuse UDOs in multiple documents.

Similar to Report Variables and the Variable Editor (Chapter 18), the User Object dialog box has two tabs, a Definition tab in which you define the object name, type, and qualification as well as the Formula tab in which you apply the calculation or transformation, as shown in Figure 22-9. If you will be creating UDOs, I recommend

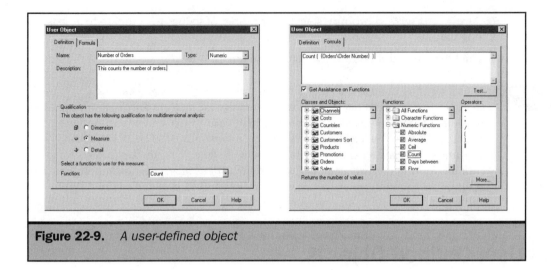

Figure 22-9.   *A user-defined object*

reading Chapters 8 and 10 to understand some of the options here. If you designate an object to be a measure, you specify two aggregates: the projection aggregate that is used in the report calculations and the SQL aggregate that is used on the server. The projection aggregate is the function on the Definition tab. The SQL aggregate is the numeric function on the Formula tab.

From the Formula tab, if you select the option Get Assistance On Functions, BusinessObjects will prompt you to enter any required parameters.

Summary

Much of the power in BusinessObjects lies in its robust query capabilities. It can handle complex database schemas by allowing you to generate multiple SQL statements to present one seamless report. In some cases, such as multipass SQL, you may never realize this happens. In other queries, you may explicitly combine queries with a UNION operator. As you create complex queries, be aware that queries may run slower and you should ideally test your query logic with small data sets. In some cases, there is no way around the performance issues; it's a complex business question answered with complex SQL. In other instances, you may be able to construct the query in ways that help the processing, or the DBA may be able to do some additional tuning.

The Complete Reference

Chapter 23

WebIntelligence

WebIntelligence (WebI) is the thin-client product for interactive reporting and analysis. As shown in Figure 16-1, when you use the BusinessObjects full client (or two-tier mode), your PC does most of the report processing. With WebI, a central WebI server or node will do most of the processing. Your browser simply presents the results to you. InfoView is the entry to WebI and is a portal to content from WebI, the Internet, and corporate documents. Some users may access only InfoView to retrieve and view reports. If you want to refresh, modify, or create reports, however, you will also need access to WebI. This chapter builds on concepts presented in other chapters in Part III of this book.

Navigating InfoView

InfoView is Business Objects' portal solution. It allows you to interact with the BusinessObjects repository to view and retrieve corporate documents or personal documents. The repository allows you to store non-WebI and non-BusinessObjects documents such as Word, Excel, and PDF files, making it a powerful mechanism for managing and measuring business performance.

To log into InfoView, you only need a browser and a web site address or URL. No additional software needs to be installed on your PC. The specific web site address for the InfoView start page will vary from company to company. Also, your company may have customized the login page. The following screen shows the default InfoView login:

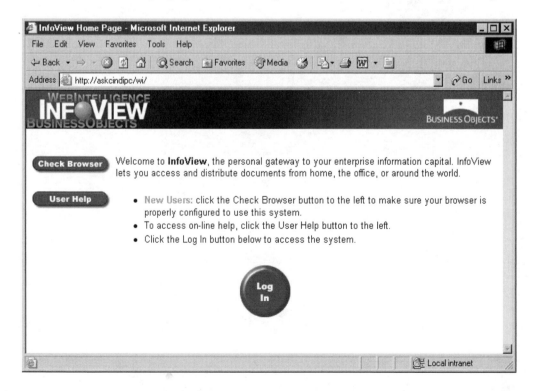

If your company has a standard browser and version, you can Log In. If your company uses multiple browsers and different versions, click Check Browser to determine if your browser is compatible with WebI. As you perform different actions within InfoView and WebI, the different browser types, components, and versions affect the actions you can perform. For example, in the next section, you will choose how InfoView should present BusinessObjects documents. If you choose the setting Enhanced Document Format, it requires ActiveX controls; if you use Netscape as your browser, you must first install a plug-in. If you have Internet Explorer (IE), you must have version 4 or higher. Similarly, when you create a new document, WebI uses a Java Virtual Machine (JVM). This is one component within your browser. If the JVM within your browser is not supported, you may receive errors when trying to create a new document. The Check Browser will highlight any versions or components that may later cause a problem.

Logging In

When you log into InfoView, you are validating your username and password against the same BusinessObjects repository, security domain used for the full client, as described in Chapter 16. To log into InfoView:

1. Set your browser to your company's WebI URL and click Log In. The Enter Network Password dialog box appears. This dialog box is generic for any web servers, so don't let the name of the dialog box mislead you.

2. Enter your BusinessObjects username and Password assigned to you by the BusinessObjects supervisor. Both are case sensitive.

3. If you want your password saved in an encrypted temporary file, called a cookie, check the box Save this password in your password list.

4. Click OK to complete the login. If you enter an incorrect password, the dialog box will reappear but will not explicitly tell you that the password was incorrect. After three incorrect attempts, the web page will display a message, "Your login

has been disabled by your supervisor." This is the BusinessObjects supervisor, not to be confused with your boss.

If you are also a BusinessObjects full-client user, note that with InfoView, there is no possibility to select a security domain. If your company has multiple security domains, then you may have multiple WebI servers to access each security domain. If so, then you access the different WebI servers through different URLs or web addresses.

The first time you log into the BusinessObjects repository either via WebI or BusinessObjects, you may be prompted to change your password. You also will receive this prompt if the BusinessObjects supervisor requires you to change your password on a periodic basis, for example, every 90 days. For more information on passwords, refer to Chapter 16, "About Passwords."

 Depending on how the designer has defined the universe connections, in some cases, your BusinessObjects password and universe data source must be the same or you will receive an error upon query refresh.

My InfoView

Your initial InfoView page may display a default Welcome screen, a list of documents, or a customized page called My InfoView that contains a mix of lists, documents, and web sites, as shown in Figure 23-1. The BusinessObjects general supervisor sets these defaults, which you can further customize, as explained in the next section.

The Navigation bar along the left of the page allows you to view different lists of documents, search for particular documents, log out, or access online help. The Navigation bar remains the same throughout your InfoView session. A tooltip appears as you move your cursor over each menu option.

The options in the Top bar change depending on what page you are viewing or whether or not you are viewing a list of documents, creating a document, or analyzing

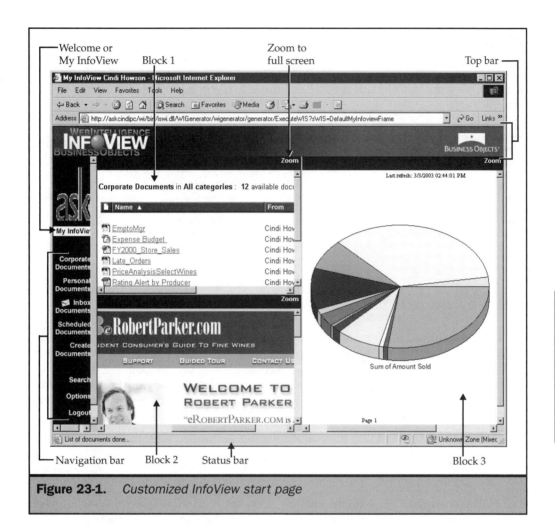

Figure 23-1. *Customized InfoView start page*

an individual document. When you first access My InfoView, the Top bar does not display any menu options. You must first select Zoom from one of the blocks to display a list, web site, or individual document in full screen. As you view a list of documents, the Top bar allows you to upload another document, delete a document, and search for documents. In some respects, the Top bar is similar to the pull-down menus in full-client BusinessObjects.

As you perform various actions, the Status bar at the bottom of your browser will indicate progress or problems.

Options

The first time you work with InfoView, you need to modify several options to ensure you display and build reports in the desired format. To modify your default settings, select Options in the Navigation bar on the left.

Start Page

You can specify the initial contents of the start page. If you have the security profile General Supervisor, then you can customize the start page for all the users in your group. Check the box Default New User Profile to have these changes applied to all new users.

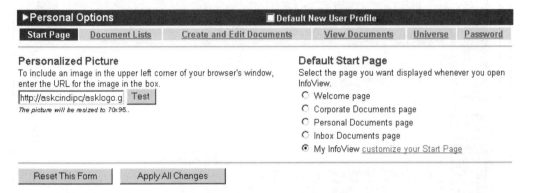

The Personalized Picture appears above the Welcome or My InfoView option in the Navigation bar. In Figure 23-1, this is the company logo ASK. The picture can be either a local file on your PC or an image from a web site. If you are customizing the default start page for new users, specify a file on the server that is accessible to all users. InfoView automatically resizes the picture to 70 by 95 pixels, so if your picture is larger than this, the results will be skewed.

To display a picture in the Navigation bar:

1. Enter the URL as **http://*webserver/filename.gif*.** The file type can also be JPG or BMP.

2. Click Test to display the picture in the Navigation bar.

3. If you are satisfied with the change, click Apply All Changes. InfoView displays a message at the bottom of the page, "Status: User options have been saved."

The Default Start Page allows you to customize the contents of the page that appears when you first log into InfoView using the following:

■ **Welcome page**   A generic page that displays options similar to the selections in the Navigation bar.

■ **Corporate Documents page**   Lists the corporate documents to which you have access in the BusinessObjects repository, document domain. Report authors publish documents to Corporate Documents by selecting File | Publish To in BusinessObjects; or selecting Upload or Publish from the Top bar within InfoView.

■ **Personal Documents page**   Lists documents that you have created with WebI or that you have specifically uploaded.

■ **Inbox Documents**   Lists documents that other users have sent you or that Broadcast Agent has distributed to you.

■ **My InfoView**   Allows you to further customize the appearance of your start page, displaying each of the various document lists, individual documents, or web sites, as shown in Figure 23-1.

To customize My InfoView:

1. First select the radio button My InfoView and then click the hyperlink "customize your start page."

  If you click the link to customize your start page without first clicking the radio button, My InfoView, your customizations are not saved.

2. InfoView displays several screen layouts, as shown next. Each section of a page is referred to as a block. In the following screen, the three-block screen is selected that corresponds to Figure 23-1:

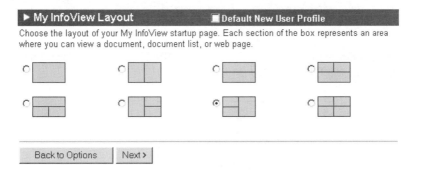

3. Click Next > to specify the contents for the first block. For each block, you select the contents, as shown in Figure 23-2. When displaying a list, you can filter the list by categories, sort it by a particular column, and select to display the list in Compressed mode or Expanded mode. These list options are covered in the next section. As you customize each block, the block number whose contents you are specifying appears above the layout.

4. InfoView allows you to select from six different block types, as shown in the next drop-down menu. As you select a different block type, the My InfoView Contents page changes to reflect the corresponding selections. For example, if you change the block type to a Corporate Document, you are prompted

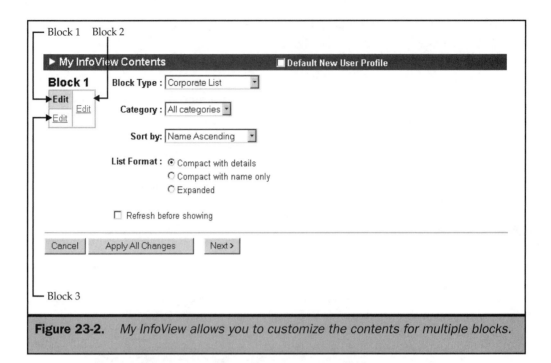

Figure 23-2.   *My InfoView allows you to customize the contents for multiple blocks.*

to enter a Document Name. If you change the block type to Web Page, you are
prompted for a URL Location.

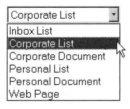

Caution   *Although InfoView allows you to access filenames that contain spaces, My InfoView in
WebI 2.7 does not. If you select any filenames that contain spaces in the name, you will
later receive an error in applying the changes. InfoView does not have a rename function.
Instead, you will have to resave or republish the file under a new filename with no spaces.*

5. To specify the Block Type for the remaining blocks, select Next > or click the
   Edit hyperlink within the block.

6. When you have set all the Block Types, click Apply All Changes. InfoView displays
   the status at the bottom of the page, "User options have been saved." If you had
   a Welcome option on the Navigation bar previously, this now displays My
   InfoView, as shown in Figure 23-1.

Document List

To change the way a list of documents appears, select Options and then Document Lists. Options for each list appear as shown in Figure 23-3. These settings affect the lists when you select a list from the Navigation bar; they do not affect how a list is displayed in My InfoView. You set the list appearance within My InfoView when you set the block contents; in Figure 23-2, the corporate document list is set to compact with details.

As you select lists from the Navigation bar, you can choose to display a compact list or an expanded list. The compact list displays the name of the document, the author, the date last modified, and the file size. Expanded mode shows a description of the document (when an author specifies one) and includes some additional menu options depending on the type of document. The following shows expanded information for the document WinePrice. The Expanded check box acts as a toggle for which menu option appears on the Top bar. If you have selected Expanded as your default display option, then Compact later appears on the Top bar. If you leave the Expanded box unchecked, then an option to Expand the display appears on the Top bar.

 WinePrice
Description: Average Wine Price for USA Wines
Feb 05 2003 14:29:40 - Document size: 13 K
Load into spreadsheet Edit Publish Send to users Delete Properties

Default Category allows you to further filter the list of documents displayed. The BusinessObjects supervisor may create the categories, or report authors create them

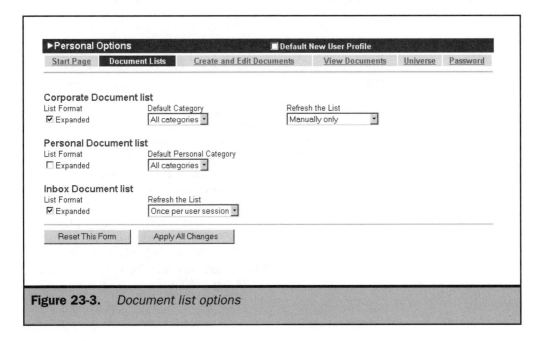

Figure 23-3.   *Document list options*

when publishing standard reports. If your document domain contains hundreds of documents, then further filter the list by selecting individual categories. If you later find you need a document from another category, you can change the filter from the main document list. The category option here is only an *initial* filter. For both the corporate documents and inbox documents, you can specify how often the list is refreshed:

- The list is manually refreshed when you choose Refresh from the Top bar.
- Every visit to the list rereads the list of available documents from the repository.
- Once per user session reads the list from the repository the first time you access a particular list during the session.

Fetching a long list of documents from the repository can be quite slow, so I would avoid the Every Visit option. For example, let's say you log into the repository at 8 A.M. There are ten documents available. During the day, other users publish five new documents to the corporate documents list. When you select Corporate Documents from the Navigation bar, if you have selected the option Once Per User Session, then the list that appears to you will continue to display the original list of ten documents generated at 8 A.M., even though 15 documents now exist in the repository. To see the five new documents, select Refresh from the Top bar.

Creating and Editing Documents

In simply retrieving and viewing documents, you are working with InfoView. When you create and edit documents from InfoView, you choose what type of document you want to create:

- WebI thin client, which creates a .wqy file
- BusinessObjects three-tier mode or Zero Administration BusinessObjects (ZABO), which creates a .rep file

You select which application to use via the Create and Edit Document options shown in Figure 23-4. If the BusinessObjects supervisor has not granted you access to BusinessObjects, then this option does not appear. When you select BusinessObjects, either your local version of BusinessObjects will launch or the product will install. If BusinessObjects is installed on your PC and you choose this option for creating documents, then InfoView launches the locally installed software but will use the WebI server to communicate to the data source; it launches the product in three-tier mode. If, however, you do not have BusinessObjects installed and you choose this option for creating documents, InfoView will install BusinessObjects the first time. This software is permanently installed on your computer. The size of the downloaded files is approximately 6MB, which expands to 20MB upon installation. When you execute a query via three-tier mode, the WebI server provides the database connectivity to the source RDBMS; in full-client mode, you must have the connectivity software also locally installed.

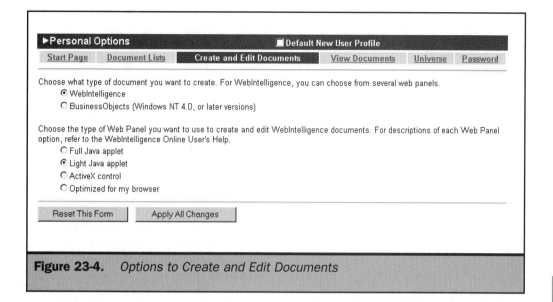

Figure 23-4. *Options to Create and Edit Documents*

You also can choose to use WebI to create new documents. Whereas InfoView allows you to view documents, WebI allows you to create and edit WebI documents through applets, which are mini-applications that get installed dynamically on your PC. For security reasons, some companies do not allow applets to cross firewalls. As an applet is an application, it can be slow to download, but not as slow as the full BusinessObjects, because it is significantly smaller. For performance reasons, WebI offers both a full applet and a light applet. If you are accessing WebI over a corporate intranet with a fast network, use the full applet. If you access WebI via dial-up or a slow network, then you may want to use the light applet. For Internet Explorer browsers, WebI is available as an ActiveX control. If you select the radio button Optimized For My Browser in Figure 23-4, ActiveX is automatically used for Internet Explorer browsers and the Full Java applet is used for Netscape browsers. The primary difference between the three options is in appearance and ease of navigation. Table 23-1 summarizes the differences among the different Web Panels.

Note *WebI allows you to edit WebI documents only; to edit BusinessObjects documents, you must use BusinessObjects.*

Viewing Documents

When you view a WebI document (.wqy), the document is automatically presented in HTML format. When you view a BusinessObjects document (.rep), you can decide if you want to open BusinessObjects or if you want to use InfoView to view the document. If you select InfoView, the document will be converted to a different format for viewing.

Function	Full Java Applet	Light Java Applet	ActiveX Control
Object help text	Automatically displayed	Toggle display	Toggle display
Scope of Analysis	Specify one to three levels or custom	Custom only	Specify one to three levels or custom
Drill mode	Via check box on main panel or settings panel	Enabled in Settings panel	Via check box
Block type	Multiple types on main toolbar	One chart button invokes an additional dialog box to select a new block type	One chart button invokes a drop-down menu
Nested conditions with AND/OR	Via toolbar with Shift Left, Shift Right buttons or drag-and-drop	Via drag-and-drop only	Via toolbar with Shift Left, Shift Right buttons or drag-and-drop
Tooltips	Yes	No	Yes
Right-click pop-up menus	No	No	Yes

Table 23-1.   *Summary of Differences in Applets and ActiveX*

For large, complex documents and busy WebI servers, this conversion can be slow. For smaller documents, converting the document to another format may be faster than launching BusinessObjects. If you do not have access to BusinessObjects, you must convert them to display the results. Figures 23-5 thru 23-7 show the difference between one report viewed in HTML format versus the same report in Enhanced document and PDF format. You can compare the appearance of this report in the three different viewing formats to that of the full-client version of the same report shown in Figure 16-3.

Note   *This conversion is for presentation purposes only and does not affect the original file format, which remains as* document.rep.

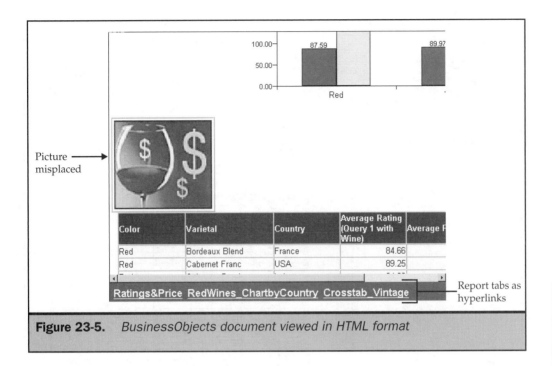

Picture misplaced

Report tabs as hyperlinks

Figure 23-5. *BusinessObjects document viewed in HTML format*

From the View Options page, select the desired format for viewing BusinessObjects documents:

- **Standard HTML format**   Documents that contain multiple report tabs are parsed into separate HTML pages that you navigate through hyperlinks. There are no options to control the print layout. Figure 23-5 shows a BusinessObjects document in HTML format.

- **Enhanced document format**   Uses an ActiveX viewer to display the document similar to how it appears in Report Manager in the full client. If your browser is something other than Internet Explorer and you select enhanced document format for viewing BusinessObjects .rep files, you will be prompted to install a document reader plug-in. You navigate a document with multiple reports via a Sections Tree on the left of the page, similar to the Report Manager Map within BusinessObjects. You also have an additional toolbar that allows you to change the view from actual size to fit to window. The printing with the enhanced document format matches more closely how the report is formatted as it is displayed. For example, in Figure 23-6, the Enhanced document version correctly displays the picture of the wine glass to the left of the bar chart, whereas the HTML version (Figure 23-5) moves the wine glass to beneath the chart. Through a button on the toolbar, you also can change the print setup and layout.

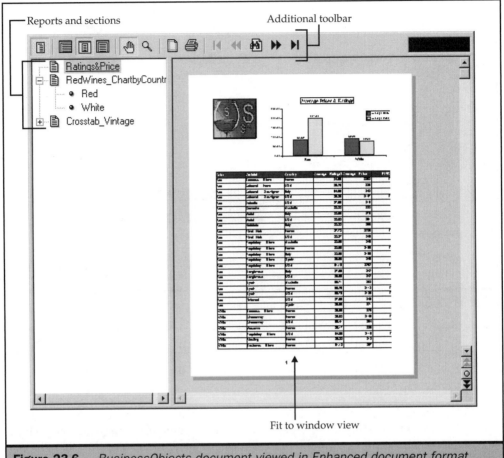

Figure 23-6. *BusinessObjects document viewed in Enhanced document format*

- **PDF Acrobat Reader** Adobe Acrobat is a third-party document viewer that must be installed on your PC. For report tabs, Adobe Acrobat will use a hyperlink for each. Sections within a master/detail report appear as bookmarks that you can display in the frame on the left. As with the enhanced document format, you can choose to display the report to fit in the window or as the actual size. The print quality is better than standard HTML and similar to enhanced document format. The Acrobat Reader also includes a search icon that allows you to search for text within a report; this option is not available in other viewing formats. Figure 23-7 shows the same BusinessObjects viewed with Adobe Acrobat.

- **Optimized for my browser** If you have Netscape, reports are displayed in HTML format; if you have Internet Explorer, reports are displayed with the ActiveX viewer.

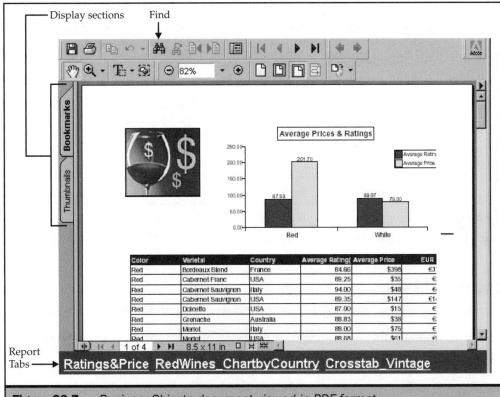

Figure 23-7.   *BusinessObjects document viewed in PDF format*

Universe

Universe options allow you to specify how the list of universes appears when you create a new document. These options are shown in Figure 23-8.

Compact mode shows the name of the universe, the universe domain it comes from, and the date last modified. Expanded mode displays this information, but in addition, it displays the universe description, in which some designers provide meaningful help text. For whichever initial mode you specify here, there is a corresponding menu option (Expand or Compact) on the Top bar to toggle the display. You also can specify a default universe when you often create reports with only one universe. Make sure that you first select the radio button Default Universe, and then select the universe. If you select the universe without also clicking this radio button, the change will not take effect. If you ever need to create reports based on a different universe or based on an OLAP data source, then you must modify the universe options to again display a list.

By default, the list of available universes is refreshed when you first select to Create Documents with the setting Once Per User Session. You can suppress this initial check by changing the setting to Manually Only. With this setting, you must explicitly select Refresh List from the Top bar when viewing a list of universes.

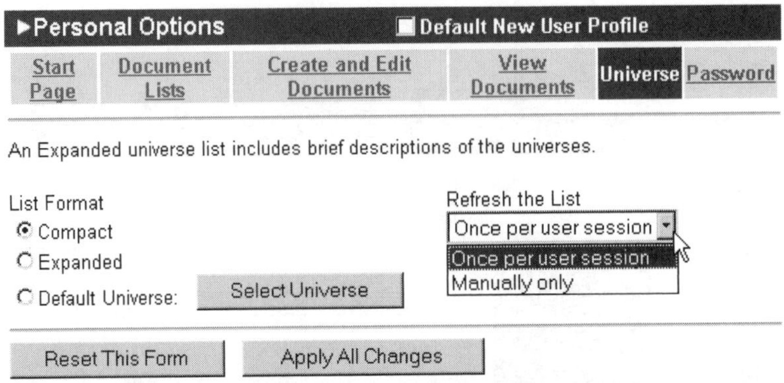

▶Personal Options   ■ Default New User Profile

| Start Page | Document Lists | Create and Edit Documents | View Documents | Universe | Password |

An Expanded universe list includes brief descriptions of the universes.

List Format
- ⦿ Compact
- ○ Expanded
- ○ Default Universe: Select Universe

Refresh the List
[Once per user session ▾]
Once per user session
Manually only

Reset This Form   Apply All Changes

Figure 23-8. *Universe display options*

Document Lists

From the Navigation bar on the left, you select which list of documents to view:

■ **Corporate Documents page**   Lists the corporate documents to which you have access in the BusinessObjects repository, document domain. Report authors publish documents to Corporate Documents by selecting File | Publish To in BusinessObjects; or by selecting Upload or Publish from the Top bar within InfoView.

■ **Personal Documents page**   Lists documents that you have created with WebI or that you have specifically uploaded.

■ **Inbox Documents**   Lists documents that other users have sent you or that Broadcast Agent has distributed to you.

■ **Scheduled Documents**   Lists documents that you have scheduled through Broadcast Agent. If the document refreshed successfully, you will see it under Inbox Documents. If it has not yet run, you will see it as a Pending Job under this list.

The BusinessObjects repository, document domain allows you to store different document types. Each document type has a different icon, as shown in the following table. Certain document types allow you to perform additional functions. For example, from the list of documents, you can load data from a WebI document directly into a spreadsheet; however, you cannot do this with a BusinessObjects document. For BusinessObjects documents, you can download them from the repository to your local disk. This has the same functionality as selecting File | Retrieve From from the BusinessObjects pull-down menus (see Chapter 16, "Repository Documents").

Document Icon	Document Type
	WebI
	BusinessObjects
	PDF
	Excel
	WebI OLAP

The options you set under Options | Document Lists determine if the initial list is displayed in Compact or Expanded mode or if the list shows only certain categories or all. When you view a document list in Compact mode, you can sort the list by type, name, author, last refresh date, and size. The primary sort order is flagged with a triangle next to the column heading. To sort in descending order, click the column heading again until a downward triangle appears. For example, in the following, the document list would be sorted in descending date order:

To have hyperlinks appear beneath a document name that allows you to perform additional actions, view the list in Expanded mode by selecting Expand from the Top bar.

USAWinePrice (Document)
Description: Average Wine Price for USA Wines
Feb 08 2003 15:14:43 - From: Cindi Howson - Document size: 13 K
Load into spreadsheet Save Send to users Edit Delete Properties

Finding Documents

Some document lists can be quite long, and simply sorting the list is not enough to help you find the desired document. InfoView provides you with several additional ways to find a document through Categories and Search from the Navigation bar.

Categories provide a way of grouping documents. They may relate to particular work processes, business units, functions, or projects. Report authors can create a category when they publish a BusinessObjects document to Corporate Documents; from within InfoView, you must explicitly define a category before you publish a document to a category. The BusinessObjects supervisor must grant you the rights to maintain categories. To create a category from within InfoView:

1. Select Categories from the Corporate Documents list.

2. The Category Management screen appears. In the Category box, enter a name for the new category.

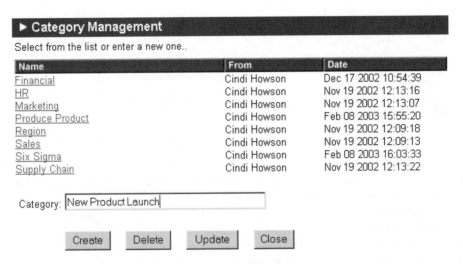

3. Click Create. InfoView gives you a status message, "New category successfully created."

4. Click Close to return to the Corporate Documents list.

To filter the list of documents for one particular category, select the drop-down menu labeled Categories: from the Top bar.

You also can search for documents by name, author, date, or keywords by selecting Search from the Navigation bar. The Search options are shown in Figure 23-9. First select in which list you want to search, Corporate Documents, Personal Documents, or Inbox

> ▶ **Search for document(s)**
>
> Search in: ⦿ Corporate Documents page
> ○ Personal Documents page
> ○ Inbox Documents page
>
> Document name contains: [   ]
>
> Author name contains: [   ]
>
> Keywords: [   ]
>
> Date between: [MM] / [DD] / [YYYY] and [MM] / [DD] / [YYYY]
>
> Order by: ⦿ Document name
> ○ Author name
> ○ Document size

Figure 23-9.   *Search for documents*

Documents. InfoView will then filter that list according to the additional search criteria you enter. The search criteria are not case sensitive and will match partial words.

- **Document name**   Searches within the entire document name. You do not need to specify any additional wildcards. For example, if you enter Budget, you would find the documents Expense Budget, Current Year Budget By Region.

- **Author name**   For WebI reports, this is the username. The username is also used for non-WebI/BusinessObjects documents that have been uploaded to the repository. In BusinessObjects, the login name initially used to create the document appears under File | Properties; however, the author name in the repository is the person who published or uploaded the document.

- **Keywords**   Must be explicitly assigned when a document is saved and are more precise than categories. For example, you may have a Category called Financial, but then assign the keywords "expense, budget, actual" to an expense variance report.

- **Date between**   Used to search for documents last modified during the specified date range.

Note   *The Search For box on the Top bar searches only the document name. The tooltip suggests that it looks for keywords, but it does not. Therefore, use the Search option from the Navigation bar on the left if you want to search for keywords.*

Uploading a Document

You can publish BusinessObjects full-client reports from within BusinessObjects by selecting File | Publish To or from within InfoView by selecting Upload from the Top bar. If you are viewing Personal Documents when you select Upload, then the document is uploaded into your personal list. To upload to Corporate Documents, ensure you are viewing the Corporate Documents list. You use this same procedure to upload non-BusinessObjects documents such as spreadsheets or Word documents that relate to business intelligence:

1. Select Upload from the Top bar.

2. Enter the filename from your local PC/network drive or click Browse to navigate the file directory.

3. Enter a document name to be used for storing the document in the repository. If you wish to use the document in My InfoView, ensure the name contains no spaces.

4. Enter a document description that will display when users view a list in Expanded mode or when they select Properties.

5. Specify the categories to which the document should be assigned for search purposes. Use CTRL-click to assign a document to more than one category.

6. Enter keywords that allow more precise searching. Keywords are not case sensitive and do need to be separated with commas. Note that to later assign a keyword, you must re-upload a file.

7. If you have access to multiple document domains, select the domain to which you want to upload this document.

8. Select the groups that should have access to this document.

9. If a document with the same name exists in the repository, click the radio button Yes to overwrite it. If you select No, the document will not be uploaded.

10. Click Publish to upload the document and return to the list.

Document Properties

From within a list of documents, you can also view a document's properties if the list is displayed in Expanded mode. To display the list in Expanded mode, select Expanded from the Top bar. Additional hyperlinks appear beneath each document name. Select the Properties link to view the document properties. The document properties page displays information such as the name and description of the document. From here, you can modify the categories to which the document is assigned. The keywords are also displayed but cannot be modified. The only way to modify keywords is to resave the document. For WebI and BusinessObjects documents, the Document Properties will also give information on the Data Providers, as shown in the next screen.

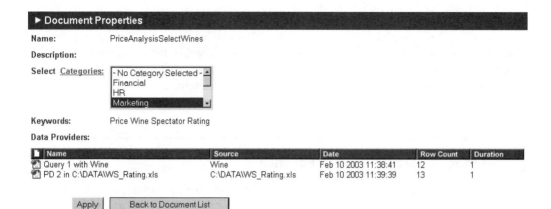

- **Name**   Displays the name of the query and the data provider type. For queries against a universe, the default name is Query N, in which N is a numeric value for the number of queries in the document. Through BusinessObjects, you can change the query name for full-client documents through Data Manager (Data | View Data, Definition tab); you cannot change the name of a query file for WebI documents. In the preceding screen, the second data provider is from a personal data file.

- **Source**   Lists the name of the universe or personal data file used to generate the query. Details for OLAP data sources are not displayed.

- **Date**   Displays the last date the query was refreshed.

- **Row Count**   Displays the number of rows retrieved from the source RDBMS as part of the result set. Duration is the time to execute the query and fetch the rows.

Viewing Documents

InfoView handles viewing documents differently depending on the type of document. If you view a spreadsheet or PDF document, then the document is displayed in a frame within the browser. When you view a BusinessObjects document, BusinessObjects may launch or you may view the report in HTML, enhanced document format, or PDF (see the earlier "Viewing Documents" section). When you view a WebI document, InfoView displays the document in HTML format.

Viewing BusinessObjects Documents in Enhanced Document Format

If you view a document created with BusinessObjects, the options you set for View Documents determine how the report is displayed. The report is displayed in BusinessObjects, HTML, Enhanced document format, or PDF. (Refer to earlier Figures 23-5, 23-6, and 23-7 for a comparison of the viewing formats.) This section describes viewing a document in Enhanced document format. InfoView provides you with an additional toolbar that controls the viewing options.

Table 23-2 describes the purpose of each button in viewing a document in Enhanced format.

Button	Name	Function
	Show/Hide Sections Tree	Creates a frame to display additional report tabs or sections in a master/detail report similar to the Map view within Report Manager.
	Normal Size	Displays the report in actual size.
	Fit To Window	Zooms out to fit the entire contents of the report in one window.
	Fit Width To Window	Zooms out to fit the page width to the screen.
	Panning	Allows you to drag a document up or down within a window to scroll through pages.
	Zooming	Zoom increases the display size. To zoom out, right-click within the document to call a pop-up menu, then select Zoom Out.
	Page Setup	Calls the Page Setup dialog that allows you to select paper size, print orientation, and margins.
	Print	Presents a Print dialog box that lets you choose to print multiple copies of a report or certain pages within the report.
	Begin	Returns to the first page of the current report.
	Previous	Returns to the previous page of the current report.
	Go To Page	Calls a Go To Page dialog that allows you to enter a specific page number to scroll to.

Table 23-2. *Enhanced Document Format Toolbar*

Button	Name	Function
▶▶	Next	Moves to the next page in the current report.
▶▎	End	Displays the last page of the current report.

Table 23-2. *Enhanced Document Format Toolbar* (continued)

WebI Documents

Viewing a WebI document (Figure 23-10) is different than viewing a BusinessObjects document via InfoView. In earlier Figure 23-6, the BusinessObjects documents had multiple report tabs and multiple blocks within a report. In WebI 2.*x*, a document can contain only one report and one block style. This changes significantly in version 6.0

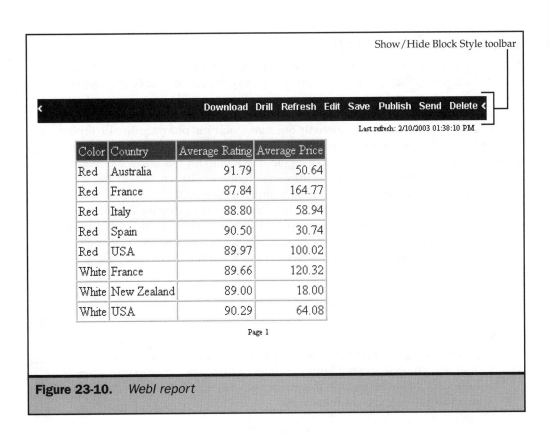

Show/Hide Block Style toolbar

Download Drill Refresh Edit Save Publish Send Delete

Last refresh: 2/10/2003 01:38:10 PM

Color	Country	Average Rating	Average Price
Red	Australia	91.79	50.64
Red	France	87.84	164.77
Red	Italy	88.80	58.94
Red	Spain	90.50	30.74
Red	USA	89.97	100.02
White	France	89.66	120.32
White	New Zealand	89.00	18.00
White	USA	90.29	64.08

Page 1

Figure 23-10. *WebI report*

(see Chapter 24). You can, however, modify the block style while viewing the document by selecting < from the Top bar.

When viewing a WebI document, the Top bar provides you with additional options to download the data to a spreadsheet or to enable Drill mode.

For particularly long reports, a Page count appears on the Top bar.

You can go directly to a specific page by entering a page number in the box, or use one of these:

Icon	Function
	Return to the first page
	Move to the preceding page
	Move to the next page
	Go to the last page of the report

Changing the Block Type

When a report author creates a query, the author specifies the initial block type as a table, a financial report, a form, or a chart. You can modify the block style of WebI reports while viewing the document. Certain formats such as master/detail and crosstab are available only from the Web Panel or while editing the document. An option for pie charts appears only when the tabular block contains only one dimension and one measure. To display the block style buttons while viewing the report, click the arrow at the far-right end of the Top bar. This arrow acts as a toggle. The tooltip for this arrow tells you it will Show/Hide Turn To Chart Bar. It shows the toolbar to turn to other table styles in addition to chart styles (so don't let the tooltip confuse you).

The vertical toolbar appears to the right of the document display. As you move your mouse over each button, a tooltip describes a block type. The list of available buttons will change depending on the type of block you are currently viewing.

Figure 23-11 shows some popular block types. Chapter 16 covers block types in more detail.

- **Tabular**   The default block type is similar to a spreadsheet style. Object names appear as column headings, and the data values as rows.

- **Financial**   Transposes the row and column headings. This is similar to BusinessObjects' Format | Rotate Table. This block type is useful for analyzing data that has a limited number of rows but many columns—for example, if you have many measures and only a few products for which you want to analyze the measures.

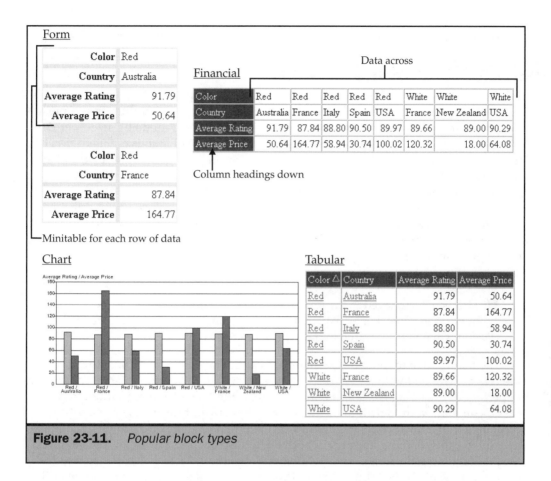

Figure 23-11. *Popular block types*

- **Form** Transposes the row and column headings but creates a minitable for each row of data. The Form block type is useful for contact or product lists. This block type is unique to WebI and not available in BusinessObjects.

- **Charts** Allow you to visually analyze the data to identify patterns. WebI supports a number of chart formats, including bar, line, polar, scatter, and pie. When the block type is a chart, two additional buttons appear on the Block Type bar to alter if and where a legend is displayed.

Button	Function
	Removes the legend.
	Displays the legend to the right of the chart.

You can specify or modify additional chart settings while editing a document.

Analyzing Data with Drill Mode

While InfoView allows you to view and refresh fixed reports, WebI enables you to create new queries and to analyze data in Drill mode. A report author may save a document in Drill mode, or you may explicitly enable Drill mode by selecting Drill from the Top bar. A standard report gives you an overview of *what* is going on; Drill mode allows you to explore *why, when,* and *where* by analyzing measures by different dimensions or levels of detail. For more information on the concepts of multidimensional analysis, refer to Chapter 19.

Drill mode formats the dimension objects with a hyperlink to allow you to drill down. Column headings may have a drill-up icon. It also adds a drill section in the report page, providing drop-down boxes for each dimension (see Figure 23-12). A drop-down box appears for each dimension:

■ That is displayed in the report and specified as a result object in the Web Panel.

■ That is not displayed in the report but that was retrieved using Scope of Analysis in the Web Panel. For an explanation of how more data can exist in the microcube than what you see in the initial report, refer to Figure 19-2.

The hand shape of the mouse cursor indicates when you can drill. Additionally, the cell is formatted with a hyperlink. When you get to the bottom of a hierarchy, the hyperlink does not appear and the mouse cursor remains a regular pointer. In some cases, you may want to drill to the next level of detail, but this level of detail is not contained in the microcube. WebI will warn you that drilling further will generate a new query; this warning appears in both the tooltip and the status bar. For example, the Producer hierarchy runs Country ⇨ Region ⇨ Producer ⇨ Label Name. In Figure 23-12, Country appears in the tabular block. Producer is available in the microcube and appears in the Drill bar at the top section of the page. However, the Region level of the hierarchy is not in the microcube. If you attempt to drill on any members in the Country column of the table, then WebI indicates the drill action will run a new query as displayed in the tooltip and status bar:

Drill Down to Region (new query)

This drill process is slightly different in BusinessObjects. In BusinessObjects, by default you would drill to the next available level in the microcube, to Producer. In WebI, you must drill the levels sequentially and cannot skip a level. In this respect, retrieving

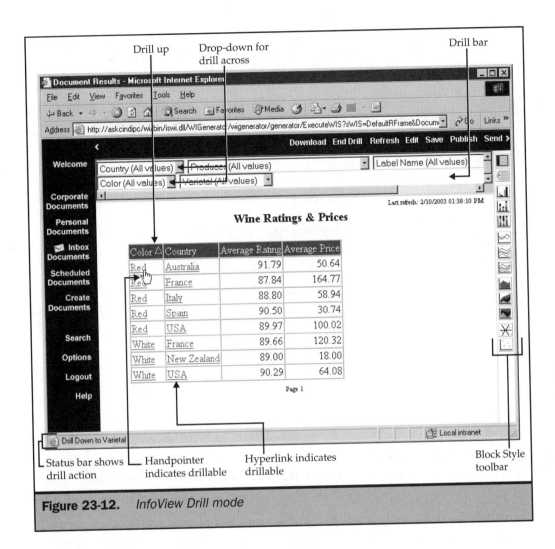

Figure 23-12.   *InfoView Drill mode*

Producer in the Scope of Analysis (but not Region) does not help the drill-down process but only provides a way of filtering the data for drill across.

To drill down on a particular column:

1. Position the hand pointer over a cell containing a hyperlink—for example, Red in Figure 23-12.

2. Click the hyperlink. The selection in the Drill bar changes from Color (All Values) to Red. The color column is removed from the table block, and WebI inserts a new column for Varietal, the next level in the hierarchy.

New column added to block

Filter on Red

Note *If you want two columns from the same hierarchy, such as Color and Varietal, to appear in the block, you edit the block in the Web Panel; the Drill bar does not contain a Move To Block option as in BusinessObjects.*

To drill up on a particular column, click the triangle that appears next to the column heading. The drill-up column will be removed from the block and replaced with the details for the next level up in the hierarchy.

Drill Down and Modify Query

If you drill down to a level of detail not contained in the microcube, WebI will prompt you to update the Scope of Analysis for that particular hierarchy. For example, if you drill down on Country with the hand pointer positioned over France, WebI prompts you to specify additional dimension objects within the Producer hierarchy and allows you to execute the query to retrieve information only for French wines or for all countries.

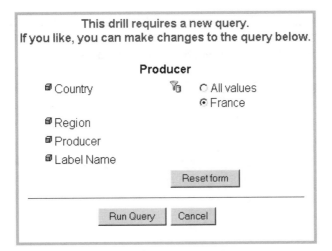

In the preceding example, the values for the additional levels within the Producer hierarchy already existed in the microcube, so WebI did not provide check boxes to modify the Scope of Analysis to include them. However, let's assume you are drilling down in a Time hierarchy on the Year member. The next level is Quarter; this dimension level will automatically be retrieved when you drill down. If you know in advance that you will want to further drill down to Month and Week, check these boxes to retrieve additional details and minimize the number of times the query must execute.

Drill Across

You also can use the drop-down boxes in the Drill bar to drill across or filter the data. For example, if you want to see the varietals, rating, and prices for a particular producer such as Chateau Margaux, click the Producer drop-down box. When you drill across, you are working against the microcube cached on the WebI server; drill across does not execute another query, it merely filters the existing result set.

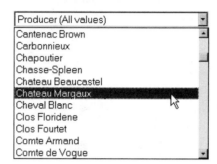

If you want to close the Drill bar and remove the hyperlinks from the cells in the report, select End Drill from the Top bar. Closing the Drill bar does not affect the query.

Refreshing a Document

The date a report was last refreshed is displayed both in the document list and in the upper-right corner of the page when viewing a document. A report author may save a document with one of two settings:

- Refreshed manually
- Refresh when opened

To manually refresh a report, select Refresh from the Top bar while viewing a document. If the document was saved with the setting to refresh upon opening, the query will execute as soon as you attempt to view it. When you refresh a query, you may be prompted to specify query conditions to ensure the correct data is returned to you (Figure 23-13). These prompts may appear within the report page or may appear only upon query execution. If you have refreshed the query at least once, then the values used in the last refresh appear in the prompt boxes.

You can either enter the values yourself, or in many cases, you can choose from a list of values. The report author determines if a list of values is displayed or not. A list of values is a pick-list generated from a query file sent to the data source; therefore, the first time you access a new list of values, there may be a delay while the list of values query executes and the pick-list appears.

The main difference between WebI prompts and BusinessObjects is that in WebI the list of values is displayed on the same screen as the prompt message. Notice that in

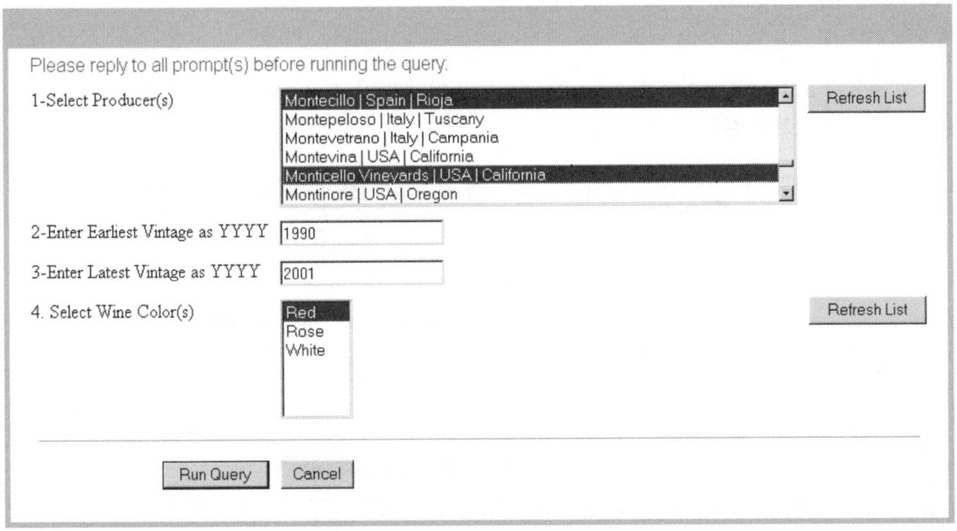

Figure 23-13. *Refresh a query with prompts*

Figure 23-13, the Producer list of values has been customized to display the producer name, country, and region. The universe designer specifies the list of values customization. For lists that change frequently, click Refresh List to reexecute the list of values query. A customized list of values may contain an additional prompt to limit the rows returned for particularly long lists. For example, when refreshing a list of Customer IDs, you may first be prompted to select a Country. When selecting the values from a long list, you can skip ahead to find a particular beginning letter in the list. First, position your mouse within the list, then press the desired letter to skip ahead to.

Once you have entered the prompt selections, click Run Query to execute the query and retrieve the updated results.

Saving Results

When you refresh a query, the new results are not saved in the document file until you explicitly save the document or republish it to Corporate Documents. When you refresh a corporate document, you save the new results to your personal document list. To save the document:

1. Select Save from the Top bar. InfoView displays the Save as personal document page.

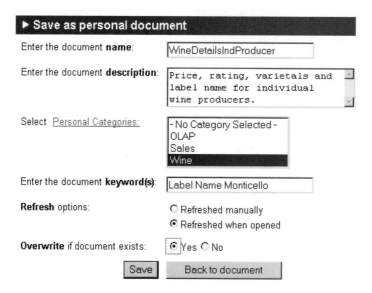

2. Enter a document name. If you wish to replace an existing personal document, then you must enter the exact name of the existing document; the current name is not provided for you. The name is not case sensitive. If you wish to use the document in My InfoView, ensure the name contains no spaces.

3. Enter a document description that will display when you view the list of personal documents in Expanded mode or when you select Properties.

4. Specify personal categories to which the document should be assigned for search purposes. These categories are different from Corporate Categories. Use CTRL-click to assign a document to more than one category.

5. Enter keywords that allow more precise searching. Keywords are not case sensitive and do need to be separated with commas. Note that to later assign a keyword, you must resave a file.

6. Specify the refresh options for the next time you open the document. If you want to keep the last result set and not execute the query again, select Refreshed Manually.

7. To replace the last version of the document with the updated result set, click the radio button Yes to overwrite the previous version. If you select No and the document exists, you will be warned that "This name already exists: use a different name or allow overwrite."

8. Click Save to save the document with the new result set to your personal document list.

Editing/Creating a Document

From within WebI, you can create documents that access a universe or an OLAP data source.

To create a new document, select Create Documents from the Navigation bar. If you have specified in your options to create documents based on a default universe, then the Web Panel appears. Otherwise, a list of universes appears in either Compact or Expanded mode. When viewing a list of universes in Compact mode, you can sort the list by universe name, the domain name from which the universe comes, or the date last modified.

Universes	OLAP Data Sources

17 Available universes. This list was last refreshed: **Feb 11 2003 14:29:52**.

Name ▲	From	Date
AcctRec	Universe	Oct 17 2002 16:53:18
Audit (audit)	Universe	Dec 09 2002 21:31:38
Bank Account (DebitCre)	Universe	Nov 03 2002 12:17:14

To display a meaningful description for the universes, select Expand from the Top bar. The universe designer maintains the universe description and may use this to communicate universe changes. The following list of universes is displayed in Expanded mode:

Store   Universe
Feb 04 2003 16:33:56

Test Fashion (TestFash)   Universe
Test Fashion universe with a subset of objects from the sample EFashion universe.
Feb 11 2003 14:29:47

Wine   Universe
The Wine universe provides rating and price information on a sample set of wines.

Rating information has been provided by eRobertParker.com. Mr. Parker provides "independent, accurate, critical commentaries and opinions on fine wines and fine wine values through the publication The Wine Advocate. The Wine Advocate has over 40,000 subscribers, in every state in the United States, and in over 37 foreign countries. Today, virtually every knowledgeable observer agrees that The Wine Advocate exerts the most significant influence on the serious wine consumer's buying habits and trends not only in America, but in France, England, Switzerland, Japan, Taiwan, Singapore, Russia, Mexico, Brazil, and China. In addition to doing the writing and tasting for The Wine Advocate, which is published bi-monthly in Parkton, Maryland, Mr. Parker has been a contributing editor for Food and Wine Magazine."

Price information has been provided by winealert.com, an internet company that surveys retailers, distributors, and wholesalers to help consumers find the best wine prices.
Jan 28 2003 08:44:23

To create a document based on a particular universe, select the universe name from the list. WebI displays the Web Panel shown in Figure 23-14. If you work with the BusinessObjects full client, you'll notice that some of the functionality that is split between the Slice and Dice Panel and the Query Panel is merged in the Web Panel. Via the Web Panel, you construct the query, but also, the default report layout. The exact appearance of your Web Panel will vary depending on whether you use the Java applet, Light applet, or ActiveX controls set through Options | Create and Edit Documents (see Figure 23-4). The Web Panel throughout this section uses the Full Java applet. The buttons in Table 23-3 affect what is displayed in the Web Panel and allow you to format the initial block type.

Note   *If you use the Light Java applet to create and edit WebI documents, not all the buttons are available in the toolbar.*

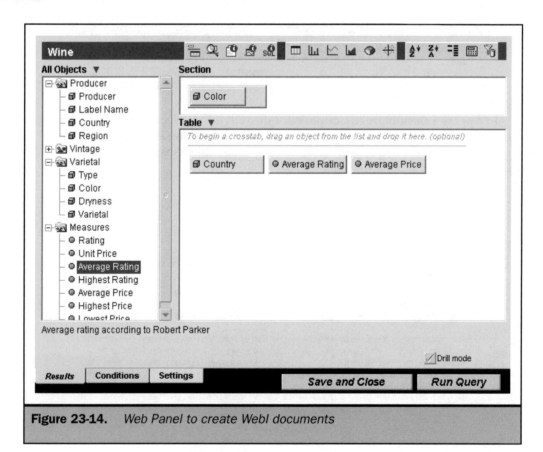

Figure 23-14.   *Web Panel to create WebI documents*

Button	Name	Function
	Show/Hide Sections	Toggle to display or hide the section window for creating a master/detail report.
	Custom Scope of Analysis	Allows you to retrieve additional dimensions for drilling.
	Document Settings	Similar to selecting the Settings tab, accesses the Document Settings page to control page headers and footers.
	Block Settings	Access the Block Settings page to format the color of a block and to control break headers.
	View Query SQL	Displays the syntax of the SQL SELECT statement.
	Block Types	Opens another button menu to select different block types.
	Bar Charts	Opens a dialog to select additional chart formats such as stacked bar, mixed line and bar, and 3-D.
	Line Charts	Opens a dialog to select additional line chart styles.
	Area Charts	Opens a dialog box to select additional area chart styles.
	Pie Charts	Opens a dialog box to select additional pie chart styles.
	Radar Charts	Opens a dialog box to select additional radar chart styles such as polar and scatter.
	Ascending Sort	Sorts the results in ascending order, A–Z for character fields or 1–10 for numeric fields.
	Descending Sort	Sorts the results in descending order, Z–A for character fields or 10–1 for numeric fields.

Table 23-3.   *Buttons in the Web Panel Toolbar*

Button	Name	Function
	Break	Inserts a break when a dimension value changes.
	Calculations	Inserts a calculation and opens a dialog box to select Sum, Count, Average, Minimum, Maximum, and Percentage.
	Conditions	Adds a condition to the result object and invokes the conditions page.
	Shift Right	Appears on the Conditions page and allows you to indent AND or OR connectors to create nested conditions. See Chapter 22, "Specifying Sets of Data."
	Shift Left	Appears on the Conditions page and allows you to indent AND or OR connectors to create nested conditions.

Table 23-3. *Buttons in the Web Panel Toolbar* (continued)

The All Objects frame on the left of the Web Panel are all objects available within the universe. As you select an object, the description appears at the bottom of the Web Panel and provides information on how to use the objects in a query or for measures, as well as how the object is calculated. The Section pane of the Web Panel allows you to create a master/detail report. For example, you can specify Color as a section heading to create separate mini-tables or chart blocks for each wine color. To make an object a section header, as shown in earlier Figure 23-14, drag the object to the Section pane. The Table pane of the Web Panel displays the results objects, or columns of data in a tabular report. To add an object to a query or report, you can either drag objects from the All Objects frame to the Table window or double-click the object name.

Scope of Analysis

You use Scope of Analysis in conjunction with Drill mode. Scope of Analysis allows you to retrieve additional dimensions that may not appear as columns in the initial report. When you drill down on the higher-level dimension in the report, lower-level details that you specified in Scope of Analysis already exist in the microcube; WebI does not execute a new query to perform the drill down. To display the Scope of Analysis window, click the Scope of Analysis button from the toolbar. Result objects appear with a rectangle in the Scope of Analysis window. For example, *Quarter* in the following screen is a result object. To retrieve an additional dimension object, drag it from the All Objects window to the Scope of Analysis window. These objects appear with the standard dimension symbol and shadow box. For example, *Year, Month,* and *Week* will be retrieved in the query but will not appear in the initial table. Note that the order of the objects in the Scope of Analysis window is hierarchical from top to bottom.

In WebI 2.x, you cannot skip levels within a hierarchy when drilling. For example, you cannot drill from Quarter to Week. Therefore, be sure to include the sequential levels within the Scope of Analysis.

To display the report in Drill mode, click the Drill mode box at the bottom-right corner of the page. Drill mode adds a Drill bar to the report window and formats dimension members with hyperlinks to enable drill down to the dimension details you specify in Scope of Analysis.

Conditions

Once you have chosen the result objects, select the Conditions tab to limit the data returned or displayed in the initial report. If you want to add a condition on a result object, you also can click the Conditions button from the toolbar; this navigates you to the Condition page and automatically inserts the selected result object into the Query Conditions pane. The Conditions page (Figure 23-15) allows you to set both query conditions and document filters. Query conditions limit the size of the result set from the data source. They append a WHERE clause to the SQL statement. A Condition object is denoted with a filter icon in the All Objects window. These are predefined query conditions specified by the universe designer. Document filters limit the data displayed in the initial report, although more data still exists in the microcube. Use query conditions to select data by your area of interest; use document filters to further analyze different subsets of this data. For example, in the Wine universe, assume you are looking only for Red Wines produced after 1980. You want to analyze wines from different countries but want to start your analyses with those from France. To set these conditions:

1. Drag *Color* to the Query Conditions window. Leave the operator as Equal to.

2. As the Operand, select Enter A Constant and enter **Red.**

3. Drag *Vintage* to the Query Conditions window. Change the operator to `Greater than or equal to`.

4. In the Operand box, select Enter a constant and enter **1980**.

5. Drag *Country* to the Document Filters window. Once you add a document filter, note that the Conditions tab displays a filter icon.

6. For the *Country* Operand, select Show list of values. Select France and click OK to close the list of values box.

7. Click Run Query to execute the query and display the results.

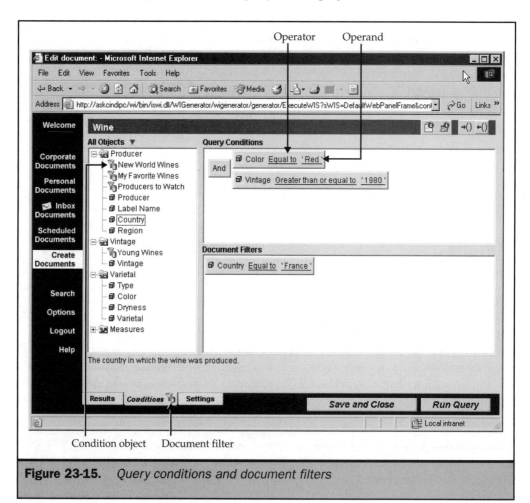

Figure 23-15. *Query conditions and document filters*

To change the document filter to view the results for a different country:

1. Select Edit from the Top bar.
2. Select the Conditions tab.
3. Modify the Document Filters.
4. Click Apply Format. This filters the report display without reexecuting the query against the RDBMS.

To remove a condition, drag the object from the Query Conditions or Document Filters window back to the All Objects window.

If you want to make the condition interactive, for the operand, click the drop-down menu to specify either Prompt list of values or Enter a prompt. With Prompt list of values, the prompt and list of values are displayed on the same screen, as shown in Figure 23-13. With Enter a prompt, a list of values is not displayed even if one is associated with this particular object in the universe. Unless the list of values is exceedingly long, it is better to select Prompt list of values for more accurate query results. WebI provides you with a default prompt in the box that you can modify. You can have the prompt value displayed when viewing the report results by selecting Settings | Document | Show prompts within the report.

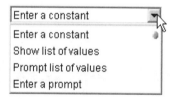

For more information on query conditions, refer to Chapter 21, "Conditions," or Chapter 22.

Breaks, Sorts, and Calculations

Breaks allow you to group sets of data and further analyze them within mini-tables. You can apply calculations such as Sum, Count, Average, Minimum, Maximum, or Percentage to an entire table or to each break level. In BusinessObjects, you apply breaks after you execute a query either via the Slice and Dice Panel or via Format | Breaks. In WebI, you define the breaks and calculations from the same panel you use to build the query. As discussed in Chapter 18, "Breaks," the break and sort orders are the same; you do not need to explicitly add the sorts. In Figure 23-16, Color contains both the first sort level and the first break level. In WebI, all sorts are done within the microcube. There is no option to perform the sort on the server. To ensure that the calculations are added for each break level, insert the breaks first, then insert the calculations.

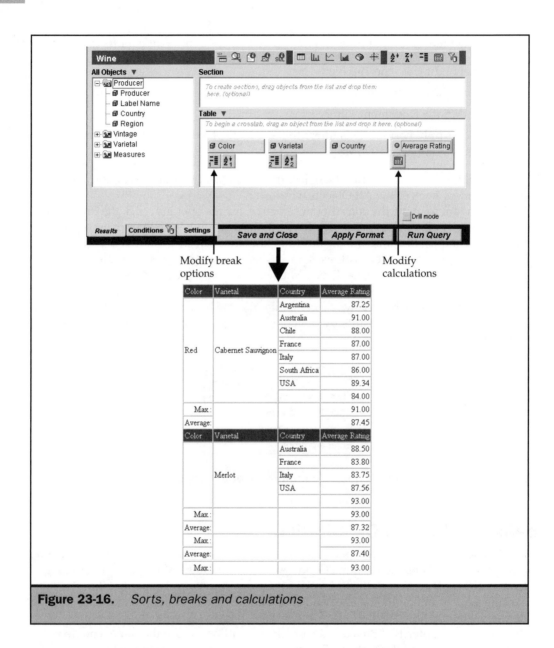

Figure 23-16.   *Sorts, breaks and calculations*

To insert a sort, break, or calculation on an object, first select the object from the Table pane, then click the appropriate button on the toolbar. Alternatively, you can drag the button from the toolbar to the specific object. To modify one of these settings, click the button beneath the object. For example, WebI sets the default calculation as Sum. It does not make sense to Sum wine ratings. To add a break on Color and then change the calculation to display an Average and a Maximum:

1. Drag the Break button from to the toolbar to the *Color* object in the Table pane.

2. Drag the Calculation button from the toolbar to the *Average Rating* object.

3. Double-click the Calculation button beneath the *Average Rating* object. As you select functions beneath the objects, WebI will show the button is selected by adding a gray box to the button. If you select the object rather than the button, a gray box appears around the object name. Double-clicking an object name invokes the cell settings.

4. WebI displays the Calculation dialog. Note that the default calculation type is Sum. Click the Sum check box to remove the check. Click the Average and Maximum check boxes.

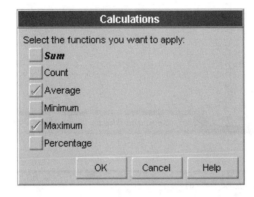

5. Click OK to close the Calculation dialog box.

6. Click Apply Format to display the report as it appears in Figure 23-16. You do not need to reexecute the query, as sorts, breaks, and calculations affect only the report appearance and not the SQL query.

Settings

There are two types of settings that control the appearance of your report: document settings and individual block settings. You can view and modify these settings by selecting the Setting tab or clicking the Document Settings or Block Settings buttons from the toolbar.

Figure 23-17 shows the *document* settings. Note in the right window, WebI displays the report structure similar to BusinessObjects Report Manager, Structure view. In this figure, the black boxes or markers indicate that the entire document is selected. If you click an individual report component in the structure window, such as the Title or Table, WebI will display the settings for that component, either block settings, cell settings, or section settings.

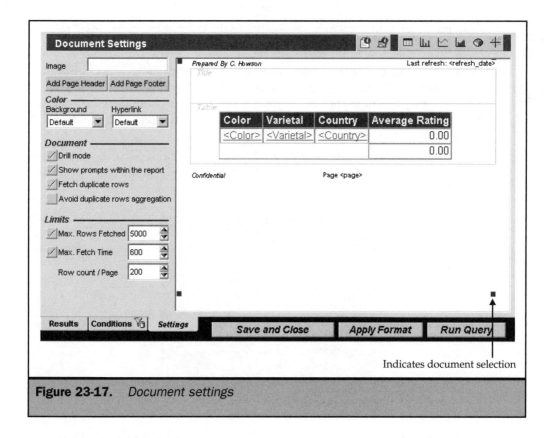

Figure 23-17. *Document settings*

Document Settings

Document settings affect the appearance of the entire document, the initial view of the document in WebI, and certain query settings.

- **Image**   Specifies a background image for your document. You can use a file from the WebI server or from your local disk. To use a local file, use file://C:*directory**imagefile.bmp,* where *directory* is the path to the file and *imagefile* is the name of the file.

By default, WebI provides a default page header that displays the last refresh data and a footer that provides the page number. You can provide additional headers:

- **Add Page Header**   Inserts a cell at the top left of the page. When you click this button, you are prompted with a text box—for example, to enter the document name. You can then modify the color, alignment, and font for the Page Header. The Page Header appears when you view and print a report. To return to document settings, click anywhere within the document in the right window, but ensure you are not selecting a specific report component.

- **Add Page Footer** Inserts a cell in the bottom left of the page. You may want to use the footer to provide a document classification such as Confidential.

In the Color section of the Document settings, you specify the default background color and hyperlink color. By default, the background color of a web page is white. To alter the color, click the drop-down box to select a different color from the palette. The Document settings alter the way the initial report is presented:

- **Drill Mode** Formats dimension values with hyperlinks and creates a Drill bar above the report. These settings have the same functionality as selecting Drill mode from the Web Panel or the Top bar while viewing a report.

- **Show Prompts Within The Report** Creates an additional section while viewing a report that displays the prompt value used as a condition for the query. If the prompt uses the list of values, you will also have a drop-down box to select a different value and a Refresh List button. This option also adds a button to the report view that lets you refresh the query.

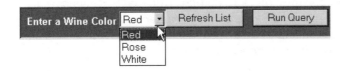

- **Fetch Duplicate Rows** This is the default setting, and this box is normally checked. When you remove the check, WebI adds DISTINCT to the SQL statement. When your report contains measures that use an aggregate function such as SUM, by default all duplicate rows are grouped into one summary row with the GROUP BY clause, and this setting should not be used. However, if you are creating a list report of product names or customer names, you may receive duplicate names for each occurrence in the source table. Set this option to retrieve only distinct rows.

- **Avoid Duplicate Rows Aggregation** Works in conjunction with projection aggregates (see Chapter 19, "How Is the Data Aggregated?") and affects how information is aggregated from the result set to the report display. As you remove result objects from the report display or as you add additional details in the scope of analysis, WebI will use the object's projection aggregates to dynamically calculate the measures in a report. If you need to see the individual rows from a query result (either to understand the data or to download it to a spreadsheet), set this option. This option does not affect the SQL.

The universe designer may set limits for the number of rows that can be retrieved in one query or how long a query can execute. If you exceed these limits, your report will display partial results. You can modify the Row Count / Page to accommodate the number of rows displayed on one page. This affects both the display and printed report.

Block Settings

You modify block settings by selecting Block Settings from the Web Panel toolbar. You also can modify block settings by selecting the individual report components from the Settings tab:

- Title Block Settings
- Sections
- Table Settings
- Chart Settings
- Cell Settings

The following screen shows the Title Block Settings. In the structure window, the black handle markers are now on the Title block and not the entire document, as shown in Figure 23-17. The border settings have been modified to illustrate the effect of changing the Border, Padding, and Spacing. To modify the format for the title text, click the title text rather than the entire block to display Title Cell Settings. For all of the individual cell settings, you can modify the color, alignment, and font as you would in any MS Windows application and as described in Chapter 17. Table 23-4 describes the unique settings to format different report components.

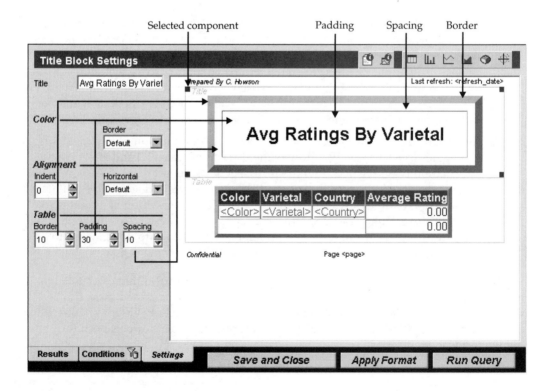

Report Component	Formatting Option	Explanation
Title Block Settings	Title	Allows you to enter a report title in the text box.
	Border	The number within this box allows you to set the thickness of the line added to the block. If you do not want any border, enter **0** or scroll down to select 0.
	Padding	This number determines the distance between the text and inner border created with the Spacing setting. If Spacing is set to 0, it is the distance to the border.
	Spacing	Creates an inner box in addition to the border.
Section Cell Settings	Show As Index	Creates an additional frame or window with hyperlinks to navigate each section. Each section is then displayed as a separate page instead of one long page with multiple section headings.
	Repeat On Each Page	This is the default setting for sections. If you use the section cell as an index, set this option as well so that the section value prints on the report page.
Block Settings	Header, Each New Block	When using breaks, repeats the column headings for each miniblock created.
	Header, Each New Page	Repeats the column headings when a block spans more than one page.
	Header, Each Row	Repeats the column headings for every row of data.

Table 23-4. *Settings to Format Report Components*

Report Component	Formatting Option	Explanation
Chart Settings	Chart, 3D Look	Similar to selecting a 3D Bar Chart from the Block Style dialog box.
	Zero-Based axis	Forces the axis to start at zero.
	Flip Horizontal/Vertical	Transposes the X and Y axes to display bars horizontally instead of vertically.
	Axis Legend	To display a legend beneath the chart, select Horizontal from the drop-down. To display a legend to the right of the chart, select Vertical. Also available from the vertical toolbar while viewing the report (Table 23-2).
Cell Settings	Header	When you select a header cell, it displays the object name as it appears in the universe. For long object names, you can enter a shorter column heading in the Header box.
	Format	When you select a measure cell, the default format for the number of decimal places, thousands separator, currency, and so on, is set by the universe designer. To override this format, select the measure cell and click the Format drop-down box. Select Custom to define your own format (see Chapter 17, "Number").

Table 23-4.   *Settings to Format Report Components* (continued)

OLAP Data Source

When you create a new document, you can choose to access an OLAP data source. If this is the first time you are using WebI to access the OLAP data source, you need to define a connection, as shown in the next screen and described in the subsequent table.

▶ Create OLAP Data Source

OLAP Data Source name: `Essbase Softdrink`
Server information
        OLAP Server: `Essbase` ▾
        Server Name: `ASK`
        Description: `|`

| Save | Reset | Back |

Prompt	Explanation
OLAP Data Source Name	The name that appears to you when you choose to create a new document from an OLAP server.
OLAP Server	The type of OLAP database or server you are accessing—for example, Essbase or Microsoft OLAP Services. The corresponding OLAP connectivity packs must be installed on the WebI server.
Server Name	The name of the MOLAP server.
Description	Optional description. You can leave this blank, as it does not appear elsewhere in WebI.

As discussed in Chapter 13, "MOLAP Cubes," and Chapter 21, "OLAP Access," BusinessObjects uses the OLAP Panel to build the query; once you build the query, you perform most of the sorting and formatting offline in BusinessObjects. The workflow for WebI is significantly different and better leverages the power of the MOLAP server. All your sorts, ranking, and filters are server-based. You drill within a formatted grid or chart. Also, WebI allows you to drill from a cube through to the details in a relational database, a functionality not yet available in the full client.

Figure 23-18 shows the Hyperion Essbase Sample database. The OLAP Report shows a grid of the first two dimensions in the outline (Year and Product). The grand total for the Year has been explicitly added to the grid. The Query Panel shows the current grid selections and filters. When you first launch an OLAP Report, by default, the numbers displayed in the grid are for the first child in the Measure dimension. In Figure 23-18, this selection has been changed to display the Sales measure. Figure 23-18 also shows the more robust formatting available via WebI's OLAP as you can have both a table and a chart displayed simultaneously.

To drill down, you click the + next to a member. For example, to drill from Qtr1 down to Jan, Feb, Mar, click the + next to Qtr1. To drill up, click the – next to any member. The grid and the chart drills are synchronized. When you drill to month in the grid, the chart reflects the same monthly details. Beneath the chart, you also can filter the data via the Row drop-down box. For example, in Figure 23-18, Sales for all products for the year are displayed in the bar chart. To focus on Qtr4, select the Row drop-down and choose Qtr4. The bar chart will display Qtr4 data, while the grid will continue to display details for all four quarters.

You add additional dimensions to the grid by dragging them from the Query Panel to the grid. As you drag dimensions, watch the status bar to ensure you are dragging them to the appropriate place in the grid. The status bar will display either Move To Row or Move To Column. You also can add a dimension to the table by selecting the children of a particular dimension, as explained in the later section "Filtering Data by Members and Values."

Table 23-5 describes the purpose of each button on the OLAP toolbar. Several buttons allow you to select from an additional drop-down menu. If you click the button, the first option in the menu is the default and is selected.

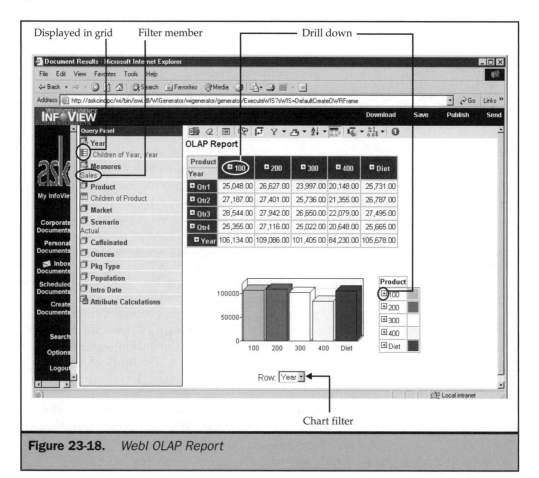

Figure 23-18.   *WebI OLAP Report*

Button	Name	Description
	Create Printable Version	Opens a second browser session to print the currently displayed grid or chart.
	Clear Query	Resets all filters and displays only the first two dimensions in the grid.
	View	Allows you to close the Query Panel in the left or to suppress the display of a report title.
	Drill Through	Allows you to drill from the summary MOLAP cube to details in a relational database. The universe designer must enable drill-through from a MOLAP cube to a detailed universe and reports.
	Swap Axes	Switches the columns and rows in a tabular report.
	Value Filter	Allows you to filter measure values via different operators. You filter dimension members via selections in the Query Panel.
	Rank	Provides a drop-down box to perform server-based rankings according to top or bottom performers.
	Sort	Provides a drop-down menu to sort values.
	Turn Empty Cell Suppression On or Off	Toggle to suppress empty cells.
	Layout Menu	Allows you to display a chart, mixed chart, or grid, and to select additional chart styles.

Table 23-5.   *OLAP Panel Buttons*

Button	Name	Description
	Formatting Menu	Format measures, parent/child indents, aliases.
	Report Information	Displays database and query selections in the left frame. To close the information frame and redisplay the Query Panel, click the X in the Report Information.

Table 23-5.   *OLAP Panel Buttons* (continued)

Figure 23-18 shows the numeric codes for each product. To display the longer alias names:

1. Select the Formatting menu from the toolbar and choose Alias from the drop-down box.
2. This opens a frame on the left titled Format Alias Table. Use the drop-down box to select the alias table; this is typically Default, but your Essbase Administrator may create additional alias tables.

3. Click OK to close the dialog box.

Now the product description, Colas, appears rather than the numeric ID 100.

Filtering Data by Members and Values

You can filter your data according to individual members, their relationships, or values for measures. You can filter data even when it does not appear in the grid or chart. In Figure 23-18, Sales (under the Measures dimension) and Actual (under the Scenario dimension) were used as filters; however, only the children of product and year are displayed in the report. To add a filter on the Market dimension to show data for the East region:

1. In the Query Panel, double-click Market. WebI displays the Select Members dialog box. The first drop-down box in this dialog allows you to view the outline by members or levels. When you view it by levels, you also see a count for the number of members within a particular level.

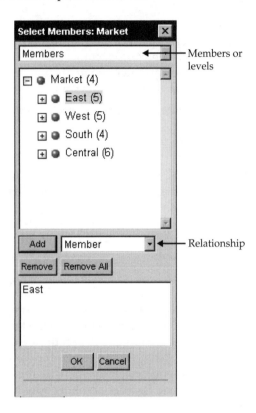

2. Highlight East.

3. From the second drop-down box, you can specify the relationship. Leave the selection as Member and click Add.

This filter selection will now appear in the Query Panel.

Value-based filters allow you to filter individual columns by values. When you have multiple rows, the filter applies to the innermost row. For example, in Figure 23-18, you want to see only Colas, Product 100, with Sales greater than 26000. The quarters appear as the row dimension. To filter Colas according to Sales for a particular Quarter:

1. Select the Colas or 100 column by clicking one of the values in this column. Do not select the column heading.

2. Click the Value Filter drop-down menu from the toolbar and select Custom. You also could select an operator from the drop-down menu to filter the values according to the cell value you select in a grid. If you click the Value Filter icon without selecting the drop-down menu, then your table is filtered for greater than the selected cell or first cell in the column.

3. WebI opens a Value Filter dialog box. Select > in the first drop-down and then enter **26000**.

4. Click OK.

The rows for Qtr1 and Qtr4 will be suppressed, as these are < 26000. A filter statement is added to the Year dimension in the Query Panel. The filter does not apply to the months but only to the quarters.

 Note   *Even though the filter applies to the Colas-100 column, the quarters for the other products are also suppressed.*

Rank

Rank allows you to select the top or bottom values according to a particular column. Like the Value Filter, Rank looks at the innermost row in the table. In the following example, Product is the innermost row, so the rank will select the top or bottom products. If Market were the innermost column, rank would select the top- or bottom-performing markets. The Rank default is Top 10. If you click Rank, it ranks the data according to the Top 10 of whatever column you selected. For more ranking options, click the drop-down arrow next to the Rank button.

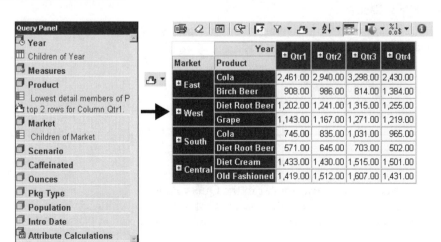

To rank products according to the two most profitable products for Qtr1 as shown in the preceding illustration:

1. Select the column Qtr1. Be sure to select the values and not the column name.

2. Click the Rank menu. Select Custom from the drop-down menu.

3. This opens the Rank dialog. In the first drop-down, select Top. In the second box, enter a value **2**.

4. Click OK to close the dialog box and rank the products. A rank icon appears in the Query Panel beneath the Product dimension.

Notice in the preceding report that the top two products in the East region are Cola and Birch Beer, whereas the top two products in the West region are different; in Qtr1, the profit for Grape soft drink was higher than Birch Beer.

Drill Through

Drill through is a powerful feature available only via WebI and not available in BusinessObjects. It allows you to explore the data in a summary MOLAP cube and then drill through to retrieve details from a relational database. The details are presented to you in a formatted WebI report. The universe designer must enable drill through for each cube (see Chapter 11). You specify the drill through intersection, which gets passed as a condition or WHERE clause into the WebI query. If you want to use all the member values for the intersection, select the numeric measure in the table and then click Drill Through. If you want to select only one member value, select the row or column heading and then click Drill Through.

Drill Through makes sense only when you are at the lowest level of detail in the cube; there are now + signs next to the dimension members to indicate you can drill down further. In the next example, the lowest members for the Time, Product, and Market dimensions are displayed and there is no + for drilling. If you select the intersection of July, 100-10, and New York by placing your mouse on the cell value 912, then all three of these member names are used as conditions in the query. If you click in the cell containing New York, then only this member value is passed through to the conditions.

To drill through to details:

1. Select either the member name or the numeric measure for which you want to retrieve details.

2. Click Drill Through from the toolbar.

3. You are prompted to select a WebI report called a Drill Through Target. Each report may contain different result columns or block styles.

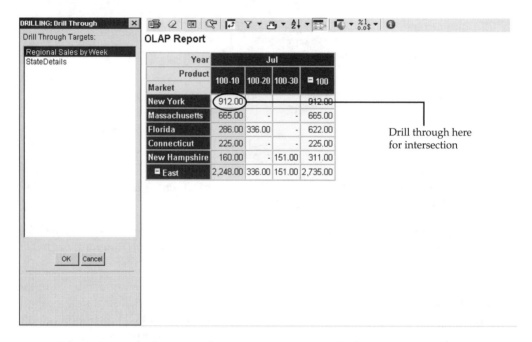

4. Click OK.

5. WebI displays the details for the drill through.

State	Product Name	Month	Week	Sales
New York	Cola	July	27.00	216.00
New York	Cola	July	28.00	182.00
New York	Cola	July	29.00	182.00
New York	Cola	July	30.00	166.00
New York	Cola	July	31.00	166.00

Page 1

You may be able to use your browser Back button to return to the OLAP Panel, but I have never had this work successfully with Essbase.

Caution *When you drill through to details, be careful in using either alias names or IDs. Ideally, the universe designer has enabled the drill-through to work with either values, but this may not be possible for all aliases. The member names—either aliases or codes—displayed in the OLAP Panel get passed through as the conditions.*

Summary

InfoView allows you to access, share, and analyze documents via a thin-client interface. When you want to refresh a query, analyze data further with drill down, or build a new query, use WebI. Version 2.*x* of WebI allows you to create single-block reports in many different block styles. As you will see in Chapter 24, the newest version of WebI brings the work flow and functionality between BusinessObjects and the web platform much closer together.

REPORTING WITH BUSINESSOBJECTS

The
Complete
Reference

Business
Objects

Chapter 24

WebIntelligence
Version 6.0

A t the time of this writing, BusinessObjects and WebIntelligence (WebI) version 6.0 were in Beta 2. WebI version 6.0 narrows the functionality gap between the two platforms, providing improved graphics, a more intuitive interface, simpler workflow, multitab and multiblock reports, and report variables and formulas. Web-based reports have never been so rich! Whereas users previously had to sacrifice functionality for thin-client computing, WebI version 6.0 removes many of those barriers and offers even more enhancements.

This chapter assumes you have worked with either BusinessObjects or WebI 2.*x* and focuses on the version differences or new steps for completing a task covered in other chapters in Part III of this book. There may be slight differences between the Beta 2 product and released product.

Two Interfaces

WebI version 6.0 comes in two different interfaces:

- Java Report Panel
- HTML Report Panel

The Java Report Panel uses an applet that gets downloaded to your browser the first time you launch the Java Report Panel, either by editing a document or choosing to create a new one. The Java Report Panel allows for the most complex and robust web-based reporting and analysis. BusinessObjects full-client or three-tier mode users will find the Java Report Panel familiar.

The HTML Report Panel uses dynamic HTML to provide a zero-footprint client. As a zero-footprint client, it's ideal for extranet deployments or slow networks. New users also may prefer a more basic interface that guides you through the process of creating a new document. The HTML Report Panel has a different interface, but also only a subset of the WebI functionality. Table 24-1 highlights some of the main differences between BusinessObjects, WebI version 2, and the different interfaces of version 6.0.

Topic	Functionality	BusinessObjects	WebI 2.*x*	WebI 6.0 Java Report Panel	WebI 6.0 HTML Report Panel
Query	List of values chunking and search within	No	No	Yes	No
Query	Hierarchical view of objects in query	Yes	No	Yes	No

Table 24-1. *Differences in the Versions and WebI Interfaces*

Topic	Functionality	BusinessObjects	WebI 2.x	WebI 6.0 Java Report Panel	WebI 6.0 HTML Report Panel
Query	Control prompt order	Workaround is to modify prompt text to include numbers	Workaround	Yes, via UP ARROW /DOWN ARROW keys	No
Query	Advanced query filters for subqueries	Yes	No	Yes	No
Query	Multiple data providers	Yes	No	No	No
Query	Custom Scope of Analysis	Yes	Yes	Yes	No
Query	User-defined objects	Yes	No	No	No
Report	Suppress empty values	No	No	Yes	No
Report	Multiblock creation	Yes	No	Yes	No
Report	Multireport creation	Yes	No	Yes	No
Report	Complex calculations and local variables	Yes	No	Yes	No
Report	Format report in structure view	Yes	No	Yes	No
Report	Relative positioning for multiblock reports	Yes	NA	Yes	NA
Report	Save as Excel	New in 6.0	No	Yes	Yes
Report	Alternate row colors in tables	No	No	Yes	No
Drill	Skip level within Scope of Analysis	Yes	No	Yes	No
Drill	Contextual drill bar	Yes	No	Yes	Yes
Drill	Drill by	Yes	No	Yes	Yes
Drill	Drill snapshot	Yes	No	Yes	No
Drill	Synchronized multiblock drilling	No	No	Yes	No

Table 24-1.   *Differences in the Versions and WebI Interfaces* (continued)

Navigating InfoView

Immediately when you open InfoView, you see the difference in graphics between InfoView versions 6.0 and 2.7. The new icons are slick and replace what previously had been plain-text menus. The Top bar displays a "skin" that you can modify from three other default skins. Items such as Corporate Documents that used to appear along the Navigation bar on the left are now nicely displayed in both the Home page and links along the bottom of each list page. Previously, if you customized My InfoView, this became your default start page and replaced the Welcome page. With version 6.0, you continue to have access to the default Home page or the customized My InfoView.

The workflow for a number of actions has been greatly improved, making them more logical and requiring fewer steps. For example, notice that Inbox documents (documents that BCA or other users have sent to you) now appear under Personal Documents, rather than as a separate menu. Under New Document, you can either create a new document or select Add A Document, replacing the former Upload menu from the Top bar.

The initial list of Corporate Documents makes better use of Categories. As shown in Figure 24-1, subcategories are new to version 6.0, allowing companies with hundreds of

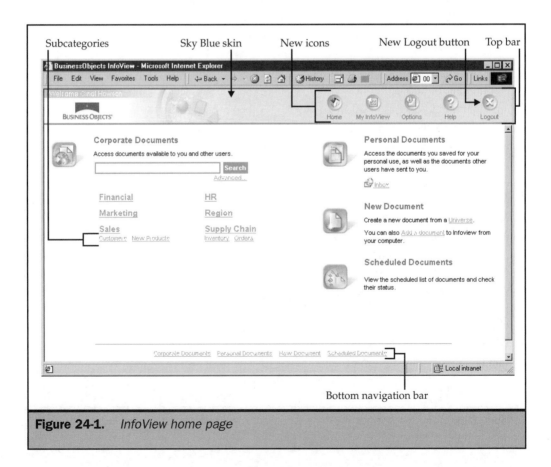

Figure 24-1.   *InfoView home page*

standard reports to better organize their documents. There is no limit to the number of subcategories you can create.

In the Top bar, two new buttons, Help and Logout, are more prominently displayed and available within all InfoView pages.

Options

Options

As with the previous version, there are still some Options that you should customize before you begin accessing the lists and documents. To modify any of the following options, select Options from the Top bar.

Display Options

From the Display page, you can specify your default start page, skins, and My InfoView settings. Skins are sets of graphic images and styles that change the appearance of the toolbars and buttons. For example, compare the default skin Sky Blue in Figure 24-1 with the following Top bar that uses a different skin, Midnight Blue. The WebI administrator can create and customize skins to display a corporate logo or corporate color scheme.

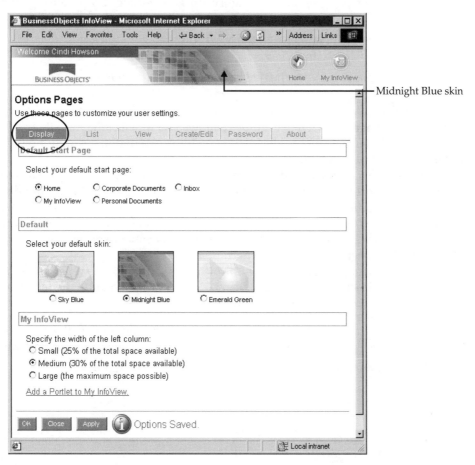

Midnight Blue skin

From the display page, you set the size of the left frame in My InfoView. By default, this frame contains a list of personal documents. You can set the size of the frame to small, medium, or large. The radio button Large sets the document list as large as possible, depending on what information appears to the right of the personal document list. You customize My InfoView by adding portlets to the page. *Portlets* are mini–portal windows that allow you to display different content within the My InfoView page. A portlet can be another web site, which you add via this page, or a document, which you add while viewing My InfoView. Previously, My InfoView was limited to four blocks within a page. With the portlet approach, the limit is what fits into the display area. This new approach provides greater flexibility over the previous block approach. With the portlets, you reorganize the layout while you are in My InfoView, not via the Options page.

You add additional document lists to My InfoView by clicking the link Add To My InfoView while viewing a particular list. Likewise, you display a document in My InfoView by selecting Add To My InfoView while viewing the document. For example, to add the list of Corporate Documents, Marketing Category to My InfoView

1. From the Home page, select the category Marketing under Corporate Documents.

2. While viewing the documents in the Marketing category, click the hyperlink Add To My InfoView.

3. My InfoView appears with the newly added list of documents.

View Options

The View Options page, shown in Figure 24-2, allows you to select the format for viewing a WebI document, actions when drilling within a WebI document, or how to view a BusinessObjects full-client document.

InfoView version 6.0 provides some additional functionality when viewing a WebI document, such as sorting and filtering data. Previously, you could sort and filter data only by editing the document and launching WebI. In Version 6.0, when you select HTML (Interactive), you can sort and filter data directly from within InfoView, without having to launch WebI to edit the document. The BusinessObjects Supervisor can remove or enable this specific functionality through permissions.

Version 6.0 documents can now have multiple blocks and multiple reports within one document, introducing new view options when you drill. Similar to the full client, you now have options to specify if you want to

■ Create a duplicate report when you start drilling. With this option, the filters and display in the original report are preserved and WebI inserts a new report tab.

■ Drill within the existing report, without inserting a new report tab.

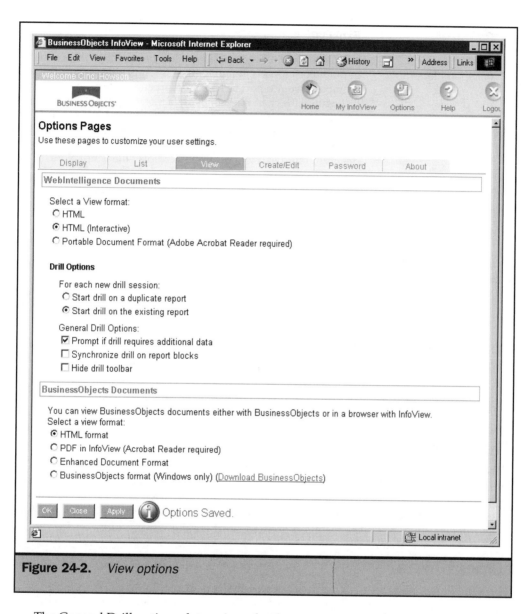

Figure 24-2. *View options*

The General Drill options determine what happens once you have initiated a drill session. These options are described in the following table:

Option	Explanation
Prompt if drill requires additional data	If a drill will launch a new query (when the additional details do not exist in the microcube), you are prompted before the query executes.

Option	Explanation
Synchronize drill on report blocks	Unique to WebI 6.0 is the ability to synchronize the drill actions in multiblock reports, set under the General Drill Options. For example, if your report has both a chart and a table, when you drill within the chart, the same drill actions apply in the table. If you drill from wine color red in a table to varietal, the detailed varietals will be displayed in both the chart and the table. If the drill is not synchronized, then the table will display the varietal details but the chart will continue to display the wine colors.
Hide drill toolbar	Previously, the only way to hide the drill toolbar from the report view was to end the drill session. Now, you can hide the drill toolbar, yet still have the drill actions within a block, either via hyperlinks, drill-up arrows, or pop-up menus.

The View options for full-client BusinessObjects documents are unchanged and explained in Chapter 23. To modify the View options:

1. Select Options from the main toolbar.

2. Click the View tab.

3. Select the desired options.

4. Click Apply at the bottom of the page. InfoView displays the status at the bottom of the page, "Options Saved." The new settings become effective only if you receive this confirmation message. You also can click OK to apply the changes and return immediately to the Home or Start page.

The About Page

About is a new page that lets you load server defaults, restoring your options to the initial settings. If you are a General Supervisor or BusinessObjects Administrator, the About page also lets you set the options as server defaults for new users. Users can continue to override these options, but this page allows you to modify their initial settings. The About page also displays the installed products and version information.

Document Lists

From the Home page, you access the different list of documents. You can access a list by clicking the icon or clicking the hyperlink. From the Home page, you navigate corporate documents by categories or subcategories. The category and subcategory names that appear on this page are ones that contain documents for which you have permission. Empty categories do not appear on this page.

If you want to view a list of corporate documents independent of their category assignment:

1. From the Home page, click the Corporate Documents hyperlink or button.

2. InfoView displays the Corporate Documents page. In addition to the categories that were displayed on the Home page, you now have two new hyperlinks: All Documents and Uncategorized Documents.

3. Select All Documents to display a full list of corporate documents to which you have access.

 If you have customized your list of Corporate Documents to access a specific category directly, click the hyperlink Corporate Documents next to the specific category to see all the categories.

 From within Corporate Documents, you can display a list of categories in a frame on the left, as shown in Figure 24-3. Click the Show Column button, in the upper-left corner, to show or hide the Categories list. This button acts as a toggle and becomes a Hide Column button when the category list is displayed. Having the categories continually displayed allows you to more quickly navigate from one category's list to another's.

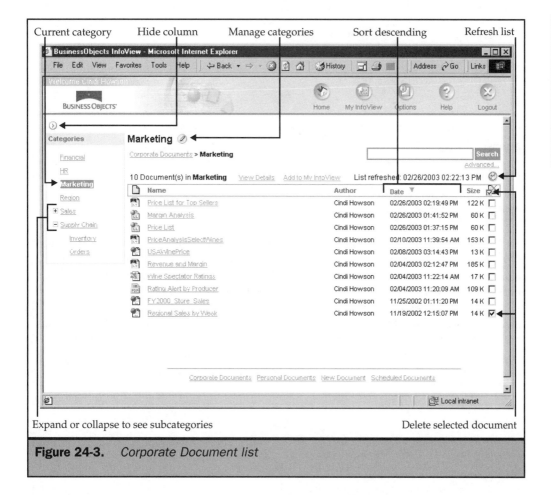

Figure 24-3.   *Corporate Document list*

REPORTING WITH BUSINESSOBJECTS

Notice in Figure 24-3 that some of the document icons have changed. WebI 6.0 uses a different file format, icon, and extension than WebI 2.*x*. When you view/edit a WebI 2.*x* document, WebI 6.0 dynamically converts it to the new format. You can then choose to save the file in the new format, or if you do modify the file, to leave it in the old format. Both copies and versions remain on the server. You must explicitly delete the old version once you have converted a document to version 6.0. The following table shows the icons for the different file formats. The file format for BusinessObjects documents (.rep) has not changed, so both versions 5.*x* and 6.*x* documents show the same icon.

Document Icon	Document Type
	WebI version 2.*x*, .wqy file
	WebI version 6.0, .wid file
	BusinessObjects
	PDF

The list of available Corporate Documents can change frequently if report authors publish new documents throughout the day. Your list may be updated

- Every time you access the list
- Only when you first access the list

- When you specifically select Refresh List

You specify whether or not the list is updated on the first visit or each visit through Options | Lists. If your options are set to refresh the list only upon the first viewing of Corporate Documents, the list is maintained in a server cache. When a report author publishes a new report, click Refresh List to see the new document.

As with the previous version, you can sort any list by document name, author, date, and size. To sort the list by one of these columns, click the column name, not the triangle next to the name. An upward-pointing triangle appears next to the column heading. To change the sort order to descending, click the column heading again; the triangle points down. In Figure 24-3, the documents are sorted descending by Date.

To delete a document, check the box in the rightmost column, then click Delete Selected Document(s).

Search

The Search box searches the entire document name. For example, a Search on Margin finds:

- Margin Analysis
- Gross margin by product
- Revenue and Margin

Clicking the Advanced hyperlink below the Search button allows you to specify additional search criteria such as the document list to search within, keyword, author/ sender, and date. The Search Document(s) page in version 6.0 is similar to that of WebI 2.*x*, shown in Figure 23-7 in Chapter 23.

Categories

Categories allow you to organize documents into meaningful groups and provide an additional filtering mechanism for what otherwise may be an overwhelmingly long list of documents. For categories to be effective:

- Users and/or the administrator must define meaningful categories.
- Report authors must associate a document with a category when saving, publishing, or uploading a document.

Tip *The ability to display a list of uncategorized documents is new in Version 6.0. The administrator or support personnel should periodically view this list to ensure all documents are assigned to at least one category.*

One document can be assigned to multiple categories or subcategories. New in version 6.0 is the ability to create multiple levels of subcategories. The Categories page also provides useful information such as who created the category and the number of documents associated with a category.

To create or modify a subcategory:

1. Display Corporate Documents.

2. Click Manage Categories.

3. InfoView displays a list of Corporate Categories. To add a new category, enter a category name in the bottom text box and click Create. To add a subcategory, click the main category. In the following screen, Supply Chain is the main category; Inventory, Orders, and Suppliers are the subcategories. Enter the new subcategory in the box—for example, **Swaps**.

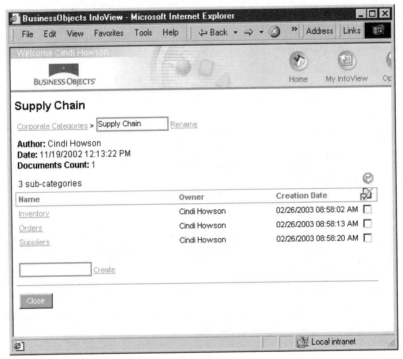

4. Click Create. InfoView confirms that the "Category was successfully created."

5. You can continue to add more categories or click Close to return to the list of corporate documents.

Close is a nifty new button at the bottom of most pages. Previously, the only way to cancel your settings was to click the browser's Back button, which may have brought you back too far. The Close button closes the current page without saving your changes and nicely returns you to the previous page.

Document Properties

The hyperlinks View List and View Details replace the Expand and Compact menu options. View Details changes the list to a two-column display that provides additional actions and details for each document. With View Details, you see keywords if they are available or the first few words of a description. To see the full description, click the Properties hyperlink beneath the document name, as shown in Figure 24-4.

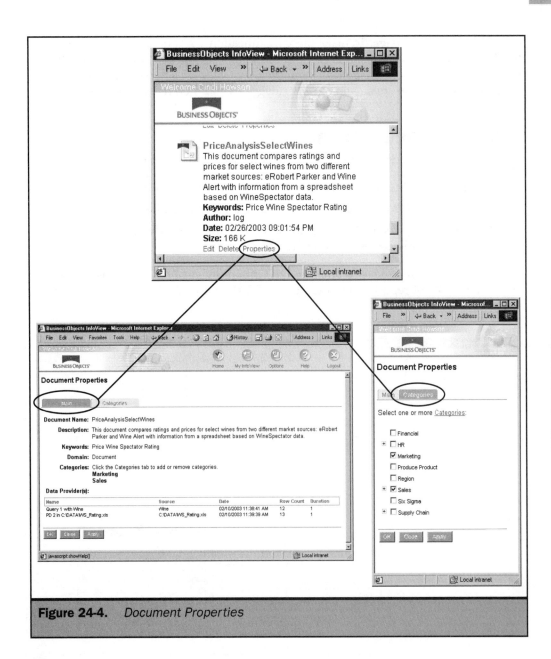

Figure 24-4. *Document Properties*

Note

The Author displayed in the Document Properties is the person who published the document to the Corporate Documents; it may not be the author who originally created the document as listed under File | Properties in BusinessObjects.

The Document Properties page now has two tabs, Main and Categories. The Main page is unchanged from the previous version. You cannot modify the keywords or the description from this page. To make these modifications, you must edit and then resave the document. From the Categories tab, you can assign a document to additional categories by checking the appropriate boxes. If you click the Categories hyperlink at the top of the page, you also can create and modify categories and then reassign the document.

Viewing Documents

When viewing a WebI document in InfoView, you have three ways to view the document:

- Standard HTML, which allows for drill but not sort and filter
- Interactive HTML, which allows you to drill, sort, and filter a report
- PDF format, which allows you to view a document in Adobe Acrobat, and therefore does not include drill, filter, or sort

You set your default view mode through Options | View. This section assumes you are viewing a WebI report using Interactive HTML. Figure 24-5 shows a multiblock,

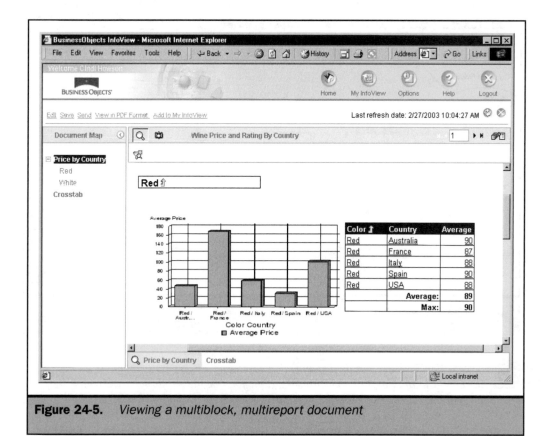

Figure 24-5. *Viewing a multiblock, multireport document*

multireport document in interactive HTML. You navigate the report in much the same way you do in the full client. To see another report tab, you can select it from the Document Map or click the tab on the bottom of the screen. Table 24-2 describes the buttons available to you when viewing a document.

Button	Name	Explanation
	Refresh	Executes the query and refreshes the data in the microcube.
	Close	Closes the view of the current document and returns you to the previous document list.
	Show/Hide Report Map	This button appears in the top-left corner of your page. Use the report map to navigate sections in a master/detail report or to select reports in a document with multiple report tabs.
	Show/Hide Prompt	This button is similar to the preceding one but appears in the top-right corner of your page. If your query contains prompts to filter the data upon refresh, you can show or hide the prompt frame.
	Drill	Adds navigation arrows on column headings for drill up and down and hyperlinks to dimension values.
	Add Filter	Creates a drill bar that allows you to filter a document by a particular dimension. This filter icon appears only when you enable Drill mode by first clicking Drill. You also can filter data when you are not in Drill mode, but this is done via a pop-up menu, not this button.
	Snapshot	Creates a copy of the report with the current drill selections. This icon appears only when your report is in Drill mode.
	Page Navigation	WebI processes each page as you request it for more efficient network traffic and faster analysis. You can enter a page number in the box or use the arrows to scroll to the first, next, previous, or last page.
	Toggle to Draft Mode	With slower network connections, high graphics can be slow to convert and display. Draft mode allows you to display a report more quickly. It does not affect print quality.

Table 24-2.   *Buttons for Navigating a Document in InfoView*

Sort and Filter

When viewing a WebI 6.0 document in InfoView Interactive HTML, you can sort dimension and detail columns without launching the WebI report panel. InfoView Filter and Sort are not available for measure columns; use WebI for this. The Sort applies only to the currently selected block and does not synchronize the sort order for other blocks within the same report. For example, in the table block in Figure 24-5, to add a sort to the Country column:

1. Hold your mouse over the Country column.

2. A pop-up menu appears. Select Sort | Descending.

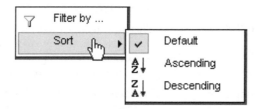

3. InfoView redraws the table with the new sort order; the X-axis legend in the chart block remains the same.

Filters, on the other hand, are global. When you add a filter on a table, the chart data is also filtered. When you select Filter by in the pop-up menu, InfoView creates a Dynamic Filters frame. The Filter By option in the pop-up menu appears only when you are not in Drill mode. To add a filter on Country:

1. Hold your mouse over the Country column in the table.

2. From the pop-up menu, select Filter By. The following Dynamic Filters window appears to the left of your report window:

3. If you have selected the wrong column or decide you do not want to filter the data, click Close Filter to close the Dynamic Filters frame. Otherwise, select the dimension values by which you want to filter the table. Use CTRL-click to select multiple values.

4. Click Apply. The Dynamic Filters window closes automatically. InfoView redraws both the table and the chart with the subset of data.

From within InfoView, you cannot apply a Filter directly to a chart, but if you filter a table within a multiblock report that contains a chart, the chart data is also filtered.

From within InfoView, you can filter multiple dimension columns, but you will get an overview of all the filters only when you edit the document. To remove a filter from an individual column:

1. Position your mouse over the column.

2. Select Filter By from the pop-up menu.

3. Click Remove.

HTML Interactive is only available for documents created with WebI 6.0, using either the Java Report Panel or the HTML Report Panel. For documents created with either BusinessObjects or earlier versions of WebI, the Sort and Filter menus will not appear. Filter By does not appear when your report is displayed in Drill mode.

Drill

When you first view a report, it may open in Drill mode or you may enable Drill mode by selecting Drill from the toolbar. In your Options, you specify if you want Drill mode to create a new report or if you want to drill within the existing report.

The new drill interface is much more intuitive than in WebI 2.x and behaves more like the full client. You now can customize the drill bar, select Drill By from a pop-up menu, and select drill filters to include in a drill-through query. For more information on these options, refer to Chapter 19.

Refresh

A report author can save a document with a setting to automatically refresh the data when you view the document. Alternatively, you can refresh the document on demand, by clicking Refresh.

When you refresh a document, you may be prompted to enter information or select values to restrict the amount of data returned in the query. When you click Refresh from the Top bar, a prompt page appears that displays the prompt values from the last query refresh (Figure 24-6). You also can display the prompt frame by clicking the Show Prompt icon in the upper-right corner. Within the prompt frame, click Advanced to see the prompt page.

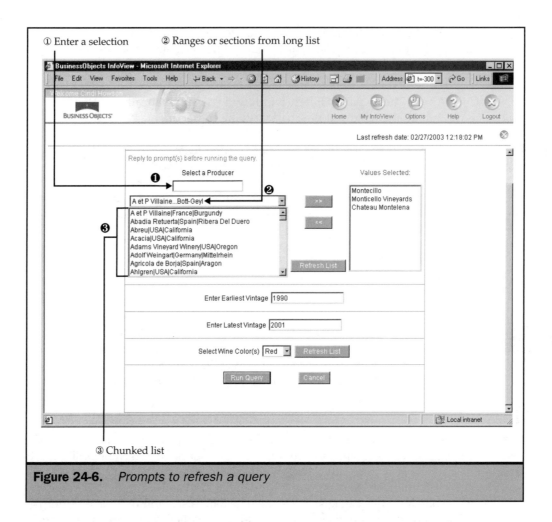

Figure 24-6.   *Prompts to refresh a query*

In version 6.0, report authors have additional control over how prompts, lists of values, and the last condition values interact when you refresh the query. The report author can require you to select and enter new values each time you refresh the query, or he or she can provide you with defaults. Refer to "Conditions and Query Filters" later in this chapter for more information on how to set prompt options in a query.

Figure 24-6 shows a query with multiple prompts. The prompt on producer allows you to select values from a customized list of values. For a long list of values, the list is now chunked into multiple pages for improved performance. This affects how you search for a particular dimension value, as you no longer scroll through one long list. Notice in Figure 24-6, there are three boxes that relate to Producer. Box 1 allows you to type in the name of a particular producer. The report author must enable this or can force a selection from the list of values. Box 2 contains a drop-down menu that provides a list of ranges or chunks. Box 3 provides a subset from the list of values, based on your selection in box 2. Box 4 contains the values you have selected. You must click >> from the list in box 3 to add your selections to the query conditions and box 4.

Figure 24-7 shows two chunks from the long producer list in Figure 24-6. The first chunk shown contains a list of producers from Chateau Mendoza through and including Domaine Bastide Blanche. You can select any producers that appear within this alphabetical range from box 3. The second chunk shown is the last alphabetical chunk from White Oak to Zonin. The size of the scrollable chunk is set by the WebI administrator. (From the WebI Administration Console, select WIReportServer, then set the List of Values Batch Size.)

Notice in Figure 24-6, the report author has forced a selection from the list of values on wine color; there is not another box that allows you to enter the color as there was for producer.

| Tip | *For long list of values, there is a new Find button available via Edit Query in the WebI Report Panel.* |

REPORTING WITH BUSINESSOBJECTS

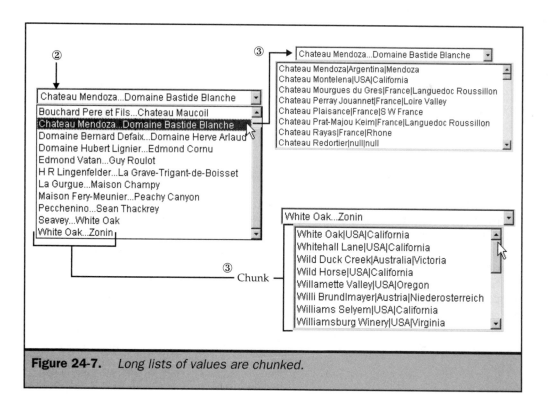

Figure 24-7. *Long lists of values are chunked.*

Saving

After refreshing a query, sorting results, or creating a snapshot on a drill scenario, you save your query. The save options are greatly improved over the previous release, and the save process is a prime example of how Business Objects has improved the work flow. When you click the Save hyperlink from within the Report view, you are presented with an additional page to choose where you want to save the document. Save as a corporate document and Save to my computer are new. Previously, to save a corporate document required save, then publish; there was no export to Excel.

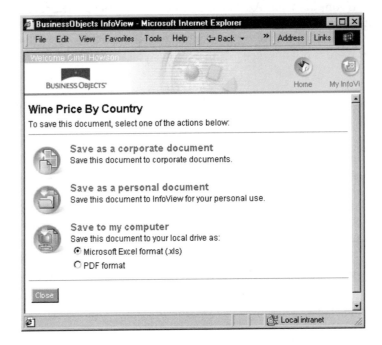

When you choose to save the document as a personal document or as a corporate document, you will find many of the options covered in Chapter 23, "Saving Results." InfoView finally prompts you with the current document name; you no longer need to remember it. For Refresh options, you still have Manually or When Opened and in addition have the new Scheduled Refresh.

Save To Excel is nothing short of wonderful. All formatting, section cells, and subtotals are preserved. The subtotals contain values and do not contain Excel formulas. Charts are converted to Excel charts that can be modified, as shown next.

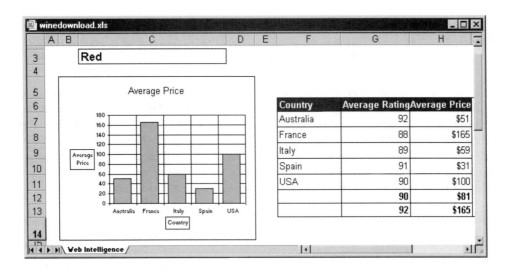

Editing/Creating a Document with the Java Report Panel

Up until this point, all your analysis and navigation have been within the InfoView portal. You did need any additional software or applets to do the sort, filter, drill, refresh, and save. If you want to edit the query, change the block style, or insert breaks or calculations, you must edit the document and launch WebI. If you have selected the Java Report Panel as the option to create/edit documents, your browser opens a second window and displays the Java Report Panel. Don't let the name confuse you; within the Java Report Panel there is a Query page and a Report page. If you are used to the full client, you will enjoy the familiarity of building the query in one screen (like the Query Panel, Chapter 21) and then specifying report options in a separate panel (like Report Manager, Chapter 16, or the Slice and Dice Panel, Chapter 18).

Also new in version 6.0 is a completely thin client called the HTML Report Panel that uses dynamic HTML. It runs within the same browser session as InfoView. This version is ideal for extranet applications and for slow networks. The disadvantage is a less graphical interface, with no drag-and-drop. The HTML Report Panel can create and edit single-block, single-report documents only. The screens in this chapter use the Java version of the Report Panel, which automatically downloads a 1.0MB applet the first time you launch WebI. The applet is 2.8MB when uncompressed.

The Java Report Panel launches when you

- Select New Document from the Home page, then select the universe
- Select Edit when viewing an existing document
- Select Edit when viewing a list of documents in detail mode

If you know you want to modify a document, you can bypass viewing the document in InfoView that first converts the document to HTML. From the list of documents, select View Details, then click Edit for the document you want to modify.

Figure 24-8 shows the Java version of the Edit Query tab from within the Java Report Panel. The Java Report Panel opens a second browser session. This allows you to continue to view existing documents and navigate lists within the InfoView browser, while creating and modifying queries in the second browser session. You can launch multiple Java Report Panels from the InfoView browser, allowing you to edit and create multiple documents via multiple browser windows. Be careful with this, though; if you log out from the InfoView browser window, it leaves you with a stray Java Report Panel.

Caution *Do not close the InfoView browser window without first saving your work and closing the Java Report Panels.*

You build a query in the same way you build a query in the full client (see Chapter 21), dragging and dropping objects from the All Objects pane to the Results, Conditions, or Scope of Analysis pane. You remove objects also by dragging them away from the Results or Query Filters pane back to the All Objects pane; there is no right-click to

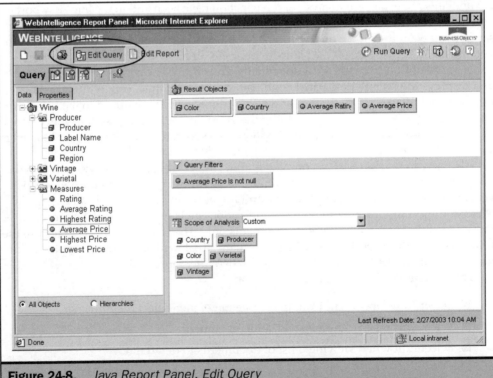

Figure 24-8. *Java Report Panel, Edit Query*

remove them. Predefined conditions are displayed along with regular objects. New in version 6.0 is the ability to view objects sorted by custom hierarchies, defined by the universe designer. This is particularly useful for adding objects to Scope of Analysis. Click the Hierarchies radio button in the bottom left of the panel. You now can skip levels in the hierarchy—for example, Year to Month, skipping Quarter—something not possible in WebI 2.x. Table 24-3 describes the additional buttons available from the toolbar.

Button	Name	Function
	New Document	Creates a new document on the current universe. To select a different universe, return to the InfoView browser window and select Create Documents.
	Save	Saves the current document. This button is active only from the Edit Report window.
	Export to PDF	Exports the report to PDF for printing, allowing you to specify print orientation and page settings.
	Edit Query	Displays the Edit Query page.
	Edit Report	Displays the Edit Report page.
	Run Query	Executes the query. You must run the query to save any changes you make in the Edit Query page.
	Purge Data	Purges data from the microcube.
	Show User Settings	Launches a User Settings dialog box that allows you to display a grid.
	Show Me How	Lists demonstration files to teach you how to use most common WebI actions.
	Help	Offers contextual help.
	Show/Hide Manager	Toggles to show or hide the list of classes and objects within the Edit Query page or the list of variables and formulas within Edit Report.
	Show/Hide Filter Pane	Toggles to close the filter pane where you specify query conditions. Closing the pane does not remove the filters.
	Show/Hide Scope of Analysis Pane	Toggles to show or hide the Scope of Analysis pane to retrieve additional results for drill-down and drill-by within the microcube.

Table 24-3. *Buttons Available in Edit Query*

REPORTING WITH BUSINESSOBJECTS

Button	Name	Function
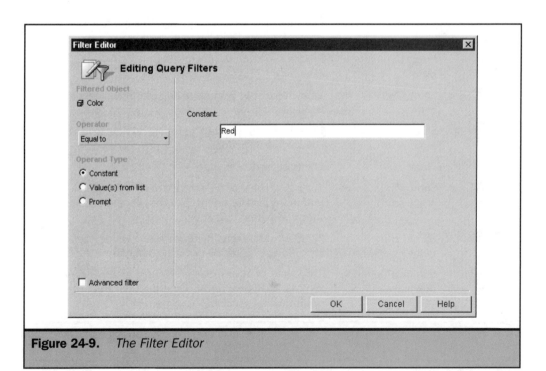	Add Quick Filter	Allows you to add a simple filter to a result object. Displays a list of values.
	View SQL	Displays the SQL.

Table 24-3. *Buttons Available in Edit Query* (continued)

Conditions and Query Filters

Conditions have been renamed Query Filters in version 6.0 Adding query filters is much more intuitive through a new Filter Editor, shown in Figure 24-9. The Filter Editor appears whenever you drag an object from the All Objects pane to the Query Filters pane. Equal to is now the default Operator and Constant is the default Operand. To change the operator, click the drop-down arrow next to Equal to (or whatever operator is currently selected). Operators and Operands are explained in Chapter 21, Tables 21-2 and 21-3.

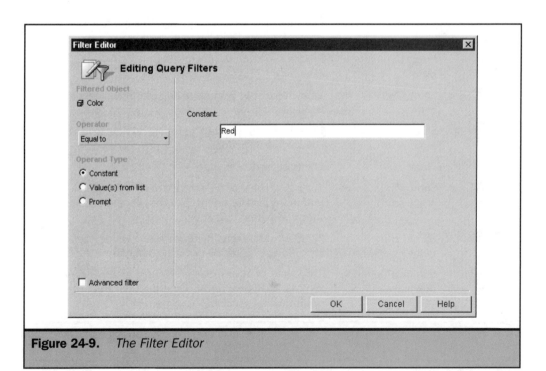

Figure 24-9. *The Filter Editor*

When you change the operand from Constant to Values From List, the Filter Editor displays the list of values. Here, you can manually enter a value or select from the list. Long lists of values are chunked as described in the earlier section "Refresh" and Figure 24-7. There is a new Find button to help you limit the list to values that contain a particular pattern. For example, to find all Producers that have the word Chateau in their name:

1. From the Edit Query page, drag Producer from All Objects to Query Filters.

2. Use the drop-down menu to change the operator from `Equal to` to `In List`.

3. Select the radio button Values From List.

4. Enter **Chateau** in the Find box.

 Note   *The Search text is case sensitive.*

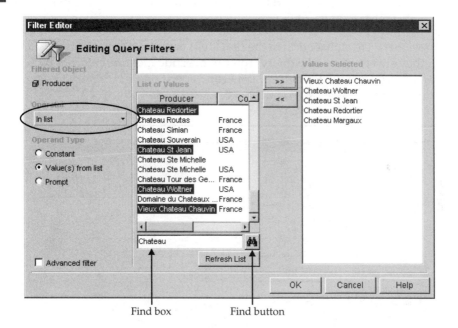

Find box   Find button

5. Click the binoculars icon. The resulting list of values is filtered. To remove a search filter, delete the text, Chateau, from the find box and click the binoculars again.

6. Select the values you want to act as the query conditions and then click >> to add these values to the Values Selected box.

7. Click OK to close the Filter Editor.

Note   *The Find button searches only the first column in a customized list of values. For example, in the preceding Filter Editor dialog, entering USA will not find any producers.*

Conditioning with a Prompt

When you change the Operand Type to Prompt, you have additional control over how users can respond to the prompt (see Figure 24-10).

■ **Prompt with List of Values** Displays the list of values when users execute the query, as shown earlier in Figure 24-7.

■ **Keep last value(s) selected** Displays the last values used so that report readers do not constantly have to reselect the same values. You can change the last value used.

■ **Set default value(s)** Allows you to set the initial condition values, although you can still change them upon query refresh.

■ **Select only from list** Disables the text box; users must select from the list and cannot manually enter a condition value. This option helps ensure that you receive results rather than no rows from entering an incorrect condition value.

Prompts that were alphabetical in the previous version now appear in the same order in which they are entered in the query. You can override the prompt order by selecting the Properties tab from the Edit Query panel and specifying the Prompt Order with the up and down buttons, as shown on the next page.

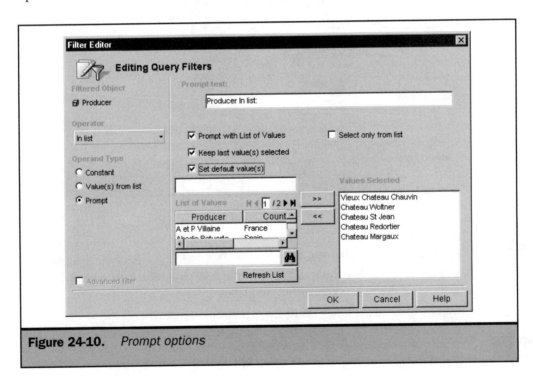

Figure 24-10. *Prompt options*

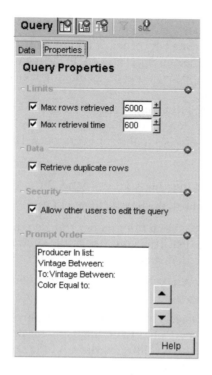

Nested Conditions

Nesting conditions also uses a drag-and-drop technique, rather than the shift left and right menu commands. In the following example, to nest Country and Vintage, you drag Vintage to appear to the right of Country. When it is properly positioned, a blue box shadow appears around the other object that you are nesting it with and a small blue box appears to the left. When the conditions are all on the same level—that is, not nested—an outline box appears around the set of conditions. To change the connector from And to Or, double-click the connector.

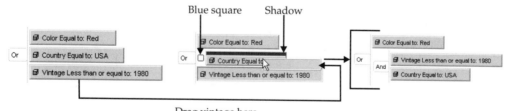

Drag vintage here

Subqueries

In BusinessObjects, you create a subquery by selecting the operand Create a subquery ANY. Selecting this operand inserts a new query tab in the Query Panel.

In WebI version 6.0, you create a subquery by clicking the Advanced filter box in the Filter Editor shown in the lower-left corner of Figure 24-10. This then allows you to add conditions that apply just to the one object and not to the main query. All the conditions—main and subquery—now appear in one pane, making it easier to get an overview of the results you are selecting.

For example, in the EFASHION universe, you want to know revenue in 2001 for *SKU numbers* that were promoted in 2000. *Year=2001* applies to the main query; *Year=2000* and *Promotion=Y* applies to the subquery only. This is similar to Figure 21-7 in Chapter 21.

1. Drag *SKU Number* to the Query Filters pane.

2. In the Filter Editor, check the box Advanced Filter.

3. WebI prompts you to enter a filter name. You also can choose to exclude the filter values from the list. This will change the subquery from `In` to `Not In`. Click OK to close the dialog box.

4. WebI adds a filter icon next to the object that contains the subquery and adds an up arrow that allows you to show/hide the conditions for the subquery.

5. Drag *Year* from All Objects to the Query Filters pane, beneath *SKU Number*. *SKU Number* or whatever object you are using for the subquery comparison will be highlighted with a yellow shadow. A blue shadow means you are adding *Year* as a regular condition to the main query. Enter the condition value, in this example **2000**. Click OK to close the Filter Editor.

6. Drag the object *Promotion (y/n)* to beneath *SKU Number*. Enter the condition value **y** and click OK to close the Filter Editor. Your final condition values should appear as follows:

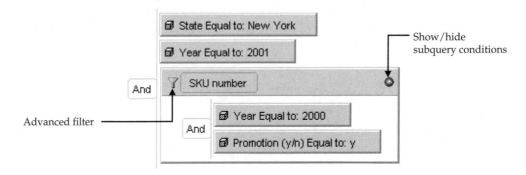

To change the filter name or the exclude setting, double-click the filter icon next to the condition object.

Formatting a Report

Once you are done defining the results, conditions, and scope of analysis, you Run the Query and the Edit Report panel shown in Figure 24-11. This panel also appears when you select Edit while viewing document details or an individual document from within InfoView.

When you display the Report Manager, the Report page contains four new tabs that allow you to modify the report. If you do not see these tabs on your screen, click the Show/Hide Manager.

- **Data**   Allows you to drag and drop objects from the variables list to the report window and to specific blocks within the report.

- **Templates**   Allows you to change the block style of an existing block or to add a new block to create a multiblock report. You also use the Templates tab to insert free-standing cells—for example, for a report title or to show page numbers.

- **Properties**   Controls the formatting for different document components. Within the Properties tab, there is an additional vertical toolbar that, for example, lets you set break options, the size of a chart, and the text for column headings. There is a new table property that allows you to format alternate rows of data for easier reading.

- **Map**   Displays a list of individual reports and sections in a master/detail report.

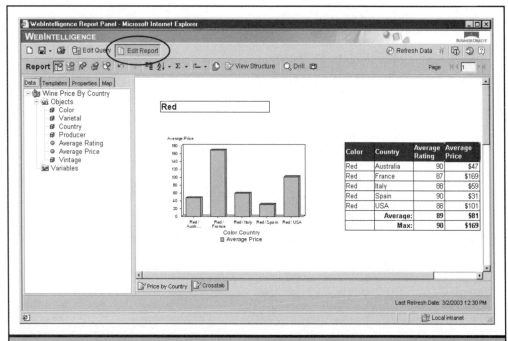

Figure 24-11.   *Report page of the Java Report Panel*

Specifying a Block Style

Templates enable you to insert a new report tab, modify an existing block style, or insert a new block in an existing report. You modify blocks by dragging the desired template style onto the existing block or onto an empty space for a new block. For example, to convert the bar chart in Figure 24-11 to a pie chart:

1. From within the Report page, Report Manager, select the Templates tab.

2. Expand the Chart folder by clicking the + sign to see the different chart types.

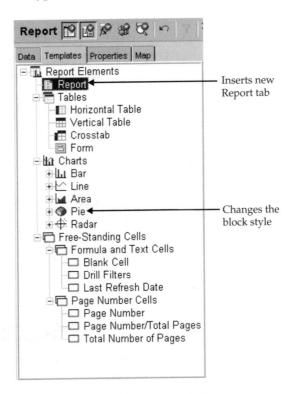

3. Expand the Pie folder to see the different styles of pie charts.

4. Select 3D Pie and drag it to the bar chart in the report window. The bar chart in Figure 24-11 now appears as a pie chart.

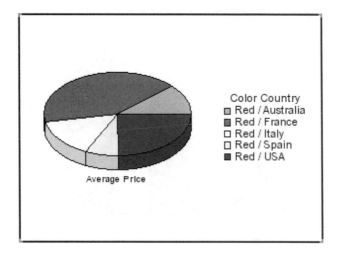

You can also select Turn To from the pop-up menu to convert an existing block. To select the entire block, click just above the block until a gray shadow appears around the block. Then right-click to select Turn To from the pop-up menu. You then select the new block format via a dialog box.

The Second Y Axis

When you chart two different measures that have different ranges of values, you may need to display the values across two Y axes. This version does not specifically allow you to add a second Y axis for line charts, but you can use a mixed bar and line chart to create a second Y axis.

1. From within the Report page, select the Templates tab.

2. Under Report Elements, select Report and drag it to the report windows. WebI inserts a new report tab. You can change the name of the report tab by selecting the Properties tab, Report Properties, then Name.

3. Under Charts, expand the folder Bar, then select Vertical Bar and Line.

4. WebI inserts a blank chart similar to what appears when you select View Structure from the toolbar.

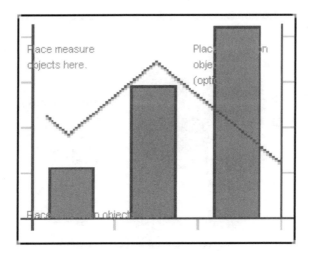

5. From the Report Manager pane, select the Data tab. Drag the dimension object (in this example, Country) to the X axis. Drag the first measure, Average Ratings, to the first Y axis. Drag the second measure, Average Price, to the second Y axis. The structure now appears as follows:

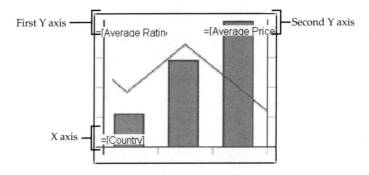

The formatted chart should look like this:

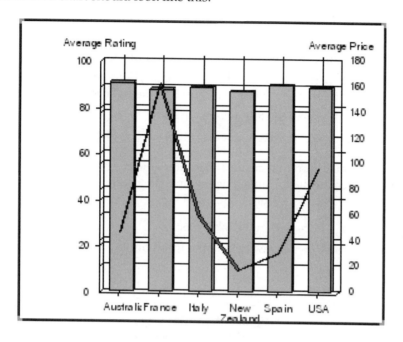

Note   *You cannot modify the scale of the Y axis. For example, it would be more meaningful to set the Y axis for ratings to start at 80, to better see the range of ratings from 80 to 100. You also cannot specify particular line styles.*

Variables and Formulas

Many companies say one of the key reasons their users would not use WebI 2.x rather than two-tier or three-tier mode BusinessObjects was the absence of formulas and report variables. Version 6.0 addresses many of those needs. A few functions are not available in this release, so you will need to evaluate which functions essential to particular users are missing. For some of the missing functions, there are workarounds. For example, although `Var` and `VarP` are not available, you can use arithmetic operators to calculate the variance between two measures. Cumulative aggregates `RunningSum` and the `Where` qualifier are two popular functions that were not available in the beta 2.

The formula syntax is slightly different between WebI 6.0 and BusinessObjects in the following ways:

- Variables within formulas use brackets [ ] to enclose variable names, compared with the < > that are used in the full-client formula syntax.
- The function `Concatenation` is not available, but you can use + rather than the ampersand (&) used in the full client.
- `If then else` uses the following syntax:

    `If (boolean_expr; value_if_true; value_if_false)`

To create a formula, you first create a placeholder in the block (either a cell or a column) and then create the formula. For example, to insert a formula that flags higher wine ratings in the table block from Figure 24-11:

1. Click Average Price within the table block.

2. Click the drop-down arrow next to the Insert button on the toolbar, and select Insert Column After.

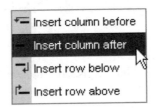

3. Select the blank cell in the newly inserted column.

4. From the toolbar, select Show/Hide Formula Editor. Alternatively, you can right-click in the new column and select Formula Editor from the pop-up menu.

5. Enter the formula **=If([Average Rating]>90;"High Rating";"")**, as shown next.

Formula editor   Variable editor   Validate

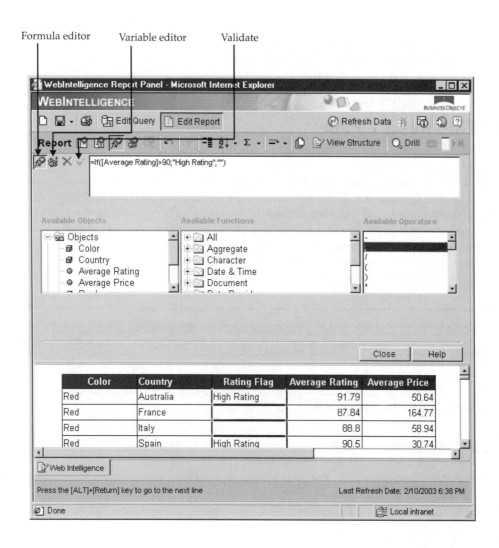

6. Click the check mark to validate the formula. If your formula contains errors, WebI will give you the position number of the error. When the formula syntax is validated, select Close to insert the formula into the block.

7. Select the column heading cell. With either the Formula Toolbar or the Formula Editor displayed, enter the text **Rating Flag** in the formula box. When entering fixed text or constants, you do not preface the text with = or you will receive a validation error.

To save this formula as a variable, click Create Variable from the Formula Editor toolbar. You will be prompted to enter a name and select an object qualification. For more information on creating variables, refer to Chapter 18, "Using Formulas as Variables."

The HTML Report Panel

Unlike the Java Report Panel that opens a second browser window, the HTML Report Panel launches within the current InfoView browser window. Figure 24-12 shows the HTML Report Panel. To add objects to the result pane, you click >>; drag-and-drop is not available. Use the tabs at the top to navigate through the steps of building a query, defining conditions, and then formatting the report. Also note in Figure 24-12 that the Scope of Analysis does not allow Custom; you can only choose to drill down by a level for the Result objects currently selected. While the HTML Report Panel may lack the complexity, buttons, and capabilities in the Java Report Panel, it is a zero-footprint interface, ideal for slow networks or extranet deployments.

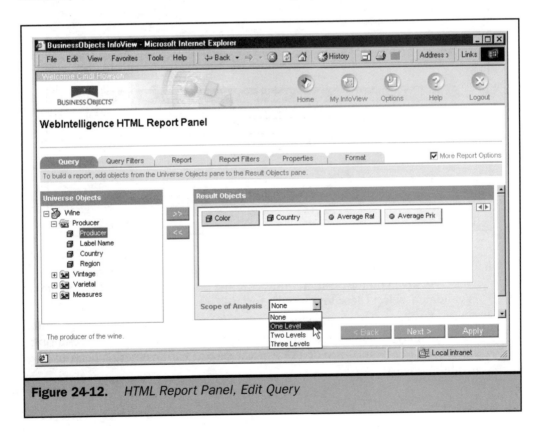

Figure 24-12.   *HTML Report Panel, Edit Query*

Note	*If you try to edit a multiblock report with the HTML Report Panel, you will receive an error message that the block is too complex to edit. You must use the Java Report Panel to edit multiblock reports. Select Options	Create/Edit. Under WebI Documents, select the Java Report Panel.*

Summary

For all the power that has made the BusinessObjects full client a market leader, much of the power is now in WebI version 6.0. Web-based reporting has never been so intuitive and robust, with mixed-block reports, multireport documents, an intuitive drill bar, and the ability to create formulas and reports. While the HTML Report Panel may lack some of these features, companies with extranet deployments will enjoy the zero-footprint client that helps you navigate the query and report building process. For companies who have been waiting for more functionality in WebI, now just may be the time to migrate more full client users to WebI. It's true, you still can't create user objects, but hey, that gives one more reason to ensure the objects are built into the universe, right?

REPORTING WITH
BUSINESSOBJECTS

The Complete Reference

Bibliography

729

BOB: BusinessObjects Query Tools Forum (www.forumtopics.com/busobj/about.php).

BusinessObjects Online Technical Support (www.techsupport.businessobjects.com).

Change, Dr. Daniel T. "CWM Enablement Showcase: Warehouse Meta Data Interchange made Easy Using CWM." *TDWI What Works, Volume 11*.

DataPro. "1999–2001 Business Intelligence and Data Warehousing User Survey." December 13, 1999.

Eckerson, Wayne. "Analytic Applications: Build or Buy." TDWI Business Intelligence Strategies Program, November 5–6, 2002.

Groff, James. *SQL: The Complete Reference*. McGraw-Hill/Osborne, 2002.

Howson, Cindi. "Business Objects Improves Web-Based OLAP Access." *TDWI Flashpoint*, January 2002.

Howson, Cindi. "Marketing the Data Warehouse." The Data Warehouse Institute, November 2003.

Howson, Cindi. "Path to Enlightenment." *Intelligent Enterprise*, April 2002.

IBM DB2 Warehouse Manager (www.ibm.com).

Loney, Kevin. *Oracle 9i: The Complete Reference*. McGraw-Hill/Osborne, 2002.

McKnight, William. "How to Justify a Data Warehouse Using ROI." The Data Warehouse Institute, February 2003.

Meta Integration (www.metaintegration.net).

Mishra, Sanjay. *Mastering Oracle SQL*. O'Reilly, April 2002.

Morris, Henry, et. al. "The Financial Impact of Business Analytics, An IDC ROI Study." December 2002.

Object Management Group (www.omg.com).

Pense, Nigel, The OLAP Report (www.olapreport.com).

Powell, Thomas. *HTML: The Complete Reference*. McGraw-Hill/Osborne, 2001.

Schauer, Val. "Business Objects." *DM Review,* January 2003.

Solutionselling.com.

Sparacino, Frank. "Business intelligence industry update." First Analysis, January 3, 2002.

Stoller, Don. "Turning your Business Intelligence Investment into a Profit Center." TDWI Business Intelligence Strategies Program, November 5–6, 2002.

Vesset, Dan. "Trends in the Market for Business Intelligence Software." *DM Review,* August 2001.

Watson, Hugh, et. al. "Current Practices in Data Warehousing."

Wu, Jonathon. "Calculating ROI for Business Intelligence Projects." Base Consulting, December 12, 2000.

Zurich North America (www.zurichna.com).

Index